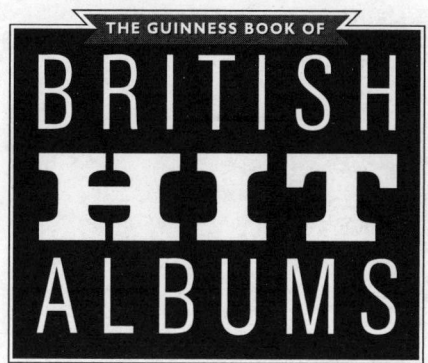

THE GUINNESS BOOK OF

BRITISH
HIT
ALBUMS

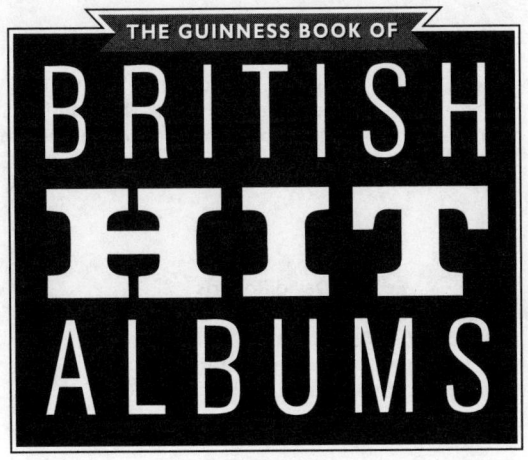

THE GUINNESS BOOK OF

BRITISH HIT ALBUMS

PAUL GAMBACCINI
TIM RICE
JONATHAN RICE

EDITION 7

GRR Editorial Associate: Tony Brown

GUINNESS PUBLISHING

ACKNOWLEDGEMENTS

Special thanks to Eileen Heinink, Jan Rice, Alex Rice, Tony Vickers, Neil Warwick, Jimmy Brown and Samantha King. We also want to thank New Musical Express and CIN for their charts and many record companies for their patient help.

Editor: David Roberts
Deputy Editor and Picture Researcher: Hal Norman
Editorial Assistant: Helen Rodger
Design: Ad Vantage, Sarah Silvé
Computer Systems Manager: Alex Reid

First edition 1983
Second edition 1986
Third edition 1988
Fourth edition 1990
Fifth Edition 1992
Sixth edition 1994
Seventh edition 1996
Reprint 10 9 8 7 6 5 4 3 2 1

Published in Great Britain by
Guinness Publishing Ltd,
33 London Road, Enfield,
Middlesex

Printed and bound in Great Britain by The Bath Press, Bath

A catalogue record for this book is available from the British Library

ISBN 0-85112-619-7

INTRODUCTION

If the twin themes of the British music business during 1994–95 were summed up in the titles of previous hit albums, they would be *Boom Boom* and *Alone*. The 1992 John Lee Hooker blues title applies to the astonishing increase in sales enjoyed in the two-year period, while the Nana Mouskouri hit from 1986 relates to the growing tendency of all major record-buying countries, including the United Kingdom, to concentrate on local talent.

ROBSON & JEROME unchained

The sales sensation of late 1995 exemplifies both points perfectly. Robson Green and Jerome Flynn broke all previous records for reaching the million mark, and then the two million, in the shortest time period. They only required the final 48 days of the year to hit the two million level with *Robson & Jerome*. This sales stunner spent the last six weeks of the year and the first of 1996 at number one, to become the only debut album to spend its initial seven chart weeks on top. By the end of January 1996 it was expected to breeze past Kylie Minogue's *Kylie* (oddly, another debut disc titled after the first name of the artist) to become the best-selling album of all time on an independent label.

These are fantastic feats. Mention them to someone abroad and the response is likely to be 'Who are they?' It's slightly unfair to dismiss the international chances of *Robson & Jerome* completely, since as a late-1995 release it awaited promotion abroad, but since the duo's singles success (two of the top three of the year) had not been duplicated in other countries, the album containing these tracks was hardly likely to set the planet on fire.

Yet we pat Green and Flynn on the back, rather than snigger, because their fate is illustrative of the growing parochialism of popular music. The counterpart to *Robson & Jerome* at the top of the US Albums of the Year list was *Cracked Rear View* by Hootie and the Blowfish, which streaked past 11 million sales in the States alone without finishing in the UK Top 100 for the year. A typical reaction here would be 'What are Blowfish?' America's second best for 1995, *The Hits* by Garth Brooks, staggered to an 88 finish in Britain. The third, *II* by Boyz II Men, was not among the 100 top UK sellers, nor was the fourth, *Hell Freezes Over* by the Eagles. The tendency to favour local talent was even pronounced in Germany, the largest continental market, where the only artist with two hit albums in mid-December was Herbert Gronemeyer.

Who's Hootie?

INTRODUCTION

As with individual acts, so with trends. Album sales in 1995 were a staggering 25% up on 1994, which in turn had seen an improvement over 1993. Part of the reason for the upturn was an increase in the number of British acts that caught the public fancy. Neither Black Grape, Oasis, Portishead, Pulp nor Supergrass had entered the album chart before the end of 1993 but were all in the Top 50 of 1995. Elastica and Leftfield just missed. Several of these artists were commonly listed with Blur and Eternal, who reached new heights in 1994–95, as examples of 'Britpop'. (High achievers like Take That and East 17, plus Irish first timers Boyzone, were frequently assigned to the new category of Boy Band.)

The leaders of this pack were strictly local heroes. Of course, emerging talent usually finds favour in its home country before it succeeds anywhere else, and it is to be assumed that some home-grown heroes will eventually travel. But there is no doubt that Britpop was a Britflop abroad. Record industry legend Maurice Oberstein, the former head of CBS and PolyGram who is now spending his retirement in Florida, called Britpop 'a cul-de-sac . . . so typically chi-chi, a 'Winchester Cathedral'-type attitudinal thing.'

True enough. *The Great Escape* by Blur, for example, only registered one week in the American Top 200. The real British breakthrough in America was by Bush with their long-running hit *Sixteen Stone*, which finally rocked the US Top Ten at the beginning of 1996. Japan continued to tear its hair out for Shampoo. Both Bush and Shampoo were virtually unknown in Britpop-obsessed Britain.

In fact, the international hit albums from these isles were almost exclusively by acts to which the UK pop press no longer pays regular attention. The Beatles were the best-selling British act on Earth in 1995 as they began an imaginative release schedule designed to last through 1996, though the prospect of any artist's out-takes, even those by the biggest band in history, outselling everything new is somewhat disturbing. The Rolling Stones were the biggest-drawing live attraction, registering all ten of the world's largest crowds during 1995, according to *Amusement Weekly*. Elton John was the top UK male vocalist in the world for the two-year period, based on the sales of his *Lion King* soundtrack, the new studio album, *Made In England*, and the compilation, *Love Songs*. These three artists, plus Queen, occupied the top four positions in the mid-December Eurochart. All are British; all had their first hit albums over two decades ago.

To demonstrate further that it is vintage rather than new British artists who appealed to world audiences in 1994–95, Pink Floyd had an international number one with *The Division Bell* and Eric Clapton had the second American chart topper of his career with *From The Cradle*. Sade and Sting scored worldwide with greatest hits sets, and Annie Lennox turned heads, if not to stone, with *Medusa*.

Virtually the only artists of any nationality to sell large numbers of albums across borders are ones who were doing so ten years ago or earlier. Prominent exceptions include Mariah Carey, Celine Dion and Enya, who have emerged as consistent world favourites, and Seal, who has pleased everywhere with his two albums. The only recent global group breakout has been that of the Cranberries. As can best be calculated, the Irish group's *No Need To Argue* was the best-selling album by non-Americans during 1995. The Cranberries spent more weeks on the British chart during 1994–95 than any act except R.E.M. who pipped them by just one week. The quartet had only managed one week on chart in 1993.

The search for a future British favourite inevitably leads to Oasis. To show again how quickly the music scene changes, the only Oasis in our last edition included

Were there a Brit Award for Export, this could have been a contender

Mary Hopkin, Julian Lloyd Webber and Peter Skellern, and peaked at 14 in 1984 with their only hit, their eponymous album. In two years the new band of that name has completely eclipsed the earlier act. *Definitely Maybe* went platinum in 1994 and added more than a half million further sales in the following 12 months. This latter figure, combined with the 1,840,000-plus units of *(What's The Story) Morning Glory?*, made the Gallaghers' group the best-selling act of 1995. Oasis showed signs of registering an important international breakthrough in 1996, beginning the year in the Eurochart Top Ten and climbing the American table.

Part of the health of the UK albums field is due to the increased action in the compilation market. In the introduction to our last edition we wrote 'The Top 50 compilations of 1993 were contained in the top 171 of the overall chart . . . which is presented to the trade but rarely seen by the public.' We thought that was impressive, but this time we invite you to change the 171 to 131. The weekly slice of the album pie has increased to 25% and is still growing. This is directly attributable to the continued boom in dance singles. Since many dance hits are by artists who have yet to record albums or do so infrequently, the compilation is the most efficient way to buy a group of dance hits on album quickly and economically.

The other major factor in the health of compilation discs is continued clever programming and marketing. Even the major labels are now keen to include on editions of *Now That's What I Call Music!* not only current hit singles but tracks considered sure bets to succeed. It was once assumed that giving a compilation CD an album's most popular track would destroy the individual artist's sales. This fear has been forgotten. *Now That's What I Call Music! 32* emerged as the compilation chart champ of 1995, besting even 30 and 31, but *NOW!* had a contender series in *The Best* (fill in the genre) *Album In The World . . . Ever!* The most popular of these was *Rock Ballads* but even *Punk* and *Classical* found favour.

The success in recycling proven product like this is encouraging from the balance sheet point of view, and it makes building a library of top tracks easier, but it is rather like relying on older buyers to repurchase their vinyl favourites on CD. These processes can only be taken so far before one notices the lack of fresh food to nourish the beast. It is hoped that maturing mid-1990s acts such as multiple-Grammy nominee Alanis Morissette, Oasis, and even Herbert Gronemeyer can develop into true international stars in a way in which their late-1980s and early-1990s predecessors have almost to a man and woman been unable. Then next edition we can celebrate not only *Boom Boom* but *All Around The World* (Jason Donovan, 1993), instead of *The World Won't Listen* (Smiths, 1987).

PAUL GAMBACCINI   JONATHAN RICE   TIM RICE

1958

In 1948 CBS introduced the long-playing microgroove recording to America. It was devised by Peter Goldmark who, it is said, had had enough of getting up several times during one piece of music to change several 78s. He thought there had to be a market for a single disc that could contain an entire symphony or sonata.

The 18 albums that hit the chart in the last eight weeks of 1958, the first weeks of *Melody Maker*'s Top Ten chart (the first LP chart published in the UK), demonstrated that Goldmark's invention had other applications. None of the 18 best-sellers was a classical orchestral performance! Thirteen were by adult male performers with wide audience appeal and five were of show business origin – that is, stage, screen or television.

The soundtrack to *South Pacific* was number one for each of the eight weeks, a prelude to its equally total domination of the 1959 lists. The man with the most LPs to chart was Frank Sinatra, who touched the Top Ten four times. Elvis Presley had the most total weeks on chart, that is to say a sum of the runs of each of his hit LPs. Both *Elvis' Golden Records* and *King Creole* were on every one of the eight charts.

The other artists who contributed to the all-male domain were Perry Como, Russ Conway, Mario Lanza, the American satirist Tom Lehrer, and Johnny Mathis. Perhaps Lanza was the closest to what Goldmark had in mind: one side of his disc was the soundtrack to the film about the classical tenor Enrico Caruso, *The Great Caruso*.

8

1959

It can be whispered in reverent awe or shouted from the rooftops, but the achievement is so great that it cannot be conveyed in casual conversation: the original soundtrack to the film *South Pacific* was at number one for the entire year 1959. This family favourite led the list for every one of the 52 weeks, a feat which has never been matched, though later discs would surpass it in sales. *South Pacific* boasted a wide range of memorable music, from the love ballad *Some Enchanted Evening* (an American number one for Perry Como) to the novelty tune *Happy Talk* (eventually a UK number one for Captain Sensible).

Film soundtracks were still the leading money-spinners in the LP market of 1959. The form was only a decade old, and soundtracks, Broadway cast performances and classical works were still the most logical initial uses of Peter Goldmark's invention, requiring the additional space a long player could provide. The movie versions of *Gigi* and *The King And I* were notable winners in 1959, as was the New York stage production of *West Side Story*.

Rock-and-roll vocalists, previously content with singles, made further inroads into the album field, but Frank Sinatra still scored the most weeks on chart for a solo singer. Elvis Presley was a close second, registering an impressive success with *Elvis' Golden Records*. The chart appearance of two LPs by Cliff Richard was the best 1959 showing by a young Briton.

Curtain Up!, a compilation of stars from the London Palladium hosted by Bruce Forsyth, enjoyed a 13-week run, but the most impressive performance by a show business star was that of Peter Sellers, who spent 32 weeks in the Top Ten with two solo LPs and a further five with his colleagues the Goons.

1960

*S*outh Pacific dominated the album charts one more time in 1960, though not to the extent it had in 1959. It was in the best-sellers for every one of the 53 charts of the year, the only title to achieve that run, but it did occasionally let other discs take the top spot. Number one on the very first *Record Retailer* album chart, that of 10 March, was *The Explosive Freddy Cannon*, which fell in fragments the following week after giving Cannon the distinction of being the first rock-and-roll singer to have a number one LP in the UK. Even the second, Elvis Presley, who had been a more likely contender for that honour, only managed one week at the summit, scoring with *Elvis Is Back*. The other disc to interrupt the *South Pacific* streak was *Down Drury Lane To Memory Lane*, a nostalgic effort by the studio group 101 Strings.

Rock and roll made great progress in the long playing market in 1960. The previous year only four rockers had charted in the entire 12 months. This time five of the top six acts were rock stars, though the majority of chart artists were still not of this nature. Presley pipped Peter Sellers as the individual with most weeks on the chart, though Sellers would have ranked above Presley if the computation included his additional appearances with the Goons and Sophia Loren, not, one must add, on the same disc.

American guitarist Duane Eddy's surprisingly strong showing in fourth place should not be overlooked.

Commercial success does not guarantee artistic immortality, as the George Mitchell Minstrels have proved. Their *Black And White Minstrel Show* was an enormous success on television, record and stage, but an entire generation has grown up in, shall we say, the dark about their achievements.

9

1961

*T*he *Black And White Minstrel Show* was the only album to stay in the chart for the whole of 1961. It accumulated seven weeks at number one in four separate visits, while *Another Black And White Minstrel Show* had a single mighty eight-week run at the top. Mass audiences loved the old-time performances of the Minstrels, many of whom blacked up to sing vintage popular songs. It was the dated nature of their material, as well as increased sophistication concerning racial matters, which spelled an end to large scale interest in the group in the late sixties.

Elvis Presley was the outstanding artist for the second consecutive year, enjoying 22 weeks at number one with the soundtrack to *GI Blues*. The granddaddy of film favourites, *South Pacific*, put in a final nine weeks at the peak before retiring. It was a bumper year for original cast recordings of stage musicals, with a strong emphasis on the London stage. *Oliver*, *Sound Of Music* and *Stop The World I Want To Get Off* all had lengthy runs with British rosters. The year saw hit honours for the well-remembered *Beyond The Fringe* and the completely forgotten *King Kong*. Even the London cast of *Bye Bye Birdie* flew out of the wings and into the charts.

Frank Sinatra continued his series of fine years, entering the Top 20 with seven titles on four different labels. Cliff Richard had three new top two successes and one happy hangover from 1960, *Me And My Shadows. 21 Today* was his first number one, though his mates beat him to the top by six weeks with their debut disc *The Shadows*.

1962

Elvis Presley and the George Mitchell Minstrels overachieved again in 1962. The King of rock and roll notched up 18 weeks at number one with his *Blue Hawaii* soundtrack, more time at the top than any other long player that year, and he ruled the roost for six more weeks with *Pot Luck*. The Minstrels led the list with their new release, *On Stage With The George Mitchell Minstrels*, and then encored with their 1960 issue, the original *Black And White Minstrel Show*. Their three albums tallied a total of 109 weeks in the chart, the first time any act had hit the century.

Compared to these two artists the rest of the field failed to flame, though *South Pacific* again managed to appear in every one of the 52 charts. The new film sensation was *West Side Story*, surpassing its significant stage sales to pace the pack for 12 weeks. Four other multi-media successes were the soundtrack to *It's Trad Dad*, the original cast album of the London production *Blitz*, and two Dorothy Provine sets inspired by her television series *The Roaring Twenties*. Further evidence of the taste for trad was the appearance of a budget album, *The Best Of Ball, Barber And Bilk*, at number one for two weeks. Chris Barber and Acker Bilk had appeared together on two fast-selling packages in 1961, sans Kenny Ball.

The Shadows achieved the fabulous feat of nabbing their second number one with their second effort, *Out Of The Shadows*. They shared credit on Cliff Richard's table-topping *The Young Ones*. Cliff managed to top the Shads in weeks on chart thanks to his subsequent release, the literally timed and titled *32 Minutes And 17 Seconds*.

1963

Beatlemania spread like a flash fire in 1963, and the album chart showed its effects. The Fab Four's *Please Please Me* seized the top spot on 11 May and held it for 30 consecutive weeks, to be replaced only by *With The Beatles*, which kept clear for a further 21. The Liverpudlians had come from nowhere to hold the premier position for one week shy of a full year. It was nothing short of a musical revolution: from their arrival until 1968, only one non-rock album would have a look in at number one. A field that had been the domain of the soundtrack and cast album overnight became ruled by rock. It was hard to believe that 1963 had begun with *The Black And White Minstrel Show* still in the lead. With a couple of notable exceptions, the film and stage market dried up.

Cliff Richard was the weeks on chart champ this time, his total fed by three new successes. The second highest figures were achieved equally by Elvis Presley and Buddy Holly. The Pelvis began twitching in anxiety as the soundtracks to three bad films did progressively worse. Holly, dead for four years, had always been a strong album seller, but really surged in 1963 when the poignantly-titled collection *Reminiscing* joined the list of his other posthumous best sellers.

Frank Ifield proved a one-year though not a one-hit wonder, reaching number three with two releases. He never came close again. Frank Sinatra rebounded with three top tenners, including a team-up with Count Basie that went to number two.

1964

The Beatles and Rolling Stones monopolised the number one position during 1964, making it the purest year for rock music in terms of holding the top spot. The only 12 weeks John, Paul, George and Ringo were not ahead with either *With The Beatles*, *A Hard Day's Night* or *Beatles For Sale*, their chief competition was in front with the debut disc *The Rolling Stones*. The fresh triumphs of *A Hard Day's Night* and *Beatles For Sale* gave the Beatles four number ones in four releases, a 100 per cent success ratio they maintained through all of their 11 official international outings, though two other issues, a 1966 UK compilation and the *Yellow Submarine* soundtrack on which they played only a part, fell short of the top. No other act has hit number one every time with as many records.

The Fab Four's quartet of hit LPs gave them 104 weeks on chart, the first time a century had been achieved by a rock act. But even they were outdistanced by Jim Reeves. The American country singer had enjoyed two big albums to accompany his two strong singles in the first half of the year. After he died in a plane crash in July, nine further packages made the chart, six in a four-week period. Gentleman Jim accumulated 115 weeks on chart in all, a record that would stand until 1968.

Third in the weeks on chart category was Roy Orbison, who enjoyed the distinction of seeing his *In Dreams* set on every chart of the year, a feat attained for the second consecutive year by *West Side Story*. Cliff Richard had only one new album, below average for his early years, and Elvis Presley slipped seriously as none of his three long players reached the Top Three.

11

1965

For the three middle years of the sixties only the Beatles, Rolling Stones, Bob Dylan and *The Sound Of Music* reached number one, trading off in a seemingly endless sequence. The first three were the rock artists who came to represent the spirit of the decade, while the last was a show business phenomenon that came, saw, conquered, and wouldn't go away.

The Beatles began the year on top with *Beatles For Sale* and ended it there with *Rubber Soul*, having spent much of the summer there as well with *Help*. Bob Dylan had the second highest total of chart-toppers, two, succeeding *The Freewheelin' Bob Dylan* with his own *Bringing It All Back Home*, but his most impressive statistic was his 112 weeks on chart. Much of his back catalogue charted in late 1964 and 1965. Though primarily considered an album artist, he also logged five Top 30 singles in 1965, his peak year.

Dylan's dear friend Joan Baez shared his success, with three charters to follow her 1964 debut. Her winners included *Joan Baez*, *Joan Baez No. 5* and *Farewell Angelina*, but no sign of Joan Baez Nos. 2, 3 or 4.

Though Miss Baez was the front-running credited female vocalist, Julie

Andrews accounted for the greatest grosses with her soundtracks. *Mary Poppins* spent the most weeks on chart of any 1965 title, 50, and *The Sound Of Music* began a run to rival that of *South Pacific*, accumulating its first 20 weeks at number one.

Sir Winston Churchill, who had died early in the year, had a posthumous Top Ten LP, *The Voice Of Sir Winston Churchill.*

1966

Cash register tills were still alive to *The Sound Of Music* in 1966. If the Beatles or Rolling Stones didn't have a new album, the star soundtrack of the 60s kept the number

one position warm. It followed *Rubber Soul* and preceded *Aftermath*; it moved back in the aftermath of *Aftermath* and before *Revolver*. When the latter Beatles album had shot its bolt, Julie Andrews and company skipped back to the top for the last three months of the year.

The Sound Of Music was the only album to spend all of 1966 in the best sellers. It was as big an international phenomenon as a UK success. *Time* reported that it had sold seven million copies by Christmas, outmoving all other stage or screen sets, even the legendary *South Pacific*.

The musical version of the Von Trapp family story was a timely purchase in any season, not linked to fad or fashion. The Beatles' unprecedented popularity, on the other hand, had made every one of their new discs an immediate must purchase. A short period of colossal concentrated sale would then be followed by a chart decline. Hence *Revolver*, a summer number one, was almost gone by Christmas. Parlophone, wanting a Beatles product for the major marketing month of the year, issued *A Collection Of Beatles Oldies* in December. However, the fans weren't fooled. It peaked at seven, a commercial miscalculation.

The Beach Boys spent more weeks on the chart than anyone in 1966, with five long players accumulating 95 weeks between them. This success reflected their four consecutive Top Three singles. One album, the classic *Pet Sounds*, did much better in Britain than America, reaching number two.

The other album artist of note was Herb Alpert, who garnered 89 weeks, but while his Tijuana Brass LPs loitered on the list they did not reach the highest chart positions.

1967

History remembers 1967 as the year of flower power and psychedelia. The only real evidence of this in the upper echelons of the LP charts was the tremendous success of the Beatles' landmark *Sergeant Pepper's Lonely Hearts Club Band* and the considerable achievement of *Are You Experienced* by the Jimi Hendrix Experience.

Sergeant Pepper, chosen the best rock album of all time in two international critics' polls, spent exactly half the year at number one. The other 26 weeks were divided between the recurrent *The Sound Of Music* and the first-time sets by the distinctly unpsychedelic Monkees. In a year when they had six hit singles and a cult television show, the 'fabricated four' reached the top with *The Monkees* and *More Of The Monkees*.

With only those four albums going all the way in 1967, it was a major achievement to get to number two. Hendrix and band did. Cream did respectably but not quite as well, earning Top Ten placings with their first two cartons of *Fresh Cream* and *Disraeli Gears*. The Rolling Stones surprisingly peaked at three with *Between The Buttons*.

It was a fine year for easy listening and soul. In addition to *Best Of The Beach Boys*, records that rode the roster for all 52 weeks included the soundtracks of *The Sound Of Music* and *Dr Zhivago* and *Going Places* by Herb Alpert and the Tijuana Brass. Alpert led overall by a toot with 101 weeks on chart, though the Beach Boys were a close second with 97. Tom Jones had three Top Ten issues and the Dubliners, Irish singers enjoying a year of British popularity, had two.

This was the best year on record for Geno Washington, an outstanding live soul attraction. Otis Redding and the Four Tops also had strong chart performances, but they would do even better in 1968.

1968

The album chart lost its sense of discipline in 1968. In previous years the number of different artists who had reached number one, not counting performers on film soundtracks, could be counted on the fingers of a sawmill operator's hand. This time no fewer than a dozen different acts went all the way, with occasional further appearances by *The Sound Of Music*.

The nature of the chart-toppers changed, too. Recently the number one spot had been the property of the world's outstanding rock talents. In 1968 Val Doonican, Tom Jones and Andy Williams managed to head the hordes. The Small Faces and Scott Walker enjoyed their only number one LPs, and Simon and Garfunkel their first.

The Four Tops, Otis Redding, and Diana Ross and the Supremes broke the all-white stranglehold on the top spot. The only black faces to have been there before were the made-up ones of the George Mitchell Minstrels. Sadly, Redding's number one was achieved posthumously. Four albums charted after his death, two studio sets, a compilation, and a live LP.

For the fifth time in six seasons, the Fab Four had the Christmas number one, this year with the double disc *The Beatles*, often referred to as *The White Album*. The Rolling Stones could reach no higher than three for the second straight year. Bob Dylan, on the other hand, had a marvellous comeback from his motorcycle mishap, spending 13 weeks at number one with *John Wesley Harding*.

Tom Jones had 135 weeks on the chart, the highest total yet achieved in any calendar year. Otis Redding also broke the previous high, set by another aeroplane casualty, Jim Reeves, by tallying 121 weeks.

In the How Great Thou Were department, Elvis Presley only had one week on the chart in 1968, as did the George Mitchell Minstrels. Even the Mothers Of Invention did better than both of them put together.

1969

For the third time the Beatles began and ended a year with different albums at number one. Their double LP *The Beatles* ushered 1969 in and *Abbey Road* showed it out. The 11 straight weeks the latter disc spent on top just before Christmas was the longest consecutive stint by any record since *Sergeant Pepper*. *Abbey Road* returned in the last week of the year, marking the fifth occasion in 1969 when a former number one encored at that position. This statistic demonstrates the instability of the chart during these 12 months.

Familiar faces atop the heap included Bob Dylan, who successfully flirted with country music in *Nashville Skyline*, the Rolling Stones, who managed a week out front with *Let It Bleed*, and Elvis Presley, who scored a glorious comeback with *From Elvis In Memphis*. Other rock luminaries who led the list included Cream, whose farewell set *Goodbye* had three separate appearances at number one, the Moody Blues, who scored the first of their three toppers, and Jethro Tull, making their only stand-out stint with *Stand Up*.

But one cannot overlook the achievement of the easy listening mogul Ray Conniff, who spent three weeks ahead of the herd without the benefit of a hit single. Jim Reeves astonished all by registering the only number one of his career five years after his death. It should be noted, however, that his *According To My Heart* was a budget album.

Best Of The Seekers bested all competition on five separate occasions. The Australians had the most weeks on chart with a comparatively feeble total of 66, three ahead of Simon and Garfunkel, who tallied their total without the benefit of a new release.

One LP most chartologists might not have remembered as a number one which did get there was *Diana Ross And The Supremes Join The Temptations*. One LP most chartologists might have thought of as a number one which did not get there was the Who's rock opera *Tommy*, which had to settle for the second spot.

14

1970

Simon and Garfunkel were the mighty men of the new decade's first year. Britain's best-selling album of the seventies, *Bridge Over Troubled Water*, dominated the chart, spending 23 weeks at number one. The closest competitors, *Abbey Road* and *Led Zeppelin III*, managed five weeks each. The S&G catalogue also sold handsomely in the wake of *Water*, giving the duo an astonishing 167 weeks on the chart in a single year, easily smashing Tom Jones' record of 135.

With the exception of the compilations *Motown Chartbusters Vol 3 & 4* and the Christmas number one, *Andy Williams' Greatest Hits*, every chart-topper was by a rock artist. The Beatles began their break-up year with *Abbey Road* and parted with their spring smash *Let It Be*. Fab Four fans obviously didn't want to say goodbye, buying enough various Beatle albums to give the group 122 weeks in the chart, the highest total of any year in their career. In parallel fashion, the greatest American star of the sixties, Bob Dylan, also had his last two number one LPs in 1970, *Self Portrait* and *New Morning*.

It was a banner year for what was then called progressive music. The Moody Blues had a number one and an admirable 115 weeks on the chart. Led Zeppelin flew over all followers with both *II* and *III*. Pink Floyd exploded with a real mother, *Atom Heart Mother*, and Black Sabbath won hosannas for heavy metal with their powerful *Paranoid*.

The outstanding performance by an artist in a supporting role was by Johnny Cash. Though he did not get to number one, the former Sun star did notch up 125 weeks on the chart as four albums entered on the heels of his phenomenally successful *Johnny Cash At San Quentin*.

1971

Bridge Over Troubled Water was the outstanding album of yet another year, accumulating 17 weeks at number one, more than any other title. It was the only LP to appear on every one of the year's weekly tabulations.

Simon and Garfunkel works spent a total of 102 weeks on the chart during 1971, a sum exceeded only by the product of the prolific Andy Williams. The long-time hit-maker was at the peak of his career courtesy of his popular television series, and two different titles, *Greatest Hits* and *Home Loving Man*, reached number one for him during the 12-month period. No other artist had more than one chart-topper this year, although three lots of uncredited session singers and instrumentalists did go all the way with budget compilations of cover versions. If anyone was involved with more than one of these productions, they have wisely remained silent.

Two ex-Beatles fronted the flock with solo albums, Paul McCartney with *Ram* and John Lennon with *Imagine*, though additional credits were given to Linda McCartney and the Plastic Ono Band, respectively. *Sticky Fingers*, the Rolling Stones' first effort on their eponymous label, gave them a one-for-one record. They continued their 100 per cent performance until their 1974 issue, *It's Only Rock And Roll*, only hit number two.

The Stones' competitors for the title of the World's Greatest Live Rock and Roll Band, the Who, scored their only chart-topper ever, *Who's Next*, while after a year of dominating the singles scene T. Rex managed an album number one in *Electric Warrior*. Other acts enjoying outstanding years included Led Zeppelin, Rod Stewart, James Taylor, and the veteran Frank Sinatra. Only the *My Way* man and Elvis Presley were still going strong from the original crew of 1958.

1972

Marc Bolan and a load of other people dominated the album charts in 1972. The T. Rex phenomenon was a manifestation of genuine fan fervour. The appearance of five Various Artist LPs at number one was a triumph of marketing.

The year began with *Electric Warrior* retaining the top spot. In May a double re-issue, *My People Were Fair . . . /Prophets Seers And Sages*, grabbed the glory for a week, bearing the original label credit of Tyrannosaurus Rex. That an artist's old material released under an obsolete name could get to number one indicated the

15

frenzied following T. Rex had at the time. The following set, *Bolan Boogie*, also went all the way.

Bolan's boys were one of four attractions to spend between 80 and 90 weeks on the chart in 1972. Cat Stevens did best with 89 in a year when no one hit the century.

Rod Stewart had his second good year as *Never A Dull Moment* went to number one and *Every Picture Tells A Story* continued a long run. These were the first two of six consecutive toppers by the leader of the Faces. That group's *A Nod's As Good As A Wink* reached the second slot in 1972, narrowly missing an unusual double for Stewart.

No artist had ever scored number ones as a soloist and a group member in the same year, though Cliff Richard had made it on his own and with the Shadows backing him. Paul Simon came close, touching the top with his solo debut in 1972, but *Bridge Over Troubled Water* had, by then, finished making occasional appearances at number one.

Outside of the *Concert For Bangladesh* triple album, the Various Artists compilations that led the list for 27 weeks, over half the year, were assembled by marketing firms for television advertising. This innovation in merchandising started a packaging trend that has stayed strong ever since. Sales of this type of disc generally offered no indication of how popular taste in music was changing, as success was attributable to the impact of the commercial rather than the music itself.

16

1973

avid Bowie and Max Bygraves have never shared the concert stage, but they certainly were together in the 1973 album charts. The innovatory space rocker had six hit LPs that year, the singalong star five. Two of Bowie's efforts, *Aladdin Sane* and *Pin Ups*, were number ones, while the resuscitated *Hunky Dory* soared to three. Bygraves scored three Top Ten entries with his everybody-join-in approach to medleys of old favourites.

The Rise And Fall Of Ziggy Stardust And The Spiders From Mars had broken Bowie big in 1972. Now he ruled the album chart, accumulating an unprecedented 182 weeks on the list during 1973 with six different titles. This sum shattered the mark of 167 weeks set by Simon and Garfunkel in 1970. Ironically, the defunct duo still managed to total 104 weeks in 1973, three years after their break-up, with the potent pairing of *Greatest Hits* and *Bridge Over Troubled Water.*

The siblings from the States, the Carpenters, managed 88 weeks in the list to tie Max Bygraves for third, though the positions reached were less impressive. Elton John and Slade both achieved two number ones, Gilbert O'Sullivan his only one and Roxy Music their first. Rod Stewart nabbed one as a soloist and another as a member of the Faces, completing the odd double that had eluded him in 1972.

Perhaps the most telling statistic of the year is that 20 different albums reached number one. This new high suggested that even the outstanding artists were not dominating the charts as firmly as in the sixties, and that marketing departments had learned how to achieve great sales in a limited time period.

1974

Two artists who were already strong in 1973, the Carpenters and Elton John, surged in 1974. Richard and Karen accumulated 17 weeks at number one in four summit visits with *The Singles 1969–73*, the highest total since *Bridge Over Troubled Water*. The bespectacled pianist, who had scored two number ones the previous 12 months, bagged another brace this time, reigning with *Caribou* and the Christmas number one *Elton John's Greatest Hits*.

Another keyboard wizard did a double. For the second successive year the previously unknown feat of hitting the heights both as a soloist and a group member was achieved. Rick Wakeman's last album with Yes, *Tales From Topographic Oceans* was the year's first number one. That spring the synthesizer star topped the table again with his own *Journey To The Centre Of The Earth*.

Dramatic evidence that the albums and singles charts had grown far apart was offered in September. Mike Oldfield held the first two long-player disc positions with his new release, *Hergest Ridge*, and his 1973 classic, *Tubular Bells*. Simultaneously the Osmonds were at one and two in the seven-inch stakes with their own *Love Me For A Reason* and Donny and Marie's *I'm Leaving It All Up To You*. Oldfield and Osmonds – two more contrasting acts could hardly be imagined.

David Bowie narrowly nudged the Carpenters in the weeks on chart table in 1974, 107 to 106. In the process he picked up his third career number one, *Diamond Dogs*.

The Beatles were close behind with 104, thanks to the year-long persistence of their 1973 compilations, *1962–66* and *1967–70*. Paul McCartney was doubtless more pleased by the seven-week tenure at the top by Wings' *Band On The Run*.

17

1975

The album and singles charts showed greater similarities in 1975 than in the immediate past. The three best-selling singles of the year were by the Bay City Rollers, Rod Stewart and the Stylistics, and all three artists also achieved number one LPs. *Best Of The Stylistics* spent more weeks in the Top Ten than any other disc, a statistic that startles until one recalls it benefited from a mighty marketing campaign that included considerable television advertising.

Other greatest hits albums that went to the summit courtesy of blurbs on the box included anthologies by Perry Como, Engelbert Humperdinck, Tom Jones and Jim Reeves; mass appeal singers logically benefited most from mass advertising. The one collection that went to number one naturally as a result of the artist's current popularity rather than artificial stimulus was *Elton John's Greatest Hits*. By landing the laurels for the last five weeks of 1974 and the first five of 1975, the Pinner prodigy matched the Stylistics' ten weeks over two calendar years. Elton was out front on his own with his total of 105 weeks on the chart, approached only by the slow-to-fade Simon and Garfunkel, whose back catalogue stayed around for 100 more seven-day spells.

The year ended with Queen's *A Night At The Opera* ruling. It included the Christmas number one single, *Bohemian Rhapsody*. Status Quo, Led Zeppelin and Pink Floyd all lent the number one spot a heavier touch during the course of 1975. Max Boyce translated his Welsh superstardom into disc sales with the first ever comedy number one.

1976

B eware of Greeks bearing gift tokens. There must have been a lot of them about in 1976, because Demis Roussos came from out of the Aegean blue to spend more weeks in the album chart than any other artist. The man-mountain scaled the survey with two Top Five entries, *Happy To Be* and *Forever And Ever*, in reaching his total of 84 weeks, one more than Queen, two more than John Denver, and three more than Pink Floyd. Roussos also topped the singles chart with his *Roussos Phenomenon* EP, the first time an Extended Play disc triumphed in that table.

The low magnitude of the leading weeks on chart total suggests that no artist stood out as David Bowie had only recently. This was indeed the case, as only Led Zeppelin zapped two number ones in 1976, both of which stayed on top for only one week. Were there a trend it would appear to have been in Greatest Hits compilations, with number one packages coming from Perry Como, Roy Orbison, Slim Whitman, Abba, the Beach Boys, and Glen Campbell. The legendary guitar star Bert Weedon actually made it all the way with a set of other people's hits. This information should not suggest that Weedon, Whitman, Como, Campbell or even the Beach Boys were enjoying a renaissance in singles sales, merely that television advertising of the Greatest Hits LP had reached the peak of its success. Only the 11 weeks spent at number one by *Abba's Greatest Hits*, the highest sum of list leading weeks in 1976, reflected fame on 45. Indeed, the Super Swedes were enjoying their best year on the singles chart.

Rock Follies and *Stupidity* (by Dr Feelgood) both reached the top without benefit of a hit single. For *Rock Follies* the feat was doubly distinctive: the Andy Mackay–Howard Schuman score was the first television soundtrack ever to top the album chart.

18

1977

M arketing was the main matter when it came to getting to number one in 1977. Clever campaigns, with a heavy emphasis on television advertising, succeeded in helping several artists who had gone cold back to glory.

Slim Whitman, who had registered one hit single in 20 years, was once again brilliantly promoted to the premier long-player position by United Artists marketing. The Beatles had their first weeks of supremacy since *Let It Be* with an extremely after-the-fact live album. Connie Francis and Bread, both of whom had fallen flat for some time, had number one compilations. The roll call of artists who vaulted to Valhalla with TV anthologies reads like a Hall of Fame: Johnny Mathis, Elvis Presley, Cliff Richard, Diana Ross and the Supremes, the Shadows, and Frank Sinatra. By its very nature this plethora of platters could only be issued once, so 1977 was the peak of this kind of catalogue culling.

Abba were on top for a total of ten weeks, more than any other act or compilation. The Sex Pistols made history with their debut disc, *Never Mind The Bollocks Here's The Sex Pistols*, number one for two weeks in November despite some retail reluctance to display the provocative title. It was the first New Wave number one.

Pink Floyd bested Abba for most weeks on chart, 108 to 106, on the basis of their new number two, *Animals*, and their still-selling back list. In the year of his death Elvis Presley accumulated 95 weeks with an unprecedented 18 titles, almost all re-entries.

1978

Two film soundtracks proved it was still possible for albums to achieve lengthy runs at number one, television advertising campaigns and a diverging market notwithstanding. *Saturday Night Fever* stayed on top for 18 weeks, the longest uninterrupted reign since that of *Sergeant Pepper's Lonely Hearts Club Band*, and indeed there were fewer number one LPs in 1978, eight, than in any year since 1967, the time of the classic Beatles release.

Grease was the other movie megahit, spending 13 weeks atop the greasy pole. Since John Travolta starred in both films, one might assume he was on the number one for 31 weeks of the year, the most by any artist since the cast of *The Sound Of Music* achieved the same figure in 1966. But though Travolta was shown on the cover of *Fever*, earning a royalty, he did not figure in the music. The Bee Gees, whose tunes dominated the motion picture, did not appear on the screen. The real winner was the Robert Stigwood Organisation, which issued both films and discs.

Boney M, who enjoyed a pair of chart-topping singles in 1978, also enjoyed their most successful LP, *Night Flight To Venus*. Abba earned seven more number one weeks with *The Album* and managed 112 weeks on chart during the year, clearly outdistancing all competition. Fleetwood Mac's *Rumours*, America's top record of 1977, finally managed seven days at the summit in Britain.

19

1979

Nineteen different albums played musical chairs with the number one position in 1979, more than twice the total of toppers the previous year. No piece of product could compete with RSO's 1978 soundtracks in terms of length of stay there. *The Best Disco Album In The World*, a Warner Brothers compilation released at the height of the disco craze and supported by television advertising, managed the longest stint, six weeks. Indeed, Warners as a company may have been the sales star of the year, managing to place three consecutive number ones at the top in their first week of release. Certainly the artists involved – Led Zeppelin, Gary Numan and Boney M – could not have been appealing to the same buyers.

The real star performers of 1979 were Abba, Blondie and the Electric Light Orchestra. The first two names each achieved two number ones, spending totals of seven and five weeks ahead respectively. Gary Numan did nab one winner under his own name and another in his group identity, Tubeway Army, but each of those only stayed in the lead for one week.

ELO's mark of merit was the 112 weeks spent on the chart by their various albums, including the number one *Discovery*. The Jeff Lynne-led ensemble had their finest 12 months, enjoying four Top Ten singles as well. The only act to approach ELO in weeks on chart was Blondie with an exact century; Earth Wind and Fire trailed in third with 68.

Bat Out Of Hell by Meat Loaf and Jeff Wayne's *War Of The Worlds* each spent the entire year on the chart as they headed for two of the longest runs in recent times. Neither album ever reached number one, but both ultimately outsold almost every disc that did in 1979.

1980

Twenty-three different albums led the list at some point during 1980, the most in any single year to date. The number one position was like New England's fabled weather: if you didn't like it, you could stick around for an hour and it would change. Johnny Mathis, Genesis and Rose Royce appeared in quick succession, and if the rapid variation from easy listening to rock to soul wasn't enough for the catholic consumer, Sky followed with a kind of classical and pop hybrid that was impossible to categorise.

With more number one albums in a year than David Bowie has had images in a career, staying in front for even a month was an achievement. The Pretenders made it with their eponymous debut disc, and Roxy Music were champs for four weeks in two stints with *Flesh And Blood*. The star performers of the year were Police and Abba. The Bleach Boys had their second number one LP, *Zenyatta Mondatta*, and scored 116 on chart in total, far in front of the 70-week sum of runner-up AC/DC. The Scandinavian sensations once again had chart-toppers early and late in a year, registering in January with *Greatest Hits Volume 2* and beginning a nine-week rule in November with *Super Trouper*.

An extremely odd circumstance characterised the spring. For the entire season, albums had two-week runs at number one and were then replaced. Seven LPs were in the spring string. The previous record for consecutive two-week reigns had been a mere two, so this development was certainly curious if ultimately unimportant.

1981

To find the top album artists of 1981 one didn't have to look far beyond the letter 'A' in alphabetical browser bins. Abba began and ended the year at number one with *Super Trouper* and *The Visitors*, extending their string of chart-topping LPs to seven. Adam and the Ants were the breakout act of the year, accumulating 12 weeks at the very top with *Kings Of The Wild Frontier*, the longest leading stint. *Kings* was also one of five long players to stay the course for the entire year. It was joined by previous Adam material and the end-of-year release *Prince Charming* to give the Ants 87 weeks on the chart, a total topped only by Barry Manilow. The American balladeer bettered the Ant total by five weeks. Personal appearances and heavy promotion gave him a career peak in Britain several years after he had done his best at home.

One had to look hard to find evidence of the growth of technopop, the synthesized sound making great inroads in the singles market. *Dare* by the Human League was the nation's best-seller for one week, but this was before the fourth single from the set, *Don't You Want Me,* became the year's Christmas number one and propelled its parent back up the charts in 1982. Ultravox, important pioneers of technopop, re-entered for another 48 weeks with *Vienna* on the strength of the single of the same name.

There were oddities, as always. *The Royal Wedding* of Prince Charles to Lady Diana Spencer was number one for a fortnight, twice as long as Motorhead managed with their equally live *No Sleep Till Hammersmith*, but the Royals never challenged the heavy metal merchants to a battle of the bands.

1982

Remember my name', Irene Cara advised in the title tune of the film *Fame*, 'I'm gonna live forever.' Well, almost. *Fame* itself proved to be more enduring than any of the young people in it.

When the BBC began broadcasting the American television series *Fame*, a spin-off from the Alan Parker movie, Cara's original version of the song, a US hit in 1980, zoomed to the top of the UK singles chart. It was actually only the beginning of a phenomenon.

BBC Records' *The Kids From Fame* television cast collection proceeded to lead the list itself. Fuelled by two Top Ten singles, this album sold over 850,000 copies by December, surpassing even the previous year's *Royal Wedding* to become the BBC's best-selling long player.

RCA had leased the album because BBC1 could only plug vinyl with the BBC label, and they needed to establish the singing actors as a recording act. Mission accomplished, RCA issued a second TV platter, *The Kids From Fame Again*, and this also made the Top Three.

The sales success of the *Kids From Fame* was peculiar to Britain. In contrast, the only LP that outsold theirs in the UK in 1982 was by a worldwide star. *Love Songs* by Barbra Streisand was the year's best seller. That it did so well was perhaps surprising, since it was a make-do collection with only two new songs assembled in lieu of new product.

ABC distinguished themselves by spending their first-ever week on the chart at number one with *The Lexicon Of Love*. The debut marked another first, the initial joint number one on the album chart. *The Lexicon Of Love* shared the spotlight with – yes – *Fame*.

21

1983

Two of the greatest stars of the early seventies stood out this year, but whereas one, David Bowie, had already set album chart standards, Michael Jackson had previously been best known as a singles artist. He managed to reach number five in 1979 with *Off The Wall*, his solo album start on Epic, but nothing prepared the world for what happened in 1983.

Thriller first entered the sweepstakes in December 1982, but by the end of its first month of release had only climbed to 15. It was only with the release of the second single from the set, *Billie Jean*, that the platter peaked. It went all the way three times for a total of seven weeks and was the year's best seller. Michael enjoyed three further weeks at number one when Motown's repackaged *18 Greatest Hits* proved popular during the summer. The llama lover totalled 123 weeks on chart.

This year, however, David Bowie achieved a total eclipse of the chart, setting a new mark with 198. This staggering sum beat his old record of 182, established a full decade earlier in 1973. Nearly all his success this year came in the wake of *Let's Dance*, which entered at number one. Thirteen Bowie titles in all appeared in the 53 charts of 1983. Ten Bowie albums were in the week of 16 July, the year's greatest monopoly.

Phil Collins racked up 78 weeks on chart on his own and also did very well with Genesis. Meat Loaf followed closely with 76. Mighty sales figures were accumulated by Paul Young and Lionel Richie. Richard Clayderman, the French pianist cleverly promoted in both print and television, enjoyed two of the year's Top 100 and amassed 66 weeks on chart. He was far and away 1983's most successful instrumentalist.

Thirteen of the year's 20 top albums were by groups. Culture Club were number one for five weeks with *Colour By Numbers* and *Men At Work* toiled the same time at the top with *Business As Usual*. Duran Duran only managed one week ahead of the field with *Seven And The Ragged Tiger* but did stockpile 105 weeks on chart, more than any group save Dire Straits, who garnered 107 without issuing any new material. Twenty-three different titles reached number one during 1983, more than in any previous calendar year.

Bonnie Tyler was the only female artist to spend even a single week ahead of the field, though Alison 'Alf' Moyet was the featured vocalist with two-week champs Yazoo. Barbra Streisand was the woman winner in weeks on chart with 57, but most of these were the final flings of 1982's list leader, *Love Songs*. The most noteworthy variety of female achievement from a chart-watcher's point of view was the faddish popularity of a new form – the workout album. Two of the year's Top 100 were of this sort, *Jane Fonda's Workout Record* and Felicity Kendal's *Shape Up And Dance (Volume 1)*. Jackie Genova also charted with an exercise exemplar.

1984

The face that dominated music advertising on television in George Orwell's dreaded year turned out not to be Big Brother but a pig. The porker was the meaty mascot of the EMI/Virgin anthologies *Now That's What I Call Music*. The first *Now* ended 1983 and began 1984 at number one. The second moved into the sty in the sky in April and the third checked in during August. The three double albums spent a total of 15 of the year's 52 weeks on top, more than any individual act managed to achieve. *Now 4* did well enough in its mere month of release to be one of 1984's Top Ten but was kept out of number one by CBS/WEA's even more lucrative imitative compilation *The Hits Album/The Hits Tape*.

Television advertising also played a prominent part in the success of the longest-running number one of the year, the late Bob Marley and the Wailers' *Legend* (12 weeks). The top-selling album of 1984 was *Can't Slow Down* by Lionel Richie. Though it was only number one for a fortnight it was near the top most of the year. The Motown marvel was one of an astonishing seven albums to stay on the chart for the entire year along with *Can't Slow Down*, Michael Jackson's *Thriller*, Paul Young's *No Parlez*, Meat Loaf's *Bat Out Of Hell*, Queen's *Greatest Hits* and U2's *Live: Under A Blood Red Sky*.

Billy Joel had the most albums on chart in a single week, six. Nik Kershaw managed two of the year's Top 50, Elton John two of the Top 100. Michael Jackson had a trio of best sellers, *Off The Wall* continuing its revival and *18 Greatest Hits* being a compilation shared with the Jackson Five. Jackson wound up with 136 weeks on chart. He was the year's top weekly act.

Other groups with noteworthy performances included U2, who totalled an even 100 weeks on chart; Queen, who had two of the year's Top 50; and Wham!, whose *Make It Big* was one of the year's Top Five. The Smiths scored two Top Tens on the independent Rough Trade label and *Welcome To The Pleasuredome* by Frankie Goes To Hollywood gave ZTT its first week at number one.

It was not a great year for female soloists. None reached number one, though women did make the top spot as members of Eurythmics and the Thompson Twins. Sade had the biggest seller by a woman, *Diamond Life*, while Elaine Paige had two of the year's Top 100. Barbra Streisand accumulated 67 weeks on chart to lead the ladies.

Instrumentalists fared poorly. Richard Clayderman was the only non-vocalist in the year's Top 100. The independent compilation company Street Sounds attained 15 charters during the year. The devotional artist Bryn Yemm had three new albums in, more than any other British act. 1984 was itself a star. It was the first year to have three hit LPs named after it. The artists were Eurythmics, Van Halen and Rick Wakeman.

1985

The long distance runner wasn't lonely in 1985. Nine albums remained on the chart for the entire 52 weeks, and four acts accumulated totals in excess of 100 weeks on chart. Astonishing records were set. After a series of UK stadium dates Bruce Springsteen placed his entire catalogue of seven albums in the Top 50. Never before had an artist with that large a body of work got the lot that high. Springsteen finished the year with a total of 177 weeks on chart, the third-best figure ever. *Born In The USA* was one of the nine discs that saw the year through. It wound up the number four seller of 1985. Competing with the Boss for the title of Male Artist of the Year, Phil Collins finished with fewer weeks on chart, a still spectacular 131, but managed to nab the number two spot of the year-end tabulation with *No Jacket Required*.

Madonna was clearly the female artist of 1985; her *Like A Virgin* (the third best-selling set of the year) and her retitled first album both entered the Top 50. As noteworthy as her own success was the extremely strong showing by female artists in general. Seven of the year's Top 20 were either by female soloists or outfits with female vocalists. Sade's two albums both finished in the Top 20.

Dire Straits and U2 vied for Group of Year honours. Mark Knopfler's lot put in a special claim with the year's number one, *Brothers In Arms*. 1985 was the third successive year in which Dire Straits exceeded 100 weeks on chart, a feat previously performed only by Simon and Garfunkel. During the three-year period 1983–85, Mark's men leapt from 33rd to 8th on the all-time list. Despite their achievements they were slightly pipped in weeks on chart by U2, 168 to 158. The Irish band were also on a prolonged hot streak, having vaulted from 20 to 375 weeks on chart in three years.

Richard Clayderman retained his laurels as leading solo instrumentalist, but James Last bounced back as the top orchestra. It was also a good year for what might be called up-market material, with Andrew Lloyd Webber's *Requiem*, Leonard

Bernstein's operatic version of *West Side Story* and the Anderson/Rice/Ulvaeus *Chess* all in 1985's Top 100.

The most successful broadcasting and charity event of all time, Live Aid, achieved another distinction as the single happening that has most influenced the album chart. In the 27 July chart nine albums by acts in the concert re-entered the Top 100, four after a long absence, and 21 previously peaked packages suddenly surged.

The craze of 1984, the TV compilations of recent and current hits, abated only slightly, with three EMI/Virgin *Now* packages in the year-end Top Ten and two CBS/WEA *Hits* collections in the Top 20.

Meat Loaf's *Bat Out Of Hell* fell from favour, but still managed to add 31 weeks on chart to equal *The Sound Of Music* as the all-time longest-running chart LP.

1986

Were there a pinball machine of the album chart it would have tilted this year as Dire Straits amassed an unprecedented 217 listed weeks, an average of over four placings per week.

That *Brothers In Arms* was the year's number two in sales, slipping down just one place from 1985's top spot, was remarkable enough. That Mark Knopfler's band was so popular that a substantial part of Dire Straits' back catalogue resided in the best sellers was astounding.

There was another artist, however, who accounted for three of the Top 100 of 1986. Madonna sold stacks of all three of her releases, and *True Blue* was the year's number one. All told she spent 125 weeks on chart, by far the highest figure ever achieved by a woman. 1985 debutante Whitney Houston's first album was 1986's number five set of the year.

In the rich-get-richer category old friends Phil Collins and Queen excelled themselves, Collins moving up to third in the annual weeks on chart listing. Though his total fell from 131 to 113 he made amends by sharing Genesis' 28 weeks. Queen broke through the century mark for the first time while staying in the Top Ten artists list for the third consecutive year. Paul Simon's *Graceland* was the year's number four.

Madonna and Collins were the only two solo artists in the year-end weeks on chart Top Ten. The LP list seemed the province of the big groups in 1986, with Simple Minds enjoying their biggest year and U2 finishing in the charmed circle for the fourth year in succession, even though they had no new issues. Talking Heads put in their finest career outing, while A-Ha and Five Star cut impressive figures in their first full year of activity. The *Now* and *Hits* series stayed strong.

1987

Whatever you thought of the charts in 1987, you had to agree it was a *Bad* year. Lightning struck a second time for Michael Jackson as he once again achieved a year-end number one. The main difference was that whereas the champ of 1983, *Thriller*, had started slowly in 1982 and grown gradually, *Bad* was a massive number one in its first week and retained its edge to finish several lengths in front. The new set was only the second package in history to debut at number one in both the UK and US charts. The first was another of this year's giants, *Whitney*, which wound up at number three for 1987.

Bad, in contrast, seemed to pose no threat to *Thriller*, far and away the most successful LP ever released. Its global sales at about 40 million were well ahead of the immediate runners-up, including *Rumours* by Fleetwood Mac, but that 1977 phenomenon had its own reason to celebrate ten years later. During the course of 1987 it overtook *Bat Out Of Hell* to become the longest runner in chart chronicles.

The reappearance of *Rumours* can be largely attributed to the continued growth of the compact disc market which gave a new lease of life to many classic albums. Collectors who already had black vinyl copies bought CD versions for their superior sound. The Beatles benefited most clearly from this. All of their original studio sets were issued on CD in 1987, and all charted. The 20th anniversary of *Sergeant Pepper's Lonely Hearts Club Band* attracted massive media attention and boosted the classic package back to the Top Three.

Though Madonna did not have one of the year's Top Ten sellers she was the most charted artist of 1987, her albums making 127 appearances. This tally exceeded the record for a female artist she herself set only the previous year.

U2 and Queen followed the champ with 126 and 117 weeks respectively, both continuing their lengthy run of strong showings and improving on their fine 1986 figures. Dire Straits did well, too, their 84 weeks giving them a career total of exactly 900, the top total of acts still recording.

The Phantom Of The Opera made history by becoming the first original cast recording to top the UK chart. In this respect *My Fair Lady* may have been unlucky. In the very first chart of 1958 and peaking at number two, it may have been a number one had its earlier sales been tabulated.

1988

For the sixth consecutive year the three acts with the most weeks on chart totalled at least 100. Seven of 1988's ten top stars had been in the charmed circle before, six of them the previous year. Michael Jackson, who paced the pack with 116 weeks, was returning to the leaders for the first time since 1984.

Jacko's joyride came courtesy of *Bad*, on the chart all year, and a variety of back items including *Thriller* and Motown repackages. In his case the progress from one year to the next looked like a week-to-week sequence, with 1987's number one slipping two places to number three on the 1988 year end tally. *Bad* was constantly in the public eye thanks to Jackson's personal appearances at open air venues and a steady stream of hit singles. The promotion paid off. Britain was the one major country where *Bad* outsold *Thriller*, and the artist topped the table of weeks on chart for the first time.

The second-place finishers on both the sales and weeks on chart list were vinyl veterans. Cliff Richard, who had the year's number one single, *Mistletoe And Wine*, also had the runner-up album, *Private Collection*. It was the first time he had finished in the top two in both chart categories. Fleetwood Mac, who had undergone a telephone book's worth of personnel changes since their album chart breakthrough in 1968, scored their first annual century with 107 weeks, second only to Jackson. They, too, were helped by touring, and scored two of the year's 30 best sellers, *Tango In The Night* and *Greatest Hits*. The Pet Shop Boys were the third act to accumulate 100 weeks on chart, doing best with *Introspective*.

In addition to the two groups mentioned above, U2, Dire Straits, Whitney Houston and Luther Vandross repeated in the year's Top Ten acts. Whitney now had 200 weeks on chart with only two albums for an astonishing average of 100 weeks per release. This was still unlikely to impress U2 and Dire Straits, who continued their winning ways and seemed to guarantee they would finish ahead of Queen as the top album acts of the eighties.

The most amazing achievement by a new artist belonged to Kylie Minogue. Before January 1988 she had never released an album in Britain. At the end of the year she had the top title of the 12 months, *Kylie*. This was the first time a solo artist had scored the year's top seller with a debut disc. The teen market didn't just support Stock–Aitken–Waterman acts. The fresh-faced trio Bros wound up at number four with their debut issue, *Push*. Another new act who came in the Top Ten sellers in famous fashion was Tracy Chapman, whose career took off after she appeared before a live global television audience at the Nelson Mandela Birthday Concert.

Compilations took up so many of the top positions in the album chart that the industry decided they would be segregated in future and have their own list in 1989. This meant that the performance of the *Now! That's What I Call Music* series in placing editions 11, 12 and 13 in the year-end top 15 would never be repeated. Even compilation soundtracks like the phenomenal *Dirty Dancing* would be separated out. As the year ended observers wondered if new artists would actually benefit from the new order, in which product by individual acts would overnight chart higher than it would have in 1988. Would the illusion of success become a reality?

1989

The cosy feeling old friends gave the album chart in 1988 was displaced by the excitement of new acquaintances a year later. Jason Donovan, a co-star of Kylie Minogue on television's soap opera *Neighbours*, repeated his fellow Australian's feat of having the best-selling LP of the year with a premiere performance. His *Ten Good Reasons* outshone even Simply Red's long-burning *A New Flame*.

The continued shift in sales from singles to albums was dramatically underscored this year when four LPs but no 45s sold over a million copies. Including sales in all configurations, the year's number one single, *Ride On Time* by Black Box, managed 849,116 units. *Ten Good Reasons* shifted 1,450,500. Indeed, the seven top albums of the year outsold every single. It was thus important financially as well as for image that the young Stock-Aitken-Waterman favourites did well on both sides. Kylie and Jason were each in the 1989 Top Ten on both charts, with Miss Minogue enjoying the year's number six album, *Enjoy Yourself*.

Kylie was one of eight acts to finish in the year's Top Ten acts who had not been in the previous list. Recalling that in 1988 only four names were non-repeaters gives an indication of the progress of new talent in 1989. Guns N' Roses made the most impressive showing, leading the lot with 85 weeks on chart. This figure, achieved by *Appetite For Destruction* and *GN'R Lies*, was admittedly below the century, the first time since 1982 that the year's top tally was short of 100. Nonetheless it was a major achievement for a heavy metal act. Strong sellers in this genre had traditionally opened strongly and faded quickly.

Erasure finished second in the weeks-on-chart sweepstakes, moving up from fourth the year before. Third in the table was what might be called a veteran newcomer, Gloria Estefan. In a masterful piece of public relations her group Miami Sound Machine groomed her as its focal point and then gave her joint and finally sole billing. The strategy succeeded spectacularly with the year's number four seller *Anything For You* by Gloria Estefan and Miami Sound Machine, and the number five, *Cuts Both Ways*, credited merely to Gloria Estefan.

Another notable newcomer to the top acts list was the Scottish band Deacon Blue, who finished fourth. Bobby Brown, 1989's top singles star, made his album table bow at number ten. The late Roy Orbison experienced a phenomenal posthumous comeback, appearing in the Top Ten acts list for the first time since 1964. A quarter of a century was by far the longest gap between visits to this charmed circle.

The fastest-selling work in 1989 was released late in the year. Phil Collins' . . . *But Seriously* managed to chalk up sales of over one million in only six weeks, beginning a long run at number one and setting itself up for continued chart domination in early 1990. Here was a case where the change of decades would be bridged by a single strong record. This had not been the case when the 70s met the 80s, when Greatest Hits acts by Abba and Rod Stewart took turns at the top. The *South Pacific* film soundtrack had welded 1959 and 1960 together, and the Beatles' *Abbey Road* had both seen out 1969 and welcomed 1970. . . . *But Seriously* now joined these giants.

1990

Classic stars and classical music dominated 1990. Phil Collins spent a further ten weeks at number one at the beginning of the year with his late 1989 smash . . . *But Seriously*. Its total of 15 weeks at the top was the thirteenth longest run at number one in chart history. . . . *But Seriously* remained on the register all year long and wound up 1990's best seller. Collins had another of the year's Top Ten, *Serious Hits Live*, and discs by the singing drummer from Genesis spent more weeks on chart (85) than those of any other artist.

Collins was the outstanding male star to have dominated the field. Elton John was the only other artist to have two of the year's ten best sellers. His *Very Best Of Elton John* and *Sleeping With The Past* were both number ones, making him the only act to have two chart toppers in 1990.

Luciano Pavarotti followed with $1^{1}/3$ number ones, pacing the pack with his own *Essential Pavarotti* and as one of the 'three tenors' *In Concert*. José Carreras and Placido Domingo joined the inimitable Italian on the latter live recording. It was the first time three chart acts had joined forces to achieve a number one album as a trio. Jazzmen Kenny Ball, Chris Barber and Acker Bilk had gone to the top in 1962, but this was before Ball had charted on his own. By beating *In Concert* to number one with his own compilation, Luciano Pavarotti became the first classical artist to achieve a number one.

The top instrumentalist of the year was Nigel Kennedy, whose performance of Vivaldi's *Four Seasons* gave him the year's twelfth best seller and was the main factor in his finishing fourth on the most weeks on chart list. His total of 66 was the highest ever by a classical artist.

The year's stand-out female star, Madonna, added to her historic achievements. Her *Immaculate Collection* was 1990's number two in sales. By leading the list for the last six weeks of the year, she took her career total to 16 weeks in pole position, overtaking Barbra Streisand as the woman with the most weeks at number one. Various Madonna titles accumulated 53 weeks on chart to regain for her the distinction as most charted woman that she had last enjoyed in 1987. Tina Turner shared her weeks on chart total, thanks to the long-running *Foreign Affair*, but trailed her in sales.

UB40 were the group with most weeks on chart, due in large measure to *Labour Of Love II*, but they were surpassed in sales by the Carpenters. Richard and Karen's *Only Yesterday* was one of the year's ten best sellers. The success of this catalogue promotion surprised the music business, especially since much of the material had been included in the 1974 number one *The Singles 1969–73*. The seven-week list-leading leasehold of *Only Yesterday* moved the Carpenters to a tie with Cliff Richard for eighth position on the most weeks at number one list.

David Bowie also made noteworthy career progress. *ChangesBowie* was his seventh album to enter the chart at number one. Nobody else had debuted at the top as often. Bowie moved into a three-way tie for fifth in the most number one albums category.

Special note should be taken of the achievement of Michael Bolton, whose *Soul Provider* never got higher than number four in any weekly chart, yet finished fifth for the year. In contrast, Prince was number one first week out with *Graffiti Bridge*, yet didn't even finish in the top 75 sellers of 1991. The American number one of the year, MC Hammer's *Please Hammer Don't Hurt 'Em*, was Britain's number 36, as good evidence as any that the massive sales enjoyed by rap artists in the US were not being duplicated in the UK.

1991

The brightest stars this year were the ones in the title of Simply Red's album, the best seller of the year and their fourth top two hit in as many releases. As exciting as the achievements of Mick Hucknall's group were, with *Stars* enjoying a long Top Five run and returning to number one as *A New Flame* had done two years earlier, Simply Red could not be said to have loomed large over the year. No act did. The weeks on chart winner for 1991, Michael Bolton, amassed the lowest total, 63, since Elvis Presley triumphed with 51 in 1960.

Whereas both Phil Collins and Elton John had each scored two of the year's Top Ten sellers in 1990, no artist achieved the feat in the following 12 months. Queen came closest, with three out of the Top 40. Even before Freddie Mercury's death the quartet had tallied two number ones this calendar year, making them the only act to have more than one. *Innuendo* led the list for a fortnight in February and *Greatest Hits II* debuted at number one in November. The double gave Queen a career total of eight number ones, the third highest total in history, tying them with Abba and Led Zeppelin behind the Beatles (12) and the Rolling Stones (9).

Greatest Hits II returned to the top after Mercury passed away and stayed there through the holidays for a total of five weeks as head of the hits. It was the second highest figure for the year, Eurythmics' *Greatest Hits* having been number one for ten weeks. The latter disc was the year's best seller until the holiday period, when it was finally eclipsed by *Stars*.

Simply Red, Eurythmics and Queen had 1991's best sellers, but other groups merited attention. Roxette had most weeks on chart by a duo or group (62), just one shy of Michael Bolton's winning figure. After their first half-dozen chart albums peaked short of the Top Ten, R.E.M. got lucky with number seven, going all the way with *Out Of Time* and winding up with one of the Top Ten of the year. The Doors broke on through with four items when Oliver Stone's film biography of Jim Morrison was released.

The year's greatest chart disappointments were also most registered by groups. Simple Minds and U2 broke their strings of consecutive number one releases at four and three, respectively. Dire Straits opened at number one with *On Every Street*, but its solitary seven days at the summit were a fleeting moment compared to the 14 weeks their preceding studio set, *Brothers In Arms*, had enjoyed.

The only one of 1990's Top Ten to repeat in 1991 was Madonna's *Immaculate Collection*. She again accumulated the most weeks on chart by a female artist. However, in a reversal of their 1990 two-woman race, Tina Turner outsold her, with *Simply The Best* finishing the year at number four, the best showing by any soloist. Cher was also in the year-end Top Ten. She nabbed the first number one of her 26-year chart career, *Love Hurts*.

The memory of the slow start by *Thriller* warned one from hasty judgment of Michael Jackson's work, but it certainly appeared from its first five weeks on the market that *Dangerous* was truly in peril compared to its immediate predecessors. After debuting at number one the set made way for the return of *Queen's Greatest Hits II*. By Christmas Jackson had the odd distinction of also being outsold by another Michael – Crawford.

No instrumentalists were in the year-end Top 50. Luciano Pavarotti was there with *Essential Pavarotti II* and as part of the 'three tenors' *In Concert*. For the second consecutive year Michael Bolton had one of the year's Top Ten sellers without ever getting to number one. Proving that there are always new records to be set, *Circle Of One* by Oleta Adams was the first album to re-enter the chart at number one.

1992

This year cash registers joined the lead vocalists of rock bands in singing. Seventies groups, eighties outfits and newly emerging bands came together to give metal music in various forms its greatest domination of the weeks on chart table to date.

The leader of the list was Queen, who tallied 128 weeks on chart with various titles. The reason for their resurgence was, of course, the death in December 1991 of front man Freddie Mercury. Public affection for him and respect for the group could not be overestimated. There have been several tragic demises in rock history, but one has to go back to 1964 to find a deceased artist leading the weeks on chart list. In that instance the star, Jim Reeves, presented a very different form of material, country and western. It is worth noting that the top American star of the early nineties, Garth Brooks, specialised in a genre of modern country that did not initially make a massive impact in Britain.

With their 1992 performance Queen moved to within a tiara's distance of the King, Elvis Presley, for fourth place in the all-time most weeks on chart list. They had managed to rank that high in the countdown without ever having previously topped the 12-month table. Despite being dead for 15 years Presley was still putting up a good fight, scoring yet another posthumous hit.

The special and sad circumstances of Queen's success did not keep any particular pop singer from leading the list. The number two act was another rock band, Guns N' Roses, who accumulated 121 weeks in the tally they had led in 1989 with a mere 85. Their *Use Your Illusion II* slightly outperformed *Use Your Illusion I*, mainly because, at the time of their original release in late 1991, the second set had included a track that had recently been a Top Three single, 'You Could Be Mine'. Top Ten singles from the two albums continued to be issued during 1992.

There were four other rock acts in the year-end Top Ten. U2 returned to the list for the first time since 1989. R.E.M. climbed to seventh from their 1991 debut position of ten. Nirvana brought the Seattle sound to the UK in blissful fashion with *Nevermind* in the best sellers list all 53 chart weeks of the year. Genesis also saw the year through with their number one hit *We Can't Dance*. Simple Minds did not finish in the Top Ten for weeks on chart but were in the Top Ten for sales, with their *Glittering Prize 81–92* winding up the year's number four.

The top-selling disc of the year was *Stars* by Simply Red. For the first time in history, one album managed to be the best seller of two consecutive years. Back catalogue sales gave the group 77 weeks on chart, the third-highest total behind Queen and Guns N' Roses. Simply Red were one of seven acts with a figure higher than Michael Bolton's 1991 winning total of 63.

Bolton was not inactive in 1992, finishing at seven in the sales survey with *Timeless (The Classics)*, but he could not beat the top two male vocalists of the year, who had both begun their careers at Motown. Lionel Richie was still there, returning from a six-year break with a case study of making a little go a long way. *Back To Front*, a collection of greatest hits with new material, was the second-highest selling album of the year and his first number one since 1984. Michael Jackson's *Dangerous* was the year's number five in sales. He did outdistance Richie in terms of weeks on chart, as his other albums contributed to his constant presence.

Anyone guessing the identity of the top female vocalist of the year would probably have started with Annie Lennox, whose award-winning *Diva* was a number one that sold well enough to finish as the year's number six hit and even returned to the top spot after a half-year absence. Enya would also be a reasonable guess, as she was the woman with the most weeks on chart. However, the actual best-selling female artist was Cher, whose *Greatest Hits* was the third biggest record of the year. It was a comment on her star status in Britain that this CD was not a factor in America, just as 'The Shoop Shoop Song' was a number one in the UK and not even a Top 20 hit in the US.

Every year produces its own oddities. 1992 was the tenth anniversary of Madness' only number one album, *Complete Madness*, so it was appropriate they should come out of retirement to visit the top spot again with another compilation, *Divine Madness*. Abba also managed the ten-year trick with *Gold*, their first number one since 1982's *The Singles – The First Ten Years*.

One had to go back even further for the first half of Mike Oldfield's feat. *Tubular Bells II* was the number one follow-up to his 1973 original, which had reached the top the following year after the success of *Hergest Ridge*. The 18-year gap between a number one album and its number one sequel was by far the longest time between chart-topping numerically-related albums of original material. Indeed, the only previous such exercise in titles to result in a brace of number ones, *Rolling Stones* and *Rolling Stones No. 2*, involved only a seven-month wait.

1993

M eat Loaf swooped like a bat out of chart hell this year, scoring his first number one in a dozen years. *Bat Out Of Hell II – Back Into Hell* was the official sequel to the 1978 classic *Bat Out Of Hell* and reached the top spot denied the original. (Although many trivia contest competitors might be caught out on this point, Meat Loaf's only previous number one was *Dead Ringer*.) *Bat Out Of Hell II* overtook hits from earlier in the year, including the leading compilation, *The Bodyguard*, to become the best-selling title of 1993. The *Bat* man also rejuvenated sales of his back catalogue, with both the 15-year-old album and the anthology *Hits Out Of Hell* winding up in the year's Top 100 sellers.

Unusually for this era, the availability of the single 'I'd Do Anything For Love (But I Won't Do That)' on *Bat Out Of Hell II* did not seem to diminish sales of either CD. It has become customary for singles to plummet when they appear on album, but this one stayed at number one for seven weeks and gave Meat Loaf the number one single as well as album of the year.

The Meat treats all came in the final third of the year, but they still managed to combine for 58 weeks on chart. This total, the highest number for a male vocalist, was also achieved by works of Eric Clapton, most notably his *Unplugged* hit. R.E.M. continued their progress in the annual table, leading the list for the first time with 97 weeks. Their biggest hit was *Automatic For The People*, the year's second-best seller. By any account, R.E.M. were the leading group of 1993. Guns N' Roses and Nirvana were also repeaters from the previous year's winners' circle.

If one included Tina Turner, the leading female artist on this table, as a rock artist, then eight of the top ten, indeed eight of the top nine, were of this musical style. This was the greatest domination any musical style had achieved in the weeks on chart computation. When one considers that the ninth act in the top nine was Abba, charting strictly with collections of old hits, one could be excused for thinking that rock was the only form of music that was selling. In fact considerable sales were being enjoyed by rave and other forms of dance music, but these were via anthologies that were listed in the compilation chart. Though they might be experiencing strong singles sales, most record makers in these styles were either not making albums or not selling them in large numbers.

Although Tina Turner was the first female in the weeks on chart list, several women enjoyed better-selling albums. Dina Carroll was a Top Ten stalwart with her debut disc, *So Close*, then number three hit of the year. Diana Ross came in fifth in the 1993 sales chart with *One Woman – The Ultimate Collection* and Mariah Carey anchored the Top Ten with *Music Box*. Annie Lennox managed another year in the best sellers with *Diva*, which climbed back to number one the week of 6 March. Twenty-five other discs had occupied the peak place since *Diva* debuted there on 18 April 1992, giving it the distinction of longest gap between weeks at number one.

Special note must be made of the achievement of Take That, who were the only act to place two titles in the Top 20. Simply Red earned further plaudits this year when their *Stars* passed the three million mark in sales. Cliff Richard won congratulations again when his new work debuted at number one, 32 years after his first appearance at the summit with *21 Today*. This was far and away the longest spread of number ones, although Cliff did appear to be running out of titles: the 1993 issue was simply called *The Album*.

An unusual feature of the album chart late in the year was the presence of two albums called *Duets*. Both releases, by Elton John and Frank Sinatra with various vocal partners, made the Top Five of the weekly chart, with Elton doing best overall. Several stars charted with *Unplugged* soundtracks from MTV programmes, though Rod Stewart had the wit to expand his title to include . . . *And Seated*.

1994

This year it was official: *Greatest Hits* is no longer a sufficiently imaginative title for a career retrospective. Seven of 1994's top 20 sellers were artist anthologies of hit singles, and none were merely called *Greatest Hits*. The number one of the year was *Cross Road – The Best Of Bon Jovi*, which held off *Carry On Up The Charts – The Best Of The Beautiful South*. Wet Wet Wet finished sixth for the year with their 1993 holdover hit *End Of Part One (Their Greatest Hits)*. This disc spurted to the top months after release when 'Love Is All Around', itself not on the album, became a long-running number one single.

Sting called his compilation *Fields Of Gold – The Best Of Sting*, Cyndi Lauper went for *Twelve Deadly Cyns . . . And Then Some*, and Deacon Blue chose *Our Town – Greatest Hits*. Cliff Richard needed neither dashes nor ellipsis dots to sell well with *The Hit List*.

Just missing the Top 20 of the year were two collections with the most intriguing titles of all. Diana Ross got dramatic with *One Woman – The Ultimate Collection*, while New Order were witty with *? (The Best Of)*. *Big Ones* was one big hit for Aerosmith and *Carnival Of Hits* rode the chart roller coaster for Judith Durham and the Seekers. When acts like the Seekers, who hadn't charted a new album since 1968, make the year-end Top 100, one senses the absence of a great number of important new releases.

Indeed, this was a year for new artists to develop out of the spotlight while veterans anthologised themselves. The CD that would win the Album of the Year Grammy Award in America was by Tony Bennett, so no fresh breeze was blowing from a westerly direction. Eternal, Blur and East 17 were the young acts in the year-end Top Ten, and all were British. The only 1990s star from

MARIAH CAREY was unusually fresh in 94

TONY BENNETT who won three 1962 Grammy Awards for "I Left My Heart In San Francisco" and won the Album of the Year prize 32 years later

the States to finish in the charmed circle was Mariah Carey, whose *Music Box* was the number three of the year and the best-selling album of original material.

Carey was the top female vocalist of the year in the weeks on chart table, too. Diana Ross was the only other female artist to finish in this top ten. For the second year running the top three of weeks on chart stars did not include a British act. Meat Loaf led the list with 75 weeks, a tribute to the enduring popularity of 1993's number one *Bat Out Of Hell II – Back Into Hell* and its 1978 predecessor. Nirvana followed closely with 69 weeks, a melancholy salute to Kurt Cobain, who fatally shot himself in April. R.E.M. rounded out the all-American top three.

Meat Loaf may have been the top male vocalist in terms of chart longevity, but Jimmy Nail came top in sales of a single album. *Crocodile Shoes*, the year's number 12, was his success. One had to go all the way down to 26 to find the next male vocalist, and that gentleman, Julio Iglesias, was neither British nor fresh. The male soloist who once dominated popular music had virtually disappeared.

One of the vanishing breed, Elton John, had the world number one of the year in the form of the soundtrack to the animated Disney film *The Lion King*, but because several cast members were heard on the disc it was bizarrely included in the compilation chart in Britain. Artists with even longer spans of hits than Elton did well this year, including Pink Floyd, number five for 1994 with their world number one *The Division Bell*, and the Beatles, whose *Live At The BBC* was their first Top Ten album of previously unreleased material since 1977.

José Carreras, Placido Domingo and Luciano Pavarotti, who had hit number one in 1990, sold more millions in this new World Cup year with *The 3 Tenors In Concert 1994*. In almost any other year the classical number one would have been by the Monks of the Benedictine Monastery of Santo Domingo de Silos, whose Canto Gregoriano consisted of chants recorded in Spain during the 1970s. In what may well be the first case of employees appearing in the chart at the same time as their boss, the monks charted simultaneously with The Pope. It is doubtful whether the monks in the 1970s or the Beatles in the BBC Paris Studio in the early 1960s, would have taken seriously an oracle predicting multi-million international sales success in 1994.

1995

Robson Green and Jerome Flynn soldier soldiered to the top of the album chart in November of this year and broke all speed records for hitting both one and two million sales. Their middle-of-the-road balladeering made no concession to fashion, and their multiple platinum discs more than compensated for a lack of Brit awards when it came to interior decoration. *Robson & Jerome* was the best-selling album of 1995 and even outsold the number one single of the year, 'Unchained Melody/White Cliffs of Dover', which was also Green and Flynn's.

Life did not have quite the longevity of Stars

PULP were no longer common people when they moved to a *Different Class*

In launching their surprise attack at the end of the year the television 'squaddies' put expected chart champs Oasis in the shade. By shifting over 1.84 million of the year's number two, *(What's The Story) Morning Glory?* and a further half million-plus on the 1994 issue *Definitely Maybe*, the Gallagher gang were still the best-selling group of the year. Their persistent sales helped vault them over Simply Red, who had the year's number four, *Life*. Although this was hardly death, it was a marked come-down from the last outing by Mick Hucknall's mob. *Stars* had been the first album to be the best seller for two calendar years, in its case 1991 and 1992.

Other groups to figure in the Top Ten sellers of the year were Queen, Wet Wet Wet, Blur and Pulp. The first mentioned was *Made In Heaven*, assembled around vocals recorded before Freddie Mercury's death in 1991. In *Picture This*, Wet Wet Wet finally had a studio album of their own that included their long-running 1994 number one single, 'Love Is All Around'. Blur broke out with *The Great Escape* after winning multiple prizes at the Brit Awards. For Pulp, however, *Different Class* was a different level of experience. They had long laboured with-out chart reward, and when it came in 1995 it was sufficient to also boost *His 'N' Hers* into the year-end Top 100.

None of the groups in the sales Top Ten were in the top three of the weeks on chart list. The longevity leaders were the Cranberries, who lingered for 96 weeks with their new hit *No Need To Argue* and their 1993 release *Everybody Else Is*

THE COLOUR OF MY LOVE

DION

CELINE DION is the most successful French Canadian artist of all time in Britain and internationally

Doing It So Why Can't We? Second on the list were R.E.M. who remained for 86 weeks with *Monster* and *Automatic For the People*. This put their totals for the last four years at 70–97–65–85, a remarkably consistent performance at a time when almost all artists take one or two years off between releases and temporarily vanish from the charts. The third highest weeks on chart total this year was achieved by Bon Jovi with 80, which would have been enough for first in 1994.

Celine Dion was unquestionably the female artist of the year. *The Colour Of My Love* was the number three of the year, and she had more weeks on chart than any other woman. Madonna was her chief competitor, both in sales with *Something To Remember* and in time spent in the Top 75. Both women should be cheered that they had more weeks on chart than any male vocalist. Neither boy nor man was in the Top Ten in this department, although Michael Jackson and Paul Weller did finish in the Top Ten sales.

For the second consecutive year, the Beatles had one of the Top 20 albums. This would be the chronological equivalent of Bing Crosby, chart champion of the 1930s, having two awesome albums in the 1960s; he didn't. An audience search for spiritual satisfaction led to both *Pan Pipe Moods* by Free The Spirit and *Chants And Dances Of The Native Americans* by Sacred Spirit finishing in

Clever marketing enabled *Pan Pipe Moods* by FREE THE SPIRIT to capitalise on the record buying public's search for spiritual satisfaction

the Top 50 of the year. In cases like these, hit singles were not required to sell large numbers of albums.

Vanessa-Mae was the top-selling classical artist of the year with *The Violin Player*, unless one succumbed to the trendy temptation to categorise her as 'classical crossover', which would leave Anthony Way at the top with the TV soundtrack *The Choir*. He was allowed no time to gloat, however, his own follow-up also being labelled 'classical crossover'.

THE CHARTS

If ever a week went by without a chart being compiled, the previous week's chart was used again for the purposes of all the statistics and information contained in this book. The dates used throughout corre-spond to the Saturday ending the week in which the chart was published. So for example, Abba's *Waterloo* album entered the chart in the week ending 8 June 1974, making their first day of chart action 2 June 1974.

The charts used in compiling this book are:

8 Nov 58	First album chart published by *Melody Maker*. It is a Top Ten.
27 Jun 59	Newspaper strike. No chart published until 8 August, so the 20 June chart is repeated throughout.
26 Mar 60	First *Record Retailer* chart published, a Top 20. We have taken our information from the *Record Retailer* from this date onwards, although the *Melody Maker* chart continued.
14 Apr 66	Chart becomes a Top 30.
8 Dec 66	Chart becomes a Top 40.
12 Feb 69	Chart drops back to a Top 15.
8 Mar 69	Incorrect chart published. Correct chart calculated by back-tracking from following week's listings.
11 Jun 69	Chart becomes a Top 20 again.
25 Jun 69	Chart becomes a Top 40 again.
9 Aug 69	Chart is a Top 32 (!) for this one week only.
11 Oct 69	Chart drops back to a Top 25.
8 Nov 69	Chart varies from a Top 20 to a Top 24 until 24 Jan 70.
31 Jan 70	Chart lists from 47 to 77 albums each week until 9 Jan 71.
9 Jan 71	*Record Retailer* becomes *Record And Tape Retailer*.
16 Jan 71	Chart stabilises as a Top 50.
6 Feb 71	Postal strike means no chart published until 3 Apr 71. 30 Jan chart repeated throughout.
7 Aug 71	The Full Price chart (the one we've been using) is combined with the previously separate Budget chart. This means there is a sudden influx of budget-label albums onto the chart.
8 Jan 72	Chart reverts to full price albums only, so the budget albums disappear as suddenly as they appeared.
18 Mar 72	*Record And Tape Retailer* becomes *Music Week*.
13 Jan 73	Chart is a Top 24 for this week only.
5 Jan 74	Chart is a Top 42 for this week only.
5 Jul 75	Chart becomes a Top 60.
14 Jan 78	Chart is a Top 30 for this week only.
2 Dec 78	Chart becomes a Top 75.
13 Oct 79	Two consecutive weeks' charts published simultaneously as a result of speedy new chart compilation system which enables *Music Week* to catch up a week. Until this date, the publica-tion of the chart had been more than a week after the sur-vey period. Both charts of this date are included in our calculations.
8 Aug 81	Chart becomes a Top 100.
14 Jan 89	Chart splits in two, and becomes a Top 75 'Artist Albums' and a Top 20 'Compilation Albums'. For this book, the Artist Albums chart is considered the main chart, but we record sep-arately the activities of the Compilations chart.

HIT ALBUMS

ALPHABETICALLY BY ARTIST

The combined sales of *Definitely Maybe* and *(What's The Story) Morning Glory?*
made OASIS (left to right: Paul 'Guigsy' McGuigan, Paul 'Bonehead' Arthurs,
Liam Gallagher, Alan White, Noel Gallagher) the best-selling act of 1995. The picture was taken in late 1995 when the band were in Paris for the MTV awards.

The information given in this part of the book is as follows:

DATE the album first hit the chart, the album **TITLE, LABEL, CATALOGUE NUMBER,** the **HIGHEST POSITION** it reached on the chart, and the **TOTAL WEEKS** it remained on the chart. Number one albums are highlighted with a **STAR** ★ and Top Ten albums with a **DOT** ●. A **DAGGER** † indicates the album is still on the chart on 30 December 1995, the final chart included in our calculations for this edition.

For the purposes of this book, an album is considered a re-issue if it hits the chart for a second time with a new catalogue number. From the time when albums began to be produced in both mono and stereo versions (around 1966), we list only the stereo catalogue number. Cassette sales and – since the mid-80s – CD sales, have become rapidly more significant in the compilation of the album charts, and the catalogue numbers listed reflected this.

Describing a recording act in one sentence is often fraught with danger, but we have attempted to do so above each act's list of hits. Although we are aware that many of the 'vocalists' thus described also play an instrument, we have only mentioned this fact where the artist's instrumental skills were an important factor in the album's success.

We have credited hit albums in combination with other chart acts to both artists' lists. So, for example, you will find *The Cream Of Eric Clapton* listed twice, once under Eric Clapton and once under Cream. There is no separate entry for them as a combined act, and the weeks that record spent on the chart are credited to both acts.

This edition of *The Guinness Book of British Hit Albums* includes a photo of each of the Top 30 acts of all time, as listed in the Most Weeks On Chart table in Part Three (page 429). All of these photos are numbered according to their position in the chart and are accompanied by the symbol

...which in this case indicates that Abba are number 19 in the Top 30 acts of all time.

British Hit Albums Part One

Date of chart entry/Title & catalogue no./Peak position reached/Weeks on chart

★ Number One   ● Top Ten   † still on chart at 30 Dec 1995   ☐ credited to act billed in footnote

AALIYAH *US, female vocalist* — **6 wks**

| 23 Jul 94 | **AGE AIN'T NOTHING BUT A NUMBER** *Jive CHIP 149* ....**23** | 6 wks |

AARONSON - *See HAGAR, SCHON, AARONSON, SHRIEVE*

ABBA *Sweden / Norway, male / female vocal / instrumental group* — **635 wks**

8 Jun 74	**WATERLOO** *Epic EPC 80179*..................................**28**	2 wks
31 Jan 76	**ABBA** *Epic EPC 80835*...**13**	10 wks
10 Apr 76	★ **GREATEST HITS** *Epic EPC 69218* **1**	130 wks
27 Nov 76	★ **ARRIVAL** *Epic EPC 86018* **1**	92 wks
4 Feb 78	★ **THE ALBUM** *Epic EPC 86052* **1**	61 wks
19 May 79	★ **VOULEZ-VOUS** *Epic EPC 86086* **1**	43 wks
10 Nov 79	★ **GREATEST HITS VOLUME 2** *Epic EPC 10017* **1**	63 wks
22 Nov 80	★ **SUPER TROUPER** *Epic EPC 10022* **1**	43 wks
19 Dec 81	★ **THE VISITORS** *Epic EPC 10032*.............................**1**	21 wks
20 Nov 82	★ **THE SINGLES THE FIRST TEN YEARS** *Epic ABBA 10*.......**1**	22 wks
19 Nov 83	**THANK YOU FOR THE MUSIC** *Epic EPC 10043* **17**	12 wks
19 Nov 88	**ABSOLUTE ABBA** *Telstar STAR 2329* **70**	7 wks
3 Oct 92	★ **GOLD - GREATEST HITS** *Polydor 5170072*................**1**	115 wks
5 Jun 93	**MORE ABBA GOLD - MORE ABBA HITS** *Polydor 5193532*....**14**	14 wks

Russ ABBOT *UK, male vocalist* — **16 wks**

| 5 Nov 83 | **RUSS ABBOT'S MADHOUSE** *Ronco RTL 2096* ....**41** | 7 wks |
| 23 Nov 85 | **I LOVE A PARTY** *K-Tel ONE 1313* ....**12** | 9 wks |

Gregory ABBOTT *US, male vocalist* — **5 wks**

| 10 Jan 87 | **SHAKE YOU DOWN** *CBS 4500611* ....**53** | 5 wks |

ABC *UK, male vocal / instrumental group* — **90 wks**

3 Jul 82	★ **THE LEXICON OF LOVE** *Neutron NTRS 1*....................**1**	50 wks
26 Nov 83	**BEAUTY STAB** *Neutron NTRL 2* **12**	13 wks
26 Oct 85	**HOW TO BE A ZILLIONAIRE** *Neutron NTRH 3* **28**	3 wks
24 Oct 87	● **ALPHABET CITY** *Neutron NTRH 4* **7**	10 wks
28 Oct 89	**UP** *Neutron 838646 1* **58**	1 wk
21 Apr 90	● **ABSOLUTELY** *Neutron 8429671* **7**	12 wks
24 Aug 91	**ABRACADABRA** *Parlophone PCS 7355* **50**	1 wk

Group was UK / US, male / female for third album.

Paula ABDUL *US, female vocalist* — **51 wks**

15 Apr 89	● **FOREVER YOUR GIRL** *Siren SRNLP 19* **3**	39 wks
10 Nov 90	**SHUT UP AND DANCE (THE DANCE MIXES)**	
	Virgin America VUSLP 28 ....**40**	2 wks
27 Jul 91	● **SPELLBOUND** *Virgin America VUSLP 33*.....................**4**	9 wks
1 Jul 95	**HEAD OVER HEELS** *Virgin America CDVUS 90* **61**	1 wk

A.B.'S *Japan, instrumental group* — **2 wks**

| 14 Apr 84 | **DEJA VU** *Street Sounds XKHAN 503* ....**80** | 2 wks |

ACADEMY OF ST MARTIN IN THE FIELDS – *See Neville MARRINER and the ACADEMY OF ST MARTIN IN THE FIELDS*

TOP 30 № 19

Of all groups, only the
Beatles have had more
weeks at number one
than ABBA.

(Simon Fowler/LFI)

ACCEPT *Germany, male vocal / instrumental group* **5 wks**

7 May 83	**RESTLESS AND WILD** Heavy Metal Worldwid HMILP 6	**98**	2 wks
30 Mar 85	**METAL HEART** Portrait PRT 26358	**50**	1 wk
15 Feb 86	**KAIZOKU-BAN** Portrait PRT 5916	**91**	1 wk
3 May 86	**RUSSIAN ROULETTE** Portrait PRT 26893	**80**	1 wk

AC/DC *Australia / UK, male vocal / instrumental group* **248 wks**

5 Nov 77	**LET THERE BE ROCK** Atlantic K 50366	**17**	5 wks
20 May 78	**POWERAGE** Atlantic K 50483	**26**	9 wks
28 Oct 78	**IF YOU WANT BLOOD YOU'VE GOT IT** Atlantic K 50532	**13**	58 wks
18 Aug 79	● **HIGHWAY TO HELL** Atlantic K 50628	**8**	32 wks
9 Aug 80	★ **BACK IN BLACK** Atlantic K 50735	**1**	40 wks
5 Dec 81	● **FOR THOSE ABOUT TO ROCK** Atlantic K 50851	**3**	29 wks
3 Sep 83	● **FLICK OF THE SWITCH** Atlantic 7801001	**4**	9 wks
13 Jul 85	● **FLY ON THE WALL** Atlantic 781263	**7**	10 wks
7 Jun 86	**WHO MADE WHO** Atlantic WX 57	**11**	12 wks
13 Feb 88	● **BLOW UP YOUR VIDEO** Atlantic WX 144	**2**	14 wks
6 Oct 90	● **THE RAZOR'S EDGE** Atco WX 364	**4**	18 wks
7 Nov 92	● **LIVE** Atco 7567922152	**5**	7 wks
7 Oct 95	● **BALLBREAKER** East West 7559617802	**6**	5 wks

ACE OF BASE *Sweden, male / female vocal / instrumental group* **39 wks**

19 Jun 93	★ **HAPPY NATION** London 5177492	**1**	38 wks
2 Dec 95	**THE BRIDGE** London 5296552	**66**	1 wk

Happy Nation changed its catalogue number to 5214722 during its chart run.

Bryan ADAMS *Canada, male vocalist / instrumentalist – guitar* **245 wks**

2 Mar 85	● **RECKLESS** A & M AMA 5013	**7**	115 wks
24 Aug 85	**YOU WANT IT, YOU GOT IT** A & M AMLH 64864	**78**	5 wks
15 Mar 86	**CUTS LIKE A KNIFE** A & M AMLH 64919	**21**	6 wks
11 Apr 87	● **INTO THE FIRE** A & M AMA 3907	**10**	21 wks
5 Oct 91	★ **WAKING UP THE NEIGHBOURS** A & M 3971641	**1**	54 wks
20 Nov 93	★ **SO FAR SO GOOD** A & M 5401572	**1**	40 wks
6 Aug 94	**LIVE! LIVE! LIVE!** A & M 3970942	**17**	4 wks

Oleta ADAMS *US, female vocalist / instrumentalist – piano* **34 wks**

26 May 90	★ **CIRCLE OF ONE** Fontana 8427441	**1**	26 wks
7 Aug 93	● **EVOLUTION** Fontana 5149652	**10**	7 wks
4 Nov 95	**MOVING ON** Fontana 5285302	**59**	1 wk

Cliff ADAMS SINGERS *UK, male / female vocal group* **20 wks**

16 Apr 60	**SING SOMETHING SIMPLE** Pye MPL 28013	**15**	4 wks
24 Nov 62	**SING SOMETHING SIMPLE** Pye Golden Guinea GGL 0150	**15**	2 wks
20 Nov 76	**SING SOMETHING SIMPLE '76** Warwick WW 5016/17	**23**	8 wks
25 Dec 82	**SING SOMETHING SIMPLE** Ronco RTD 2087	**39**	6 wks

All the identically titled albums are different.

ADAMSKI *UK, male multi–instrumentalist / producer* **16 wks**

9 Dec 89	**LIVE AND DIRECT** MCA MCL 1900	**47**	11 wks
13 Oct 90	● **DOCTOR ADAMSKI'S MUSICAL PHARMACY** MCA MCG 6107	**8**	5 wks

King Sunny ADE and his AFRICAN BEATS
Nigeria, male vocalist and male vocal / instrumental group **1 wk**

9 Jul 83	**SYNCHRO SYSTEM** Island ILPS 9737	**93**	1 wk

ADEVA *US, female vocalist* **24 wks**

9 Sep 89	● **ADEVA** Cooltempo ICTLP 13	**6**	24 wks

A
43

ADICTS *UK, male vocal / instrumental group* **1 wk**

4 Dec 82   **SOUND OF MUSIC** *Razor RAZ 2* 99   1 wk

ADIEMUS *UK, male instrumental duo* **4 wks**

1 Jul 95   **SONGS OF SANCTUARY** *Virgin CDVE 925* 38   4 wks
All tracks feature Miriam Stockley and the London Philharmonic Orchestra.

Larry ADLER *US, male instrumentalist – harmonica* **18 wks**

6 Aug 94 ● **THE GLORY OF GERSHWIN** *Mercury 5227272* ....**2**   18 wks

ADORABLE *UK, male vocal / instrumental group* **1 wk**

13 Mar 93   **AGAINST PERFECTION** *Creation CRECD 138* ....**70**   1 wk

ADVENTURES *UK, male / female vocal / instrumental group* **11 wks**

21 May 88   **THE SEA OF LOVE** *Elektra EKT 45* ....**30**   10 wks
17 Mar 90   **TRADING SECRETS WITH THE MOON** *Elektra EKT 63* ....**64**   1 wk

ADVERTS *UK, male / female vocal / instrumental group* **1 wk**

11 Mar 78   **CROSSING THE RED SEA WITH THE ADVERTS** *Bright BRL 201* ....**38**   1 wk

AEROSMITH *US, male vocal / instrumental group* **94 wks**

5 Sep 87   **PERMANENT VACATION** *Geffen WX 126* ....**37**   14 wks
23 Sep 89 ● **PUMP** *Geffen WX 304* ....**3**   26 wks
1 May 93 ● **GET A GRIP** *Geffen GED 24444* ....**2**   38 wks
12 Nov 94 ● **BIG ONES** *Geffen GED 24546* ....**7**   16 wks
Pump changed its catalogue number to GEF 24245 during its chart run.

A
44

AFGHAN WHIGS *US, male vocal / instrumental group* **1 wk**

16 Oct 93   **GENTLEMEN** *Blast First BFFP 90CD* ....**58**   1 wk

AFRICAN BEATS – *See King Sunny ADE and his AFRICAN BEATS*

AFTER THE FIRE *UK, male vocal / instrumental group* **4 wks**

13 Oct 79   **LASER LOVE** *CBS 83795* ....**57**   1 wk
1 Nov 80   **80 F** *Epic EPC 84545* ....**69**   1 wk
3 Apr 82   **BATTERIES NOT INCLUDED** *CBS 85566* ....**82**   2 wks

A-HA *Norway, male vocal / instrumental group* **143 wks**

9 Nov 85 ● **HUNTING HIGH AND LOW** *Warner Bros. WX 30* ....**2**   78 wks
18 Oct 86 ● **SCOUNDREL DAYS** *Warner Bros. WX 62* ....**2**   29 wks
14 May 88 ● **STAY ON THESE ROADS** *Warner Bros. WX 166* ....**2**   19 wks
2 Nov 90   **EAST OF THE SUN WEST OF THE MOON** *Warner Bros. WX 378* ..**12**   4 wks
16 Nov 91   **HEADLINES AND DEADLINES – THE HITS OF A-HA**
          Warner Bros. WX 450 ....**12**   10 wks
26 Jun 93   **MEMORIAL BEACH** *Warner Bros. 9362452292* ....**17**   3 wks

AIRHEAD *UK, male vocal / instrumental group* **7 wks**

1 Feb 92   **BOING** *Korova 9031746792* ....**29**   7 wks

ALARM *UK, male vocal / instrumental group* **29 wks**

25 Feb 84 ● **DECLARATION** *IRS IRSA 7044* ....**6**   11 wks
26 Oct 85   **STRENGTH** *IRS MIRF 1004* ....**18**   6 wks
14 Nov 87   **EYE OF THE HURRICANE** *IRS MIRG 1023* ....**23**   4 wks

5 Nov 88	**ELECTRIC FOLKLORE LIVE** *IRS MIRMC 5001*	**62**	2 wks
30 Sep 89	**CHANGE** *IRS EIRSAX 1020*	**13**	3 wks
24 Nov 90	**STANDARDS** *IRS EIRSA 1043*	**47**	1 wk
4 May 91	**RAW** *IRS EIRSA 1055*	**33**	2 wks

John ALDISS – *See LONDON PHILHARMONIC CHOIR*

ALEXANDER BROTHERS *UK, male vocal duo*   **1 wk**

10 Dec 66	**THESE ARE MY MOUNTAINS** *Pye GGL 0375*	**29**	1 wk

ALICE IN CHAINS *US, male vocal / instrumental group*   **20 wks**

24 Oct 92	**DIRT** *Columbia 4723302*	**42**	13 wks
5 Feb 94	● **JAR OF FLIES / SAP** *Columbia 4757132*	**4**	5 wks
18 Nov 95	**ALICE IN CHAINS** *Columbia 4811149*	**37**	2 wks

ALIEN SEX FIEND *UK, male / female vocal / instrumental group*   **1 wk**

12 Oct 85	**MAXIMUM SECURITY** *Anagram GRAM 24*	**100**	1 wk

ALL ABOUT EVE *UK, male / female vocal / instrumental group*   **37 wks**

27 Feb 88	● **ALL ABOUT EVE** *Mercury MERH 119*	**7**	29 wks
28 Oct 89	● **SCARLET AND OTHER STORIES** *Mercury 838965 1*	**9**	4 wks
7 Sep 91	**TOUCHED BY JESUS** *Vertigo 510461*	**17**	3 wks
7 Nov 92	**ULTRAVIOLET** *MCA MCD 10712*	**46**	1 wk

ALLEN – *See FOSTER and ALLEN*

Ed ALLEYNE-JOHNSON *UK, male instrumentalist – violin*   **1 wk**

18 Jun 94	**ULTRAVIOLET** *Equation EQCD 002*	**68**	1 wk

ALL-4-ONE *US, male vocal group*   **5 wks**

23 Jul 94	**ALL-4-ONE** *Atlantic 7567825882*	**25**	5 wks

Mose ALLISON *US, male vocalist / instrumentalist – piano*   **1 wk**

4 Jun 66	**MOSE ALIVE** *Atlantic 587007*	**30**	1 wk

ALLMAN BROTHERS BAND *US, male vocal / instrumental group*   **4 wks**

6 Oct 73	**BROTHERS AND SISTERS** *Warner Bros. K 47507*	**42**	3 wks
6 Mar 76	**THE ROAD GOES ON FOREVER** *Capricorn 2637 101*	**54**	1 wk

ALMIGHTY *UK, male vocal / instrumental group*   **11 wks**

20 Oct 90	**BLOOD FIRE AND LIVE** *Polydor 8471071*	**62**	1 wk
30 Mar 91	**SOUL DESTRUCTION** *Polydor 8479611*	**22**	4 wks
17 Apr 93	● **POWERTRIPPIN'** *Polydor 5191042*	**5**	4 wks
8 Oct 94	**CRANK** *Chrysalis CDCHRZ 6086*	**15**	2 wks

Marc ALMOND *UK, male vocalist*   **25 wks**

16 Oct 82	**UNTITLED** *Some Bizzare BZA 13* 1	**42**	4 wks
20 Aug 83	**TORMENT AND TORREROS** *Some Bizzare BIZL 4* 1	**28**	5 wks
10 Nov 84	**VERMIN IN ERMINE** *Some Bizzare BIZL 8*	**36**	2 wks
5 Oct 85	**STORIES OF JOHNNY** *Some Bizzare FAITH 1*	**22**	3 wks
18 Apr 87	**MOTHER FIST AND HER FIVE DAUGHTERS** *Some Bizzare FAITH 2* 2	**41**	2 wks
8 Oct 88	**THE STARS WE ARE** *Parlophone PCS 7324*	**41**	5 wks
16 Jun 90	**ENCHANTED** *Some Bizzare PCS 7344*	**52**	1 wk
26 Oct 91	**TENEMENT SYMPHONY** *Some Bizzare WX 442*	**39**	3 wks

1 Marc and the Mambas   2 Marc Almond and the Willing Sinners

A
45

Herb ALPERT and the TIJUANA BRASS
US, male band leader / instrumentalist – trumpet   **312 wks**

29 Jan 66	● **GOING PLACES** Pye NPL 28065...**4**	138 wks
23 Apr 66	● **WHIPPED CREAM AND OTHER DELIGHTS** Pye NPL 28058..............**2**	42 wks
28 May 66	**WHAT NOW MY LOVE** Pye NPL 28077 ....**18**	17 wks
11 Feb 67	● **S.R.O.** Pye NSPL 28088...**5**	26 wks
15 Jul 67	**SOUNDS LIKE** A & M AMLS 900...**21**	10 wks
3 Feb 68	**NINTH** A & M AMLS 905...**26**	9 wks
29 Jun 68	● **BEAT OF THE BRASS** A & M AMLS 916 ....**4**	21 wks
9 Aug 69	**WARM** A & M AMLS 937...**30**	4 wks
14 Mar 70	**THE BRASS ARE COMIN'** A & M AMLS 962.............................**40**	1 wk
30 May 70	● **GREATEST HITS** A & M AMLS 980.......................................**8**	27 wks
27 Jun 70	**DOWN MEXICO WAY** A & M AMLS 974..................................**64**	1 wk
13 Nov 71	**AMERICA** A & M AMLB 1000..**45**	1 wk
12 Nov 77	**40 GREATEST** K-Tel NE 1005..**45**	2 wks
17 Nov 79	**RISE** A & M AMLH 64790 [1] **37**	7 wks
4 Apr 87	**KEEP YOUR EYE ON ME** Breakout AMA 5125 [1] **79**	3 wks
28 Sep 91	**THE VERY BEST OF HERB ALPERT** A & M 3971651 [1] **34**	3 wks

[1] Herb Alpert

On 29 Jun 67 Going Places and What Now My Love changed labels and numbers to A & M AMLS 965 and AMLS 977 respectively.

ALT *Ireland / New Zealand / UK, male vocal / instrumental group*   **1 wk**

24 Jun 95	**ALTITUDE** Parlophone CDPCS 7377..**67**	1 wk

ALTERED IMAGES *UK, female / male vocal / instrumental group*   **40 wks**

19 Sep 81	**HAPPY BIRTHDAY** Epic EPC 84893.......................................**26**	21 wks
15 May 82	**PINKY BLUE** Epic EPC 85665..**12**	10 wks
25 Jun 83	**BITE** Epic EPC 25413...**16**	9 wks

ALTERN 8 *UK, male instrumental / production duo*   **4 wks**

25 Jul 92	**FULL ON ... MASK HYSTERIA** Network TOPCD 1 ....**11**	4 wks

AMAZULU *UK, female vocal group*   **1 wk**

6 Dec 88	**AMAZULU** Island ILPS 9851..**97**	1 wk

AMEN CORNER *UK, male vocal / instrumental group*   **8 wks**

30 Mar 68	**ROUND AMEN CORNER** Deram SML 1021 ....**26**	7 wks
1 Nov 69	**EXPLOSIVE COMPANY** Immediate IMSP 023 ....**19**	1 wk

AMERICA *US, male vocal / instrumental group*   **22 wks**

22 Jan 72	**AMERICA** Warner Bros. K 46093 ....**14**	13 wks
9 Dec 72	**HOMECOMING** Warner Bros. K 46180...................................**21**	5 wks
10 Nov 73	**HAT TRICK** Warner Bros. K 56016.......................................**41**	3 wks
7 Feb 76	**HISTORY – AMERICA'S GREATEST HITS** Warner Bros. K 56169....**60**	1 wk

AMERICAN MUSIC CLUB *US, male vocal / instrumental group*   **3 wks**

27 Mar 93	**MERCURY** Virgin CDV 2708...**41**	2 wks
24 Sep 94	**SAN FRANCISCO** Virgin CDV 2752..**72**	1 wk

Tori AMOS *US, female vocalist*   **32 wks**

18 Jan 92	**LITTLE EARTHQUAKES** East West 7567823582..............................**14**	19 wks
12 Feb 94	★ **UNDER THE PINK** East West 7567825672 ....**1**	13 wks

AMPS *US, male / female vocal / instrumental group*   **1 wk**

11 Nov 95	**PACER** 4AD CAD 5016CD..**60**	1 wk

AND WHY NOT *UK, male vocal group* **3 wks**

| 10 Mar 90 | **MOVE YOUR SKIN** *Island ILPS 9935*.................................**24** | 3 wks |

Carleen ANDERSON *US, female vocalist* **5 wks**

| 13 Nov 93 | **DUSKY SAPPHO EP** *Circa YRCDG 108* ....**38** | 1 wk |
| 18 Jun 94 | **TRUE SPIRIT** *Circa CIRCDX 30* ....**12** | 4 wks |

Ian ANDERSON *UK, male vocalist / instrumentalist – flute* **1 wk**

| 26 Nov 83 | **WALK INTO LIGHT** *Chrysalis CDL 1443* ....**78** | 1 wk |

Jon ANDERSON *UK, male vocalist* **19 wks**

24 Jul 76	● **OLIAS OF SUNHILLOW** *Atlantic K 50261*....................**8**	10 wks
15 Nov 80	**SONG OF SEVEN** *Atlantic K 50756*................................**38**	3 wks
5 Jun 82	**ANIMATION** *Polydor POLD 5044* **43**	6 wks

See also Jon and Vangelis; Anderson Bruford Wakeman Howe.

Laurie ANDERSON *US, female vocalist / multi–instrumentalist* **8 wks**

| 1 May 82 | **BIG SCIENCE** *Warner Bros. K 57002*.............................**29** | 6 wks |
| 10 Mar 84 | **MISTER HEARTBREAK** *Warner Bros. 9250771* ....**93** | 2 wks |

Lynn ANDERSON *US, female vocalist* **1 wk**

| 17 Apr 71 | **ROSE GARDEN** *CBS 64333* ....**45** | 1 wk |

Moira ANDERSON *UK, female vocalist* **6 wks**

| 20 Jun 70 | **THESE ARE MY SONGS** *Decca SKL 5016*........................**50** | 1 wk |
| 5 Dec 81 | **GOLDEN MEMORIES** *Warwick WW 5107* 1 ....**46** | 5 wks |

1 Harry Secombe and Moira Anderson

ANDERSON BRUFORD WAKEMAN HOWE
UK, male vocal / instrumental group **6 wks**

| 8 Jul 89 | **ANDERSON BRUFORD WAKEMAN HOWE** *Arista 209970* ....**14** | 6 wks |

See also Jon Anderson; Rick Wakeman; Steve Howe.

John ANDERSON ORCHESTRA *Ireland, orchestra* **5 wks**

| 25 Nov 95 | **PAN PIPES - ROMANCE OF IRELAND** *MCA MCD 60004*................**56** | 5 wks |

Julie ANDREWS *UK, female vocalist* **5 wks**

| 16 Jul 83 | **LOVE ME TENDER** *Peach River JULIE 1* ....**63** | 5 wks |

ANGELIC UPSTARTS *UK, male vocal / instrumental group* **20 wks**

18 Aug 79	**TEENAGE WARNING** *Warner Bros. K 50634* **29**	7 wks
12 Apr 80	**WE'VE GOTTA GET OUT OF THIS PLACE** *Warner Bros. K 56806* ..**54**	3 wks
7 Jun 81	**2,000,000 VOICES** *Zonophone ZONO 104* **32**	3 wks
26 Sep 81	**ANGELIC UPSTARTS** *Zonophone ZEM 102* **27**	7 wks

ANIMAL NIGHTLIFE *UK, male vocal / instrumental group* **6 wks**

| 24 Aug 85 | **SHANGRI-LA** *Island ILPS 9830*......................................**36** | 6 wks |

ANIMALS *UK, male vocal / instrumental group* **86 wks**

| 14 Nov 64 | ● **THE ANIMALS** *Columbia 33SX 1669*..............................**6** | 20 wks |
| 22 May 65 | ● **ANIMAL TRACKS** *Columbia 33SX 1708* ....**6** | 26 wks |

A
47

16 Apr 66	● **MOST OF THE ANIMALS** Columbia 33SX 6035	**4**	20 wks
28 May 66	● **ANIMALISMS** Decca LK 4797	**4**	17 wks
25 Sep 71	**MOST OF THE ANIMALS (re-issue)** MFP 5218	**18**	3 wks

ANNIHILATOR UK, male vocal / instrumental group — **1 wk**

| 11 Aug 90 | **NEVER NEVERLAND** Roadrunner RR 93741 | **48** | 1 wk |

Adam ANT UK, male vocalist — **155 wks**

15 Nov 80	★ **KINGS OF THE WILD FRONTIER** CBS 84549 [1]	**1**	66 wks
17 Jan 81	**DIRK WEARS WHITE SOX** Do It RIDE 3 [1]	**16**	29 wks
14 Nov 81	● **PRINCE CHARMING** CBS 85268 [1]	**2**	21 wks
23 Oct 82	● **FRIEND OR FOE** CBS 25040	**5**	12 wks
19 Nov 83	**STRIP** CBS 25705	**20**	8 wks
14 Sep 85	**VIVE LE ROCK** CBS 26583	**42**	3 wks
24 Mar 90	**MANNERS AND PHYSIQUE** MCA MCG 6068	**19**	3 wks
28 Aug 93	● **ANTMUSIC - THE VERY BEST OF ADAM ANT** Arcade ARC 3100052	**6**	11 wks
15 Apr 95	**WONDERFUL** EMI CDEMC 3687	**24**	2 wks

[1] Adam and the Ants

ANTHRAX US, male vocal / instrumental group — **22 wks**

18 Apr 87	**AMONG THE LIVING** Island ILPS 9865	**18**	5 wks
24 Sep 88	**STATE OF EUPHORIA** Island ILPS 9916	**12**	4 wks
8 Sep 90	**PERSISTENCE OF TIME** Island ILPS 9967	**13**	5 wks
20 Jul 91	**ATTACK OF THE KILLER B'S** Island ILPS 9980	**13**	5 wks
29 May 93	**SOUND OF WHITE NOISE** Elektra 7559614302	**14**	3 wks

ANTI-PASTI UK, male vocal / instrumental group — **7 wks**

| 15 Aug 81 | **THE LAST CALL** Rondelet ABOUT 5 | **31** | 7 wks |

ANTI-NOWHERE LEAGUE UK, male vocal / instrumental group — **12 wks**

| 22 May 82 | **WE ARE . . . THE LEAGUE** WXYZ LMNOP 1 | **24** | 11 wks |
| 5 Nov 83 | **LIVE IN YUGOSLAVIA** I.D. NOSE 3 | **88** | 1 wk |

ANTS – See Adam ANT

APACHE INDIAN UK, male rapper — **2 wks**

| 6 Feb 93 | **NO RESERVATIONS** Island CID 8001 | **36** | 2 wks |

APHEX TWIN UK, male producer – Richard James — **7 wks**

19 Mar 94	**SELECTED AMBIENT WORKS VOLUME II** Warp WARPCD 21	**11**	3 wks
11 Feb 95	**CLASSICS** R & S RS 94035CD	**24**	2 wks
6 May 95	**. . . I CARE BECAUSE YOU DO** Warp WARPCD 30	**24**	2 wks

Carmine APPICE – See Jeff BECK, Tim BOGERT and Carmine APPICE

Kim APPLEBY UK, female vocalist — **13 wks**

| 8 Dec 90 | **KIM APPLEBY** Parlophone PCS 7348 | **23** | 13 wks |

See also Mel and Kim.

APRIL WINE Canada, male vocal / instrumental group — **8 wks**

| 15 Mar 80 | **HARDER . . . FASTER** Capitol EST 12013 | **34** | 5 wks |
| 24 Jan 81 | **THE NATURE OF THE BEAST** Capitol EST 12125 | **48** | 3 wks |

ARCADIA UK, male vocal / instrumental group — **10 wks**

| 7 Dec 85 | **SO RED THE ROSE** Parlophone Odeon PCSD 101 | **30** | 10 wks |

Tasmin ARCHER *UK, female vocalist*

42 wks

| 31 Oct 92 | ● **GREAT EXPECTATIONS** *EMI CDEMC 3624* | ......8 | 42 wks |

Tina ARENA *Australia, female vocalist*

10 wks

| 20 May 95 | **DON'T ASK** *Columbia 4778862* | ......11 | 10 wks |

ARGENT *UK, male vocal / instrumental group*

9 wks

| 29 Apr 72 | **ALL TOGETHER NOW** *Epic EPC 64962* | ......13 | 8 wks |
| 31 Mar 73 | **IN DEEP** *Epic EPC 65475* | ......49 | 1 wk |

Joan ARMATRADING *UK, female vocalist*

193 wks

4 Sep 76	**JOAN ARMATRADING** *A & M AMLH 64588*	12	27 wks
1 Oct 77	● **SHOW SOME EMOTION** *A & M AMLH 68433*	6	11 wks
14 Oct 78	**TO THE LIMIT** *A & M AMLH 64732*	13	10 wks
24 May 80	● **ME MYSELF I** *A & M AMLH 64809*	5	23 wks
12 Sep 81	● **WALK UNDER LADDERS** *A & M AMLH 64876*	6	29 wks
12 Mar 83	● **THE KEY** *A & M AMLX 64912*	10	14 wks
26 Nov 83	**TRACK RECORD** *A & M JA 2001*	18	32 wks
16 Feb 85	**SECRET SECRETS** *A & M AMA 5040*	14	12 wks
24 May 86	**SLEIGHT OF HAND** *A & M AMA 5130*	34	6 wks
16 Jul 88	**THE SHOUTING STAGE** *A & M AMA 5211*	28	10 wks
16 Jun 90	**HEARTS AND FLOWERS** *A & M 3952981*	29	4 wks
16 Mar 91	● **THE VERY BEST OF JOAN ARMATRADING** *A & M 3971221*	9	11 wks
20 Jun 92	**SQUARE THE CIRCLE** *A & M 3953882*	34	2 wks
10 Jun 95	**WHAT'S INSIDE** *RCA 74321272692*	48	2 wks

ARMOURY SHOW *UK, male vocal / instrumental group*

1 wk

| 21 Sep 85 | **WAITING FOR THE FLOODS** *Parlophone ARM 1* | ......57 | 1 wk |

Louis ARMSTRONG
US, male band leader vocalist / instrumentalist – trumpet / cornet

29 wks

22 Oct 60	**SATCHMO PLAYS KING OLIVER** *Audio Fidelity AFLP 1930*	20	1 wk
28 Oct 61	**JAZZ CLASSICS** *Ace of Hearts AH 7*	20	1 wk
27 Jun 64	**HELLO DOLLY** *London HAR 8190*	11	6 wks
16 Nov 68	**WHAT A WONDERFUL WORLD** *Stateside SSL 10247*	37	3 wks
20 Feb 82	**THE VERY BEST OF LOUIS ARMSTRONG** *Warwick WW 5112*	30	3 wks
21 May 94	**THE ULTIMATE COLLECTION** *Bluebird 74321197062*	48	3 wks
17 Dec 94	● **WE HAVE ALL THE TIME IN THE WORLD – THE VERY BEST OF LOUIS ARMSTRONG** *EMI CDEMTV 89*	10	12 wks

ARRESTED DEVELOPMENT
US, male / female vocal / instrumental group

40 wks

31 Oct 92	● **3 YEARS, 5 MONTHS AND 2 DAYS IN THE LIFE OF . . .** *Cooltempo CCD 1929*	3	34 wks
10 Apr 93	**UNPLUGGED** *Cooltempo CTCD 33*	40	3 wks
18 Jun 94	**ZINGALAMDUNI** *Cooltempo CTCD 42*	16	3 wks

Steve ARRINGTON *US, male vocalist*

11 wks

| 13 Apr 85 | **DANCIN' IN THE KEY OF LIFE** *Atlantic 781245* | ......41 | 11 wks |

ART OF NOISE *UK, male / female instrumental duo*

37 wks

3 Nov 84	**(WHO'S AFRAID OF) THE ART OF NOISE** *ZTT ZTTIQ 2*	27	17 wks
26 Apr 86	**IN VISIBLE SILENCE** *Chrysalis WOL 2*	18	15 wks
10 Oct 87	**IN NO SENSE / NONSENSE** *China WOL 4*	55	2 wks
3 Dec 88	**THE BEST OF THE ART OF NOISE** *China 837 367 1*	55	3 wks

Act was a male / female instrumental group for first two albums.

Davey ARTHUR – *See FUREYS and Davey ARTHUR*

ASAP *UK, male vocal / instrumental group*   **1 wk**

4 Nov 89	**SILVER AND GOLD** *EMI EMC 3566*	70	1 wk

ASHFORD and SIMPSON *US, male / female vocal duo*   **6 wks**

16 Feb 85	**SOLID** *Capitol SASH 1*	42	6 wks

ASIA *UK, male vocal / instrumental group*   **50 wks**

10 Apr 82	**ASIA** *Geffen GEF 85577*	11	38 wks
20 Aug 83	● **ALPHA** *Geffen GEF 25508*	5	11 wks
14 Dec 85	**ASTRA** *Geffen GEF 26413*	68	1 wk

ASSOCIATES *UK, male vocal / instrumental group*   **28 wks**

22 May 82	● **SULK** *Associates ASCL 1*	10	20 wks
16 Feb 85	**PERHAPS** *WEA WX 9*	23	7 wks
31 Mar 90	**WILD AND LONELY** *Circa CIRCA 11*	71	1 wk

Act was a duo for the first album.

Rick ASTLEY *UK, male vocalist*   **62 wks**

28 Nov 87	★ **WHENEVER YOU NEED SOMEBODY** *RCA PL 71529*	1	34 wks
10 Dec 88	● **HOLD ME IN YOUR ARMS** *RCA PL 71932*	8	19 wks
2 Mar 91	● **FREE** *RCA PL 74896*	9	9 wks

ASWAD *UK, male vocal / instrumental group*   **60 wks**

24 Jul 82	**NOT SATISFIED** *CBS 85666*	50	6 wks
10 Dec 83	**LIVE AND DIRECT** *Island IMA 6*	57	16 wks
3 Nov 84	**REBEL SOULS** *Island ILPS 9780*	48	2 wks
28 Jun 86	**TO THE TOP** *Simba SIMBALP 2*	71	3 wks
9 Apr 88	● **DISTANT THUNDER** *Mango ILPS 9895*	10	15 wks
3 Dec 86	**RENAISSANCE** *Stylus SMR 866*	52	8 wks
22 Sep 90	**TOO WICKED** *Mango MLPS 1054*	51	2 wks
9 Jul 94	**RISE AND SHINE** *Bubblin' BUBBCD 1*	38	5 wks
12 Aug 95	**GREATEST HITS** *Bubblin' BUBBCD 4*	20	3 wks

ATHLETICO SPIZZ 80 *UK, male vocal / instrumental group*   **5 wks**

26 Jul 80	**DO A RUNNER** *A & M AMLE 68514*	27	5 wks

Chet ATKINS *US, male instrumentalist – guitar*   **16 wks**

18 Mar 61	**THE OTHER CHET ATKINS** *RCA RD 27194*	20	1 wk
17 Jun 61	**CHET ATKINS' WORKSHOP** *RCA RD 27214*	19	1 wk
20 Feb 63	**CARIBBEAN GUITAR** *RCA RD 7519*	17	3 wks
24 Nov 90	**NECK AND NECK** *CBS 4674351* ⓵	41	11 wks

⓵ Chet Atkins and Mark Knopfler

Rowan ATKINSON *UK, male comedian*   **9 wks**

7 Feb 81	**LIVE IN BELFAST** *Arista SPART 1150*	44	9 wks

ATLANTIC STARR *US, male / female vocal / instrumental group*   **15 wks**

15 Jun 85	**AS THE BAND TURNS** *A & M AMA 5019*	64	3 wks
11 Jul 87	**ALL IN THE NAME OF LOVE** *WEA WX 115*	48	12 wks

ATOMIC ROOSTER *UK, male vocal / instrumental group*   **13 wks**

13 Jun 70	**ATOMIC ROOSTER** *B & C CAS 1010*	49	1 wk
16 Jan 71	**DEATH WALKS BEHIND YOU** *Charisma CAS 1026*	12	8 wks
21 Aug 71	**IN HEARING OF ATOMIC ROOSTER** *Pegasus PEG 1*	18	4 wks

ATTRACTIONS – *See Elvis COSTELLO and the ATTRACTIONS*

AU PAIRS *UK, female / male vocal / instrumental group*   **10 wks**

| 6 Jun 81 | **PLAYING WITH A DIFFERENT SEX** *Human HUMAN 1* ....**33** | 7 wks |
| 4 Sep 82 | **SENSE AND SENSUALITY** *Kamera KAM 010* ....**79** | 3 wks |

Brian AUGER TRINITY – *See Julie DRISCOLL and the Brian AUGER TRINITY*

Patti AUSTIN *US, female vocalist*   **1 wk**

| 26 Sep 81 | **EVERY HOME SHOULD HAVE ONE** *Qwest K 56931* ....**99** | 1 wk |

AUTEURS *UK, male / female vocal / instrumental group*   **3 wks**

| 6 Mar 93 | **NEW WAVE** *Hut CDHUT 7* ....**35** | 2 wks |
| 21 May 94 | **NOW I'M A COWBOY** *Hut CDHUT 16* ....**27** | 1 wk |

AVERAGE WHITE BAND *UK, male vocal / instrumental group*   **50 wks**

1 Mar 75	● **AVERAGE WHITE BAND** *Atlantic K 50058* **6**	14 wks
5 Jul 75	**CUT THE CAKE** *Atlantic K 50146* **28**	4 wks
31 Jul 76	**SOUL SEARCHING TIME** *Atlantic K 50272* **60**	1 wk
10 Mar 79	**I FEEL NO FRET** *RCA XL 13063* **15**	15 wks
31 May 80	**SHINE** *RCA XL 13123* **14**	13 wks
2 Apr 94	**LET'S GO ROUND AGAIN – THE BEST OF**	
	THE AVERAGE WHITE BAND *The Hit Label AHLCD 15* **38**	3 wks

Roy AYERS *US, male vocalist / instrumentalist – vibraphone*   **2 wks**

| 26 Oct 85 | **YOU MIGHT BE SURPRISED** *CBS 26653* ....**91** | 2 wks |

Pam AYRES *UK, female vocalist*   **29 wks**

| 27 Mar 76 | **SOME OF ME POEMS AND SONGS** *Galaxy GAL 6003* ....**13** | 23 wks |
| 11 Dec 76 | **SOME MORE OF ME POEMS AND SONGS** *Galaxy GAL 6010* ......**23** | 6 wks |

Charles AZNAVOUR *France, male vocalist*   **21 wks**

29 Jun 74	**AZNAVOUR SINGS AZNAVOUR VOLUME 3** *Barclay 80472* **23**	7 wks
7 Sep 74	● **A TAPESTRY OF DREAMS** *Barclay 90003* **9**	13 wks
2 Aug 80	**HIS GREATEST LOVE SONGS** *K-Tel NE 1078*................**73**	1 wk

AZTEC CAMERA *UK, male vocal / instrumental group*   **76 wks**

23 Apr 83	**HIGH LAND HARD RAIN** *Rough Trade ROUGH 47*..........**22**	18 wks
29 Sep 84	**KNIFE** *WEA WX 8* **14**	6 wks
21 Nov 87	● **LOVE** *WEA WX 128* **10**	43 wks
16 Jun 90	**STRAY** *WEA WX 350* **22**	7 wks
29 May 93	**DREAMLAND** *WEA 4509924922*........................**21**	2 wks

Derek B *UK, male rapper*   **9 wks**

| 28 May 88 | **BULLET FROM A GUN** *Tuff Audio DRKLP 1* ....**11** | 9 wks |

Eric B. and RAKIM *US, male vocal / instrumental duo*   **10 wks**

| 12 Sep 87 | **PAID IN FULL** *Fourth & Broadway BRLP 514* ....**85** | 4 wks |
| 6 Aug 88 | **FOLLOW THE LEADER** *MCA MCG 6031*............................**25** | 4 wks |

British Hit Albums Part One
Date of chart entry/Title & catalogue no./Peak position reached/Weeks on chart
★ Number One ● Top Ten † still on chart at 30 Dec 1995 ☐ credited to act billed in footnote

| 7 Jul 90 | **LET THE RHYTHM HIT 'EM** MCA MCG 6097 | **58** | 1 wk |
| 11 Jul 92 | **DON'T SWEAT THE TECHNIQUE** MCA MCAD 10594 | **73** | 1 wk |

B BOYS US, male vocal / instrumental group   **1 wk**

| 28 Jan 84 | **CUTTIN' HERBIE** Streetwave X KHAN 501 | **90** | 1 wk |

BABES IN TOYLAND US, female vocal / instrumental group   **3 wks**

| 5 Sep 92 | **FONTANELLE** Southern 185012 | **24** | 2 wks |
| 3 Jul 93 | **PAINKILLER** Southern 185122 | **53** | 1 wk |

BABY ANIMALS Australia, male vocal / instrumental group   **1 wk**

| 14 Mar 92 | **BABY ANIMALS** Imago PD 90580 | **70** | 1 wk |

BACCARA Spain, female vocal duo   **6 wks**

| 4 Mar 78 | **BACCARA** RCA PL 28316 | **26** | 6 wks |

Burt BACHARACH US, orchestra and chorus   **43 wks**

22 May 65	● **HIT MAKER - BURT BACHARACH** London HAR 8233	**3**	18 wks
28 Nov 70	**REACH OUT** A & M AMLS 908	**52**	3 wks
3 Apr 71	● **PORTRAIT IN MUSIC** A & M AMLS 2010	**5**	22 wks

BACHELORS Ireland, male vocal group   **103 wks**

27 Jun 64	● **THE BACHELORS AND 16 GREAT SONGS** Decca LK 4614	**2**	44 wks
9 Oct 65	**MORE GREAT SONG HITS FROM THE BACHELORS** Decca LK 4721	**15**	6 wks
9 Jul 66	**HITS OF THE SIXTIES** Decca TXL 102	**12**	9 wks
5 Nov 66	**BACHELORS' GIRLS** Decca LK 4827	**24**	8 wks
1 Jul 67	**GOLDEN ALL TIME HITS** Decca SKL 4849	**19**	7 wks
14 Jun 69	● **WORLD OF THE BACHELORS** Decca SPA 2	**8**	18 wks
23 Aug 69	**WORLD OF THE BACHELORS VOLUME 2** Decca SPA 22	**11**	7 wks
22 Dec 79	**25 GOLDEN GREATS** Warwick WW 5068	**38**	4 wks

BACHMAN-TURNER OVERDRIVE
Canada, male vocal / instrumental group   **13 wks**

| 14 Dec 74 | **NOT FRAGILE** Mercury 9100 007 | **12** | 13 wks |

BACK TO THE PLANET UK, male vocal / instrumental group   **2 wks**

| 18 Sep 93 | **MIND AND SOUL COLLABORATORS** Parallel ALLCD 2 | **32** | 2 wks |

BACKBEAT BAND US, male vocal / instrumental group   **2 wks**

| 16 Apr 94 | **BACKBEAT (film soundtrack)** Virgin CDV 2729 | **39** | 2 wks |

BAD BOYS INC. UK, male vocal group   **6 wks**

| 18 Jun 94 | **BAD BOYS INC.** A & M 5402002 | **13** | 6 wks |

BAD COMPANY UK, male vocal / instrumental group   **87 wks**

15 Jun 74	● **BAD COMPANY** Island ILPS 9279	**3**	25 wks
12 Apr 75	● **STRAIGHT SHOOTER** Island ILPS 9304	**3**	27 wks
21 Feb 76	● **RUN WITH THE PACK** Island ILPS 9346	**4**	12 wks
19 Mar 77	**BURNIN' SKY** Island ILPS 9441	**17**	8 wks

17 Mar 79	● **DESOLATION ANGELS** Swansong SSK 59408	**10**	9 wks
28 Aug 82	**ROUGH DIAMONDS** Swansong SSK 59419	**15**	6 wks

BAD ENGLISH UK / US, male vocal / instrumental group   **2 wks**

16 Sep 89	**BAD ENGLISH** Epic 4634471	**74**	1 wk
19 Oct 91	**BACKLASH** Epic 4685691	**64**	1 wk

BAD MANNERS UK, male vocal / instrumental group   **44 wks**

26 Apr 80	**SKA 'N' B** Magnet MAG 5033	**34**	13 wks
29 Nov 80	**LOONEE TUNES** Magnet MAG 5038	**36**	12 wks
24 Oct 81	**GOSH IT'S BAD MANNERS** Magnet MAGL 5043	**18**	12 wks
27 Nov 82	**FORGING AHEAD** Magnet MAGL 5050	**78**	1 wk
7 May 83	**THE HEIGHT OF BAD MANNERS** Telstar STAR 2229	**23**	6 wks

BAD NEWS UK, male vocal group   **1 wk**

24 Oct 87	**BAD NEWS** EMI EMC 3535	**69**	1 wk

BAD SEEDS – See Nick CAVE featuring the BAD SEEDS

Angelo BADALAMENTI Italy, male arranger   **25 wks**

17 Nov 90	**MUSIC FROM 'TWIN PEAKS'** Warner Bros. 7599263161	**27**	25 wks

BADLANDS UK, male vocal / instrumental group   **3 wks**

24 Jun 89	**BADLANDS** WEA 7819661	**39**	2 wks
22 Jun 91	**VOODOO HIGHWAY** Atlantic 7567822511	**74**	1 wk

Joan BAEZ US, female vocalist   **88 wks**

18 Jul 64	● **JOAN BAEZ IN CONCERT VOLUME 2** Fontana TFL 6033	**8**	19 wks
15 May 65	● **JOAN BAEZ NO. 5** Fontana TFL 6043	**3**	27 wks
19 Jun 65	● **JOAN BAEZ** Fontana TFL 6002	**9**	13 wks
27 Nov 65	● **FAREWELL ANGELINA** Fontana TFL 6058	**5**	23 wks
19 Jul 69	**JOAN BAEZ ON VANGUARD** Vanguard SVXL 100	**15**	5 wks
3 Apr 71	**FIRST TEN YEARS** Vanguard 6635 003	**41**	1 wk

Philip BAILEY US, male vocalist   **17 wks**

30 Mar 85	**CHINESE WALL** CBS 26161	**29**	17 wks

Anita BAKER US, female vocalist   **81 wks**

3 May 86	**RAPTURE** Elektra EKT 37	**13**	47 wks
29 Oct 88	● **GIVING YOU THE BEST THAT I GOT** Elektra EKT 49	**9**	20 wks
14 Jul 90	● **COMPOSITIONS** Elektra EKT 72	**7**	9 wks
24 Sep 94	**RHYTHM OF LOVE** Elektra 7559615552	**14**	5 wks

Ginger BAKER'S AIR FORCE
UK, male vocal / instrumental group   **1 wk**

13 Jun 70	**GINGER BAKER'S AIR FORCE** Polydor 266 2001	**37**	1 wk

See also Baker–Gurvitz Army.

BAKER-GURVITZ ARMY UK, male vocal / instrumental group   **5 wks**

22 Feb 75	**BAKER-GURVITZ ARMY** Vertigo 9103 201	**22**	5 wks

See also Ginger Baker's Air Force.

BALAAM AND THE ANGEL UK, male / vocal instrumental group   **2 wks**

16 Aug 86	**THE GREATEST STORY EVER TOLD** Virgin V 2377	**67**	2 wks

**B
53**

Kenny BALL *UK, male vocalist / instrumentalist – trumpet*　　**50 wks**

25 Aug 62	★ BEST OF BALL, BARBER AND BILK		
	Pye Golden Guinea GGL 0131 [1]	1	24 wks
7 Sep 63	● KENNY BALL'S GOLDEN HITS Pye Golden Guinea GGL 0209	4	26 wks

[1] Kenny Ball, Chris Barber and Acker Bilk

Michael BALL *UK, male vocalist*　　**34 wks**

30 May 92	★ MICHAEL BALL Polydor 5113302	1	10 wks
17 Jul 93	● ALWAYS Polydor 5196662	3	11 wks
13 Aug 94	● ONE CAREFUL OWNER Columbia 4772802	7	6 wks
19 Nov 94	THE BEST OF MICHAEL BALL PolyGram TV 5238912	25	7 wks

BANANARAMA *UK, female vocal group*　　**97 wks**

19 Mar 83	● DEEP SEA SKIVING London RAMA 1	7	16 wks
28 Apr 84	BANANARAMA London RAMA 2	16	11 wks
19 Jul 86	TRUE CONFESSIONS London RAMA 3	46	5 wks
19 Sep 87	WOW! London RAMA 4	26	26 wks
22 Oct 88	● THE GREATEST HITS COLLECTION London RAMA 5	3	37 wks
25 May 91	POP LIFE London 8282461	42	1 wk
10 Apr 93	PLEASE YOURSELF London 8283572	46	1 wk

BANCO DE GAIA *UK, male multi-instrumentalist – Toby Marks*　　**4 wks**

12 Mar 94	MAYA Planet Dog BARKCD 3	34	2 wks
13 May 95	LAST TRAIN TO LHASA Planet Dog BARKCD 0115	31	2 wks

BAND *Canada / US, male vocal / instrumental group*　　**18 wks**

31 Jan 70	THE BAND Capitol EST 132	25	11 wks
3 Oct 70	STAGE FRIGHT Capitol EA SW 425	15	6 wks
27 Nov 71	CAHOOTS Capitol EAST 651	41	1 wk

BAND AID – *See Midge URE*

BANDERAS *UK, female vocal / instrumental duo*　　**3 wks**

13 Apr 91	RIPE London 8282471	40	3 wks

BANGLES *US, female vocal / instrumental group*　　**97 wks**

16 Mar 85	ALL OVER THE PLACE CBS 26015	86	1 wk
15 Mar 86	● DIFFERENT LIGHT CBS 26659	3	47 wks
10 Dec 88	● EVERYTHING CBS 4629791	5	26 wks
9 Jun 90	● GREATEST HITS CBS 4667691	4	23 wks

Tony BANKS *UK, male instrumentalist – keyboards*　　**7 wks**

20 Oct 79	A CURIOUS FEELING Charisma CAS 1148	21	5 wks
25 Jun 83	THE FUGITIVE Charisma TBLP 1	50	2 wks

BANSHEES – *See SIOUXSIE and the BANSHEES*

Chris BARBER *UK, male vocalist / instrumentalist – trombone*　　**88 wks**

24 Sep 60	CHRIS BARBER BAND BOX NO. 2 Columbia 33SCX 3277	17	1 wk
5 Nov 60	ELITE SYNCOPATIONS Columbia 33SX 1245	18	1 wk
12 Nov 60	BEST OF CHRIS BARBER Ace Of Clubs ACL 1037	17	1 wk
27 May 61	● BEST OF BARBER AND BILK VOLUME 1		
	Pye Golden Guinea GGL 0075 [1]	4	43 wks
11 Nov 61	● BEST OF BARBER AND BILK VOLUME 2		
	Pye Golden Guinea GGL 0096 [1]	8	18 wks
25 Aug 62	★ BEST OF BALL, BARBER AND BILK		
	Pye Golden Guinea GGL 0131 [2]	1	24 wks

[1] Chris Barber and Acker Bilk　[2] Kenny Ball, Chris Barber and Acker Bilk

BARCLAY JAMES HARVEST UK, male vocal / instrumental group 42 wks

14 Dec 74	BARCLAY JAMES HARVEST LIVE Polydor 2683 052	40	2 wks
18 Oct 75	TIME HONOURED GHOST Polydor 2383 361	32	3 wks
23 Oct 76	OCTOBERON Polydor 2442 144	19	4 wks
1 Oct 77	GONE TO EARTH Polydor 2442 148	30	7 wks
21 Oct 78	BARCLAY JAMES HARVEST XII Polydor POLD 5006	31	2 wks
23 May 81	TURN OF THE TIDE Polydor POLD 5040	55	2 wks
24 Jul 82	A CONCERT FOR THE PEOPLE (BERLIN) Polydor POLD 5052	15	11 wks
28 May 83	RING OF CHANGES Polydor POLH 3	36	4 wks
14 Apr 84	VICTIMS OF CIRCUMSTANCE Polydor POLD 5135	33	6 wks
14 Feb 87	FACE TO FACE Polydor POLD 5209	65	1 wk

BARENAKED LADIES Canada, male vocal / instrumental group 1 wk

27 Aug 94	MAYBE YOU SHOULD DRIVE Reprise 9362457092	57	1 wk

Daniel BARENBOIM – See John WILLIAMS and Daniel BARENBOIM

Wild Willy BARRETT – See John OTWAY and Wild Willy BARRETT

Syd BARRETT UK, male vocalist / instrumentalist – guitar 1 wk

7 Feb 70	MADCAP LAUGHS Harvest SHVL 765	40	1 wk

BARRON KNIGHTS UK, male vocal / instrumental group 22 wks

2 Dec 78	NIGHT GALLERY Epic EPC 83221	15	13 wks
1 Dec 79	TEACH THE WORLD TO LAUGH Epic EPC 83891	51	4 wks
13 Dec 80	JUST A GIGGLE Epic EPC 84550	45	5 wks

John BARRY UK, male arranger / conductor 17 wks

29 Jan 72	THE PERSUADERS CBS 64816	18	9 wks
20 Apr 91	DANCES WITH WOLVES (film soundtrack) Epic 4675911	45	8 wks

BASIA Poland, female vocalist 4 wks

13 Feb 88	TIME AND TIDE Portrait 4502631	61	3 wks
3 Mar 90	LONDON WARSAW NEW YORK Epic 4632821	68	1 wk

Count BASIE US, male orchestra leader / instrumentalist – piano 24 wks

16 Apr 60	CHAIRMAN OF THE BOARD Columbia 33SX 1209	17	1 wk
23 Feb 63	● SINATRA - BASIE Reprise R 1008 [1]	2	23 wks

[1] Frank Sinatra and Count Basie

Toni BASIL US, female vocalist 16 wks

6 Feb 82	WORD OF MOUTH Radialchoice BASIL 1	15	16 wks

Shirley BASSEY UK, female vocalist 284 wks

28 Jan 61	FABULOUS SHIRLEY BASSEY Columbia 33SX 1178	12	2 wks
25 Feb 61	● SHIRLEY Columbia 33SX 1286	9	10 wks
17 Feb 62	SHIRLEY BASSEY Columbia 33SX 1382	14	11 wks
15 Dec 62	LET'S FACE THE MUSIC Columbia 33SX 1454 [1]	12	7 wks
4 Dec 65	SHIRLEY BASSEY AT THE PIGALLE Columbia 33SX 1787	15	7 wks
27 Aug 66	I'VE GOT A SONG FOR YOU United Artists ULP 1142	26	1 wk
17 Feb 68	TWELVE OF THOSE SONGS Columbia SCX 6204	38	3 wks
7 Dec 68	GOLDEN HITS OF SHIRLEY BASSEY Columbia SCX 6294	28	40 wks
11 Jul 70	LIVE AT THE TALK OF THE TOWN United Artists UAS 29095	38	6 wks
29 Aug 70	● SOMETHING United Artists UAS 29100	5	28 wks
15 May 71	● SOMETHING ELSE United Artists UAG 29149	7	9 wks
2 Oct 71	BIG SPENDER Sunset SLS 50262	27	8 wks
30 Oct 71	IT'S MAGIC Starline SRS 5082	32	1 wk

B
55

6 Nov 71	THE FABULOUS SHIRLEY BASSEY *MFP 1398*....................................**48**	1 wk
4 Dec 71	WHAT NOW MY LOVE *MFP 5230* **17**	5 wks
8 Jan 72	THE SHIRLEY BASSEY COLLECTION *United Artists UAD 60013/4*..**37**	1 wk
19 Feb 72	I CAPRICORN *United Artists UAS 29246* **13**	11 wks
29 Nov 72	AND I LOVE YOU SO *United Artists UAS 29385*.....................**24**	9 wks
2 Jun 73	● NEVER NEVER NEVER *United Artists UAG 29471* **10**	10 wks
15 Mar 75	● THE SHIRLEY BASSEY SINGLES ALBUM	
	United Artists UAS 29728 ....**2**	23 wks
1 Nov 75	GOOD, BAD BUT BEAUTIFUL *United Artists UAS 29881* **13**	7 wks
15 May 76	LOVE, LIFE AND FEELINGS *United Artists UAS 29944* **13**	5 wks
4 Dec 76	THOUGHTS OF LOVE *United Artists UAS 30011* **15**	9 wks
25 Jun 77	YOU TAKE MY HEART AWAY *United Artists UAS 30037* **34**	5 wks
4 Nov 78	● 25TH ANNIVERSARY ALBUM *United Artists SBTV 601 4748* **3**	12 wks
12 May 79	THE MAGIC IS YOU *United Artists UATV 30230*.....................**40**	5 wks
17 Jul 82	LOVE SONGS *Applause APKL 1163* **48**	5 wks
20 Oct 84	I AM WHAT I AM *Towerbell TOWLP 7* **25**	18 wks
18 May 91	KEEP THE MUSIC PLAYING *Dino DINTV 21* **25**	7 wks
5 Dec 92	THE BEST OF SHIRLEY BASSEY *Dino DINCD 49* **27**	5 wks
4 Dec 93	SHIRLEY BASSEY SINGS ANDREW LLOYD WEBBER	
	Premier CDDPR 114 ....**34**	5 wks
11 Nov 95	SHIRLEY BASSEY SINGS THE MOVIES *PolyGram TV 5293992* ..**24†**	8 wks

1 Shirley Bassey with the Nelson Riddle Orchestra

BASS-O-MATIC *UK, male multi–instrumentalist*   **2 wks**

13 Oct 90	SET THE CONTROLS FOR THE HEART OF THE BASS	
	Virgin V 2641 ....**57**	2 wks

Mike BATT – See *Justin HAYWARD*

BAUHAUS *UK, male vocal/instrumental group*   **24 wks**

15 Nov 80	IN THE FLAT FIELD *4AD CAD 13* **72**	1 wk
24 Oct 81	MASK *Beggars Banquet BEGA 29*.....................................**30**	5 wks
30 Oct 82	● THE SKY'S GONE OUT *Beggars Banquet BEGA 42*.........................**4**	6 wks
23 Jul 83	BURNING FROM THE INSIDE *Beggars Banquet BEGA 45* **13**	10 wks
30 Nov 85	1979–1983 *Beggars Banquet BEGA 64* **36**	2 wks

BAY CITY ROLLERS *UK, male vocal/instrumental group*   **127 wks**

12 Oct 74	★ ROLLIN' *Bell BELLS 244* **1**	62 wks
3 May 75	★ ONCE UPON A STAR *Bell SYBEL 8001* **1**	37 wks
13 Dec 75	● WOULDN'T YOU LIKE IT *Bell SYBEL 8002* **3**	12 wks
25 Sep 76	● DEDICATION *Bell SYBEL 8005*.......................................**4**	12 wks
13 Aug 77	IT'S A GAME *Arista SPARTY 1009* **18**	4 wks

BBC SYMPHONY ORCHESTRA, SINGERS and CHORUS
UK, orchestra/choir and audience   **6 wks**

4 Oct 69	LAST NIGHT OF THE PROMS *Philips SFM 23033* **36**	1 wk
11 Dec 82	HIGHLIGHTS - LAST NIGHT OF THE PROMS '82 *K-Tel NE 1198*....**69**	5 wks

Last Night Of The Proms *was conducted by Colin Davis and* Highlights Last Night Of The Proms '82 *by James Loughran.*

BBC WELSH CHORUS – See *Aled JONES*

BBM *UK, male vocal/instrumental group*   **4 wks**

18 Jun 94	● AROUND THE NEXT DREAM *Virgin CDV 2745*................................**9**	4 wks

BEACH BOYS *US, male vocal/instrumental group*   **558 wks**

25 Sep 65	SURFIN' USA *Capitol T 1890*..**17**	7 wks
19 Feb 66	● BEACH BOYS PARTY *Capitol T 2398* **3**	14 wks
16 Apr 66	● BEACH BOYS TODAY *Capitol T 2269*.......................................**6**	25 wks
9 Jul 66	● PET SOUNDS *Capitol T 2458*...**2**	39 wks
16 Jul 66	● SUMMER DAYS *Capitol T 2354* **4**	22 wks

B
56

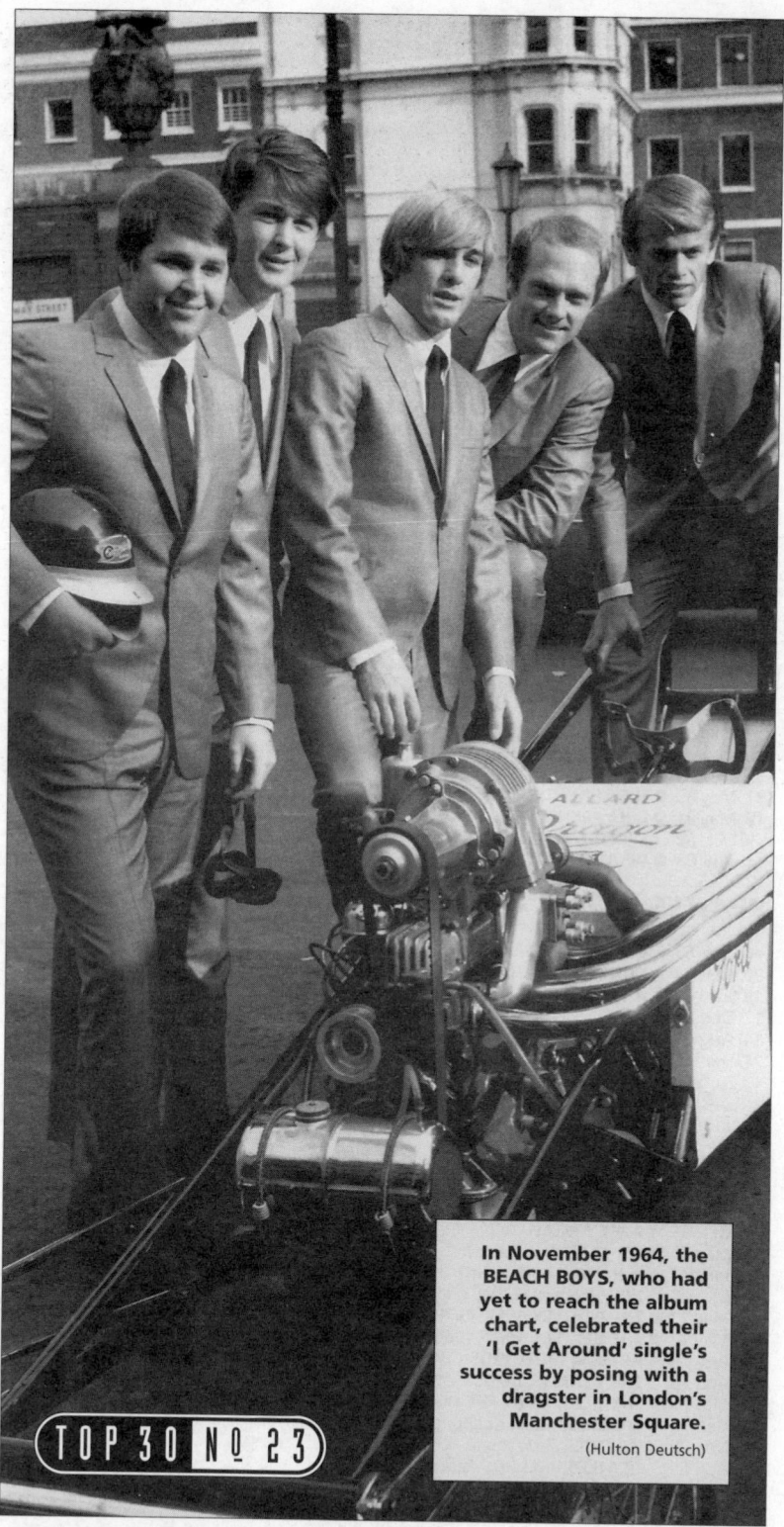

In November 1964, the BEACH BOYS, who had yet to reach the album chart, celebrated their 'I Get Around' single's success by posing with a dragster in London's Manchester Square.

(Hulton Deutsch)

TOP 30 № 23

12 Nov 66	● **BEST OF THE BEACH BOYS** *Capitol T 20865*	2	142 wks
11 Mar 67	**SURFER GIRL** *Capitol T 1981*	13	14 wks
21 Oct 67	● **BEST OF THE BEACH BOYS VOLUME 2** *Capitol ST 20956*	3	39 wks
18 Nov 67	● **SMILEY SMILE** *Capitol ST 9001*	9	8 wks
16 Mar 68	● **WILD HONEY** *Capitol ST 2859*	7	15 wks
21 Sep 68	**FRIENDS** *Capitol ST 2895*	13	8 wks
23 Nov 68	● **BEST OF THE BEACH BOYS VOLUME 3** *Capitol ST 21142*	9	12 wks
29 Mar 69	● **20 / 20** *Capitol EST 133*	3	10 wks
19 Sep 70	● **GREATEST HITS** *Capitol T 21628*	5	30 wks
5 Dec 70	**SUNFLOWER** *Stateside SSL 8251*	29	6 wks
27 Nov 71	**SURF'S UP** *Stateside SLS 10313*	15	7 wks
24 Jun 72	**CARL AND THE PASSIONS / SO TOUGH** *Reprise K 44184*	25	1 wk
17 Feb 73	**HOLLAND** *Reprise K 54008*	20	7 wks
10 Jul 76	★ **20 GOLDEN GREATS** *Capitol EMTV 1*	1	86 wks
24 Jul 76	**15 BIG ONES** *Reprise K 54079*	31	3 wks
7 May 77	**THE BEACH BOYS LOVE YOU** *Reprise K 54087*	28	1 wk
21 Apr 79	**LA (LIGHT ALBUM)** *Caribou CRB 86081*	32	6 wks
12 Apr 80	**KEEPING THE SUMMER ALIVE** *Caribou CRB 86109*	54	3 wks
30 Jul 83	★ **THE VERY BEST OF THE BEACH BOYS** *Capitol BBTV 1867193*	1	17 wks
22 Jun 85	**THE BEACH BOYS** *Caribou CRB 26378*	60	2 wks
23 Jun 90	◒ **SUMMER DREAMS** *Capitol EMTVD 51*	2	27 wks
1 Jul 95	**THE BEST OF THE BEACH BOYS** *Capitol CDESTVD 3*	25	6 wks
16 Sep 95	**PET SOUNDS (re-issue)** *Fame CDFA 3298*	70	1 wk

The two Best Of The Beach Boys *albums are different.*

BEASTIE BOYS *US, male vocal group*   **59 wks**

31 Jan 87	● **LICENCE TO ILL** *Def Jam 450062*	7	40 wks
5 Aug 89	**PAUL'S BOUTIQUE** *Capitol EST 2102*	44	2 wks
4 Jun 94	● **ILL COMMUNICATION** *Capitol CDEST 2229*	10	15 wks
10 Jun 95	**ROOT DOWN EP** *Capitol CDEST 2262*	23	2 wks

**B
58**

BEAT *UK, male vocal / instrumental group*   **69 wks**

31 May 80	● **JUST CAN'T STOP IT** *Go-Feet BEAT 001*	3	32 wks
16 May 81	● **WHA'PPEN** *Go-Feet BEAT 3*	3	18 wks
9 Oct 82	**SPECIAL BEAT SERVICE** *Go-Feet BEAT 5*	21	6 wks
11 Jun 83	● **WHAT IS BEAT? (THE BEST OF THE BEAT)** *Go-Feet BEAT 6*	10	13 wks

BEATLES *UK, male vocal / instrumental group*   **1160 wks**

6 Apr 63	★ **PLEASE PLEASE ME** *Parlophone PMC 1202*	1	70 wks
30 Nov 63	★ **WITH THE BEATLES** *Parlophone PMC 1206*	1	51 wks
18 Jul 64	★ **A HARD DAY'S NIGHT** *Parlophone PMC 1230*	1	38 wks
12 Dec 64	★ **BEATLES FOR SALE** *Parlophone PMC 1240*	1	46 wks
14 Aug 65	★ **HELP** *Parlophone PMC 1255*	1	37 wks
11 Dec 65	★ **RUBBER SOUL** *Parlophone PMC 1267*	1	42 wks
13 Aug 66	★ **REVOLVER** *Parlophone PMC 7009*	1	34 wks
10 Dec 66	● **A COLLECTION OF BEATLES OLDIES** *Parlophone PMC 7016*	7	34 wks
3 Jun 67	★ **SERGEANT PEPPER'S LONELY HEARTS CLUB BAND** *Parlophone PCS 7027*	1	148 wks
13 Jan 68	**MAGICAL MYSTERY TOUR (import)** *Capitol SMAL 2835*	31	2 wks
7 Dec 68	★ **THE BEATLES** *Apple PCS 7067/8*	1	22 wks
1 Feb 69	● **YELLOW SUBMARINE** *Apple PCS 7070*	3	10 wks
4 Oct 69	★ **ABBEY ROAD** *Apple PCS 7088*	1	81 wks
23 May 70	★ **LET IT BE** *Apple PXS 1*	1	59 wks
16 Jan 71	**A HARD DAY'S NIGHT (re-issue)** *Parlophone PCS 3058*	30	1 wk
24 Jul 71	**HELP (re-issue)** *Parlophone PCS 3071*	33	2 wks
5 May 73	● **THE BEATLES 1967–1970** *Apple PCSP 718*	2	113 wks
5 May 73	● **THE BEATLES 1962–1966** *Apple PCSP 717*	3	148 wks
26 Jun 76	**ROCK 'N' ROLL MUSIC** *Parlophone PCSP 719*	11	15 wks
21 Aug 76	**THE BEATLES TAPES** *Polydor 2683 068*	45	1 wk
21 May 77	★ **THE BEATLES AT THE HOLLYWOOD BOWL** *Parlophone EMTV 4*	1	17 wks
17 Dec 77	● **LOVE SONGS** *Parlophone PCSP 721*	7	17 wks
3 Nov 79	**RARITIES** *Parlophone PCM 1001*	71	1 wk
15 Nov 80	**BEATLES BALLADS** *Parlophone PCS 7214*	17	16 wks
30 Oct 82	● **20 GREATEST HITS** *Parlophone PCTC 260*	10	30 wks
7 Mar 87	**PLEASE PLEASE ME (re-issue)** *Parlophone CDP 746 4352*	32	4 wks

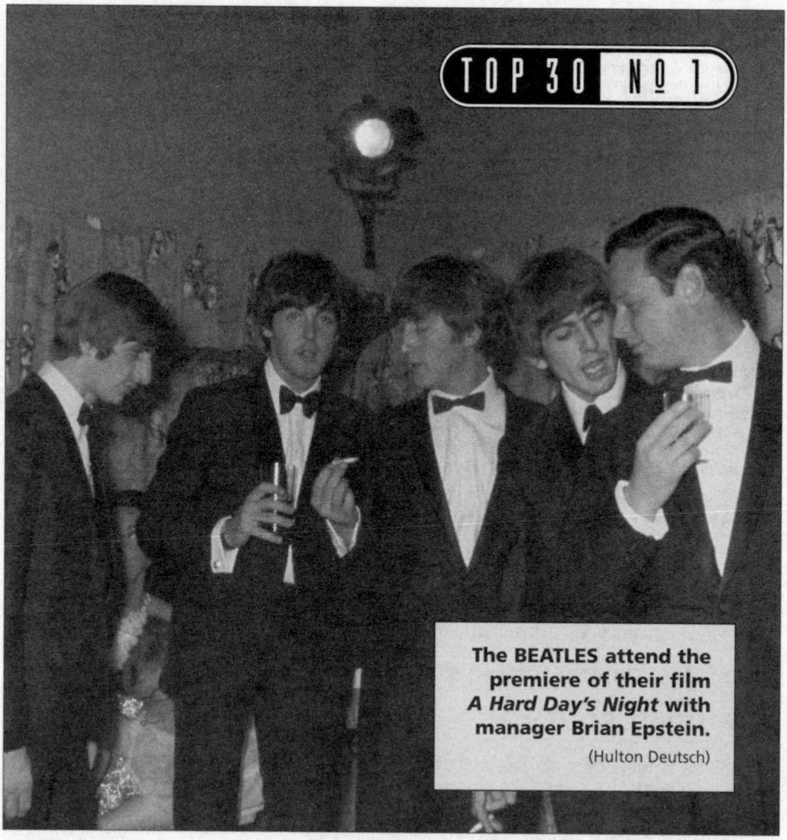

TOP 30 | Nº 1

The BEATLES attend the premiere of their film *A Hard Day's Night* with manager Brian Epstein.

(Hulton Deutsch)

B 59

Carry On Up The Charts - The Best of the BEAUTIFUL SOUTH was the number two hit of 1994.

(LFI)

7 Mar 87	**WITH THE BEATLES (re-issue)** *Parlophone CDP 746 4362* **40**	2 wks
7 Mar 87	**A HARD DAY'S NIGHT (2nd re-issue)** *Parlophone CDP 7464372* **30**	4 wks
7 Mar 87	**BEATLES FOR SALE (re-issue)** *Parlophone CDP 746 4382* **45**	2 wks
9 May 87	**HELP (2nd re-issue)** *Parlophone CDP 7464392* **61**	2 wks
9 May 87	**RUBBER SOUL (re-issue)** *Parlophone CDP 746 4402* **60**	3 wks
9 May 87	**REVOLVER (re-issue)** *Parlophone CDP 746 4412* **55**	5 wks
6 Jun 87	● **SERGEANT PEPPER'S LONELY HEARTS CLUB BAND (re-issue)**	
	Parlophone CDP 7464422....................................**3†**	26 wks
5 Sep 87	**THE BEATLES (re-issue)** *Parlophone CDS 746 4439* **18**	2 wks
5 Sep 87	**YELLOW SUBMARINE (re-issue)** *Parlophone CDP 746 4452* **60**	1 wk
3 Oct 87	**MAGICAL MYSTERY TOUR (re-issue)** *Parlophone PCTC 255*.......**52**	1 wk
31 Oct 87	**ABBEY ROAD (re-issue)** *Parlophone CDP 746 4462* **30**	2 wks
31 Oct 87	**LET IT BE (re-issue)** *Parlophone CDP 746 4472* **50**	1 wk
19 Mar 88	**PAST MASTERS VOLUME 1** *Parlophone CDBPM 1* **49**	1 wk
19 Mar 88	**PAST MASTERS VOLUME 2** *Parlophone CDBPM 2* **46**	1 wk
2 Oct 93	● **THE BEATLES 1962-1966 (re-issue)** *Parlophone BEACD 2511* .....**3†**	23 wks
2 Oct 93	● **THE BEATLES 1967-1970 (re-issue)** *Parlophone BEACD 2512*.....**4†**	20 wks
10 Dec 94	★ **LIVE AT THE BBC** *Apple CDS 8317962* **1**	20 wks
2 Dec 95	● **ANTHOLOGY 1** *Apple CDPCSP 727*...........................**2†**	5 wks

Yellow Submarine featured several tracks by the George Martin Orchestra. The albums recharted in 1987 and 1993 after being made available as compact discs.

BEATMASTERS *UK, male / female instrumental group*   **10 wks**

1 Jul 89	**ANYWAYAWANNA** *Rhythm King LEFTLP 10*......................**30**	10 wks

BEATS INTERNATIONAL
UK, male / female vocal / instrumental group   **15 wks**

14 Apr 90	**LET THEM EAT BINGO** *Go.Beat 8421961*.........................**17**	15 wks

BEAUTIFUL SOUTH *UK, male / female vocal / instrumental group*   **145 wks**

4 Nov 89	● **WELCOME TO THE BEAUTIFUL SOUTH** *Go! Discs AGOLP 16* **2**	23 wks
10 Nov 90	● **CHOKE** *Go! Discs 8282331* **2**	22 wks
11 Apr 92	● **0898** *Go! Discs 8283102* **4**	17 wks
9 Apr 94	● **MIAOW** *Go! Discs 8285072* **6**	24 wks
19 Nov 94	★ **CARRY ON UP THE CHARTS – THE BEST OF**	
	THE BEAUTIFUL SOUTH *Go! Discs 8285722* ....**1†**	59 wks

BE-BOP DELUXE *UK, male vocal / instrumental group*   **28 wks**

31 Jan 76	**SUNBURST FINISH** *Harvest SHSP 4053*....................**17**	12 wks
25 Sep 76	**MODERN MUSIC** *Harvest SHSP 4058* **12**	6 wks
6 Aug 77	● **LIVE! IN THE AIR AGE** *Harvest SHVL 816* **10**	5 wks
25 Feb 78	**DRASTIC PLASTIC** *Harvest SHSP 4091* **22**	5 wks

BECK *US, male vocalist*   **3 wks**

2 Apr 94	**MELLOW GOLD** *Geffen GED 24634* **41**	3 wks

Jeff BECK *UK, male vocal / instrumentalist – guitar*   **14 wks**

13 Sep 69	**BECK-OLA** *Columbia SCX 6351* **39**	1 wk
28 Apr 73	**JEFF BECK, TIM BOGERT AND CARMINE APPICE**	
	Epic EPC 65455 [1] **28**	3 wks
24 Jul 76	**WIRED** *CBS 86012*....................**38**	5 wks
19 Jul 80	**THERE AND BACK** *Epic EPC 83288*..........................**38**	4 wks
17 Aug 85	**FLASH** *Epic EPC 26112* **83**	1 wk

[1] Jeff Beck, Tim Bogert and Carmine Appice

BEE GEES *UK / Australia, male vocal / instrumental group*   **239 wks**

12 Aug 67	● **BEE GEES FIRST** *Polydor 583012* **8**	26 wks
24 Feb 68	**HORIZONTAL** *Polydor 582020*............................**16**	15 wks
28 Sep 68	● **IDEA** *Polydor 583036* **4**	18 wks
5 Apr 69	● **ODESSA** *Polydor 583049/50* **10**	1 wk

8 Nov 69	● **BEST OF THE BEE GEES** Polydor 583063	**7**	22	wks
9 May 70	**CUCUMBER CASTLE** Polydor 2383010	**57**	2	wks
17 Feb 79	★ **SPIRITS HAVING FLOWN** RSO RSBG 001	**1**	33	wks
10 Nov 79	● **BEE GEES GREATEST** RSO RSDX 001	**6**	25	wks
7 Nov 81	**LIVING EYES** RSO RSBG 002	**73**	8	wks
3 Oct 87	● **E.S.P.** Warner Bros. WX 83	**5**	24	wks
29 Apr 89	**ONE** Warner Bros. WX 252	**29**	3	wks
17 Nov 90	● **THE VERY BEST OF THE BEE GEES** Polydor 8473391	**8**	44	wks
6 Apr 91	**HIGH CIVILISATION** Warner Bros. WX 417	**24**	5	wks
25 Sep 93	**SIZE ISN'T EVERYTHING** Polydor 5199452	**23**	13	wks

All albums from Cucumber Castle onwards group were UK only.

Sir Thomas BEECHAM *UK, conductor*   **2 wks**

26 Mar 60	**CARMEN** HMV ALP 1762/4	**18**	2	wks

Full credit on sleeve reads 'Orchestre National de la Radio Diffusion Française, conducted by Sir Thomas Beecham'.

BELL BIV DEVOE *US, male vocal group*   **5 wks**

1 Sep 90	**POISON** MCA MCG 6094	**35**	5	wks

BELLAMY BROTHERS *US, male vocal duo*   **6 wks**

19 Jun 76	**BELLAMY BROTHERS** Warner Bros. K 56242	**21**	6	wks

Regina BELLE *US, female vocalist*   **5 wks**

1 Aug 87	**ALL BY MYSELF** CBS 450 9981	**53**	4	wks
16 Sep 89	**STAY WITH ME** CBS 465132 1	**62**	1	wk

BELLE STARS *UK, female vocal / instrumental group*   **12 wks**

5 Feb 83	**THE BELLE STARS** Stiff SEEZ 45	**15**	12	wks

BELLY *US, male / female vocal / instrumental group*   **13 wks**

13 Feb 93	● **STAR** 4AD 3002CD	**2**	10	wks
25 Feb 95	● **KING** 4AD CADD 5004CD	**6**	3	wks

Pierre BELMONDE *France, male instrumentalist – panpipes*   **10 wks**

7 Jun 80	**THEMES FOR DREAMS** K-Tel ONE 1077	**13**	10	wks

BELMONTS – *See DION and the BELMONTS*

BELOVED *UK, male vocal / instrumental duo*   **28 wks**

3 Mar 90	**HAPPINESS** East West WX 299	**14**	14	wks
1 Dec 90	**BLISSED OUT** East West WX 383	**38**	2	wks
20 Feb 93	● **CONSCIENCE** East West 4509914832	**2**	12	wks

Pat BENATAR *US, female vocalist*   **84 wks**

25 Jul 81	**PRECIOUS TIME** Chrysalis CHR 1346	**30**	7	wks
13 Nov 82	**GET NERVOUS** Chrysalis CHR 1396	**73**	6	wks
15 Oct 83	**LIVE FROM EARTH** Chrysalis CHR 1451	**60**	5	wks
17 Nov 84	**TROPICO** Chrysalis CHR 1471	**31**	25	wks
24 Aug 85	**IN THE HEAT OF THE NIGHT** Chrysalis CHR 1236	**98**	1	wk
7 Dec 85	**SEVEN THE HARD WAY** Chrysalis CHR 1507	**69**	4	wks
7 Nov 87	● **BEST SHOTS** Chrysalis PATV 1	**6**	19	wks
16 Jul 88	**WIDE AWAKE IN DREAMLAND** Chrysalis CDL 1628	**11**	14	wks
4 May 91	**TRUE LOVE** Chrysalis CHR 1805	**40**	3	wks

Cliff BENNETT and the REBEL ROUSERS
UK, male vocal / instrumental group   **3 wks**

22 Oct 66	**DRIVIN' ME WILD** MFP 1121	**25**	3	wks

B
61

Tony BENNETT US, male vocalist   **63 wks**

29 May 65	**I LEFT MY HEART IN SAN FRANCISCO** CBS BPG 62201 ....**13**	14 wks
19 Feb 66 ●	**A STRING OF TONY'S HITS** CBS DP 66010 ....**9**	13 wks
10 Jun 67	**TONY'S GREATEST HITS** CBS SBPG 62821 ....**14**	24 wks
23 Sep 67	**TONY MAKES IT HAPPEN** CBS SBPG 63055 ....**31**	3 wks
23 Mar 68	**FOR ONCE IN MY LIFE** CBS SBPG 63166 ....**29**	5 wks
26 Feb 77	**THE VERY BEST OF TONY BENNETT – 20 GREATEST HITS** Warwick PA 5021 ....**23**	4 wks

George BENSON US, male vocalist / instrumentalist – guitar   **269 wks**

19 Mar 77	**IN FLIGHT** Warner Bros. K 56237 ....**19**	23 wks
18 Feb 78	**WEEKEND IN L.A.** Warner Bros. K 66074 ....**47**	1 wk
24 Mar 79	**LIVING INSIDE YOUR LOVE** Warner Bros. K 66085 ....**24**	14 wks
26 Jul 80 ●	**GIVE ME THE NIGHT** Warner Bros. K 56823 ....**3**	40 wks
14 Nov 81	**GEORGE BENSON COLLECTION** Warner Bros. K 66107 ....**19**	35 wks
11 Jun 83 ●	**IN YOUR EYES** Warner Bros. 9237441 ....**3**	53 wks
26 Jan 85 ●	**20 / 20** Warner Bros. 9251781 ....**9**	19 wks
19 Oct 85 ★	**THE LOVE SONGS** K-Tel NE 1308 ....**1**	26 wks
6 Sep 86	**WHILE THE CITY SLEEPS . . .** Warner Bros. WX 55 ....**13**	27 wks
11 Jul 87	**COLLABORATION** Warner Bros. WX 91 [1] **47**	6 wks
10 Sep 88	**TWICE THE LOVE** Warner Bros. WX 160 ....**16**	10 wks
8 Jul 89	**TENDERLY** Warner Bros. WX 263 ....**52**	3 wks
26 Oct 91	**MIDNIGHT MOODS – THE LOVE COLLECTION** Telstar STAR 2450 ....**25**	12 wks

[1] George Benson and Earl Klugh

BERLIN US, male / female vocal / instrumental group   **11 wks**

17 Jan 87	**COUNT THREE AND PRAY** Mercury MER 101 ....**32**	11 wks

BERLIN PHILHARMONIC ORCHESTRA – See Herbert VON KARAJAN

B
62

Shelley BERMAN US, male comedian   **4 wks**

19 Nov 60	**INSIDE SHELLEY BERMAN** Capitol CLP 1300 ....**12**	4 wks

Leonard BERNSTEIN US, male conductor   **2 wks**

10 Feb 90	**BERNSTEIN IN BERLIN - BEETHOVEN'S 9TH** Deutsche Grammophon **54**	2 wks

Leonard BERNSTEIN'S WEST SIDE STORY – See STUDIO CAST RECORDINGS

Chuck BERRY US, male vocalist / instrumentalist – guitar   **53 wks**

25 May 63	**CHUCK BERRY** Pye International NPL 28024 ....**12**	16 wks
5 Oct 63 ●	**CHUCK BERRY ON STAGE** Pye International NPL 28027 ....**6**	11 wks
7 Dec 63 ●	**MORE CHUCK BERRY** Pye International NPL 28028 ....**9**	8 wks
30 May 64 ●	**HIS LATEST AND GREATEST** Pye NPL 28037 ....**8**	7 wks
3 Oct 64	**YOU NEVER CAN TELL** Pye NPL 29039 ....**18**	2 wks
12 Feb 77 ●	**MOTORVATIN'** Chess 9288 690 ....**7**	9 wks

Mike BERRY UK, male vocalist   **3 wks**

24 Jan 81	**THE SUNSHINE OF YOUR SMILE** Polydor 2383 592 ....**63**	3 wks

Nick BERRY UK, male vocalist   **8 wks**

20 Dec 86	**NICK BERRY** BBC REB 618 ....**99**	1 wk
21 Nov 92	**NICK BERRY** Columbia 4727182 ....**28**	7 wks

The two identically titled albums are different.

BEVERLEY-PHILLIPS ORCHESTRA UK, orchestra   **9 wks**

9 Oct 76	**GOLD ON SILVER** Warwick WW 5018 ....**22**	9 wks

Frankie BEVERLY – *See MAZE featuring Frankie BEVERLY*

B-52s *US, male / female vocal / instrumental group*   **69 wks**

4 Aug 79	**B-52S** *Island ILPS 9580*	22	12 wks
13 Sep 80	**WILD PLANET** *Island ILPS 9622*	18	4 wks
11 Jul 81	**THE PARTY MIX ALBUM** *Island IPM 1001*	36	5 wks
27 Feb 82	**MESOPOTAMIA** *EMI ISSP 4006*	18	6 wks
21 May 83	**WHAMMY!** *Island ILPS 9759*	33	4 wks
8 Aug 87	**BOUNCING OFF THE SATELLITES** *Island ILPS 9871*	74	2 wks
29 Jul 89	● **COSMIC THING** *Reprise WX 283*	8	27 wks
14 Jul 90	**THE BEST OF THE B-52S – DANCE THIS MESS AROUND** *Island ILPS 9959*	36	3 wks
11 Jul 92	● **GOOD STUFF** *Reprise 7599269432*	8	6 wks

BIBLE *UK, male vocal / instrumental group*   **2 wks**

2 Jan 88	**EUREKA** *Cooltempo CHR 1646*	71	1 wk
7 Oct 89	**THE BIBLE** *Ensign CHEN 12*	67	1 wk

BIG AUDIO DYNAMITE *UK, male vocal / instrumental group*   **43 wks**

16 Nov 85	**THIS IS BIG AUDIO DYNAMITE** *CBS 26714*	27	27 wks
8 Nov 86	**NO. 10 UPPING STREET** *CBS 450 1371*	11	8 wks
9 Jul 88	**TIGHTEN UP VOL. 88** *CBS 4611991*	33	3 wks
16 Sep 89	**MEGATOP PHOENIX** *CBS 4657901*	26	3 wks
2 Nov 90	**KOOL-AID** *CBS 4674661*	55	1 wk
17 Aug 91	**THE GLOBE** *Columbia 4677061*	63	1 wk

BIG BEN BANJO BAND *UK, male instrumental group*   **1 wk**

17 Dec 60	**MORE MINSTREL MELODIES** *Columbia 33SX 1254*	20	1 wk

BIG COUNTRY *UK, male vocal / instrumental group*   **147 wks**

6 Aug 83	● **THE CROSSING** *Mercury MERH 27*	3	80 wks
27 Oct 84	★ **STEELTOWN** *Mercury MERH 49*	1	21 wks
12 Jul 86	● **THE SEER** *Mercury MERH 87*	2	16 wks
8 Oct 88	● **PEACE IN OUR TIME** *Mercury MERH 130*	9	6 wks
26 May 90	● **THROUGH A BIG COUNTRY – GREATEST HITS** *Mercury 8460221*	2	17 wks
28 Sep 91	**NO PLACE LIKE HOME** *Vertigo 5102301*	28	2 wks
3 Apr 93	**THE BUFFALO SKINNERS** *Compulsion CDNOIS 2*	25	2 wks
18 Jun 94	**WITHOUT THE AID OF A SAFETY NET (LIVE)** *Compulsion CDNOIS 5*	35	1 wk
24 Jun 95	**WHY THE LONG FACE** *Transatlantic TRACD 109*	48	2 wks

BIG DADDY KANE *US, male vocalist*   **3 wks**

30 Sep 89	**IT'S A BIG DADDY THING** *Cold Chillin' WX 305*	37	3 wks

BIG DISH *UK, male vocal / instrumental group*   **3 wks**

11 Oct 86	**SWIMMER** *Virgin V 2374*	85	1 wk
23 Feb 91	**SATELLITES** *East West WX 400*	43	2 wks

BIG FUN *UK, male vocal group*   **11 wks**

12 May 90	● **A POCKETFUL OF DREAMS** *Jive FUN 1*	7	11 wks

BIG ROLL BAND – *See Zoot MONEY and the BIG ROLL BAND*

BIG SOUND – *See Simon DUPREE and the BIG SOUND*

Mr. Acker BILK
UK, male band leader; vocalist / instrumentalist – clarinet   **161 wks**

19 Mar 60	● **SEVEN AGES OF ACKER** *Columbia 33SX 1205*	6	6 wks

9 Apr 60	**ACKER BILK'S OMNIBUS** Pye NJL 22 ....**14**	3 wks
4 Mar 61	**ACKER** Columbia 33SX 1248 ....**17**	1 wk
1 Apr 61	**GOLDEN TREASURY OF BILK** Columbia 33SX 1304....................**11**	6 wks
27 May 61	● **BEST OF BARBER AND BILK VOLUME 1**	
	Pye Golden Guinea GGL 0075 [1] **4**	43 wks
11 Nov 61	● **BEST OF BARBER AND BILK VOLUME 2**	
	Pye Golden Guinea GGL 0096 [1] **8**	18 wks
26 May 62	● **STRANGER ON THE SHORE** Columbia 33SX 1407 ....**6**	28 wks
25 Aug 62	★ **BEST OF BALL, BARBER AND BILK**	
	Pye Golden Guinea GGL 0131 [2] **1**	24 wks
4 May 63	**A TASTE OF HONEY** Columbia 33SX 1493.........................**17**	4 wks
9 Oct 76	**THE ONE FOR ME** Pye NSPX 41052 ....**38**	6 wks
4 Jun 77	● **SHEER MAGIC** Warwick WW 5028.................................**5**	8 wks
11 Nov 78	**EVERGREEN** Warwick PW 5045 ....**17**	14 wks

[1] Chris Barber and Acker Bilk [2] Kenny Ball, Chris Barber and Acker Bilk

BIOHAZARD US, male vocal/instrumental group — **1 wk**

| 14 May 94 | **STATE OF THE WORLD ADDRESS** Warner Bros. 9362455952 ....**72** | 1 wk |

BIOSPHERE Norway, male instrumentalist – Gier Jenssen, keyboards — **1 wk**

| 5 Mar 94 | **PATASHNIK** Apollo AMB 3927CDX...............................**50** | 1 wk |

BIRDLAND UK, male vocal/instrumental group — **1 wk**

| 2 Mar 91 | **BIRDLAND** Lazy LAZY 25...**44** | 1 wk |

BIRTHDAY PARTY Australia, male vocal/instrumental group — **3 wks**

| 24 Jul 82 | **JUNKYARD** 4AD CAD 207 ....**73** | 3 wks |

Stephen BISHOP US, male instrumentalist – piano — **3 wks**

| 1 Apr 72 | **GRIEG AND SCHUMANN PIANO CONCERTOS** Philips 6500 166 ..**34** | 3 wks |

BIZARRE INC UK, male/female vocal instrumental group — **2 wks**

| 7 Nov 92 | **ENERGIQUE** Vinyl Solution STEAM 47CD............................**41** | 2 wks |

BJÖRK Iceland, female vocalist — **85 wks**

| 17 Jul 93 | ● **DEBUT** One Little Indian TPLP 31CD ....**3** | 63 wks |
| 24 Jun 95 | ● **POST** One Little Indian TPLP 51CD ....**21†** | 22 wks |

BLACK Ireland, male vocalist/instrumentalist – Colin Vearncombe — **29 wks**

26 Sep 87	● **WONDERFUL LIFE** A & M AMA 5165 ....**3**	23 wks
29 Oct 88	**COMEDY** A & M AMA 5222 ....**32**	4 wks
1 Jun 91	**BLACK** A & M 3971261 ....**42**	2 wks

Cilla BLACK UK, female vocalist — **63 wks**

13 Feb 65	● **CILLA** Parlophone PMC 1243......................................**5**	11 wks
14 May 66	● **CILLA SINGS A RAINBOW** Parlophone PMC 7004 ....**4**	15 wks
13 Apr 68	● **SHER-OO** Parlophone PCS 7041..................................**7**	11 wks
30 Nov 68	**BEST OF CILLA BLACK** Parlophone PCS 7065...................**21**	11 wks
25 Jul 70	**SWEET INSPIRATION** Parlophone PCS 7103 ....**42**	4 wks
29 Jan 83	**THE VERY BEST OF CILLA BLACK** Parlophone EMTV 38 ....**20**	9 wks
2 Oct 93	**THROUGH THE YEARS** Columbia 4746502 ....**41**	2 wks

Frank BLACK US, male vocalist — **5 wks**

| 20 Mar 93 | ● **FRANK BLACK** 4AD CAD 3004CD..................................**9** | 3 wks |
| 4 Jun 94 | **TEENAGER OF THE YEAR** 4AD DAD 4009CD ....**21** | 2 wks |

Mary BLACK Ireland, female vocalist — **6 wks**

| 3 Jul 93 | **THE HOLY GROUND** Grapevine GRACD 11 ....**58** | 2 wks |
| 16 Sep 95 | **CIRCUS** Grapevine GRACD 014 ....**16** | 4 wks |

BLACK BOX *Italy, male / female vocal / instrumental group*   **30 wks**

5 May 90	**DREAMLAND** Deconstruction PL 74572	...**14**	30 wks

BLACK CROWES *US, male vocal / instrumental group*   **22 wks**

24 Aug 91	**SHAKE YOUR MONEY MAKER** Def American 8425151	...**36**	11 wks
23 May 92	● **SOUTHERN HARMONY AND MUSICAL COMPANION**		
	Def American 5122632	...**2**	7 wks
12 Nov 94	● **AMORICA** American 74321241942	...**8**	4 wks

BLACK DOG *UK, male instrumental group*   **2 wks**

28 Jan 95	**SPANNERS** Warp PUPCD 1	...**30**	2 wks

BLACK GRAPE *UK, male vocal / instrumental group*   **20 wks**

19 Aug 95	★ **IT'S GREAT WHEN YOU'RE STRAIGHT...YEAH!**		
	Radioactive RAD 11224	...**1†**	20 wks

BLACK LACE *UK, male vocal / instrumental group*   **26 wks**

8 Dec 84	● **PARTY PARTY - 16 GREAT PARTY ICEBREAKERS**		
	Telstar STAR 2250	...**4**	14 wks
7 Dec 85	**PARTY PARTY 2** Telstar STAR 2266	...**18**	6 wks
6 Dec 86	**PARTY CRAZY** Telstar STAR 2288	...**58**	6 wks

BLACK, ROCK and RON *US, male rap group*   **1 wk**

22 Apr 89	**STOP THE WORLD** Supreme SU 5	...**72**	1 wk

BLACK SABBATH *UK / US, male vocal / instrumental group*   **213 wks**

7 Mar 70	● **BLACK SABBATH** Vertigo VO 6	...**8**	42 wks
26 Sep 70	★ **PARANOID** Vertigo 6360 011	...**1**	27 wks
21 Aug 71	● **MASTER OF REALITY** Vertigo 6360 050	...**5**	13 wks
30 Sep 72	● **BLACK SABBATH VOLUME 4** Vertigo 6360 071	...**8**	10 wks
8 Dec 73	● **SABBATH BLOODY SABBATH** WWA WWA 005	...**4**	11 wks
27 Sep 75	● **SABOTAGE** NEMS 9119 001	...**7**	7 wks
7 Feb 76	**WE SOLD OUR SOUL FOR ROCK 'N' ROLL** NEMS 6641 335	...**35**	5 wks
6 Nov 76	**TECHNICAL ECSTASY** Vertigo 9102 750	...**13**	6 wks
14 Oct 78	**NEVER SAY DIE** Vertigo 9102 751	...**12**	6 wks
26 Apr 80	● **HEAVEN AND HELL** Vertigo 9102 752	...**9**	22 wks
5 Jul 80	● **BLACK SABBATH LIVE AT LAST** NEMS BS 001	...**5**	15 wks
27 Sep 80	**PARANOID (re-issue)** NEMS NEL 6003	...**54**	2 wks
14 Nov 81	**MOB RULES** Mercury 6V02119	...**12**	14 wks
22 Jan 83	**LIVE EVIL** Vertigo SAB 10	...**13**	11 wks
24 Sep 83	● **BORN AGAIN** Vertigo VERL 8	...**4**	7 wks
1 Mar 86	**SEVENTH STAR** Vertigo VERH 29 [1]	...**27**	5 wks
28 Nov 87	**THE ETERNAL IDOL** Vertigo VERH 51	...**66**	1 wk
29 Apr 89	**HEADLESS CROSS** IRS EIRSA 1002	...**31**	2 wks
1 Sep 90	**TYR** IRS EIRSA 1038	...**24**	3 wks
4 Jul 92	**DEHUMANIZER** IRS EIRSCD 1064	...**28**	2 wks
12 Feb 94	**CROSS PURPOSES** IRS EIRSCD 1067	...**41**	1 wk
17 Jun 95	**FORBIDDEN** IRS EIRSCD 1072	...**71**	1 wk

[1] Black Sabbath featuring Tony Iommi

BLACK UHURU *Jamaica, male / female vocal / instrumental group*   **22 wks**

13 Jun 81	**RED** Island ILPS 9625	...**28**	13 wks
22 Aug 81	**BLACK UHURU** Virgin VX 1004	...**81**	2 wks
19 Jun 82	**CHILL OUT** Island ILPS 9701	...**38**	6 wks
25 Aug 84	**ANTHEM** Island ILPS 9773	...**90**	1 wk

Band of the BLACK WATCH *UK, military band*   **13 wks**

7 Feb 76	**SCOTCH ON THE ROCKS** Spark SRLM 503	...**11**	13 wks

B
65

BLACK WIDOW *UK, male vocal / instrumental group*   **2 wks**

| 4 Apr 70 | **SACRIFICE** CBS 63948 | .... | **32** | 2 wks |

BLACKFOOT *US, male vocal / instrumental group*   **22 wks**

18 Jul 81	**MARAUDER** Atco K 50799	....	**38**	12 wks
11 Sep 82	**HIGHWAY SONG BLACKFOOT LIVE** Atco K 50910	......	**14**	6 wks
21 May 83	**SIOGO** Atco 7900801	....	**28**	3 wks
29 Sep 84	**VERTICAL SMILES** Atco 790218	....	**82**	1 wk

BLACKHEARTS – *See Joan JETT and the BLACKHEARTS*

Ritchie BLACKMORE'S RAINBOW – *See RAINBOW*

BLACKSTREET *US, male vocal group*   **6 wks**

| 9 Jul 94 | **BLACKSTREET** Interscope 6544923512 | .... | **35** | 6 wks |

Howard BLAKE conducting the SINFONIA OF LONDON
UK, conductor and orchestra   **12 wks**

| 22 Dec 84 | **THE SNOWMAN** CBS 71116 | .... | **54** | 12 wks |

Narration by Bernard Cribbins.

BLANCMANGE *UK, male vocal / instrumental duo*   **57 wks**

9 Oct 82	**HAPPY FAMILIES** London SH 8552	....	**30**	38 wks
26 May 84	● **MANGE TOUT** London SH 8554	....	**8**	17 wks
26 Oct 85	**BELIEVE YOU ME** London LONLP 10	....	**54**	2 wks

Mary J. BLIGE *US, female vocalist*   **4 wks**

| 20 Mar 93 | **WHAT'S THE 411** Uptown UPTD 10681 | .... | **53** | 1 wk |
| 17 Dec 94 | **MY LIFE** Uptown UPTD 11156 | .... | **59** | 3 wks |

BLIND FAITH *UK, male vocal / instrumental group*   **10 wks**

| 13 Sep 69 | ★ **BLIND FAITH** Polydor 583059 | .... | **1** | 10 wks |

BLIND MELON *US, male vocal / instrumental group*   **4 wks**

| 22 Jan 94 | **BLIND MELON** Capitol CDEST 2188 | .... | **53** | 3 wks |
| 19 Aug 95 | **SOUP** Capitol CDEST 2261 | .... | **48** | 1 wk |

BLITZ *UK, male vocal / instrumental group*   **3 wks**

| 6 Nov 82 | **VOICE OF A GENERATION** No Future PUNK 1 | .... | **27** | 3 wks |

BLIZZARD OF OZ – *See Ozzy OSBOURNE*

BLOCKHEADS – *See Ian DURY and the BLOCKHEADS*

BLODWYN PIG *UK, male vocal / instrumental group*   **11 wks**

| 16 Aug 69 | ● **AHEAD RINGS OUT** Island ILPS 9101 | .... | **9** | 4 wks |
| 25 Apr 70 | ● **GETTING TO THIS** Island ILPS 9122 | .... | **8** | 7 wks |

BLONDIE *US / UK, female / male vocal / instrumental group*   **294 wks**

4 Mar 78	● **PLASTIC LETTERS** Chrysalis CHR 1166	....	**10**	54 wks
23 Sep 78	★ **PARALLEL LINES** Chrysalis CDL 1192	....	**1**	105 wks
10 Mar 79	**BLONDIE** Chrysalis CHR 1165	....	**75**	1 wk
13 Oct 79	★ **EAT TO THE BEAT** Chrysalis CDL 1225	....	**1**	38 wks
29 Nov 80	● **AUTOAMERICAN** Chrysalis CDL 1290	....	**3**	16 wks

31 Oct 81	● BEST OF BLONDIE *Chrysalis CDLTV 1*...................................**4**	40 wks
5 Jun 82	● THE HUNTER *Chrysalis CDL 1384*.................................**9**	12 wks
17 Dec 88	ONCE MORE INTO THE BLEACH *Chrysalis CJB 2* 1 ....**50**	4 wks
16 Mar 91	● THE COMPLETE PICTURE - THE VERY BEST OF	
	DEBORAH HARRY AND BLONDIE *Chrysalis CHR 1817* 1 ....**3**	22 wks
29 Jul 95	BEAUTIFUL - THE REMIX ALBUM *Chrysalis CDCHR 6105* **25**	2 wks

1 Deborah Harry and Blondie

BLOOD SWEAT AND TEARS
US / Canada, male vocal / instrumental group   **21 wks**

13 Jul 68	CHILD IS FATHER TO THE MAN *CBS 63296* **40**	1 wk
12 Apr 69	BLOOD SWEAT AND TEARS *CBS 63504* **15**	8 wks
8 Aug 70	BLOOD SWEAT AND TEARS 3 *CBS 64024* **14**	12 wks

BLOW MONKEYS *UK, male vocal / instrumental group*   **27 wks**

19 Apr 86	ANIMAL MAGIC *RCA PL 70910* **21**	8 wks
25 Apr 87	SHE WAS ONLY A GROCER'S DAUGHTER *RCA PL 71245* **20**	8 wks
11 Feb 89	WHOOPS! THERE GOES THE NEIGHBOURHOOD *RCA PL 71858* .**46**	2 wks
26 Aug 89	● CHOICES *RCA PL 74191* **5**	9 wks

BLOWING FREE *UK, male instrumental duo*   **13 wks**

29 Jul 95	● SAX MOODS *Dino DINCD 106* **6**	13 wks

BLUE AEROPLANES *UK, male / female vocal / instrumental group*   **5 wks**

24 Feb 90	SWAGGER *Ensign CHEN 13*..**54**	1 wk
17 Aug 91	BEATSONGS *Ensign CHEN 21* **33**	3 wks
12 Mar 94	LIFE MODEL *Beggars Banquet BBQCD 143* **59**	1 wk

BLUE MURDER *US, male vocal / instrumental group*   **3 wks**

6 May 89	BLUE MURDER *Geffen WX 245* **45**	3 wks

BLUE NILE *UK, male vocal / instrumental group*   **6 wks**

19 May 84	A WALK ACROSS THE ROOFTOPS *Linn LKH 1*......................**80**	2 wks
21 Oct 89	HATS *Linn LKH 2*...**12**	4 wks

BLUE OYSTER CULT *US, male vocal / instrumental group*   **40 wks**

3 Jul 76	AGENTS OF FORTUNE *CBS 81385* **26**	10 wks
4 Feb 78	SPECTRES *CBS 86050*..**60**	1 wk
28 Oct 78	SOME ENCHANTED EVENING *CBS 86074* **18**	4 wks
18 Aug 79	MIRRORS *CBS 86087*...**46**	5 wks
19 Jul 80	CULTOSAURUS ERECTUS *CBS 86120* **12**	7 wks
25 Jul 81	FIRE OF UNKNOWN ORIGIN *CBS 85137* **29**	7 wks
22 May 82	EXTRATERRESTRIAL LIVE *CBS 22203* **39**	5 wks
19 Nov 83	THE REVOLUTION BY NIGHT *CBS 25686*..........................**95**	1 wk

BLUE PEARL *UK / US, male / female vocal / instrumental group*   **2 wks**

1 Dec 90	NAKED *Big Life BLR LP4* **58**	2 wks

BLUE RONDO A LA TURK *UK, male vocal / instrumental group*   **2 wks**

6 Nov 82	CHEWING THE FAT *Diable Noir V 2240* **80**	2 wks

BLUEBELLS *UK, male vocal / instrumental group*   **15 wks**

11 Aug 84	SISTERS *London LONLP 1* **22**	10 wks
17 Apr 93	THE SINGLES COLLECTION *London 8284052* **27**	5 wks

BLUES BAND *UK, male vocal / instrumental group*   **18 wks**

8 Mar 80	OFFICIAL BOOTLEG ALBUM *Arista BBBP 101* **40**	9 wks

B
67

| 18 Oct 80 | **READY** Arista BB 2 | 36 | 6 wks |
| 17 Oct 81 | **ITCHY FEET** Arista BB 3 | 60 | 3 wks |

BLUR UK, male vocal / instrumental group   **119 wks**

7 Sep 91	● **LEISURE** Food FOODLP 6	7	9 wks
22 May 93	**MODERN LIFE IS RUBBISH** Food FOODCD 9	15	11 wks
7 May 94	★ **PARKLIFE** Food FOODCD 10	1	84 wks
23 Sep 95	★ **THE GREAT ESCAPE** Food FOODCD 14	1†	15 wks

B M EX UK, male production / instrumental group   **2 wks**

| 30 Jan 93 | **APPOLONIA** Union City UCRCD 14 | 17 | 2 wks |

BODINES UK, male vocal / instrumental group   **1 wk**

| 29 Aug 87 | **PLAYED** Pop BODL 2001 | 94 | 1 wk |

BODY COUNT US, male vocal / instrumental group   **2 wks**

| 17 Sep 94 | **BORN DEAD** Rhyme Syndicate RSYND 2 | 15 | 2 wks |

Tim BOGERT – See Jeff BECK

Suzy BOGGUSS US, female vocalist   **1 wk**

| 25 Sep 93 | **SOMETHING UP MY SLEEVE** Liberty CDEST 221 | 69 | 1 wk |

Marc BOLAN – See T. REX

BOLSHOI UK, male vocal / instrumental group   **1 wk**

| 3 Oct 87 | **LINDY'S PARTY** Beggars Banquet BEGA 86 | 100 | 1 wk |

Michael BOLTON US, male vocalist   **196 wks**

17 Mar 90	● **SOUL PROVIDER** CBS 4653431	4	72 wks
11 Aug 90	**THE HUNGER** CBS 4601631	44	5 wks
18 May 91	● **TIME LOVE AND TENDERNESS** Columbia 4678121	2	57 wks
10 Oct 92	● **TIMELESS (THE CLASSICS)** Columbia 4723022	3	24 wks
27 Nov 93	● **THE ONE THING** Columbia 4743552	4	24 wks
30 Sep 95	● **GREATEST HITS 1985-1995** Columbia 4810022	2†	14 wks

BOMB THE BASS UK, male producer – Tim Simenon   **16 wks**

22 Oct 88	**INTO THE DRAGON** Rhythm King DOOD 1	18	10 wks
31 Aug 91	**UNKNOWN TERRITORY** Rhythm King 4687740	19	4 wks
15 Apr 95	**CLEAR** Fourth & Broadway BRCD 611	22	2 wks

BOMBALURINA featuring Timmy MALLETT
UK, male vocalist   **5 wks**

| 15 Dec 90 | **HUGGIN' AN' A KISSIN'** Polydor 8476481 | 55 | 5 wks |

BON JOVI US, male vocal / instrumental group   **340 wks**

28 Apr 84	**BON JOVI** Vertigo VERL 14	71	3 wks
11 May 85	**7800° FAHRENHEIT** Vertigo VERL 24	28	12 wks
20 Sep 86	● **SLIPPERY WHEN WET** Vertigo VERH 38	6	122 wks
1 Oct 88	★ **NEW JERSEY** Vertigo VERH 62	1	46 wks
14 Nov 92	★ **KEEP THE FAITH** Jambco 5141972	1	70 wks
22 Oct 94	★ **CROSS ROAD - THE BEST OF BON JOVI** Jambco 5229362	1†	60 wks
1 Jul 95	★ **THESE DAYS** Mercury 5282482	1†	27 wks

See Jon Bon Jovi.

B 68

BLUR took home four awards and a bottle at the 1995 Brits.

(Mirror Syndication)

Jon Bon Jovi, shown playing for free in Covent Garden, has led BON JOVI to four consecutive number ones.

(Mirror Syndication)

Jon BON JOVI US, male vocalist   **23 wks**

25 Aug 90 ● **BLAZE OF GLORY / YOUNG GUNS II (film soundtrack)**
         Vertigo 8464731 ....**2**   23 wks

See Bon Jovi.

Graham BOND UK, male vocalist / instrumentalist – keyboards   **2 wks**

20 Jun 70   **SOLID BOND** Warner Bros. WS 3001 ....**40**   2 wks

Gary U.S. BONDS US, male vocalist   **8 wks**

22 Aug 81   **DEDICATION** EMI America AML 3017 ....**43**   3 wks
10 Jul 82   **ON THE LINE** EMI America AML 3022 ....**55**   5 wks

BONEY M Jamaica / Montserrat / Antillies, male / female vocal group   **140 wks**

23 Apr 77   **TAKE THE HEAT OFF ME** Atlantic K 50314 ....**40**   15 wks
6 Aug 77   **LOVE FOR SALE** Atlantic K 50385 ....**60**   1 wk
29 Jul 78 ★ **NIGHT FLIGHT TO VENUS** Atlantic/Hansa K 50498..........**1**   65 wks
29 Sep 79 ★ **OCEANS OF FANTASY** Atlantic/Hansa K 50610 ....**1**   18 wks
12 Apr 80 ★ **THE MAGIC OF BONEY M** Atlantic/Hansa BMTV 1 ....**1**   26 wks
6 Sep 86   **THE BEST OF 10 YEARS** Stylus SMR 621 ....**35**   5 wks
27 Mar 93   **THE GREATEST HITS** Telstar TCD 2656.......................**14**   10 wks

BONFIRE Germany, male vocal / instrumental group   **1 wk**

21 Oct 89   **POINT BLANK** MSA ZL 74249 ....**74**   1 wk

Graham BONNET UK, male vocalist   **3 wks**

7 Nov 81   **LINE UP** Mercury 6302151 ....**62**   3 wks

BONNIE – See DELANEY and BONNIE and FRIENDS

BONZO DOG DOO-DAH BAND
UK, male vocal / instrumental group   **4 wks**

18 Jan 69   **DOUGHNUT IN GRANNY'S GREENHOUSE** Liberty LBS 83158 ......**40**   1 wk
30 Aug 69   **TADPOLES** Liberty LBS 83257 ....**36**   1 wk
22 Jun 74   **THE HISTORY OF THE BONZOS** United Artists UAD 60071 ....**41**   2 wks

Betty BOO UK, female vocalist   **25 wks**

22 Sep 90 ● **BOOMANIA** Rhythm King LEFTLP 12 ....**4**   24 wks
24 Oct 92   **GRRR! IT'S BETTY BOO** WEA 4509909082 ....**62**   1 wk

BOO RADLEYS UK, male vocal / instrumental group   **26 wks**

4 Apr 92   **EVERYTHING'S ALRIGHT FOREVER** Creation CRECD 120..............**55**   1 wk
28 Aug 93   **GIANT STEPS** Creation CRECD 149............................**17**   4 wks
8 Apr 95 ★ **WAKE UP!** Creation CRECD 179 ....**1**   21 wks

BOO-YAA T.R.I.B.E. US, male rap group   **1 wk**

14 Apr 90   **NEW FUNKY NATION** Fourth & Broadway ....**74**   1 wk

BOOGIE DOWN PRODUCTIONS US, male rapper   **9 wks**

18 Jan 88   **BY ALL MEANS NECESSARY** Jive HIP 63 ....**38**   3 wks
22 Jul 89   **GHETTO MUSIC** Jive HIP 80.....................................**32**   4 wks
25 Aug 90   **EDUTAINMENT** Jive HIP 100 ....**52**   2 wks

BOOKER T. and the MG'S US, male instrumental group   **5 wks**

25 Jul 64   **GREEN ONIONS** London HAK 8182 ....**11**   4 wks

11 Jul 70	**MCLEMORE AVENUE** Stax SXATS 1031	70	1 wk

BOOMTOWN RATS *Ireland, male vocal / instrumental group*   **96 wks**

17 Sep 77	**BOOMTOWN RATS** Ensign ENVY 1	18	11 wks
8 Jul 78	● **TONIC FOR THE TROOPS** Ensign ENVY 3	8	44 wks
3 Nov 79	● **THE FINE ART OF SURFACING** Ensign ENROX 11	7	26 wks
24 Jan 81	● **MONDO BONGO** Mercury 6359 042	6	7 wks
3 Apr 82	**V DEEP** Mercury 6359 082	64	5 wks
9 Jul 94	● **LOUDMOUTH - THE BEST OF THE BOOMTOWN RATS AND BOB GELDOF** Vertigo 5222852 [1]	10	3 wks

[1] Boomtown Rats and Bob Geldof

Pat BOONE *US, male vocalist*   **12 wks**

22 Nov 58	● **STARDUST** London HAD 2127	10	1 wk
28 May 60	**HYMNS WE HAVE LOVED** London HAD 2228	12	2 wks
25 Jun 60	**HYMNS WE LOVE** London HAD 2092	14	1 wk
24 Apr 76	**PAT BOONE ORIGINALS** ABC ABSD 301	16	8 wks

BOOTZILLA ORCHESTRA – *See Malcolm McLAREN*

BOSTON *US, male vocal / instrumental group*   **44 wks**

5 Feb 77	**BOSTON** Epic EPC 81611	11	20 wks
9 Sep 78	● **DON'T LOOK BACK** Epic EPC 86057	9	10 wks
4 Apr 81	**BOSTON** Epic EPC 32038	58	2 wks
18 Oct 86	**THIRD STAGE** MCA MCG 6017	37	11 wks
25 Jun 94	**WALK ON** MCA MCD 10973	56	1 wk

The two eponymous albums are different.

Judy BOUCHER *UK, female vocalist*   **1 wk**

25 Apr 87	**CAN'T BE WITH YOU TONIGHT** Orbitone OLP 024	95	1 wk

B 71

BOW WOW WOW *UK, male / female vocal / instrumental group*   **38 wks**

24 Oct 81	**SEE JUNGLE! SEE JUNGLE! GO JOIN YOUR GANG YEAH CITY ALL OVER! GO APE CRAZY** RCA RCALP 00273000	26	32 wks
7 Aug 82	**I WANT CANDY** EMI EMC 3416	26	6 wks

David BOWIE *UK, male vocalist*   **903 wks**

1 Jul 72	● **THE RISE AND FALL OF ZIGGY STARDUST AND THE SPIDERS FROM MARS** RCA Victor SF 8287	5	106 wks
23 Sep 72	● **HUNKY DORY** RCA Victor SF 8244	3	69 wks
25 Nov 72	**SPACE ODDITY** RCA Victor LSP 4813	17	37 wks
25 Nov 72	**THE MAN WHO SOLD THE WORLD** RCA Victor LSP 4816	26	22 wks
5 May 73	★ **ALADDIN SANE** RCA Victor RS 1001	1	47 wks
3 Nov 73	★ **PIN-UPS** RCA Victor RS 1003	1	21 wks
8 Jun 74	★ **DIAMOND DOGS** RCA Victor APLI 0576	1	17 wks
16 Nov 74	● **DAVID LIVE** RCA Victor APL 2 0771	2	12 wks
5 Apr 75	● **YOUNG AMERICANS** RCA Victor RS 1006	2	12 wks
7 Feb 76	● **STATION TO STATION** RCA Victor APLI 1327	5	16 wks
12 Jun 76	● **CHANGESONEBOWIE** RCA Victor RS 1055	2	28 wks
29 Jan 77	● **LOW** RCA Victor PL 12030	2	18 wks
29 Oct 77	● **HEROES** RCA Victor PL 12522	3	18 wks
14 Oct 78	● **STAGE** RCA Victor PL 02913	5	10 wks
9 Jun 79	● **LODGER** RCA BOW LP 1	4	17 wks
27 Sep 80	★ **SCARY MONSTERS AND SUPER CREEPS** RCA BOW LP 2	1	32 wks
10 Jan 81	● **VERY BEST OF DAVID BOWIE** K-Tel NE 1111	3	20 wks
17 Jan 81	**HUNKY DORY (re-issue)** RCA International INTS 5064	32	51 wks
31 Jan 81	**THE RISE AND FALL OF ZIGGY STARDUST AND THE SPIDERS FROM MARS (re-issue)** RCA International INTS 5063	33	62 wks
28 Nov 81	**CHANGESTWOBOWIE** RCA BOW LP 3	24	17 wks
6 Mar 82	**ALADDIN SANE (re-issue)** RCA International INTS 5067	49	24 wks
14 Jan 83	**RARE** RCA PL 45406	34	11 wks

TOP 30 № 6

In mid-July 1983 DAVID BOWIE had ten albums in the chart simultaneously, a figure only ever surpassed by Elvis Presley.

(Solo/Joe Bangay Photography)

23 Apr 83	★ LETS DANCE *EMI America AML 3029*	**1**	56	wks
30 Apr 83	PIN-UPS (re-issue) *RCA International INTS 5236*	**57**	15	wks
30 Apr 83	THE MAN WHO SOLD THE WORLD (re-issue)			
	RCA International INTS 5237	**64**	8	wks
14 May 83	DIAMOND DOGS (re-issue) *RCA International INTS 5068*	**60**	14	wks
11 Jun 83	HEROES (re-issue) *RCA International INTS 5066*	**75**	8	wks
11 Jun 83	LOW (re-issue) *RCA International INTS 5065*	**85**	5	wks
20 Aug 83	GOLDEN YEARS *RCA BOWLP 4*	**33**	5	wks
5 Nov 83	ZIGGY STARDUST – THE MOTION PICTURE *RCA PL 84862*	**17**	6	wks
28 Apr 84	FAME AND FASHION (ALL TIME GREATEST HITS)			
	RCA PL 84919	**40**	6	wks
19 May 84	LOVE YOU TILL TUESDAY *Deram BOWIE 1*	**53**	4	wks
6 Oct 84	★ TONIGHT *EMI America DB 1*	**1**	19	wks
2 May 87	● NEVER LET ME DOWN *EMI America AMLS 3117*	**6**	16	wks
24 Mar 90	★ CHANGESBOWIE *EMI DBTV 1*	**1**	29	wks
14 Apr 90	HUNKY DORY (2nd re-issue) *EMI EMC 3572*	**39**	2	wks
14 Apr 90	THE MAN WHO SOLD THE WORLD (2nd re-issue)			
	EMI EMC 3573	**66**	1	wk
14 Apr 90	SPACE ODDITY (re-issue) *EMI EMC 3571*	**64**	1	wk
23 Jun 90	THE RISE AND FALL OF ZIGGY STARDUST AND THE SPIDERS			
	FROM MARS (2nd re-issue) *EMI EMC 3577*	**25**	4	wks
28 Jul 90	ALADDIN SANE (2nd re-issue) *EMI EMC 3579*	**43**	1	wk
28 Jul 90	PIN-UPS (2nd re-issue) *EMI EMC 3580*	**52**	1	wk
27 Oct 90	DIAMOND DOGS (2nd re-issue) *EMI EMC 3584*	**67**	1	wk
4 May 91	YOUNG AMERICANS (re-issue) *EMI EMD 1021*	**54**	1	wk
4 May 91	STATION TO STATION (re-issue) *EMI EMD 1020*	**57**	1	wk
7 Sep 91	LOW (2nd re-issue) *EMI EMD 1027*	**64**	1	wk
17 Apr 93	★ BLACK TIE WHITE NOISE *Arista 74321136972*	**1**	11	wks
20 Nov 93	● THE SINGLES COLLECTION *EMI CDEM 1512*	**9**	15	wks
7 May 94	SANTA MONICA '72 *Trident GY 002*	**74**	1	wk
7 Oct 95	● OUTSIDE *RCA 74321310662*	**8**	4	wks

BOXCAR WILLIE *US, male vocalist* **12 wks**

31 May 80	● KING OF THE ROAD *Warwick WW 5084*	**5**	12	wks

B
73

BOY GEORGE *UK, male vocalist* **15 wks**

27 Jun 87	SOLD *Virgin V 2430*	**29**	6	wks
13 Apr 91	THE MARTYR MANTRAS *More Protein CUMLP 1* [1]	**60**	1	wk
2 Oct 93	AT WORST . . . THE BEST OF BOY GEORGE AND			
	CULTURE CLUB *Virgin VTCD 19* [2]	**24**	5	wks
12 Mar 94	THE DEVIL IN SISTER GEORGE *Virgin VSCDG 1490*	**26**	2	wks
3 Jun 95	CHEAPNESS AND BEAUTY *Virgin CDV 2780*	**44**	1	wk

[1] Boy George and Culture Club [1] Jesus Loves You

BOY MEETS GIRL *US, male / female vocal / instrumental duo* **1 wk**

4 Feb 89	REEL LIFE *RCA PL 88414*	**74**	1	wk

Max BOYCE *UK, male vocalist / comedian* **105 wks**

5 Jul 75	LIVE AT TREORCHY *One Up OU 2033*	**21**	32	wks
1 Nov 75	★ WE ALL HAD DOCTORS' PAPERS *EMI MB 101*	**1**	17	wks
20 Nov 76	● THE INCREDIBLE PLAN *EMI MB 102*	**9**	12	wks
7 Jan 78	THE ROAD AND THE MILES *EMI MB 103*	**50**	3	wks
11 Mar 78	LIVE AT TREORCHY (re-issue) *One Up OU 54043*	**42**	6	wks
27 May 78	● I KNOW COS I WAS THERE *EMI MAX 1001*	**6**	14	wks
13 Oct 79	NOT THAT I'M BIASED *EMI MAX 1002*	**27**	13	wks
15 Nov 80	ME AND BILLY WILLIAMS *EMI MAX 1003*	**37**	8	wks

BOYS *UK, male vocal / instrumental group* **1 wk**

1 Oct 77	THE BOYS *NEMS NEL 6001*	**50**	1	wk

BOYZ II MEN *US, male vocal group* **23 wks**

31 Oct 92	● COOLEYHIGHHARMONY *Motown 5300892*	**7**	18	wks
24 Sep 94	II *Motown 5304312*	**17**	5	wks

BOYZONE *Ireland, male vocal group*   **18 wks**

2 Sep 95 ★ **SAID AND DONE** *Polydor 5278012* ....**1†**   18 wks

BRAD *US, male vocal / instrumental group*   **1 wk**

15 May 93   **SHAME** *Epic 4735962* ....**72**   1 wk

Paul BRADY *Ireland, male vocalist / instrumentalist – guitar*   **1 wk**

6 Apr 91   **TRICK OR TREAT** *Fontana 8484541* ....**62**   1 wk

Billy BRAGG *UK, male vocalist*   **77 wks**

21 Jan 84   **LIFE'S A RIOT WITH SPY VS SPY** *Utility UTIL 1* ....**30**   30 wks
20 Oct 84   **BREWING UP WITH BILLY BRAGG** *Go! Discs AGOLP 4* ....**16**   21 wks
4 Oct 86 ● **TALKING WITH THE TAXMAN ABOUT POETRY**
            Go! Discs AGOLP 6 ....**8**   8 wks
13 Jun 87   **BACK TO BASICS** *Go! Discs AGOLP 8* ....**37**   4 wks
1 Oct 88   **WORKERS PLAYTIME** *Go! Discs AGOLP 15* ....**17**   4 wks
12 May 90   **THE INTERNATIONALE** *Utility UTIL 11*.......................**34**   4 wks
28 Sep 91 ● **DON'T TRY THIS AT HOME** *Go! Discs 8282791* ....**8**   6 wks

Wilfrld BRAMBELL and Harry H. CORBETT
UK, male comic duo   **34 wks**

23 Mar 63 ● **STEPTOE AND SON** *Pye NPL 18081* ....**4**   28 wks
11 Jan 64   **STEPTOE AND SON** *Pye GGL 0217*..................................**14**   5 wks
14 Mar 64   **MORE** *UNK Pye NPL 18090*..**19**   1 wk

First two albums are different.

BRAND NEW HEAVIES
UK / US, male / female vocal / instrumental group   **67 wks**

14 Mar 92   **BRAND NEW HEAVIES** *London 8283002* ....**25**   16 wks
5 Sep 92   **HEAVY RHYME EXPERIENCE** *Acid Jazz 8283352*............................**38**   2 wks
16 Apr 94 ● **BROTHER SISTER** *ffrr 8284902* ....**4**   48 wks
12 Nov 94   **ORIGINAL FLAVA** *Acid Jazz JAZIDCD 114*......................**64**   1 wk

BRAND X *UK, male vocal / instrumental group*   **6 wks**

21 May 77   **MOROCCAN ROLL** *Charisma CAS 1126* ....**37**   5 wks
11 Sep 82   **IS THERE ANYTHING ABOUT?** *CBS 85967* ....**93**   1 wk

Laura BRANIGAN *US, female vocalist*   **18 wks**

18 Aug 84   **SELF CONTROL** *Atlantic 780147* ....**16**   14 wks
24 Aug 85   **HOLD ME** *Atlantic 7812651*.......................................**64**   4 wks

BRASS CONSTRUCTION *US, male vocal / instrumental group*   **12 wks**

20 Mar 76 ● **BRASS CONSTRUCTION** *United Artists UAS 29923* ....**9**   11 wks
30 Jun 84   **RENEGADES** *Capitol EJ 24 0160*.....................................**94**   1 wk

Los BRAVOS *Spain / Germany, male vocal / instrumental group*   **1 wk**

8 Oct 64   **BLACK IS BLACK** *Decca LK 4822* ....**29**   1 wk

Toni BRAXTON *US, female vocalist*   **31 wks**

29 Jan 94 ● **TONI BRAXTON** *LaFace 74321162682* ....**4**   31 wks

BREAD *US, male vocal / instrumental group*   **179 wks**

26 Sep 70   **ON THE WATERS** *Elektra 2469005* ....**34**   5 wks

18 Mar 72	● BABY I'M A WANT-YOU Elektra K 42100	9	19 wks
28 Oct 72	● BEST OF BREAD Elektra K 42115	7	100 wks
27 Jul 74	THE BEST OF BREAD VOLUME 2 Elektra K 42161	48	1 wk
29 Jan 77	LOST WITHOUT YOUR LOVE Elektra K 52044	17	6 wks
5 Nov 77	★ THE SOUND OF BREAD Elektra K 52062	1	46 wks
28 Nov 87	THE VERY BEST OF BREAD Telstar STAR 2303	84	2 wks

BREAK MACHINE US, male vocal group

16 wks

| 9 Jun 84 | BREAK MACHINE Record Shack SOHOLP 3 | 17 | 16 wks |

BREATHE UK, male vocal / instrumental group

5 wks

| 8 Oct 88 | ALL THAT JAZZ Siren SRNLP 12 | 22 | 5 wks |

BREEDERS US, female / male vocal / instrumental group

8 wks

| 9 Jun 90 | POD 4AD CAD 0006 | 22 | 3 wks |
| 11 Sep 93 | ● LAST SPLASH 4AD CAD 3014CD | 5 | 5 wks |

Maire BRENNAN Ireland, female vocalist

2 wks

| 13 Jun 92 | MAIRE RCA PD 75358 | 53 | 2 wks |

Adrian BRETT UK, male instrumentalist – flute

11 wks

| 10 Nov 79 | ECHOES OF GOLD Warwick WW 5062 | 19 | 11 wks |

Paul BRETT UK, male instrumentalist – guitar

7 wks

| 19 Jul 80 | ROMANTIC GUITAR K-Tel ONE 1079 | 24 | 7 wks |

B
75

Edie BRICKELL and the NEW BOHEMIANS
US, female / male vocal / instrumental group

19 wks

4 Feb 89	SHOOTING RUBBERBANDS AT THE STARS Geffen WX 215	25	17 wks
10 Nov 90	GHOST OF A DOG Geffen WX 386	63	1 wk
3 Sep 94	PICTURE PERFECT MORNING Geffen GED 24715 [1]	59	1 wk

[1] Edie Brickell

BRIGHOUSE AND RASTRICK BRASS BAND
UK, male brass band

11 wks

| 28 Jan 78 | ● FLORAL DANCE Logo 1001 | 10 | 11 wks |

Sarah BRIGHTMAN UK, female vocalist

8 wks

17 Jun 89	THE SONGS THAT GOT AWAY Really Useful 839116 1	48	2 wks
8 Aug 92	AMIGOS PARA SIEMPRE East West 4509902562 [1]	53	4 wks
11 Nov 95	THE UNEXPECTED SONGS - SURRENDER Really Useful 5277022	45	2 wks

[1] José Carreras and Sarah Brightman

See also Andrew Lloyd Webber.

BRILLIANT UK, male / female vocal / instrumental group

1 wk

| 20 Sep 86 | KISS THE LIPS OF LIFE Food BRILL 1 | 83 | 1 wk |

Johnny BRISTOL US, male vocalist

7 wks

| 5 Oct 74 | HANG ON IN THERE BABY MGM 2315 303 | 12 | 7 wks |

BRODSKY QUARTET – See Elvis COSTELLO and the ATTRACTIONS

June BRONHILL and Thomas ROUND
Australia / UK, female / male vocal duo **1 wk**

18 Jun 60	**LILAC TIME** HMV CLP 1248	17	1 wk

BRONSKI BEAT *UK, male vocal / instrumental group* **65 wks**

20 Oct 84	● **THE AGE OF CONSENT** Forbidden Fruit BITLP 1	4	53 wks
21 Sep 85	**HUNDREDS AND THOUSANDS** Forbidden Fruit BITLP 2	24	6 wks
10 May 86	**TRUTHDARE DOUBLEDARE** Forbidden Fruit BITLP 3	18	6 wks

Elkie BROOKS *UK, female vocalist* **214 wks**

18 Jun 77	**TWO DAYS AWAY** A & M AMLH 68409	16	20 wks
13 May 78	**SHOOTING STAR** A & M AMLH 64695	20	13 wks
13 Oct 79	**LIVE AND LEARN** A & M AMLH 68509	34	6 wks
14 Nov 81	● **PEARLS** A & M ELK 1981	2	79 wks
13 Nov 82	● **PEARLS II** A & M ELK 1982	5	25 wks
14 Jul 84	**MINUTES** A & M AML 68565	35	7 wks
8 Dec 84	**SCREEN GEMS** EMI SCREEN 1	35	11 wks
6 Dec 86	● **NO MORE THE FOOL** Legend LMA 1	5	23 wks
27 Dec 86	● **THE VERY BEST OF ELKIE BROOKS** Telstar STAR 2284	10	18 wks
11 Jun 88	**BOOKBINDER'S KID** Legend LMA 3	57	3 wks
18 Nov 89	**INSPIRATIONS** Telstar STAR 2354	58	3 wks
13 Mar 93	**ROUND MIDNIGHT** Castle Communications CTVCD 113	27	4 wks
16 Apr 94	**NOTHIN' BUT THE BLUES** Castle Communications CTVCD 127	58	2 wks

Garth BROOKS *US, male vocalist* **39 wks**

15 Feb 92	**ROPIN' THE WIND** Capitol CDESTU 2162	41	2 wks
12 Feb 94	● **IN PIECES** Capitol CDEST 2212	2	11 wks
24 Dec 94	**THE HITS** Capitol CDP 8320812	11	21 wks
2 Dec 95	**FRESH HORSES** Capitol CDGB 1	22†	5 wks

B
76

Nigel BROOKS SINGERS *UK, male / female vocal choir* **17 wks**

| 29 Nov 75 | ● **SONGS OF JOY** K-Tel NE 706 | 5 | 16 wks |
| 5 Jun 76 | **20 ALL TIME EUROVISION FAVOURITES** K-Tel NE 712 | 44 | 1 wk |

BROS *UK, male vocal / instrumental duo* **69 wks**

9 Apr 88	● **PUSH** CBS 460629 1	2	54 wks
28 Oct 89	● **THE TIME** CBS 465918 1	4	13 wks
12 Oct 91	**CHANGING FACES** Columbia 4688171	18	2 wks

Act was a group for first album.

BROTHER BEYOND *UK, male vocal / instrumental group* **24 wks**

| 26 Nov 88 | ● **GET EVEN** Parlophone PCS 7327 | 9 | 23 wks |
| 25 Nov 89 | **TRUST** Parlophone PCS 7337 | 60 | 1 wk |

BROTHERHOOD OF MAN *UK, male / female vocal group* **40 wks**

24 Apr 76	**LOVE AND KISSES FROM** Pye NSPL 18490	20	8 wks
12 Aug 78	**B FOR BROTHERHOOD** Pye NSPL 18567	18	9 wks
7 Oct 78	● **BROTHERHOOD OF MAN** K-Tel BML 7980	6	15 wks
29 Nov 80	**SING 20 NUMBER ONE HITS** Warwick WW 5087	14	8 wks

BROTHERS JOHNSON *US, male vocal / instrumental duo* **22 wks**

19 Aug 78	**BLAM!!** A & M AMLH 64714	48	8 wks
23 Feb 80	**LIGHT UP THE NIGHT** A & M AMLK 63716	22	12 wks
18 Jul 81	**WINNERS** A & M AMLK 63724	42	2 wks

Edgar BROUGHTON BAND *UK, male vocal / instrumental group* **6 wks**

| 20 Jun 70 | **SING BROTHER SING** Harvest SHVL 772 | 18 | 4 wks |

By the end of 1995 BOYZONE had enjoyed four top three singles from their number one debut album.
(Solo/Mail Newspapers)

MARIAH CAREY has funded a camp for Underprivileged children in upstate New York.
(LFI)

5 Jun 71   **THE EDGAR BROUGHTON BAND** Harvest SHVL 791 ....**28**   2 wks

Bobby BROWN US, male vocalist   65 wks

28 Jan 89	● **DON'T BE CRUEL** MCA MCF 3425 ....**3**	41 wks
5 Aug 89	**KING OF STAGE** CA MCL 1886 ....**40**	6 wks
2 Dec 89	**DANCE! . . . YA KNOW IT!** MCA MCG 6074...............**26**	10 wks
5 Sep 92	**BOBBY** MCA MCAD 10695 ....**11**	5 wks
5 Aug 95	**TWO CAN PLAY THAT GAME** MCA MCD 11334............**24**	3 wks

Crazy World Of Arthur BROWN
UK, male vocal / instrumental group   16 wks

6 Jul 68   ● **CRAZY WORLD OF ARTHUR BROWN** Track 612005 ....**2**   16 wks

Dennis BROWN Jamaica, male vocalist   6 wks

26 Jun 82   **LOVE HAS FOUND ITS WAY** A & M AMLH 64886 ....**72**   6 wks

James BROWN US, male vocalist   51 wks

18 Oct 86	**GRAVITY** Scotti Bros. SCT 57108 ....**85**	3 wks
25 Jun 88	**I'M REAL** Scotti Bros. POLD 5230 ....**27**	5 wks
10 Oct 88	**BEST OF JAMES BROWN – GODFATHER OF SOUL** K-Tel NE 1376 ....**17**	21 wks
16 Nov 91	**SEX MACHINE – THE VERY BEST OF JAMES BROWN** Polydor 8458281 ....**19**	22 wks

Joe BROWN UK, male vocalist / instrumentalist – guitar   47 wks

1 Sep 62	● **A PICTURE OF YOU** Pye Golden Guinea GGL 0146............**3**	39 wks
25 May 63	**JOE BROWN – LIVE** Piccadilly NPL 38006 ....**14**	8 wks

Roy 'Chubby' BROWN UK, male comedian   6 wks

25 Nov 95   **TAKE FAT AND PARTY** PolyStar 5297842 ....**29†**   6 wks

Sam BROWN UK, female vocalist   30 wks

11 Mar 89	● **STOP** A & M AMA 5195 ....**4**	18 wks
14 Apr 90	**APRIL MOON** A & M AMA 9014.....................**38**	12 wks

Jackson BROWNE US, male vocalist   36 wks

4 Dec 76	**THE PRETENDER** Asylum K 53048 ....**26**	5 wks
21 Jan 78	**RUNNING ON EMPTY** Asylum K 53070 ....**28**	7 wks
12 Jul 80	**HOLD OUT** Asylum K 52226.....................**44**	5 wks
13 Aug 83	**LAWYERS IN LOVE** Asylum 9602681 ....**37**	7 wks
8 Mar 86	**LIVES IN THE BALANCE** Asylum EKT 31 ....**36**	7 wks
17 Jun 89	**WORLD IN MOTION** Elektra EKT 50.................**39**	2 wks
6 Nov 93	**I'M ALIVE** Elektra 7559615242 ....**35**	3 wks

BROWNSTONE US, female vocal group   13 wks

29 Apr 95   **FROM THE BOTTOM UP** MJJ 4773622 ....**18**   13 wks

Dave BRUBECK US, male instrumental group   17 wks

25 Jun 60	**TIME OUT** Fontana TFL 5085 [1] **11**	1 wk
7 Apr 62	**TIME FURTHER OUT** Fontana TFL 5161 ....**12**	16 wks

[1] Dave Brubeck Quartet

Jack BRUCE UK, male vocalist / instrumentalist – bass   9 wks

27 Sep 69   ● **SONGS FOR A TAILOR** Polydor 583058 ....**6**   9 wks

BRUFORD – See ANDERSON BRUFORD WAKEMAN HOWE

B 78

Peabo BRYSON – *See Roberta FLACK*

BT *US, male producer – Brian Transeau*   **2 wks**

21 Oct 95   **IMA** *Perfecto 0630123452* ....**45**   2 wks

Lindsey BUCKINGHAM *US, male vocalist*   **1 wk**

8 Aug 92   **OUT OF THE CRADLE** *Mercury 5126582* ....**51**   1 wk

Jeff BUCKLEY *US, male vocalist*   **6 wks**

27 Aug 94   **GRACE** *Columbia 4759282* ....**50**   6 wks

BUCKS FIZZ *UK, male / female vocal group*   **80 wks**

8 Aug 81	**BUCKS FIZZ** *RCA RCALP 5050* **14**	28 wks
18 May 82 ●	**ARE YOU READY?** *RCA RCALP 8000* **10**	23 wks
19 Mar 83	**HAND CUT** *RCA RCALP 6100* **17**	13 wks
3 Dec 83	**GREATEST HITS** *RCA RCA PL 70022* **25**	13 wks
24 Nov 84	**I HEAR TALK** *RCA PL 70397* **66**	2 wks
13 Dec 86	**THE WRITING ON THE WALL** *Polydor POHL 30* **89**	1 wk

Harold BUDD/Liz FRASER/Robin GUTHRIE/
Simon RAYMONDE *UK, male / female vocal / instrumental group*   **2 wks**

22 Nov 86   **THE MOON AND THE MELODIES** *4AD CAD 611* ....**46**   2 wks

See also Cocteau Twins.

BUDGIE *UK, male vocal / instrumental group*   **10 wks**

8 Jun 74	**IN FOR THE KILL** *MCA MCF 2546* **29**	3 wks
27 Sep 75	**BANDOLIER** *MCA MCF 2723* **36**	4 wks
31 Oct 81	**NIGHT FLIGHT** *RCA RCALP 6003* **68**	2 wks
23 Oct 82	**DELIVER US FROM EVIL** *RCA RCALP 6054* **62**	1 wk

BUFFALO TOM *US, male vocal / instrumental group*   **5 wks**

14 Mar 92	**LET ME COME OVER** *Situation Two SITU 36CD* **49**	1 wk
9 Oct 93	**(BIG RED LETTER DAY)** *Beggars Banquet BBQCD 142* **17**	3 wks
22 Jul 95	**SLEEPY EYED** *Beggars Banquet BBQCD 177*.....................**31**	1 wk

BUGGLES *UK, male vocal / instrumental duo*   **6 wks**

16 Feb 80   **THE AGE OF PLASTIC** *Island ILPS 9585* ....**27**   6 wks

BUNNYMEN – *See ECHO and the BUNNYMEN*

Eric BURDON and WAR
UK, male vocalist and US, male vocal / instrumental group   **2 wks**

3 Oct 70   **ERIC BURDON DECLARES WAR** *Polydor 2310041* ....**50**   2 wks

Jean-Jacques BURNEL
UK, male vocalist / instrumentalist– bass guitar   **6 wks**

21 Apr 79	**EUROMAN COMETH** *United Artists UAG 30214* **40**	5 wks
3 Dec 83	**FIRE AND WATER** *Epic EPC 25707* 1 ....**94**	1 wk

1 Dave Greenfield and Jean-Jacques Burnel

Kate BUSH *UK, female vocalist*   **278 wks**

11 Mar 78 ●	**THE KICK INSIDE** *EMI EMC 3223* **3**	70 wks
25 Nov 78 ●	**LIONHEART** *EMI EMA 787*.................................**6**	36 wks
20 Sep 80 ★	**NEVER FOR EVER** *EMI EMA 7964*.......................**1**	23 wks

25 Sep 82	● **THE DREAMING** *EMI EMC 3419* **3**	10 wks
28 Sep 85	★ **HOUNDS OF LOVE** *EMI KAB 1* **1**	51 wks
22 Nov 86	★ **THE WHOLE STORY** *EMI KBTV 1* **1**	53 wks
28 Oct 89	● **THE SENSUAL WORLD** *EMI EMD 1010* **2**	20 wks
13 Nov 93	● **THE RED SHOES** *EMI CDEMD 1047* **2**	15 wks

BUTLER – *See McALMONT and BUTLER*

Jonathan BUTLER
South Africa, male vocalist / instrumentalist – guitar　　　**14 wks**

12 Sep 87	**JONATHAN BUTLER** *Jive HIP 46* **12**	11 wks
4 Feb 89	**MORE THAN FRIENDS** *Jive HIP 70*.......................**29**	3 wks

BUTTHOLE SURFERS *UK, male vocal / instrumental group*　　**2 wks**

16 Mar 91	**PIOUHGD** *Rough Trade R 20812601* **68**	1 wk
3 Apr 93	**INDEPENDENT WORM SALOON** *Capitol CDEST 2192* **73**	1 wk

BUZZCOCKS *UK, male vocal / instrumental group*　　**23 wks**

25 Mar 78	**ANOTHER MUSIC IN A DIFFERENT KITCHEN** *United Artists UAG 30159* **15**	11 wks
7 Oct 78	**LOVE BITES** *United Artists UAG 30184* **13**	9 wks
6 Oct 79	**A DIFFERENT KIND OF TENSION** *United Artists UAG 30260* **26**	3 wks

BY ALL MEANS *US, male / female vocal group*　　**1 wk**

16 Jul 88	**BY ALL MEANS** *Fourth & Broadway BRLP 520* **80**	1 wk

Max BYGRAVES *UK, male vocalist*　　**176 wks**

23 Sep 72	● **SING ALONG WITH MAX** *Pye NSPL 18361* **4**	44 wks
2 Dec 72	**SING ALONG WITH MAX VOLUME 2** *Pye NSPL 18383* **11**	23 wks
5 May 73	● **SINGALONGAMAX VOLUME 3** *Pye NSPL 18401* **5**	30 wks
29 Sep 73	● **SINGALONGAMAX VOLUME 4** *Pye NSPL 18410* **7**	12 wks
15 Dec 73	**SINGALONGPARTY SONG** *Pye NSPL 18419* **15**	6 wks
12 Oct 74	**YOU MAKE ME FEEL LIKE SINGING A SONG** *Pye NSPL 18436*....**39**	3 wks
7 Dec 74	**SINGALONGAXMAS** *Pye NSPL 18439* **21**	6 wks
13 Nov 76	● **100 GOLDEN GREATS** *Ronco RTDX 2019* **3**	21 wks
28 Oct 78	**LINGALONGAMAX** *Ronco RPL 2033* **39**	5 wks
16 Dec 78	**THE SONG AND DANCE MEN** *Pye NSPL 18574* **67**	1 wk
19 Aug 89	● **SINGALONGAWARYEARS** *Parkfield Music PMLP 5001* **5**	19 wks
25 Nov 89	**SINGALONGAWARYEARS VOLUME 2** *Parkfield Music PMLP 5006* **33**	6 wks

Charlie BYRD – *See Stan GETZ and Charlie BYRD*

Donald BYRD *US, male vocalist / instrumentalist – trumpet*　**3 wks**

10 Oct 81	**LOVE BYRD** *Elektra K 52301*.......................**70**	3 wks

BYRDS *US, male vocal / instrumental group*　　**42 wks**

28 Aug 65	● **MR. TAMBOURINE MAN** *CBS BPG 62571* **7**	12 wks
9 Apr 66	**TURN, TURN, TURN** *CBS BPG 62652* **11**	5 wks
1 Oct 66	**5TH DIMENSION** *CBS BPG 62783* **27**	2 wks
22 Apr 67	**YOUNGER THAN YESTERDAY** *CBS SBPG 62988* **37**	4 wks
4 May 68	**THE NOTORIOUS BYRD BROTHERS** *CBS 63169* **12**	11 wks
24 May 69	**DR. BYRDS AND MR. HYDE** *CBS 63545* **15**	1 wk
14 Feb 70	**BALLAD OF EASY RIDER** *CBS 63795*.......................**41**	1 wk
28 Nov 70	**UNTITLED** *CBS 66253* **11**	4 wks
14 Apr 73	**BYRDS** *Asylum SYLA 8754*.......................**31**	1 wk
19 May 73	**HISTORY OF THE BYRDS** *CBS 68242* **47**	1 wk

David BYRNE *UK, male vocalist*　　**17 wks**

21 Feb 81	**MY LIFE IN THE BUSH OF GHOSTS** *Polydor EGLP 48* 1 ....**29**	8 wks

21 Oct 89	**REI MOMO** Warner Bros. WX 319	52	2 wks
14 Mar 92	**UH–OH** Luaka Bop 7599267992	26	5 wks
4 Jun 94	**DAVID BYRNE** Luaka Bop 9362455582	44	2 wks

[1] Brian Eno and David Byrne

C&C MUSIC FACTORY/CLIVILLES and COLE
US, male / female vocal / instrumental group; US male production duo;   **14 wks**

| 9 Feb 91 | ● **GONNA MAKE YOU SWEAT** Columbia 4678141 [1] | 8 | 13 wks |
| 28 Mar 92 | **GREATEST REMIXES VOLUME 1** Columbia 4694462 [2] | 45 | 1 wk |

[1] C&C Music Factory [2] Clivilles and Cole

Montserrat CABALLE Spain, female vocalist   **11 wks**

22 Oct 88	**BARCELONA** Polydor POLH 44 [1]	15	8 wks
8 Aug 92	**FROM THE OFFICIAL BARCELONA GAMES CEREMONY**		
	RCA Red Seal 09026612042 [2]	41	3 wks

[1] Freddie Mercury and Montserrat Caballe [2] Placido Domingo, José Carreras and Montserrat Caballe

CABARET VOLTAIRE UK, male vocal / instrumental group   **11 wks**

26 Jun 82	**2 X 45** Rough Trade ROUGH 42	98	1 wk
13 Aug 83	**THE CRACKDOWN** Some Bizzare CV 1	31	5 wks
10 Nov 84	**MICRO-PHONIES** Some Bizzare CV 2	69	1 wk
3 Aug 85	**DRINKING GASOLINE** Some Bizzare CVM 1	71	2 wks
26 Oct 85	**THE COVENANT, THE SWORD AND THE ARM OF THE LORD**		
	Some Bizzare CV 3	57	2 wks

CACTUS WORLD NEWS Ireland, male vocal / instrumental group   **2 wks**

| 24 May 86 | **URBAN BEACHES** MCA MCG 6005 | 56 | 2 wks |

John CALE - See Lou REED

JJ CALE US, male vocalist / instrumentalist - guitar   **24 wks**

2 Oct 76	**TROUBADOUR** Island ISA 5011	53	1 wk
25 Aug 79	**5** Shelter ISA 5018	40	6 wks
21 Feb 81	**SHADES** Shelter ISA 5021	44	7 wks
20 Mar 82	**GRASSHOPPER** Shelter IFA 5022	36	5 wks
24 Sep 83	**#8** Mercury MERL 22	47	3 wks
26 Sep 92	**NUMBER 10** Silvertone ORECD 523	58	2 wks

Maria CALLAS Greece, female vocalist   **7 wks**

| 20 Jun 87 | **THE MARIA CALLAS COLLECTION** Stylus SMR 732 | 50 | 7 wks |

CAMEL UK, male vocal / instrumental group   **47 wks**

24 May 75	**THE SNOW GOOSE** Decca SKL 5207	22	13 wks
17 Apr 76	**MOON MADNESS** Decca TXS 115	15	6 wks
17 Sep 77	**RAIN DANCES** Decca TXS 124	20	8 wks
14 Oct 78	**BREATHLESS** Decca TXS 132	26	1 wk
27 Oct 79	**I CAN SEE YOUR HOUSE FROM HERE** Decca TXS 137	45	3 wks
31 Jan 81	**NUDE** Decca SKL 5323	34	7 wks
15 May 82	**THE SINGLE FACTOR** Decca SKL 5328	57	5 wks
21 Apr 84	**STATIONARY TRAVELLER** Decca SKL 5334	57	4 wks

British Hit Albums Part One

Date of chart entry/Title & catalogue no./Peak position reached/Weeks on chart

★ Number One ● Top Ten † still on chart at 30 Dec 1995 □ credited to act billed in footnote

CAMEO US, male vocal / instrumental group   47 wks

10 Aug 85	SINGLE LIFE Club JABH 11	66	12 wks
18 Oct 86 ●	WORD UP Club JABH 19	7	34 wks
26 Nov 88	MACHISMO Club 836002 1	86	1 wk

Ali CAMPBELL UK, male vocalist   11 wks

| 17 Jun 95 ● | BIG LOVE Kuff CDV 2783 | 6 | 11 wks |

Glen CAMPBELL US, male vocalist   184 wks

31 Jan 70	GLEN CAMPBELL LIVE Capitol SB 21444	16	14 wks
28 Feb 70	BOBBIE GENTRY AND GLEN CAMPBELL Capitol ST 2928 [1]	50	1 wk
30 May 70	TRY A LITTLE KINDNESS Capitol ESW 389	37	10 wks
12 Dec 70	THE GLEN CAMPBELL ALBUM Capitol ST 22493	16	5 wks
27 Nov 71 ●	GREATEST HITS Capitol ST 21885	8	113 wks
25 Oct 75	RHINESTONE COWBOY Capitol ESW 11430	38	9 wks
20 Nov 76 ★	20 GOLDEN GREATS Capitol EMTV 2	1	27 wks
23 Apr 77	SOUTHERN NIGHTS Capitol EST 11601	51	1 wk
22 Jul 89	THE COMPLETE GLEN CAMPBELL Stylus SMR 979	47	4 wks

[1] Bobbie Gentry and Glen Campbell

CANNED HEAT US, male vocal / instrumental group   40 wks

29 Jun 68 ●	BOOGIE WITH CANNED HEAT Liberty LBL 83103	5	21 wks
14 Feb 70 ●	CANNED HEAT COOKBOOK Liberty LBS 83303	8	12 wks
4 Jul 70	CANNED HEAT '70 CONCERT Liberty LBS 83333	15	3 wks
10 Oct 70	FUTURE BLUES Liberty LBS 83364	27	4 wks

Freddy CANNON US, male vocalist   11 wks

| 27 Feb 60 ★ | THE EXPLOSIVE FREDDY CANNON Top Rank 25/108 | 1 | 11 wks |

CAPERCAILLIE UK / Ireland, male / female vocal / instrumental group   6 wks

25 Sep 93	SECRET PEOPLE Arista 74321162742	40	3 wks
17 Sep 94	CAPERCAILLIE Survival 74321229112	61	1 wk
4 Nov 95	TO THE MOON Survival SURCD 019	41	2 wks

CAPPELLA UK / Italy, male / female vocal / instrumental group   9 wks

| 26 Mar 94 ● | U GOT 2 KNOW Internal Dance CAPPC 1 | 10 | 9 wks |

CAPTAIN BEEFHEART and his MAGIC BAND
US, male vocal / instrumental group   16 wks

6 Dec 69	TROUT MASK REPLICA Straight STS 1053	21	1 wk
23 Jan 71	LICK MY DECALS OFF BABY Straight STS 1063	20	10 wks
29 May 71	MIRROR MAN Buddah 2365 002	49	1 wk
19 Feb 72	THE SPOTLIGHT KID Reprise K 44162	44	2 wks
18 Sep 82	ICE CREAM FOR CROW Virgin V 2337	90	2 wks

CAPTAIN SENSIBLE UK, male vocalist   3 wks

| 11 Sep 82 | WOMEN AND CAPTAIN FIRST A & M AMLH 68548 | 64 | 3 wks |

CAPTAIN and TENNILLE US, male / female vocal / instrumental duo 6 wks

| 22 Mar 80 | MAKE YOUR MOVE Casablanca CAL 2060 | 33 | 6 wks |

CARPENTER

KAREN 1950–1983 A STAR ON EARTH – A STAR IN HEAVEN

Despite the death of Karen, the CARPENTERS continued to chart with compilations and previously unreleased material.

(LFI)

TOP 30 № 21

CARAVAN *UK, male vocal / instrumental group* **2 wks**

30 Aug 75	**CUNNING STUNTS** Decca SKL 5210	50	1 wk
15 May 76	**BLIND DOG AT ST. DUNSTAN'S** BTM BTM 1007	53	1 wk

CARCASS *UK, male vocal / instrumental group* **1 wk**

6 Nov 93	**HEARTWORK** Earache MOSH 097CD	67	1 wk

CARDIGANS *Sweden, male / female vocal / instrumental group* **2 wks**

8 Jul 95	**LIFE** Stockholm 5235562	58	2 wks

Mariah CAREY *US, female vocalist* **187 wks**

15 Sep 90	● **MARIAH CAREY** CBS 4668151	6	40 wks
26 Oct 91	● **EMOTIONS** Columbia 4688511	4	40 wks
18 Jul 92	● **MTV UNPLUGGED EP** Columbia 4718692	3	10 wks
11 Sep 93	★ **MUSIC BOX** Columbia 4742702	1	77 wks
19 Nov 94	**MERRY CHRISTMAS** Columbia 4773422	32	7 wks
7 Oct 95	★ **DAYDREAM** Columbia 4813672	1†	13 wks

Belinda CARLISLE *US, female vocalist* **149 wks**

2 Jan 88	● **HEAVEN ON EARTH** Virgin V 2496..............................	4	54 wks
4 Nov 89	● **RUNAWAY HORSES** Virgin V 2599..............................	4	39 wks
26 Oct 91	● **LIVE YOUR LIFE BE FREE** Virgin V 2680	7	16 wks
19 Sep 92	★ **THE BEST OF BELINDA VOLUME 1** Virgin BELCD 1........	1	35 wks
23 Oct 93	● **REAL** Virgin CDV 2725	9	5 wks

CARMEL *UK, female / male vocal / instrumental group* **11 wks**

1 Oct 83	**CARMEL** Red Flame RFM 9	94	2 wks
24 Mar 84	**THE DRUM IS EVERYTHING** London SH 8555	19	8 wks
27 Sep 86	**THE FALLING** London LONLP 17....................................	88	1 wk

Eric CARMEN *US, male vocalist* **1 wk**

15 May 76	**ERIC CARMEN** Arista ARTY 120	58	1 wk

Kim CARNES *US, female vocalist* **16 wks**

20 Jun 81	**MISTAKEN IDENTITY** EMI America AML 3018	26	16 wks

Mary-Chapin CARPENTER *US, female vocalist* **5 wks**

29 Oct 94	**STONES IN THE ROAD** Columbia CK 64327	26	5 wks

CARPENTERS *US, male / female vocal / instrumental duo* **574 wks**

23 Jan 71	**CLOSE TO YOU** A & M AMLS 998..................................	23	82 wks
30 Oct 71	**THE CARPENTERS** A & M AMLS 63502	12	36 wks
15 Apr 72	**TICKET TO RIDE** A & M AMLS 64342	20	3 wks
23 Sep 72	**A SONG FOR YOU** A & M AMLS 63511	13	37 wks
7 Jul 73	● **NOW AND THEN** A & M AMLH 63519	2	65 wks
26 Jan 74	★ **THE SINGLES 1969-1973** A & M AMLH 63601	1	125 wks
28 Jun 75	★ **HORIZON** A & M AMLK 64530	1	27 wks
23 Aug 75	**TICKET TO RIDE** (re-issue) Hamlet AMLP 8001	35	2 wks
3 Jul 76	● **A KIND OF HUSH** A & M AMLK 64581..........................	3	15 wks
8 Jan 77	**LIVE AT THE PALLADIUM** A & M AMLS 68403..................	28	3 wks
8 Oct 77	**PASSAGE** A & M AMLK 64703	12	12 wks
2 Dec 78	● **THE SINGLES 1974–1978** A & M AMLT 19748	2	27 wks
27 Jun 81	**MADE IN AMERICA** A & M AMLK 63723	12	10 wks
15 Oct 83	● **VOICE OF THE HEART** A & M AMLX 64954....................	6	19 wks
20 Oct 84	● **YESTERDAY ONCE MORE** EMI/A & M SING 1................	10	26 wks
13 Jan 90	**LOVELINES** A & M AMA 3931..	73	1 wk
31 Mar 90	★ **ONLY YESTERDAY** A & M AMA 1990	1	74 wks

15 Oct 94	**INTERPRETATIONS** A & M 5402512 ....**29**	10 wks

Vikki CARR US, female vocalist
12 wks

22 Jul 67	**WAY OF TODAY** Liberty SLBY 1331 ....**31**	2 wks
12 Aug 67	**IT MUST BE HIM** Liberty LBS 83037 ....**12**	10 wks

José CARRERAS Spain, male vocalist
136 wks

1 Oct 88	**JOSÉ CARRERAS COLLECTION** Stylus SMR 860 ....**90**	4 wks
23 Dec 89	**JOSÉ CARRERAS SINGS ANDREW LLOYD WEBBER**	
	WEA WX 325 ....**42**	6 wks
1 Sep 90	★ **IN CONCERT** Decca 4304331 [1] **1**	78 wks
23 Feb 91	**THE ESSENTIAL JOSÉ CARRERAS** Philips 4326921 ....**24**	9 wks
6 Apr 91	**HOLLYWOOD GOLDEN CLASSICS** East West WX 416.......**47**	3 wks
8 Aug 92	**FROM THE BARCELONA GAMES CEREMONY**	
	RCA Red Seal 09026612042 [2] **41**	3 wks
8 Aug 92	**AMIGOS PARA SIEMPRE** East West 4509902562 [3] **53**	4 wks
16 Oct 93	**WITH A SONG IN MY HEART** Teldec 4509923692 ....**73**	1 wk
25 Dec 93	**CHRISTMAS IN VIENNA** Sony Classical SK 53358 [4] **71**	2 wks
10 Sep 94	★ **THE THREE TENORS IN CONCERT 1994** Teldec 4509962002 [5] **1**	26 wks

[1] Luciano Pavarotti, Placido Domingo and José Carreras [2] Placido Domingo, José Carreras and Montserrat Caballe [3] José Carreras and Sarah Brightman [4] Placido Domingo, Diana Ross and José Carreras [5] José Carreras, Placido Domingo and Luciano Pavrotti with Mehta

Dina CARROLL UK, female vocalist
63 wks

30 Jan 93	● **SO CLOSE** A & M 5400342...**2**	63 wks

Jasper CARROTT UK, male comedian
66 wks

18 Oct 75	● **RABBITS ON AND ON** DJM DJLPS 462 ....**10**	7 wks
6 Nov 76	**CARROTT IN NOTTS** DJM DJF 20482 ....**56**	1 wk
25 Nov 78	**THE BEST OF JASPER CARROTT** DJM DJF 20549 ....**38**	13 wks
20 Oct 79	**THE UNRECORDED JASPER CARROTT** DJM DJF 20560 ...**19**	15 wks
19 Sep 81	**BEAT THE CARROTT** DJM DJF 20575 ....**13**	16 wks
25 Dec 82	**CARROTT'S LIB** DJM DJF 20580 ....**80**	3 wks
19 Nov 83	**THE STUN (CARROTT TELLS ALL)** DJF 20582 ....**57**	8 wks
7 Feb 87	**COSMIC CARROTT** Portrait LAUGH 1 ....**66**	3 wks

CARS US, male vocal / instrumental group
72 wks

2 Dec 78	**CARS** Elektra K 52088 ....**29**	15 wks
7 Jul 79	**CANDY-O** Elektra K 52148 ....**30**	6 wks
6 Oct 84	**HEARTBEAT CITY** Elektra 960296................................**25**	30 wks
9 Nov 85	**THE CARS GREATEST HITS** Elektra EKT 25 ....**27**	19 wks
5 Sep 87	**DOOR TO DOOR** Elektra EKT 42.................................**72**	2 wks

CARTER – THE UNSTOPPABLE SEX MACHINE
UK, male vocal / instrumental duo
39 wks

2 Mar 91	● **30 SOMETHING** Rough Trade R2011 2702.....................**8**	9 wks
21 Sep 91	**101 DAMNATIONS** Big Cat ABB 101 ....**29**	6 wks
1 Feb 92	**30 SOMETHING (re-issue)** Chrysalis CHR 1897 ....**21**	4 wks
16 May 92	★ **1992 – THE LOVE ALBUM** Chrysalis CCD 1946 ....**1**	9 wks
18 Sep 93	● **POST HISTORIC MONSTERS** Chrysalis CDCHR 7090 ....**5**	4 wks
26 Mar 94	**STARRY EYED AND BOLLOCK NAKED** Chrysalis CDCHR 6069......**22**	2 wks
18 Feb 95	● **WORRY BOMB** Chrysalis CDCHRX 6096 ....**9**	3 wks
14 Oct 95	**STRAW DONKEY. . . THE SINGLES** Chrysalis CDCHR 6110 ....**37**	2 wks

Johnny CASH US, male vocalist
290 wks

23 Jul 66	**EVERYBODY LOVES A NUT** CBS BPG 62717 ....**28**	1 wk
4 May 68	**FROM SEA TO SHINING SEA** CBS 62972 ....**40**	1 wk
6 Jul 68	**OLD GOLDEN THROAT** CBS 63316 ....**37**	2 wks
24 Aug 68	● **JOHNNY CASH AT FOLSOM PRISON** CBS 63308 ....**8**	53 wks
23 Aug 69	● **JOHNNY CASH AT SAN QUENTIN** CBS 63629 ....**2**	114 wks
4 Oct 69	**GREATEST HITS VOLUME 1** CBS 63062 ....**23**	25 wks
7 Mar 70	● **HELLO I'M JOHNNY CASH** CBS 63796...........................**6**	16 wks

C
85

15 Aug 70	● **WORLD OF JOHNNY CASH** CBS 66237 ....**5**	31 wks
12 Dec 70	**THE JOHNNY CASH SHOW** CBS 64089 ....**18**	6 wks
18 Sep 71	**MAN IN BLACK** CBS 64331 ....**18**	7 wks
13 Nov 71	**JOHNNY CASH** Hallmark SHM 739.....................**43**	2 wks
20 May 72	● **A THING CALLED LOVE** CBS 64898 ....**8**	11 wks
14 Oct 72	**STAR PORTRAIT** CBS 67201 ....**16**	7 wks
10 Jul 76	**ONE PIECE AT A TIME** CBS 81416 ....**49**	3 wks
9 Oct 76	**THE BEST OF JOHNNY CASH** CBS 10000 ....**48**	2 wks
2 Sep 78	**ITCHY FEET** CBS 10009 ....**36**	4 wks
27 Aug 94	**THE MAN IN BLACK – THE DEFINITIVE COLLECTION** Columbia MOODCD 35.....................**15**	5 wks

CASHFLOW *US, male vocal / instrumental group* **3 wks**

28 Jun 86	**CASHFLOW** Club JABH 17.....................**33**	3 wks

CASHMERE *US, male vocal / instrumental group* **5 wks**

2 Mar 85	**CASHMERE** Fourth & Broadway BRLP 503.....................**63**	5 wks

David CASSIDY *US, male vocalist* **94 wks**

20 May 72	● **CHERISH** Bell BELLS 210.....................**2**	43 wks
24 Feb 73	● **ROCK ME BABY** Bell BELLS 218 ....**2**	20 wks
24 Nov 73	★ **DREAMS ARE NOTHIN' MORE THAN WISHES** Bell BELLS 231 ......**1**	13 wks
3 Aug 74	● **CASSIDY LIVE** Bell BELLS 243 ....**9**	7 wks
9 Aug 75	**THE HIGHER THEY CLIMB** RCA Victor RS 1012.....................**22**	5 wks
8 Jun 85	**ROMANCE** Arista 206 983 ....**20**	6 wks

CAST *UK, male vocal / instrumental group* **4 wks**

28 Oct 95	● **ALL CHANGE** Polydor 5293122.....................**7**	4 wks

CATHERINE WHEEL *UK, male vocal / instrumental group* **2 wks**

29 Feb 92	**FERMENT** Fontana 5109032 ....**36**	1 wk
31 Jul 93	**CHROME** Fontana 5180392 ....**58**	1 wk

Nick CAVE and the BAD SEEDS
Australia, male vocalist with male vocal / instrumental group **12 wks**

2 Jun 84	**FROM HER TO ETERNITY** Mute STUMM 17 ....**40**	3 wks
15 Jun 85	**THE FIRST BORN IS DEAD** Mute STUMM 21 ....**53**	1 wk
30 Aug 86	**KICKING AGAINST THE PRICKS** Mute STUMM 28 ....**89**	1 wk
1 Oct 88	**TENDER PREY** Mute STUMM 52.....................**67**	1 wk
28 Apr 90	**THE GOOD SON** Mute STUMM 76 ....**47**	1 wk
9 May 92	**HENRY'S DREAM** Mute CDSTUMM 92 ....**29**	2 wks
18 Sep 93	**LIVE SEEDS** Mute CDSTUMM 122 ....**67**	1 wk
30 Apr 94	**LET LOVE IN** Mute LCDSTUMM 123.....................**12**	2 wks

CAVEMAN *UK, male rap duo* **2 wks**

13 Apr 91	**POSITIVE REACTION** Profile FILER 406 ....**43**	2 wks

CCS *UK, male vocal / instrumental group* **5 wks**

8 Apr 72	**CCS** RAK SRAK 503.....................**23**	5 wks

CENTRAL LINE *UK, male vocal / instrumental group* **5 wks**

13 Feb 82	**BREAKING POINT** Mercury MERA 001.....................**64**	5 wks

CERRONE *France, male producer / multi–instrumentalist* **1 wk**

30 Sep 78	**SUPERNATURE** Atlantic K 50431 ....**60**	1 wk

ALPHABETICALLY BY ARTIST

A CERTAIN RATIO *UK, male vocal / instrumental group*   **3 wks**

30 Jan 82   **SEXTET** *Factory FACT 55* ....**53**   3 wks

Peter CETERA *US, male vocalist*   **4 wks**

13 Sep 86   **SOLITUDE / SOLITAIRE** *Full Moon 9254741*.....................**56**   4 wks

Richard CHAMBERLAIN *US, male vocalist*   **8 wks**

16 Mar 63 ● **RICHARD CHAMBERLAIN SINGS** *MGM C 923* ....**8**   8 wks

CHAMELEONS *UK, male vocal / instrumental group*   **4 wks**

25 May 85   **WHAT DOES ANYTHING MEAN? BASICALLY** *Statik STAT LP 22*..**60**   2 wks
20 Sep 86   **STRANGE TIMES** *Geffen 924 1191*................................**44**   2 wks

CHAMPAIGN *US, male / female vocal / instrumental group*   **4 wks**

27 Jun 81   **HOW 'BOUT US** *CBS 84927* ....**38**   4 wks

CHANGE *US, male / female vocal / instrumental group*   **23 wks**

19 May 84   **CHANGE OF HEART** *WEA WX 5*...........................**34**   17 wks
27 Apr 85   **TURN ON THE RADIO** *Cooltempo CHR 1504*..............**39**   6 wks

Michael CHAPMAN *UK, male vocalist*   **1 wk**

21 Mar 70   **FULLY QUALIFIED SURVIVOR** *Harvest SHVL 764* ....**45**   1 wk

Tracy CHAPMAN *US, female vocalist*   **103 wks**

21 May 88 ★ **TRACY CHAPMAN** *Elektra EKT 44* ....**1**   84 wks
14 Oct 89 ★ **CROSSROADS** *Elektra EKT 61*............................**1**   16 wks
9 May 92   **MATTERS OF THE HEART** *Elektra 7559612152* ....**19**   3 wks

CHAPTERHOUSE *UK, male vocal / instrumental group*   **3 wks**

11 May 91   **WHIRLPOOL** *Dedicated DEDLP 001* ....**23**   3 wks

CHAQUITO ORCHESTRA
UK, orchestra arranged and conducted by Johnny Gregory   **2 wks**

24 Feb 68   **THIS IS CHAQUITO** *Fontana SFXL 50* [1] ....**36**   1 wk
4 Mar 72   **THRILLER THEMES** *Philips 6308 087* ....**48**   1 wk

[1] Chaquito and Quedo Brass

CHARGE GBH *UK, male vocal / instrumental group*   **6 wks**

14 Aug 82   **CITY BABY ATTACKED BY RATS** *Clay CLAYLP 4* ....**17**   6 wks

CHARLATANS *UK, male vocal / instrumental group*   **33 wks**

20 Oct 90 ★ **SOME FRIENDLY** *Situation Two SITU 30* ....**1**   17 wks
4 Apr 92   **BETWEEN 10TH AND 11TH** *Situation Two SITU 37CD* ....**21**   4 wks
2 Apr 94 ● **UP TO OUR HIPS** *Beggars Banquet BBQCD 147* ....**8**   3 wks
9 Sep 95 ★ **THE CHARLATANS** *Beggars Banquet BBQCD 174* ....**1**   9 wks

CHARLENE *US, female vocalist*   **4 wks**

17 Jul 82   **I'VE NEVER BEEN TO ME** *Motown STML 12171* ....**43**   4 wks

Ray CHARLES *US, male vocalist / instrumentalist – piano*   **45 wks**

28 Jul 62 ● **MODERN SOUNDS IN COUNTRY AND WESTERN MUSIC**
HMV CLP 1580........................**6**   16 wks

On 12 October 1995, CARRERAS DOMINGO PAVAROTTI, confounding non-opera lovers by lining up as Domingo Carreras Pavarotti, announced their 1996 world tour.

(Mirror Syndication)

TOP 30 № 28

The 1993 Grammy Awards were harvest time for ERIC CLAPTON, whose multiple win included Best Album for *Unplugged*.

(Hulton Deutsch)

23 Feb 63	**MODERN SOUNDS IN COUNTRY AND WESTERN MUSIC**		
	VOLUME 2 HMV CLP 1613 ....**15**	5 wks
20 Jul 63	**GREATEST HITS** HMV CLP 1626 ....**16**	5 wks
5 Oct 68	**GREATEST HITS VOLUME 2** Stateside SSL 10241 ....**24**	8 wks
19 Jul 80	**HEART TO HEART – 20 HOT HITS** London RAY TV 1 ....**29**	5 wks
24 Mar 90	**THE COLLECTION** Arcade RCLP 101 ....**36**	3 wks
13 Mar 93	**RAY CHARLES THE LIVING LEGEND** Arcade ARC 94642 ....**48**	3 wks

Tina CHARLES UK, female vocalist   **7 wks**

3 Dec 77	**HEART 'N' SOUL** CBS 82180 ....**35**	7 wks

CHARLES and EDDIE US, male vocal duo   **15 wks**

12 Dec 92	**DUOPHONIC** Capitol CDESTU 2186...........**19**	15 wks

CHAS and DAVE UK, male vocal / instrumental duo   **101 wks**

5 Dec 81	**CHAS AND DAVE'S CHRISTMAS JAMBOREE BAG**	
	Warwick WW 5166 ....**25**	15 wks
17 Apr 82	**MUSTN'T GRUMBLE** Rockney 909 ....**35**	11 wks
8 Jan 83	**JOB LOT** Rockney ROC 910 ....**59**	15 wks
15 Oct 83	● **CHAS AND DAVE'S KNEES UP - JAMBOREE BAG NO. 2**	
	Warwick WW 5166 ....**7**	17 wks
11 Aug 84	**WELL PLEASED** Rockney ROC 912 ....**27**	10 wks
17 Nov 84	**CHAS AND DAVE'S GREATEST HITS** Rockney ROC 913 ....**16**	10 wks
15 Dec 84	**CHAS AND DAVE'S CHRISTMAS JAMBOREE BAG (re-issue)**	
	Rockney ROCM 001 ....**87**	1 wk
9 Nov 85	**JAMBOREE BAG NUMBER 3** Rockney ROC 914 ....**15**	13 wks
13 Dec 86	**CHAS AND DAVE'S CHRISTMAS CAROL ALBUM**	
	Telstar STAR 2293 ....**37**	4 wks
29 Apr 95	● **STREET PARTY** Telstar TCD 2765...........**3**	5 wks

CHEAP TRICK US, male vocal / instrumental group   **15 wks**

24 Feb 79	**CHEAP TRICK AT BUDOKAN** Epic EPC 86083 ....**29**	9 wks
6 Oct 79	**DREAM POLICE** Epic EPC 83522 ....**41**	5 wks
5 Jun 82	**ONE ON ONE** Epic EPC 85740 ....**95**	1 wk

CHECK 1–2 – See Craig McLACHLAN and CHECK 1–2

Chubby CHECKER US, male vocalist   **7 wks**

27 Jan 62	**TWIST WITH CHUBBY CHECKER** Columbia 33SX 1315 ....**13**	4 wks
3 Mar 62	**FOR TWISTERS ONLY** Columbia 33SX 1341...........**17**	3 wks

CHEMICAL BROTHERS UK, male instrumental / production duo   **17 wks**

8 Jul 95	● **EXIT PLANET DUST** Junior Boy's Own XDUSTCD 1 ....**9**	17 wks

CHER US, female vocalist   **212 wks**

2 Oct 65	● **ALL I REALLY WANT TO DO** Liberty LBY 3058 ....**7**	9 wks
7 May 66	**SONNY SIDE OF CHER** Liberty LBY 3072 ....**11**	11 wks
16 Jan 88	**CHER** Geffen WX 132...........**26**	22 wks
22 Jul 89	● **HEART OF STONE** Geffen GEF 24239 ....**7**	82 wks
29 Jun 91	★ **LOVE HURTS** Geffen GEF 24427 ....**1**	51 wks
21 Nov 92	★ **GREATEST HITS 1965–1992** Geffen GED 24439 ....**1**	30 wks
18 Nov 95	**IT'S A MAN'S WORLD** WEA 0630126702 ....**28†**	7 wks

The catalogue number for Heart Of Stone changed from WX 262 during the album's run. See also Sonny and Cher.

CHERELLE US, female vocalist   **9 wks**

25 Jan 86	**HIGH PRIORITY** Tabu TBU 26699 ....**17**	9 wks

C
89

Neneh CHERRY US, female vocalist · **45 wks**

| 17 Jun 89 | ● RAW LIKE SUSHI Circa CIRCA 8 ....2 | 43 wks |
| 7 Nov 92 | HOMEBREW Circa CIRCD 25 ....27 | 2 wks |

CHIC US, male / female vocal / instrumental group · **47 wks**

3 Feb 79	● C'EST CHIC Atlantic K 50565....................2	24 wks
18 Aug 79	RISQUE Atlantic K 50634 29	12 wks
15 Dec 79	THE BEST OF CHIC Atlantic K 50686 30	8 wks
5 Dec 87	FREAK OUT Telstar STAR 2319 [1] 72	3 wks

[1] Chic and Sister Sledge

See also Compilation Albums – Dino.

CHICAGO US, male vocal / instrumental group · **117 wks**

27 Sep 69	● CHICAGO TRANSIT AUTHORITY CBS 66221 [1] 9	14 wks
4 Apr 70	● CHICAGO CBS 66233 6	27 wks
3 Apr 71	CHICAGO 3 CBS 66260 31	1 wk
30 Sep 72	CHICAGO 5 CBS 69108 24	2 wks
23 Oct 76	CHICAGO X CBS 86010 21	11 wks
2 Oct 82	CHICAGO 16 Full Moon K 99235 44	9 wks
4 Dec 82	LOVE SONGS TV TVA 6 42	8 wks
1 Dec 84	CHICAGO 17 Full Moon 925060 24	20 wks
25 Nov 89	● THE HEART OF CHICAGO Reprise WX 328 6	25 wks

[1] Chicago Transit Authority

CHICKEN SHACK UK, male / female vocal / instrumental group · **9 wks**

| 22 Jul 68 | 40 BLUE FINGERS FRESHLY PACKED Blue Horizon 763203..........12 | 8 wks |
| 15 Feb 69 | ● OK KEN? Blue Horizon 763209 ....9 | 1 wk |

CHIEFTAINS Ireland, male vocal / instrumental group · **21 wks**

28 Mar 87	JAMES GALWAY AND THE CHIEFTAINS IN IRELAND RCA Red Seal RL 85798 [1] 32	5 wks
2 Jul 88	IRISH HEARTBEAT Mercury MERH 124 [2] 18	7 wks
4 Feb 95	THE LONG BLACK VEIL RCA 74321251672....................17	9 wks

[1] James Galway and the Chieftains [2] Van Morrison and the Chieftains

Toni CHILDS US, female vocalist · **1 wk**

| 29 Apr 89 | UNION A & M AMA 5175 ....73 | 1 wk |

CHIMES UK, male / female vocal / instrumental group · **19 wks**

| 23 Jun 90 | THE CHIMES CBS 4664811....................17 | 19 wks |

CHINA BLACK UK, male vocal / instrumental duo · **4 wks**

| 11 Mar 95 | BORN Wild Card 5237552 ....27 | 4 wks |

CHINA CRISIS UK, male vocal / instrumental group · **68 wks**

20 Nov 82	DIFFICULT SHAPES AND PASSIVE RHYTHMS Virgin V 2243 21	18 wks
12 Nov 83	WORKING WITH FIRE AND STEEL – POSSIBLE POP SONGS VOLUME 2 Virgin V 2286 20	16 wks
11 May 85	● FLAUNT THE IMPERFECTION Virgin V 2342 9	22 wks
6 Dec 86	WHAT PRICE PARADISE Virgin V 2410 63	6 wks
13 May 89	DIARY OF A HOLLOW HORSE Virgin V 2567 58	2 wks
15 Sep 90	CHINA CRISIS COLLECTION Virgin V 2613....................32	4 wks

CHORDS UK, male vocal / instrumental group · **3 wks**

| 24 May 80 | SO FAR AWAY Polydor POLS 1019....................30 | 3 wks |

C
90

CHRISTIANS *UK, male vocal / instrumental group* **96 wks**

31 Oct 87	● THE CHRISTIANS *Island ILPS 9876*	**2**	68 wks
27 Jan 90	★ COLOUR *Island ILPS 9948*..	**1**	17 wks
10 Oct 92	HAPPY IN HELL *Island CID 9996*..	**18**	3 wks
20 Nov 93	THE BEST OF THE CHRISTIANS *Island CIDTV 6*	**22**	8 wks

Tony CHRISTIE *UK, male vocalist* **10 wks**

24 Jul 71	I DID WHAT I DID FOR MARIA *MCA MKPS 2016*	**37**	1 wk
17 Feb 73	WITH LOVING FEELING *MCA MUPS 468*...........................	**19**	2 wks
31 May 75	TONY CHRISTIE – LIVE *MCA MCF 2703*.............................	**33**	3 wks
6 Nov 76	BEST OF TONY CHRISTIE *MCA MCF 2769*.........................	**28**	4 wks

CHRON GEN *UK, male vocal / instrumental group* **3 wks**

3 Apr 82	CHRONIC GENERATION *Secret SEC 3*	**53**	3 wks

CHUMBAWAMBA *UK, male / female vocal / instrumental group* **3 wks**

7 May 94	ANARCHY *One Little Indian TPLP 46CD*..............................	**29**	2 wks
4 Nov 95	SWINGIN' WITH RAYMOND *One Little Indian TPLP 66CDS*	**70**	1 wk

Sir Winston CHURCHILL *UK, male statesman* **8 wks**

13 Feb 65	● THE VOICE OF CHURCHILL *Decca LXT 6200*	**6**	8 wks

CICCONE YOUTH – *See SONIC YOUTH*

CINDERELLA *US, male vocal / instrumental group* **8 wks**

23 Jul 88	LONG COLD WINTER *Vertigo VERH 59*	**30**	6 wks
1 Dec 90	HEARTBREAK STATION *Vertigo 8480181*	**36**	2 wks

CITY BEAT BAND – *See PRINCE CHARLES and the CITY BEAT BAND*

Gary CLAIL ON-U SOUND SYSTEM
UK, male vocalist / producer **2 wks**

4 May 91	EMOTIONAL HOOLIGAN *Perfecto PL 74965*.....................	**35**	2 wks

CLANCY BROTHERS and Tommy MAKEM
Ireland, male vocal / instrumental group and male vocalist **5 wks**

16 Apr 66	ISN'T IT GRAND BOYS *CBS BPG 62674*	**22**	5 wks

CLANNAD *Ireland, male / female vocal / instrumental group* **136 wks**

2 Apr 83	MAGICAL RING *RCA RCALP 6072*	**26**	21 wks
12 May 84	LEGEND (MUSIC FROM ROBIN OF SHERWOOD) *RCA PL 70188*..	**15**	40 wks
2 Jun 84	MAGICAL RING (re-issue) *RCA PL 70003*............................	**91**	1 wk
26 Oct 85	MACALLA *RCA PL 70894*..	**33**	24 wks
7 Nov 87	SIRIUS *RCA PL 71513*..	**34**	4 wks
11 Feb 89	ATLANTIC REALM *BBC REB 727*	**41**	3 wks
6 May 89	● PASTPRESENT *RCA PL 74074*	**5**	25 wks
20 Oct 90	ANAM *RCA PL 74762*	**14**	7 wks
15 May 93	● BANBA *RCA 74321139612*..	**5**	11 wks

Pastpresent changed its catalogue number to 74321289812 during its chart run.

Eric CLAPTON *UK, male vocalist / instrumentalist – guitar* **475 wks**

30 Jul 66	● BLUES BREAKERS *Decca LK 4804* [1]	**6**	17 wks
5 Sep 70	ERIC CLAPTON *Polydor 2383021*	**17**	8 wks
26 Aug 72	HISTORY OF ERIC CLAPTON *Polydor 2659 2478 027*.....................	**20**	6 wks
24 Mar 73	IN CONCERT *RSO 2659020* [2]	**36**	1 wk
24 Aug 74	● 461 OCEAN BOULEVARD *RSO 2479 118*..............................	**3**	19 wks

C
91

12 Apr 75	THERE'S ONE IN EVERY CROWD *RSO 2479 132* **15**	8 wks
13 Sep 75	E.C. WAS HERE *RSO 2394 160* **14**	6 wks
11 Sep 76	● NO REASON TO CRY *RSO 2479 179*.....................................**8**	7 wks
26 Nov 77	SLOWHAND *RSO 2479 201* **23**	13 wks
9 Dec 78	BACKLESS *RSO RSD 5001* **18**	12 wks
10 May 80	● JUST ONE NIGHT *RSO RSDX 2* **3**	12 wks
7 Mar 81	ANOTHER TICKET *RSO RSD 5008* **18**	8 wks
24 Apr 82	TIME PIECES – THE BEST OF ERIC CLAPTON *RSO RSD 5010* **20**	14 wks
19 Feb 83	MONEY & CIGARETTES *Duck W 3773*....................................**13**	17 wks
9 Jun 84	BACKTRACKIN' *Starblend ERIC 1*...**29**	16 wks
23 Mar 85	● BEHIND THE SUN *Duck 9251661* **8**	14 wks
6 Dec 86	● AUGUST *Duck WX 71* **3**	46 wks
26 Sep 87	● THE CREAM OF ERIC CLAPTON *Polydor ECTV 1* [3] **3**	104 wks
18 Nov 89	● JOURNEYMAN *Duck WX 322* **2**	32 wks
26 Oct 91	24 NIGHTS *Duck WX 373* **17**	7 wks
12 Sep 92	● UNPLUGGED *Duck 9362450242* **2**	90 wks
24 Sep 94	★ FROM THE CRADLE *Duck 9362457352* **1**	18 wks

[1] John Mayall and Eric Clapton [2] Derek and the Dominos [3] Eric Clapton and Cream

From 9 Jul 93 The Cream Of Eric Clapton *was repackaged and was available as* The Best Of Eric Clapton.

Louis CLARK – *See ROYAL PHILHARMONIC ORCHESTRA*

Gary CLARK *UK, male vocalist*   **2 wks**

8 May 93	TEN SHORT SONGS ABOUT LOVE *Circa CIRCD 23*..........................**25**	2 wks

Petula CLARK *UK, female vocalist*   **43 wks**

30 Jul 66	I COULDN'T LIVE WITHOUT YOUR LOVE *Pye NPL 18148* **11**	10 wks
4 Feb 67	HIT PARADE *Pye NPL 18159* **18**	13 wks
18 Feb 67	COLOUR MY WORLD *Pye NSPL 18171*.....................................**16**	9 wks
7 Oct 67	THESE ARE MY SONGS *Pye NSPL 18197*..................................**38**	3 wks
6 Apr 68	THE OTHER MAN'S GRASS IS ALWAYS GREENER *Pye NSPL 18211* **37**	1 wk
5 Feb 77	20 ALL TIME GREATEST *K-Tel NE 945*.....................................**18**	7 wks

C
92

Dave CLARK FIVE *UK, male vocal / instrumental group*   **31 wks**

18 Apr 64	● A SESSION WITH THE DAVE CLARK FIVE *Columbia 33SX 1598* **3**	8 wks
14 Aug 65	● CATCH US IF YOU CAN *Columbia 33SX 1756*.................................**8**	8 wks
4 Mar 78	● 25 THUMPING GREAT HITS *Polydor POLTV 7*..................................**7**	10 wks
17 Apr 93	GLAD ALL OVER AGAIN *EMI CDEMTV 75* **28**	5 wks

Gilby CLARKE *US, male instrumentalist – guitar*   **1 wk**

6 Aug 94	PAWNSHOP GUITARS *Virgin America CDVUS 76* **39**	1 wk

John Cooper CLARKE *UK, male vocalist*   **9 wks**

19 Apr 80	SNAP CRACKLE AND BOP *Epic EPC 84083*....................................**26**	7 wks
5 Jun 82	ZIP STYLE METHOD *Epic EPC 85667* **97**	2 wks

Stanley CLARKE *US, male vocal / instrumentalist – bass*   **2 wks**

12 Jul 80	ROCKS PEBBLES AND SAND *Epic EPC 84342* **42**	2 wks

CLASH *UK, male vocal / instrumental group*   **107 wks**

30 Apr 77	CLASH *CBS 82000*...**12**	16 wks
25 Nov 78	● GIVE 'EM ENOUGH ROPE *CBS 82431* **2**	14 wks
22 Dec 79	● LONDON CALLING *CBS CLASH 3* **9**	20 wks
20 Dec 80	SANDINISTA *CBS FSLN 1* **19**	9 wks
22 May 82	● COMBAT ROCK *CBS FMLN 2* **2**	23 wks
16 Nov 85	CUT THE CRAP *CBS 26601* **16**	3 wks
2 Apr 88	● THE STORY OF THE CLASH *CBS 460244 1*................................**7**	20 wks
16 Nov 91	THE SINGLES *Columbia 4689461* **68**	2 wks

CLASSIX NOUVEAUX UK, male vocal / instrumental group   **6 wks**

30 May 81	**NIGHT PEOPLE** Liberty LBG 30325	66	2 wks
24 Apr 82	**LA VERITE** Liberty LBG 30346	44	4 wks

Richard CLAYDERMAN France, male instrumentalist – piano   **209 wks**

13 Nov 82 ●	**RICHARD CLAYDERMAN** Decca SKL 5329..........................	2	64 wks
8 Oct 83	**THE MUSIC OF RICHARD CLAYDERMAN** Decca SKL 5333	21	28 wks
24 Nov 84	**THE MUSIC OF LOVE** Decca SKL 5340	28	21 wks
1 Dec 84	**CHRISTMAS** Decca SKL 5337	53	5 wks
23 Nov 85	**THE CLASSIC TOUCH** Decca SKL 5343	17	18 wks
22 Nov 86	**HOLLYWOOD AND BROADWAY** Decca SKL 5344	28	9 wks
28 Nov 87	**SONGS OF LOVE** Decca SKL 5345	19	13 wks
3 Dec 88	**A LITTLE NIGHT MUSIC** Decca Delphine 8281251	52	5 wks
25 Nov 89	**THE LOVE SONGS OF ANDREW LLOYD WEBBER** Decca Delphine 8281751	18	10 wks
24 Nov 90	**MY CLASSIC COLLECTION** Decca Delphine 8282281.............	29	7 wks
9 Nov 91	**TOGETHER AT LAST** Delphine/Polydor 5115251 [1]	14	15 wks
14 Nov 92	**THE VERY BEST OF RICHARD CLAYDERMAN** Decca Delphine 8283362 [2]	47	5 wks
19 Nov 94	**IN HARMONY** Polydor 5238242 [1]	28	7 wks
25 Nov 95	**THE CARPENTERS COLLECTION** PolyGram TV 8286882	65	2 wks

[1] Richard Clayderman and James Last [2] Richard Clayderman with the Royal Philmarnomic Orchestra

CLAYTOWN TROUPE UK, male vocal / instrumental group   **1 wk**

21 Oct 89	**THROUGH THE VEIL** Island ILPS 9933....................	72	1 wk

CLIMAX BLUES BAND UK, male vocal / instrumental group   **1 wk**

13 Nov 76	**GOLD PLATED** BTM 1009	56	1 wk

CLIMIE FISHER UK, male vocal / instrumental duo   **38 wks**

13 Feb 88	**EVERYTHING** EMI EMC 3538..........................	14	36 wks
21 Oct 89	**COMING IN FOR THE KILL** EMI EMC 3565	35	2 wks

Patsy CLINE US, female vocalist   **22 wks**

19 Jan 91	**SWEET DREAMS** MCA MCG 6003	18	10 wks
19 Jan 91	**DREAMING** Platinum Music PLAT 303	55	4 wks
5 Sep 92	**THE DEFINITIVE PATSY CLINE** Arcade ARC 94992..........	11	8 wks

CLIVILLES & COLE – See C&C MUSIC FACTORY/CLIVILLES & COLE

CLOCK UK, male / female vocal / instrumental group   **2 wks**

23 Sep 95	**IT'S TIME . . .** Media MCD 11355	27	2 wks

Luis COBOS Spain, male orchestra leader   **1 wk**

21 Apr 90	**OPERA EXTRAVAGANZA** Epic MOOD 12	72	1 wk

Eddie COCHRAN US, male vocalist / instrumentalist – guitar   **47 wks**

30 Jul 60	**SINGING TO MY BABY** London HAU 2093...................	19	1 wk
1 Oct 60 ●	**EDDIE COCHRAN MEMORIAL ALBUM** London HAG 2267............	9	12 wks
12 Jan 63	**CHERISHED MEMORIES** Liberty LBY 1109	15	3 wks
20 Apr 63	**EDDIE COCHRAN MEMORIAL ALBUM (re-issue)** Liberty LBY 1127	11	18 wks
19 Oct 63	**SINGING TO MY BABY (re-issue)** Liberty LBY 1158	20	1 wk
9 May 70	**VERY BEST OF EDDIE COCHRAN** Liberty LBS 83337..........	34	3 wks
18 Aug 79	**THE EDDIE COCHRAN SINGLES ALBUM** United Artists UAK 30244	39	6 wks

16 Apr 88 **C'MON EVERYBODY** *Liberty ECR 1* 53   3 wks

Brenda COCHRANE *Ireland, female vocalist*   **14 wks**

14 Apr 90 **THE VOICE** *Polydor 8431411* 14   11 wks
6 Apr 91 **IN DREAMS** *Polydor 8490341* 55   3 wks

Joe COCKER *UK, male vocalist*   **62 wks**

26 Sep 70 **MAD DOGS AND ENGLISHMEN** *A & M AMLS 6002* 16   8 wks
6 May 72 **JOE COCKER / WITH A LITTLE HELP FROM MY FRIENDS**
     Double Back TOOFA 1/2 29   4 wks
30 Jun 84 **A CIVILISED MAN** *Capitol EJ 240139 1* 100   1 wk
11 Apr 92 **NIGHT CALLS** *Capitol CDESTU 2167* 25   14 wks
27 Jun 92 ● **THE LEGEND THE ESSENTIAL COLLECTION**
     PolyGram TV 5154112...4   20 wks
17 Sep 94 ● **HAVE A LITTLE FAITH** *Capitol CDEST 2233* 9   15 wks

COCKNEY REBEL *– See Steve HARLEY and COCKNEY REBEL*

COCKNEY REJECTS *UK, male vocal / instrumental group*   **17 wks**

15 Mar 80 **GREATEST HITS VOLUME 1** *Zonophone ZONO 101* 22   11 wks
25 Oct 80 **GREATEST HITS VOLUME 2** *Zonophone ZONO 102* 23   3 wks
18 Apr 81 **GREATEST HITS VOLUME 3 (LIVE AND LOUD)**
     Zonophone ZEM 101 27   3 wks

COCONUTS *– See Kid CREOLE and the COCONUTS*

COCTEAU TWINS *UK, male / female vocal / instrumental group*   **42 wks**

29 Oct 83 **HEAD OVER HEELS** *4AD CAD 313* 51   15 wks
24 Nov 84 **TREASURE** *4AD CAD 412*...29   8 wks
26 Apr 86 ● **VICTORIALAND** *4AD CAD 602* 10   7 wks
1 Oct 88 **BLUE BELL KNOLL** *4AD CAD 807*....................................15   4 wks
22 Sep 90 ● **HEAVEN OR LAS VEGAS** *4AD CAD 0012* 7   5 wks
30 Oct 93 **FOUR CALENDAR CAFE** *Fontana 5182592* 13   3 wks

See also Harold Budd / Liz Fraser / Robin Guthrie / Simon Raymonde, the latter three being the Cocteau Twins.

Leonard COHEN *Canada, male vocalist*   **150 wks**

31 Aug 68 **SONGS OF LEONARD COHEN** *CBS 63241* 13   71 wks
3 May 69 ● **SONGS FROM A ROOM** *CBS 63587* 2   26 wks
24 Apr 71 ● **SONGS OF LOVE AND HATE** *CBS 69004* 4   18 wks
28 Sep 74 **NEW SKIN FOR THE OLD CEREMONY** *CBS 69087*..................24   3 wks
10 Dec 77 **DEATH OF A LADIES' MAN** *CBS 86042*............................35   5 wks
16 Feb 85 **VARIOUS POSITIONS** *CBS 26222* 52   6 wks
27 Feb 88 **I'M YOUR MAN** *CBS 460642 1* 48   13 wks
6 Aug 88 **GREATEST HITS** *CBS 32644* 99   1 wk
5 Dec 92 **THE FUTURE** *Columbia 4724982* 36   3 wks
6 Aug 94 **COHEN LIVE** *Columbia 4771712* 35   4 wks

Marc COHN *UK, male vocalist / instrumentalist – piano*   **23 wks**

29 Jun 91 **MARC COHN** *Atlantic 7567821781* 27   20 wks
12 Jun 93 **THE RAINY SEASON** *Atlantic 7567824912* 24   3 wks

COLDCUT *UK, male production duo*   **4 wks**

29 Apr 89 **WHAT'S THAT NOISE** *Ahead Of Our Time CCUTLP 1* 20   4 wks

Lloyd COLE *UK, male vocalist*   **88 wks**

20 Oct 84 **RATTLESNAKES** *Polydor LCLP 1* [1] 13   30 wks
30 Nov 85 ● **EASY PIECES** *Polydor LCLP 2* [1] 5   18 wks
7 Nov 87 ● **MAINSTREAM** *Polydor LCLP 3* [1] 9   20 wks

8 Apr 89	**19841989** Polydor 837736 1 `1`	**14**	7 wks
3 Mar 90	**LLOYD COLE** Polydor 8419071	**11**	6 wks
28 Sep 91	**DON'T GET WEIRD ON ME BABE** Polydor 5110931	**21**	3 wks
23 Oct 93	**BAD VIBES** Fontana 5183182	**38**	2 wks
7 Oct 95	**LOVE STORY** Fontana 5285292	**27**	2 wks

`1` Lloyd Cole and the Commotions

Nat 'King' COLE US, male vocalist   **126 wks**

19 Aug 61	**STRING ALONG WITH NAT 'KING' COLE** Encore ENC 102 ....**12**		9 wks
20 Oct 62	● **NAT 'KING' COLE SINGS AND THE GEORGE SHEARING**		
	QUINTET PLAYS Capitol W 1675 `1` **8**		7 wks
27 Mar 65	**UNFORGETTABLE NAT 'KING' COLE** Capitol W 20664 ....**11**		8 wks
7 Dec 68	● **BEST OF NAT 'KING' COLE** Capitol ST 21139 ....**5**		18 wks
5 Dec 70	**BEST OF NAT 'KING' COLE VOLUME 2** Capitol ST 21687..........**39**		2 wks
27 Nov 71	**WHITE CHRISTMAS** MFP 5224 `2` **45**		1 wk
8 Apr 78	★ **20 GOLDEN GREATS** Capitol EMTV 9 ....**1**		37 wks
20 Nov 82	● **GREATEST LOVE SONGS** Capitol EMTV 35 ....**7**		26 wks
26 Nov 88	**CHRISTMAS WITH NAT 'KING' COLE** Stylus SMR 868..................**25**		9 wks
23 Nov 91	**UNFORGETTABLE NAT 'KING' COLE** EMI EMTV 61 ....**23**		9 wks

`1` Nat 'King' Cole and the George Shearing Quintet `2` Nat 'King' Cole and Dean Martin
The two Unforgettable Nat 'King' Cole *albums are different.*

Natalie COLE US, female vocalist   **65 wks**

17 Sep 83	● **UNFORGETTABLE: A MUSICAL TRIBUTE TO NAT 'KING' COLE**		
	CBS 10042 `1` **5**		16 wks
7 May 88	**EVERLASTING** Manhattan MTL 1012............................**62**		4 wks
20 May 89	● **GOOD TO BE BACK** EMI-USA MTL 1042 ....**10**		12 wks
27 Jul 91	**UNFORGETTABLE – WITH LOVE** Elektra EKT 91............................**11**		29 wks
26 Jun 93	**TAKE A LOOK** Elektra 7559614962............................**16**		4 wks

`1` Johnny Mathis and Natalie Cole

Ansil COLLINS – *See DAVE and Ansil COLLINS*

Edwyn COLLINS UK, male vocalist   **8 wks**

22 Jul 95	● **GORGEOUS GEORGE** Setanta AHOAON 058 ....**8**		8 wks

Joan COLLINS – *See Anthony NEWLEY, Peter SELLERS, Joan COLLINS*

Judy COLLINS US, female vocalist   **18 wks**

10 Apr 71	**WHALES AND NIGHTINGALES** Elektra EKS 75010 ....**37**		2 wks
31 May 75	● **JUDITH** Elektra K 52019 ....**7**		12 wks
14 Dec 85	**AMAZING GRACE** Telstar STAR 2265............................**34**		4 wks

Phil COLLINS UK, male vocalist / instrumentalist – drums   **756 wks**

21 Feb 81	★ **FACE VALUE** Virgin V 2185 ....**1**		274 wks
13 Nov 82	● **HELLO I MUST BE GOING** Virgin V 2252............................**2**		163 wks
2 Mar 85	★ **NO JACKET REQUIRED** Virgin V 2345 ....**1**		176 wks
2 Dec 89	★ **. . . BUT SERIOUSLY** Virgin V 2620............................**1**		72 wks
17 Nov 90	● **SERIOUS HITS . . . LIVE!** Virgin PCLP 1 ....**2**		50 wks
20 Nov 93	★ **BOTH SIDES** Virgin CDV 2800 ....**1**		21 wks

Willie COLLINS US, male vocalist   **1 wk**

14 Jun 86	**WHERE YOU GONNA BE TONIGHT?** Capitol EST 2012 ....**97**		1 wk

COLOR ME BADD US, male vocal group   **22 wks**

24 Aug 91	● **CMB** Giant WX 425............................**3**		22 wks

COLOSSEUM UK, male vocal / instrumental group   **14 wks**

17 May 69	**COLOSSEUM** Fontana S 5510 ....**15**		1 wk

C
95

TOP 30 № 13

Mike Rutherford and
Tony Banks of Genesis
were real pussycats
about giving PHIL
COLLINS time to pursue
his solo career.
(LFI)

22 Nov 69	**VALENTYNE SUITE** Vertigo VO 1	**15**	2 wks
5 Dec 70	**DAUGHTER OF TIME** Vertigo 6360 017	**23**	5 wks
26 Jun 71	**COLOSSEUM LIVE** Bronze ICD 1	**17**	6 wks

COLOUR FIELD UK, male vocal/instrumental group   **8 wks**

4 May 85	**VIRGINS AND PHILISTINES** Chrysalis CHR 1480	**12**	7 wks
4 Apr 87	**DECEPTION** Chrysalis CDL 1546	**95**	1 wk

COLOURBOX UK, male vocal/instrumental group   **2 wks**

24 Aug 85	**COLOURBOX** 4AD CAD 508	**67**	2 wks

Alice COLTRANE – See SANTANA

Shawn COLVIN US, female vocalist   **1 wk**

17 Sep 94	**COVER GIRL** Columbia 4772402	**67**	1 wk

COMETS – See Bill HALEY and his COMETS

COMIC RELIEF UK, charity ensemble of comedians   **8 wks**

10 May 86	● **UTTERLY UTTERLY LIVE!** WEA WX 51	**10**	8 wks

COMMITMENTS Ireland, male/female vocal/instrumental group   **131 wks**

26 Oct 91	● **THE COMMITMENTS (film soundtrack)** MCA MCA 10286	**4**	120 wks
25 Apr 92	**THE COMMITMENTS VOLUME 2** MCA MCAD 10506	**13**	11 wks

COMMODORES US/UK, male vocal/instrumental group   **129 wks**

13 May 78	**LIVE** Motown TMSP 6007	**60**	1 wk
10 Jun 78	● **NATURAL HIGH** Motown STML 12087	**8**	23 wks
2 Dec 78	**GREATEST HITS** Motown STML 12100	**19**	16 wks
18 Aug 79	**MIDNIGHT MAGIC** Motown STMA 8032	**15**	25 wks
28 Jun 80	**HEROES** Motown STMA 8034	**50**	5 wks
18 Jul 81	**IN THE POCKET** Motown STML 12156	**69**	5 wks
14 Aug 82	● **LOVE SONGS** K-Tel NE 1171	**5**	28 wks
23 Feb 85	**NIGHTSHIFT** Motown ZL 72343	**13**	10 wks
9 Nov 85	**THE VERY BEST OF THE COMMODORES** Telstar STAR 2249	**25**	13 wks
6 May 95	**THE VERY BEST** Motown 5305472	**26**	3 wks

Group were US only for first seven albums.

COMMOTIONS – See Lloyd COLE

COMMUNARDS UK, male vocal/instrumental duo   **74 wks**

2 Aug 86	● **COMMUNARDS** London LONLP 18	**7**	45 wks
17 Oct 87	● **RED** London LONLP 39	**4**	29 wks

Perry COMO US, male vocalist   **191 wks**

8 Nov 58	● **DEAR PERRY** RCA RD 27078	**6**	5 wks
31 Jan 59	● **COMO'S GOLDEN RECORDS** RCA RD 27100	**4**	5 wks
10 Apr 71	**IT'S IMPOSSIBLE** RCA Victor SF 8175	**13**	13 wks
7 Jul 73	★ **AND I LOVE YOU SO** RCA Victor SF 8360	**1**	109 wks
24 Aug 74	**PERRY** RCA Victor APLI 0585	**26**	3 wks
19 Apr 75	**MEMORIES ARE MADE OF HITS** RCA Victor RS 1005	**14**	16 wks
25 Oct 75	★ **40 GREATEST HITS** K-Tel NE 700	**1**	34 wks
3 Dec 83	**FOR THE GOOD TIMES** Telstar STAR 2235	**41**	6 wks

COMPILATION ALBUMS – See VARIOUS ARTISTS

COMPULSION Ireland/Holland, male vocal/instrumental group   **1 wk**

9 Apr 94	**COMFORTER** One Little Indian TPLP 59CDL	**59**	1 wk

COMSAT ANGELS *UK, male vocal / instrumental group* — **9 wks**

5 Sep 81	**SLEEP NO MORE** Polydor POLS 1038	51	5 wks
18 Sep 82	**FICTION** Polydor POLS 1075	94	2 wks
8 Oct 83	**LAND** Jive HIP 8	91	2 wks

CONNELLS *US, male vocal / instrumental group* — **2 wks**

9 Sep 95	**RING** London 8286602	36	2 wks

Harry CONNICK Jr *US, male vocalist / instrumentalist – piano* — **67 wks**

22 Sep 90 ●	**WE ARE IN LOVE** CBS 4667361	7	46 wks
26 Oct 91	**BLUE LIGHT RED LIGHT** Columbia 4690871	16	11 wks
30 Jan 93	**25** Columbia 4728092	35	2 wks
12 Jun 93	**FOREVER FOR NOW** Columbia 4738732	32	5 wks
27 Aug 94	**SHE** Columbia 4768162	21	3 wks

Ray CONNIFF *US, male orchestra leader* — **96 wks**

28 May 60	**IT'S THE TALK OF THE TOWN** Philips BBL 7354	15	1 wk
25 Jun 60	**S'AWFUL NICE** Philips BBL 7281	13	1 wk
26 Nov 60 ●	**HI-FI COMPANION ALBUM** Philips BET 101	3	44 wks
20 May 61	**MEMORIES ARE MADE OF THIS** Philips BBL 7439	14	4 wks
29 Dec 62	**WE WISH YOU A MERRY CHRISTMAS** CBS BPG 62092	12	1 wk
29 Dec 62	**'S WONDERFUL 'S MARVELLOUS** CBS DPG 66001	18	3 wks
16 Apr 66	**HI-FI COMPANION ALBUM (re-issue)** CBS DP 66011	24	4 wks
9 Sep 67	**SOMEWHERE MY LOVE** CBS SBPG 62740	34	3 wks
21 Jun 69 ★	**HIS ORCHESTRA, HIS CHORUS, HIS SINGERS, HIS SOUND** CBS SPR 27	1	16 wks
23 May 70	**BRIDGE OVER TROUBLED WATER** CBS 64020	30	14 wks
12 Jun 71	**LOVE STORY** CBS 64294	34	1 wk
19 Feb 72	**I'D LIKE TO TEACH THE WORLD TO SING** CBS 64449	17	4 wks

C 98

Billy CONNOLLY *UK, male vocalist* — **108 wks**

20 Jul 74 ●	**SOLO CONCERT** Transatlantic TRA 279	8	33 wks
18 Jan 75 ●	**COP YER WHACK OF THIS** Polydor 2383 310	10	29 wks
20 Sep 75	**WORDS AND MUSIC** Transatlantic TRA SAM 32	34	10 wks
6 Dec 75 ●	**GET RIGHT INTAE HIM** Polydor 2383 368	6	14 wks
11 Dec 76	**ATLANTIC BRIDGE** Polydor 2383 419	20	9 wks
28 Jan 78	**RAW MEAT FOR THE BALCONY** Polydor 2383 463	57	3 wks
5 Dec 81	**PICK OF BILLY CONNOLLY** Polydor POLTV 15	23	8 wks
5 Dec 87	**BILLY AND ALBERT** 10 DIX 65	81	2 wks

CONSOLIDATED *US, male vocal / instrumental group* — **1 wk**

30 Jul 94	**BUSINESS OF PUNISHMENT** London 8285142	53	1 wk

Russ CONWAY *UK, male instrumentalist – piano* — **69 wks**

22 Nov 58 ●	**PACK UP YOUR TROUBLES** Columbia 33SX 1120	9	5 wks
2 May 59 ●	**SONGS TO SING IN YOUR BATH** Columbia 33SX 1149	8	10 wks
19 Sep 59 ●	**FAMILY FAVOURITES** Columbia 33SX 1169	3	16 wks
19 Dec 59 ●	**TIME TO CELEBRATE** Columbia 33SX 1197	3	7 wks
26 Mar 60 ●	**MY CONCERTO FOR YOU** Columbia 33SX 1214	5	17 wks
17 Dec 60 ●	**PARTY TIME** Columbia 33SX 1279	7	11 wks
23 Apr 77	**RUSS CONWAY PRESENTS 24 PIANO GREATS** Ronco RTL 2022	25	3 wks

Ry COODER *US, male vocalist / instrumentalist – guitar* — **33 wks**

11 Aug 79	**BOP TILL YOU DROP** Warner Bros. K 56691	36	9 wks
18 Oct 80	**BORDER LINE** Warner Bros. K 56864	35	6 wks
24 Apr 82	**THE SLIDE AREA** Warner Bros. K 56976	18	12 wks
14 Nov 87	**GET RHYTHM** Warner Bros. WX 121	75	3 wks
9 Apr 94	**TALKING TIMBUKTU** World Circuit WCD 040 [1]	44	3 wks

[1] Ali Farka Touri and Ry Cooder

ALPHABETICALLY BY ARTIST

Peter COOK and Dudley MOORE UK, male comedy duo   **34 wks**

21 May 66	**ONCE MOORE WITH COOK** Decca LK 4785	25	1 wk
18 Sep 76	**DEREK AND CLIVE LIVE** Island ILPS 9434	12	25 wks
24 Dec 77	**COME AGAIN** Virgin V 2094	18	8 wks

See also Dudley Moore.

Sam COOKE US, male vocalist   **27 wks**

26 Apr 86	● **THE MAN AND HIS MUSIC** RCA PL 87127	8	27 wks

COOKIE CREW UK, female vocal duo   **4 wks**

6 May 89	**BORN THIS WAY!** London 828134 1	24	4 wks

COOL NOTES UK, male / female vocal / instrumental group   **2 wks**

9 Nov 85	**HAVE A GOOD FOREVER** Abstract Dance ADLP 1	66	2 wks

Rita COOLIDGE US, female vocalist   **44 wks**

6 Aug 77	● **ANYTIME ANYWHERE** A & M AMLH 64616	6	28 wks
6 May 78	**NATURAL ACT** A & M AMLH 64690 [1]	35	4 wks
8 Jul 78	**LOVE ME AGAIN** A & M AMLH 64699	51	1 wk
14 Mar 81	● **VERY BEST OF** A & M AMLH 68520	6	11 wks

[1] Kris Kristofferson and Rita Coolidge

COOLIO US, male rapper   **8 wks**

29 Oct 94	**IT TAKES A THIEF** Tommy Boy TBCD 1083	67	1 wk
18 Nov 95	**GANGSTA'S PARADISE** Tommy Boy TBCD 1141	18†	7 wks

Alice COOPER US, male vocalist   **127 wks**

5 Feb 72	**KILLER** Warner Bros. K 56005	27	18 wks
22 Jul 72	● **SCHOOL'S OUT** Warner Bros. K 56007	4	20 wks
9 Sep 72	**LOVE IT TO DEATH** Warner Bros. K 46177	28	7 wks
24 Mar 73	★ **BILLION DOLLAR BABIES** Warner Bros. K 56013	1	23 wks
12 Jan 74	**MUSCLE OF LOVE** Warner Bros. K 56018	34	4 wks
15 Mar 75	**WELCOME TO MY NIGHTMARE** Anchor ANCL 2011	19	8 wks
24 Jul 76	**ALICE COOPER GOES TO HELL** Warner Bros. K 56171	23	7 wks
28 May 77	**LACE AND WHISKY** Warner Bros. K 56365	33	3 wks
23 Dec 78	**FROM THE INSIDE** Warner Bros. K 56577	68	3 wks
17 May 80	**FLUSH THE FASHION** Warner Bros. K 56805	56	3 wks
12 Sep 81	**SPECIAL FORCES** Warner Bros. K 56927	96	1 wk
12 Nov 83	**DADA** Warner Bros. 9239691	93	1 wk
1 Nov 86	**CONSTRICTOR** MCA MCF 3341	41	2 wks
7 Nov 87	**RAISE YOUR FIST AND YELL** MCA MCF 3392	48	3 wks
26 Aug 89	● **TRASH** Epic 465130 1	2	12 wks
13 Jul 91	● **HEY STOOPID** Epic 4684161	4	7 wks
18 Jun 94	● **THE LAST TEMPTATION** Epic 4765949	6	5 wks

Alice Cooper was US, male vocal / instrumental group for first five albums.

Julian COPE UK, male vocalist   **34 wks**

3 Mar 84	**WORLD SHUT YOUR MOUTH** Mercury MERL 37	40	4 wks
24 Nov 84	**FRIED** Mercury MERL 48	87	1 wk
14 Mar 87	**SAINT JULIAN** Island ILPS 9861	11	10 wks
29 Oct 88	**MY NATION UNDERGROUND** Island ILPS 9918	42	2 wks
16 Mar 91	**PEGGY SUICIDE** Island ILPSD 9977	23	7 wks
15 Aug 92	**FLOORED GENIUS – THE BEST OF JULIAN COPE** Island CID 8000 [1]	22	3 wks
31 Oct 92	**JEHOVAKILL** Island 5140522	20	2 wks
16 Jul 94	**AUTOGEDDON** Echo ECHCD 1	16	3 wks
9 Sep 95	**JULIAN COPE PRESENTS 20 MOTHERS** Echo ECHCD 5	20	2 wks

[1] Julian Cope and the Teardrop Explodes

Harry H. CORBETT – *See Wilfrid BRAMBELL and Harry H. CORBETT*

CORDUROY *UK, male vocal / instrumental group*   **1 wk**

8 Oct 94   **OUT OF HERE** *Acid Jazz JAZIDCD 107* ....**73**   1   wk

---

Hugh CORNWELL *UK, male vocalist*   **1 wk**

18 Jun 88   **WOLF** *Virgin V 2420* ....**98**   1   wk

CORO DE MUNJES DEL MONASTERIO BENEDICTINO DE SANTO DOMINGO DE SILOS *Spain, monastic choir*   **28 wks**

5 Mar 94 ● **CANTO GREGORIANO** *EMI Classics CMS 5652172* ....**7**   25 wks
17 Dec 94   **CANTO NOEL** *EMI Classics CDC 5552172* ....**53**   3 wks

---

CORONA *Brazil / Italy, male / female vocal / instrumental duo*   **7 wks**

20 May 95   **THE RHYTHM OF THE NIGHT** *Eternal 0630103312*.........................**18**   7 wks

---

CORRIES *UK, male vocal / instrumental duo*   **5 wks**

9 May 70   **SCOTTISH LOVE SONGS** *Fontana 6309004* ....**46**   4 wks
16 Sep 72   **SOUND OF PIBROCH** *Columbia SCX 6511* ....**39**   1 wk

---

COSMIC BABY *Germany, male producer*   **1 wk**

23 Apr 94   **THINKING ABOUT MYSELF** *Logic 74321196052*..............................**60**   1 wk

---

Elvis COSTELLO
UK, male vocalist and male vocal / instrumental group   **203 wks**

6 Aug 77	**MY AIM IS TRUE** *Stiff SEEZ 3* [1]	**14**	12 wks
1 Apr 78	● **THIS YEAR'S MODEL** *Radar RAD 3* [1]	**4**	14 wks
20 Jan 79	● **ARMED FORCES** *Radar RAD 14*	**2**	28 wks
23 Feb 80	● **GET HAPPY** *F-Beat XXLP 1*	**2**	14 wks
31 Jan 81	● **TRUST** *F-Beat XXLP 11* [1]	**9**	7 wks
31 Oct 81	● **ALMOST BLUE** *F-Beat XXLP 13*	**7**	18 wks
10 Jul 82	● **IMPERIAL BEDROOM** *F-Beat XXLP 17*	**6**	12 wks
6 Aug 83	● **PUNCH THE CLOCK** *F-Beat XXLP 19*	**3**	13 wks
7 Jul 84	● **GOODBYE CRUEL WORLD** *F-Beat ZL 70317*	**10**	10 wks
20 Apr 85	● **THE BEST OF ELVIS COSTELLO – THE MAN** *Telstar STAR 2247* [1] 8		25 wks
1 Mar 86	**KING OF AMERICA** *F-Beat ZL 70496* [2]	**11**	9 wks
27 Sep 86	**BLOOD AND CHOCOLATE** *Imp XFIEND 80*	**16**	5 wks
18 Feb 89	● **SPIKE** *Warner Bros. WX 238* [1]	**5**	16 wks
28 Oct 89	**GIRLS GIRLS GIRLS** *Demon DFIEND 160* [1]	**67**	1 wk
25 May 91	● **MIGHTY LIKE A ROSE** *Warner Bros. WX 419* [1]	**5**	6 wks
30 Jan 93	**THE JULIET LETTERS** *Warner Bros. 9362451802* [3]	**18**	3 wks
19 Mar 94	● **BRUTAL YOUTH** *Warner Bros. 9362455352*	**2**	5 wks
12 Nov 94	**THE VERY BEST OF ELVIS COSTELLO AND THE ATTRACTIONS** *Demon DPAM 13* [1]	**57**	2 wks
27 May 95	**KOJAK VARIETY** *Warner Bros. 9362459032*	**21**	2 wks
12 Aug 95	**KING OF AMERICA (re-issue)** *Demon DPAM 11*	**71**	1 wk

[1] Elvis Costello and the Attractions   [2] Costello Show   [3] Elvis Costello and the Brodsky Quartet

John COUGAR – *See John Cougar MELLENCAMP*

Phil COULTER *Ireland, male orchestra leader / instrumentalist – piano*   **15 wks**

13 Oct 84   **SEA OF TRANQUILLITY** *K-Tel Ireland KLP 185* ....**46**   14 wks
18 May 85   **PHIL COULTER'S IRELAND** *K-Tel ONE 1296* ....**86**   1 wk

---

COUNTING CROWS *US, male vocal / instrumental group*   **36 wks**

12 Mar 94   **AUGUST AND EVERYTHING AFTER** *Geffen GED 24528* ....**16**   36 wks

The CRANBERRIES, with lead singer Dolores O'Riordan, had the most weeks on chart in 1995.

(Andrew Catlin/LFI)

C
101

David COVERDALE *UK, male vocalist*   **1 wk**

27 Feb 82	**NORTHWINDS** *Purple TTS 3513* **78**	1 wk

See also Coverdale Page.

COVERDALE PAGE *UK, male vocal / instrumental duo*   **8 wks**

27 Mar 93	● **COVERDALE PAGE** *EMI CDEMD 1041* **4**	8 wks

See also David Coverdale; Jimmy Page.

COWBOY JUNKIES *US, male / female vocal / instrumental group*   **7 wks**

24 Mar 90	**THE CAUTION HORSES** *RCA PL 90450*.......**33**	4 wks
15 Feb 92	**BLACK EYED MAN** *RCA PD 90620*...............**21**	3 wks

CRACKER *US, male vocal / instrumental group*   **2 wks**

25 Jun 94	**KEROSENE HAT** *Virgin America CDVUS 67* **44**	2 wks

CRAMPS *US, male / female vocal / instrumental group*   **13 wks**

25 Jun 83	**OFF THE BONE** *Illegal ILP 012*....................**44**	4 wks
26 Nov 83	**SMELL OF FEMALE** *Big Beat NED 6*...........**74**	2 wks
1 Mar 86	**A DATE WITH ELVIS** *Big Beat WIKA 46*......**34**	6 wks
24 Feb 90	**STAY SICK!** *Enigma ENVLP 1001* **62**	1 wk

CRANBERRIES *Ireland, male / female vocal / instrumental group*   **150 wks**

13 Mar 93	★ **EVERYBODY ELSE IS DOING IT, SO WHY CAN'T WE** *Island CID 8003* **1**	86 wks
15 Oct 94	● **NO NEED TO ARGUE** *Island CID 8029* ....**2†**	64 wks

CRANES *UK, male vocal / instrumental group*   **2 wks**

28 Sep 91	**WINGS OF JOY** *Dedicated DEDLP 003*.........**52**	1 wk
8 May 93	**FOREVER** *Dedicated DEDCD 009* **40**	1 wk

CRASH TEST DUMMIES
Canada, male / female vocal / instrumental group   **23 wks**

14 May 94	● **GOD SHUFFLED HIS FEET** *RCA 74321201522* **2**	23 wks

CRASS *UK, male vocal / instrumental group*   **2 wks**

28 Aug 82	**CHRIST THE ALBUM** *Crass BOLLOX 2U2* **26**	2 wks

Beverley CRAVEN *UK, female vocalist / instrumentalist – piano*   **65 wks**

2 Mar 91	● **BEVERLEY CRAVEN** *Columbia 4670531* **3**	52 wks
9 Oct 93	● **LOVE SCENES** *Epic 4745172* **4**	13 wks

Michael CRAWFORD *UK, male vocalist*   **70 wks**

28 Nov 87	**SONGS FROM THE STAGE AND SCREEN** *Telstar STAR 2308* [1] ..**12**	13 wks
2 Dec 89	**WITH LOVE** *Telstar STAR 2340* **31**	7 wks
9 Nov 91	● **PERFORMS ANDREW LLOYD WEBBER** *Telstar STAR 2544* **3**	36 wks
13 Nov 93	**A TOUCH OF MUSIC IN THE NIGHT** *Telstar TCD 2676*...........**12**	11 wks
19 Nov 94	**THE LOVE SONGS ALBUM** *Telstar TCD 2748* **64**	3 wks

[1] Michael Crawford and the London Symphony Orchestra

Randy CRAWFORD *US, female vocalist*   **151 wks**

28 Jun 80	● **NOW WE MAY BEGIN** *Warner Bros. K 56791* **10**	16 wks
16 May 81	● **SECRET COMBINATION** *Warner Bros. K 56904*.........**2**	60 wks

12 Jun 82	● **WINDSONG** Warner Bros. K 57011 ....**7**	17	wks
22 Oct 83	**NIGHTLINE** Warner Bros. 9239761 ....**37**	4	wks
13 Oct 84	● **MISS RANDY CRAWFORD – THE GREATEST HITS** K-Tel NE 1281 ..**10**	17	wks
28 Jun 86	**ABSTRACT EMOTIONS** Warner Bros. WX 46 ....**14**	10	wks
10 Oct 87	**THE LOVE SONGS** Telstar STAR 2299 ....**27**	13	wks
21 Oct 89	**RICH AND POOR** Warner Bros. WX 308...............................**63**	1	wk
27 Mar 93	● **THE VERY BEST OF RANDY CRAWFORD** Dino DINCD 58...............**8**	13	wks

Robert CRAY BAND US, male vocal / instrumental group   **53 wks**

12 Oct 85	**FALSE ACCUSATIONS** Demon FIEND 43 ....**68**	1	wk
15 Nov 86	**STRONG PERSUADER** Mercury MERH 97 ....**34**	28	wks
3 Sep 88	**DON'T BE AFRAID OF THE DARK** Mercury MERH 129 ....**13**	12	wks
22 Sep 90	**MIDNIGHT STROLL** Mercury 8466521 ....**19**	7	wks
12 Sep 92	**I WAS WARNED** Mercury 5127212...**29**	3	wks
16 Oct 93	**SHAME AND SIN** Mercury 5185172 ....**48**	1	wk
20 May 95	**SOME RAINY MORNING** Mercury 5269282 [1] **63**	1	wk

[1] Robert Cray

CRAZY HORSE – See Neil YOUNG

CRAZY WORLD – See Crazy World of Arthur BROWN

CREAM UK, male vocal / instrumental group   **286 wks**

24 Dec 66	● **FRESH CREAM** Reaction 593001...**6**	17	wks
18 Nov 67	● **DISRAELI GEARS** Reaction 594003 ....**5**	42	wks
17 Aug 68	● **WHEELS OF FIRE (DOUBLE)** Polydor 583-031/2 ....**3**	26	wks
17 Aug 68	● **WHEELS OF FIRE (SINGLE)** Polydor 583033 ....**7**	13	wks
8 Feb 69	● **FRESH CREAM (re-issue)** Reaction 594001 ....**7**	2	wks
15 Mar 69	★ **GOODBYE** Polydor 583053 ....**1**	28	wks
8 Nov 69	● **BEST OF CREAM** Polydor 583060 ....**6**	34	wks
4 Jul 70	● **LIVE CREAM** Polydor 2383016 ....**4**	15	wks
24 Jun 72	**LIVE CREAM VOLUME 2** Polydor 2383 119 ....**15**	5	wks
26 Sep 87	● **THE CREAM OF ERIC CLAPTON** Polydor ECTV [1] **3**	104	wks

[1] Eric Clapton and Cream

From 9 Jul 93 The Cream Of Eric Clapton was repackaged and was available as The Best Of Eric Clapton.

CREATURES UK, male / female vocal / instrumental duo   **9 wks**

28 May 83	**FEAST** Wonderland SHELP 1 ....**17**	9	wks

CREDIT TO THE NATION UK, male rap group   **3 wks**

9 Apr 94	**TAKE DIS** One Little Indian TPLP 44CDH **20**	3	wks

CREEDENCE CLEARWATER REVIVAL
US, male vocal / instrumental group   **65 wks**

24 Jan 70	**GREEN RIVER** Liberty LBS 83273 ....**20**	6	wks
28 Mar 70	● **WILLY AND THE POOR BOYS** Liberty LBS 83338 ....**10**	24	wks
2 May 70	**BAYOU COUNTRY** Liberty LBS 83261 ....**62**	1	wk
12 Sep 70	★ **COSMO'S FACTORY** Liberty LBS 83388 ....**1**	15	wks
23 Jan 71	**PENDULUM** Liberty LBG 83400...**23**	12	wks
30 Jun 79	**GREATEST HITS** Fantasy FT 558 ....**35**	5	wks
19 Oct 85	**THE CREEDENCE COLLECTION** Impression IMDP 3 ....**68**	2	wks

CREME – See GODLEY and CREME

Kid CREOLE and the COCONUTS
US, male / female vocal / instrumental group   **54 wks**

22 May 82	● **TROPICAL GANGSTERS** Ze ILPS 7016 ....**3**	40	wks
26 Jun 82	**FRESH FRUIT IN FOREIGN PLACES** Ze ILPS 7014..........................**99**	1	wk
17 Sep 83	**DOPPELGANGER** Island ILPS 9743 ....**21**	6	wks

15 Sep 84   **CRE–OLE** *Island IMA 13* ....**21**   7 wks

Bernard CRIBBINS – *See Howard BLAKE conducting the SINFONIA OF LONDON*

CRICKETS   US, male vocal / instrumental group   **34 wks**

25 Mar 61   **IN STYLE WITH THE CRICKETS** *Coral LVA 9142* ....**13**   7 wks
27 Oct 62 ● **BOBBY VEE MEETS THE CRICKETS** *Liberty LBY 1086* [1] ....**2**   27 wks

[1] Bobby Vee and the Crickets

See also Buddy Holly and the Crickets.

Bing CROSBY   US, male vocalist   **42 wks**

 8 Oct 60 ● **JOIN BING AND SING ALONG** *Warner Bros. WM 4021* ....**7**   11 wks
21 Dec 74   **WHITE CHRISTMAS** *MCA MCF 2568* ....**45**   3 wks
20 Sep 75   **THAT'S WHAT LIFE IS ALL ABOUT** *United Artists UAG 2973* ....**28**   6 wks
 5 Nov 77   **THE BEST OF BING** *MCA MCF 2540* ....**41**   7 wks
 5 Nov 77 ● **LIVE AT THE LONDON PALLADIUM** *K-Tel NE 951* ....**9**   2 wks
17 Dec 77   **SEASONS** *Polydor 2442 151* ....**25**   7 wks
 5 May 79   **SONGS OF A LIFETIME** *Philips 6641 923*................................**29**   3 wks
14 Dec 91   **CHRISTMAS WITH BING CROSBY** *Telstar STAR 2468* ....**66**   3 wks

David CROSBY   US, male vocalist   **12 wks**

24 Apr 71   **IF ONLY I COULD REMEMBER MY NAME** *Atlantic 2401005* ....**12**   7 wks
13 May 72   **GRAHAM NASH AND DAVID CROSBY** *Atlantic K 50011* [1] ....**13**   5 wks

[1] Graham Nash and David Crosby

See also Crosby, Stills, Nash and Young.

CROSBY, STILLS, NASH and YOUNG
US / UK / Canada, male vocal / instrumental group   **93 wks**

23 Aug 69   **CROSBY, STILLS AND NASH** *Atlantic 588189* [1] ....**25**   5 wks
30 May 70 ● **DEJA VU** *Atlantic 2401001* ....**5**   61 wks
22 May 71 ● **FOUR-WAY STREET** *Atlantic 2956 004*.................................**5**   12 wks
21 May 74   **SO FAR** *Atlantic K 50023* ....**25**   6 wks
 9 Jul 77   **CSN** *Atlantic K 50369* [1] ....**23**   9 wks

[1] Crosby, Stills and Nash

CROSS   UK / US, male vocal / instrumental group   **2 wks**

 6 Feb 88   **SHOVE IT** *Virgin V 2477*..**58**   2 wks

Christopher CROSS   US, male vocalist   **93 wks**

21 Feb 81   **CHRISTOPHER CROSS** *Warner Bros. K 56789* ....**14**   77 wks
19 Feb 83 ● **ANOTHER PAGE** *Warner Bros. W 3757* ....**4**   16 wks

Sheryl CROW   US, female vocalist   **50 wks**

12 Feb 94 ● **TUESDAY NIGHT MUSIC CLUB** *A & M 5401262* ....**8**   50 wks

CROWDED HOUSE
Australia / New Zealand, male vocal / instrumental group   **117 wks**

13 Jul 91 ● **WOODFACE** *Capitol EST 2144* ....**6**   85 wks
23 Oct 93 ● **TOGETHER ALONE** *Capitol CDESTU 2215* ....**4**   32 wks

CROWN HEIGHTS AFFAIR   US, male vocal / instrumental group   **3 wks**

23 Sep 78   **DREAM WORLD** *Philips 6372 754*..**40**   3 wks

CRUSADERS   US, male vocal / instrumental group   **30 wks**

21 Jul 79 ● **STREET LIFE** *MCA MCF 3008*..**10**   16 wks

19 Jul 80	**RHAPSODY AND BLUE** MCA MCG 4010	40	5 wks
12 Sep 81	**STANDING TALL** MCA MCF 3122	47	5 wks
7 Apr 84	**GHETTO BLASTER** MCA MCF 3176	46	4 wks

Bobby CRUSH *UK, male instrumentalist piano*   **12 wks**

25 Nov 72	**BOBBY CRUSH** Philips 6308 135	15	7 wks
18 Dec 82	**THE BOBBY CRUSH INCREDIBLE DOUBLE DECKER** *Warwick WW 5126/7*	53	5 wks

CUD *UK, male vocal / instrumental group*   **2 wks**

11 Jul 92	**ASQUARIUS** A & M 3953902	30	1 wk
23 Apr 94	**SHOWBIZ** A & M 5402112	46	1 wk

CUDDLES – *See Keith HARRIS, ORVILLE and CUDDLES*

CULT *UK, male vocal / instrumental group*   **85 wks**

18 Jun 83	**SOUTHERN DEATH CULT** Beggars Banquet BEGA 46 [1]	43	3 wks
8 Sep 84	**DREAMTIME** Beggars Banquet BEGA 57	21	8 wks
26 Oct 85	● **LOVE** Beggars Banquet BEGA 65	4	22 wks
18 Apr 87	● **ELECTRIC** Beggars Banquet BEGA 80	4	27 wks
22 Apr 89	● **SONIC TEMPLE** Beggars Banquet BEGA 98	3	11 wks
5 Oct 91	● **CEREMONY** Beggars Banquet BEGA 122	9	4 wks
13 Feb 93	★ **PURE CULT** Beggars Banquet BEGACD 130	1	8 wks
22 Oct 94	**CULT** Beggars Banquet BBQCD 164	21	2 wks

[1] Southern Death Cult

CULT JAM – *See LISA LISA and CULT JAM with FULL FORCE*

CULTURE *Jamaica, male vocal / instrumental group*   **1 wk**

1 Apr 78	**TWO SEVENS CLASH** Lightning LIP 1	60	1 wk

CULTURE BEAT
UK / US / Germany, male / female vocal / instrumental group   **10 wks**

25 Sep 93	**SERENITY** Dance Pool 4741012	13	10 wks

CULTURE CLUB *UK, male vocal / instrumental group*   **149 wks**

16 Oct 82	● **KISSING TO BE CLEVER** Virgin V 2232	5	59 wks
22 Oct 83	★ **COLOUR BY NUMBERS** Virgin V 2285	1	56 wks
3 Nov 84	● **WAKING UP WITH THE HOUSE ON FIRE** Virgin V 2330	2	13 wks
12 Apr 86	● **FROM LUXURY TO HEARTACHE** Virgin V 2380	10	6 wks
18 Apr 87	● **THIS TIME** Virgin VTV 1	8	10 wks
2 Oct 93	**AT WORST . . . THE BEST OF BOY GEORGE AND CULTURE CLUB** Virgin VYCD 19 [1]	24	5 wks

[1] Boy George and Culture Club

CURE *UK, male vocal / instrumental group*   **192 wks**

2 Jun 79	**THREE IMAGINARY BOYS** Fiction FIX 001	44	3 wks
3 May 80	**17 SECONDS** Fiction FIX 004	20	10 wks
25 Apr 81	**FAITH** Fiction FIX 6	14	8 wks
15 May 82	● **PORNOGRAPHY** Fiction FIX D7	8	9 wks
3 Sep 83	**BOYS DON'T CRY** Fiction SPELP 26	71	7 wks
24 Dec 83	**JAPANESE WHISPERS** Fiction FIXM 8	26	14 wks
12 May 84	● **THE TOP** Fiction FIXS 9	10	10 wks
3 Nov 84	**CONCERT – THE CURE LIVE** Fiction FIXH 10	26	4 wks
7 Sep 85	● **THE HEAD ON THE DOOR** Fiction FIXH 11	7	13 wks
31 May 86	● **STANDING ON A BEACH – THE SINGLES** Fiction FIXH 12	4	35 wks
6 Jun 87	● **KISS ME KISS ME KISS ME** Fiction FIXH 13	6	15 wks
13 May 89	● **DISINTEGRATION** Fiction FIXH 14	3	26 wks
17 Nov 90	● **MIXED UP** Fiction 8470991	8	17 wks
6 Apr 91	● **ENTREAT** Fiction FIXH 17	10	5 wks

2 May 92 ★ **WISH** Fiction FIXCD 20	**1**	13	wks
25 Sep 93 **SHOW** Fiction FIXCD 25	**29**	2	wks
6 Nov 93 **PARIS** Fiction FIXCD 26	**56**	1	wk

The compact disc version of FIXH 12 was titled Staring At The Sea.

CURIOSITY KILLED THE CAT *UK, male vocal/instrumental group* **27 wks**

| 9 May 87 ★ **KEEP YOUR DISTANCE** Mercury CATLP 1 | **1** | 24 | wks |
| 4 Oct 89 **GETAHEAD** Mercury 842010 1 | **29** | 3 | wks |

CURVE *UK, male/female vocal/instrumental duo* **6 wks**

21 Mar 92 **DOPPELGANGER** Anxious ANXCD 77	**11**	3	wks
19 Jun 93 **RADIO SESSIONS** Anxious ANXCD 80	**72**	1	wk
25 Sep 93 **CUCKOO** Anxious ANXCD 81	**23**	2	wks

CURVED AIR *UK, male/female vocal/instrumental group* **32 wks**

5 Dec 70 ● **AIR CONDITIONING** Warner Bros. WSX 3012	**8**	21	wks
9 Oct 71 **CURVED AIR** Warner Bros. K 46092	**11**	6	wks
13 May 72 **PHANTASMAGORIA** Reprise K 46158	**20**	5	wks

Adge CUTLER – *See WURZELS*

CUTTING CREW *UK/Canada, male vocal/instrumental group* **6 wks**

| 29 Nov 86 **BROADCAST** Siren SIRENLP 7 | **41** | 6 | wks |

CYPRESS HILL *US, male rap group* **53 wks**

| 7 Aug 93 **BLACK SUNDAY** Ruffhouse 4740752 | **13** | 49 | wks |
| 11 Nov 95 **III (TEMPLES OF BOOM)** Columbia 4781279 | **11** | 4 | wks |

Billy Ray CYRUS *US, male vocalist* **10 wks**

| 29 Aug 92 ● **SOME GAVE ALL** Mercury 5106352 | **9** | 10 | wks |

Holger CZUKAY – *See David SYLVIAN*

D. MOB *UK, male producer, Danny D* **11 wks**

| 11 Nov 89 **A LITTLE BIT OF THIS A LITTLE BIT OF THAT** ffrr 8281591 | **46** | 11 | wks |

D:REAM *UK, male vocal/instrumental duo* **41 wks**

| 30 Oct 93 ● **D:REAM ON VOLUME 1** Magnet 4509933712 | **5** | 37 | wks |
| 30 Sep 95 ● **WORLD** Magnet 0630117962 | **5** | 4 | wks |

For second album D:ream was just Peter Cunnah.

D-TRAIN *US, male vocalist/multi–instrumentalist, Hubert Eaves* **4 wks**

| 8 May 82 **D-TRAIN** Epic EPC 85683 | **72** | 4 | wks |

DAINTEES – *See Martin STEPHENSON and the DAINTEES*

DAISY CHAINSAW *UK, male/female vocal/instrumental group* **1 wk**

| 10 Oct 92 **ELEVENTEEN** Deva TPLP 100CD | **62** | 1 | wk |

DAKOTAS – *See Billy J. KRAMER and the DAKOTAS*

British Hit Albums Part One

Date of chart entry/Title & catalogue no./Peak position reached/Weeks on chart

★ Number One   ● Top Ten   † still on chart at 30 Dec 1995   ☐ credited to act billed in footnote

DALEK I *UK, male vocal / instrumental group* **2 wks**

| 9 Aug 80 | **COMPASS KUMPAS** *Backdoor OPEN 1* .... | **54** | 2 wks |

DALI'S CAR *UK, male vocal / instrumental duo* **1 wk**

| 1 Dec 84 | **THE WAKING HOUR** *Paradox DOXLP 1* .... | **84** | 1 wk |

Roger DALTREY *UK, male vocalist* **24 wks**

26 Jul 75	**RIDE A ROCK HORSE** *Polydor 2660 111*	**14**	10 wks
4 Jun 77	**ONE OF THE BOYS** *Polydor 2442 146*	**45**	1 wk
23 Aug 80	**MCVICAR (film soundtrack)** *Polydor POLD 5034*	**39**	11 wks
2 Nov 85	**UNDER A RAGING MOON** *10 DIX 17*	**52**	2 wks

Glen DALY *UK, male vocalist* **2 wks**

| 20 Nov 71 | **GLASGOW NIGHT OUT** *Golden Guinea GGL 0479* .... | **28** | 2 wks |

DAMNED *UK, male vocal / instrumental group* **54 wks**

12 Mar 77	**DAMNED DAMNED DAMNED** *Stiff SEEZ 1*	**36**	10 wks
17 Nov 79	**MACHINE GUN ETIQUETTE** *Chiswick CWK 3011*	**31**	5 wks
29 Nov 80	**THE BLACK ALBUM** *Chiswick CWK 3015*	**29**	3 wks
28 Nov 81	**BEST OF** *Chiswick DAM 1*	**43**	12 wks
23 Oct 82	**STRAWBERRIES** *Bronze BRON 542*	**15**	4 wks
27 Jul 85	**PHANTASMAGORIA** *MCA MCF 3275*	**11**	17 wks
13 Dec 86	**ANYTHING** *MCA MCG 6015*	**40**	2 wks
12 Dec 87	**LIGHT AT THE END OF THE TUNNEL** *MCA MCSP 312*	**87**	1 wk

Vic DAMONE *US, male vocalist* **8 wks**

| 25 Apr 81 | **NOW!** *RCA INTS 5080* .... | **28** | 7 wks |
| 2 Apr 83 | **VIC DAMONE SINGS THE GREAT SONGS** *CBS 32261* .... | **87** | 1 wk |

DANA *Ireland, female vocalist* **2 wks**

| 27 Dec 80 | **EVERYTHING IS BEAUTIFUL** *Warwick WW 5099* .... | **43** | 2 wks |

Suzanne DANDO *UK, female exercise instructor* **1 wk**

| 17 Mar 84 | **SHAPE UP AND DANCE WITH SUZANNE DANDO** *Lifestyle LEG 21* .... | **87** | 1 wk |

D'ANGELO *US, male vocalist* **2 wks**

| 28 Oct 95 | **BROWN SUGAR** *Cooltempo CTCD 46* .... | **57** | 2 wks |

Charlie DANIELS BAND *US, male vocal / instrumental group* **1 wk**

| 10 Nov 79 | **MILLION MILE REFLECTIONS** *Epic EPC 83446* .... | **74** | 1 wk |

DANNY WILSON *UK, male vocal / instrumental group* **11 wks**

30 Apr 88	**MEET DANNY WILSON** *Virgin V 2419*	**65**	5 wks
29 Jul 89	**BEEBOP MOPTOP** *Virgin V 2594*	**24**	5 wks
31 Aug 91	**SWEET DANNY WILSON** *Virgin V 2669*	**54**	1 wk

DANSE SOCIETY *UK, male vocal / instrumental group* **4 wks**

| 11 Feb 84 | **HEAVEN IS WAITING** *Society 205 972* .... | **39** | 4 wks |

Stephen DANTE *UK, male vocalist* **1 wk**

3 Sep 88	**FIND OUT** Cooltempo CTLP 6 87	1 wk

Terence Trent D'ARBY *US, male vocalist* **96 wks**

25 Jul 87 ★	**INTRODUCING THE HARDLINE ACCORDING TO**		
	TERENCE TRENT D'ARBY CBS 4509111...**1**	67 wks
4 Nov 89	**NEITHER FISH NOR FLESH** CBS 4658091.....................................**12**	5 wks
15 May 93 ●	**SYMPHONY OR DAMN** Columbia 4735612 ....**4**	19 wks
29 Apr 95	**TERENCE TRENT D'ARBY'S VIBRATOR** Columbia 4785052 ....**11**	5 wks

DARE *UK, male vocal / instrumental group* **1 wk**

14 Sep 91	**BLOOD FROM STONE** A & M 3953601 ....**48**	1 wk

Bobby DARIN *US, male vocalist* **15 wks**

19 Mar 60 ●	**THIS IS DARIN** London HA 2235 ....**4**	8 wks
9 Apr 60	**THAT'S ALL** London HAE 2172 ....**15**	1 wk
5 Oct 85	**THE LEGEND OF BOBBY DARIN – HIS GREATEST HITS**	
	Stylus SMR 8504 ....**39**	6 wks

DARLING BUDS *UK, male / female vocal / instrumental group* **3 wks**

18 Feb 89	**POP SAID** Epic 462894 1 ....**23**	3 wks

DARTS *UK, male / female vocal / instrumental group* **57 wks**

3 Dec 77 ●	**DARTS** Magnet MAG 5020 ....**9**	22 wks
3 Jun 78	**EVERYONE PLAYS DARTS** Magnet MAG 5022......................**12**	18 wks
18 Nov 78 ●	**AMAZING DARTS** K-Tel/Magnet DLP 7981 ....**8**	13 wks
6 Oct 79	**DART ATTACK** Magnet MAG 5030......................................**38**	4 wks

DAVE and Ansil COLLINS *Jamaica, male vocal duo* **2 wks**

7 Aug 71	**DOUBLE BARREL** Trojan TBL 162 ....**41**	2 wks

F.R. DAVID *France, male vocalist* **6 wks**

7 May 83	**WORDS** Carrere CAL 145 ....**46**	6 wks

Windsor DAVIES – See Don ESTELLE and Windsor DAVIES

Carl DAVIS and the ROYAL LIVERPOOL
PHILHARMONIC ORCHESTRA *US, male conductor and orchestra* **4 wks**

19 Oct 91	**PAUL McCARTNEY'S LIVERPOOL ORATORIO**	
	EMI Classics PAUL 1..**36**	4 wks

Colin DAVIS – See BBC SYMPHONY ORCHESTRA

Miles DAVIS *US, male instrumentalist – trumpet* **6 wks**

11 Jul 70	**BITCHES BREW** CBS 66236 ....**71**	1 wk
15 Jun 85	**YOU'RE UNDER ARREST** CBS 26447 ....**88**	1 wk
18 Oct 86	**TUTU** Warner Bros. 925490 1...**74**	2 wks
3 Jun 89	**AMANDLA** Warner Bros. WX 250.......................................**49**	2 wks

Sammy DAVIS Jr *US, male vocalist* **1 wk**

13 Apr 63	**SAMMY DAVIS JR. AT THE COCONUT GROVE** Reprise R 6063/2..**19**	1 wk

Spencer DAVIS GROUP *UK, male vocal / instrumental group* **47 wks**

8 Jan 66 ●	**THEIR 1ST LP** Fontana TL 5242 ....**6**	9 wks

| 22 Jan 66 | ● **THE 2ND LP** Fontana TL 5295 | **3** | 18 wks |
| 11 Sep 66 | ● **AUTUMN '66** Fontana TL 5359 | **4** | 20 wks |

DAWN US, male / female vocal group   **2 wks**

| 4 May 74 | **GOLDEN RIBBONS** Bell BELLS 236 | **46** | 2 wks |

Doris DAY US, female vocalist   **35 wks**

6 Jan 79	**20 GOLDEN GREATS** Warwick PR 5053	**12**	11 wks
11 Nov 89	**A PORTRAIT OF DORIS DAY** Stylus SMR 984	**32**	9 wks
6 Nov 93	**GREATEST HITS** Telstar TCD 2659	**14**	12 wks
10 Dec 94	**THE LOVE ALBUM** Vision VIS CD2	**64**	3 wks

Taylor DAYNE US, female vocalist   **17 wks**

| 5 Mar 88 | **TELL IT TO MY HEART** Arista 208898 | **24** | 17 wks |

Chris DE BURGH Ireland, male vocalist   **265 wks**

12 Sep 81	**BEST MOVES** A & M AMLH 68532	**65**	4 wks
9 Oct 82	**THE GETAWAY** A & M AMLH 68549	**30**	16 wks
19 May 84	**MAN ON THE LINE** A & M AMLX 65002	**11**	24 wks
29 Dec 84	● **THE VERY BEST OF CHRIS DE BURGH** Telstar STAR 2248	**6**	70 wks
24 Aug 85	**SPANISH TRAIN AND OTHER STORIES** A & M AMLH 68343	**78**	3 wks
7 Jun 86	● **INTO THE LIGHT** A & M AM 5121	**2**	59 wks
4 Oct 86	**CRUSADER** A & M AMLH 64746	**72**	1 wk
15 Oct 88	★ **FLYING COLOURS** A & M AMA 5224	**1**	30 wks
4 Nov 89	● **FROM A SPARK TO A FLAME – THE VERY BEST OF CHRIS DE BURGH** A & M CDBLP 100	**4**	29 wks
22 Sep 90	**HIGH ON EMOTION LIVE FROM DUBLIN** A & M 3970861	**15**	6 wks
9 May 92	● **POWER OF TEN** A & M 3971882	**3**	10 wks
28 May 94	● **THIS WAY UP** A & M 5402332	**5**	6 wks
18 Nov 95	**BEAUTIFUL DREAMS** A & M 5404322	**33†**	7 wks

D
109

DE LA SOUL US, male rap / sampling group   **69 wks**

25 Mar 89	**3 FEET HIGH AND RISING** Big Life DLSLP 1	**13**	56 wks
25 May 91	● **DE LA SOUL IS DEAD** Big Life BLRLP 8	**7**	11 wks
9 Oct 93	**BUHLOONE MINDSTATE** Big Life BLRCD 25	**37**	2 wks

Waldo DE LOS RIOS Argentina, orchestra   **26 wks**

| 1 May 71 | ● **SYMPHONIES FOR THE SEVENTIES** A & M AMLS 2014 | **6** | 26 wks |

Manitas DE PLATA Spain, male instrumentalist – guitar   **1 wk**

| 29 Jul 67 | **FLAMENCO GUITAR** Philips SBL 7786 | **40** | 1 wk |

DEACON BLUE UK, male / female vocal / instrumental group   **214 wks**

6 Jun 87	**RAINTOWN** CBS 4505491	**14**	77 wks
15 Apr 89	★ **WHEN THE WORLD KNOWS YOUR NAME** CBS 4633211	**1**	54 wks
22 Sep 90	● **OOH LAS VEGAS** CBS 4672421	**3**	8 wks
15 Jun 91	● **FELLOW HOODLUMS** Columbia 4685501	**2**	27 wks
13 Mar 93	● **WHATEVER YOU SAY SAY NOTHING** Columbia 4735272	**4**	10 wks
16 Apr 94	★ **OUR TOWN – GREATEST HITS** Columbia 4766422	**1**	38 wks

DEAD CAN DANCE Australia, male / female vocal / instrumental duo   **1 wk**

| 25 Sep 93 | **INTO THE LABYRINTH** 4AD CAD 3013CD | **47** | 1 wk |

DEAD KENNEDYS US, male vocal / instrumental group   **8 wks**

| 13 Sep 80 | **FRESH FRUIT FOR ROTTING VEGETABLES** Cherry Red BRED 10 | **33** | 6 wks |
| 4 Jul 87 | **GIVE ME CONVENIENCE** Alternative Tentacles VIRUS 5 | **84** | 2 wks |

DEAD OR ALIVE *UK, male vocal / instrumental group*   **22 wks**

28 Apr 84	**SOPHISTICATED BOOM BOOM** Epic EPC 25835 ....**29**	3 wks
25 May 85 ●	**YOUTHQUAKE** Epic EPC 26420 ....**9**	15 wks
14 Feb 87	**MAD, BAD AND DANGEROUS TO KNOW** Epic 450 2571 ....**27**	4 wks

DEAN – *See JAN and DEAN*

Hazell DEAN *UK, female vocalist*   **3 wks**

22 Oct 88	**ALWAYS** EMI EMC 3546...**38**	3 wks

DeBARGE *US, male / female vocal group*   **2 wks**

25 May 85	**RHYTHM OF THE NIGHT** Gordy ZL 72340 ....**94**	2 wks

Kiki DEE *UK, female vocalist*   **11 wks**

26 Mar 77	**KIKI DEE** Rocket ROLA 3 ....**24**	5 wks
18 Jul 81	**PERFECT TIMING** Ariola ARL 5050..**47**	4 wks
9 Apr 94	**THE VERY BEST OF KIKI DEE** PolyGram TV 516728 ....**62**	2 wks

Dave DEE, DOZY, BEAKY, MICK and TICH
UK, male vocal / instrumental group   **15 wks**

2 Jul 66	**DAVE DEE, DOZY, BEAKY, MICK AND TICH** Fontana STL 5350 ..**11**	10 wks
7 Jan 67	**IF MUSIC BE THE FOOD OF LOVE . . . PREPARE FOR**	
	INDIGESTION Fontana STL 5388 ....**27**	5 wks

DEEE-LITE *US, male / female vocal / instrumental group*   **19 wks**

8 Sep 90	**WORLD CLIQUE** Elektra EKT 77 ....**14**	18 wks
4 Jul 92	**INFINITY WITHIN** Elektra 7559613132..**37**	1 wk

DEEP FOREST *France, male instrumental duo*   **16 wks**

26 Feb 94	**DEEP FOREST** Columbia 4741782..**15**	11 wks
3 Jun 95	**BOHEME** Columbia 4786232 ....**12**	5 wks

DEEP PURPLE *UK, male vocal / instrumental group*   **274 wks**

24 Jan 70	**CONCERTO FOR GROUP AND ORCHESTRA** Harvest SHVL 767 ....**26**	4 wks
20 Jun 70 ●	**DEEP PURPLE IN ROCK** Harvest SHVL 777 ....**4**	68 wks
18 Sep 71 ★	**FIREBALL** Harvest SHVL 793 ....**1**	25 wks
15 Apr 72 ★	**MACHINE HEAD** Purple TPSA 7504 ....**1**	24 wks
6 Jan 73	**MADE IN JAPAN** Purple TPSP 351 ....**16**	14 wks
17 Feb 73 ●	**WHO DO WE THINK WE ARE** Purple TPSA 7508 ....**4**	11 wks
2 Mar 74 ●	**BURN** Purple TPA 3505...**3**	21 wks
23 Nov 74 ●	**STORM BRINGER** Purple TPS 3508 ....**6**	12 wks
5 Jul 75	**24 CARAT PURPLE** Purple TPSM 2002 ....**14**	17 wks
22 Nov 75	**COME TASTE THE BAND** Purple TPSA 7515 ....**19**	4 wks
27 Nov 76	**DEEP PURPLE LIVE** Purple TPSA 7517 ....**12**	6 wks
21 Apr 79	**THE MARK II PURPLE SINGLES** Purple TPS 3514 ....**24**	6 wks
19 Jul 80 ★	**DEEPEST PURPLE** Harvest EMTV 25 ....**1**	15 wks
13 Dec 80	**IN CONCERT** Harvest SHDW 4121/4122 ....**30**	8 wks
4 Sep 82	**DEEP PURPLE LIVE IN LONDON** Harvest SHSP 4124 ....**23**	5 wks
10 Nov 84 ●	**PERFECT STRANGERS** Polydor POLH 16 ....**5**	15 wks
29 Jun 85	**THE ANTHOLOGY** Harvest PUR 1 ....**50**	3 wks
24 Jan 87 ●	**THE HOUSE OF BLUE LIGHT** Polydor POLH 32 ....**10**	9 wks
16 Jul 88	**NOBODY'S PERFECT** Polydor PODV 10 ....**38**	2 wks
2 Nov 90	**SLAVES AND MASTERS** RCA PL 90535 ....**45**	2 wks
7 Aug 93	**THE BATTLE RAGES ON . . .** RCA 74321154202 ....**21**	3 wks

DEF LEPPARD *UK, male vocal / instrumental group*   **169 wks**

22 Mar 80	**ON THROUGH THE NIGHT** Vertigo 9102 040 ....**15**	8 wks

25 Jul 81	**HIGH 'N' DRY** Vertigo 6359 045	26	8 wks
12 Mar 83	**PYROMANIA** Vertigo VERS 2	18	8 wks
29 Aug 87	★ **HYSTERIA** Bludgeon Riffola HYSLP 1	1	101 wks
11 Apr 92	★ **ADRENALIZE** Bludgeon Riffola 5109782	1	30 wks
16 Oct 93	● **RETRO ACTIVE** Bludgeon Riffola 5183052	6	5 wks
4 Nov 95	● **VAULT – GREATEST HITS 1980-1995** Bludgeon Riffola 5286572	3†	9 wks

DEFINITION OF SOUND UK, male rap group
4 wks

29 Jun 91	**LOVE AND LIFE** Circa CIRCA 14	38	3 wks

DEICIDE US, male vocal / instrumental group
1 wk

13 May 95	**ONCE UPON THE CROSS** Roadrunner RR 89492	66	1 wk

Desmond DEKKER Jamaica, male vocalist
4 wks

5 Jul 69	**THIS IS DESMOND DEKKER** Trojan TTL 4	27	4 wks

DEL AMITRI UK, male vocal / instrumental group
89 wks

24 Feb 90	● **WAKING HOURS** A & M AMA 9006	6	44 wks
13 Jun 92	● **CHANGE EVERYTHING** A & M 3953852	2	20 wks
11 Mar 95	● **TWISTED** A & M 5403112	3	25 wks

DE'LACY US, male / female vocal / instrumental group
1 wk

1 Jul 95	**HIDEAWAY** Slip 'n' Slide SLIP 023	53	1 wk

DELANEY and BONNIE and FRIENDS
US / UK, male / female vocal / instrumental group
3 wks

6 Jun 70	**ON TOUR** Atlantic 2400013	39	3 wks

DEMON UK, male vocal / instrumental group
5 wks

14 Aug 82	**THE UNEXPECTED GUEST** Carrere CAL 139	47	3 wks
2 Jul 83	**THE PLAGUE** Clay CLAY LP 6	73	2 wks

Chaka DEMUS and PLIERS
Jamaica, male vocal / instrumental duo
30 wks

10 Jul 93	★ **TEASE ME** Mango CIDM 1102	1	30 wks

Cathy DENNIS UK, female vocalist
35 wks

10 Aug 91	● **MOVE TO THIS** Polydor 8495031	3	31 wks
23 Jan 93	● **INTO THE SKYLINE** Polydor 5139352	8	4 wks

Sandy DENNY UK, female vocalist
2 wks

2 Oct 71	**THE NORTH STAR GRASSMAN AND THE RAVENS** Island ILPS 9165	31	2 wks

John DENVER US, male vocalist
240 wks

17 Mar 73	**ROCKY MOUNTAIN HIGH** RCA SF 2308	11	15 wks
2 Jun 73	**POEMS, PRAYERS AND PROMISES** RCA SF 8219	19	5 wks
23 Jun 73	**RHYMES AND REASONS** RCA Victor SF 8348	21	5 wks
30 Mar 74	● **THE BEST OF JOHN DENVER** RCA Victor APLI 0374	7	69 wks
7 Sep 74	● **BACK HOME AGAIN** RCA Victor APLI 0548	3	29 wks
22 Mar 75	**AN EVENING WITH JOHN DENVER** RCA Victor LSA 3211/12	31	4 wks
11 Oct 75	**WIND SONG** RCA Victor APLI 1183	14	21 wks
15 May 76	● **LIVE IN LONDON** RCA Victor RS 1050	2	29 wks
4 Sep 76	● **SPIRIT** RCA Victor APLI 1694	9	11 wks
19 Mar 77	● **BEST OF JOHN DENVER VOLUME 2** RCA Victor PL 42120	9	9 wks
11 Feb 78	**I WANT TO LIVE** RCA PL 12561	25	5 wks

21 Apr 79	JOHN DENVER *RCA Victor PL 13075*	68	1	wk
28 Nov 81	PERHAPS LOVE *CBS 73592* 1	17	21	wks
22 Oct 83	IT'S ABOUT TIME *RCA RCALP 6087*	90	2	wks
1 Dec 84	JOHN DENVER COLLECTION *Telstar STAR 2253*	20	11	wks
23 Aug 86	ONE WORLD *RCA PL 85811*	91	3	wks

1 Placido Domingo and John Denver

Karl DENVER *UK, male vocalist* · 27 wks

| 23 Dec 61 | ● WIMOWEH *Ace Of Clubs ACL 1098* | 7 | 27 wks |

DEPECHE MODE *UK, male vocal / instrumental group* · 159 wks

14 Nov 81	● SPEAK AND SPELL *Mute STUMM 5*	10	33	wks
9 Oct 82	● A BROKEN FRAME *Mute STUMM 9*	8	11	wks
3 Sep 83	● CONSTRUCTION TIME AGAIN *Mute STUMM 13*	6	12	wks
6 Sep 84	● SOME GREAT REWARD *Mute STUMM 19*	5	12	wks
26 Oct 85	● THE SINGLES 81–85 *Mute MUTEL 1*	6	22	wks
29 Mar 86	● BLACK CELEBRATION *Mute STUMM 26*	4	11	wks
10 Oct 87	● MUSIC FOR THE MASSES *Mute STUMM 47*	10	4	wks
25 Mar 89	● 101 *Mute STUMM 101*	5	8	wks
31 Mar 90	● VIOLATOR *Mute STUMM 64*	2	30	wks
3 Apr 93	★ SONGS OF FAITH AND DEVOTION *Mute CDSTUMM 106*	1	16	wks

DEREK AND CLIVE – See Peter COOK and Dudley MOORE

DEREK and the DOMINOS – See Eric CLAPTON

DES'REE *UK, female vocalist* · 11 wks

| 29 Feb 92 | MIND ADVENTURES *Dusted Sound 4712632* | 26 | 5 | wks |
| 21 May 94 | I AIN'T MOVIN' *Dusted Sound 4758432* | 13 | 6 | wks |

DESTROYERS – See George THOROGOOD and the DESTROYERS

Marcella DETROIT *US, female vocalist* · 5 wks

| 9 Apr 94 | JEWEL *London 8284912* | 15 | 5 wks |

DETROIT SPINNERS *US, male vocal group* · 3 wks

| 14 May 77 | DETROIT SPINNERS' SMASH HITS *Atlantic K 50363* | 37 | 3 wks |

DEUCE *UK, male / female vocal group* · 2 wks

| 9 Sep 95 | ON THE LOOSE *London 8286642* | 18 | 2 wks |

Sidney DEVINE *UK, male vocalist* · 11 wks

| 10 Apr 76 | DOUBLE DEVINE *Philips 6625 019* | 14 | 10 | wks |
| 11 Dec 76 | DEVINE TIME *Philips 6308 283* | 49 | 1 | wk |

DEVO *US, male vocal / instrumental group* · 22 wks

16 Sep 78	Q: ARE WE NOT MEN? A: NO WE ARE DEVO! *Virgin V 2106*	12	7	wks
23 Jun 79	DUTY NOW FOR THE FUTURE *Virgin V 2125*	49	6	wks
24 May 80	FREEDOM OF CHOICE *Virgin V 2162*	47	5	wks
5 Sep 81	NEW TRADITIONALISTS *Virgin V 2191*	50	4	wks

Howard DEVOTO *UK, male vocalist* · 2 wks

| 6 Aug 83 | JERKY VERSIONS OF THE DREAM *Virgin V 2272* | 57 | 2 wks |

DEXY'S MIDNIGHT RUNNERS
UK, male / female vocal / instrumental group · 79 wks

| 26 Jul 80 | ● SEARCHING FOR THE YOUNG SOUL REBELS *Parlophone PCS 7213* | 6 | 10 wks |

7 Aug 82	● **TOO–RYE–AY** Mercury MERS 5	2	46 wks
26 Mar 83	**GENO** EMI EMS 1007	79	2 wks
21 Sep 85	**DON'T STAND ME DOWN** Mercury MERH 56	22	6 wks
8 Jun 91	**THE VERY BEST OF DEXY'S MIDNIGHT RUNNERS** Mercury 8464601	12	15 wks

Group was all male for first album.

Jim DIAMOND *UK, male vocalist* **5 wks**

22 May 93	**JIM DIAMOND** PolyGram TV 8438472	16	5 wks

Neil DIAMOND *US, male vocalist* **535 wks**

3 Apr 71	**TAP ROOT MANUSCRIPT** Uni UNLS 117	19	12 wks
3 Apr 71	**GOLD** Uni UNLS 116	23	11 wks
11 Dec 71	**STONES** Uni UNLS 121	18	14 wks
5 Aug 72	● **MOODS** Uni UNLS 128	7	19 wks
12 Jan 74	**HOT AUGUST NIGHT** Uni ULD 1	32	2 wks
16 Feb 74	**JONATHAN LIVINGSTON SEAGULL** CBS 69047	35	1 wk
9 Mar 74	**RAINBOW** MCA MCF 2529	39	5 wks
29 Jul 74	**HIS 12 GREATEST HITS** MCA MCF 2550	13	78 wks
9 Nov 74	**SERENADE** CBS 69067	11	14 wks
10 Jul 76	● **BEAUTIFUL NOISE** CBS 86004	10	26 wks
12 Mar 77	● **LOVE AT THE GREEK** CBS 95001	3	32 wks
6 Aug 77	**HOT AUGUST NIGHT (re-issue)** MCA MCSP 255	60	1 wk
17 Dec 77	**I'M GLAD YOU'RE HERE WITH ME TONIGHT** CBS 86044	16	12 wks
25 Nov 78	● **20 GOLDEN GREATS** MCA EMTV 14	2	29 wks
6 Jan 79	**YOU DON'T BRING ME FLOWERS** CBS 86077	15	23 wks
19 Jan 80	**SEPTEMBER MORN** CBS 86096	14	11 wks
22 Nov 80	● **THE JAZZ SINGER (film soundtrack)** Capitol EAST 12120	3	110 wks
28 Feb 81	**LOVE SONGS** MCA MCF 3092	43	6 wks
5 Dec 81	**THE WAY TO THE SKY** CBS 85343	39	13 wks
19 Jun 82	**12 GREATEST HITS VOLUME 2** CBS 85844	32	8 wks
13 Nov 82	**HEARTLIGHT** CBS 25073	43	10 wks
10 Dec 83	**THE VERY BEST OF NEIL DIAMOND** K-Tel NE 1265	33	11 wks
28 Jul 84	● **PRIMITIVE** CBS 86306	7	10 wks
24 May 86	**HEADED FOR THE FUTURE** CBS 26952	36	8 wks
28 Nov 87	**HOT AUGUST NIGHT 2** CBS 460 4081	74	4 wks
25 Feb 89	**THE BEST YEARS OF OUR LIVES** CBS 463201 1	42	6 wks
9 Nov 91	**LOVESCAPE** Columbia 4688901	36	13 wks
4 Jul 92	★ **THE GREATEST HITS 1966–1992** Columbia 4715022	1	30 wks
28 Nov 92	**THE CHRISTMAS ALBUM** Columbia 4724102	50	6 wks
9 Oct 93	**UP ON THE ROOF – SONGS FROM THE BRILL BUILDING** Columbia 4743562	28	10 wks

DIAMOND HEAD *UK, male vocal / instrumental group* **9 wks**

23 Oct 82	**BORROWED TIME** MCA DH 1001	24	5 wks
24 Sep 83	**CANTERBURY** MCA DH 1002	32	4 wks

DICKIES *US, male vocal / instrumental group* **19 wks**

17 Feb 79	**THE INCREDIBLE SHRINKING DICKIES** A & M AMLE 64742	18	17 wks
24 Nov 79	**DAWN OF THE DICKIES** A & M AMLE 68510	60	2 wks

Bruce DICKINSON *UK, male vocalist* **12 wks**

19 May 90	**TATTOOED MILLIONAIRE** EMI EMC 3574	14	9 wks
18 Jun 94	**BALLS TO PICASSO** EMI CDEMX 1057	21	3 wks

Barbara DICKSON *UK, female vocalist* **142 wks**

18 Jun 77	**MORNING COMES QUICKLY** RSO 2394 188	58	1 wk
12 Apr 80	● **THE BARBARA DICKSON ALBUM** Epic EPC 84088	7	12 wks
16 May 81	**YOU KNOW IT'S ME** Epic EPC 84551	39	6 wks
6 Feb 82	● **ALL FOR A SONG** Epic EPC 10030	3	37 wks
24 Sep 83	**TELL ME IT'S NOT TRUE** Legacy LLM 101	100	1 wk
23 Jun 84	**HEARTBEATS** Epic EPC 25706	21	8 wks

Having apparently failed an audition for Zorro in 1967, the young NEIL DIAMOND contemplates a career in the album charts.
(Hulton Deutsch)

TOP 30 | NO_ 25

CELINE DION, a 1993 Grammy winner, had the third best-selling UK album of 1995.
(LFI)

12 Jan 85	● **THE BARBARA DICKSON SONGBOOK** K-Tel NE 1287	**5**	19 wks
23 Nov 85	**GOLD** K-Tel ONE 1312	**11**	18 wks
15 Nov 86	**THE VERY BEST OF BARBARA DICKSON** Telstar STAR 2276	**78**	8 wks
29 Nov 86	**THE RIGHT MOMENT** K-Tel ONE 1335	**39**	8 wks
6 May 89	**COMING ALIVE AGAIN** Telstar STAR 2349	**30**	7 wks
15 Aug 92	**DON'T THINK TWICE IT'S ALL RIGHT** Columbia MOODCD 25	**32**	5 wks
28 Nov 92	**THE BEST OF ELAINE PAIGE AND BARBARA DICKSON**		
	Telstar TCD 2632 [1]	**22**	9 wks
5 Mar 94	**PARCEL OF ROGUES** Castle Communications CTVCD 126	**30**	3 wks

[1] Elaine Paige and Barbara Dickson

Tell Me It's Not True *is a mini–album featuring songs from the musical* Blood Brothers.

Bo DIDDLEY US, male vocalist / instrumentalist – guitar   **16 wks**

5 Oct 63	**BO DIDDLEY** Pye International NPL 28026	**11**	8 wks
9 Oct 63	**BO DIDDLEY IS A GUNSLINGER** Pye NJL 33	**20**	1 wk
30 Nov 63	**BO DIDDLEY RIDES AGAIN** Pye International NPL 28029	**19**	1 wk
15 Feb 64	**BO DIDDLEY'S BEACH PARTY** Pye NPL 28032	**13**	6 wks

DIESEL PARK WEST UK, male vocal / instrumental group   **3 wks**

11 Feb 89	**SHAKESPEARE ALABAMA** Food FOODLP 2	**55**	2 wks
15 Feb 92	**DECENCY** Food FOODCD 7	**57**	1 wk

DIFFORD and TILBROOK UK, male vocal / instrumental duo   **3 wks**

14 Jul 84	**DIFFORD AND TILBROOK** A & M AMLX 64985	**47**	3 wks

DIGITAL UNDERGROUND US, male vocal / instrumental group   **2 wks**

7 Apr 90	**SEX PACKETS** BCM BCM 377LP	**59**	1 wk
30 Jun 90	**DOWUTCHYALIKE / PACKET MAN** BCM BCM 463X	**59**	1 wk

Richard DIMBLEBY UK, male broadcaster   **5 wks**

4 Jun 66	**VOICE OF RICHARD DIMBLEBY** MFP 1087	**14**	5 wks

DINOSAUR JR US, male vocalist / multi–instrumentalist – J. Mascis   **7 wks**

2 Mar 91	**GREEN MIND** Blanco Y Negro BYN 24	**36**	2 wks
20 Feb 93	● **WHERE YOU BEEN** Blanco Y Negro 4509916272	**10**	3 wks
10 Sep 94	**WITHOUT A SOUND** Blanco Y Negro 4509969332	**24**	2 wks

DIO UK / US, male vocal / instrumental group   **48 wks**

11 Jun 83	**HOLY DIVER** Vertigo VERS 5	**13**	15 wks
21 Jul 84	● **THE LAST IN LINE** Vertigo VERL 16	**4**	14 wks
7 Sep 85	● **SACRED HEART** Vertigo VERH 30	**4**	6 wks
5 Jul 86	**INTERMISSION** Vertigo VERB 40	**22**	5 wks
22 Aug 87	● **DREAM EVIL** Vertigo VERH 46	**8**	5 wks
26 May 90	**LOCK UP THE WOLVES** Vertigo 8460331	**28**	3 wks

Celine DION Canada, female vocalist   **69 wks**

5 Mar 94	★ **THE COLOUR OF MY LOVE** Epic 4747432	**1†**	58 wks
16 Sep 95	**UNISON** Epic 4672032	**56**	2 wks
7 Oct 95	● **D'EUX** Epic 4802862	**7**	9 wks

DION and the BELMONTS US, male vocal group   **5 wks**

12 Apr 80	**20 GOLDEN GREATS** K-Tel NE 1057	**31**	5 wks

DIRE STRAITS UK, male vocal / instrumental group   **1082 wks**

22 Jul 78	● **DIRE STRAITS** Vertigo 9102 021	**5**	130 wks
23 Jun 79	● **COMMUNIQUE** Vertigo 9102 031	**5**	32 wks

D
115

25 Oct 80 ● **MAKIN' MOVIES** Vertigo 6359 034 ....**4**   249 wks
2 Oct 82 ★ **LOVE OVER GOLD** Vertigo 6359 109 ....**1**   198 wks
24 Mar 84 ● **ALCHEMY – DIRE STRAITS LIVE** Vertigo VERY 11.....................**3**   163 wks
25 May 85 ★ **BROTHERS IN ARMS** Vertigo VERH 25 ....**1**   203 wks
29 Oct 88 ★ **MONEY FOR NOTHING** Vertigo VERH 64 ....**1**   64 wks
21 Sep 91 ★ **ON EVERY STREET** Vertigo 5101601 ....**1**   35 wks
22 May 93 ● **ON THE NIGHT** Vertigo 5147662.................................**4**   7 wks
8 Jul 95   **LIVE AT THE BBC** Windsong WINCD 072X ....**71**   1 wk

DISCHARGE UK, male vocal / instrumental group   **5 wks**

15 May 82   **HEAR NOTHING, SEE NOTHING, SAY NOTHING** Clay CLAYLP 3 ..**40**   5 wks

DISCIPLES OF SOUL – See LITTLE STEVEN

DISPOSABLE HEROES OF HIPHOPRISY
US, male rap / instrumental duo   **3 wks**

16 May 92   **HYPOCRISY IS THE GREATEST LUXURY**
            Fourth & Broadway BRCD 584.......................................**40**   3 wks

Sacha DISTEL France, male vocalist   **14 wks**

2 May 70   **SACHA DISTEL** Warner Bros. WS 3003 ....**21**   14 wks

DIVINYLS Australia, male / female vocal / instrumental duo   **1 wk**

20 Jul 91   **DIVINYLS** Virgin America VUSLP 30.............................**59**   1 wk

DJ JAZZY JEFF and FRESH PRINCE US, male rap duo   **10 wks**

28 Feb 87   **ROCK THE HOUSE** Champion CHAMP 1004 ....**97**   1 wk
21 May 88   **HE'S THE DJ, I'M THE RAPPER** Jive HIP 61......................**68**   2 wks
14 Sep 91   **HOMEBASE** Jive HIP 116 ....**69**   1 wk
11 Dec 93   **CODE RED** Jive CHIP 140 1 ....**50**   6 wks

1 Jazzy Jeff and Fresh Prince

DJ KRUSH Japan, male producer   **2 wks**

3 Sep 94   **BAD BROTHERS** Island IMCD 8024 1 ....**58**   1 wk
11 Nov 95   **MEISO** Mo Wax MW 039CD ....**64**   1 wk

1 Ronny Jordan meets DJ Krush

DR. FEELGOOD UK, male vocal / instrumental group   **33 wks**

18 Oct 75   **MALPRACTICE** United Artists UAS 29880 ....**17**   6 wks
2 Oct 76 ★ **STUPIDITY** United Artists UAS 29990 ....**1**   9 wks
4 Jun 77 ● **SNEAKIN' SUSPICION** United Artists UAS 30075 ....**10**   6 wks
8 Oct 77   **BE SEEING YOU** United Artists UAS 30123 ....**55**   3 wks
7 Oct 78   **PRIVATE PRACTICE** United Artists UAG 30184 ....**41**   5 wks
2 Jun 79   **AS IT HAPPENS** United Artists UAK 30239 ....**42**   4 wks

DR. HOOK US, male vocal / instrumental group   **149 wks**

25 Jun 76 ● **A LITTLE BIT MORE** Capitol E-ST 23795.........................**5**   42 wks
29 Oct 77   **MAKING LOVE AND MUSIC** Capitol EST 11632....................**39**   4 wks
27 Oct 79   **PLEASURE AND PAIN** Capitol EAST 11859 ....**47**   6 wks
17 Nov 79   **SOMETIMES YOU WIN** Capitol EST 12018 ....**14**   44 wks
29 Nov 80   **RISING** Mercury 6302 076 ....**44**   5 wks
6 Dec 80 ● **DR. HOOK'S GREATEST HITS** Capitol EST 26037 ....**2**   28 wks
14 Nov 81   **DR. HOOK LIVE IN THE UK** Capitol EST 26706...................**90**   1 wk
13 Jun 92 ● **COMPLETELY HOOKED – THE BEST OF DR. HOOK**
            Capitol CDESTV 2 ....**3**   19 wks

DOCTOR and the MEDICS
UK, male / female vocal / instrumental group   **3 wks**

21 Jun 86   **LAUGHING AT THE PIECES** MCA MIRG 1010 ....**25**   3 wks

Ken DODD *UK, male vocalist*   **36 wks**

25 Dec 65	● **TEARS OF HAPPINESS** Columbia 33SX 1793	**6**	12 wks
23 Jul 66	**HITS FOR NOW AND ALWAYS** Columbia SX 6060	**14**	11 wks
14 Jan 67	**FOR SOMEONE SPECIAL** Columbia SCX 6224	**40**	1 wk
29 Nov 80	● **20 GOLDEN GREATS OF KEN DODD** Warwick WW 5098	**8**	12 wks

DODGY *UK, male vocal / instrumental group*   **12 wks**

5 Jun 93	**THE DODGY ALBUM** A & M 5400822	**75**	1 wk
5 Nov 94	**HOMEGROWN** A & M 5402822	**28**	11 wks

DOGS D'AMOUR *UK, male vocal / instrumental group*   **12 wks**

22 Oct 88	**IN THE DYNAMITE JET SALOON** China WOL 8	**97**	1 wk
25 Mar 89	**A GRAVEYARD OF EMPTY BOTTLES** China 8390740	**16**	4 wks
30 Sep 89	**ERROL FLYNN** China 8397001	**22**	3 wks
6 Oct 90	**STRAIGHT** China 8437961	**32**	2 wks
7 Sep 91	**DOG'S HITS AND THE BOOTLEG ALBUM** China WOL 1020	**58**	1 wk
15 May 93	**. . . MORE UNCHARTED HEIGHTS OF DISGRACE** China WOLCD 1032	**30**	1 wk

DOKKEN *US, male vocal / instrumental group*   **1 wk**

21 Nov 87	**BACK FOR THE ATTACK** Elektra EKT 43	**96**	1 wk

Thomas DOLBY *UK, male vocalist / instrumentalist – keyboards*   **29 wks**

22 May 82	**THE GOLDEN AGE OF WIRELESS** Venice In Peril VIP 1001	**65**	10 wks
18 Feb 84	**THE FLAT EARTH** Parlophone Odeon PCS 2400341	**14**	14 wks
7 May 88	**ALIENS ATE MY BUICK** Manhattan MTL 1020	**30**	3 wks
8 Aug 92	**ASTRONAUTS AND HERETICS** Virgin CDV 2701	**35**	2 wks

DOLLAR *UK, male / female vocal duo*   **28 wks**

15 Sep 79	**SHOOTING STARS** Carrere CAL 111	**36**	8 wks
24 Apr 82	**THE VERY BEST OF DOLLAR** Carrere CAL 3001	**31**	9 wks
30 Oct 82	**THE DOLLAR ALBUM** WEA DTV 1	**18**	11 wks

Placido DOMINGO *Spain, male vocalist*   **189 wks**

28 Nov 81	**PERHAPS LOVE** CBS 73592 ⓵	**17**	21 wks
21 May 83	**MY LIFE FOR A SONG** CBS 73683	**31**	8 wks
27 Dec 86	**PLACIDO DOMINGO COLLECTION** Stylus SMR 625	**30**	14 wks
23 Apr 88	**GREATEST LOVE SONGS** CBS 44701	**63**	2 wks
17 Jun 89	**GOYA . . . A LIFE IN A SONG** CBS 463294 1	**36**	4 wks
17 Jun 89	**THE ESSENTIAL DOMINGO** Deutsche Grammophon PDTV 1	**20**	8 wks
1 Sep 90	★ **IN CONCERT** Decca 4304331 ⓶	**1**	78 wks
24 Nov 90	**BE MY LOVE . . . AN ALBUM OF LOVE** EMI EMTV 54 ⓷	**14**	12 wks
7 Dec 91	**THE BROADWAY I LOVE** East West 9031755901	**45**	6 wks
13 Jun 92	**DOMINGO: ARIAS AND SPANISH SONGS** Deutsche Grammophon 4371122	**47**	3 wks
8 Aug 92	**FROM THE OFFICIAL BARCELONA GAMES CEREMONY** RCA Red Seal 09026612042 ⓸	**41**	3 wks
25 Dec 93	**CHRISTMAS IN VIENNA** Sony Classical SK 53358 ⓹	**71**	2 wks
10 Sep 94	★ **THE THREE TENORS IN CONCERT 1994** Teldec 4509962002 ⓺	**1**	26 wks
10 Dec 94	**CHRISTMAS IN VIENNA II** Sony Classical SK 64304 ⓻	**60**	2 wks

⓵ Placido Domingo and John Denver ⓶ José Carreras, Placido Domingo and Luciano Pavarotti ⓷ Placido Domingo featuring The London Symphony Orchestra ⓸ Placido Domingo, José Carreras and Montserrat Caballe ⓹ Placido Domingo, Diana Ross and José Carreras ⓺ José Carreras, Placido Domingo and Luciano Pavarotti with Mehta ⓻ Dionne Warwick Placido Domingo

See also Andrew Lloyd Webber.

Fats DOMINO *US, male vocalist / instrumentalist – piano*   **1 wk**

16 May 70	**VERY BEST OF FATS DOMINO** Liberty LBS 83331	**56**	1 wk

Lonnie DONEGAN *UK, male vocalist*   **29 wks**

1 Sep 62	● **GOLDEN AGE OF DONEGAN** *Pye Golden Guinea GGL 0135* **3**	23 wks
9 Feb 63	**GOLDEN AGE OF DONEGAN VOLUME 2**	
	Pye Golden Guinea GGL 0170 ....**15**	3 wks
25 Feb 78	**PUTTING ON THE STYLE** *Chrysalis CHR 1158* **51**	3 wks

DONOVAN *UK, male vocalist*   **73 wks**

5 Jun 65	● **WHAT'S BIN DID AND WHAT'S BIN HID** *Pye NPL 18117* **3**	16 wks
6 Nov 65	**FAIRY TALE** *Pye NPL 18128* **20**	2 wks
8 Jul 67	**SUNSHINE SUPERMAN** *Pye NPL 18181* **25**	7 wks
14 Oct 67	● **UNIVERSAL SOLDIER** *Marble Arch MAL 718* **5**	18 wks
11 May 68	**A GIFT FROM A FLOWER TO A GARDEN** *Pye NSPL 20000*...........**13**	14 wks
12 Sep 70	**OPEN ROAD** *Dawn DNLS 3009* **30**	4 wks
24 Mar 73	**COSMIC WHEELS** *Epic EPC 65450* **15**	12 wks

Jason DONOVAN *Australia, male vocalist*   **99 wks**

13 May 89	★ **TEN GOOD REASONS** *PWL HF 7* **1**	54 wks
9 Jun 90	● **BETWEEN THE LINES** *PWL HF 14* **2**	26 wks
28 Sep 91	● **GREATEST HITS** *PWL HF 20* **9**	17 wks
11 Sep 93	**ALL AROUND THE WORLD** *Polydor 8477452* **27**	2 wks

See also Stage Cast Recordings – Joseph And The Amazing Technicolour Dreamcoat.

DOOBIE BROTHERS *US, male vocal / instrumental group*   **30 wks**

30 Mar 74	**WHAT WERE ONCE VICES ARE NOW HABITS**	
	Warner Bros. K 56206 ....**19**	10 wks
17 May 75	**STAMPEDE** *Warner Bros. K 56094* **14**	11 wks
10 Apr 76	**TAKIN' IT TO THE STREETS** *Warner Bros. K 56196*.............**42**	2 wks
17 Sep 77	**LIVING ON THE FAULT LINE** *Warner Bros. K 56383* **25**	5 wks
11 Oct 80	**ONE STEP CLOSER** *Warner Bros. K 56824*...................**53**	2 wks

DOOLEYS *UK, male / female vocal / instrumental group*   **27 wks**

30 Jun 79	● **THE BEST OF THE DOOLEYS** *GTO GTTV 038* **6**	21 wks
3 Nov 79	**THE CHOSEN FEW** *GTO GTLP 040* **56**	4 wks
25 Oct 80	**FULL HOUSE** *GTO GTTV 050* **54**	2 wks

Val DOONICAN *Ireland, male vocalist*   **170 wks**

12 Dec 64	● **LUCKY 13 SHADES OF VAL DOONICAN** *Decca LK 4648* **2**	27 wks
3 Dec 66	● **GENTLE SHADES OF VAL DOONICAN** *Decca LK 4831* **5**	52 wks
2 Dec 67	★ **VAL DOONICAN ROCKS BUT GENTLY** *Pye NSPL 18204* **1**	23 wks
30 Nov 68	● **VAL** *Pye NSPL 18236* **6**	11 wks
14 Jun 69	● **WORLD OF VAL DOONICAN** *Decca SPA 3* **2**	31 wks
13 Dec 69	**SOUNDS GENTLE** *Pye NSPL 18321* **22**	9 wks
19 Dec 70	**THE MAGIC OF VAL DOONICAN** *Philips 6642 003* **34**	3 wks
27 Nov 71	**THIS IS VAL DOONICAN** *Philips 6382 017*...................**40**	1 wk
22 Feb 75	**I LOVE COUNTRY MUSIC** *Philips 9299261* **37**	2 wks
21 May 77	**SOME OF MY BEST FRIENDS ARE SONGS** *Philips 6641 607* **29**	5 wks
24 Mar 90	**SONGS FROM MY SKETCH BOOK** *Parkfield PMLP 5014*...............**33**	6 wks

DOORS *US, male vocal / instrumental group*   **85 wks**

28 Sep 68	**WAITING FOR THE SUN** *Elektra EKS7 4024* **16**	10 wks
11 Apr 70	**MORRISON HOTEL** *Elektra EKS 75007*......................**12**	8 wks
26 Sep 70	**ABSOLUTELY LIVE** *Elektra 2665 002* **69**	1 wk
31 Jul 71	**L.A. WOMAN** *Elektra K 42090* **28**	4 wks
1 Apr 72	**WEIRD SCENES INSIDE THE GOLD MINE** *Elektra K 62009* **50**	1 wk
29 Oct 83	**ALIVE, SHE CRIED** *Elektra 9602691* **36**	5 wks
4 Jul 87	**LIVE AT THE HOLLYWOOD BOWL** *Elektra EKT 40* **51**	3 wks
6 Apr 91	**THE DOORS (film soundtrack)** *Elektra EKT 85* **11**	17 wks
20 Apr 91	**BEST OF THE DOORS** *Elektra EKT 21*.......................**17**	18 wks
20 Apr 91	**THE DOORS** *Elektra K 42012*...............................**43**	13 wks
1 Jun 91	**IN CONCERT** *Elektra EKT 88* **24**	5 wks

Lee DORSEY US, male vocalist — **4 wks**

17 Dec 66	**NEW LEE DORSEY** Stateside SSL 10192	**34**	4 wks

DOUBLE Switzerland, male vocal / instrumental duo — **4 wks**

8 Mar 86	**BLUE** Polydor POLD 5187	**69**	4 wks

DOUBLE TROUBLE – See Stevie Ray VAUGHAN and DOUBLE TROUBLE

DOUBLE TROUBLE UK, male production duo — **1 wk**

4 Aug 90	**AS ONE** Desire LULP 6	**73**	1 wk

Craig DOUGLAS UK, male vocalist — **2 wks**

6 Aug 60	**CRAIG DOUGLAS** Top Rank BUY 049	**17**	2 wks

DOWN US, male vocal / instrumental group — **1 wk**

30 Sep 95	**NOLA** Atlantic 7559618302	**68**	1 wk

Will DOWNING US, male vocalist — **28 wks**

26 Mar 88	**WILL DOWNING** Fourth & Broadway BRLP 518	**20**	23 wks
18 Nov 89	**COME TOGETHER AS ONE** Fourth & Broadway BRLP 538	**36**	2 wks
6 Apr 91	**A DREAM FULFILLED** Fourth & Broadway BRLP 565	**43**	3 wks

DREAD ZEPPELIN UK, male vocal / instrumental group — **2 wks**

11 Aug 90	**UN–LED–ED** IRS EIRSA 1042	**71**	2 wks

DREADZONE UK, male instrumental group — **3 wks**

10 Jun 95	**SECOND LIGHT** Virgin CDV 2778	**37**	3 wks

DREAM ACADEMY UK, male / female vocal / instrumental group — **2 wks**

12 Oct 85	**THE DREAM ACADEMY** Blanco Y Negro BYN 6	**58**	2 wks

DREAM THEATER US, male vocal / instrumental group — **1 wk**

15 Oct 94	**AWAKE** East West 7567901262	**65**	1 wk

DREAM WARRIORS Canada, male rap group — **7 wks**

16 Feb 91	**AND NOW THE LEGACY BEGINS** Fourth & Broadway BRLP 560	**18**	7 wks

DREAMERS – See FREDDIE and the DREAMERS

DRIFTERS US, male vocal group — **88 wks**

18 May 68	**GOLDEN HITS** Atlantic 588103	**27**	7 wks
10 Jun 72	**GOLDEN HITS (re-issue)** Atlantic K 40018	**26**	8 wks
8 Nov 75	● **24 ORIGINAL HITS** Atlantic K 60106	**2**	34 wks
13 Dec 75	**LOVE GAMES** Bell BELLS 246	**51**	1 wk
18 Oct 86	**THE VERY BEST OF THE DRIFTERS** Telstar STAR 2280	**24**	15 wks
14 Mar 87	**STAND BY ME (THE ULTIMATE COLLECTION)** Atlantic WX 90 ⒈	**14**	8 wks
20 Oct 90	**THE BEST OF BEN E. KING AND THE DRIFTERS** Telstar STAR 2373 ⒈	**15**	16 wks

⒈ Ben E. King and the Drifters

Julie DRISCOLL and the Brian AUGER TRINITY
UK, female / male vocal / instrumental group — **13 wks**

8 Jun 68	**OPEN** Marmalade 608002	**12**	13 wks

D
119

DRIZABONE UK, male instrumental / production duo   1 wk

19 Nov 94   **CONSPIRACY** Fourth & Broadway BRCD 593 ....**72**   1 wk

DRUGSTORE UK / US / Brazil, male / female vocal / instrumental group   2 wks

8 Apr 95   **DRUGSTORE** Honey 8286170 ....**31**   2 wks

DRUM CLUB UK, male instrumental / production duo   1 wk

20 Aug 94   **DRUMS ARE DANGEROUS** Butterfly BFLCD 10 ....**53**   1 wk

DUBLINERS Ireland, male vocal / instrumental group   88 wks

13 May 67   ● **A DROP OF THE HARD STUFF** Major Minor MMLP 3 ....**5**   41 wks
9 Sep 67   **BEST OF THE DUBLINERS** Transatlantic TRA 158 ....**25**   11 wks
7 Oct 67   ● **MORE OF THE HARD STUFF** Major Minor MMLP 5 ....**8**   23 wks
2 Mar 68   **DRINKIN' AND COURTIN'** Major Minor SMLP 14 ....**31**   3 wks
25 Apr 87   **THE DUBLINERS 25 YEARS CELEBRATION** Stylus SMR 731 ....**43**   10 wks

DUBSTAR UK, male / female vocal / instrumental group   2 wks

21 Oct 95   **DISGRACEFUL** Food FOODCDX 13 ....**33**   2 wks

Stephen 'Tin Tin' DUFFY UK, male vocalist   7 wks

20 Apr 85   **THE UPS AND DOWNS** 10 DIX 5 ....**35**   7 wks

George DUKE US, male vocalist / instrumentalist – keyboards   4 wks

26 Jul 80   **BRAZILIAN LOVE AFFAIR** Epic EPC 84311 ....**33**   4 wks

DUKES – See Steve EARLE

Candy DULFER Holland, female instrumentalist – saxophone   11 wks

18 Aug 90   **SAXUALITY** RCA PL 74661 ....**27**   9 wks
13 Mar 93   **SAX-A-GO-GO** Ariola 4321111812 ....**56**   2 wks

DUNCAN – See PJ and DUNCAN

Simon DUPREE and the BIG SOUND
UK, male vocal / instrumental group   1 wk

16 Aug 67   **WITHOUT RESERVATIONS** Parlophone PCS 7029 ....**39**   1 wk

DURAN DURAN UK, male vocal / instrumental group   372 wks

27 Jun 81   ● **DURAN DURAN** EMI EMC 3372 ....**3**   118 wks
22 May 82   ● **RIO** EMI EMC 3411 ....**2**   109 wks
3 Dec 83   ★ **SEVEN AND THE RAGGED TIGER** EMI DD 1 ....**1**   47 wks
24 Nov 84   ● **ARENA** Parlophone DD 2 ....**6**   31 wks
6 Dec 86   **NOTORIOUS** EMI DDN 331 ....**16**   16 wks
29 Oct 88   **BIG THING** EMI DDB 33 ....**15**   5 wks
25 Nov 89   ● **DECADE** EMI DDX 10 ....**5**   16 wks
1 Sep 90   ● **LIBERTY** Parlophone PCSD 112 ....**8**   4 wks
27 Feb 93   ● **DURAN DURAN (THE WEDDING ALBUM)** Parlophone CDDB 34 ..**4**   23 wks
8 Apr 95   **THANK YOU** Parlophone CDDDB 36 ....**12**   3 wks

Group were UK / US from 1990 and were billed as Duranduran on EMI DDB 33.

Deanna DURBIN Canada, female vocalist   4 wks

30 Jan 82   **THE BEST OF DEANNA DURBIN** MCA International MCL 1634 ....**84**   4 wks

Judith DURHAM – See SEEKERS

TOP 30 № 4

Mark Knopfler and
DIRE STRAITS have never
missed the Top Ten with
official releases.

(LFI)

D
121

TOP 30 № 20

It is late April 1965, and
BOB DYLAN is discussing
the release of *Bringing
It All Back Home.*

(Hulton Deutsch)

Ian DURY and the BLOCKHEADS
UK, male vocal / instrumental group   **118 wks**

22 Oct 77	● **NEW BOOTS AND PANTIES!!** *Stiff SEEZ 4* **5**	90 wks
2 Jun 79	● **DO IT YOURSELF** *Stiff SEEZ 14* **2**	18 wks
6 Dec 80	**LAUGHTER** *Stiff SEEZ 30* **48**	4 wks
10 Oct 81	**LORD UPMINSTER** *Polydor POLD 5042* **53**	4 wks
4 Feb 84	**4,000 WEEKS HOLIDAY** *Polydor POLD 5112* [1] **54**	2 wks

[1] Ian Dury and the Music Students

Bob DYLAN *US, male vocalist*   **575 wks**

23 May 64	★ **THE FREEWHEELIN' BOB DYLAN** *CBS BPG 62193* **1**	49 wks
11 Jul 64	● **THE TIMES THEY ARE A–CHANGIN'** *CBS BPG 62251* **4**	20 wks
21 Nov 64	● **ANOTHER SIDE OF BOB DYLAN** *CBS BPG 62429*..................**8**	19 wks
8 May 65	**BOB DYLAN** *CBS BPG 62022* **13**	6 wks
15 May 65	★ **BRINGING IT ALL BACK HOME** *CBS BPG 62515*..................**1**	29 wks
9 Oct 65	● **HIGHWAY 61 REVISITED** *CBS BPG 62572* **4**	15 wks
20 Aug 66	● **BLONDE ON BLONDE** *CBS DDP 66012* **3**	15 wks
14 Jan 67	● **GREATEST HITS** *CBS SBPG 62847* **6**	82 wks
2 Mar 68	★ **JOHN WESLEY HARDING** *CBS SBPG 63252*......................**1**	29 wks
17 May 69	★ **NASHVILLE SKYLINE** *CBS 63601* **1**	42 wks
11 Jul 70	★ **SELF PORTRAIT** *CBS 66250* **1**	15 wks
28 Nov 70	★ **NEW MORNING** *CBS 69001* **1**	18 wks
25 Dec 71	**MORE BOB DYLAN GREATEST HITS** *CBS 67238/9* **12**	15 wks
29 Sep 73	**PAT GARRETT AND BILLY THE KID (film soundtrack)**	
	CBS 69042 ....**29**	11 wks
23 Feb 74	● **PLANET WAVES** *Island ILPS 9261* **7**	8 wks
13 Jul 74	● **BEFORE THE FLOOD** *Asylum IDBD 1* **8**	7 wks
15 Feb 75	● **BLOOD ON THE TRACKS** *CBS 69097* **4**	16 wks
26 Jul 75	● **THE BASEMENT TAPES** *CBS 88147*......................................**8**	10 wks
31 Jan 76	● **DESIRE** *CBS 86003* **3**	35 wks
9 Oct 76	● **HARD RAIN** *CBS 86016* **3**	7 wks
1 Jul 78	● **STREET LEGAL** *CBS 86067* **2**	20 wks
26 May 79	● **BOB DYLAN AT BUDOKAN** *CBS 96004* **4**	19 wks
8 Sep 79	● **SLOW TRAIN COMING** *CBS 86095* **2**	13 wks
28 Jun 80	● **SAVED** *CBS 86113*..**3**	8 wks
29 Aug 81	● **SHOT OF LOVE** *CBS 85178*..**6**	8 wks
12 Nov 83	● **INFIDELS** *CBS 25539*..**9**	12 wks
15 Dec 84	**REAL LIVE** *CBS 26334* **54**	2 wks
22 Jun 85	**EMPIRE BURLESQUE** *CBS 86313* **11**	6 wks
2 Aug 86	**KNOCKED OUT LOADED** *CBS 86326* **35**	5 wks
23 Apr 88	**GREATEST HITS VOLUME 3** *CBS 460907 1* **47**	3 wks
25 Jun 88	**DOWN IN THE GROOVE** *CBS 460267 1* **32**	3 wks
18 Feb 89	**DYLAN AND THE DEAD** *CBS 463381 1* [1] **38**	3 wks
14 Oct 89	● **OH MERCY** *CBS 465800 1* **6**	7 wks
22 Sep 90	**UNDER THE RED SKY** *CBS 4671881* **13**	3 wks
13 Apr 91	**THE BOOTLEG SERIES VOLUMES 1–3** *Columbia 4680861* **32**	5 wks
14 Nov 92	**GOOD AS I BEEN TO YOU** *Columbia 4727102* **18**	3 wks
20 Nov 93	**WORLD GONE WRONG** *Columbia 474 8572*......................**35**	2 wks
29 Apr 95	● **UNPLUGGED** *Columbia 4783742* **10**	5 wks

[1] Bob Dylan and the Grateful Dead

E STREET BAND - *See Bruce SPRINGSTEEN*

EAGLES *US, male vocal / instrumental group*   **340 wks**

27 Apr 74	**ON THE BORDER** *Asylum SYL 9016* **28**	9 wks
12 Jul 75	● **ONE OF THESE NIGHTS** *Asylum SYLA 8759* **8**	41 wks
12 Jul 75	**DESPERADO** *Asylum SYLL 9011* **39**	9 wks
6 Mar 76	● **THEIR GREATEST HITS 1971–1975** *Asylum K 53017* **2**	77 wks
25 Dec 76	● **HOTEL CALIFORNIA** *Asylum K 53051* **2**	67 wks

D
122

13 Oct 79	● THE LONG RUN *Asylum K 52181*	4	16	wks
22 Nov 80	LIVE *Asylum K 62032*	24	13	wks
18 May 85	● BEST OF EAGLES *Asylum EKT 5*	8	74	wks
23 Jul 94	● THE VERY BEST OF EAGLES *Elektra 9548323752*	4	24	wks
19 Nov 94	HELL FREEZES OVER *Geffen GED 24725*	28	11	wks

Steve EARLE and the DUKES
US, male vocal / instrumental group   **15 wks**

4 Jul 87	EXIT 0 *MCA MCF 3379* [1]	77	2	wks
19 Nov 88	COPPERHEAD ROAD *MCA MCF 3426*	42	8	wks
7 Jul 90	THE HARD WAY *MCA MCG 6095*	22	4	wks
19 Oct 91	SHUT UP AND DIE LIKE AN AVIATOR *MCA MCA 10315*	62	1	wk

[1] Steve Earle

EARTH WIND AND FIRE *US, male vocal / instrumental group*   **160 wks**

21 Jan 78	ALL 'N' ALL *CBS 86051*	13	23	wks
16 Dec 78	● THE BEST OF EARTH WIND AND FIRE VOLUME 1 *CBS 83284*	6	42	wks
23 Jun 79	● I AM *CBS 86084*	5	41	wks
1 Nov 80	● FACES *CBS 88498*	10	6	wks
14 Nov 81	RAISE *CBS 85272*	14	22	wks
19 Feb 83	POWERLIGHT *CBS 25120*	22	7	wks
10 May 86	● THE COLLECTION *K-Tel NE 1322*	5	13	wks
28 Nov 92	THE VERY BEST OF EARTH WIND AND FIRE *Telstar TCD 2631*	40	6	wks

EARTHLING *UK, male vocal / instrumental duo*   **1 wk**

3 Jun 95	RADAR *Cooltempo CTCD 44*	66	1	wk

EAST OF EDEN *UK, male vocal / instrumental group*   **2 wks**

14 Mar 70	SNAFU *Deram SML 1050*	29	2	wks

E
123

EAST 17 *UK, male vocal group*   **75 wks**

27 Feb 93	★ WALTHAMSTOW *London 8283732*	1	33	wks
29 Oct 94	● STEAM *London 8285422*	3	36	wks
25 Nov 95	● UP ALL NIGHT *London 8286992*	7†	6	wks

Walthamstow *changed its catalogue number to 8284262 during its chart run.*

EASTERHOUSE *UK, male vocal / instrumental group*   **1 wk**

28 Jun 86	CONTENDERS *Rough Trade ROUGH 94*	91	1	wk

Sheena EASTON *UK, female vocalist*   **37 wks**

31 Jan 81	TAKE MY TIME *EMI EMC 3354*	17	19	wks
3 Oct 81	YOU COULD HAVE BEEN WITH ME *EMI EMC 3378*	33	6	wks
25 Sep 82	MADNESS, MONEY AND MUSIC *EMI EMC 3414*	44	4	wks
15 Oct 83	BEST KEPT SECRET *EMI EMC 1077951*	99	1	wk
4 Mar 89	THE LOVER IN ME *MCA MCG 6036*	30	7	wks

Clint EASTWOOD and General SAINT
Jamaica, male vocal duo   **3 wks**

6 Feb 82	TWO BAD DJ *Greensleeves GREL 24*	99	2	wks
28 May 83	STOP THAT TRAIN *Greensleeves GREL 53*	98	1	wk

EAT STATIC *UK, male instrumental duo*   **4 wks**

15 May 93	ABDUCTION *Planet Dog BARKCD 1*	62	1	wk
25 Jun 94	IMPLANT *Planet Dog BARKCD 005*	13	3	wks

ECHO and the BUNNYMEN *UK, male vocal / instrumental group*   **89 wks**

26 Jul 80	CROCODILES *Korova KODE 1*	17	6	wks

6 Jun 81 ● **HEAVEN UP HERE** *Korova KODE 3*....................**10**	16	wks
12 Feb 83 ● **PORCUPINE** *Korova KODE 6* **2**	17	wks
12 May 84 ● **OCEAN RAIN** *Korova KODE 8*......................**4**	26	wks
23 Nov 85 ● **SONGS TO LEARN & SING** *Korova KODE 13* **6**	15	wks
18 Jul 87 ● **ECHO AND THE BUNNYMEN** *WEA WX 108* **4**	9	wks

ECHOBELLY *UK / Sweden, male / female vocal / instrumental group* **12 wks**

3 Sep 94 ● **EVERYONE'S GOT ONE** *Fauve FAUV 3CD* **8**	3	wks
30 Sep 95 ● **ON** *Fauve FAUV 6CD*..................................**4**	9	wks

EDDIE and the HOT RODS *UK, male vocal / instrumental group* **5 wks**

18 Dec 76 **TEENAGE DEPRESSION** *Island ILPS 9457* **43**	1	wk
3 Dec 77 **LIFE ON THE LINE** *Island ILPS 9509* **27**	3	wks
24 Mar 79 **THRILLER** *Island ILPS 9563*.............................**50**	1	wk

Duane EDDY *US, male instrumentalist – guitar* **88 wks**

6 Jun 59 ● **HAVE TWANGY GUITAR WILL TRAVEL** *London HAW 2160*...........**6**	3	wks
31 Oct 59 ● **SPECIALLY FOR YOU** *London HAW 2191* **6**	8	wks
19 Mar 60 ● **THE TWANG'S THE THANG** *London HAW 2236*...............**2**	25	wks
26 Nov 60 **SONGS OF OUR HERITAGE** *London HAW 2285* **13**	5	wks
1 Apr 61 ● **A MILLION DOLLARS' WORTH OF TWANG** *London HAW 2325* **5**	19	wks
9 Jun 62 **A MILLION DOLLARS' WORTH OF TWANG VOLUME 2** *London HAW 2435*...............**18**	1	wk
21 Jul 62 ● **TWISTIN' AND TWANGIN'** *RCA RD 27264* **8**	12	wks
8 Dec 62 **TWANGY GUITAR – SILKY STRINGS** *RCA RD 7510* **13**	11	wks
16 Mar 63 **DANCE WITH THE GUITAR MAN** *RCA RD 7545* **14**	4	wks

EDMONTON SYMPHONY ORCHESTRA – *See PROCOL HARUM*

E
124

Dave EDMUNDS *UK, male vocalist / instrumentalist – guitar* **21 wks**

23 Jun 79 **REPEAT WHEN NECESSARY** *Swansong SSK 59409* **39**	12	wks
18 Apr 81 **TWANGIN'** *Swansong SSK 59411* **37**	4	wks
3 Apr 82 **DE7** *Arista SPART 1184*..................................**60**	3	wks
30 Apr 83 **INFORMATION** *Arista 205 348* **92**	2	wks

Dennis EDWARDS *US, male vocalist* **1 wk**

14 Apr 84 **DON'T LOOK ANY FURTHER** *Gordy ZL 72148* **91**	1	wk

EEK-A-MOUSE *Jamaica, male vocalist* **3 wks**

14 Aug 82 **SKIDIP** *Greensleeves GREL 41* **61**	3	wks

801 *UK, male vocal / instrumental group* **2 wks**

20 Nov 76 **801 LIVE** *Island ILPS 9444* **52**	2	wks

808 STATE *UK, male instrumental group* **18 wks**

16 Dec 89 **NINETY** *ZTT ZTT 2* **57**	5	wks
16 Mar 91 ● **EX:EL** *ZTT ZTT 6* **4**	10	wks
13 Feb 93 **GORGEOUS** *ZTT 4509911002* **17**	3	wks

EIGHTH WONDER *UK, male / female vocal / instrumental group* **4 wks**

23 Jul 88 **FEARLESS** *CBS 460628 1* **47**	4	wks

ELASTICA *UK, female / male vocal / instrumental group* **25 wks**

25 Mar 95 ★ **ELASTICA** *Deceptive BLUFF 014CD*......................**1**	25	wks

ELECTRAFIXION *UK, male vocal / instrumental group* **2 wks**

7 Oct 95 **BURNED** *Spacejunk 0630112482*..........................**38**	2	wks

ELECTRIBE 101 *UK / Germany, male / female vocal / instrumental group* **4 wks**

20 Oct 90	**ELECTRIBAL MEMORIES** Mercury 8429651 ....**26**	3 wks

ELECTRIC BOYS *Sweden, male vocal / instrumental group* **1 wk**

6 Jun 92	**GROOVUS MAXIMUS** Vertigo 5122552..............................**61**	1 wk

ELECTRIC LIGHT ORCHESTRA
UK, male vocal / instrumental group **381 wks**

12 Aug 72	**ELECTRIC LIGHT ORCHESTRA** Harvest SHVL 797 ....**32**	4 wks
31 Mar 73	**ELO 2** Harvest SHVL 806 ....**35**	1 wk
11 Dec 76	● **A NEW WORLD RECORD** United Artists UAG 30017 ....**6**	100 wks
12 Nov 77	● **OUT OF THE BLUE** United Artists UAR 100 ....**4**	108 wks
6 Jan 79	**THREE LIGHT YEARS** Jet JET BX 1 ....**38**	9 wks
16 Jun 79	★ **DISCOVERY** Jet JET LX 500 ....**1**	46 wks
1 Dec 79	● **ELO'S GREATEST HITS** Jet JET LX 525 ....**7**	18 wks
8 Aug 81	★ **TIME** Jet JETLP 236 ....**1**	32 wks
2 Jul 83	● **SECRET MESSAGES** Jet JET LX 527 ....**4**	15 wks
15 Mar 86	● **BALANCE OF POWER** Epic EPC 26467 ....**9**	12 wks
16 Dec 89	**THE GREATEST HITS** Telstar STAR 2370.......................**23**	21 wks
1 Jun 91	**ELECTRIC LIGHT ORCHESTRA PART 2** Telstar STAR 2503 [1] **34**	4 wks
2 Jul 94	● **THE VERY BEST OF THE ELECTRIC LIGHT ORCHESTRA** Dino DINCD 90 ....**4**	11 wks

[1] ELO Part 2

A New World Record *changed label number to JET LP 200 and* Out Of The Blue *changed to JET DP 400 during their chart runs. The Greatest Hits* was also issued under the title The Very Best Of Electric Light Orchestra, *with the same track listings and catalogue number.*

ELECTRIC SUN – *See Uli Jon ROTH and ELECTRIC SUN*

E
125

ELECTRIC WIND ENSEMBLE *UK, male instrumental group* **9 wks**

18 Feb 84	**HAUNTING MELODIES** Nouveau Music NML 1007........................**28**	9 wks

ELECTRONIC *UK, male vocal / instrumental duo* **16 wks**

8 Jun 91	● **ELECTRONIC** Factory FACT 290 ....**2**	16 wks

Danny ELFMAN *US, male orchestra leader* **6 wks**

12 Aug 89	**BATMAN** Warner Bros. WX 287 ....**45**	6 wks

Duke ELLINGTON *US, orchestra* **2 wks**

8 Apr 61	**NUT CRACKER SUITE** Philips BBL 7418 ....**11**	2 wks

Ben ELTON *UK, male comedian* **2 wks**

14 Nov 87	**MOTORMOUTH** Mercury BENLP 1 ....**86**	2 wks

EMERSON, LAKE and POWELL
UK, male vocal / instrumental group **5 wks**

14 Jun 86	**EMERSON, LAKE AND POWELL** Polydor POLD 5191 ....**35**	5 wks

See also Greg Lake; Cozy Powell; Emerson, Lake and Palmer.

EMERSON, LAKE and PALMER *UK, male instrumental group* **135 wks**

5 Dec 70	● **EMERSON, LAKE AND PALMER** Island ILPS 9132 ....**4**	28 wks
19 Jun 71	★ **TARKUS** Island ILPS 9155 ....**1**	17 wks
4 Dec 71	● **PICTURES AT AN EXHIBITION** Island HELP 1 ....**3**	5 wks
8 Jul 72	● **TRILOGY** Island ILPS 9186 ....**2**	29 wks

22 Dec 73 ● **BRAIN SALAD SURGERY** *Manticore K 53501* ....**2**   17 wks
24 Aug 74 ● **WELCOME BACK MY FRIENDS TO THE SHOW THAT NEVER**
ENDS – LADIES AND GENTLEMEN: EMERSON, LAKE
AND PALMER *Manticore K 63500* ....**5**   5 wks

See also Greg Lake; Emerson, Lake and Powell.

EMF *UK, male vocal / instrumental group*   **22 wks**

18 May 91 ● **SCHUBERT DIP** *Parlophone PCS 7353*..................................**3**   19 wks
10 Oct 92   **STIGMA** *Parlophone CDPCSD 122*..............................**19**   2 wks
18 Mar 95   **CHA CHA CHA** *Parlophone CDPCSD 165* ....**30**   1 wk

An EMOTIONAL FISH *UK, male vocal / instrumental group*   **3 wks**

25 Aug 90   **AN EMOTIONAL FISH** *East West WX 359* ....**40**   3 wks

EN VOGUE *US, female vocal group*   **42 wks**

2 Jun 90   **BORN TO SING** *Atlantic 7567820841* ....**23**   13 wks
23 May 92 ● **FUNKY DIVAS** *East West America 7567921212*..................**4**   29 wks

ENERGY ORCHARD *Ireland, male vocal / instrumental group*   **2 wks**

12 May 90   **ENERGY ORCHARD** *MCA MCG 6083* ....**53**   2 wks

ENGLAND FOOTBALL WORLD CUP SQUAD
UK, male football team vocalists   **18 wks**

16 May 70 ● **THE WORLD BEATERS SING THE WORLD BEATERS**
Pye NSPL 18337 ....**4**   8 wks
15 May 82   **THIS TIME** *K-Tel NE 1169*.....................................**37**   10 wks

ENGLISH CHAMBER ORCHESTRA – See *John WILLIAMS; Nigel KENNEDY;*
Andrew LLOYD WEBBER; Kiri TE KANAWA

ENIGMA *UK, male vocal / instrumental group*   **3 wks**

5 Sep 81   **AIN'T NO STOPPIN'** *Creole CRX 1* ....**80**   3 wks

ENIGMA *Romania, male producer*   **111 wks**

22 Dec 90 ★ **MCMXC AD** *Virgin International VIR 11* ....**1**   76 wks
19 Feb 94 ★ **THE CROSS OF CHANGES** *Virgin International CDVIR 20* ....**1**   35 wks

Brian ENO *UK, male instrumentalist   keyboards*   **16 wks**

9 Mar 74   **HERE COME THE WARM JETS** *Island ILPS 9268* ....**26**   2 wks
21 Oct 78   **MUSIC FOR FILMS** *Polydor 2310 623*...................................**55**   1 wk
21 Feb 81   **MY LIFE IN THE BUSH OF GHOSTS** *Polydor EGLP 48* [1] ....**29**   8 wks
8 May 82   **AMBIENT FOUR ON LAND** *EG EGED 20* ....**93**   1 wk
12 Sep 92   **NERVE NET** *Opal 9362450332*...................................**70**   1 wk
24 Sep 94   **WAH WAH** *Fontana 5228272* [2] ....**11**   2 wks
14 Oct 95   **SPINNER** *All Saints ASCD 023* [3] ....**71**   1 wk

[1] Brian Eno and David Byrne [2] James and Brian Eno [3] Brian Eno and Jah Wobble

ENUFF Z'NUFF *US, male vocal / instrumental group*   **1 wk**

13 Apr 91   **STRENGTH** *Atco 7567916381* ....**56**   1 wk

ENYA *Ireland, female vocalist / instrumentalist – keyboards*   **209 wks**

6 Jun 87   **ENYA** *BBC REB 605*...**69**   4 wks
15 Oct 88 ● **WATERMARK** *WEA WX 199* ....**5**   92 wks
16 Nov 91 ★ **SHEPHERD MOONS** *WEA WX 431* ....**1**   90 wks
28 Nov 92 ● **THE CELTS** *WEA 4509911672* ....**10**   18 wks
2 Dec 95 ● **THE MEMORY OF TREES** *WEA 0630128792* ....**5†**   5 wks

The Celts is a repackaged and re–issued version of Enya.

EPMD *US, male rap duo*   **1 wk**

| 16 Feb 91 | **BUSINESS AS USUAL** Def Jam 4676971 | 69 | 1 | wk |

EQUALS *UK, male vocal / instrumental group*   **10 wks**

| 18 Nov 67 | ● **UNEQUALLED EQUALS** President PTL 1006 | 10 | 9 | wks |
| 9 Mar 68 | **EQUALS EXPLOSION** President PTLS 1015 | 32 | 1 | wk |

ERASURE *UK, male vocal / instrumental duo*   **311 wks**

14 Jun 86	**WONDERLAND** Mute STUMM 25	71	7	wks
11 Apr 87	● **THE CIRCUS** Mute STUMM 35	6	107	wks
30 Apr 88	★ **THE INNOCENTS** Mute STUMM 55	1	78	wks
28 Oct 89	★ **WILD!** Mute STUMM 75	1	48	wks
26 Oct 91	★ **CHORUS** Mute STUMM 95	1	25	wks
28 Nov 92	★ **POP! – THE FIRST 20 HITS** Mute CDMUTEL 2	1	26	wks
28 May 94	★ **I SAY I SAY I SAY** Mute LCDSTUMM 115	1	15	wks
4 Nov 95	**ERASURE** Mute CDSTUMM 145	14†	5	wks

David ESSEX *UK, male vocalist*   **164 wks**

24 Nov 73	● **ROCK ON** CBS 65823	7	22	wks
19 Oct 74	● **DAVID ESSEX** CBS 69088	2	24	wks
27 Sep 75	● **ALL THE FUN OF THE FAIR** CBS 69160	3	20	wks
5 Jun 76	**ON TOUR** CBS 95000	51	1	wk
30 Oct 76	**OUT ON THE STREET** CBS 86017	31	9	wks
8 Oct 77	**GOLD AND IVORY** CBS 86038	29	4	wks
6 Jan 79	**DAVID ESSEX ALBUM** CBS 10011	29	7	wks
31 Mar 79	**IMPERIAL WIZARD** Mercury 9109 616	12	9	wks
12 Jun 80	**HOT LOVE** Mercury 6359 017	75	1	wk
19 Jun 82	**STAGE–STRUCK** Mercury MERS 4	31	15	wks
27 Nov 82	**THE VERY BEST OF DAVID ESSEX** TV TVA 4	37	11	wks
15 Oct 83	**MUTINY** Mercury MERH 30	39	4	wks
17 Dec 83	**THE WHISPER** Mercury MERH 34	67	6	wks
6 Dec 86	**CENTRE STAGE** K–Tel ONE 1333	82	4	wks
19 Oct 91	**HIS GREATEST HITS** Mercury 5103081	13	13	wks
10 Apr 93	● **COVER SHOT** PolyGram TV 5145632	3	8	wks
22 Oct 94	**BACK TO BACK** PolyGram TV 5237902	33	2	wks
9 Dec 95	**MISSING YOU** PolyGram TV 5295822	45†	4	wks

Mutiny is a studio recording of a musical that was not staged until 1985. Both this album and the eventual stage production starred David Essex and Frank Finlay.

Gloria ESTEFAN *US, female vocalist*   **232 wks**

19 Nov 88	★ **ANYTHING FOR YOU** Epic 4631251 [1]	1	54	wks
5 Aug 89	★ **CUTS BOTH WAYS** Epic 4651451	1	64	wks
16 Feb 91	● **INTO THE LIGHT** Epic 4677821	2	36	wks
14 Nov 92	● **GREATEST HITS** Epic 4723322	2	47	wks
10 Jul 93	**MI TIERRA** Epic 4737992	11	11	wks
29 Oct 94	● **HOLD ME THRILL ME KISS ME** Epic 4774162	5	19	wks
21 Oct 95	**ABRIENDO PUERTAS** Epic 4809922	70	1	wk

[1] Miami Sound Machine

Don ESTELLE and Windsor DAVIES *UK, male vocal duo*   **8 wks**

| 10 Jan 76 | ● **SING LOFTY** EMI EMC 3102 | 10 | 8 | wks |

ETERNAL *UK, female vocal group*   **84 wks**

| 11 Dec 93 | ● **ALWAYS AND FOREVER** EMI CDEMD 1053 | 2 | 76 | wks |
| 11 Nov 95 | ● **POWER OF A WOMAN** EMI CDEMD 1053 | 6† | 8 | wks |

Melissa ETHERIDGE *US, female vocalist*   **2 wks**

| 30 Sep 89 | **BRAVE AND CRAZY** Island ILPS 9939 | 63 | 1 | wk |

9 May 92   **NEVER ENOUGH** *Island CID 9990* ....**56**   1   wk

EUROPE *Sweden, male vocal / instrumental group*   **43 wks**

22 Nov 86	● **THE FINAL COUNTDOWN** *Epic EPC 26808*......................**9**	37	wks
17 Sep 88	**OUT OF THIS WORLD** *Epic 4624491*.........................**12**	5	wks
19 Oct 91	**PRISONERS IN PARADISE** *Epic 4687551* **61**	1	wk

EUROPEANS *UK, male vocal / instrumental group*   **1 wk**

11 Feb 84   **LIVE** *A & M SCOT 1* ....**100**   1   wk

EURYTHMICS *UK, female / male vocal / instrumental duo*   **425 wks**

12 Feb 83	● **SWEET DREAMS (ARE MADE OF THIS)** *RCA RCALP 6063* **3**	60	wks
26 Nov 83	★ **TOUCH** *RCA PL 70109*..**1**	48	wks
9 Jun 84	**TOUCH DANCE** *RCA PG 70354* **31**	5	wks
24 Nov 84	**1984 (FOR THE LOVE OF BIG BROTHER)** *Virgin V 1984*.........**23**	17	wks
11 May 85	● **BE YOURSELF TONIGHT** *RCA PL 70711* **3**	80	wks
12 Jul 86	● **REVENGE** *RCA PL 71050* **3**	52	wks
21 Nov 87	● **SAVAGE** *RCA PL 71555* **7**	33	wks
23 Sep 89	★ **WE TOO ARE ONE** *RCA PL 74251* **1**	32	wks
30 Mar 91	★ **GREATEST HITS** *RCA PL 74856* **1**	91	wks
27 Nov 93	**EURYTHMICS LIVE 1983–1989** *RCA 74321171452*.......................**22**	7	wks

Phil EVERLY *US, male vocalist*   **1 wk**

7 May 83   **PHIL EVERLY** *Capitol EST 27670* ....**61**   1   wk

See also the Everly Brothers.

EVERLY BROTHERS *US, male vocal duo*   **123 wks**

2 Jul 60	● **IT'S EVERLY TIME** *Warner Bros. WM 4006* **2**	23	wks
15 Oct 60	● **FABULOUS STYLE OF THE EVERLY BROTHERS** *London HAA 2266* ..**4**	11	wks
4 Mar 61	● **A DATE WITH THE EVERLY BROTHERS** *Warner Bros. WM 4028* **3**	14	wks
21 Jul 62	**INSTANT PARTY** *Warner Bros. WM 4061* **20**	1	wk
12 Sep 70	● **ORIGINAL GREATEST HITS** *CBS 66255* **7**	16	wks
8 Jun 74	**THE VERY BEST OF THE EVERLY BROTHERS** *Warner Bros. K 46008* **43**	1	wk
29 Nov 75	● **WALK RIGHT BACK WITH THE EVERLYS** *Warner Bros. K 56118* ..**10**	10	wks
9 Apr 77	**LIVING LEGENDS** *Warwick WW 5027* **12**	10	wks
18 Dec 82	**LOVE HURTS** *K-Tel NE 1197* **22**	22	wks
7 Jan 84	**EVERLY BROTHERS REUNION CONCERT** *Impression IMDP 1* **47**	6	wks
3 Nov 84	**THE EVERLY BROTHERS** *Mercury MERH 44* **36**	4	wks
29 May 93	**GOLDEN YEARS OF THE EVERLY BROTHERS – THEIR 24**		
	GREATEST HITS *Warner Bros. 9548319922* **26**	5	wks

See also Phil Everly.

EVERYTHING BUT THE GIRL
UK, male / female vocal / instrumental duo   **77 wks**

16 Jun 84	**EDEN** *Blanco Y Negro BYN 2*.................................**14**	22	wks
27 Apr 85	● **LOVE NOT MONEY** *Blanco Y Negro BYN 3* **10**	9	wks
6 Sep 86	**BABY THE STARS SHINE BRIGHT** *Blanco Y Negro BYN 9*...........**22**	9	wks
12 Mar 88	**IDLEWILD** *Blanco Y Negro BYN 14*..........................**13**	9	wks
6 Aug 88	**IDLEWILD (re–issue)** *Blanco Y Negro BYN 16* **21**	6	wks
17 Feb 90	● **THE LANGUAGE OF LOVE** *Blanco Y Negro BYN 21* **10**	6	wks
5 Oct 91	**WORLDWIDE** *Blanco Y Negro BYN 25* **29**	5	wks
22 May 93	● **HOME MOVIES – THE BEST OF EVERYTHING BUT THE GIRL**		
	Blanco Y Negro 4509923192 ....**5**	8	wks
25 Jun 94	**AMPLIFIED HEART** *Blanco Y Negro 4509964822* **20**	3	wks

EXODUS *US, male vocal / instrumental group*   **1 wk**

11 Feb 89   **FABULOUS DISASTER** *Music For Nations MFN 90* ....**67**   1   wk

EXPLOITED *UK, male vocal / instrumental group*   **26 wks**

16 May 81   **PUNK'S NOT DEAD** *Secret SEC 1* ....**20**   11   wks

| 14 Nov 81 | **EXPLOITED LIVE** *Superville EXPLP 2001* | **52** | 3 wks |
| 19 Jun 82 | **TROOPS OF TOMORROW** *Secret SEC 8* | **17** | 12 wks |

EXTREME *US, male vocal / instrumental group*   **75 wks**

1 Jun 91	**EXTREME II PORNOGRAFFITI** *A & M 3953131*	**12**	61 wks
26 Sep 92	● **III SIDES TO EVERY STORY** *A & M 5400062*	**2**	11 wks
11 Feb 95	● **WAITING FOR THE PUNCHLINE** *A & M 5403052*	**10**	3 wks

EYC *US, male vocal group*   **5 wks**

| 16 Apr 94 | **EXPRESS YOURSELF CLEARLY** *MCA MCD 11061* | **14** | 5 wks |

F.A.B. *UK, male producers*   **3 wks**

| 10 Nov 90 | **POWER THEMES 90** *Telstar STAR 2430* | **53** | 3 wks |

FACES *UK, male vocal / instrumental group*   **57 wks**

4 Apr 70	**FIRST STEP** *Warner Bros. WS 3000*	**45**	1 wk
8 May 71	**LONG PLAYER** *Warner Bros. W 3011*	**31**	7 wks
25 Dec 71	● **A NOD'S AS GOOD AS A WINK . . . TO A BLIND HORSE** *Warner Bros. K 56006*	**2**	22 wks
21 Apr 73	★ **OOH–LA–LA** *Warner Bros. K 56011*	**1**	13 wks
26 Jan 74	● **OVERTURE AND BEGINNERS** *Mercury 9100 001* [1]	**3**	7 wks
21 May 77	**THE BEST OF THE FACES** *Riva RVLP 3*	**24**	6 wks
7 Nov 92	**THE BEST OF ROD STEWART AND THE FACES 1971–1975** *Mercury 5141802* [1]	**58**	1 wk

[1] Rod Stewart and the Faces

See also Rod Stewart.

Donald FAGEN *US, male vocalist*   **25 wks**

| 20 Oct 82 | **THE NIGHTFLY** *Warner Bros. 923696* | **44** | 16 wks |
| 5 Jun 93 | ● **KAMAKIRIAD** *Reprise 9362452302* | **3** | 9 wks |

FAIRGROUND ATTRACTION
UK, male / female vocal / instrumental group   **54 wks**

| 28 May 88 | ● **THE FIRST OF A MILLION KISSES** *RCA PL 71696* | **2** | 52 wks |
| 30 Jun 90 | **AY FOND KISS** *RCA PL 74596* | **55** | 2 wks |

Group were male only on last album.

FAIRPORT CONVENTION
UK, male / female vocal / instrumental group   **41 wks**

2 Aug 69	**UNHALFBRICKING** *Island ILPS 9102*	**12**	8 wks
17 Jan 70	**LIEGE AND LIEF** *Island ILPS 9115*	**17**	15 wks
18 Jul 70	**FULL HOUSE** *Island ILPS 9130*	**13**	11 wks
3 Jul 71	● **ANGEL DELIGHT** *Island ILPS 9162*	**8**	5 wks
12 Jul 75	**RISING FOR THE MOON** *Island ILPS 9313*	**52**	1 wk
28 Jan 89	**RED AND GOLD** *New Routes RUE 002*	**74**	1 wk

Adam FAITH *UK, male vocalist*   **46 wks**

19 Nov 60	● **ADAM** *Parlophone PMC 1128*	**6**	36 wks
11 Feb 61	**BEAT GIRL (film soundtrack)** *Columbia 33SX 1225*	**11**	3 wks
24 Mar 62	**ADAM FAITH** *Parlophone PMC 1162*	**20**	1 wk
25 Sep 65	**FAITH ALIVE** *Parlophone PMC 1249*	**19**	1 wk

| 19 Dec 81 | **20 GOLDEN GREATS** Warwick WW 5113 | **61** | 3 wks |
| 27 Nov 93 | **MIDNIGHT POSTCARDS** PolyGram TV 8213982 | **43** | 2 wks |

FAITH BROTHERS UK, male vocal / instrumental group · **1 wk**

| 9 Nov 85 | **EVENTIDE** Siren SIRENLP 1 | **66** | 1 wk |

FAITH NO MORE US, male vocal / instrumental group · **70 wks**

17 Feb 90	**THE REAL THING** Slash 8281541	**30**	35 wks
16 Feb 91	**LIVE AT THE BRIXTON ACADEMY** Slash 8282381	**20**	4 wks
20 Jun 92	● **ANGEL DUST** Slash 8283212	**2**	25 wks
25 Mar 95	● **KING FOR A DAY FOOL FOR A LIFETIME** Slash 8285602	**5**	6 wks

Marianne FAITHFULL UK, female vocalist · **19 wks**

5 Jun 65	**COME MY WAY** Decca LK 4688	**12**	7 wks
5 Jun 65	**MARIANNE FAITHFULL** Decca LK 4689	**15**	2 wks
24 Nov 79	**BROKEN ENGLISH** Island M1	**57**	3 wks
17 Oct 81	**DANGEROUS ACQUAINTANCES** Island ILPS 9648	**45**	4 wks
26 Mar 83	**A CHILD'S ADVENTURE** Island ILPS 9734	**99**	1 wk
8 Aug 87	**STRANGE WEATHER** Island ILPS 9874	**78**	2 wks

FALCO Austria, male vocalist · **15 wks**

| 26 Apr 86 | **FALCO 3** A & M AMA 5105 | **32** | 15 wks |

FALL UK, male vocal / instrumental group · **31 wks**

20 Mar 82	**HEX ENDUCTION HOUR** Kamera KAM 005	**71**	3 wks
20 Oct 84	**THE WONDERFUL AND FRIGHTENING WORLD OF . . .** Beggars Banquet BEGA 58	**62**	2 wks
5 Oct 85	**THE NATION'S SAVING GRACE** Beggars Banquet BEGA 67	**54**	2 wks
11 Oct 86	**BEND SINISTER** Beggars Banquet BEGA 75	**36**	3 wks
12 Mar 88	**THE FRENZ EXPERIMENT** Beggars Banquet BEGA 91	**19**	4 wks
12 Nov 88	**I AM KURIOUS, ORANJ** Beggars Banquet BEGA 96	**54**	2 wks
8 Jul 89	**SEMINAL LIVE** Beggars Banquet BBL 102	**40**	2 wks
3 Mar 90	**EXTRICATE** Cog Sinister 8422041	**31**	3 wks
15 Sep 90	**458489** Beggars Banquet BEGA 111	**44**	2 wks
4 May 91	**SHIFT WORK** Cog Sinister 8485941	**17**	2 wks
28 Mar 92	**CODE: SELFISH** Cog Sinister 5121622	**21**	1 wk
8 May 93	● **INFOTAINMENT SCAN** Permanent PERMCD 12	**9**	3 wks
14 May 94	**MIDDLE CLASS REVOLT** Permanent PERMCD 16	**48**	1 wk
11 Mar 95	**CEREBRAL CAUSTIC** Permanent PERMCD 30	**67**	1 wk

Agnetha FALTSKOG Sweden, female vocalist · **17 wks**

11 Jun 83	**WRAP YOUR ARMS AROUND ME** Epic EPC 25505	**18**	13 wks
4 May 85	**EYES OF A WOMAN** Epic EPC 26446	**38**	3 wks
12 Mar 88	**I STAND ALONE** WEA WX 150	**72**	1 wk

Georgie FAME UK, male vocalist · **72 wks**

17 Oct 64	**FAME AT LAST** Columbia 33SX 1638	**15**	8 wks
14 May 66	● **SWEET THINGS** Columbia SX 6043	**6**	22 wks
15 Oct 66	● **SOUND VENTURE** Columbia SX 6076	**9**	9 wks
11 Mar 67	**HALL OF FAME** Columbia SX 6120	**12**	18 wks
1 Jul 67	**TWO FACES OF FAME** CBS SBPG 63018	**22**	15 wks

FAMILY UK, male vocal / instrumental group · **41 wks**

10 Aug 68	**MUSIC IN THE DOLLS HOUSE** Reprise RLP 6312	**35**	3 wks
22 Mar 69	● **FAMILY ENTERTAINMENT** Reprise RSLP 6340	**6**	3 wks
7 Feb 70	**A SONG FOR ME** Reprise RSLP 9001	**4**	13 wks
28 Nov 70	● **ANYWAY** Reprise RSX 9005	**7**	7 wks
20 Nov 71	**FEARLESS** Reprise K 54003	**14**	2 wks
30 Sep 72	**BANDSTAND** Reprise K 54006	**15**	10 wks
29 Sep 73	**IT'S ONLY A MOVIE** Raft RA 58501	**30**	3 wks

FAMILY CAT *UK, male vocal / instrumental group* **1 wk**

4 Jul 92   **FURTHEST FROM THE SUN** *Dedicated DEDCD 007* ....**55** 1 wk

FAMILY STAND *US, male / female vocal / instrumental group* **3 wks**

19 May 90   **CHAIN** *Atlantic WX 349* ....**52** 3 wks

FAMILY STONE – *See SLY and the FAMILY STONE*

Chris FARLOWE *UK, male vocalist* **3 wks**

2 Apr 66   **14 THINGS TO THINK ABOUT** *Immediate IMLP 005* ....**19** 1 wk
10 Dec 66   **THE ART OF CHRIS FARLOWE** *Immediate IMLP 006* ....**37** 2 wks

FARM *UK, male vocal / instrumental group* **17 wks**

16 Mar 91 ★ **SPARTACUS** *Produce MILKLP 1* ....**1** 17 wks

FARMERS BOYS *UK, male vocal / instrumental group* **1 wk**

29 Oct 83   **GET OUT AND WALK** *EMI EMC 1077991*....................**49** 1 wk

John FARNHAM *Australia, male vocalist* **9 wks**

11 Jul 87   **WHISPERING JACK** *RCA PL 71224* ....**35** 9 wks

FARRAR – *See MARVIN, WELCH and FARRAR*

FASHION *UK, male vocal / instrumental group* **17 wks**

3 Jul 82 ● **FABRIQUE** *Arista SPART 1185* ....**10** 16 wks
16 Jun 84   **TWILIGHT OF IDOLS** *De Stijl EPC 25909* ....**69** 1 wk

FASTER PUSSYCAT *US, male vocal / instrumental group* **3 wks**

16 Sep 89   **WAKE ME WHEN IT'S OVER** *Elektra EKT 64* ....**35** 2 wks
22 Aug 92   **WHIPPED** *Elektra 7559611242* ....**58** 1 wk

FASTWAY *UK, male vocal / instrumental group* **2 wks**

30 Apr 83   **FASTWAY** *CBS 25359* ....**43** 2 wks

FAT BOYS *US, male rap group* **5 wks**

3 Oct 87   **CRUSHIN'** *Urban URBLP 3* ....**49** 4 wks
30 Jul 88   **COMING BACK HARD AGAIN** *Urban URBLP 13* ....**98** 1 wk

FAT LADY SINGS *UK, male vocal / instrumental group* **1 wk**

18 May 91   **TWIST** *East West WX 418*..**50** 1 wk

FAT LARRY'S BAND *US, male vocal / instrumental group* **4 wks**

9 Oct 82   **BREAKIN' OUT** *Virgin V 2229* ....**58** 4 wks

FATBACK BAND *US, male vocal / instrumental group* **7 wks**

6 Mar 76   **RAISING HELL** *Polydor 2391 203* ....**19** 6 wks
4 Jul 87   **FATBACK LIVE** *Start STL 12*..**80** 1 wk

FATHER ABRAHAM and the SMURFS
Holland, male vocalist as himself and Smurfs **11 wks**

25 Nov 78   **FATHER ABRAHAM IN SMURFLAND** *Decca SMURF 1*...................**19** 11 wks

FATHER KILCOYNE – See POPE JOHN PAUL II

FATIMA MANSIONS Ireland, male vocal/instrumental group   **1 wk**

| 6 Jun 92 | **VALHALLA AVENUE** Radioactive KWCD 18 ....**52** | 1 | wk |

FBI – See REDHEAD KINGPIN and the FBI

FEAR FACTORY US, male vocal/instrumental group   **1 wk**

| 1 Jul 95 | **DEMANUFACTURE** Roadrunner RR 89565....................**27** | 1 | wk |

Phil FEARON and GALAXY
UK, male/female vocal/instrumental group   **9 wks**

| 25 Aug 84 | ● **PHIL FEARON AND GALAXY** Ensign ENCL 2 ....**8** | 8 | wks |
| 14 Sep 85 | **THIS KIND OF LOVE** Ensign ENCL 4....................**98** | 1 | wk |

Wilton FELDER US, male instrumentalist tenor sax   **3 wks**

| 23 Feb 85 | **SECRETS** MCA MCF 3237....................**77** | 3 | wks |

Also featuring Bobby Womack and introducing Alltrina Grayson.

José FELICIANO US, male vocalist/instrumentalist – guitar   **40 wks**

2 Nov 68	● **FELICIANO** RCA Victor SF 7946 ....**6**	36	wks
29 Nov 69	**JOSÉ FELICIANO** RCA Victor SF 8044....................**29**	2	wks
14 Feb 70	**10 TO 23** RCA SF 7946 ....**38**	1	wk
22 Aug 70	**FIREWORKS** RCA SF 8124 ....**65**	1	wk

F
132

FELIX UK, male producer   **4 wks**

| 10 Apr 93 | **#1** Deconstruction 74321137002 ....**26** | 4 | wks |

Julie FELIX US, female vocalist   **4 wks**

| 11 Sep 66 | **CHANGES** Fontana TL 5368....................**27** | 4 | wks |

Bryan FERRY UK, male vocalist   **293 wks**

3 Nov 73	● **THESE FOOLISH THINGS** Island ILPS 9249....................**5**	42	wks
20 Jul 74	● **ANOTHER TIME, ANOTHER PLACE** Island ILPS 9284 ....**4**	25	wks
2 Oct 76	**LET'S STICK TOGETHER** Island ILPSX 1 ....**19**	5	wks
5 Mar 77	● **IN YOUR MIND** Polydor 2302 055 ....**5**	17	wks
30 Sep 78	**THE BRIDE STRIPPED BARE** Polydor POLD 5003 ....**13**	5	wks
15 Jun 85	★ **BOYS AND GIRLS** EG EGLP 62 ....**1**	44	wks
26 Apr 86	★ **STREET LIFE – 20 GREAT HITS** EG EGTV 1 [1] **1**	77	wks
14 Nov 87	● **BETE NOIRE** Virgin V 2474 ....**9**	16	wks
19 Nov 88	● **THE ULTIMATE COLLECTION** EG EGTV 2 [1] **6**	35	wks
3 Apr 93	● **TAXI** Virgin CDV 2700....................**2**	14	wks
17 Sep 94	**MAMOUNA** Virgin CDV 2751 ....**11**	4	wks
4 Nov 95	**MORE THAN THIS – THE BEST OF BRYAN FERRY AND ROXY MUSIC** Virgin CDV 2791 [1] ....**15†**	9	wks

[1] Bryan Ferry and Roxy Music

FFWD UK/Germany, male instrumental group   **1 wk**

| 13 Aug 94 | **FFWD** Inter INTA 001CD....................**48** | 1 | wk |

Brad FIDEL Germany, male arranger   **7 wks**

| 31 Aug 91 | **TERMINATOR 2 (film soundtrack)** Vareses Sarabande VS 5335 ..**26** | 7 | wks |

Gracie FIELDS UK, female vocalist   **3 wks**

| 20 Dec 75 | **THE GOLDEN YEARS** Warwick WW 5007 ....**48** | 3 | wks |

FIELDS OF THE NEPHILIM
UK, male vocal / instrumental group   **9 wks**

30 May 87	**DAWNRAZOR** *Situation 2 SITU 18*	**62**	2 wks
17 Sep 88	**THE NEPHILIM** *Situation 2 SITU 22*	**14**	3 wks
6 Oct 90	**ELIZIUM** *Beggars Banquet BEGA 115*...	**22**	2 wks
6 Apr 91	**EARTH INFERNO** *Beggars Banquet BEGA 120*............................	**39**	2 wks

52ND STREET *UK, male / female vocal / instrumental group*   **1 wk**

19 Apr 86	**CHILDREN OF THE NIGHT** *10 DIX 25*...	**71**	1 wk

FINE YOUNG CANNIBALS
UK, male vocal / instrumental group   **94 wks**

21 Dec 85	**FINE YOUNG CANNIBALS** *London LONLP 16*...............................	**11**	27 wks
18 Feb 89	★ **THE RAW AND THE COOKED** *London 8280691*	**1**	66 wks
15 Dec 90	**FYC** *London 8282211* [1]..	**61**	1 wk

[1] FYC

FYC *is a remix album of* The Raw And The Cooked.

Frank FINLAY – *See David ESSEX*

FINN *New Zealand, male vocal / instrumental duo*   **3 wks**

28 Oct 95	**FINN** *Parlophone CDFINN 1*	**15**	3 wks

See also Tim Finn.

Tim FINN *New Zealand, male vocalist*   **2 wks**

10 Jul 93	**BEFORE AND AFTER** *Capitol CDEST 2202*	**29**	2 wks

See also Finn.

FIRM *UK, male vocal / instrumental group*   **8 wks**

2 Mar 85	**THE FIRM** *Atlantic 7812391*..	**15**	5 wks
5 Apr 86	**MEAN BUSINESS** *Atlantic WX 35*	**46**	3 wks

FIRST CIRCLE *US, male vocal / instrumental group*   **2 wks**

2 May 87	**BOYS' NIGHT OUT** *EMI America AML 3118*	**70**	2 wks

FISCHER-Z *UK, male vocal / instrumental group*   **1 wk**

23 Jun 79	**WORD SALAD** *United Artists UAG 30232*	**66**	1 wk

FISH *UK, male vocalist*   **15 wks**

10 Feb 90	● **VIGIL IN A WILDERNESS OF MIRRORS** *EMI EMD 1015*	**5**	6 wks
9 Nov 91	**INTERNAL EXILE** *Polydor 5110491*..	**21**	3 wks
30 Jan 93	**SONGS FROM THE MIRROR** *Polydor 5174992*	**46**	2 wks
11 Jun 94	**SUITS** *Dick Bros. DDICK 004CD*	**18**	2 wks
16 Sep 95	**YANG** *Dick Bros. DDICK 012CD*	**52**	1 wk
16 Sep 95	**YIN** *Dick Bros. DDICK 011CD*...	**58**	1 wk

FISHBONE *US, male vocal / instrumental group*   **1 wk**

13 Jul 91	**THE REALITY OF MY SURROUNDINGS** *Columbia 4676151*	**75**	1 wk

Ella FITZGERALD *US, female vocalist*   **31 wks**

11 Jun 60	**ELLA SINGS GERSHWIN** *Brunswick LA 8648*	**13**	3 wks
18 Jun 60	**ELLA AT THE OPERA HOUSE** *Columbia 3SX 10126*	**16**	1 wk
23 Jul 60	**ELLA SINGS GERSHWIN VOLUME 5** *HMV CLP 1353*......................	**18**	2 wks

F

133

10 May 80	THE INCOMPARABLE ELLA *Polydor POLTV 9*	**40**	7 wks
27 Feb 88	A PORTRAIT OF ELLA FITZGERALD *Stylus SMR 847*	**42**	10 wks
19 Nov 94	ESSENTIAL ELLA *PolyGram TV 5239902*	**35**	8 wks

FIVE PENNY PIECE *UK, male / female vocal / instrumental group* **6 wks**

| 24 Mar 73 | MAKING TRACKS *Columbia SCX 6536* | **37** | 1 wk |
| 3 Jul 76 | ● KING COTTON *EMI EMC 3129* | **9** | 5 wks |

FIVE STAR *UK, male / female vocal group* **153 wks**

3 Aug 85	LUXURY OF LIFE *Tent PL 70735*	**12**	70 wks
30 Aug 86	★ SILK AND STEEL *Tent PL 71100*	**1**	58 wks
26 Sep 87	● BETWEEN THE LINES *Tent PL 71505*	**7**	17 wks
27 Aug 88	ROCK THE WORLD *Tent PL 71747*	**17**	5 wks
21 Oct 89	GREATEST HITS *Tent PL 74080*	**53**	3 wks

FIVE THIRTY *UK, male vocal / instrumental group* **1 wk**

| 31 Aug 91 | BED *East West WX 530* | **57** | 1 wk |

FIXX *UK, male vocal / instrumental group* **7 wks**

| 22 May 82 | SHUTTERED ROOM *MCA FX 1001* | **54** | 6 wks |
| 21 May 83 | REACH THE BEACH *MCA FX 1002* | **91** | 1 wk |

Roberta FLACK *US, female vocalist* **45 wks**

15 Jul 72	FIRST TAKE *Atlantic K 40040*	**47**	2 wks
13 Oct 73	KILLING ME SOFTLY *Atlantic K 50021*	**40**	2 wks
7 Jun 80	ROBERTA FLACK AND DONNY HATHAWAY		
	Atlantic K 50696 [1]	**31**	7 wks
17 Sep 83	BORN TO LOVE *Capitol EST 7122841* [2]	**15**	10 wks
31 Mar 84	GREATEST HITS *K-Tel NE 1269*	**35**	14 wks
19 Feb 94	● SOFTLY WITH THESE SONGS – THE BEST OF ROBERTA FLACK		
	Atlantic 7567824982	**7**	10 wks

[1] Roberta Flack and Donny Hathaway [2] Peabo Bryson and Roberta Flack

FLASH AND THE PAN *Australia, male vocal / instrumental group* **2 wks**

| 16 Jul 83 | PAN–ORAMA *Easy Beat EASLP 100* | **69** | 2 wks |

FLEETWOOD MAC
UK / US, male / female vocal / instrumental group **795 wks**

2 Mar 68	● FLEETWOOD MAC *Blue Horizon BPG 763200*	**4**	37 wks
7 Sep 68	● MR. WONDERFUL *Blue Horizon 763205*	**10**	11 wks
30 Aug 69	PIOUS BIRD OF GOOD OMEN *Blue Horizon 763215*	**18**	4 wks
4 Oct 69	● THEN PLAY ON *Reprise RSLP 9000*	**6**	11 wks
10 Oct 70	KILN HOUSE *Reprise RSLP 9004*	**39**	2 wks
19 Feb 72	GREATEST HITS *CBS 69011*	**36**	14 wks
6 Nov 76	FLEETWOOD MAC *Reprise K 54043*	**23**	19 wks
26 Feb 77	★ RUMOURS *Warner Bros. K 56344*	**1**	443 wks
27 Oct 79	★ TUSK *Warner Bros. K 66088*	**1**	26 wks
13 Dec 80	FLEETWOOD MAC LIVE *Warner Bros. K 66097*	**31**	9 wks
10 Jul 82	● MIRAGE *Warner Bros. K 56592*	**5**	39 wks
25 Apr 87	★ TANGO IN THE NIGHT *Warner Bros. WX 65*	**1**	109 wks
3 Dec 88	● GREATEST HITS *Warner Bros. WX 221*	**3**	47 wks
21 Apr 90	★ BEHIND THE MASK *Warner Bros. WX 335*	**1**	21 wks
23 Sep 95	LIVE AT THE BBC *Essential EDFCD 297*	**48**	2 wks
21 Oct 95	TIME *Warner Bros. 9362459202*	**47**	1 wk

Group were UK and male only for first six albums and for Live At The BBC in 95. All the above albums are different, although some are identically titled. Greatest Hits in 72 changed its catalogue number to 4607041 during its chart run.

Berni FLINT *UK, male vocalist* **6 wks**

| 2 Jul 77 | I DON'T WANT TO PUT A HOLD ON YOU *EMI EMC 3184* | **37** | 6 wks |

FLOATERS *US, male vocal / instrumental group*   **8 wks**

20 Aug 77   **FLOATERS** *ABC ABCL 5229* ....**17**   8 wks

FLOCK *UK, male vocal / instrumental group*   **2 wks**

2 May 70   **FLOCK** *CBS 63733* ....**59**   2 wks

A FLOCK OF SEAGULLS *UK, male vocal / instrumental group*   **59 wks**

17 Apr 82   **A FLOCK OF SEAGULLS** *Jive HOP 201*...............**32**   44 wks
7 May 83   **LISTEN** *Jive HIP 4* ....**16**   10 wks
1 Sep 84   **THE STORY OF A YOUNG HEART** *Jive HIP 14* ....**30**   5 wks

FLOWERED UP *UK, male vocal / instrumental group*   **3 wks**

7 Sep 91   **A LIFE WITH BRIAN** *London 8282441* ....**23**   3 wks

Eddie FLOYD *US, male vocalist*   **5 wks**

29 Apr 67   **KNOCK ON WOOD** *Stax 589006*.....................**36**   5 wks

FLUKE *UK, male instrumental / vocal group*   **2 wks**

23 Oct 93   **SIX WHEELS ON MY WAGON** *Circa CIRCDX 27*...........**41**   1 wk
19 Aug 95   **OTO** *Circa CIRCD 31* ....**44**   1 wk

A FLUX OF PINK INDIANS
UK, male vocal / instrumental group   **2 wks**

5 Feb 83   **STRIVE TO SURVIVE CAUSING LEAST SUFFERING POSSIBLE**
            Spiderleg SDL 8 ....**79**   2 wks

FLYING LIZARDS *UK, male / female vocal / instrumental group*   **3 wks**

16 Feb 80   **FLYING LIZARDS** *Virgin V 2150* ....**60**   3 wks

FLYING PICKETS *UK, male vocal group*   **22 wks**

17 Dec 83   **LIVE AT THE ALBANY EMPIRE** *AVM AVMLP 0001* ....**48**   11 wks
9 Jun 84   **LOST BOYS** *10 DIX 4* ....**11**   11 wks

Jerome FLYNN – *See Robson GREEN and Jerome FLYNN*

FM *UK, male vocal / instrumental group*   **3 wks**

20 Sep 86   **INDISCREET** *Portrait PRT 26827* ....**76**   1 wk
14 Oct 89   **TOUGH IT OUT** *Epic 465589 1* ....**34**   2 wks

FOCUS *Holland, male instrumental group*   **65 wks**

11 Nov 72 ● **MOVING WAVES** *Polydor 2931 002* ....**2**   34 wks
2 Dec 72 ● **FOCUS 3** *Polydor 2383 016* ....**6**   15 wks
20 Oct 73   **FOCUS AT THE RAINBOW** *Polydor 2442 118* ....**23**   5 wks
25 May 74   **HAMBURGER CONCERTO** *Polydor 2442 124* ....**20**   5 wks
9 Aug 75   **FOCUS** *Polydor 2384 070* ....**23**   6 wks

Dan FOGELBERG *US, male vocalist*   **3 wks**

29 Mar 80   **PHOENIX** *Epic EPC 83317*..........................**42**   3 wks

John FOGERTY *US, male vocalist / instrumentalist – guitar*   **11 wks**

16 Feb 85   **CENTERFIELD** *Warner Bros. 9252031* ....**48**   11 wks

F
135

Ellen FOLEY US, female vocalist — 3 wks

17 Nov 79	**NIGHT OUT** Epic EPC 83718	**68**	1 wk
4 Apr 81	**SPIRIT OF ST. LOUIS** Epic EPC 84809	**57**	2 wks

Jane FONDA US, female exercise instructor — 51 wks

29 Jan 83	● **JANE FONDA'S WORKOUT RECORD** CBS 88581	**7**	47 wks
22 Sep 84	**JANE FONDA'S WORKOUT RECORD: NEW AND IMPROVED** CBS 88640	**60**	4 wks

Wayne FONTANA and the MINDBENDERS
UK, male vocalist and male vocal/instrumental group — 1 wk

20 Feb 65	**WAYNE FONTANA AND THE MINDBENDERS** Fontana TL 5230	**18**	1 wk

See also the Mindbenders.

FOO FIGHTERS US, male vocal/instrumental group — 16 wks

8 Jul 95	● **FOO FIGHTERS** Roswell CDSET 2266	**3**	16 wks

Steve FORBERT US, male vocalist — 3 wks

9 Jun 79	**ALIVE ON ARRIVAL** Epic EPC 83308	**56**	1 wk
24 Nov 79	**JACK RABBIT SLIM** Epic EPC 83879	**54**	2 wks

Clinton FORD UK, male vocalist — 4 wks

26 May 62	**CLINTON FORD** Oriole PS 40021	**16**	4 wks

Lita FORD US, female vocalist — 4 wks

26 May 84	**DANCIN' ON THE EDGE** Vertigo VERL 13	**96**	1 wk
23 Jun 90	**STILETTO** RCA PL 82090	**66**	1 wk
25 Jan 92	**DANGEROUS CURVES** RCA PD 90592	**51**	2 wks

Julia FORDHAM UK, female vocalist — 36 wks

18 Jun 88	**JULIA FORDHAM** Circa CIRCA 4	**20**	22 wks
21 Oct 89	**PORCELAIN** Circa CIRCA 10	**13**	5 wks
2 Nov 91	**SWEPT** Circa CIRCA 18	**33**	6 wks
21 May 94	**FALLING FORWARD** Circa CIRCD 28	**21**	3 wks

FOREIGNER UK/US, male vocal/instrumental group — 126 wks

26 Aug 78	**DOUBLE VISION** Atlantic K 50476	**32**	5 wks
25 Jul 81	● **4** Atlantic K 50796	**5**	62 wks
18 Dec 82	**RECORDS** Atlantic A 0999	**58**	11 wks
22 Dec 84	★ **AGENT PROVOCATEUR** Atlantic 7819991	**1**	32 wks
19 Dec 87	**INSIDE INFORMATION** Atlantic WX 143	**64**	7 wks
6 Jul 91	**UNUSUAL HEAT** Atlantic WX 424	**56**	1 wk
2 May 92	**THE VERY BEST OF FOREIGNER** Atlantic 7567805112	**19**	7 wks
12 Nov 94	**MR. MOONLIGHT** Arista 74321232852	**59**	1 wk

49ers Italy, male producer – Gianfranco Bortolotti — 5 wks

10 Mar 90	**THE 49ERS** Fourth & Broadway BRLP 547	**51**	5 wks

FOSTER and ALLEN Ireland, male vocal duo — 162 wks

14 May 83	**MAGGIE** Ritz RITZLP 0012	**72**	6 wks
5 Nov 83	**I WILL LOVE YOU ALL OF MY LIFE** Ritz RITZLP 0015	**71**	6 wks
17 Nov 84	**THE VERY BEST OF FOSTER AND ALLEN** Ritz RITZ LPTV 1	**18**	18 wks
29 Mar 86	**AFTER ALL THESE YEARS** Ritz RITZLP 0032	**82**	2 wks
25 Oct 86	**REMINISCING** Stylus SMR 623	**11**	15 wks

ERASURE was the slowest starting but longest lasting of Vince Clarke's recording configurations.

(LFI)

It is May 1968, and FLEETWOOD MAC (left to right: Mick Fleetwood, Peter Green, Jeremy Spencer and John McVie) are in the charts with their first album.

(Hulton Deutsch)

TOP 30 № 10

TOP 30 № 29

GENESIS are shown in 1979, without Peter Gabriel and with a lot of cows.

(Jill Furmanousky/LFI)

27 Jun 87	**LOVE SONGS – THE VERY BEST OF FOSTER AND ALLEN VOLUME 2** *Ritz RITZLP 0036*	**92**	1 wk
10 Oct 87	**REFLECTIONS** *Stylus SMR 739*	**16**	16 wks
30 Apr 88	**REMEMBER YOU'RE MINE** *Stylus SMR 853*	**16**	15 wks
28 Oct 89	**THE MAGIC OF FOSTER AND ALLEN** *Stylus SMR 989*	**29**	12 wks
9 Dec 89	**THE FOSTER AND ALLEN CHRISTMAS ALBUM** *Stylus SMR 995*	**40**	4 wks
10 Nov 90	**SOUVENIRS** *Telstar STAR 2457*	**15**	12 wks
8 Dec 90	**THE CHRISTMAS COLLECTION** *Telstar STAR 2459*	**44**	4 wks
2 Nov 91	**MEMORIES** *Telstar STAR 2527*	**18**	11 wks
31 Oct 92	**HEART STRINGS** *Telstar TCD 2608*	**37**	10 wks
23 Oct 93	**BY REQUEST** *Telstar TCD 2670*	**14**	12 wks
5 Nov 94	**SONGS WE LOVE TO SING** *Telstar TCD 2741*	**41**	9 wks
4 Nov 95	**100 GOLDEN GREATS** *Telstar TCD 2791*	**30†**	9 wks

FOTHERINGAY UK, male/female vocal/instrumental group **6 wks**

11 Jul 70	**FOTHERINGAY** *Island ILPS 9125*	**18**	6 wks

4 NON BLONDES US, female/male vocal/instrumental group **18 wks**

17 Jul 93	● **BIGGER, BETTER, FASTER, MORE!** *Interscope 7567921122*	**4**	18 wks

4 OF US Ireland, male vocal/instrumental group **1 wk**

20 Mar 93	**MAN ALIVE** *Columbia 4723262*	**64**	1 wk

FOUR PENNIES UK, male vocal/instrumental group **5 wks**

7 Nov 64	**TWO SIDES OF FOUR PENNIES** *Philips BL 7642*	**13**	5 wks

FOUR SEASONS US, male vocal group **62 wks**

6 Jul 63	**SHERRY** *Stateside SL 10033*	**20**	1 wk
10 Apr 71	**EDIZIONE D'ORO** *Philips 6640002*	**11**	7 wks
20 Nov 71	**THE BIG ONES** *Philips 6336208*	**37**	1 wk
6 Mar 76	**THE FOUR SEASONS STORY** *Private Stock DAPS 1001*	**20**	8 wks
6 Mar 76	**WHO LOVES YOU** *Warner Bros. K 56179*	**12**	17 wks
20 Nov 76	● **GREATEST HITS** *K-Tel NE 942*	**4**	6 wks
21 May 88	**THE COLLECTION** *Telstar STAR 2320*	**38**	9 wks
7 Mar 92	● **THE VERY BEST OF FRANKIE VALLI AND THE FOUR SEASONS** *PolyGram TV 5131192* [1]	**7**	13 wks

[1] Frankie Valli and the Four Seasons

4-SKINS UK, male vocal/instrumental group **4 wks**

17 Apr 82	**THE GOOD, THE BAD AND THE 4-SKINS** *Secret SEC 4*	**80**	4 wks

FOUR TOPS US, male vocal group **255 wks**

19 Nov 66	● **FOUR TOPS ON TOP** *Tamla Motown TML 11037*	**9**	23 wks
11 Feb 67	● **FOUR TOPS LIVE!** *Tamla Motown STML 11041*	**4**	72 wks
25 Nov 67	● **REACH OUT** *Tamla Motown STML 11056*	**4**	34 wks
20 Jan 68	★ **GREATEST HITS** *Tamla Motown STML 11061*	**1**	67 wks
8 Feb 69	**YESTERDAY'S DREAMS** *Tamla Motown STML 11087*	**37**	1 wk
27 Jun 70	**STILL WATERS RUN DEEP** *Tamla Motown STML 11149*	**29**	8 wks
29 May 71	● **MAGNIFICENT SEVEN** *Tamla Motown STML 11179* [1]	**6**	11 wks
27 Nov 71	**FOUR TOPS' GREATEST HITS VOLUME 2** *Tamla Motown STML 11195*	**25**	10 wks
10 Nov 73	**THE FOUR TOPS STORY 1964–72** *Tamla Motown TMSP 11241/2*	**35**	5 wks
13 Feb 82	**THE BEST OF THE FOUR TOPS** *K-Tel NE 1160*	**13**	13 wks
8 Dec 90	**THEIR GREATEST HITS** *Telstar STAR 2437*	**47**	6 wks
19 Sep 92	**THE SINGLES COLLECTION** *PolyGram TV 5157102*	**11**	5 wks

[1] Supremes and Four Tops

FOX UK, male/female vocal instrumental group **8 wks**

17 May 75	● **FOX** *GTO GTLP 001*	**7**	8 wks

Samantha FOX *UK, female vocalist*   **18 wks**

26 Jul 86	**TOUCH ME** *Jive HIP 39*	**17**	10 wks
1 Aug 87	**SAMANTHA FOX** *Jive HIP 48*	**22**	6 wks
18 Feb 89	**I WANNA HAVE SOME FUN** *Jive HIP 72*	**46**	2 wks

Bruce FOXTON *UK, male vocalist*   **4 wks**

12 May 84	**TOUCH SENSITIVE** *Arista 206 251*	**68**	4 wks

John FOXX *UK, male vocalist*   **17 wks**

2 Feb 80	**METAMATIX** *Metalbeat V 2146*	**18**	7 wks
3 Oct 81	**THE GARDEN** *Virgin V 2194*	**24**	6 wks
8 Oct 83	**THE GOLDEN SECTION** *Virgin V 2233*	**27**	3 wks
5 Oct 85	**IN MYSTERIOUS WAYS** *Virgin V 2355*	**85**	1 wk

FRAGGLES *UK / US, puppets*   **4 wks**

21 Apr 84	**FRAGGLE ROCK** *RCA PL 70221*	**38**	4 wks

Peter FRAMPTON *UK, male vocalist / instrumentalist – guitar*   **49 wks**

22 May 76	● **FRAMPTON COMES ALIVE** *A & M AMLM 63703*	**6**	39 wks
18 Jun 77	**I'M IN YOU** *A & M AMLK 64039*	**19**	10 wks

Connie FRANCIS *US, female vocalist*   **31 wks**

26 Mar 60	**ROCK 'N' ROLL MILLION SELLERS** *MGM C 804*	**12**	1 wk
11 Feb 61	**CONNIE'S GREATEST HITS** *MGM C 831*	**16**	3 wks
18 Jun 77	★ **20 ALL TIME GREATS** *Polydor 2391 290*	**1**	22 wks
24 Apr 93	**THE SINGLES COLLECTION** *PolyGram TV 5191312*	**12**	5 wks

FRANK AND WALTERS *Ireland, male vocal / instrumental group*   **1 wk**

7 Nov 92	**TRAINS, BOATS AND PLANES** *Setanta 8283692*	**36**	1 wk

FRANKIE GOES TO HOLLYWOOD
UK, male vocal / instrumental group   **91 wks**

10 Nov 84	★ **WELCOME TO THE PLEASUREDOME** *ZTT ZTTIQ 1*	**1**	63 wks
1 Nov 86	● **LIVERPOOL** *ZTT ZTTIQ 8*	**5**	13 wks
30 Oct 93	● **BANG! – THE GREATEST HITS OF FRANKIE GOES TO HOLLYWOOD** *ZTT 4509939122*	**4**	15 wks

Aretha FRANKLIN *US, female vocalist*   **66 wks**

12 Aug 67	**I NEVER LOVED A MAN** *Atlantic 587006*	**36**	2 wks
13 Apr 68	**LADY SOUL** *Atlantic 588099*	**25**	18 wks
14 Sep 68	● **ARETHA NOW** *Atlantic 588114*	**6**	11 wks
18 Jan 86	**WHO'S ZOOMIN' WHO?** *Arista 2072 02*	**49**	12 wks
24 May 86	**THE FIRST LADY OF SOUL** *Stylus SMR 8506*	**89**	1 wk
8 Nov 86	**ARETHA** *Arista 208 020*	**51**	13 wks
3 Jun 89	**THROUGH THE STORM** *Arista 209842*	**46**	1 wk
19 Mar 94	**GREATEST HITS 1980 – 1994** *Arista 74321162022*	**27**	3 wks
29 Oct 94	**QUEEN OF SOUL – THE VERY BEST OF ARETHA FRANKLIN** *Atlantic 8122713962*	**20**	5 wks

Rodney FRANKLIN *US, male instrumentalist – piano*   **2 wks**

24 May 80	**YOU'LL NEVER KNOW** *CBS 83812*	**64**	2 wks

Liz FRASER – *See Harold BUDD/Liz FRASER/Robin GUTHRIE/Simon RAYMONDE*

FRAZIER CHORUS *UK, male / female vocal / instrumental group*   **2 wks**

20 May 89	**SUE** *Virgin V 2578*	**56**	1 wk

16 Mar 91   **RAY** *Virgin VFC 2654* ....**66**   1 wk

FREAK OF NATURE *US / Denmark, male vocal / instrumental group*   **1 wk**

1 Oct 94   **GATHERING OF FREAKS** *Music For Nations CDMFN 169*..............**66**   1 wk

FREAK POWER *UK / Canada, male vocal / instrumental group*   **5 wks**

15 Apr 95   **DRIVE–THRU BOOTY** *Fourth & Broadway BRCDX 606* ....**11**   5 wks

FREDDIE and the DREAMERS
UK, male vocal / instrumental group   **26 wks**

9 Nov 63 ● **FREDDIE AND THE DREAMERS** *Columbia 33SX 1577*.....................**5**   26 wks

FREDERICK – *See NINA and FREDERICK*

FREE *UK, male vocal / instrumental group*   **71 wks**

11 Jul 70 ● **FIRE AND WATER** *Island ILPS 9120* ....**2**   18 wks
23 Jan 71   **HIGHWAY** *Island ILPS 9138* ....**41**   10 wks
26 Jun 71 ● **FREE LIVE!** *Island ILPS 9160* ....**4**   12 wks
17 Jun 72 ● **FREE AT LAST** *Island ILPS 9192* ....**9**   9 wks
3 Feb 73 ● **HEARTBREAKER** *Island ILPS 9217*.......................................**9**   7 wks
16 Mar 74 ● **THE FREE STORY** *Island ISLD 4* ....**2**   6 wks
2 Mar 91 ● **THE BEST OF FREE – ALL RIGHT NOW** *Island ILPTV 2*....................**9**   9 wks

FREE THE SPIRIT *UK, male instrumental duo*   **32 wks**

4 Feb 95 ● **PAN PIPE MOODS** *PolyGram TV 5271972* ....**2**   23 wks
4 Nov 95   **PAN PIPE MOODS TWO** *PolyGram TV 5293952* ....**18†**   9 wks

FREEEZ *UK, male vocal / instrumental group*   **18 wks**

7 Feb 81   **SOUTHERN FREEEZ** *Beggars Banquet BEGA 22* ....**17**   15 wks
22 Oct 83   **GONNA GET YOU** *Beggars Banquet BEGA 48* ....**46**   3 wks

FREHLEY'S COMET *US, male vocal / instrumental group*   **1 wk**

18 Jun 88   **SECOND SIGHT** *Atlantic 781862 1* ....**79**   1 wk

FRESH PRINCE – *See DJ JAZZY JEFF and FRESH PRINCE*

Glenn FREY *US, male vocalist*   **9 wks**

6 Jul 85   **THE ALLNIGHTER** *MCA MCF 3277* ....**31**   9 wks

FRIDA *Norway, female vocalist*   **8 wks**

18 Sep 82   **SOMETHING'S GOING ON** *Epic EPC 85966*................................**18**   7 wks
20 Oct 84   **SHINE** *Epic EPC 26178* ....**67**   1 wk

Dean FRIEDMAN *US, male vocalist*   **14 wks**

21 Oct 78   **WELL, WELL, SAID THE ROCKING CHAIR** *Lifesong LSLP 6019* ....**21**   14 wks

Robert FRIPP *UK, male vocalist / instrumentalist – guitar*   **3 wks**

12 May 79   **EXPOSURE** *Polydor EGLP 101* ....**71**   1 wk
17 Jul 93   **THE FIRST DAY** *Virgin CDVX 2712* 1 ....**21**   2 wks

1 David Sylvian and Robert Fripp

FRONT 242 *Belgium / US, male vocal / instrumental group*   **3 wks**

2 Feb 91   **TYRANNY FOR YOU** *RRE RRE 011* ....**49**   1 wk

| 22 May 93 | **06:21:03:11 UP EVIL** *RRE RRE 021CD* | .....44 | 1 wk |
| 4 Sep 93 | **05:22:09:12 OFF** *RRE RRE 022CD* | .....46 | 1 wk |

FUGAZI *UK, male vocal / instrumental group* — **5 wks**

21 Sep 91	**STEADY DIET OF NOTHING** *Dischord DISCHORD 60*	63	1 wk
19 Jun 93	**IN ON THE KILLTAKER** *Dischord DIS 70CD*	24	2 wks
13 May 95	**RED MEDICINE** *Dischord DIS 90CD*	18	2 wks

FULL FORCE – See LISA LISA and CULT JAM with FULL FORCE

FUN BOY THREE *UK, male vocal / instrumental group* — **40 wks**

| 20 Mar 82 | ● **FUNBOY THREE** *Chrysalis CHR 1383* | .....7 | 20 wks |
| 19 Feb 83 | **WAITING** *Chrysalis CHR 1417* | .....14 | 20 wks |

FUN DA MENTAL *UK, male rap group* — **1 wk**

| 25 Jun 94 | **SEIZE THE TIME** *Nation NATCD 33* | .....74 | 1 wk |

FUNK FEDERATION – See Arlene PHILLIPS

FUNKADELIC *US, male vocal / instrumental group* — **5 wks**

| 23 Dec 78 | **ONE NATION UNDER A GROOVE** *Warner Bros. K 56539* | .....56 | 5 wks |

FUNKDOOBIEST *US, male rap group* — **1 wk**

| 15 Jul 95 | **BROTHAS DOOBIE** *Epic 4783812* | .....62 | 1 wk |

FUNKY BUNCH – See MARKY MARK and the FUNKY BUNCH

FUREYS and Davey ARTHUR
Ireland / UK, male vocal / instrumental group — **38 wks**

8 May 82	**WHEN YOU WERE SWEET SIXTEEN** *Ritz RITZLP 0004*	99	1 wk
10 Nov 84	**GOLDEN DAYS** *K–Tel ONE 1283*	17	19 wks
26 Oct 85	**AT THE END OF THE DAY** *K-Tel ONE 1310*	35	11 wks
21 Nov 87	**FUREYS FINEST** *Telstar HSTAR 2311*	65	7 wks

FURIOUS FIVE – See GRANDMASTER FLASH and the FURIOUS FIVE

Billy FURY *UK, male vocalist* — **51 wks**

4 Jun 60	**THE SOUND OF FURY** *Decca LF 1329*	18	2 wks
23 Sep 61	● **HALFWAY TO PARADISE** *Ace Of Clubs ACL 1083*	5	9 wks
11 May 63	● **BILLY** *Decca LK 4533*	6	21 wks
26 Oct 63	**WE WANT BILLY** *Decca LK 4548*	14	2 wks
19 Feb 83	**HIT PARADE** *Decca TAB 37*	44	15 wks
26 Mar 83	**THE ONE AND ONLY** *Polydor POLD 5069*	54	2 wks

FUSE *Canada, male instrumentalist keyboards, Richie Hawtin* — **1 wk**

| 19 Jun 93 | **DIMENSION INTRUSION** *Warp WARPCD 12* | .....63 | 1 wk |

See also Plastik Man.

FUTURE SOUND OF LONDON *UK, male instrumental duo* — **8 wks**

18 Jul 92	● **ACCELERATOR** *Jumpin' & Pumpin' CDTOT 2*	75	1 wk
4 Jun 94	● **LIFEFORMS** *Virgin CDV 2722*	6	5 wks
17 Dec 94	**ISDN** *Virgin CDV 2755*	62	1 wk
17 Jun 95	**ISDN (REMIX)** *Virgin CDVX 2755*	44	1 wk

FUZZBOX – See WE'VE GOT A FUZZBOX AND WE'RE GONNA USE IT

FYC – See FINE YOUNG CANNIBALS

F 141

G

Kenny G US, *male instrumentalist – saxophone*   **44 wks**

17 Mar 84	**G FORCE** *Arista 206 168*	**56**	5	wks
8 Aug 87	**DUOTONES** *Arista 207 792*	**28**	5	wks
14 Apr 90	**MONTAGE** *Arista 210621*	**32**	7	wks
15 May 93	● **BREATHLESS** *Arista 07822186462*	**4**	27	wks

Warren G US, *male rapper*   **6 wks**

6 Aug 94	**REGULATE . . . G FUNK ERA** *RAL 5233352*	**25**	6	wks

Peter GABRIEL UK, *male vocalist*   **202 wks**

12 Mar 77	● **PETER GABRIEL** *Charisma CDS 4006*	**7**	19	wks
17 Jun 78	● **PETER GABRIEL** *Charisma CDS 4013*	**10**	8	wks
7 Jun 80	★ **PETER GABRIEL** *Charisma CDS 4019*	**1**	18	wks
18 Sep 82	● **PETER GABRIEL** *Charisma PG 4*	**6**	16	wks
18 Jun 83	● **PETER GABRIEL PLAYS LIVE** *Charisma PGDL 1*	**8**	9	wks
30 Apr 85	**BIRDY (film soundtrack)** *Charisma CAS 1167*	**51**	3	wks
31 May 86	★ **SO** *Virgin PG 5*	**1**	76	wks
17 Jun 89	**PASSION** *Virgin RWLP 1*	**29**	5	wks
1 Dec 90	**SHAKING THE TREE – GOLDEN GREATS** *Virgin PGTV 6*	**11**	15	wks
10 Oct 92	● **US** *Realworld PGCD 7*	**2**	29	wks
10 Sep 94	● **SECRET WORLD LIVE** *Realworld PGDCD 8*	**10**	4	wks

First four albums are different.

GABRIELLE UK, *female vocalist*   **22 wks**

30 Oct 93	● **FIND YOUR WAY** *Go.Beat 8284412*	**9**	22	wks

GALAXY – *See Phil FEARON and GALAXY*

GALLAGHER and LYLE UK, *male vocal / instrumental duo*   **44 wks**

28 Feb 76	● **BREAKAWAY** *A & M AMLH 68348*	**6**	35	wks
29 Jan 77	**LOVE ON THE AIRWAYS** *A & M AMLH 64620*	**19**	9	wks

Rory GALLAGHER UK, *male vocalist / instrumentalist – guitar*   **43 wks**

29 May 71	**RORY GALLAGHER** *Polydor 2383044*	**32**	2	wks
4 Dec 71	**DEUCE** *Polydor 2383076*	**39**	1	wk
20 May 72	● **LIVE IN EUROPE** *Polydor 2383 112*	**9**	15	wks
24 Feb 73	**BLUE PRINT** *Polydor 2383 189*	**12**	7	wks
17 Nov 73	**TATTOO** *Polydor 2383 230*	**32**	3	wks
27 Jul 74	**IRISH TOUR '74** *Polydor 2659 031*	**36**	2	wks
30 Oct 76	**CALLING CARD** *Chrysalis CHR 1124*	**32**	1	wk
22 Sep 79	**TOP PRIORITY** *Chrysalis CHR 1235*	**56**	4	wks
8 Nov 80	**STAGE STRUCK** *Chrysalis CHR 1280*	**40**	3	wks
8 May 82	**JINX** *Chrysalis CHR 1359*	**68**	5	wks

GALLIANO UK, *male / female vocal / instrumental group*   **15 wks**

20 Jun 92	**A JOYFUL NOISE UNTO THE CREATOR** *Talkin Loud 8480802*	**28**	3	wks
11 Jun 94	● **THE PLOT THICKENS** *Talkin Loud 5224522*	**7**	12	wks

GALLON DRUNK UK, *male vocal / instrumental group*   **1 wk**

13 Mar 93	**FROM THE HEART OF TOWN** *Clawfist HUNKACDL 005*	**67**	1	wk

James GALWAY *UK, male instrumentalist – flute*   **95 wks**

27 May 78	**THE MAGIC FLUTE OF JAMES GALWAY** RCA Red Seal LRLI 5131 **43**	6 wks
1 Jul 78	**THE MAN WITH THE GOLDEN FLUTE** RCA Red Seal LRLI 5127 ....**52**	3 wks
9 Sep 78	● **JAMES GALWAY PLAYS SONGS FOR ANNIE**	
	RCA Red Seal RL 25163..**7**	40 wks
15 Dec 79	**SONGS OF THE SEASHORE** Solar RL 25253 ....**39**	6 wks
31 May 80	**SOMETIMES WHEN WE TOUCH** RCA PL 25296 [1] **15**	14 wks
18 Dec 82	**THE JAMES GALWAY COLLECTION** Telstar STAR 2224 ....**41**	8 wks
8 Dec 84	**IN THE PINK** RCA Red Seal RL 85315 [2] **62**	6 wks
28 Mar 87	**JAMES GALWAY AND THE CHIEFTAINS IN IRELAND**	
	RCA Red Seal RL 85798 [3] **32**	5 wks
17 Apr 93	**THE ESSENTIAL FLUTE OF JAMES GALWAY**	
	RCA Victor 74321133852 ....**30**	5 wks
18 Feb 95	**I WILL ALWAYS LOVE YOU** RCA Victor 74321262212 ....**59**	2 wks

[1] Cleo Laine and James Galway [2] James Galway and Henry Mancini with the National Philharmonic Orchestra [3] James Galway and the Chieftains

GANG OF FOUR *UK, male vocal / instrumental group*   **9 wks**

13 Oct 79	**ENTERTAINMENT** EMI EMC 3313 ....**45**	3 wks
21 Mar 81	**SOLID GOLD** EMI EMC 3364 ....**52**	2 wks
29 May 82	**SONGS OF THE FREE** EMI EMC 3412.....................................**61**	4 wks

GANG STARR *US, male rap group*   **6 wks**

26 Jan 91	**STEP IN THE ARENA** Cooltempo ZCTLP 21 ....**36**	3 wks
12 Mar 94	**HARD TO EARN** Cooltempo CTCD 38 ....**29**	3 wks

GAP BAND *US, male vocal / instrumental group*   **3 wks**

7 Feb 87	**GAP BAND 8** Total Experience FL 89992 ....**47**	3 wks

GARBAGE *US / UK, male / female vocal / instrumental group*   **8 wks**

14 Oct 95	**GARBAGE** Mushroom D 31450......................................**12†**	8 wks

Art GARFUNKEL *US, male vocalist*   **58 wks**

13 Oct 73	**ANGEL CLARE** CBS 69021 ....**14**	7 wks
1 Nov 75	● **BREAKAWAY** CBS 86002...**7**	10 wks
18 Mar 78	**WATER MARK** CBS 86054.....................................**25**	5 wks
21 Apr 79	● **FATE FOR BREAKFAST** CBS 86082 ....**2**	20 wks
19 Sep 81	**SCISSORS CUT** CBS 85259 ....**51**	3 wks
17 Nov 84	**THE ART GARFUNKEL ALBUM** CBS 10046 ....**12**	13 wks

See also Simon and Garfunkel.

Judy GARLAND *US, female vocalist*   **3 wks**

3 Mar 62	**JUDY AT CARNEGIE HALL** Capitol W 1569 ....**13**	3 wks

Errol GARNER *US, male instrumentalist – piano*   **1 wk**

14 Jul 62	**CLOSE UP IN SWING** Philips BBL 7579 ....**20**	1 wk

Lesley GARRETT *UK, female vocalist*   **13 wks**

12 Feb 94	**THE ALBUM** Telstar TCD 2709..............................**25**	7 wks
18 Nov 95	**SOPRANO IN RED** Silva Classics SILKTVCD 1 ....**59**	6 wks

David GATES *US, male vocalist*   **4 wks**

31 May 75	**NEVER LET HER GO** Elektra K 52012.................................**32**	1 wk
29 Jul 78	**GOODBYE GIRL** Elektra K 52091 ....**28**	3 wks

British Hit Albums Part One

Date of chart entry/Title & catalogue no./Peak position reached/Weeks on chart

★ Number One   ● Top Ten   † still on chart at 30 Dec 1995   □ credited to act billed in footnote

Marvin GAYE US, male vocalist — 174 wks

Date	Title	Peak	Weeks
16 Mar 68	**GREATEST HITS** Tamla Motown STML 11065	40	1 wk
22 Aug 70	**GREATEST HITS** Tamla Motown STML 11153 [1]	60	4 wks
19 Jan 71	● **DIANA AND MARVIN** Tamla Motown STMA 8015 [2]	6	43 wks
10 Nov 73	**LET'S GET IT ON** Tamla Motown STMA 8013	39	1 wk
15 May 76	**I WANT YOU** Tamla Motown STML 12025	22	5 wks
30 Oct 76	**THE BEST OF MARVIN GAYE** Tamla Motown STML 12042	56	1 wk
28 Feb 81	**IN OUR LIFETIME** Motown STML 12149	48	4 wks
29 Aug 81	**DIANA AND MARVIN (re-issue)** Motown STMS 5001 [2]	78	2 wks
20 Nov 82	● **MIDNIGHT LOVE** CBS 85977	10	16 wks
12 Nov 83	**GREATEST HITS** Telstar STAR 2234	13	61 wks
15 Jun 85	**DREAM OF A LIFETIME** CBS 26239	46	4 wks
12 Nov 88	**LOVE SONGS** Telstar STAR 2331 [3]	69	9 wks
2 Nov 90	**LOVE SONGS** Telstar STAR 2427	39	5 wks
9 Apr 94	● **THE VERY BEST OF MARVIN GAYE** Motown 5302922	3	18 wks

[1] Marvin Gaye and Tammi Terrell [2] Diana Ross and Marvin Gaye [3] Marvin Gaye and Smokey Robinson

The Greatest Hits albums are different.

GAYE BYKERS ON ACID UK, male vocal / instrumental group — 1 wk

Date	Title	Peak	Weeks
14 Nov 87	**DRILL YOUR OWN HOLE** Virgin V 2478	95	1 wk

Crystal GAYLE US, female vocalist — 25 wks

Date	Title	Peak	Weeks
21 Jan 78	**WE MUST BELIEVE IN MAGIC** United Artists UAG 30108	15	7 wks
23 Sep 78	**WHEN I DREAM** United Artists UAG 30169	25	8 wks
22 Mar 80	● **THE CRYSTAL GAYLE SINGLES ALBUM** United Artists UAG 30287	7	10 wks

Michelle GAYLE UK, female vocalist — 10 wks

Date	Title	Peak	Weeks
22 Oct 94	**MICHELLE GAYLE** RCA 74321234122	30	10 wks

Gloria GAYNOR US, female vocalist — 17 wks

Date	Title	Peak	Weeks
8 Mar 75	**NEVER CAN SAY GOODBYE** MGM 2315 321	32	8 wks
24 Mar 79	**LOVE TRACKS** Polydor 2391 385	31	7 wks
16 Aug 86	**THE POWER OF GLORIA GAYNOR** Stylus SMR 618	81	2 wks

J. GEILS BAND US, male vocal / instrumental group — 15 wks

Date	Title	Peak	Weeks
27 Feb 82	**FREEZE FRAME** EMI America AML 3020	12	15 wks

Bob GELDOF Ireland, male vocalist — 10 wks

Date	Title	Peak	Weeks
6 Dec 86	**DEEP IN THE HEART OF NOWHERE** Mercury BOBLP 1	79	1 wk
4 Aug 90	**THE VEGETARIANS OF LOVE** Mercury 8462501	21	6 wks
9 Jul 94	● **LOUDMOUTH – THE BEST OF THE BOOMTOWN RATS AND BOB GELDOF** Vertigo 5222832 [1]	10	3 wks

[1] Boomtown Rats and Bob Geldof

GENE UK, male vocal / instrumental group — 6 wks

Date	Title	Peak	Weeks
1 Apr 95	● **OLYMPIAN** Costermonger 5274462	8	6 wks

GENE LOVES JEZEBEL UK, male vocal / instrumental group — 5 wks

Date	Title	Peak	Weeks
19 Jul 87	**DISCOVER** Beggars Banquet BEGA 73	32	4 wks

| 24 Oct 87 | **HOUSE OF DOLLS** Beggars Banquet BEGA 87 | **81** | 1 wk |

GENERATION X *UK, male vocal / instrumental group* **9 wks**

| 8 Apr 78 | **GENERATION X** Chrysalis CHR 1169 | **29** | 4 wks |
| 17 Feb 79 | **VALLEY OF THE DOLLS** Chrysalis CHR 1193 | **51** | 5 wks |

GENESIS *UK, male vocal / instrumental group* **468 wks**

14 Oct 72	**FOXTROT** Charisma CAS 1058	**12**	7 wks
11 Aug 73	● **GENESIS LIVE** Charisma CLASS 1	**9**	10 wks
20 Oct 73	● **SELLING ENGLAND BY THE POUND** Charisma CAS 1074	**3**	21 wks
11 May 74	**NURSERY CRYME** Charisma CAS 1052	**39**	1 wk
7 Dec 74	● **THE LAMB LIES DOWN ON BROADWAY** Charisma CGS 101	**10**	6 wks
28 Feb 76	● **A TRICK OF THE TAIL** Charisma CDS 4001	**3**	39 wks
15 Jan 77	● **WIND AND WUTHERING** Charisma CDS 4005	**7**	22 wks
29 Oct 77	● **SECONDS OUT** Charisma GE 2001	**4**	17 wks
15 Apr 78	● **AND THEN THERE WERE THREE** Charisma CDS 4010	**3**	32 wks
5 Apr 80	★ **DUKE** Charisma CBR 101	**1**	30 wks
26 Sep 81	★ **ABACAB** Charisma CBR 102	**1**	27 wks
12 Jun 82	● **3 SIDES LIVE** Charisma GE 2002	**2**	19 wks
15 Oct 83	★ **GENESIS** Charisma GENLP 1	**1**	51 wks
31 Mar 84	**NURSERY CRYME (re-issue)** Charisma CHC 22	**68**	1 wk
21 Apr 84	**TRESPASS** Charisma CHC 12	**98**	1 wk
21 Jun 86	★ **INVISIBLE TOUCH** Charisma GENLP 2	**1**	96 wks
23 Nov 91	★ **WE CAN'T DANCE** Virgin GENLP 3	**1**	61 wks
28 Nov 92	● **LIVE – THE WAY WE WALK VOLUME 1: THE SHORTS** Virgin GENCD 4	**3**	18 wks
23 Jan 93	★ **LIVE – THE WAY WE WALK VOLUME 2: THE LONGS** Virgin GENCD 5	**1**	9 wks

GENIUS/GZA *US, male rapper* **1 wk**

| 2 Dec 95 | **LIQUID SWORDS** Geffen GED 24813 | **73** | 1 wk |

Jackie GENOVA *UK, female exercise instructor* **2 wks**

| 21 May 83 | **WORK THAT BODY** Island ILPS 9732 | **74** | 2 wks |

Bobbie GENTRY *US, female vocalist* **2 wks**

| 25 Oct 69 | **TOUCH 'EM WITH LOVE** Capitol EST 155 | **21** | 1 wk |
| 28 Feb 70 | **BOBBIE GENTRY AND GLEN CAMPBELL** Capitol ST 2928 [1] | **50** | 1 wk |

[1] Bobbie Gentry and Glen Campbell

Lowell GEORGE *US, male vocalist / instrumentalist – guitar* **1 wk**

| 21 Apr 79 | **THANKS BUT I'LL EAT IT HERE** Warner Bros. K 56487 | **71** | 1 wk |

Robin GEORGE *UK, male vocal / instrumentalist – guitar* **3 wks**

| 2 Mar 85 | **DANGEROUS MUSIC** Bronze BRON 554 | **65** | 3 wks |

GEORGIA SATELLITES *US, male vocal / instrumental group* **9 wks**

| 7 Feb 87 | **GEORGIA SATELLITES** Elektra 980 4961 | **52** | 7 wks |
| 2 Jul 88 | **OPEN ALL NIGHT** Elektra EKT 47 | **39** | 2 wks |

GERRY and the PACEMAKERS
UK, male vocal / instrumental group **29 wks**

| 26 Oct 63 | ● **HOW DO YOU LIKE IT?** Columbia 33SX 1546 | **2** | 28 wks |
| 6 Feb 65 | **FERRY CROSS THE MERSEY** Columbia 33SX 1676 | **19** | 1 wk |

Stan GETZ and Charlie BYRD
US, male instrumental duo – saxophone and guitar **7 wks**

| 23 Feb 63 | **JAZZ SAMBA** Verve SULP 9013 | **15** | 7 wks |

Andy GIBB UK, male vocalist — **9 wks**

19 Aug 78	**SHADOW DANCING** RSO RSS 0001	**15**	9 wks

Barry GIBB UK, male vocalist — **2 wks**

20 Oct 84	**NOW VOYAGER** Polydor POLH 14	**85**	2 wks

Steve GIBBONS BAND UK, male vocal / instrumental group — **3 wks**

22 Oct 77	**CAUGHT IN THE ACT** Polydor 2478 112	**22**	3 wks

Debbie GIBSON US, female vocalist — **52 wks**

30 Jan 88	**OUT OF THE BLUE** Atlantic WX 139	**26**	35 wks
11 Feb 89 ●	**ELECTRIC YOUTH** Atlantic WX 231	**8**	16 wks
30 Mar 91	**ANYTHING IS POSSIBLE** Atlantic WX 399	**69**	1 wk

Don GIBSON US, male vocalist — **10 wks**

22 Mar 80	**COUNTRY NUMBER ONE** Warwick WW 5079	**13**	10 wks

GIBSON BROTHERS Martinique, male vocal / instrumental group — **3 wks**

30 Aug 80	**ON THE RIVIERA** Island ILPS 9620	**50**	3 wks

Johnny GILL US, male vocalist — **3 wks**

19 Jun 93	**PROVOCATIVE** Motown 5302062	**41**	3 wks

GILLAN UK, male vocal / instrumental group — **53 wks**

17 Jul 76	**CHILD IN TIME** Polydor 2490 136 [1]	**55**	1 wk
20 Oct 79	**MR. UNIVERSE** Acrobat ACRO 3	**11**	6 wks
16 Aug 80 ●	**GLORY ROAD** Virgin V 2171	**3**	12 wks
25 Apr 81 ●	**FUTURE SHOCK** Virgin VK 2196	**2**	13 wks
7 Nov 81	**DOUBLE TROUBLE** Virgin VGD 3506	**12**	15 wks
2 Oct 82	**MAGIC** Virgin V 2238	**17**	6 wks

[1] Ian Gillan Band

See also Ian Gillan.

Ian GILLAN UK, male vocalist — **1 wk**

28 Jul 90	**NAKED THUNDER** Teldec 9031718991	**63**	1 wk

See also Gillan.

David GILMOUR UK, male instrumentalist – guitar — **18 wks**

10 Jun 78	**DAVID GILMOUR** Harvest SHVL 817	**17**	9 wks
17 Mar 84	**ABOUT FACE** Harvest SHSP 2400791	**21**	9 wks

Gordon GILTRAP UK, male instrumentalist – guitar — **7 wks**

18 Feb 78	**PERILOUS JOURNEY** Electric TRIX 4	**29**	7 wks

GIN BLOSSOMS US, male vocal / instrumental group — **4 wks**

26 Feb 94	**NEW MISERABLE EXPERIENCE** Fontana 3954032	**53**	4 wks

GIPSY KINGS France, male vocal / instrumental group — **55 wks**

15 Apr 89	**GIPSY KINGS** Telstar STAR 2355	**16**	29 wks
25 Nov 89	**MOSAIQUE** Telstar STAR 2398	**27**	13 wks
13 Jul 91	**ESTE MUNDO** Columbia 4686481	**19**	7 wks

G
146

6 Aug 94	**GREATEST HITS** Columbia 4772422	**11**	6 wks

GIRL *UK, male vocal / instrumental group*   **6 wks**

9 Feb 80	**SHEER GREED** Jet JETLP 224..	**33**	5 wks
23 Jan 82	**WASTED YOUTH** Jet JETLP 238..	**92**	1 wk

GIRLS AT OUR BEST *UK, male / female vocal / instrumental group*   **3 wks**

7 Nov 81	**PLEASURE** Happy Birthday RVLP 1	**60**	3 wks

GIRLSCHOOL *UK, female vocal / instrumental group*   **23 wks**

5 Jul 80	**DEMOLITION** Bronze BRON 525..	**28**	10 wks
25 Apr 81	● **HIT 'N' RUN** Bronze BRON 534	**5**	6 wks
12 Jun 82	**SCREAMING BLUE MURDER** Bronze BRON 541	**27**	6 wks
12 Nov 83	**PLAY DIRTY** Bronze BRON 548..	**66**	1 wk

Gary GLITTER *UK, male vocalist*   **100 wks**

21 Oct 72	● **GLITTER** Bell BELLS 216	**8**	40 wks
16 Jun 73	● **TOUCH ME** Bell BELLS 222	**2**	33 wks
29 Jun 74	● **REMEMBER ME THIS WAY** Bell BELLS 237	**5**	14 wks
27 Mar 76	**GARY GLITTER'S GREATEST HITS** Bell BELLS 262	**33**	5 wks
14 Nov 92	**MANY HAPPY RETURNS – THE HITS** EMI CDEMTV 68	**35**	8 wks

GLITTER BAND *UK, male vocal / instrumental group*   **17 wks**

14 Sep 74	**HEY** Bell BELLS 241..	**13**	12 wks
3 May 75	**ROCK 'N' ROLL DUDES** Bell BELLS 253	**17**	4 wks
19 Jun 76	**GREATEST HITS** Bell BELLS 264	**52**	1 wk

GLOVE *UK, male vocal / instrumental group*   **3 wks**

17 Sep 83	**BLUE SUNSHINE** Wonderland SHELP 2	**35**	3 wks

GO-BETWEENS *Australia, male / female vocal / instrumental group*   **2 wks**

13 Jun 87	**TALLULAH** Beggars Banquet BEGA 81	**91**	1 wk
10 Sep 88	**16 LOVERS LANE** Beggars Banquet BEGA 95	**81**	1 wk

GO-GO'S *US, female vocal / instrumental group*   **4 wks**

21 Aug 82	**VACATION** IRS SP 70031	**75**	3 wks
18 Mar 95	**RETURN TO THE VALLEY OF THE GO-GOS** IRS EIRSCD 1071	**52**	1 wk

GO WEST *UK, male vocal / instrumental duo*   **119 wks**

13 Apr 85	● **GO WEST / BANGS AND CRASHES** Chrysalis CHR 1495	**8**	83 wks
6 Jun 87	**DANCING ON THE COUCH** Chrysalis CDL 1550...............................	**19**	5 wks
14 Nov 92	**INDIAN SUMMER** Chrysalis CDCHR 1964	**13**	16 wks
16 Oct 93	● **ACES AND KINGS – THE BEST OF GO WEST** Chrysalis CDCHR 6050..	**5**	15 wks

Bangs And Crashes *is an album of remixed versions of Go West tracks and some new material. From 31 May 1986 both records were available together as a double album.*

GOATS *US, male rap group*   **1 wk**

27 Aug 94	**NO GOATS NO GLORY** Columbia 4769372	**58**	1 wk

GOD MACHINE *US, male vocal / instrumental group*   **1 wk**

20 Feb 93	**SCENES FROM THE SECOND STOREY** Fiction 5171562	**55**	1 wk

GODFATHERS *UK, male vocal / instrumental group*   **3 wks**

13 Feb 88	**BIRTH SCHOOL WORK DEATH** Epic 460263 1..................................	**80**	2 wks

20 May 89   **MORE SONGS ABOUT LOVE AND HATE** Epic 463394 1 ....**49**   1   wk

GODLEY and CREME UK, male vocal / instrumental duo   **34 wks**

19 Nov 77	**CONSEQUENCES** Mercury CONS 017 ....**52**	1	wk
9 Sep 78	**L** Mercury 9109 611 ....**47**	2	wks
17 Oct 81	**ISMISM** Polydor POLD 5043 ....**29**	13	wks
29 Aug 87	● **CHANGING FACES – THE VERY BEST OF 10 C.C. AND**		
	GODLEY AND CREME ProTV TGCLP 1 1 ....**4**	18	wks

1   10 C.C. and Godley and Creme

Andrew GOLD US, male vocalist / instrumentalist – piano   **7 wks**

15 Apr 78   **ALL THIS AND HEAVEN TOO** Asylum K 53072................**31**   7   wks

GOLDEN EARRING Holland, male vocal / instrumental group   **4 wks**

2 Feb 74   **MOONTAN** Track 2406 112 ....**24**   4   wks

GOLDIE UK, male producer   **9 wks**

19 Aug 95   ● **TIMELESS** ffrr 8286142 ....**7**   9   wks

Glen GOLDSMITH UK, male vocalist   **9 wks**

23 Jul 88   **WHAT YOU SEE IS WHAT YOU GET** RCA PL 71750 ....**14**   9   wks

GOODBYE MR. MACKENZIE
UK, male / female vocal / instrumental group   **4 wks**

22 Apr 89	**GOOD DEEDS AND DIRTY RAGS** Capitol EST 2089 ....**26**	3	wks
16 Mar 91	**HAMMER AND TONGS** Radioactive RAR 10227..................**61**	1	wk

GOODIES UK, male vocal group   **11 wks**

8 Nov 75   **THE NEW GOODIES LP** Bradley's BRADL 1010 ....**25**   11   wks

Benny GOODMAN US, male instrumentalist – clarinet   **1 wk**

3 Apr 71   **BENNY GOODMAN TODAY** Decca DDS 3........................**49**   1   wk

Ron GOODWIN UK, orchestra   **1 wk**

2 May 70   **LEGEND OF THE GLASS MOUNTAIN** Studio Two TWO 220 ....**49**   1   wk

GOOMBAY DANCE BAND
Germany / Montserrat, male / female vocal group   **9 wks**

10 Apr 82   **SEVEN TEARS** Epic EPC 85702 ....**16**   9   wks

GOONS UK, male comedy group   **31 wks**

28 Nov 59	● **BEST OF THE GOON SHOWS** Parlophone PMC 1108 ....**8**	14	wks
17 Dec 60	**BEST OF THE GOON SHOWS VOLUME 2** Parlophone PMC 1129..**12**	6	wks
4 Nov 72	● **LAST GOON SHOW OF ALL** BBC Radio Enterprise REB 142.............**8**	11	wks

GORDON – See PETER and GORDON

Martin L. GORE UK, male vocalist / instrumentalist – keyboards   **1 wk**

24 Jun 89   **COUNTERFEIT E.P.** Mute STUMM 67 ....**51**   1   wk

Jaki GRAHAM UK, female vocalist   **10 wks**

14 Sep 85	**HEAVEN KNOWS** EMI JK 1 ....**48**	5	wks
20 Sep 86	**BREAKING AWAY** EMI EMC 3514 ....**25**	5	wks

G

148

GRAND PRIX *UK, male vocal / instrumental group*
2 wks

18 Jun 83	**SAMURAI** Chrysalis CHR 1430	65	2 wks

GRANDMASTER FLASH and the FURIOUS FIVE
US, male vocalist and male vocal group
20 wks

23 Oct 82	**THE MESSAGE** Sugar Hill SHLP 1007	77	3 wks
23 Jun 84	**GREATEST MESSAGES** Sugar Hill SHLP 5552	41	16 wks
23 Feb 85	**THEY SAID IT COULDN'T BE DONE** Elektra 9603891	95	1 wk

GRANDMASTER MELLE MEL *US, male vocalist*
5 wks

20 Oct 84	**WORK PARTY** Sugar Hill SHLP 5553	45	5 wks

Amy GRANT *US, female vocalist*
15 wks

22 Jun 91	**HEART IN MOTION** A & M 3953211	25	15 wks

David GRANT *UK, male vocalist*
7 wks

5 Nov 83	**DAVID GRANT** Chrysalis CHR 1448	32	6 wks
18 May 85	**HOPES AND DREAMS** Chrysalis CHR 1483	96	1 wk

Eddy GRANT *Guyana, male vocalist / multi-instrumentalist*
47 wks

30 May 81	**CAN'T GET ENOUGH** Ice ICELP 21	39	6 wks
27 Nov 82	● **KILLER ON THE RAMPAGE** Ice ICELP 3023	7	23 wks
17 Nov 84	**ALL THE HITS** K-Tel NE 1284	23	10 wks
1 Jul 89	**WALKING ON SUNSHINE (THE BEST OF EDDY GRANT)** Parlophone PCSD 108	20	8 wks

GRANT LEE BUFFALO *US, male vocal / instrumental group*
3 wks

10 Jul 93	**FUZZY** Slash 8283892	74	1 wk
1 Oct 94	**MIGHTY JOE MOON** Slash 8285412	24	2 wks

GRATEFUL DEAD *US, male vocal / instrumental group*
12 wks

19 Sep 70	**WORKINGMAN'S DEAD** Warner Bros. WS 1869	69	2 wks
3 Aug 74	**GRATEFUL DEAD FROM THE MARS HOTEL** Atlantic K 59302	47	1 wk
1 Nov 75	**BLUES FOR ALLAH** United Artists UAS 29895	45	1 wk
4 Sep 76	**STEAL YOUR FACE** United Artists UAS 60131/2	42	1 wk
20 Aug 77	**TERRAPIN STATION** Arista SPARTY 1016	30	1 wk
19 Sep 87	**IN THE DARK** Arista 208 564	57	3 wks
18 Feb 89	**DYLAN AND THE DEAD** CBS 4633811 [1]	38	3 wks

[1] Bob Dylan and the Grateful Dead

David GRAY and Tommy TYCHO *UK, male arrangers*
6 wks

16 Oct 76	**ARMCHAIR MELODIES** K-Tel NE 927	21	6 wks

Alltrina GRAYSON – See Wilton FELDER

GREAT WHITE *US, male vocal / instrumental group*
1 wk

9 Mar 91	**HOOKED** Capitol EST 2138	43	1 wk

Al GREEN *US, male vocalist*
25 wks

26 Apr 75	**AL GREEN'S GREATEST HITS** London SHU 8481	18	16 wks
1 Oct 88	**HI LIFE – THE BEST OF AL GREEN** K-Tel NE 1420	34	7 wks
24 Oct 92	**AL** Beechwood AGREECD 1	41	2 wks

Peter GREEN *UK, male vocalist / instrumentalist – guitar*
17 wks

9 Jul 79	**IN THE SKIES** Creole PULS 101	32	13 wks

24 May 80   **LITTLE DREAMER** *PUK PULS 102* ....**34**   4 wks

Robson GREEN and Jerome FLYNN *UK, male vocal duo*   **6 wks**

25 Nov 95 ★ **ROBSON AND JEROME** *RCA 74321323902* ....**1†**   6 wks

GREEN DAY *US, male vocal / instrumental group*   **49 wks**

5 Nov 94   **DOOKIE** *Reprise 9362457952* ....**13**   44 wks
21 Oct 95 ● **INSOMNIAC** *Reprise 936240462* ....**8**   5 wks

GREEN JELLY *US, male vocal / instrumental group*   **10 wks**

3 Jul 93   **CEREAL KILLER SOUNDTRACK** *Zoo 72445110382* ....**18**   10 wks

GREEN ON RED *US, male vocal / instrumental group*   **1 wk**

26 Oct 85   **NO FREE LUNCH** *Mercury MERM 78* ....**99**   1 wk

Dave GREENFIELD – See *Jean–Jacques BURNEL*

GREENSLADE *UK, male vocal / instrumental group*   **3 wks**

14 Sep 74   **SPYGLASS GUEST** *Warner Bros. K 56055* ....**34**   3 wks

Christina GREGG *UK, female exercise instructor*   **1 wk**

27 May 78   **MUSIC 'N' MOTION** *Warwick WW 5041* ....**51**   1 wk

GRID *UK, male instrumental duo*   **4 wks**

1 Oct 94   **EVOLVER** *Deconstruction 74321227182* ....**14**   3 wks
14 Oct 95   **MUSIC FOR DANCING** *Deconstruction 74321276702* ....**67**   1 wk

Nanci GRIFFITH *US, female vocalist*   **23 wks**

28 Mar 88   **LITTLE LOVE AFFAIRS** *MCA MCF 3413* ....**78**   1 wk
23 Sep 89   **STORMS** *MCA MCG 6066* ....**38**   3 wks
28 Sep 91   **LATE NIGHT GRANDE HOTEL** *MCA MCA 10306* ....**40**   5 wks
20 Mar 93   **OTHER VOICES / OTHER ROOMS** *MCA MCD 10796* ....**18**   6 wks
13 Nov 93   **THE BEST OF NANCI GRIFFITH** *MCA MCD 10966* ....**27**   4 wks
1 Oct 94   **FLYER** *MCA MCD 11155* ....**20**   4 wks

GROUNDHOGS *UK, male vocal / instrumental group*   **50 wks**

6 Jun 70 ● **THANK CHRIST FOR THE BOMB** *Liberty LBS 83295* ....**9**   13 wks
3 Apr 71 ● **SPLIT** *Liberty LBG 83401* ....**5**   27 wks
18 Mar 72 ● **WHO WILL SAVE THE WORLD** *United Artists UAG 29237*...............**8**   9 wks
13 Jul 74   **SOLID** *WWA WWA 004* ....**31**   1 wk

Sir Charles GROVES – See *ROYAL PHILHARMONIC ORCHESTRA*

GTR *UK, male vocal / instrumental group*   **4 wks**

19 Jul 86   **GTR** *Arista 207 716* ....**41**   4 wks

GUILDFORD CATHEDRAL CHOIR *UK, choir*   **4 wks**

10 Dec 66   **CHRISTMAS CAROLS FROM GUILDFORD CATHEDRAL**
            MFP 1104..**24**   4 wks

Record credits Barry Rose as conductor.

GUITAR CORPORATION *UK, male instrumental group*   **5 wks**

15 Feb 92   **IMAGES** *Quality Television QTVCD 002* ....**41**   5 wks

ROBSON GREEN AND JEROME FLYNN celebrate, not a ceasefire in *Soldier Soldier*, but reaching number one with their debut album.

(David Fisher/LFI)

GUN UK, male vocal / instrumental group   **21 wks**

22 Jul 89	**TAKING ON THE WORLD** A & M AMA 7007	.....**44**	10 wks
18 Apr 92	**GALLUS** A & M 3953832	.....**14**	4 wks
13 Aug 94	● **SWAGGER** A & M 5402542	.....**5**	7 wks

GUNS N' ROSES US, male vocal / instrumental group   **351 wks**

1 Aug 87	● **APPETITE FOR DESTRUCTION** Geffen WX 125	.....**5**	137 wks
17 Dec 88	**G N' R LIES . . .** Geffen WX 218	.....**22**	41 wks
28 Sep 91	● **USE YOUR ILLUSION I** Geffen GEF 24415	.....**2**	81 wks
28 Sep 91	★ **USE YOUR ILLUSION II** Geffen GEF 24420	.....**1**	82 wks
4 Dec 93	● **THE SPAGHETTI INCIDENT?** Geffen GED 24617	.....**2**	10 wks

GUNSHOT UK, male rap group   **1 wk**

19 Jun 93	**PATRIOT GAMES** Vinyl Solution STEAM 43CD	.....**60**	1 wk

David GUNSON UK, male after dinner speaker   **2 wks**

25 Dec 82	**WHAT GOES UP MIGHT COME DOWN** Big Ben BB 0012	.....**92**	2 wks

GURU US, male vocalist   **11 wks**

29 May 93	**JAZZAMATAZZ** Cooltempo CTCD 34	.....**58**	2 wks
15 Jul 95	**JAZZAMATAZZ VOLUME II – THE NEW REALITY** Cooltempo CTCD 47	.....**12**	9 wks

GURU JOSH UK, male producer   **2 wks**

14 Jul 90	**INFINITY** Deconstruction PL 74701	.....**41**	2 wks

G.U.S. (FOOTWEAR) BAND and the MORRISTOWN ORPHEUS CHOIR UK, male instrumental group and male / female vocal group   **1 wk**

3 Oct 70	**LAND OF HOPE AND GLORY** Columbia SCX 6406	.....**54**	1 wk

Arlo GUTHRIE US, male vocalist   **1 wk**

7 Mar 70	**ALICE'S RESTAURANT** Reprise RSLP 6267	.....**44**	1 wk

Gwen GUTHRIE US, female vocalist   **14 wks**

23 Aug 86	**GOOD TO GO LOVER** Boiling Point POLD 5201	.....**42**	14 wks

Robin GUTHRIE – See Harold BUDD/Liz FRASER/Robin GUTHRIE/Simon RAYMONDE

Buddy GUY US, male vocalist / instrumentalist – guitar   **9 wks**

22 Jun 91	**DAMN RIGHT I'VE GOT THE BLUES** Silvertone ORELP 516	.....**43**	5 wks
13 Mar 93	**FEELS LIKE RAIN** Silvertone ORECD 525	.....**36**	4 wks

A GUY CALLED GERALD UK, male multi–instrumentalist   **2 wks**

14 Apr 90	**AUTOMANIKK** Subscape 4664821	.....**68**	1 wk
1 Apr 95	**BLACK SECRET TECHNOLOGY** Juice Box JBCD 25	.....**64**	1 wk

GUYS 'N' DOLLS UK, male / female vocal group   **1 wk**

31 May 75	**GUYS 'N' DOLLS** Magnet MAG 5005	.....**43**	1 wk

GWENT CHORALE – See Bryn YEM

Steve HACKETT *UK, male vocalist / instrumentalist – guitar* **38 wks**

1 Nov 75	**VOYAGE OF THE ACOLYTE** *Charisma CAS 1111*	26	4 wks
6 May 78	**PLEASE DON'T TOUCH** *Charisma CDS 4012*	38	5 wks
26 May 79	**SPECTRAL MORNINGS** *Charisma CDS 4017*	22	11 wks
21 Jun 80	● **DEFECTOR** *Charisma CDS 4018*	9	7 wks
29 Aug 81	**CURED** *Charisma CDS 4021*	15	5 wks
30 Apr 83	**HIGHLY STRUNG** *Charisma HACK 1*	16	3 wks
19 Nov 83	**BAY OF KINGS** *Lamborghini LMGLP 3000*	70	1 wk
22 Sep 84	**TILL WE HAVE FACES** *Lamborghini LMGLP 4000*	54	2 wks

HADDAWAY *Trinidad, male vocalist* **16 wks**

23 Oct 93	● **HADDAWAY – THE ALBUM** *Logic 74321169222*	9	16 wks

Sammy HAGAR *US, male vocalist / instrumentalist guitar* **19 wks**

29 Sep 79	**STREET MACHINE** *Capitol EST 11983*	38	4 wks
22 Mar 80	**LOUD AND CLEAR** *Capitol EST 25330*	12	8 wks
7 Jun 80	**DANGER ZONE** *Capitol EST 12069*	25	3 wks
13 Feb 82	**STANDING HAMPTON** *Geffen GEF 85456*	84	2 wks
4 Jul 87	**SAMMY HAGAR** *Geffen WX 114*	86	2 wks

See also Hagar, Schon, Aaronson, Shrieve.

HAGAR, SCHON, AARONSON, SHRIEVE
US, male vocal / instrumental group **1 wk**

19 May 84	**THROUGH THE FIRE** *Geffen GEF 25893*	92	1 wk

See also Sammy Hagar.

Paul HAIG *UK, male vocalist* **2 wks**

22 Oct 83	**RHYTHM OF LIFE** *Crepuscule ILPS 9742*	82	2 wks

HAIRCUT 100 *UK, male vocal / instrumental group* **34 wks**

6 Mar 82	● **PELICAN WEST** *Arista HCC 100*	2	34 wks

Bill HALEY and his COMETS *US, male vocal / instrumental group* **5 wks**

18 May 68	**ROCK AROUND THE CLOCK** *Ace Of Hearts AH 13*	34	5 wks

HALF MAN HALF BISCUIT *UK, male vocal / instrumental group* **14 wks**

8 Feb 86	**BACK IN THE DHSS** *Probe Plus PROBE 4*	60	9 wks
21 Feb 87	**BACK AGAIN IN THE DHSS** *Probe Plus PROBE 8*	59	5 wks

Daryl HALL *US, male vocalist* **9 wks**

23 Aug 86	**THREE HEARTS IN THE HAPPY ENDING MACHINE** *RCA PL 87196*	26	5 wks
23 Oct 93	**SOUL ALONE** *Epic 4732912*	55	4 wks

See also Daryl Hall and John Oates.

Daryl HALL and John OATES *US, male vocal duo* **150 wks**

3 Jul 76	**HALL AND OATES** *RCA Victor APLI 1144*	56	1 wk
18 Sep 76	**BIGGER THAN BOTH OF US** *RCA Victor APLI 1467*	25	7 wks
15 Oct 77	**BEAUTY ON A BACK STREET** *RCA PL 12300*	40	2 wks
6 Feb 82	● **PRIVATE EYES** *RCA RCALP 6001*	8	21 wks

23 Oct 82	**H$_2$O** RCA RCALP 6056 ....**24**	35 wks
29 Oct 83	**ROCK 'N' SOUL (PART 1)** RCA PL 84858 ....**16**	45 wks
27 Oct 84	**BIG BAM BOOM** RCA PL 85309 ....**28**	13 wks
28 Sep 85	**LIVE AT THE APOLLO WITH DAVID RUFFIN AND**	
	EDDIE KENDRICK RCA PL 87035 ....**32**	5 wks
18 Jun 88	**OOH YEAH!** RCA 208895 ....**52**	3 wks
27 Oct 90	**CHANGE OF SEASON** Arista 210548 ....**44**	2 wks
19 Oct 91	● **THE BEST OF HALL AND OATES – LOOKING BACK**	
	Arista PL 90388 ....**9**	16 wks

See also Daryl Hall.

HALO JAMES UK, male vocal / instrumental group   **4 wks**

| 14 Apr 90 | **WITNESS** Epic 466761 ....**18** | 4 wks |

HAMBURG STUDENTS' CHOIR Germany, male vocal group   **6 wks**

| 17 Dec 60 | **HARK THE HERALD ANGELS SING** Pye GGL 0023.................**11** | 6 wks |

George HAMILTON IV US, male vocalist   **11 wks**

10 Apr 71	**CANADIAN PACIFIC** RCA SF 8062 ....**45**	1 wk
10 Feb 79	**REFLECTIONS** Lotus WH 5008...**25**	9 wks
13 Nov 82	**SONGS FOR A WINTER'S NIGHT** Ronco RTL 2082 ....**94**	1 wk

HAMMER – See MC HAMMER

Jan HAMMER Czechoslovakia, male instrumentalist – keyboards   **12 wks**

| 14 Nov 87 | **ESCAPE FROM TV** MCA MCF 3407......................................**34** | 12 wks |

Herbie HANCOCK US, male vocalist / instrumentalist – keyboards   **24 wks**

9 Sep 78	**SUNLIGHT** CBS 82240...**27**	6 wks
24 Feb 79	**FEETS DON'T FAIL ME NOW** CBS 83491 ....**28**	8 wks
27 Aug 83	**FUTURE SHOCK** CBS 25540..**27**	10 wks

Tony HANCOCK UK, male comedian   **51 wks**

9 Apr 60	● **THIS IS HANCOCK** Pye NPL 10845 ....**2**	22 wks
12 Nov 60	**PIECES OF HANCOCK** Pye NPL 18054 ....**17**	2 wks
3 Mar 62	**HANCOCK** Pye NPL 18068 ....**12**	23 wks
14 Sep 63	**THIS IS HANCOCK (re-issue)** Pye Golden Guinea GGL 0206 ....**16**	4 wks

Vernon HANDLEY – See Nigel KENNEDY

Bo HANNSON Sweden, multi–instrumentalist   **2 wks**

| 18 Nov 72 | **LORD OF THE RINGS** Charisma CAS 1059 ....**34** | 2 wks |

HANOI ROCKS Finland / UK, male vocal / instrumental group   **4 wks**

| 11 Jun 83 | **BACK TO MYSTERY CITY** Lick LICLP 1 ....**87** | 1 wk |
| 20 Oct 84 | **TWO STEPS FROM THE MOVE** CBS 26066 ....**28** | 3 wks |

John HANSON UK, male vocalist   **12 wks**

23 Apr 60	**THE STUDENT PRINCE** Pye NPL 18046..............................**17**	1 wk
2 Sep 61	● **THE STUDENT PRINCE / VAGABOND KING** Pye GGL 0086 ....**9**	7 wks
10 Dec 77	**JOHN HANSON SINGS 20 SHOWTIME GREATS** K-Tel NE 1002 ....**16**	4 wks

HAPPY MONDAYS UK, male vocal / instrumental group   **50 wks**

27 Jan 90	**BUMMED** Factory FACT 220 ....**59**	14 wks
17 Nov 90	● **PILLS 'N' THRILLS AND BELLYACHES** Factory FACT 320 ....**4**	28 wks
12 Oct 91	**LIVE** Factory FACT 322 ....**21**	3 wks

10 Oct 92	. . . YES PLEASE! *Factory FACD 420*	14	3 wks
18 Nov 95	LOADS – THE BEST OF THE HAPPY MONDAYS		
	Factory Once 5203432	41	2 wks

HAPPY PIANO – *See Brian SMITH and his HAPPY PIANO*

Paul HARDCASTLE *UK, male producer / instrumentalist – synthesizer*　　**5 wks**

| 30 Nov 85 | PAUL HARDCASTLE *Chrysalis CHR 1517* | 53 | 5 wks |

Mike HARDING *UK, male comedian*　　**24 wks**

30 Aug 75	MRS 'ARDIN'S KID *Rubber RUB 011*	24	6 wks
10 Jul 76	ONE MAN SHOW *Philips 6625 022*	19	10 wks
11 Jun 77	OLD FOUR EYES IS BACK *Philips 6308 290*	31	6 wks
24 Jun 78	CAPTAIN PARALYTIC AND THE BROWN ALE COWBOY		
	Philips 6641 798	60	2 wks

HARDY – *See LAUREL and HARDY*

Steve HARLEY and COCKNEY REBEL
UK, male vocalist and male vocal / instrumental group　　**52 wks**

22 Jun 74	● THE PSYCHOMODO *EMI EMC 3033* [1]	8	20 wks
22 Mar 75	● THE BEST YEARS OF OUR LIVES *EMI EMC 3068*	4	19 wks
14 Feb 76	TIMELESS FLIGHT *EMI EMA 775*	18	6 wks
27 Nov 76	LOVE'S A PRIMA DONNA *EMI EMC 3156*	28	3 wks
30 Jul 77	FACE TO FACE – A LIVE RECORDING *EMI EMSP 320*	40	4 wks

[1] Cockney Rebel

Roy HARPER *UK, male vocalist / instrumentalist – guitar*　　**9 wks**

9 Mar 74	VALENTINE *Harvest SHSP 4027*	27	1 wk
21 Jun 75	H.Q. *Harvest SHSP 4046*	31	2 wks
12 Mar 77	BULLINAMINGVASE *Harvest SHSP 4060*	25	2 wks
16 Mar 85	WHATEVER HAPPENED TO JUGULA?		
	Beggars Banquet BEGA 60 [1]	44	4 wks

[1] Roy Harper and Jimmy Page

Anita HARRIS *UK, female vocalist*　　**5 wks**

| 27 Jan 68 | JUST LOVING YOU *CBS SBPG 63182* | 29 | 5 wks |

Emmylou HARRIS *US, female vocalist*　　**34 wks**

14 Feb 76	ELITE HOTEL *Reprise K 54060*	17	11 wks
29 Jan 77	LUXURY LINER *Warner Bros. K 56344*	17	6 wks
4 Feb 78	QUARTER MOON IN A TEN CENT TOWN *Warner Bros. K 56433*	40	5 wks
29 Mar 80	HER BEST SONGS *K–Tel NE 1058*	36	3 wks
14 Feb 81	EVANGELINE *Warner Bros. K 56880*	53	4 wks
14 Mar 87	TRIO *Warner Bros. 9254911* [1]	60	4 wks
7 Oct 95	WRECKING BALL *Grapevine GRACD 102*	46	1 wk

[1] Dolly Parton/Emmylou Harris/Linda Ronstadt

Keith HARRIS, ORVILLE and CUDDLES
UK, male ventriloquist vocalist with dummies　　**1 wk**

| 4 Jun 83 | AT THE END OF THE RAINBOW *BBC REH 465* | 92 | 1 wk |

George HARRISON *UK, male vocalist / instrumentalist – guitar*　　**76 wks**

26 Dec 70	● ALL THINGS MUST PASS *Apple STCH 639*	4	24 wks
7 Jul 73	● LIVING IN THE MATERIAL WORLD *Apple PAS 10006*	2	12 wks
18 Oct 75	EXTRA TEXTURE (READ ALL ABOUT IT) *Apple PAS 10009*	16	4 wks
18 Dec 76	THIRTY THREE AND A THIRD *Dark Horse K 56319*	35	4 wks
17 Mar 79	GEORGE HARRISON *Dark Horse K 56562*	39	5 wks

H
155

13 Jun 81	**SOMEWHERE IN ENGLAND** Dark Horse K 56870	**13**	4 wks
14 Nov 87	● **CLOUD NINE** Dark Horse WX 123	**10**	23 wks

Jane HARRISON *UK, female operatic vocalist* — **1 wk**

4 Feb 89	**NEW DAY** Stylus SMR 869	**70**	1 wk

Deborah HARRY *US, female vocalist* — **53 wks**

8 Aug 81	● **KOO KOO** Chrysalis CHR 1347 [1]	**6**	7 wks
29 Nov 86	**ROCKBIRD** Chrysalis CHR 1540 [1]	**31**	11 wks
17 Dec 88	**ONCE MORE INTO THE BLEACH** Chrysalis CJB 2 [2]	**50**	4 wks
28 Oct 89	**DEF DUMB AND BLONDE** Chrysalis CHR 1650	**12**	7 wks
16 Mar 91	● **THE COMPLETE PICTURE – THE VERY BEST OF** **DEBORAH HARRY AND BLONDIE** Chrysalis CHR 1817 [2]	**3**	22 wks
31 Jul 93	**DEBRAVATION** Chrysalis CDCHR 6033	**24**	2 wks

[1] Debbie Harry [2] Deborah Harry and Blondie

Keef HARTLEY BAND *UK, male vocal / instrumental group* — **3 wks**

5 Sep 70	**THE TIME IS NEAR** Deram SML 1071	**41**	3 wks

PJ HARVEY *UK, female vocalist* — **17 wks**

11 Apr 92	**DRY** Too Pure PURECD 10	**11**	5 wks
8 May 93	● **RID OF ME** Island CID 8002	**3**	4 wks
30 Oct 93	**4–TRACK DEMOS** Island IMCD 170	**19**	2 wks
11 Mar 95	**TO BRING YOU MY LOVE** Island CID 8035	**12**	6 wks

PJ Harvey was the name of the entire group, not just the lead singer, for the first three albums.

H
156

Richard HARVEY and FRIENDS *UK, male instrumental group* — **1 wk**

6 May 89	**EVENING FALLS** Telstar STAR 2350	**72**	1 wk

HATFIELD AND THE NORTH
UK, male / female vocal / instrumental group — **1 wk**

29 Mar 75	**ROTTERS CLUB** Virgin V 2030	**43**	1 wk

Juliana HATFIELD *US, female vocalist* — **3 wks**

14 Aug 93	**BECOME WHAT YOU ARE** Mammoth 4509935292 [1]	**44**	2 wks
8 Apr 95	**ONLY EVERYTHING** East West 4509998862	**59**	1 wk

[1] Juliana Hatfield Three

Donny HATHAWAY – See Roberta FLACK

Chesney HAWKES *UK, male vocalist* — **8 wks**

13 Apr 91	**BUDDY'S SONG**(film soundtrack) Chrysalis CHR 1812	**18**	8 wks

Sophie B. HAWKINS *US, female vocalist* — **6 wks**

1 Aug 92	**TONGUES AND TAILS** Columbia 4688232	**46**	2 wks
3 Sep 94	**WHALER** Columbia 4765122	**46**	4 wks

Ted HAWKINS *US, male vocalist / instrumentalist – guitar* — **1 wk**

18 Apr 87	**HAPPY HOUR** Windows On The World WOLP 2	**82**	1 wk

HAWKWIND *UK, male vocal / instrumental group* — **101 wks**

6 Nov 71	**IN SEARCH OF SPACE** United Artists UAS 29202	**18**	19 wks
23 Dec 72	**DOREMI FASOL LATIDO** United Artists UAS 29364	**14**	5 wks

2 Jun 73	● **SPACE RITUAL ALIVE** *United Artists UAD 60037/8*.........**9**	5 wks
21 Sep 74	**HALL OF THE MOUNTAIN GRILL** *United Artists UAG 29672* **16**	5 wks
31 May 75	**WARRIOR ON THE EDGE OF TIME** *United Artists UAG 29766* **13**	7 wks
24 Apr 76	**ROAD HAWKS** *United Artists UAK 29919* **34**	4 wks
18 Sep 76	**ASTONISHING SOUNDS, AMAZING MUSIC** *Charisma CDS 4004*..**33**	5 wks
9 Jul 77	**QUARK STRANGENESS AND CHARM** *Charisma CDS 4008* **30**	6 wks
21 Oct 78	**25 YEARS ON** *Charisma CD 4014* [1] **48**	3 wks
30 Jun 79	**PXR 5** *Charisma CDS 4016* **59**	5 wks
9 Aug 80	**LIVE 1979** *Bronze BRON 527* **15**	7 wks
8 Nov 80	**LEVITATION** *Bronze BRON 530* **21**	4 wks
24 Oct 81	**SONIC ATTACK** *RCA RCALP 5004* **19**	5 wks
22 May 82	**CHURCH OF HAWKWIND** *RCA RCALP 9004* **26**	6 wks
23 Oct 82	**CHOOSE YOUR MASQUES** *RCA RCALP 6055* **29**	5 wks
5 Nov 83	**ZONES** *Flicknife SHARP 014*............................**57**	2 wks
25 Feb 84	**HAWKWIND** *Liberty SLS 1972921* **75**	1 wk
16 Nov 85	**CHRONICLE OF THE BLACK SWORD** *Flicknife SHARP 033* **65**	2 wks
14 May 88	**THE XENON CODEX** *GWR GWLP 26* **79**	2 wks
6 Oct 90	**SPACE BANDITS** *GWR GWLP 103*.........................**70**	1 wk
23 May 92	**ELECTRIC TEPEE** *Essential ESSCD 181* **53**	1 wk
6 Nov 93	**IT IS THE BUSINESS OF THE FUTURE TO BE DANGEROUS** *Essential ESCDCD 196* **75**	1 wk

[1] Hawklords

Isaac HAYES *US, male vocalist / multi–instrumentalist*   **14 wks**

18 Dec 71	**SHAFT** *Polydor 2659 007* **17**	13 wks
12 Feb 72	**BLACK MOSES** *Stax 2628 004*...........................**38**	1 wk

HAYSI FANTAYZEE *UK, male / female vocal duo*   **5 wks**

26 Feb 83	**BATTLE HYMNS FOR CHILDREN SINGING** *Regard RGLP 6000* **53**	5 wks

Justin HAYWARD *UK, male vocalist*   **35 wks**

29 Mar 75	● **BLUE JAYS** *Threshold THS 12* [1] **4**	18 wks
5 Mar 77	**SONGWRITER** *Deram SDL 15* **28**	5 wks
19 Jul 80	**NIGHT FLIGHT** *Decca TXS 138*...........................**41**	4 wks
19 Oct 85	**MOVING MOUNTAINS** *Towerbell TOWLP 15* **78**	1 wk
28 Oct 89	**CLASSIC BLUE** *Trax MODEM 1040* [2] **47**	7 wks

[1] Justin Hayward and John Lodge [2] Justin Hayward, Mike Batt and the London Philharmonic Orchestra

Lee HAZLEWOOD – *See Nancy SINATRA*

Jeff HEALEY BAND *US, male vocal / instrumental group*   **16 wks**

14 Jan 89	**SEE THE LIGHT** *Arista 209441* **58**	7 wks
9 Jun 90	**HELL TO PAY** *Arista 210815* **18**	6 wks
28 Nov 92	**FEEL THIS** *Arista 74321120872* **72**	1 wk
18 Mar 95	**COVER TO COVER** *Arista 74321238882* **50**	2 wks

HEART *US, female / male vocal / instrumental group*   **137 wks**

22 Jan 77	**DREAMBOAT ANNIE** *Arista ARTY 139* **36**	8 wks
23 Jul 77	**LITTLE QUEEN** *Portrait PRT 82075* **34**	4 wks
19 Jun 82	**PRIVATE AUDITION** *Epic EPC 85792* **77**	2 wks
26 Oct 85	**HEART** *Capitol EJ 2403721* **19**	43 wks
6 Jun 87	● **BAD ANIMALS** *Capitol ESTU 2032* **7**	56 wks
14 Apr 90	● **BRIGADE** *Capitol ESTU 2121* **3**	20 wks
28 Sep 91	**ROCK THE HOUSE 'LIVE'** *Capitol ESTU 2154* **45**	2 wks
11 Dec 93	**DESIRE WALKS ON** *Capitol CDEST 2216* **32**	2 wks

Heart changed label number during its chart run to Capitol LOVE 1.

HEARTBREAKERS *US, male vocal / instrumental group*   **1 wk**

5 Nov 77	**L.A.M.F.** *Track 2409 218*..............................**55**	1 wk

Ted HEATH AND HIS MUSIC *UK, conductor and orchestra*   **5 wks**

21 Apr 62	**BIG BAND PERCUSSION** *Decca PFM 24004*	**17**	5 wks

HEATWAVE *UK/US, male vocal/instrumental group*   **27 wks**

11 Jun 77	**TOO HOT TO HANDLE** *GTO GTLP 013*	**46**	2 wks
6 May 78	**CENTRAL HEATING** *GTO GTLP 027*	**26**	15 wks
14 Feb 81	**CANDLES** *GTO GTLP 047*	**29**	9 wks
23 Feb 91	**GANGSTERS OF THE GROOVE** *Telstar STAR 2434*	**56**	1 wk

HEAVEN 17 *UK, male vocal/instrumental group*   **128 wks**

26 Sep 81	**PENTHOUSE AND PAVEMENT** *Virgin V 2208*	**14**	76 wks
7 May 83	● **THE LUXURY GAP** *Virgin V 2253*	**4**	36 wks
6 Oct 84	**HOW MEN ARE** *B.E.F. V 2326*	**12**	11 wks
12 Jul 86	**ENDLESS** *Virgin TCVB/CDV 2383*	**70**	2 wks
29 Nov 86	**PLEASURE ONE** *Virgin V 2400*	**78**	1 wk
20 Mar 93	**HIGHER AND HIGHER – THE BEST OF HEAVEN 17** *Virgin CDV 2717*	**31**	2 wks

HEAVY D and the BOYZ *US, male vocal/instrumental group*   **3 wks**

10 Aug 91	**A PEACEFUL JOURNEY** *MCA MCA 10289*	**40**	3 wks

HEAVY PETTIN' *UK, male vocal/instrumental group*   **4 wks**

29 Oct 83	**LETTIN' LOOSE** *Polydor HEPLP 1*	**55**	2 wks
13 Jul 85	**ROCK AIN'T DEAD** *Polydor HEPLP 2*	**81**	2 wks

HELLOWEEN *Germany, male vocal/instrumental group*   **9 wks**

17 Sep 88	**KEEPER OF THE SEVEN KEYS PART 2** *Noise International NUK 117*	**24**	5 wks
15 Apr 89	**LIVE IN THE UK** *EMI EMC 3558*	**26**	2 wks
23 Mar 91	**PINK BUBBLES GO APE** *EMI EMC 3588*	**41**	2 wks

HELMET *US, male vocal/instrumental group*   **1 wk**

2 Jul 94	**BETTY** *Interscope 6544924042*	**38**	1 wk

Jimi HENDRIX *US, male vocalist/instrumentalist – guitar*   **243 wks**

27 May 67	● **ARE YOU EXPERIENCED** *Track 612001* [1]	**2**	33 wks
16 Dec 67	● **AXIS: BOLD AS LOVE** *Track 613003* [1]	**5**	16 wks
27 Apr 68	● **SMASH HITS** *Track 613004* [1]	**4**	25 wks
18 May 68	**GET THAT FEELING** *London HA 8349* [2]	**39**	2 wks
16 Nov 68	● **ELECTRIC LADYLAND** *Track 613008/9* [1]	**6**	12 wks
4 Jul 70	● **BAND OF GYPSIES** *Track 2406001*	**6**	30 wks
3 Apr 71	● **CRY OF LOVE** *Track 2408101*	**2**	14 wks
28 Aug 71	● **EXPERIENCE** *Ember NR 5057*	**9**	6 wks
20 Nov 71	**JIMI HENDRIX AT THE ISLE OF WIGHT** *Track 2302 016*	**17**	2 wks
4 Dec 71	**RAINBOW BRIDGE** *Reprise K 44159*	**16**	8 wks
5 Feb 72	● **HENDRIX IN THE WEST** *Polydor 2302 018*	**7**	14 wks
11 Nov 72	**WAR HEROES** *Polydor 2302 020*	**23**	3 wks
21 Jul 73	**SOUNDTRACK RECORDINGS FROM THE FILM 'JIMI HENDRIX'** *Warner Bros. K 64017*	**37**	1 wk
29 Mar 75	**JIMI HENDRIX** *Polydor 2343 080*	**35**	4 wks
30 Aug 75	**CRASH LANDING** *Polydor 2310 398*	**35**	3 wks
29 Nov 75	**MIDNIGHT LIGHTNING** *Polydor 2310 415*	**46**	1 wk
14 Aug 82	**THE JIMI HENDRIX CONCERTS** *CBS 88592*	**16**	11 wks
19 Feb 83	**THE SINGLES ALBUM** *Polydor PODV 6*	**77**	4 wks
11 Mar 89	**RADIO ONE** *Castle Collectors CCSLP 212*	**30**	6 wks
3 Nov 90	● **CORNERSTONES 1967–1970** *Polydor 8472311*	**5**	16 wks
14 Nov 92	**THE ULTIMATE EXPERIENCE** *PolyGram TV 5172352*	**25**	26 wks
30 Apr 94	● **BLUES** *Polydor 5210372*	**10**	3 wks
13 Aug 94	**WOODSTOCK** *Polydor 5233842*	**32**	3 wks

[1] Jimi Hendrix Experience [2] Jimi Hendrix and Curtis Knight

H
158

Don HENLEY *US, male vocalist* **27 wks**

| 9 Mar 85 | **BUILDING THE PERFECT BEAST** Geffen GEF 25939 | 14 | 11 wks |
| 8 Jul 89 | **THE END OF INNOCENCE** Geffen WX 253 | 17 | 16 wks |

Pauline HENRY *UK, female vocalist* **1 wk**

| 19 Feb 94 | **PAULINE** Sony S2 4747442 | 45 | 1 wk |

Band and Chorus of HER MAJESTY'S GUARDS DIVISION
UK, military band **4 wks**

| 22 Nov 75 | **30 SMASH HITS OF THE WAR YEARS** Warwick WW 5006 | 38 | 4 wks |

HERD *UK, male vocal / instrumental group* **1 wk**

| 24 Feb 68 | **PARADISE LOST** Fontana STL 5458 | 38 | 1 wk |

HERMAN'S HERMITS *UK, male vocal / instrumental group* **11 wks**

18 Sep 65	**HERMAN'S HERMITS** Columbia 33SX 1727	16	2 wks
25 Sep 71	**THE MOST OF HERMAN'S HERMITS** MFP 5216	14	5 wks
8 Oct 77	**GREATEST HITS** K–Tel NE 1001	37	4 wks

Kristin HERSH *US, female vocalist* **4 wks**

| 5 Feb 94 | ● **HIPS AND MAKERS** 4AD CAD 4002CD | 7 | 4 wks |

Nick HEYWARD *UK, male vocalist* **13 wks**

| 29 Oct 83 | ● **NORTH OF A MIRACLE** Arista NORTH 1 | 10 | 13 wks |

HI JACK *US, male vocal group* **1 wk**

| 19 Oct 91 | **THE HORNS OF JERICHO** Warner Bros. 7599263861 | 54 | 1 wk |

HI TENSION *UK, male vocal / instrumental group* **4 wks**

| 6 Jan 79 | **HI TENSION** Island ILPS 9564 | 74 | 4 wks |

John HIATT *US, male vocalist* **3 wks**

7 Jul 90	**STOLEN MOMENTS** A & M 3953101	72	1 wk
11 Sep 93	**PERFECTLY GOOD GUITAR** A & M 5401302	67	1 wk
11 Nov 95	**WALK ON** Capitol CDP 8334162	74	1 wk

HIGH *UK, male vocal / instrumental group* **2 wks**

| 17 Nov 90 | **SOMEWHERE SOON** London 8282241 | 59 | 2 wks |

Benny HILL *UK, male vocalist* **8 wks**

| 11 Dec 71 | ● **WORDS AND MUSIC** Columbia SCX 6479 | 9 | 8 wks |

Vince HILL *UK, male vocalist* **10 wks**

| 20 May 67 | **EDELWEISS** Columbia SCX 6141 | 23 | 9 wks |
| 29 Apr 78 | **THAT LOVING FEELING** K–Tel NE 1017 | 51 | 1 wk |

Steve HILLAGE *UK, male vocalist / instrumentalist – guitar* **41 wks**

3 May 75	**FISH RISING** Virgin V 2031	33	3 wks
16 Oct 76	● **L** Virgin V 2066	10	12 wks
22 Oct 77	**MOTIVATION RADIO** Virgin V 2777	28	5 wks
29 Apr 78	**GREEN VIRGIN** Virgin 2098	30	8 wks

H
159

17 Feb 79	**LIVE HERALD** Virgin VGD 3502	**54**	5 wks
5 May 79	**RAINBOW DOME MUSIC** Virgin VR 1	**52**	5 wks
27 Oct 79	**OPEN** Virgin V 2135	**71**	1 wk
5 Mar 83	**FOR TO NEXT** Virgin V 2244	**48**	2 wks

HIPSWAY *UK, male vocal / instrumental group* — **23 wks**

| 19 Apr 86 | **HIPSWAY** Mercury MERH 85 | **42** | 23 wks |

Roger HODGSON *UK, male vocalist* — **4 wks**

| 20 Oct 84 | **IN THE EYE OF THE STORM** A & M AMA 5004 | **70** | 4 wks |

Gerard HOFFNUNG *UK, male comedian* — **20 wks**

| 3 Sep 60 | ● **AT THE OXFORD UNION** Decca LF 1330 | **4** | 20 wks |

Susanna HOFFS *US, female vocalist* — **2 wks**

| 6 Apr 91 | **WHEN YOU'RE A BOY** Columbia 4672021 | **56** | 2 wks |

Christopher HOGWOOD – See ACADEMY OF ANCIENT MUSIC conducted by Christopher HOGWOOD

HOLE *US, female / male vocal / instrumental group* — **6 wks**

| 12 Oct 91 | **PRETTY ON THE INSIDE** City Slang E 04071 | **59** | 1 wk |
| 23 Apr 94 | **LIVE THROUGH THIS** City Slang EFA 049352 | **13** | 5 wks |

Billie HOLIDAY *US, female vocalist* — **10 wks**

| 16 Nov 85 | **THE LEGEND OF BILLIE HOLIDAY** MCA BHTV 1 | **60** | 10 wks |

Jools HOLLAND *UK, male vocalist / instrumentalist – piano* — **1 wk**

| 5 May 90 | **WORLD OF HIS OWN** IRS EIRSA 1018 | **71** | 1 wk |

HOLLIES *UK, male vocal / instrumental group* — **150 wks**

15 Feb 64	● **STAY WITH THE HOLLIES** Parlophone PMC 1220	**2**	25 wks
2 Oct 65	● **HOLLIES** Parlophone PMC 1261	**8**	14 wks
16 Jul 66	**WOULD YOU BELIEVE** Parlophone PMC 7008	**16**	8 wks
17 Dec 66	**FOR CERTAIN BECAUSE** Parlophone PCS 17011	**23**	7 wks
17 Jun 67	**EVOLUTION** Parlophone PCS 7022	**13**	10 wks
17 Aug 68	★ **GREATEST HITS** Parlophone PCS 7057	**1**	27 wks
17 May 69	● **HOLLIES SING DYLAN** Parlophone PCS 7078	**3**	7 wks
28 Nov 70	**CONFESSIONS OF THE MIND** Parlophone PCS 7117	**30**	5 wks
16 Mar 74	**HOLLIES** Polydor 2383 262	**38**	3 wks
19 Mar 77	● **HOLLIES LIVE HITS** Polydor 2383 428	**4**	12 wks
22 Jul 78	● **20 GOLDEN GREATS** EMI EMTV 11	**2**	20 wks
1 Oct 88	**ALL THE HITS AND MORE** EMI EM 1301	**51**	5 wks
3 Apr 93	**THE AIR THAT I BREATHE – THE BEST OF THE HOLLIES** EMI CDEMTV 74	**15**	7 wks

The two albums titled Hollies are different.

Laurie HOLLOWAY – See SOUTH BANK ORCHESTRA

Buddy HOLLY and the CRICKETS
US, male vocalist, male vocal / instrumental group — **328 wks**

2 May 59	● **BUDDY HOLLY STORY** Coral LVA 9105	**2**	156 wks
15 Oct 60	● **BUDDY HOLLY STORY VOLUME 2** Coral LVA 9127	**7**	14 wks
21 Oct 61	● **THAT'LL BE THE DAY** Ace Of Hearts AH 3	**5**	14 wks
6 Apr 63	● **REMINISCING** Coral LVA 9212	**2**	31 wks
13 Jun 64	● **BUDDY HOLLY SHOWCASE** Coral LVA 9222	**3**	16 wks
26 Jun 65	**HOLLY IN THE HILLS** Coral LVA 9227	**13**	6 wks

15 Jul 67 ● **BUDDY HOLLY'S GREATEST HITS** Ace Of Hearts AH 148 ....**9**	40	wks
12 Apr 69 **GIANT** MCA MUPS 371 ....**13**	1	wk
21 Aug 71 **BUDDY HOLLY'S GREATEST HITS (re-issue)** Coral CP 8 ....**32**	6	wks
12 Jul 75 **BUDDY HOLLY'S GREATEST HITS (2nd re-issue)** Coral CDLM 8007 ....**42**	3	wks
11 Mar 78 ★ **20 GOLDEN GREATS** MCA EMTV 8 ....**1**	20	wks
8 Sep 84 **GREATEST HITS (3rd re-issue)** MCA MCL 1618..................**100**	1	wk
18 Feb 89 ● **TRUE LOVE WAYS** Telstar STAR 2339........................**8**	11	wks
20 Feb 93 ★ **WORDS OF LOVE** PolyGram TV 5144872......................**1**	9	wks

Most albums feature the Crickets on at least some tracks. See also The Crickets.

David HOLMES *UK, male producer*   **1 wk**

22 Jul 95 **THIS FILM'S CRAP LET'S SLASH THE SEATS** Go! Discs 8286312 ..**51**	1	wk

John HOLT *Jamaica, male vocalist*   **2 wks**

1 Feb 75 **A THOUSAND VOLTS OF HOLT** Trojan TRLS 75 ....**42**	2	wks

HOME *UK, male vocal / instrumental group*   **1 wk**

11 Nov 72 **DREAMER** CBS 67522 ....**41**	1	wk

HONEYDRIPPERS *UK / US, male vocal / instrumental group*   **10 wks**

1 Dec 84 **THE HONEYDRIPPERS VOLUME 1** Es Paranza 790220 ....**56**	10	wks

John Lee HOOKER *US, male vocalist*   **29 wks**

4 Feb 67 **HOUSE OF THE BLUES** Marble Arch MAL 663 ....**34**	2	wks
11 Nov 89 **THE HEALER** Silvertone ORELP 508 ....**63**	8	wks
21 Sep 91 ● **MR LUCKY** Silvertone ORELP 519......................**3**	10	wks
7 Nov 92 **BOOM BOOM** Pointblank VPBCD 12 ....**15**	4	wks
4 Mar 95 **CHILL OUT** Pointblank VPBCD 22 ....**23**	5	wks

HOOTIE and the BLOWFISH *US, male vocal / instrumental group* **11 wks**

18 Mar 95 **CRACKED REAR VIEW** Atlantic 7826132 ....**12**	11	wks

Mary HOPKIN *UK, female vocalist*   **9 wks**

1 Mar 69 ● **POSTCARD** Apple SAPCOR 5........................**3**	9	wks

Bruce HORNSBY and the RANGE
US, male vocal / instrumental group   **54 wks**

13 Sep 86 **THE WAY IT IS** RCA PL 89901 ....**16**	26	wks
14 May 88 **SCENES FROM THE SOUTHSIDE** RCA PL 86686 ....**18**	18	wks
30 Jun 90 **A NIGHT ON THE TOWN** RCA PL 82041.................**23**	7	wks
8 May 93 **HARBOR LIGHTS** RCA 07863661142.....................**32**	3	wks

HORSE *UK, female / male vocal / instrumental group*   **4 wks**

23 Jun 90 **THE SAME SKY** Echo Chamber EST 2123 ....**44**	2	wks
13 Nov 93 **GOD'S HOME MOVIE** Oxygen MCD 10935................**42**	2	wks

HORSLIPS *Ireland, male vocal / instrumental group*   **3 wks**

30 Apr 77 **THE BOOK OF INVASIONS – A CELTIC SYMPHONY** DJM DJF 20498 ....**39**	3	wks

HOT CHOCOLATE *UK, male vocal / instrumental group*   **123 wks**

15 Nov 75 **HOT CHOCOLATE** RAK SRAK 516 ....**34**	7	wks
7 Aug 76 **MAN TO MAN** RAK SRAK 522 ....**32**	7	wks
20 Nov 76 ● **GREATEST HITS** RAK SRAK 524 ....**6**	35	wks

8 Apr 78	**EVERY 1'S A WINNER** RAK SRAK 531 .... **30**	8 wks
15 Dec 79	● **20 HOTTEST HITS** RAK EMTV 22 .... **3**	19 wks
25 Sep 82	**MYSTERY** RAK SRAK 549 .... **24**	7 wks
21 Feb 87	★ **THE VERY BEST OF HOT CHOCOLATE** RAK EMTV 42 .... **1**	28 wks
20 Mar 93	★ **THEIR GREATEST HITS** EMI CDEMTV 73 .... **1**	12 wks

HOT RODS – See EDDIE and the HOT RODS

HOTHOUSE FLOWERS Ireland, male vocal/instrumental group **51 wks**

18 Jun 88	● **PEOPLE** London LONLP 58 .... **2**	19 wks
16 Jun 90	● **HOME** London 8281971 .... **5**	21 wks
20 Mar 93	● **SONGS FROM THE RAIN** London 8283502 .... **7**	11 wks

HOUSE OF LOVE UK, male vocal/instrumental group **14 wks**

10 Mar 90	● **HOUSE OF LOVE** Fontana 8422931 .... **8**	10 wks
10 Nov 90	**HOUSE OF LOVE** Fontana 8469781 .... **49**	1 wk
18 Jul 92	**BABE RAINBOW** Fontana 5125492 .... **34**	2 wks
3 Jul 93	**AUDIENCE WITH THE MIND** Fontana 5148802 .... **38**	1 wk

Identically titled albums are different.

HOUSE OF PAIN US, male rap group **7 wks**

21 Nov 92	**HOUSE OF PAIN** XL XLCD 111 .... **73**	1 wk
30 Jul 94	● **SAME AS IT EVER WAS** XL XLCD 115 .... **8**	6 wks

HOUSEMARTINS UK, male vocal/instrumental group **70 wks**

5 Jul 86	● **LONDON 0 HULL 4** Go! Discs AGOLP 7 .... **3**	41 wks
27 Dec 86	**HOUSEMARTINS' CHRISTMAS SINGLES BOX** Go! Discs GOD 816 .... **84**	1 wk
3 Oct 87	● **THE PEOPLE WHO GRINNED THEMSELVES TO DEATH** Go! Discs AGOLP 9 .... **9**	18 wks
21 May 88	● **NOW THAT'S WHAT I CALL QUITE GOOD!** Go! Discs AGOLP 11 ....**8**	10 wks

Whitney HOUSTON US, female vocalist **249 wks**

14 Dec 85	● **WHITNEY HOUSTON** Arista 206978 .... **2**	119 wks
13 Jun 87	★ **WHITNEY** Arista 208141 .... **1**	101 wks
17 Nov 90	● **I'M YOUR BABY TONIGHT** Arista 211039 .... **4**	29 wks

Steve HOWE UK, male vocalist/instrumentalist – guitar **6 wks**

15 Nov 75	**BEGINNINGS** Atlantic K 50151 .... **22**	4 wks
24 Nov 79	**STEVE HOWE ALBUM** Atlantic K 50621 .... **68**	2 wks

See also Anderson Bruford Wakeman Howe.

HUDDERSFIELD CHORAL SOCIETY UK, choir **14 wks**

13 Dec 86	**THE CAROLS ALBUM** EMI EMTV 43 .... **29**	4 wks
15 Mar 86	**THE HYMNS ALBUM** EMI EMTV 40 .... **8**	10 wks

HUE AND CRY UK, male vocal/instrumental duo **74 wks**

7 Nov 87	**SEDUCED AND ABANDONED** Circa CIRCA 2 .... **22**	11 wks
10 Dec 88	● **REMOTE/THE BITTER SUITE** Circa CIRCA 6 .... **10**	48 wks
29 Jun 91	● **STARS CRASH DOWN** Circa CIRCA 15 .... **10**	9 wks
29 Aug 92	**TRUTH AND LOVE** Fidelity FIDELCD 1 .... **33**	2 wks
10 Apr 93	**LABOURS OF LOVE – THE BEST OF HUE AND CRY** Circa HACCD 1 **27**	4 wks

Remote re-entered the chart on 16 Dec 89 when it was made available with the free album The Bitter Suite.

Alan HULL UK, male vocalist **3 wks**

28 Jul 73	**PIPEDREAM** Charisma CAS 1069 .... **29**	3 wks

H
162

British Hit Albums Part One
Date of chart entry/Title & catalogue no./Peak position reached/Weeks on chart
★ Number One   ● Top Ten   † still on chart at 30 Dec 1995   □ credited to act billed in footnote

HUMAN LEAGUE *UK, male / female vocal / instrumental group* **258 wks**

31 May 80	**TRAVELOGUE** *Virgin V 2160*	**16**	42 wks
22 Aug 81	**REPRODUCTION** *Virgin V 2133*	**34**	23 wks
24 Oct 81	★ **DARE** *Virgin V 2192*	**1**	71 wks
17 Jul 82	● **LOVE AND DANCING** *Virgin OVED 6* [1]	**3**	52 wks
19 May 84	● **HYSTERIA** *Virgin V 2315*	**3**	18 wks
20 Sep 86	● **CRASH** *Virgin V 2391*	**7**	6 wks
12 Nov 88	● **GREATEST HITS** *Virgin HLTV 1*	**3**	32 wks
22 Sep 90	**ROMANTIC?** *Virgin V 2624*	**24**	2 wks
4 Feb 95	● **OCTOPUS** *East West 4509987502*	**6**	12 wks

[1] League Unlimited Orchestra

Greatest Hits *changed its catalogue number to CDV 2792 during its chart run.*

HUMBLE PIE *UK, male vocal / instrumental group* **10 wks**

6 Sep 69	**AS SAFE AS YESTERDAY IS** *Immediate IMSP 025*	**32**	1 wk
22 Jan 72	**ROCKING AT THE FILLMORE** *A & M AMLH 63506*	**32**	2 wks
15 Apr 72	**SMOKIN'** *A & M AMLS 64342*	**28**	5 wks
7 Apr 73	**EAT IT** *A & M AMLS 6004*	**34**	2 wks

Engelbert HUMPERDINCK *UK, male vocalist* **239 wks**

20 May 67	● **RELEASE ME** *Decca SKL 4868*	**6**	58 wks
25 Nov 67	● **THE LAST WALTZ** *Decca SKL 4901*	**3**	33 wks
3 Aug 68	● **A MAN WITHOUT LOVE** *Decca SKL 4939*	**3**	45 wks
1 Mar 69	● **ENGELBERT** *Decca SKL 4985*	**3**	8 wks
6 Dec 69	● **ENGELBERT HUMPERDINCK** *Decca SKL 5030*	**5**	23 wks
11 Jul 70	**WE MADE IT HAPPEN** *Decca SKL 5054*	**17**	11 wks
18 Sep 71	**ANOTHER TIME, ANOTHER PLACE** *Decca SKL 5097*	**48**	1 wk
26 Feb 72	**LIVE AT THE RIVIERA LAS VEGAS** *Decca TXS 105*	**45**	1 wk
21 Dec 74	★ **ENGELBERT HUMPERDINCK – HIS GREATEST HITS**		
	Decca SKL 5198	**1**	34 wks
4 May 85	**GETTING SENTIMENTAL** *Telstar STAR 2254*	**35**	10 wks
4 Apr 87	**THE ENGELBERT HUMPERDINCK COLLECTION**		
	Telstar STAR 2294	**35**	9 wks
10 Jun 95	**LOVE UNCHAINED** *EMI CDEMTV 94*	**16**	6 wks

Ian HUNTER *UK, male vocalist* **26 wks**

12 Apr 75	**IAN HUNTER** *CBS 80710*	**21**	15 wks
29 May 76	**ALL AMERICAN ALIEN BOY** *CBS 81310*	**29**	4 wks
5 May 79	**YOU'RE NEVER ALONE WITH A SCHIZOPHRENIC**		
	Chrysalis CHR 1214	**49**	3 wks
26 Apr 80	**WELCOME TO THE CLUB** *Chrysalis CJT 6*	**61**	2 wks
29 Aug 81	**SHORT BACK AND SIDES** *Chrysalis CHR 1326*	**79**	2 wks

HURRAH! *UK, male vocal / instrumental group* **1 wk**

28 Feb 87	**TELL GOD I'M HERE** *Kitchenware 208 201*	**71**	1 wk

HURRICANES – *See JOHNNY and the HURRICANES*

HÜSKER DÜ *US, male vocal / instrumental group* **1 wk**

14 Feb 87	**WAREHOUSE: SONGS AND STORIES** *Warner Bros. 925 5441*	**72**	1 wk

Phyllis HYMAN *US, female vocalist* **1 wk**

20 Sep 86	**LIVING ALL ALONE** *Philadelphia International PHIL 4001*	**97**	1 wk

ICE CUBE *US, male rapper*   **10 wks**

28 Jul 90	**AMERIKKKA'S MOST WANTED** Fourth & Broadway BRLP 551 ....**48**	5 wks
9 Mar 91	**KILL AT WILL** Fourth & Broadway BRLM 572 ....**66**	3 wks
5 Dec 92	**THE PREDATOR** Fourth & Broadway BRCD 592 ....**73**	1 wk
18 Dec 93	**LETHAL INJECTION** Fourth & Broadway BRCD 609 ....**52**	1 wk

ICEHOUSE *Australia / New Zealand, male vocal / instrumental group*   **7 wks**

5 Mar 83	**LOVE IN MOTION** Chrysalis CHR 1390 ....**64**	6 wks
2 Apr 88	**MAN OF COLOURS** Chrysalis CHR 1592 ....**93**	1 wk

ICE-T *US, male rapper*   **13 wks**

21 Oct 89	**THE ICEBERG / FREEDOM OF SPEECH** Warner Bros. WX 316 ......**42**	2 wks
25 May 91	**O.G.: ORIGINAL GANGSTER** Sire WX 412 ....**38**	4 wks
3 Apr 93	**HOME INVASION** Rhyme Syndicate RSYND 1 ....**15**	7 wks

ICICLE WORKS *UK, male vocal / instrumental group*   **19 wks**

31 Mar 84	**THE ICICLE WORKS** Beggars Banquet BEGA 50 ....**24**	6 wks
28 Sep 85	**THE SMALL PRICE OF A BICYCLE** Beggars Banquet BEGA 61 ......**55**	3 wks
1 Mar 86	**SEVEN SINGLES DEEP** Beggars Banquet BEGA 71......................**52**	2 wks
21 Mar 87	**IF YOU WANT TO DEFEAT YOUR ENEMY SING HIS SONG**	
	Beggars Banquet BEGA 78...**28**	4 wks
14 May 88	**BLIND** Beggars Banquet IWA 2 ....**40**	3 wks
5 Sep 92	**THE BEST OF THE ICICLE WORKS**	
	Beggars Banquet BEGA 124CD **60**	1 wk

Billy IDOL *UK, male vocalist*   **100 wks**

8 Jun 85	● **VITAL IDOL** Chrysalis CUX 1502 ....**7**	34 wks
28 Sep 85	**REBEL YELL** Chrysalis CHR 1450 ....**36**	11 wks
1 Nov 86	● **WHIPLASH SMILE** Chrysalis CDL 1514 ....**8**	20 wks
2 Jul 88	● **IDOL SONGS: 11 OF THE BEST** Chrysalis BILTVD 1 ....**2**	25 wks
12 May 90	**CHARMED LIFE** Chrysalis CHR 1735 ....**15**	8 wks
10 Jul 93	**CYBERPUNK** Chrysalis CDCHR 6000 ....**20**	2 wks

Frank IFIELD *UK, male vocalist*   **83 wks**

16 Feb 63	● **I'LL REMEMBER YOU** Columbia 33SX 1467 ....**3**	36 wks
21 Sep 63	● **BORN FREE** Columbia 33SX 1462 ....**3**	32 wks
28 Mar 64	● **BLUE SKIES** Columbia 55SX 1588...**10**	12 wks
19 Dec 64	● **GREATEST HITS** Columbia 33SX 1633 ....**9**	3 wks

Julio IGLESIAS *Spain, male vocalist*   **159 wks**

7 Nov 81	**DE NINA A MUJER** CBS 85063 ....**43**	5 wks
28 Nov 81	● **BEGIN THE BEGUINE** CBS 85462 ....**5**	28 wks
16 Oct 82	**AMOR** CBS 25103 ....**14**	14 wks
2 Jul 83	● **JULIO** CBS 10038..**5**	17 wks
1 Sep 84	**1100 BEL AIR PLACE** CBS 86308 ....**14**	14 wks
19 Oct 85	**LIBRA** CBS 26623 ....**61**	4 wks
3 Sep 88	**NON STOP** CBS 460990 1..**33**	14 wks
1 Dec 90	**STARRY NIGHT** CBS 4672841 ....**27**	20 wks
28 May 94	● **CRAZY** Columbia 4747382 ....**6**	37 wks
12 Aug 95	● **LA CARRETERA** Columbia 4807042 ....**6**	6 wks

I-LEVEL *UK, male vocal / instrumental group*   **4 wks**

9 Jul 83	**I-LEVEL** Virgin V 2270 ....**50**	4 wks

IMAGINATION *UK, male vocal group*   **122 wks**

24 Oct 81	**BODY TALK** *R & B RBLP 1001*	**20**	53 wks
11 Sep 82	● **IN THE HEAT OF THE NIGHT** *R & B RBLP 1002*	**7**	29 wks
14 May 83	● **NIGHT DUBBING** *R & B RBDUB 1*	**9**	20 wks
12 Nov 83	**SCANDALOUS** *R & B RBLP 1004*	**25**	8 wks
12 Aug 89	● **IMAGINATION – ALL THE HITS** *Stylus SMR 985*	**4**	12 wks

IMMACULATE FOOLS *UK, male vocal / instrumental group*   **2 wks**

11 May 85	**HEARTS OF FORTUNE** *A & M AMA 5030*	**65**	2 wks

IN TUNE *UK, male instrumental duo*   **3 wks**

17 Jun 95	**ACOUSTIC MOODS** *Global Television RADCD 13*	**21**	3 wks

INCANTATION *UK, male instrumental group*   **52 wks**

11 Dec 82	● **CACHARPAYA (PANPIPES OF THE ANDES)**		
	Beggars Banquet BEGA 39	**9**	26 wks
17 Dec 83	**DANCE OF THE FLAMES** *Beggars Banquet BEGA 49*	**61**	7 wks
28 Dec 85	**BEST OF INCANTATION MUSIC FROM THE ANDES**		
	West Five CODA 19	**28**	19 wks

INCOGNITO *France / UK, male / female vocal / instrumental group*   **18 wks**

18 Apr 81	**JAZZ FUNK** *Ensign ENVY 504*	**28**	8 wks
27 Jul 91	**INSIDE LIFE** *Talkin Loud 8485461*	**44**	2 wks
4 Jul 92	**TRIBES VIBES AND SCRIBES** *Talkin Loud 5123632*	**41**	2 wks
6 Nov 93	**POSITIVITY** *Talkin Loud 5182602*	**55**	2 wks
17 Jun 95	**100 DEGREES AND RISING** *Talkin Loud 5280002*	**11**	4 wks

INCREDIBLE STRING BAND
UK, male / female vocal / instrumental group   **36 wks**

21 Oct 67	**5,000 SPIRITS OR THE LAYERS OF THE ONION**		
	Elektra EUKS 257	**26**	4 wks
6 Apr 68	● **HANGMAN'S BEAUTIFUL DAUGHTER** *Elektra EVKS7 258*	**5**	21 wks
20 Jul 68	**INCREDIBLE STRING BAND** *Elektra EKL 254*	**34**	3 wks
24 Jan 70	**CHANGING HORSES** *Elektra EKS 74057*	**30**	1 wk
9 May 70	**I LOOKED UP** *Elektra 2469002*	**30**	4 wks
31 Oct 70	**U** *Elektra 2665001*	**34**	2 wks
30 Oct 71	**LIQUID ACROBAT AS REGARDS THE AIR** *Island ILPS 9172* ...	**46**	1 wk

INDIGO GIRLS *US, female vocal / instrumental duo*   **3 wks**

11 Jun 94	**SWAMP OPHELIA** *Epic 4759312*	**66**	1 wk
15 Jul 95	**4.5** *Epic 4804392*	**43**	2 wks

INFA RIOT *UK, male vocal / instrumental group*   **4 wks**

7 Aug 82	**STILL OUT OF ORDER** *Secret SEC 7*	**42**	4 wks

James INGRAM *US, male vocalist*   **19 wks**

31 Mar 84	**IT'S YOUR NIGHT** *Qwest 9239701*	**25**	17 wks
30 Aug 86	**NEVER FELT SO GOOD** *Qwest WX 44*	**72**	2 wks

INNER CIRCLE *Jamaica, male vocal / instrumental group*   **2 wks**

29 May 93	**BAD TO THE BONE** *Magnet 9031776772*	**44**	2 wks

INNER CITY *US, male / female vocal / instrumental duo*   **39 wks**

20 May 89	● **PARADISE** *10 DIX 81*	**3**	30 wks
10 Feb 90	**PARADISE REMIXED** *10 XID 81*	**17**	6 wks

11 Jul 92	**PRAISE** Ten 4718862	**52**	1 wk
15 May 93	**TESTAMENT 93** Ten CDOVD 438	**33**	2 wks

INNOCENCE UK, male/female vocal/instrumental group   **20 wks**

10 Nov 90	**BELIEF** Cooltempo CTLP 20	**24**	19 wks
31 Oct 92	**BUILD** Cooltempo CTCD 26	**66**	1 wk

INSPIRAL CARPETS UK, male vocal/instrumental group   **36 wks**

5 May 90	● **LIFE** Cow DUNG 8..	**2**	21 wks
4 May 91	● **THE BEAST INSIDE** Cow DUNG 14	**5**	6 wks
17 Oct 92	**REVENGE OF THE GOLDFISH** Cow DUNG 19	**17**	3 wks
19 Mar 94	● **DEVIL HOPPING** Cow LDUNG 25CD..................	**10**	3 wks
30 Sep 95	**THE SINGLES** Cow CDMOOTEL 3	**17**	3 wks

INSPIRATIONAL CHOIR US, male/female choir   **4 wks**

18 Jan 86	**SWEET INSPIRATION** Portrait PRT 10048	**59**	4 wks

INSPIRATIONS UK, male instrumentalist – Neil Palmer, keyboards   **22 wks**

29 Apr 95	● **PAN PIPE INSPIRATIONS** Pure Music PMCD 7011	**10**	10 wks
23 Sep 95	● **PAN PIPE DREAMS** Pure Music PMCD 7016	**10**	8 wks
11 Nov 95	**PURE EMOTIONS** Pure Music PMCD 7023	**37**	4 wks

INTI ILLIMANI–GUAMARY
Chile, male vocal/instrumental group – panpipes   **7 wks**

17 Dec 83	**THE FLIGHT OF THE CONDOR – ORIGINAL TV SOUNDTRACK** BBC REB 440	**62**	7 wks

INVISIBLE GIRLS – See Pauline MURRAY and the INVISIBLE GIRLS

INXS Australia, male vocal/instrumental group   **228 wks**

8 Feb 86	**LISTEN LIKE THIEVES** Mercury MERH 82	**48**	15 wks
28 Nov 87	● **KICK** Mercury MERH 114	**9**	103 wks
6 Oct 90	● **X** Mercury 8466681.....................................	**2**	44 wks
16 Nov 91	● **LIVE BABY LIVE** Mercury 5105801..................	**8**	9 wks
15 Aug 92	★ **WELCOME TO WHEREVER YOU ARE** Mercury 5125072	**1**	33 wks
13 Nov 93	● **FULL MOON, DIRTY HEARTS** Mercury 5186372	**3**	8 wks
12 Nov 94	● **THE GREATEST HITS** Mercury 5262302	**3**	16 wks

Tony IOMMI – See BLACK SABBATH

IQ UK, male vocal/instrumental group   **1 wk**

22 Jun 85	**THE WAKE** Sahara SAH 136	**72**	1 wk

IRON MAIDEN UK, male vocal/instrumental group   **187 wks**

26 Apr 80	● **IRON MAIDEN** EMI EMC 3330	**4**	15 wks
28 Feb 81	**KILLERS** EMI EMC 3357	**12**	8 wks
10 Apr 82	★ **THE NUMBER OF THE BEAST** EMI EMC 3400	**1**	31 wks
28 May 83	● **PIECE OF MIND** EMI EMA 800	**3**	18 wks
15 Sep 84	● **POWERSLAVE** EMI POWER 1	**2**	13 wks
15 Jun 85	**IRON MAIDEN (re-issue)** Fame FA 4131211............	**71**	2 wks
26 Oct 85	● **LIVE AFTER DEATH** EMI RIP 1........................	**2**	14 wks
11 Oct 86	● **SOMEWHERE IN TIME** EMI EMC 3512	**3**	11 wks
20 Jun 87	**THE NUMBER OF THE BEAST (re-issue)** Fame FA 3178	**98**	1 wk
23 Apr 88	★ **SEVENTH SON OF A SEVENTH SON** EMI EMD 1006	**1**	18 wks
24 Feb 90	● **RUNNING FREE / SANCTUARY** EMI IRN 1............	**10**	4 wks
3 Mar 90	● **WOMEN IN UNIFORM / TWILIGHT ZONE** EMI IRN 2	**10**	3 wks
10 Mar 90	● **PURGATORY / MAIDEN JAPAN** EMI IRN 3	**5**	3 wks
17 Mar 90	● **RUN TO THE HILLS / THE NUMBER OF THE BEAST** EMI IRN 4	**3**	2 wks
24 Mar 90	● **FLIGHT OF ICARUS / THE TROOPER** EMI IRN 5..............	**7**	2 wks

British Hit Albums Part One

Date of chart entry/Title & catalogue no./Peak position reached/Weeks on chart

★ Number One   ● Top Ten   † still on chart at 30 Dec 1995   □ credited to act billed in footnote

31 Mar 90	**2 MINUTES TO MIDNIGHT / ACES HIGH** *EMI IRN 6*......................**11**	2 wks
7 Apr 90	● **RUNNING FREE (LIVE) / RUN TO THE HILLS (LIVE)** *EMI IRN 7* **9**	2 wks
14 Apr 90	● **WASTED YEARS / STRANGER IN A STRANGE LAND** *EMI IRN 8* **9**	2 wks
21 Apr 90	● **CAN I PLAY WITH MADNESS / THE EVIL THAT MEN DO** *EMI IRN 9*..**10**	3 wks
28 Apr 90	**THE CLAIRVOYANT / INFINITE DREAMS (LIVE)** *EMI IRN 10* **11**	2 wks
13 Oct 90	● **NO PRAYER FOR THE DYING** *EMI EMD 1017*................................**2**	14 wks
23 May 92	★ **FEAR OF THE DARK** *EMI CDEMD 1032* **1**	5 wks
3 Apr 93	● **A REAL LIVE ONE** *EMI CDEMD 1042* **3**	4 wks
30 Oct 93	**A REAL DEAD ONE** *EMI CDEMD 1048*..**12**	3 wks
20 Nov 93	**LIVE AT DONNINGTON** *EMI CDDON 1* **23**	1 wk
14 Oct 95	● **THE X FACTOR** *EMI CDEMD 1087* **8**	4 wks

Entries from Feb to Apr 1990 are double 12–inch singles made ineligible for the singles chart by their retail price.

Gregory ISAACS *Jamaica, male vocalist*   **6 wks**

12 Sep 81	**MORE GREGORY** *Charisma PREX 9* **93**	1 wk
4 Sep 82	**NIGHT NURSE** *Island ILPS 9721*..**32**	5 wks

Chris ISAAK *US, male vocalist*   **38 wks**

26 Jan 91	● **WICKED GAME** *Reprise WX 406*...**3**	30 wks
24 Apr 93	**SAN FRANCISCO DAYS** *Reprise 9362451162* **12**	5 wks
3 Jun 95	**FOREVER BLUE** *Reprise 9362458452* **27**	3 wks

ISLEY BROTHERS *US, male vocal / instrumental group*   **24 wks**

14 Dec 68	**THIS OLD HEART OF MINE** *Tamla Motown STML 11034*.................**23**	6 wks
14 Aug 76	**HARVEST FOR THE WORLD** *Epic EPC 81268*.................................**50**	5 wks
14 May 77	**GO FOR YOUR GUNS** *Epic EPC 86027* **46**	2 wks
24 Jun 78	**SHOWDOWN** *Epic EPC 86039* **50**	1 wk
5 Mar 88	**GREATEST HITS** *Telstar STAR 2306* **41**	10 wks

IT BITES *UK, male vocal / instrumental group*   **12 wks**

6 Sep 86	**THE BIG LAD IN THE WINDMILL** *Virgin V 2378*............................**35**	5 wks
2 Apr 88	**ONCE AROUND THE WORLD** *Virgin V 2456*..................................**43**	3 wks
24 Jun 89	**EAT ME IN ST. LOUIS** *Virgin V 2591* **40**	3 wks
31 Aug 91	**THANK YOU AND GOODNIGHT** *Virgin VGD 24233*.......................**59**	1 wk

IT'S A BEAUTIFUL DAY *US, male / female vocal / instrumental group* **3 wks**

23 May 70	**IT'S A BEAUTIFUL DAY** *CBS 63722* **58**	1 wk
18 Jul 70	**MARRYING MAIDEN** *CBS 66236* **45**	2 wks

IT'S IMMATERIAL *UK, male vocal / instrumental group*   **3 wks**

27 Sep 86	**LIFE'S HARD AND THEN YOU DIE** *Siren SIRENLP 4*.......................**62**	3 wks

Freddie JACKSON *US, male vocalist*   **48 wks**

18 May 85	**ROCK ME TONIGHT** *Capitol EJ 24403161* **27**	22 wks
8 Nov 86	**JUST LIKE THE FIRST TIME** *Capitol EST 2023* **30**	15 wks
30 Jul 88	**DON'T LET LOVE SLIP AWAY** *Capitol EST 2067*............................**24**	9 wks
17 Nov 90	**DO ME AGAIN** *Capitol EST 2134E* **48**	2 wks

Janet JACKSON *US, female vocalist* **198 wks**

5 Apr 86	● **CONTROL** *A & M AMA 5016*	.8	72	wks
14 Nov 87	**CONTROL – THE REMIXES** *Breakout MIXLP 1*	20	14	wks
30 Sep 89	● **RHYTHM NATION 1814** *A & M AMA 3920*	.4	43	wks
29 May 93	★ **JANET / JANET REMIXED** *Virgin CDV 2720*	.1	57	wks
14 Oct 95	● **DESIGN OF A DECADE 1986 – 1996** *A & M 5404222*	2†	12	wks

From 25 Mar 95 Janet was listed with the remix album Janet Remixed.

Jermaine JACKSON *US, male vocalist* **12 wks**

31 May 80	**LET'S GET SERIOUS** *Motown STML 12127*	22	6	wks
12 May 84	**DYNAMITE** *Arista 206 317*	57	6	wks

Joe JACKSON *UK, male vocalist* **106 wks**

17 Mar 79	**LOOK SHARP** *A & M AMLH 64743*	40	11	wks
13 Oct 79	**I'M THE MAN** *A & M AMLH 64794*	12	16	wks
18 Oct 80	**BEAT CRAZY** *A & M AMLH 64837*	42	3	wks
4 Jul 81	**JUMPIN' JIVE** *A & M AMLH 68530* [1]	14	14	wks
3 Jul 82	● **NIGHT AND DAY** *A & M AMLH 64906*	.3	27	wks
7 Apr 84	**BODY AND SOUL** *A & M AMLX 65000*	14	14	wks
5 Apr 86	**BIG WORLD** *A & M JWA 3*	41	5	wks
7 May 88	**LIVE 1980–1986** *A & M AMA 6706*	66	2	wks
29 Apr 89	**BLAZE OF GLORY** *A & M AMA 5249*	36	3	wks
15 Sep 90	● **STEPPING OUT – THE VERY BEST OF JOE JACKSON** *A & M 3970521*	.7	9	wks
11 May 91	**LAUGHTER AND LUST** *Virgin America VUSLP 34*	41	2	wks

[1] Joe Jackson's Jumpin' Jive

Michael JACKSON *US, male vocalist* **770 wks**

3 Jun 72	**GOT TO BE THERE** *Tamla Motown STML 11205*	37	5	wks
13 Jan 73	**BEN** *Tamla Motown STML 11220*	17	7	wks
29 Sep 79	● **OFF THE WALL** *Epic EPC 84368*	.5	178	wks
4 Jul 81	**BEST OF MICHAEL JACKSON** *Motown STMR 9009*	11	18	wks
18 Jul 81	**ONE DAY IN YOUR LIFE** *Motown STML 12158*	29	8	wks
11 Dec 82	★ **THRILLER** *Epic EPC 85930*	.1	173	wks
12 Feb 83	**E.T. THE EXTRA TERRESTRIAL** *MCA 7000*	82	2	wks
9 Jul 83	★ **18 GREATEST HITS** *Telstar STAR 2232* [1]	.1	58	wks
3 Dec 83	**MICHAEL JACKSON 9 SINGLE PACK** *Epic MJ 1*	66	3	wks
9 Jun 84	● **FAREWELL MY SUMMER LOVE** *Motown ZL 72227*	.9	14	wks
15 Nov 86	**DIANA ROSS. MICHAEL JACKSON. GLADYS KNIGHT. STEVIE WONDER. THEIR VERY BEST BACK TO BACK** *PrioriTyV PTVR 2* [2]	21	10	wks
12 Sep 87	★ **BAD** *Epic EPC 4502901*	.1	115	wks
31 Oct 87	**LOVE SONGS** *Telstar STAR 2298* [3]	12	24	wks
26 Dec 87	**THE MICHAEL JACKSON MIX** *Stylus SMR 745*	27	25	wks
30 Jul 88	**SOUVENIR SINGLES PACK** *Epic MJ 5*	91	1	wk
30 Nov 91	★ **DANGEROUS** *Epic 4658021*	.1	96	wks
29 Feb 92	**MOTOWN'S GREATEST HITS** *Motown 5300142*	53	2	wks
15 Aug 92	**TOUR SOUVENIR PACK** *Epic MJ 4*	32	3	wks
24 Jun 95	★ **HISTORY – PAST PRESENT AND FUTURE BOOK 1** *Epic 4747092*	1†	28	wks

[1] Michael Jackson plus the Jackson Five [2] Diana Ross/Michael Jackson/Gladys Knight/ Stevie Wonder [3] Diana Ross and Michael Jackson

Off The Wall *changed its catalogue number to 4500861 during its chart run. From 14 Jan 89, when multi–artist albums were excluded from the main chart, Love Songs was listed in the compilation albums chart. See also Various Artists – Telstar.*

Millie JACKSON *US, female vocalist* **7 wks**

18 Feb 84	**E.S.P.** *Sire 250382*	59	5	wks
6 Apr 85	**LIVE AND UNCENSORED** *Important TADLP 001*	81	2	wks

JACKSONS *US, male vocal group* **140 wks**

21 Mar 70	**DIANA ROSS PRESENTS THE JACKSON FIVE** *Tamla Motown STML 11142* [1]	16	4	wks

TOP 30 № 11

MICHAEL JACKSON
shows he wasn't bad
looking at all before he
altered his appearance.
(Andy Freeberg/LFI)

15 Aug 70	**ABC** Tamla Motown STML 11153 [1]	22	6 wks
7 Oct 72	**GREATEST HITS** Tamla Motown STML 11212 [1]	26	14 wks
18 Nov 72	**LOOKIN' THROUGH THE WINDOWS**		
	Tamla Motown STML 11214 [1]	16	8 wks
16 Jul 77	**THE JACKSONS** Epic EPC 86009	54	1 wk
3 Dec 77	**GOIN' PLACES** Epic EPC 86035	45	1 wk
5 May 79	**DESTINY** Epic EPC 83200	33	7 wks
11 Oct 80	**TRIUMPH** Epic EPC 86112	13	16 wks
12 Dec 81	**THE JACKSONS** Epic EPC 88562	53	9 wks
9 Jul 83	★ **18 GREATEST HITS** Telstar STAR 2232 [2]	1	58 wks
21 Jul 84	● **VICTORY** Epic EPC 86303	3	13 wks
1 Jul 89	**2300 JACKSON ST** Epic 463352 1	39	3 wks

[1] Jackson Five [2] Michael Jackson plus the Jackson Five

JADE US, female vocal group   **3 wks**

| 29 May 93 | **JADE TO THE MAX** Giant 74321148002 ..... | 43 | 3 wks |

Mick JAGGER UK, male vocalist   **20 wks**

16 Mar 85	● **SHE'S THE BOSS** CBS 86310	6	11 wks
26 Sep 87	**PRIMITIVE COOL** CBS 460 1231	26	5 wks
20 Feb 93	**WANDERING SPIRIT** Atlantic 7567824362	12	4 wks

JAM UK, male vocal / instrumental group   **173 wks**

28 May 77	**IN THE CITY** Polydor 2383 447	20	18 wks
26 Nov 77	**THIS IS THE MODERN WORLD** Polydor 2383 475	22	5 wks
11 Nov 78	● **ALL MOD CONS** Polydor POLD 5008	6	17 wks
24 Nov 79	● **SETTING SONS** Polydor POLD 5028	4	19 wks
6 Dec 80	● **SOUND AFFECTS** Polydor POLD 5035	2	19 wks
20 Mar 82	★ **THE GIFT** Polydor POLD 5055	1	24 wks
18 Dec 82	● **DIG THE NEW BREED** Polydor POLD 5075	2	15 wks
27 Aug 83	**IN THE CITY (re-issue)** Polydor SPELP 27	100	1 wk
22 Oct 83	● **SNAP** Polydor SNAP 1	2	30 wks
13 Jul 91	● **GREATEST HITS** Polydor 8495541	2	19 wks
18 Apr 92	**EXTRAS** Polydor 5131772	15	4 wks
6 Nov 93	**LIVE JAM** Polydor 5196672	28	2 wks

JAM and SPOON Germany, male instrumental duo   **1 wk**

| 19 Feb 94 | **TRIPOMATIC FAIRYTALES 2001** Epic 4749282 ..... | 71 | 1 wk |

JAMES UK, male vocal / instrumental group   **69 wks**

2 Aug 86	**STUTTER** Blanco Y Negro JIMLP 1	68	2 wks
8 Oct 88	**STRIP MINE** Sire JIMLP 2	90	1 wk
16 Jun 90	● **GOLD MOTHER** Fontana 8485951	2	34 wks
29 Feb 92	● **SEVEN** Fontana 5109322	2	14 wks
9 Oct 93	● **LAID** Fontana 5149432	3	16 wks
24 Sep 94	**WAH WAH** Fontana 5228272 [1]	11	2 wks

[1] James and Brian Eno

Rick JAMES US, male vocalist   **2 wks**

| 24 Jul 82 | **THROWIN' DOWN** Motown STML 12167 ..... | 93 | 2 wks |

Wendy JAMES UK, female vocalist   **1 wk**

| 20 Mar 93 | **NOW AIN'T THE TIME FOR YOUR TEARS** MCA MCD 10800 ..... | 43 | 1 wk |

JAMIROQUAI UK, male vocal / instrumental group   **58 wks**

| 26 Jun 93 | ★ **EMERGENCY ON PLANET EARTH** Sony S2 4740692 ..... | 1 | 32 wks |
| 29 Oct 94 | ● **THE RETURN OF THE SPACE COWBOY** Sony S2 4778132 ..... | 2 | 27 wks |

JAN and DEAN *US, male vocal duo* **2 wks**

12 Jul 80	**THE JAN AND DEAN STORY** *K-Tel NE 1084*	67	2 wks

JANE'S ADDICTION *US, male vocal / instrumental group* **2 wks**

8 Sep 90	**RITUAL DE LO HABITUAL** *Warner Bros. WX 306*	37	2 wks

JAPAN *UK, male vocal / instrumental group* **135 wks**

9 Feb 80	**QUIET LIFE** *Ariola Hansa AHAL 8011*	53	8 wks
15 Nov 80	**GENTLEMEN TAKE POLAROIDS** *Virgin V 2180*	45	10 wks
26 Sep 81	**ASSEMBLAGE** *Hansa HANLP 1*	26	46 wks
28 Nov 81	**TIN DRUM** *Virgin V 2209*	12	50 wks
18 Jun 83	● **OIL ON CANVAS** *Virgin VD 2513*	5	14 wks
8 Dec 84	**EXORCISING GHOSTS** *Virgin VGD 3510*	45	7 wks

Jeff JARRATT and Don REEDMAN *UK, male producers* **8 wks**

22 Nov 80	**MASTERWORKS** *K-Tel ONE 1093*	39	8 wks

Jean-Michel JARRE *France, male instrumentalist / producer* **228 wks**

20 Aug 77	● **OXYGENE** *Polydor 2310 555*	2	24 wks
16 Dec 78	**EQUINOXE** *Polydor POLD 5007*	11	26 wks
6 Jun 81	● **MAGNETIC FIELDS** *Polydor POLS 1033*	6	17 wks
15 May 82	● **THE CONCERTS IN CHINA** *Polydor PODV 3*	6	17 wks
12 Nov 83	**THE ESSENTIAL JEAN MICHEL JARRE** *Polystar PROLP 3*	14	29 wks
24 Nov 84	**ZOOLOOK** *Polydor POLH 15*	47	14 wks
12 Apr 86	● **RENDEZ–VOUS** *Polydor POLH 27*	9	38 wks
18 Jul 87	**IN CONCERT LYONS / HOUSTON** *Polydor POLH 36*	18	15 wks
8 Oct 88	● **REVOLUTIONS** *Polydor POLH 45*	2	13 wks
14 Oct 89	**JARRE LIVE** *Polydor 841258 1*	16	4 wks
23 Jun 90	**WAITING FOR COUSTEAU** *Dreyfus 8436141*	14	10 wks
26 Oct 91	**IMAGES – THE BEST OF JEAN-MICHEL JARRE** *Dreyfus 5113061*	14	12 wks
5 Jun 93	**CHRONOLOGIE** *Polydor 5193732*	11	8 wks
28 May 94	**CHRONOLOGIE PART 6** *Polydor 5195792*	60	1 wk

Al JARREAU *US, male vocalist* **37 wks**

5 Sep 81	**BREAKING AWAY** *Warner Bros. K 56917*	60	8 wks
30 Apr 83	**JARREAU** *WEA International U 0070*	39	18 wks
17 Nov 84	**HIGH CRIME** *WEA 250807*	81	1 wk
13 Sep 86	**L IS FOR LOVER** *WEA International 253 0801*	45	10 wks

JAYHAWKS *US, male / female vocal / instrumental group* **1 wk**

25 Feb 95	**TOMORROW THE GREEN GRASS** *American 74321236802*	41	1 wk

JAZZY JEFF – *See DJ JAZZY JEFF and FRESH PRINCE*

JEFFERSON AIRPLANE
US / UK, female / male vocal / instrumental group **28 wks**

28 Jun 69	**BLESS ITS POINTED LITTLE HEAD** *RCA SF 8019*	38	1 wk
7 Mar 70	**VOLUNTEERS** *RCA SF 8076*	34	7 wks
2 Oct 71	**BARK** *Grunt FTR 1001*	42	1 wk
2 Sep 72	**LONG JOHN SILVER** *Grunt FTR 1007*	30	1 wk
31 Jul 76	**SPITFIRE** *Grunt RFL 1557* [1]	30	2 wks
9 Feb 80	**FREEDOM AT POINT ZERO** *Grunt FL 13452* [1]	22	11 wks
18 Jul 87	**NO PROTECTION** *Grunt FL 86413* [2]	26	5 wks

[1] Jefferson Starship [2] Starship

JELLYBEAN *US, male instrumentalist / producer* **35 wks**

31 Oct 87	**JUST VISITING THIS PLANET** *Chrysalis CHR 1569*	15	28 wks
3 Sep 88	**ROCKS THE HOUSE!** *Chrysalis CJB 1*	16	7 wks

JELLYFISH *US, male vocal / instrumental group*   **2 wks**

22 May 93	**SPILT MILK** Charisma CDCUS 20 ....**21**	2 wks

JESUS AND MARY CHAIN *UK, male vocal / instrumental group*   **39 wks**

30 Nov 85	**PSYCHOCANDY** Blanco Y Negro BYN 7 ....**31**	10 wks
12 Sep 87	● **DARKLANDS** Blanco Y Negro BYN 11 ....**5**	7 wks
30 Apr 88	● **BARBED WIRE KISSES** Blanco Y Negro BYN 15 ....**9**	7 wks
21 Oct 89	**AUTOMATIC** Blanco Y Negro BYN 20...........................**11**	4 wks
4 Apr 92	**HONEY'S DEAD** Blanco Y Negro 9031765542...............**14**	5 wks
24 Jul 93	**THE SOUND OF SPEED** Blanco Y Negro 4509931052......**15**	3 wks
27 Aug 94	**STONED AND DETHRONED** Blanco Y Negro 4509967172...........**13**	3 wks

JESUS JONES *UK, male vocal / instrumental group*   **31 wks**

14 Oct 89	**LIQUIDIZER** Food FOODLP 3 ....**32**	3 wks
9 Feb 91	★ **DOUBT** Food FOODLP 5 ....**1**	24 wks
6 Feb 93	● **PERVERSE** Food FOODCD 8...................................**6**	4 wks

JESUS LIZARD *US, male vocal / instrumental group*   **1 wk**

10 Sep 94	**DOWN** Touch And Go TG 131CD................................**64**	1 wk

JESUS LOVES YOU – *See BOY GEORGE*

JETHRO TULL *UK, male vocal / instrumental group*   **234 wks**

J
172

2 Nov 68	● **THIS WAS** Island ILPS 9085 ....**10**	22 wks
9 Aug 69	★ **STAND UP** Island ILPS 9103 ....**1**	29 wks
9 May 70	● **BENEFIT** Island ILPS 9123 ....**3**	13 wks
3 Apr 71	● **AQUALUNG** Island ILPS 9145.................................**4**	21 wks
18 Mar 72	● **THICK AS A BRICK** Chrysalis CHR 1003 ....**5**	14 wks
15 Jul 72	● **LIVING IN THE PAST** Chrysalis CJT 1 ....**8**	11 wks
28 Jul 73	**A PASSION PLAY** Chrysalis CHR 1040 ....**13**	8 wks
2 Nov 74	**WAR CHILD** Chrysalis CHR 1067 ....**14**	4 wks
27 Sep 75	**MINSTREL IN THE GALLERY** Chrysalis CHR 1082 ....**20**	6 wks
31 Jan 76	**M.U. THE BEST OF JETHRO TULL** Chrysalis CHR 1078 ....**44**	5 wks
15 May 76	**TOO OLD TO ROCK 'N' ROLL TOO YOUNG TO DIE** Chrysalis CHR 1111 ....**25**	10 wks
19 Feb 77	**SONGS FROM THE WOOD** Chrysalis CHR 1132...............**13**	12 wks
29 Apr 78	**HEAVY HORSES** Chrysalis CHR 1175 ....**20**	10 wks
14 Oct 78	**LIVE BURSTING OUT** Chrysalis CJT 4 ....**17**	8 wks
6 Oct 79	**STORM WATCH** Chrysalis CDL 1238 ....**27**	4 wks
6 Sep 80	**A** Chrysalis CDL 1301 ....**25**	5 wks
17 Apr 82	**BROADSWORD AND THE BEAST** Chrysalis CDL 1380 ......**27**	19 wks
15 Sep 84	**UNDER WRAPS** Chrysalis CDL 1461 ....**18**	5 wks
2 Nov 85	**ORIGINAL MASTERS** Chrysalis JTTV 1 ....**63**	3 wks
19 Sep 87	**CREST OF A KNAVE** Chrysalis CDL 1590 ....**19**	10 wks
9 Jul 88	**20 YEARS OF JETHRO TULL** Chrysalis TBOX 1 ....**78**	1 wk
2 Sep 89	**ROCK ISLAND** Chrysalis CHR 1708 ....**18**	6 wks
14 Sep 91	**CATFISH RISING** Chrysalis CHR 1886 ....**27**	3 wks
26 Sep 92	**A LITTLE LIGHT MUSIC** Chrysalis CCD 1954 ....**34**	2 wks
16 Sep 95	**ROOTS TO BRANCHES** Chrysalis CDCHR 6109...............**20**	3 wks

JETS *UK, male vocal / instrumental group*   **6 wks**

10 Apr 82	**100 PERCENT COTTON** EMI EMC 3399 ....**30**	6 wks

JETS *US, male / female vocal / instrumental group*   **4 wks**

11 Apr 87	**CRUSH ON YOU** MCA MCF 3312 ....**57**	4 wks

Joan JETT and the BLACKHEARTS
US, female / male vocal / instrumental group   **7 wks**

8 May 82	**I LOVE ROCK 'N' ROLL** Epic EPC 85686.......................**25**	7 wks

ALPHABETICALLY BY ARTIST

JIVE BUNNY and the MASTERMIXERS
UK, male production / mixing group   **29 wks**

9 Dec 89 ●	JIVE BUNNY – THE ALBUM *Telstar STAR 2390*	2	22 wks
8 Dec 90	IT'S PARTY TIME *Telstar STAR 2449*	23	7 wks

JO BOXERS *UK, male vocal / instrumental group*   **5 wks**

24 Sep 83	LIKE GANGBUSTERS *RCA BOXXLP 1*	18	5 wks

JODECI *US, male vocal group*   **8 wks**

29 Jul 95 ●	THE SHOW THE AFTER PARTY THE HOTEL *Uptown MCD 11258*	4	8 wks

JOE *US, male vocalist*   **1 wk**

12 Feb 94	EVERYTHING *Vertigo 5188072*	53	1 wk

Billy JOEL *US, male vocalist*   **316 wks**

25 Mar 78	THE STRANGER *CBS 82311*	25	40 wks
25 Nov 78 ●	52ND STREET *CBS 83181*	10	43 wks
22 Mar 80 ●	GLASS HOUSES *CBS 86108*	9	24 wks
10 Oct 81	SONGS IN THE ATTIC *CBS 85273*	57	3 wks
2 Oct 82	NYLON CURTAIN *CBS 85959*	27	8 wks
10 Sep 83 ●	AN INNOCENT MAN *CBS 25554*	2	95 wks
4 Feb 84	COLD SPRING HARBOUR *CBS 32400*	95	1 wk
23 Jun 84	PIANO MAN *CBS 32002*	98	1 wk
20 Jul 85 ●	GREATEST HITS VOLUME I & VOLUME II *CBS 88666*	7	39 wks
16 Aug 86	THE BRIDGE *CBS 86323*	38	10 wks
28 Nov 87	KOHYEPT – LIVE IN LENINGRAD *CBS 460 4071*	92	1 wk
4 Nov 89 ●	STORM FRONT *CBS 4656581*	5	25 wks
14 Aug 93 ●	RIVER OF DREAMS *Columbia 4738722*	3	26 wks

Elton JOHN *UK, male vocalist / instrumentalist piano*   **801 wks**

23 May 70	ELTON JOHN *DJM DJLPS 406*	11	14 wks
16 Jan 71 ●	TUMBLEWEED CONNECTION *DJM DJLPS 410*	6	20 wks
1 May 71	THE ELTON JOHN LIVE ALBUM 17–11–70 *DJM DJLPS 414*	20	2 wks
20 May 72	MADMAN ACROSS THE WATER *DJM DJLPH 420*	41	2 wks
3 Jun 72 ●	HONKY CHATEAU *DJM DJLPH 423*	2	23 wks
10 Feb 73 ★	DON'T SHOOT ME I'M ONLY THE PIANO PLAYER		
	DJM DJLPH 427	1	42 wks
3 Nov 73 ★	GOODBYE YELLOW BRICK ROAD *DJM DJLPO 1001*	1	84 wks
13 Jul 74 ★	CARIBOU *DJM DJLPH 439*	1	18 wks
23 Nov 74 ★	ELTON JOHN'S GREATEST HITS *DJM DJLPH 442*	1	84 wks
7 Jun 75 ●	CAPTAIN FANTASTIC AND THE BROWN DIRT COWBOY		
	DJM DJLPX 1	2	24 wks
8 Nov 75 ●	ROCK OF THE WESTIES *DJM DJLPH 464*	5	12 wks
15 May 76 ●	HERE AND THERE *DJM DJLPH 473*	6	9 wks
6 Nov 76 ●	BLUE MOVES *Rocket ROSP 1*	3	15 wks
15 Oct 77 ●	GREATEST HITS VOLUME 2 *DJM DJH 20520*	6	24 wks
4 Nov 78 ●	A SINGLE MAN *Rocket TRAIN 1*	8	26 wks
20 Oct 79	VICTIM OF LOVE *Rocket HISPD 125*	41	3 wks
8 Mar 80	LADY SAMANTHA *DJM 22085*	56	2 wks
31 May 80	21 AT 33 *Rocket HISPD 126*	12	13 wks
25 Oct 80	THE VERY BEST OF ELTON JOHN *K-Tel NE 1094*	24	13 wks
30 May 81	THE FOX *Rocket TRAIN 16*	12	12 wks
17 Apr 82	JUMP UP *Rocket HISPD 127*	13	12 wks
6 Nov 82	LOVE SONGS *TV TVA 3*	39	13 wks
11 Jun 83 ●	TOO LOW FOR ZERO *Rocket HISPD 24*	7	73 wks
30 Jun 84 ●	BREAKING HEARTS *Rocket HISPD 25*	2	23 wks
16 Nov 85 ●	ICE ON FIRE *Rocket HISPD 26*	3	23 wks
15 Nov 86	LEATHER JACKETS *Rocket EJLP 1*	24	9 wks
12 Sep 87	LIVE IN AUSTRALIA *Rocket EJBXL 1* [1]	43	7 wks
16 Jul 88	REG STRIKES BACK *Rocket EJLP 3*	18	6 wks
23 Sep 89 ★	SLEEPING WITH THE PAST *Rocket 8388391*	1	42 wks

10 Nov 90 ★ **THE VERY BEST OF ELTON JOHN** Rocket 8469471 ....**1**   94 wks
27 Jun 92 ● **THE ONE** Rocket 5123602 ....**2**   18 wks
4 Dec 93 ● **DUETS** Rocket 5184782 ....**5**   18 wks
1 Apr 95 ● **MADE IN ENGLAND** Rocket 5261852 ....**3**   14 wks
18 Nov 95 ● **LOVE SONGS** Rocket 5287882 ....**4†**   7 wks

[1] Elton John and the Melbourne Symphony Orchestra

Live In Australia *reappeared in 1988 as EJLP 2; EJBXL 1 was the original 'de luxe' version. The two* Very Best Of Elton John *albums are different.*

JOHNNY HATES JAZZ UK, male vocal / instrumental group   **39 wks**

23 Jan 88 ★ **TURN BACK THE CLOCK** Virgin V 2475..............................**1**   39 wks

JOHNNY and the HURRICANES US, male instrumental group   **5 wks**

3 Dec 60   **STORMSVILLE** London HAI 2269 ....**18**   1 wk
1 Apr 61   **BIG SOUND OF JOHNNY AND THE HURRICANES**
            London HAK 2322...**14**   4 wks

Matt JOHNSON – *See The THE*

Holly JOHNSON UK, male vocalist   **17 wks**

6 May 89 ★ **BLAST** MCA MCG 6042 ....**1**   17 wks

Linton Kwesi JOHNSON Jamaica, male poet   **8 wks**

30 Jun 79   **FORCE OF VICTORY** Island ILPS 9566..............................**66**   1 wk
31 Oct 80   **BASS CULTURE** Island ILPS 9605.....................................**46**   5 wks
10 Mar 84   **MAKING HISTORY** Island ILPS 9770................................**73**   2 wks

Paul JOHNSON UK, male vocalist   **3 wks**

4 Jul 87   **PAUL JOHNSON** CBS 450640 1 ....**63**   2 wks
16 Sep 89   **PERSONAL** CBS 463284 1 ....**70**   1 wk

Brian JOHNSTONE UK, male broadcaster   **3 wks**

5 Mar 94   **AN EVENING WITH JOHNNERS** Listen For Pleasure LFP 7742 ......**46**   3 wks

Al JOLSON US, male vocalist   **11 wks**

14 Mar 81   **20 GOLDEN GREATS** MCA MCTV 4 ....**18**   7 wks
17 Dec 83   **THE AL JOLSON COLLECTION** Ronco RON LP 5 ....**67**   4 wks

JON and VANGELIS UK / Greece, male vocal / instrumental duo   **53 wks**

26 Jan 80 ● **SHORT STORIES** Polydor POLD 5030 ....**4**   11 wks
11 Jul 81   **THE FRIENDS OF MR. CAIRO** Polydor POLD 5039 ....**17**   8 wks
23 Jan 82 ● **THE FRIENDS OF MR. CAIRO (re-issue)** Polydor POLD 5053 ....**6**   15 wks
2 Jul 83   **PRIVATE COLLECTION** Polydor POLH 4 ....**22**   10 wks
11 Aug 84   **THE BEST OF JON AND VANGELIS** Polydor POLH 6 ....**42**   9 wks

See also Jon Anderson; Vangelis.

JONES – *See SMITH and JONES*

Aled JONES UK, male chorister   **141 wks**

27 Apr 85 ● **VOICES FROM THE HOLY LAND** BBC REC 564 [1] ....**6**   43 wks
29 Jun 85 ● **ALL THROUGH THE NIGHT** BBC REH 569 [1] ....**2**   44 wks
23 Nov 85   **ALED JONES WITH THE BBC WELSH CHORUS** 10/BBC AJ 1 [1] ..**11**   10 wks
22 Feb 86   **WHERE E'ER YOU WALK** 10 DIX 21 ....**36**   6 wks
12 Jul 86   **PIE JESU** 10 AJ 2..**25**   16 wks
29 Nov 86   **AN ALBUM OF HYMNS** Telstar STAR 2272 ....**18**   11 wks
14 Mar 87   **ALED (MUSIC FROM THE TV SERIES)** 10 AJ 3................................**52**   6 wks

5 Dec 87   **THE BEST OF ALED JONES** *10 AJ 5* ....**59**   5 wks

1   Aled Jones with the BBC Welsh Chorus

Glenn JONES *US, male vocalist*   **1 wk**

31 Oct 87   **GLENN JONES** *Jive HIP 51* ....**62**   1 wk

Grace JONES *US, female vocalist*   **80 wks**

30 Aug 80	**WARM LEATHERETTE** *Island ILPS 9592* **45**	2 wks
23 May 81	**NIGHTCLUBBING** *Island ILPS 9624* **35**	16 wks
20 Nov 82	**LIVING MY LIFE** *Island ILPS 9722* **15**	22 wks
9 Nov 85	**SLAVE TO THE RHYTHM** *ZTT GRACE 1* **12**	8 wks
14 Dec 85	● **ISLAND LIFE** *Island GJ 1* **4**	30 wks
29 Nov 86	**INSIDE STORY** *Manhattan MTL 1007* **61**	2 wks

Howard JONES *UK, male vocalist*   **122 wks**

17 Mar 84	★ **HUMAN'S LIB** *WEA WX 1* **1**	57 wks
8 Dec 84	● **THE 12" ALBUM** *WEA WX 14* **15**	33 wks
23 Mar 85	● **DREAM INTO ACTION** *WEA WX 15* **2**	25 wks
25 Oct 86	● **ONE TO ONE** *WEA WX 68* **10**	4 wks
1 Apr 89	**CROSS THAT LINE** *WEA WX 225* **64**	1 wk
5 Jun 93	**THE BEST OF HOWARD JONES** *East West 4509927012* **36**	2 wks

Jack JONES *US, male vocalist*   **70 wks**

29 Apr 72	● **A SONG FOR YOU** *RCA Victor SF 8228* **9**	6 wks
3 Jun 72	● **BREAD WINNERS** *RCA Victor SF 8280* **7**	36 wks
7 Apr 73	● **TOGETHER** *RCA Victor SF 8342* **8**	10 wks
23 Feb 74	● **HARBOUR** *RCA Victor APLI 0408*......................**10**	5 wks
19 Feb 77	**THE FULL LIFE** *RCA Victor PL 12067*...................**41**	5 wks
21 May 77	● **ALL TO YOURSELF** *RCA TVL 2* **10**	8 wks

J
175

Quincy JONES *US, male arranger / instrumentalist – keyboards*   **41 wks**

18 Apr 81	**THE DUDE** *A & M AMLK 63721*.............................**19**	25 wks
20 Mar 82	**THE BEST** *A & M AMLH 68542* **41**	4 wks
20 Jan 90	**BACK ON THE BLOCK** *Qwest WX 313*....................**26**	12 wks

Rickie Lee JONES *US, female vocalist*   **39 wks**

16 Jun 79	**RICKIE LEE JONES** *Warner Bros. K 56628* **18**	19 wks
8 Aug 81	**PIRATES** *Warner Bros. K 56816* **37**	11 wks
2 Jul 83	**GIRL AT HER VOLCANO** *Warner Bros. 9238051* **51**	3 wks
13 Oct 84	**THE MAGAZINE** *Warner Bros. 925117*...................**40**	4 wks
7 Oct 89	**FLYING COWBOYS** *Geffen WX 309* **50**	2 wks

Tammy JONES *UK, female vocalist*   **5 wks**

12 Jul 75   **LET ME TRY AGAIN** *Epic EPC 80853* ....**38**   5 wks

Tom JONES *UK, male vocalist*   **422 wks**

5 Jun 65	**ALONG CAME JONES** *Decca LK 6693* **11**	5 wks
8 Oct 66	**FROM THE HEART** *Decca LK 4814* **23**	8 wks
8 Apr 67	● **GREEN GREEN GRASS OF HOME** *Decca SKL 4855* **3**	49 wks
24 Jun 67	● **LIVE AT THE TALK OF THE TOWN** *Decca SKL 4874* **6**	90 wks
30 Dec 67	● **13 SMASH HITS** *Decca SKL 4909* **5**	49 wks
27 Jul 68	★ **DELILAH** *Decca SKL 4946*................................**1**	29 wks
21 Dec 68	● **HELP YOURSELF** *Decca SKL 4982* **4**	9 wks
28 Jun 69	● **THIS IS TOM JONES** *Decca SKL 5007* **2**	20 wks
15 Nov 69	● **TOM JONES LIVE IN LAS VEGAS** *Decca SKL 5032*........**2**	45 wks
25 Apr 70	● **TOM** *Decca SKL 5045* **4**	18 wks
14 Nov 70	● **I WHO HAVE NOTHING** *Decca SKL 5072*.............**10**	10 wks
29 May 71	● **SHE'S A LADY** *Decca SKL 5089*.........................**9**	7 wks
27 Nov 71	**LIVE AT CAESAR'S PALACE** *Decca 1/11/2*...............**27**	5 wks

24 Jun 72	**CLOSE UP** Decca SKL 5132..**17**	4 wks
23 Jun 73	**THE BODY AND SOUL OF TOM JONES** Decca SKL 5162..............**31**	1 wk
5 Jan 74	**GREATEST HITS** Decca SKL 5176....................................**15**	13 wks
22 Mar 75	★ **20 GREATEST HITS** Decca TJD 1/11/2 ....**1**	21 wks
7 Oct 78	**I'M COMING HOME** Lotus WH 5001 ....**12**	9 wks
16 May 87	**THE GREATEST HITS** Telstar STAR 2296 ....**16**	12 wks
13 May 89	**AT THIS MOMENT** Jive TOMTV 1 ....**34**	3 wks
8 Jul 89	**AFTER DARK** Stylus SMR 978 ....**46**	4 wks
6 Apr 91	**CARRYING A TORCH** Dover ADD 20 ....**44**	4 wks
27 Jun 92	● **THE COMPLETE TOM JONES** The Hit Label 8442862 ......**8**	6 wks
26 Nov 94	**THE LEAD AND HOW TO SWING IT** ZTT 6544924982 ....**55**	1 wk

Janis JOPLIN US, female vocalist   **7 wks**

| 17 Apr 71 | **PEARL** CBS 64188 ....**50** | 1 wk |
| 22 Jul 72 | **JANIS JOPLIN IN CONCERT** CBS 67241 ....**30** | 6 wks |

Montell JORDAN US, male vocalist   **2 wks**

| 24 Jun 95 | **THIS IS HOW WE DO IT** RAL 5271792 ....**53** | 2 wks |

Ronny JORDAN UK, male instrumentalist – guitar   **7 wks**

7 Mar 92	**THE ANTIDOTE** Island CID 9988 ....**52**	4 wks
9 Oct 93	**THE QUIET REVOLUTION** Island CID 8009....................**49**	2 wks
3 Sep 94	**BAD BROTHERS** Island IMCD 8024 1 ....**58**	1 wk

1 Ronny Jordan meets DJ Krush

JOURNEY US, male vocal / instrumental group   **30 wks**

20 Mar 82	**ESCAPE** CBS 85138..**32**	16 wks
19 Feb 83	● **FRONTIERS** CBS 25261 ....**6**	8 wks
6 Aug 83	**EVOLUTION** CBS 32342 ....**100**	1 wk
24 May 86	**RAISED ON RADIO** CBS 26902 ....**22**	5 wks

JOY DIVISION UK, male vocal / instrumental group   **32 wks**

26 Jul 80	● **CLOSER** Factory FACT 25 ....**6**	8 wks
30 Aug 80	**UNKNOWN PLEASURES** Factory FACT 10 ....**71**	1 wk
17 Oct 81	● **STILL** Factory FACT 40 ....**5**	12 wks
23 Jul 88	● **1977–1980 SUBSTANCE** Factory FAC 250 ....**7**	8 wks
1 Jul 95	**PERMANENT: JOY DIVISION 1995** London 8286242 ....**16**	3 wks

JTQ with Noel McKOY – See James TAYLOR QUARTET

JUDAS PRIEST UK, male vocal / instrumental group   **78 wks**

14 May 77	**SIN AFTER SIN** CBS 82008................................**23**	6 wks
25 Feb 78	**STAINED GLASS** CBS 82430 ....**27**	5 wks
11 Nov 78	**KILLING MACHINE** CBS 83135 ....**32**	9 wks
6 Oct 79	● **UNLEASHED IN THE EAST** CBS 83852 ....**10**	8 wks
19 Apr 80	● **BRITISH STEEL** CBS 84160................................**4**	17 wks
7 Mar 81	**POINT OF ENTRY** CBS 84834................................**14**	5 wks
17 Jul 82	**SCREAMING FOR VENGEANCE** CBS 85941 ....**11**	9 wks
28 Jan 84	**DEFENDERS OF THE FAITH** CBS 25713 ....**19**	5 wks
19 Apr 86	**TURBO** CBS 26641..**33**	4 wks
13 Jun 87	**PRIEST LIVE** CBS 450 6391 ....**47**	2 wks
28 May 88	**RAM IT DOWN** CBS 461108 1 ....**24**	5 wks
22 Sep 90	**PAINKILLER** CBS 4672901 ....**26**	2 wks
8 May 93	**METAL WORKS 73–93** Columbia 4730502 ....**37**	1 wk

JUDGE DREAD UK, male vocalist   **14 wks**

| 6 Dec 75 | **BEDTIME STORIES** Cactus CTLP 113................................**26** | 12 wks |
| 7 Mar 81 | **40 BIG ONES** Creole BIG 1 ....**51** | 2 wks |

British Hit Albums Part One

Date of chart entry/Title & catalogue no./Peak position reached/Weeks on chart

★ Number One   ● Top Ten   † still on chart at 30 Dec 1995   ☐ credited to act billed in footnote

JUICY LUCY *UK, male vocal / instrumental group* **5 wks**

18 Apr 70	**JUICY LUCY** Vertigo VO 2	**41**	4 wks
21 Nov 70	**LIE BACK AND ENJOY IT** Vertigo 6360 014	**53**	1 wk

JULUKA *South Africa, male / female vocal / instrumental group* **3 wks**

23 Jul 83	**SCATTERLINGS** Safari SHAKA 1	**50**	3 wks

JUNGLE BROTHERS *US, male rap group* **3 wks**

3 Feb 90	**DONE BY THE FORCES OF NATURE** Eternal WX 332	**41**	3 wks

JUNIOR *UK, male vocalist* **14 wks**

5 Jun 82	**JI** Mercury MERS 3	**28**	14 wks

K-KLASS *UK, male / female vocal / instrumental group* **1 wk**

4 Jun 94	**UNIVERSAL** Deconstruction CDPCSDX 149	**73**	1 wk

Joshua KADISON *US, male vocalist* **4 wks**

27 May 95	**PAINTED DESERT SERENADE** SBK SBKCD 22	**45**	4 wks

Bert KAEMPFERT *Germany, orchestra* **104 wks**

5 Mar 66	● **BYE BYE BLUES** Polydor BM 84086	**4**	22 wks
16 Apr 66	**BEST OF BERT KAEMPFERT** Polydor 84012	**27**	1 wk
28 May 66	**SWINGING SAFARI** Polydor LPHM 46384	**20**	15 wks
30 Jul 66	**STRANGERS IN THE NIGHT** Polydor LPHM 84053	**13**	26 wks
4 Feb 67	**RELAXING SOUND OF BERT KAEMPFERT** Polydor 583501	**33**	3 wks
18 Feb 67	**BERT KAEMPFERT – BEST SELLER** Polydor 583551	**25**	18 wks
29 Apr 67	**HOLD ME** Polydor 184072	**36**	5 wks
26 Aug 67	**KAEMPFERT SPECIAL** Polydor 236207	**24**	5 wks
19 Jun 71	**ORANGE COLOURED SKY** Polydor 2310091	**49**	1 wk
5 Jul 80	**SOUNDS SENSATIONAL** Polydor POLTB 10	**17**	8 wks

KAJAGOOGOO *UK, male vocal / instrumental group* **23 wks**

30 Apr 83	● **WHITE FEATHERS** EMI EMC 3433	**5**	20 wks
26 May 84	**ISLANDS** EMI KAJA 1	**35**	3 wks

Nick KAMEN *UK, male vocalist* **7 wks**

18 Apr 87	**NICK KAMEN** WEA WX 84	**34**	7 wks

KANE GANG *UK, male vocal / instrumental group* **12 wks**

23 Feb 85	**THE BAD AND LOWDOWN WORLD OF THE KANE GANG** Kitchenware KWLP 2	**21**	8 wks
8 Aug 87	**MIRACLE** Kitchenware KWLP 7	**41**	4 wks

Mick KARN *UK, male vocalist / instrumentalist – bass* **4 wks**

20 Nov 82	**TITLES** Virgin V 2249	**74**	3 wks

28 Feb 87	**DREAMS OF REASON PRODUCE MONSTERS** Virgin V 2389 ....**89**	1 wk

KATRINA and the WAVES
UK / US, female / male vocal / instrumental group   **7 wks**

8 Jun 85	**KATRINA AND THE WAVES** Capitol KTW 1 ....**28**	6 wks
10 May 86	**WAVES** Capitol EST 2010 ....**70**	1 wk

KC and the SUNSHINE BAND
UK, male vocal / instrumental group   **17 wks**

30 Aug 75	**KC AND THE SUNSHINE BAND** Jayboy JSL 9 ....**26**	7 wks
1 Mar 80	● **GREATEST HITS** TK TKR 83385 ....**10**	6 wks
27 Aug 83	**ALL IN A NIGHT'S WORK** Epic EPC 85847 ....**46**	4 wks

KEEL *US, male vocal / instrumental group*   **2 wks**

17 May 86	**THE FINAL FRONTIER** Vertigo VERH 33 ....**83**	2 wks

Howard KEEL *US, male vocalist*   **36 wks**

14 Apr 84	● **AND I LOVE YOU SO** Warwick WW 5137 ....**6**	19 wks
9 Nov 85	**REMINISCING – THE HOWARD KEEL COLLECTION**	
	Telstar STAR 2259 ....**20**	12 wks
28 Mar 88	**JUST FOR YOU** Telstar STAR 2318.......................................**51**	5 wks

R. KELLY *US, male vocalist*   **51 wks**

29 Feb 92	**BORN INTO THE 90S** Jive CHIP 123 [1] **67**	1 wk
27 Nov 93	**12–PLAY** Jive CHIP 144...**20**	44 wks
25 Nov 95	**R KELLY** Jive CHIP 166 ....**18†**	6 wks

[1] R. Kelly and Public Announcement

Felicity KENDAL *UK, female exercise instructor*   **47 wks**

19 Jun 82	**SHAPE UP AND DANCE (VOLUME 1)** Lifestyle LEG 1....................**29**	47 wks

Eddie KENDRICK – See Daryl HALL and John OATES

Brian KENNEDY *Ireland, male vocalist*   **1 wk**

31 Mar 90	**THE GREAT WAR OF WORDS** RCA PL 74475 ....**64**	1 wk

Nigel KENNEDY *UK, male instrumentalist violin*   **116 wks**

1 Mar 86	**ELGAR VIOLIN CONCERTO** EMI EMX 4120581 [1] **97**	1 wk
7 Oct 89	● **VIVALDI: FOUR SEASONS** EMI NIGE 2 [2] **3**	81 wks
5 May 90	**MENDELSSOHN / BRUCH / SCHUBERT** HMV 7496631 [3] **28**	15 wks
6 Apr 91	**BRAHMS VIOLIN CONCERTO** EMI NIGE 3............................**16**	12 wks
22 Feb 92	**JUST LISTEN . . .** EMI Classics CDNIGE 4................................**56**	1 wk
21 Nov 92	**BEETHOVEN: VIOLIN CONCERTO** EMI Classics CDC 7545742 [4] ..**40**	6 wks

[1] Nigel Kennedy with the London Philharmonic Orchestra, conducted by Vernon Handley
[2] Nigel Kennedy with the English Chamber Orchestra [3] Nigel Kennedy with Jeffrey Tate and
the English Chamber Orchestra [4] Nigel Kennedy with Klaus Tennstedt and the North German
Radio Symphony Orchestra

KENNY *UK, male vocal / instrumental group*   **1 wk**

17 Jan 76	**THE SOUND OF SUPER K** RAK SRAK 518 ....**56**	1 wk

Gerard KENNY *US, male vocalist*   **4 wks**

21 Jul 79	**MADE IT THROUGH THE RAIN** RCA Victor PL 25218.....................**19**	4 wks

Nik KERSHAW *UK, male vocalist*   **100 wks**

10 Mar 84	● **HUMAN RACING** MCA MCF 3197...**5**	61 wks

| 1 Dec 84 | ● THE RIDDLE MCA MCF 3245 ....8 | 36 wks |
| 8 Nov 86 | RADIO MUSICOLA MCA MCG 6016.................................47 | 3 wks |

Chaka KHAN US, female vocalist **44 wks**

21 Apr 84	STOMPIN' AT THE SAVOY Warner Bros. 923679 [1] 64	5 wks
20 Oct 84	I FEEL FOR YOU Warner Bros. 925 162 15	22 wks
9 Aug 86	DESTINY Warner Bros. WX 45 77	2 wks
3 Jun 89	LIFE IS A DANCE – THE REMIX PROJECT Warner Bros. WX 268..14	15 wks

[1] Rufus and Chaka Khan

Aram KHATCHATURIAN/VIENNA PHILMARMONIC ORCHESTRA Russia, male conductor / Austria – orchestra **15 wks**

| 22 Jan 72 | SPARTACUS Decca SXL 6000 ....16 | 15 wks |

KIDS FROM FAME US, male / female vocal / instrumental group **117 wks**

24 Jul 82	★ KIDS FROM FAME BBC REP 447...1	45 wks
16 Oct 82	● KIDS FROM FAME AGAIN RCA RCALP 6057 2	21 wks
26 Feb 83	● THE KIDS FROM FAME LIVE BBC KIDLP 003 8	28 wks
14 May 83	THE KIDS FROM FAME SONGS BBC KIDLP 004 14	16 wks
20 Aug 83	SING FOR YOU BBC KIDLP 005..28	7 wks

KILLING JOKE UK, male vocal / instrumental group **33 wks**

25 Oct 80	KILLING JOKE Polydor EGMD 545 39	4 wks
20 Jun 81	WHAT'S THIS FOR Malicious Damage EGMD 550..........................42	4 wks
8 May 82	REVELATIONS Malicious Damage EGMD 3 12	6 wks
27 Nov 82	'HA' – KILLING JOKE LIVE EG EGMDT 4.................................66	2 wks
23 Jul 83	FIRE DANCES EG EGMD 5...29	3 wks
9 Mar 85	NIGHT TIME EG EGLP 61 11	9 wks
22 Nov 86	BRIGHTER THAN A THOUSAND SUNS EG EGLP 66.......................54	1 wk
9 Jul 88	OUTSIDE THE GATE EG EGLP 73 92	1 wk
6 Aug 94	PANDEMONIUM Butterfly BFLCD 9 16	3 wks

KIMERA with the LONDON SYMPHONY ORCHESTRA
Korea, female vocalist with UK orchestra **4 wks**

| 26 Oct 85 | HITS ON OPERA Stylus SMR 8505.....................................38 | 4 wks |

See also London Symphony Orchestra.

KING UK, male vocal / instrumental group **32 wks**

| 9 Feb 85 | ● STEPS IN TIME CBS 26095..6 | 21 wks |
| 23 Nov 85 | BITTER SWEET CBS 86320 ....16 | 11 wks |

BB KING US, male vocalist / instrumentalist – guitar **5 wks**

| 25 Aug 79 | TAKE IT HOME MCA MCF 3010 ....60 | 5 wks |

Ben E. KING US, male vocalist **27 wks**

1 Jul 67	SPANISH HARLEM Atlantic 590001 30	3 wks
14 Mar 87	STAND BY ME (THE ULTIMATE COLLECTION) Atlantic WX 90 [1] 14	8 wks
20 Oct 90	THE BEST OF BEN E. KING AND THE DRIFTERS Telstar STAR 2373 [1] ..15	16 wks

[1] Ben E. King and the Drifters

Carole KING US, female vocalist / instrumentalist piano **102 wks**

24 Jul 71	● TAPESTRY A & M AMLS 2025 4	90 wks
15 Jan 72	MUSIC A & M AMLH 67013..18	10 wks
2 Dec 72	RHYMES AND REASONS Ode 77016 40	2 wks

Diana KING Jamaica, female vocalist　　2 wks

12 Aug 95	**TOUGHER THAN LOVE** Columbia 4777562	50	2 wks

Evelyn KING US, female vocalist　　9 wks

11 Sep 82	**GET LOOSE** RCA RCALP 3093	35	9 wks

Mark KING UK, male vocalist / instrumentalist – bass　　2 wks

21 Jul 84	**INFLUENCES** Polydor MKLP 1	77	2 wks

Solomon KING US, male vocalist　　1 wk

22 Jun 68	**SHE WEARS MY RING** Columbia SCX 6250	40	1 wk

KING CRIMSON UK, male vocal / instrumental group　　54 wks

1 Nov 69	● **IN THE COURT OF THE CRIMSON KING** Island ILPS 9111	5	18 wks
30 May 70	● **IN THE WAKE OF POSEIDON** Island ILPS 9127	4	13 wks
16 Jan 71	**LIZARD** Island ILPS 9141	30	1 wk
8 Jan 72	**ISLANDS** Island ILPS 9175	30	1 wk
7 Apr 73	**LARKS' TONGUES IN ASPIC** Island ILPS 9230	20	4 wks
13 Apr 74	**STARLESS AND BIBLE BLACK** Island ILPS 9275	28	2 wks
26 Oct 74	**RED** Island ILPS 9308	45	1 wk
10 Oct 81	**DISCIPLINE** EG EGLP 49	41	4 wks
26 Jun 82	**BEAT** EG EGLP 51	39	5 wks
31 Mar 84	**THREE OF A PERFECT PAIR** EG EGLP 55	30	4 wks
15 Apr 95	**THRAK** Virgin KCCDY 1	58	1 wk

K
180

KING KURT UK, male vocal / instrumental group　　5 wks

10 Dec 83	**OOH WALLAH WALLAH** Stiff SEEZ 52	99	1 wk
8 Mar 86	**BIG COCK** Stiff SEEZ 62	50	4 wks

The Choir of KING'S COLLEGE, CAMBRIDGE UK, choir　　3 wks

11 Dec 71	**THE WORLD OF CHRISTMAS** Argo SPAA 104	38	3 wks

KING'S X US, male vocal / instrumental group　　4 wks

1 Jul 89	**GRETCHEN GOES TO NEBRASKA** Atlantic WX 279	52	1 wk
10 Nov 90	**FAITH HOPE LOVE** Megaforce 756821451	70	1 wk
28 Mar 92	**KING'S X** Atlantic 7567805062	46	1 wk
12 Feb 94	**DOGMAN** Atlantic 7567825582	49	1 wk

KINGDOM COME US, male vocal / instrumental group　　10 wks

28 Mar 88	**KINGDOM COME** Polydor KCLP 1	43	6 wks
13 May 89	**IN YOUR FACE** Polydor 839192 1	25	4 wks

KINGMAKER UK, male vocal / instrumental group　　10 wks

19 Oct 91	**EAT YOURSELF WHOLE** Scorch CHR 1878	29	3 wks
29 May 93	**SLEEPWALKING** Scorch CDCHR 6014	15	7 wks

KINGS OF SWING ORCHESTRA Australia, orchestra　　11 wks

29 May 82	**SWITCHED ON SWING** K-Tel ONE 1166	28	11 wks

KINKS UK, male vocal / instrumental group　　129 wks

17 Oct 64	● **KINKS** Pye NPL 18096	3	25 wks
13 Mar 65	● **KINDA KINKS** Pye NPL 18112	3	15 wks
4 Dec 65	● **KINKS KONTROVERSY** Pye NPL 18131	9	12 wks
11 Sep 66	● **WELL RESPECTED KINKS** Marble Arch MAL 612	5	31 wks

5 Nov 66	**FACE TO FACE** Pye NPL 18149	**12**	11 wks
14 Oct 67	**SOMETHING ELSE** Pye NSPL 18193	**35**	2 wks
2 Dec 67	● **SUNNY AFTERNOON** Marble Arch MAL 716	**9**	11 wks
23 Oct 71	**GOLDEN HOUR OF THE KINKS** Golden Hour GH 501	**21**	4 wks
14 Oct 78	**20 GOLDEN GREATS** Ronco RPL 2031	**19**	6 wks
5 Nov 83	**KINKS GREATEST HITS – DEAD END STREET** PRT KINK 1	**96**	1 wk
16 Sep 89	**THE ULTIMATE COLLECTION** Castle Communications CTVLP 001	**35**	7 wks
18 Sep 93	**THE DEFINITIVE COLLECTION** PolyGram TV 5164652	**18**	4 wks

Kathy KIRBY UK, female vocalist   8 wks

4 Jan 64	**16 HITS FROM STARS AND GARTERS** Decca LK 5475	**11**	8 wks

KISS US, male vocal / instrumental group   67 wks

29 May 76	**DESTROYER** Casablanca CBSP 4008	**22**	5 wks
25 Jun 76	**ALIVE!** Casablanca CBSP 401	**49**	2 wks
17 Dec 77	**ALIVE** Casablanca CALD 5004	**60**	1 wk
7 Jul 79	**DYNASTY** Casablanca CALH 2051	**50**	6 wks
28 Jun 80	**UNMASKED** Mercury 6302 032	**48**	3 wks
5 Dec 81	**THE ELDER** Casablanca 6302 163	**51**	3 wks
26 Jun 82	**KILLERS** Casablanca CANL 1	**42**	6 wks
6 Nov 82	**CREATURES OF THE NIGHT** Casablanca CANL 4	**22**	4 wks
8 Oct 83	● **LICK IT UP** Vertigo VERL 9	**7**	7 wks
6 Oct 84	**ANIMALISE** Vertigo VERL 18	**11**	4 wks
5 Oct 85	**ASYLUM** Vertigo VERH 32	**12**	3 wks
7 Nov 87	● **CRAZY NIGHTS** Vertigo VERH 49	**4**	14 wks
10 Dec 88	**SMASHES, THRASHES AND HITS** Vertigo 836759 1	**62**	2 wks
4 Nov 89	**HOT IN THE SHADE** Fontana 838913 1	**35**	2 wks
23 May 92	● **REVENGE** Mercury 8480372	**10**	3 wks
29 May 93	**ALIVE III** Mercury 5148272	**24**	2 wks

KISSING THE PINK UK, male / female vocal / instrumental group   5 wks

4 Jun 83	**NAKED** Magnet KTPL 1001	**54**	5 wks

KITCHENS OF DISTINCTION UK, male vocal / instrumental group   2 wks

30 Mar 91	**STRANGE FREE WORLD** One Little Indian TPLP 19	**45**	1 wk
15 Aug 92	**DEATH OF COOL** One Little Indian TPLP 39CD	**72**	1 wk

Eartha KITT US, female vocalist   1 wk

11 Feb 61	**REVISITED** London HA 2296	**17**	1 wk

KLEEER US, male vocal / instrumental group   1 wk

6 Jul 85	**SEEEKRET** Atlantic 7812541	**96**	1 wk

KLF UK, male multi–instrumental / production duo with guest vocalists   46 wks

16 Mar 91	● **THE WHITE ROOM** KLF Communications JAMSLP 6	**3**	46 wks

Earl KLUGH – See George BENSON

KNACK US, male vocal / instrumental group   2 wks

4 Aug 79	**GET THE KNACK** Capitol EST 11948	**65**	2 wks

Curtis KNIGHT – See Jimi HENDRIX

Gladys KNIGHT and the PIPS
US, female vocalist / male vocal backing group   **115 wks**

31 May 75	**I FEEL A SONG** Buddah BDLP 4030	**20**	15 wks
28 Feb 76	● **THE BEST OF GLADYS KNIGHT AND THE PIPS** Buddah BDLH 5013	**6**	43 wks

K
181

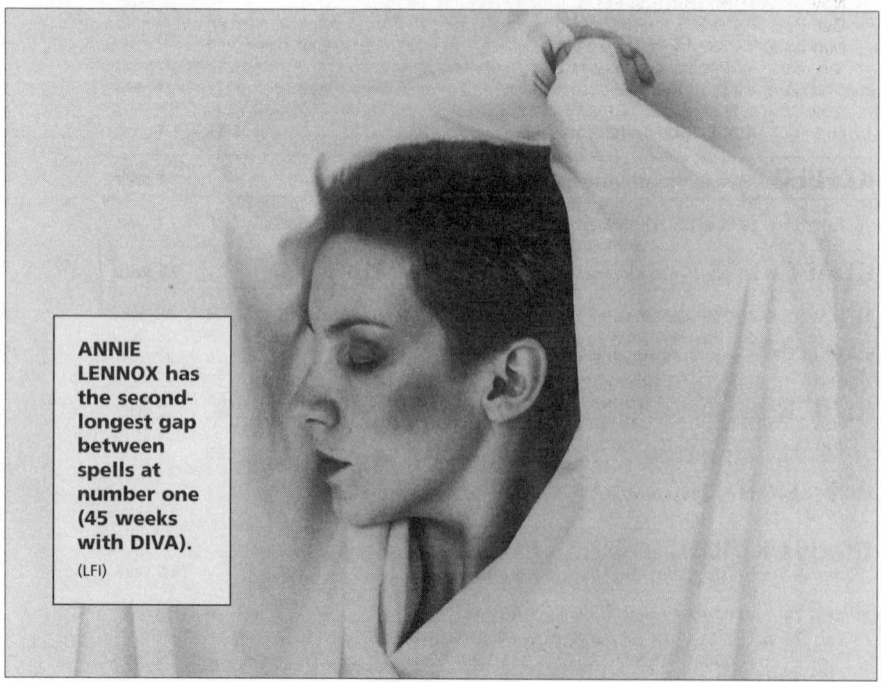

TOP 30 N⁰ 9

On 2 November 1978
ELTON JOHN returned to
live action after a
two-year break with a
performance at the
London Hilton.
(Doug Mackenzie/Hulton Deutsch)

**ANNIE
LENNOX** has
the second-
longest gap
between
spells at
number one
(45 weeks
with **DIVA**).
(LFI)

16 Jul 77	**STILL TOGETHER** Buddah BDLH 5014 42	3 wks
12 Nov 77	● **30 GREATEST** K-Tel NE 1004 ....**3**	22 wks
4 Oct 80	**A TOUCH OF LOVE** K-Tel NE 1090 ....**16**	6 wks
4 Feb 84	**THE COLLECTION - 20 GREATEST HITS** Starblend NITE 1.............**43**	5 wks
15 Nov 86	**DIANA ROSS. MICHAEL JACKSON. GLADYS KNIGHT. STEVIE WONDER. THEIR VERY BEST BACK TO BACK** PrioriTyV PTVR 2 [1] **21**	10 wks
27 Feb 88	**ALL OUR LOVE** MCA MCF 3409 ....**80**	1 wk
28 Oct 89	**THE SINGLES ALBUM** Polygram GKTV 1.......................................**13**	10 wks

[1] Diana Ross/Michael Jackson/Gladys Knight/Stevie Wonder

KNIGHTSBRIDGE STRINGS UK, male orchestra **1 wk**

25 Jun 60	**STRING SWAY** Top Rank BUY 017 ....**20**	1 wk

David KNOPFLER UK, male vocalist / instrumentalist – guitar **1 wk**

19 Nov 83	**RELEASE** Peach River DAVID 1 ....**82**	1 wk

Mark KNOPFLER UK, male vocalist / instrumentalist – guitar **25 wks**

16 Apr 83	**LOCAL HERO (film soundtrack)** Vertigo VERL 4 ....**14**	11 wks
20 Oct 84	**CAL (film soundtrack)** Vertigo VERH 17 ....**65**	3 wks
24 Nov 90	**NECK AND NECK** CBS 4674351 [1] **41**	11 wks

[1] Chet Atkins and Mark Knopfler

Frankie KNUCKLES US, male producer **2 wks**

17 Aug 91	**BEYOND THE MIX** Virgin America VUSLP 6 ....**59**	2 wks

John KONGOS South Africa, male vocalist / multi–instrumentalist **2 wks**

15 Jan 72	**KONGOS** Fly HIFLY 7 ....**29**	2 wks

KOOL AND THE GANG US, male vocal / instrumental group **115 wks**

21 Nov 81	● **SOMETHING SPECIAL** De–Lite DSR 001 ....**10**	20 wks
2 Oct 82	**AS ONE** De–Lite DSR 3...**49**	10 wks
7 May 83	● **TWICE AS KOOL** De–Lite PROLP 2 ....**4**	23 wks
14 Jan 84	**IN THE HEART** De–Lite DSR 4 ....**18**	23 wks
15 Dec 84	**EMERGENCY** De–Lite DSR 6 ....**47**	25 wks
12 Nov 88	**THE SINGLES COLLECTION** De–Lite KGTV 1.................................**28**	13 wks
27 Oct 90	**KOOL LOVE** Telstar STAR 2435 ....**50**	1 wk

KORGIS UK, male vocal / instrumental duo **4 wks**

26 Jul 80	**DUMB WAITERS** Rialto TENOR 104 ....**40**	4 wks

KRAFTWERK Germany, male vocal / instrumental group **71 wks**

17 May 75	● **AUTOBAHN** Vertigo 6360 620...**4**	18 wks
20 May 78	● **THE MAN–MACHINE** Capitol EST 11728 ....**9**	13 wks
23 May 81	**COMPUTER WORLD** EMI EMC 3370..**15**	22 wks
6 Feb 82	**TRANS–EUROPE EXPRESS** Capitol EST 11603...............................**49**	7 wks
22 Jun 85	**AUTOBAHN (re–issue)** Parlophone AUTO 1 ....**61**	3 wks
15 Nov 86	**ELECTRIC CAFE** EMI EMD 1001 ....**58**	2 wks
22 Jun 91	**THE MIX** EMI EM 1408...**15**	6 wks

Billy J. KRAMER and the DAKOTAS
UK, male vocalist, male instrumental backing group **17 wks**

16 Nov 63	**LISTEN TO BILLY J. KRAMER** Parlophone PMC 1209 ....**11**	17 wks

Lenny KRAVITZ US, male vocalist **82 wks**

26 May 90	**LET LOVE RULE** Virgin America VUSLP 10....................................**56**	4 wks

13 Apr 91	● **MAMA SAID** Virgin America VUSLP 31 ....**8**	27	wks
13 Mar 93	★ **ARE YOU GONNA GO MY WAY** Virgin America CDVUS 60 ....**1**	47	wks
23 Sep 95	● **CIRCUS** Virgin America CDVUS 86 ....**5**	4	wks

KREUZ *UK, male vocal group*   **2 wks**

18 Mar 95	**KREUZ KONTROL** Diesel DESCD 01 ....**48**	2	wks

KRIS KROSS *US, male rap duo*   **8 wks**

27 Jun 92	**TOTALLY KROSSED OUT** Columbia 4714342...................**31**	8	wks

Kris KRISTOFFERSON – See Rita COOLIDGE

KROKUS *Switzerland / Malta, male vocal / instrumental group*   **11 wks**

21 Feb 81	**HARDWARE** Ariola ARL 5064 ....**44**	4	wks
20 Feb 82	**ONE VICE AT A TIME** Arista SPART 1189 ....**28**	5	wks
16 Apr 83	**HEADHUNTER** Arista 205 255 ....**74**	2	wks

K7 *US, male vocalist*   **3 wks**

5 Feb 94	**SWING BATTA SWING** Big Life BLRCD 27..................**27**	3	wks

Charlie KUNZ *US, male instrumentalist – piano*   **11 wks**

14 Jun 69	● **THE WORLD OF CHARLIE KUNZ** Decca SPA 15 ....**9**	11	wks

L.A. GUNS *US, male / female vocal / instrumental group*   **4 wks**

5 Mar 88	**L.A. GUNS** Vertigo VERH 55 ....**73**	1	wk
30 Sep 89	**COCKED AND LOADED** Vertigo 8385921 ....**45**	2	wks
13 Jul 91	**HOLLYWOOD VAMPIRES** Mercury 8496041 ....**44**	1	wk

LA'S *UK, male vocal / instrumental group*   **19 wks**

13 Oct 90	**THE LA'S** Go! Discs 8282021 ....**30**	19	wks

Patti LaBELLE *US, female vocalist*   **17 wks**

24 May 86	**THE WINNER IN YOU** MCA MCF 3319...............................**30**	17	wks

LADYSMITH BLACK MAMBAZO
South Africa, male vocal group   **11 wks**

11 Apr 87	**SHAKA ZULU** Warner Bros. WX 94......................................**34**	11	wks

Cleo LAINE *UK, female vocalist*   **37 wks**

7 Jan 78	**BEST OF FRIENDS** RCA RS 1094 [1] **18**	22	wks
2 Dec 78	**CLEO** Arcade ADEP 37 ....**68**	1	wk
31 May 80	**SOMETIMES WHEN WE TOUCH** RCA PL 25296 [2] **15**	14	wks

[1] Cleo Laine and John Williams [2] Cleo Laine and James Galway

Frankie LAINE *US, male vocalist*   **29 wks**

24 Jun 61	● **HELL BENT FOR LEATHER** Philips BBL 7468 ....**7**	23	wks
24 Sep 77	● **THE VERY BEST OF FRANKIE LAINE** Warwick PR 5032 ....**7**	6	wks

Greg LAKE *UK, male vocalist* **3 wks**

17 Oct 81   **GREG LAKE** *Chrysalis CHR 1357* 62   3 wks

See also Emerson, Lake and Palmer; Emerson, Lake and Powell.

Annabel LAMB *UK, female vocalist* **1 wk**

28 Apr 84   **THE FLAME** *A & M AMLX 68564* 84   1 wk

LAMBRETTAS *UK, male vocal/instrumental group* **8 wks**

5 Jul 80   **BEAT BOYS IN THE JET AGE** *Rocket TRAIN 10*...............28   8 wks

LANDSCAPE *UK, male vocal/instrumental group* **12 wks**

21 Mar 81   **FROM THE TEAROOMS OF MARS TO THE HELLHOLES OF URANUS** *RCA RCALP 5003*........................13   12 wks

Ronnie LANE *UK, male vocal/instrumental group* **4 wks**

17 Aug 74   **ANYMORE FOR ANYMORE** *GM GML 1013* [1] 48   1 wk
15 Oct 77   **ROUGH MIX** *Polydor 2442147* [2] 44   3 wks

[1] Ronnie Lane and the Band Slim Chance [2] Pete Townshend and Ronnie Lane

kd lang *Canada, female vocalist* **55 wks**

28 Mar 92 ● **INGENUE** *Sire 7599268402* 3   48 wks
13 Nov 93   **EVEN COW GIRLS GET THE BLUES** *Sire 9362454332* 36   2 wks
14 Oct 95 ● **ALL YOU CAN EAT** *Warner Bros. 9362460342* 7   5 wks

Thomas LANG *UK, male vocalist* **1 wk**

20 Feb 88   **SCALLYWAG JAZ** *Epic 450996 1*.......................................92   1 wk

Mario LANZA *US, male vocalist* **63 wks**

6 Dec 58 ● **THE STUDENT PRINCE / THE GREAT CARUSO** *RCA RB 16113* 4   21 wks
23 Jul 60 ● **THE GREAT CARUSO** *RCA RB 16112* 3   15 wks
9 Jan 71   **HIS GREATEST HITS VOLUME 1** *RCA LSB 4000* 39   1 wk
5 Sep 81   **THE LEGEND OF MARIO LANZA** *K-Tel NE 1110* 29   11 wks
14 Nov 87   **A PORTRAIT OF MARIO LANZA** *Stylus SMR 741* 49   8 wks
12 Mar 94   **MARIO LANZA – THE ULTIMATE COLLECTION** *RCA Victor 74321185742* 13   7 wks

The Great Caruso side of the first album is a film soundtrack.

LARD *UK, male vocal/instrumental group* **1 wk**

6 Oct 90   **THE LAST TEMPTATION** *Alternative Tentacles VIRUS 84* 69   1 wk

James LAST *Germany, male orchestra leader* **431 wks**

15 Apr 67 ● **THIS IS JAMES LAST** *Polydor 104678* 6   48 wks
22 Jul 67   **HAMMOND A–GO–GO** *Polydor 249043* 27   10 wks
26 Aug 67   **NON–STOP DANCING** *Polydor 236203* 35   1 wk
26 Aug 67   **LOVE THIS IS MY SONG** *Polydor 583553* 32   2 wks
22 Jun 68   **JAMES LAST GOES POP** *Polydor 249160* 32   3 wks
8 Feb 69   **DANCING '68 VOLUME 1** *Polydor 249216* 40   1 wk
31 May 69   **TRUMPET A–GO–GO** *Polydor 249239* 13   1 wk
9 Aug 69   **NON–STOP DANCING '69** *Polydor 249294* 26   1 wk
24 Jan 70   **NON–STOP DANCING '69 / 2** *Polydor 249354* 27   3 wks
23 May 70   **NON–STOP DANCING** *Polydor 249370* 26   1 wk
11 Jul 70   **CLASSICS UP TO DATE** *Polydor 249371* 44   1 wk
11 Jul 70   **NON–STOP DANCING '70** *Polydor 237104* 67   1 wk
24 Oct 70   **VERY BEST OF JAMES LAST** *Polydor 2371054*...............45   4 wks
8 May 71   **NON–STOP DANCING '71** *Polydor 2371111* 21   4 wks

L
185

British Hit Albums Part One

Date of chart entry/Title & catalogue no./Peak position reached/Weeks on chart

★ Number One ● Top Ten † still on chart at 30 Dec 1995 ☐ credited to act billed in footnote

26 Jun 71	SUMMER HAPPENING *Polydor 2371133*	38	1 wk
18 Sep 71	BEACH PARTY 2 *Polydor 2371211*	47	1 wk
2 Oct 71	YESTERDAY'S MEMORIES *Contour 2870117*	17	14 wks
16 Oct 71	NON-STOP DANCING 12 *Polydor 2371141*	30	3 wks
19 Feb 72	NON-STOP DANCING 13 *Polydor 2371189*	32	2 wks
4 Mar 72	POLKA PARTY *Polydor 2371190*	22	3 wks
29 Apr 72	JAMES LAST IN CONCERT *Polydor 2371191*	13	6 wks
24 Jun 72	VOODOO PARTY *Polydor 2371235*	45	1 wk
16 Sep 72	CLASSICS UP TO DATE VOLUME 2 *Polydor 184061*	49	1 wk
30 Sep 72	LOVE MUST BE THE REASON *Polydor 2371281*	32	2 wks
27 Jan 73	THE MUSIC OF JAMES LAST *Polydor 2683010*	19	12 wks
24 Feb 73	JAMES LAST IN RUSSIA *Polydor 2371293*	12	9 wks
24 Feb 73	NON-STOP DANCING VOLUME 14 *Polydor 2371319*	27	3 wks
28 Jul 73	OLE *Polydor 2371384*	24	5 wks
1 Sep 73	NON-STOP DANCING VOLUME 15 *Polydor 2371376*	34	2 wks
20 Apr 74	NON-STOP DANCING VOLUME 16 *Polydor 2371444*	43	2 wks
29 Jun 74	IN CONCERT VOLUME 2 *Polydor 2371320*	49	1 wk
23 Nov 74	GOLDEN MEMORIES *Polydor 2371472*	39	2 wks
26 Jul 75	● TEN YEARS NON-STOP JUBILEE *Polydor 2660111*	5	16 wks
2 Aug 75	VIOLINS IN LOVE *K-Tel I*	60	1 wk
22 Nov 75	● MAKE THE PARTY LAST *Polydor 2371612*	3	19 wks
8 May 76	CLASSICS UP TO DATE VOLUME 3 *Polydor 2371538*	54	1 wk
6 May 78	EAST TO WEST *Polydor 2630092*	49	4 wks
14 Apr 79	● LAST THE WHOLE NIGHT LONG *Polydor PTD 001*	2	45 wks
23 Aug 80	THE BEST FROM 150 GOLD RECORDS *Polydor 2681 211*	56	3 wks
1 Nov 80	CLASSICS FOR DREAMING *Polydor POLTV 11*	12	18 wks
14 Feb 81	ROSES FROM THE SOUTH *Polydor 2372 051*	41	5 wks
21 Nov 81	HANSIMANIA *Polydor POLTV 14*	18	13 wks
28 Nov 81	LAST FOREVER *Polydor 2630 135*	88	2 wks
5 Mar 83	BLUEBIRD *Polydor POLD 5072*	57	3 wks
30 Apr 83	THE BEST OF MY GOLD RECORDS *Polydor PODV 7*	42	5 wks
30 Apr 83	NON-STOP DANCING '83 – PARTY POWER *Polydor POLD 5094*	56	2 wks
3 Dec 83	THE GREATEST SONGS OF THE BEATLES *Polydor POLD 5119*	52	8 wks
24 Mar 84	THE ROSE OF TRALEE AND OTHER IRISH FAVOURITES *Polydor POLD 5131*	21	11 wks
13 Oct 84	PARADISE *Polydor POLD 5163*	74	2 wks
8 Dec 84	JAMES LAST IN SCOTLAND *Polydor POLD 5166*	68	9 wks
14 Sep 85	LEAVE THE BEST TO LAST *Polydor PROLP 7*	11	27 wks
18 Apr 87	BY REQUEST *Polydor POLH 34*	22	11 wks
26 Nov 88	DANCE DANCE DANCE *Polydor JLTV 1*	38	8 wks
14 Apr 90	CLASSICS BY MOONLIGHT *Polydor 8432181*	12	12 wks
15 Jun 91	● POP SYMPHONIES *Polydor 8494291*	10	11 wks
9 Nov 91	TOGETHER AT LAST *Delphine/Polydor 5115251* ☐1	14	15 wks
12 Sep 92	VIVA ESPAÑA *PolyGram TV 5172202*	23	5 wks
20 Nov 93	JAMES LAST PLAYS ANDREW LLOYD WEBBER *Polydor 5199102*	12	10 wks
19 Nov 94	IN HARMONY *Polydor 5238242* ☐1	28	7 wks
18 Nov 95	THE VERY BEST OF JAMES LAST *Polydor 5295562*	36†	7 wks

☐1 Richard Clayderman and James Last

LATIN QUARTER *UK, male / female vocal / instrumental group* **3 wks**

1 Mar 86	MODERN TIMES *Rockin' Horse RHLP 1*	91	2 wks
6 Jun 87	MICK AND CAROLINE *Rockin' Horse 208 142*	96	1 wk

Cyndi LAUPER *US, female vocalist* **91 wks**

18 Feb 84	SHE'S SO UNUSUAL *Portrait PRT 25792*	16	32 wks
11 Oct 86	TRUE COLORS *Portrait PRT 26948*	25	12 wks
1 Jul 89	● A NIGHT TO REMEMBER *Epic 462499 1*	9	12 wks
27 Nov 93	HAT FULL OF STARS *Epic 4730542*	56	1 wk
3 Sep 94	● TWELVE DEADLY CYNS . . . AND THEN SOME *Epic 4773632*	2	34 wks

LAUREL and HARDY UK / US, male comic duo **4 wks**

6 Dec 75	**THE GOLDEN AGE OF HOLLYWOOD COMEDY** United Artists UAG 29676	55	4 wks

LAW UK / US, male vocal / instrumental duo **1 wk**

6 Apr 91	**THE LAW** Atlantic 7567821951	61	1 wk

Joey LAWRENCE US, male vocalist **3 wks**

31 Jul 93	**JOEY LAWRENCE** EMI CDEMC 3657	39	3 wks

Syd LAWRENCE UK, orchestra **9 wks**

8 Aug 70	**MORE MILLER AND OTHER BIG BAND MAGIC** Philips 6642 001	14	4 wks
25 Dec 71	**SYD LAWRENCE WITH THE GLENN MILLER SOUND** Fontana SFL 13178	31	2 wks
25 Dec 71	**MUSIC OF GLENN MILLER IN SUPER STEREO** Philips 6641017	43	2 wks
26 Feb 72	**SOMETHING OLD, SOMETHING NEW** Philips 6308 090	34	1 wk

Ronnie LAWS US, male vocalist / instrumentalist – saxophone **1 wk**

17 Oct 81	**SOLID GROUND** Liberty LBG 30336	100	1 wk

Doug LAZY US, male vocalist **1 wk**

10 Mar 90	**DOUG LAZY GETTIN' CRAZY** Atlantic 7567820661	65	1 wk

LEAGUE UNLIMITED ORCHESTRA – See HUMAN LEAGUE

L
187

LED ZEPPELIN UK, male vocal / instrumental group **441 wks**

12 Apr 69	● **LED ZEPPELIN** Atlantic 588171	6	79 wks
8 Nov 69	★ **LED ZEPPELIN 2** Atlantic 588198	1	138 wks
7 Nov 70	★ **LED ZEPPELIN 3** Atlantic 2401002	1	40 wks
27 Nov 71	★ **FOUR SYMBOLS** Atlantic K 2401012	1	66 wks
14 Apr 73	★ **HOUSES OF THE HOLY** Atlantic K 50014	1	13 wks
15 Mar 75	★ **PHYSICAL GRAFFITI** Swan Song SSK 89400	1	27 wks
24 Apr 76	★ **PRESENCE** Swan Song SSK 59402	1	14 wks
6 Nov 76	★ **THE SONG REMAINS THE SAME** Swan Song SSK 89402	1	15 wks
8 Sep 79	★ **IN THROUGH THE OUT DOOR** Swan Song SSK 59410	1	16 wks
4 Dec 82	● **CODA** Swan Song A 0051	4	7 wks
27 Oct 90	● **REMASTERS** Atlantic ZEP 1	10	23 wks
10 Nov 90	**LED ZEPPELIN** Atlantic 7567821441	48	2 wks
9 Oct 93	**BOXED SET II** Atlantic 7567824772	56	1 wk

Led Zeppelin 2 changed label / number to Atlantic K 40037 and Four Symbols changed to Atlantic K 50008 during their runs. The fourth Led Zeppelin album appeared in the chart under various guises: The Fourth Led Zeppelin Album, Runes, The New Led Zeppelin Album, Led Zeppelin 4 and Four Symbols. The two albums titled Led Zeppelin are different. (The 1990 entry was a boxed CD set of old and previously unreleased material.)

LEE – See PETERS and LEE

Brenda LEE US, female vocalist **64 wks**

24 Nov 62	**ALL THE WAY** Brunswick LAT 8383	20	2 wks
16 Feb 63	**BRENDA – THAT'S ALL** Brunswick LAT 8516	13	9 wks
13 Apr 63	● **ALL ALONE AM I** Brunswick LAT 8530	8	20 wks
16 Jul 66	**BYE BYE BLUES** Brunswick LAT 8649	21	2 wks
1 Nov 80	**LITTLE MISS DYNAMITE** Warwick WW 5083	15	11 wks
7 Jan 84	**25TH ANNIVERSARY** MCA MCLD 609	65	4 wks
30 Mar 85	**THE VERY BEST OF BRENDA LEE** MCA LETV 1	16	9 wks
15 Oct 94	**THE VERY BEST OF BRENDA LEE . . . WITH LOVE** Telstar TCD 2738	20	7 wks

Peggy LEE *US, female vocalist*   **23 wks**

4 Jun 60 ● **LATIN A LA LEE** Capitol T 1290 ....**8**	15 wks
11 Jun 60 **BEAUTY AND THE BEAT** Capitol T 1219 [1] **16**	6 wks
20 May 61 **BEST OF PEGGY LEE VOLUME 2** Brunswick LAT 8355 ....**18**	1 wk
21 Oct 61 **BLACK COFFEE** Ace of Hearts AH 5 ....**20**	1 wk

[1] Peggy Lee and George Shearing

Raymond LEFEVRE *France, orchestra*   **9 wks**

7 Oct 67 ● **RAYMOND LEFEVRE** Major Minor MMLP 4 ....**10**	7 wks
17 Feb 68 **RAYMOND LEFEVRE VOLUME 2** Major Minor SMLP 13 ....**37**	2 wks

LEFTFIELD *UK, male instrumental / production duo*   **35 wks**

11 Feb 95 ● **LEFTISM** Hard Hands HANDCD 2 ....**3**	35 wks

Tom LEHRER *US, male comic vocalist*   **26 wks**

8 Nov 58 ● **SONGS BY TOM LEHRER** Decca LF 1311 ....**7**	19 wks
25 Jun 60 ● **AN EVENING WASTED WITH TOM LEHRER** Decca LK 4332...........**7**	7 wks

LEMONHEADS *US, male vocal / instrumental group*   **30 wks**

1 Aug 92 **IT'S A SHAME ABOUT RAY** Atlantic 7567824602 ....**33**	16 wks
23 Oct 93 ● **COME ON FEEL THE LEMONHEADS** Atlantic 7567825372 ....**5**	14 wks

Group was male / female for first album.

John LENNON *UK, male vocalist*   **297 wks**

16 Jan 71 **JOHN LENNON AND THE PLASTIC ONO BAND** Apple PCS 7124 [1] **11**	11 wks
30 Oct 71 ★ **IMAGINE** Apple PAS 10004 [2] **1**	101 wks
14 Oct 72 **SOMETIME IN NEW YORK CITY** Apple PCSP 716 [3] **11**	6 wks
8 Dec 73 **MIND GAMES** Apple PCS 7165......................**13**	12 wks
19 Oct 74 ● **WALLS AND BRIDGES** Apple PCTC 253 ....**6**	10 wks
8 Mar 75 ● **ROCK 'N' ROLL** Apple PCS 7169 ....**6**	28 wks
8 Nov 75 ● **SHAVED FISH** Apple PCS 7173 ....**8**	29 wks
22 Nov 80 ★ **DOUBLE FANTASY** Geffen K 99131 [4] **1**	36 wks
20 Nov 82 ★ **THE JOHN LENNON COLLECTION** Parlophone EMTV 37...............**1**	42 wks
4 Feb 84 ● **MILK AND HONEY** Polydor POLH 5 [4] **3**	13 wks
8 Mar 86 **LIVE IN NEW YORK CITY** Parlophone PCS 7031...........................**55**	3 wks
22 Oct 88 **IMAGINE (film soundtrack)** Parlophone PCSP 722 ....**64**	6 wks

[1] John Lennon and the Plastic Ono Band [2] John Lennon and the Plastic Ono Band with the Flux Fiddlers [3] John and Yoko Lennon with the Plastic Ono Band and Elephant's Memor [4] John Lennon and Yoko Ono

Imagine *changed its label credit to Parlophone PAS 10004 between its initial chart run and later runs.* Imagine – Music From The Motion Picture *includes tracks by the Beatles. See also Beatles; Yoko Ono.*

Julian LENNON *UK, male vocalist*   **20 wks**

3 Nov 84 **VALOTTE** Charisma JLLP 1 ....**20**	15 wks
5 Apr 86 **THE SECRET VALUE OF DAYDREAMING** Charisma CAS 1171 ......**93**	1 wk
5 Oct 91 **HELP YOURSELF** Virgin V 2668 ....**42**	4 wks

Annie LENNOX *UK, female vocalist*   **114 wks**

18 Apr 92 ★ **DIVA** RCA PD 75326 ....**1**	76 wks
18 Mar 95 ★ **MEDUSA** RCA 74321257172 ....**1†**	38 wks

Deke LEONARD *UK, male vocalist / instrumentalist – guitar*   **1 wk**

13 Apr 74 **KAMIKAZE** United Artists UAG 29544..............................**50**	1 wk

L
188

Paul LEONI UK, male instrumentalist – pan flute   **19 wks**

24 Sep 83	**FLIGHTS OF FANCY** Nouveau Music NML 1002	17	19 wks

LET LOOSE UK, male vocal / instrumental group   **14 wks**

19 Nov 94	**LET LOOSE** Mercury 5260182	20	14 wks

LEVEL 42 UK, male vocal / instrumental group   **226 wks**

29 Aug 81	**LEVEL 42** Polydor POLS 1036	20	18 wks
10 Apr 82	**THE EARLY TAPES JULY–AUGUST 1980** Polydor POLS 1064	46	6 wks
18 Sep 82	**THE PURSUIT OF ACCIDENTS** Polydor POLD 5067	17	16 wks
3 Sep 83	● **STANDING IN THE LIGHT** Polydor POLD 5110	9	13 wks
13 Oct 84	**TRUE COLOURS** Polydor POLH 10	14	8 wks
6 Jul 85	**A PHYSICAL PRESENCE** Polydor POLH 23	28	5 wks
26 Oct 85	● **WORLD MACHINE** Polydor POLH 25	3	72 wks
28 Mar 87	● **RUNNING IN THE FAMILY** Polydor POLH 42	2	54 wks
1 Oct 88	● **STARING AT THE SUN** Polydor POLH 50	2	11 wks
18 Nov 89	● **LEVEL BEST** Polydor LEVTV 1	5	15 wks
14 Sep 91	● **GUARANTEED** RCA PL 75005	3	5 wks
26 Mar 94	● **FOREVER NOW** RCA 74321189962	8	3 wks

LEVELLERS UK, male vocal / instrumental group   **53 wks**

19 Oct 91	**LEVELLING THE LAND** China WOL 1022	14	30 wks
4 Sep 93	● **LEVELLERS** China WOLCD 1034	2	14 wks
9 Sep 95	★ **ZEITGEIST** China WOLCD 1064	1	9 wks

LEVERT UK, male vocal group   **1 wk**

29 Aug 87	**THE BIG THROWDOWN** Atlantic 7817731	86	1 wk

LEVITATION UK, male vocal / instrumental group   **1 wk**

16 May 92	**NEED FOR NOT** Rough Trade R 2862	45	1 wk

C J LEWIS UK, male vocalist   **2 wks**

3 Sep 94	**DOLLARS** Black Market MCD 11131	44	2 wks

Huey LEWIS and the NEWS US, male vocal / instrumental group   **94 wks**

14 Sep 85	**SPORTS** Chrysalis CHR 1412	23	24 wks
20 Sep 86	● **FORE!** Chrysalis CDL 1534	8	52 wks
6 Aug 88	**SMALL WORLD** Chrysalis CDL 1622	12	8 wks
18 May 91	**HARD AT PLAY** Chrysalis CHR 1847	39	2 wks
21 Nov 92	**THE HEART OF ROCK 'N' ROLL – BEST OF HUEY LEWIS AND THE NEWS** Chrysalis CDCHR 1934	23	8 wks

Jerry Lee LEWIS US, male vocalist / instrumentalist – piano   **6 wks**

2 Jun 62	**JERRY LEE LEWIS VOLUME 2** London HA 2440	14	6 wks

Linda LEWIS UK, female vocalist   **4 wks**

9 Aug 75	**NOT A LITTLE GIRL ANYMORE** Arista ARTY 109	40	4 wks

Ramsey LEWIS TRIO US, male instrumental trio   **4 wks**

21 May 66	**HANG ON RAMSEY** Chess CRL 4520	20	4 wks

LFO UK, male instrumental group   **2 wks**

3 Aug 91	**FREQUENCIES** Warp WARPLP 3	42	2 wks

L
189

LIGHT OF THE WORLD *UK, male vocal / instrumental group* **1 wk**

24 Jan 81   **ROUND TRIP** *Ensign ENVY 14* ....**73**   1   wk

Gordon LIGHTFOOT *Canada, male vocalist* **2 wks**

20 May 72   **DON QUIXOTE** *Reprise K 44166* ....**44**   1   wk
17 Aug 74   **SUNDOWN** *Reprise K 54020* ....**45**   1   wk

LIGHTHOUSE FAMILY *UK, male vocal / instrumental duo* **1 wk**

18 Nov 95   **OCEAN DRIVE** *Wild Card 5237872* ....**74**   1   wk

LIGHTNING SEEDS *UK, male vocal / instrumental group* **35 wks**

10 Feb 90   **CLOUDCUCKOOLAND** *Ghetto GHETT 3* ....**50**   2   wks
18 Apr 92   **SENSE** *Virgin CDV 2690* ....**53**   1   wk
17 Sep 94   **JOLLIFICATION** *Epic 4772379* ....**15†**   32   wks

LIL LOUIS *US, male producer* **5 wks**

26 Aug 89   **FRENCH KISSES** *ffrr 828170 1* ....**35**   5   wks

LIMAHL *UK, male vocalist* **3 wks**

1 Dec 84   **DON'T SUPPOSE** *EMI PLML 1* ....**63**   3   wks

Alison LIMERICK *UK, female vocalist* **2 wks**

4 Apr 92   **AND STILL I RISE** *Arista 262365*......................................**53**   2   wks

LINDISFARNE *UK, male vocal / instrumental group* **118 wks**

30 Oct 71 ★ **FOG ON THE TYNE** *Charisma CAS 1050*................................**1**   56   wks
15 Jan 72 ● **NICELY OUT OF TUNE** *Charisma CAS 1025* ....**8**   30   wks
30 Sep 72 ● **DINGLY DELL** *Charisma CAS 1057* ....**5**   10   wks
11 Aug 73   **LINDISFARNE LIVE** *Charisma CLASS 2* ....**25**   6   wks
18 Oct 75   **FINEST HOUR** *Charisma CAS 1108* ....**55**   1   wk
24 Jun 78   **BACK AND FOURTH** *Mercury 9109 609*......................**22**   11   wks
9 Dec 78   **MAGIC IN THE AIR** *Mercury 6641 877*.......................**71**   1   wk
23 Oct 82   **SLEEPLESS NIGHT** *LMP GET 1* ....**59**   3   wks

LINX *UK, male vocal / instrumental duo* **23 wks**

28 Mar 81 ● **INTUITION** *Chrysalis CHR 1332* ....**8**   19   wks
31 Oct 81   **GO AHEAD** *Chrysalis CHR 1358*......................................**35**   4   wks

LIQUID GOLD *UK, male / female vocal / instrumental group* **3 wks**

16 Aug 80   **LIQUID GOLD** *Polo POLP 101* ....**34**   3   wks

LISA – *See WENDY and LISA*

LISA LISA and CULT JAM with FULL FORCE
US, female vocalist with two US, male vocal / instrumental groups **1 wk**

21 Sep 85   **LISA LISA AND CULT JAM WITH FULL FORCE** *CBS 26593* ....**96**   1   wk

LITTLE ANGELS *UK, male vocal / instrumental group* **15 wks**

2 Mar 91   **YOUNG GODS** *Polydor 8478461* ....**17**   6   wks
6 Feb 93 ★ **JAM** *Polydor 5176422* ....**1**   5   wks
23 Apr 94   **LITTLE OF THE PAST** *Polydor 5219362*............................**20**   2   wks
2 Jul 94   **TOO POSH TO MOSH TOO GOOD TO LAST** *Essential ESSCD 213*..**18**   2   wks

LITTLE FEAT *US, male vocal / instrumental group*   **19 wks**

6 Dec 75	**THE LAST RECORD ALBUM** Warner Bros. K 56156	**36**	3 wks
21 May 77	● **TIME LOVES A HERO** Warner Bros. K 56349	**8**	11 wks
11 Mar 78	**WAITING FOR COLUMBUS** Warner Bros. K 66075	**43**	1 wk
1 Dec 79	**DOWN ON THE FARM** Warner Bros. K 56667	**46**	3 wks
8 Aug 81	**HOY HOY** Warner Bros. K 666100	**76**	1 wk

LITTLE STEVEN *US, male vocalist / instrumentalist – guitar*   **4 wks**

6 Nov 82	**MEN WITHOUT WOMEN** EMI America 3027 [1]	**73**	2 wks
6 Jun 87	**FREEDOM NO COMPROMISE** Manhattan MTL 1010	**52**	2 wks

[1] Little Steven and the Disciples of Soul

LITTLE VILLAGE *UK / US, male vocal / instrumental group*   **4 wks**

29 Feb 92	**LITTLE VILLAGE** Reprise 7599267132	**23**	4 wks

LIVE *US, male vocal / instrumental group*   **6 wks**

15 Jul 95	**THROWING COPPER** Radiocative RAD 10997	**37**	6 wks

LIVING COLOUR *US, male vocal / instrumental group*   **22 wks**

15 Sep 90	**TIME'S UP** Epic 4669201	**20**	19 wks
6 Mar 93	**STAIN** Epic 4728562	**19**	3 wks

LIVING IN A BOX *UK, male vocal / instrumental group*   **35 wks**

9 May 87	**LIVING IN A BOX** Chrysalis CDL 1547	**25**	19 wks
8 Jul 89	**GATECRASHING** Chrysalis CDI 1676	**21**	16 wks

LL COOL J *US, male rapper*   **26 wks**

15 Feb 86	**RADIO** Def Jam DEF 26745	**71**	1 wk
13 Jun 87	**BIGGER AND DEFFER** Def Jam 450 5151	**54**	19 wks
8 Jul 89	**WALKING WITH A PANTHER** Def Jam 465112 1	**43**	3 wks
13 Oct 90	**MAMA SAID KNOCK YOU OUT** Def Jam 4673151	**49**	2 wks
17 Apr 93	**14 SHOTS TO THE DOME** Def Jam 4736782	**74**	1 wk

Andrew LLOYD WEBBER *UK, male composer / producer*   **37 wks**

11 Feb 78	● **VARIATIONS** MCA MCF 2824	**2**	19 wks
23 Mar 85	● **REQUIEM** HMV ALW 1	**4**	18 wks

Variations *features cellist Julian Lloyd Webber.* Requiem *credits Placido Domingo, Sarah Brightman, Paul Miles–Kingston, Winchester Cathedral Choir and the English Chamber Orchestra conducted by Lorin Maazel.*

Julian LLOYD WEBBER *UK, male instrumentalist*   **19 wks**

14 Sep 85	**PIECES** Polydor PROLP 6	**59**	5 wks
21 Feb 87	**ELGAR CELLO CONCERTO** Philips 416 3541	**94**	1 wk
27 Oct 90	**LLOYD WEBBER PLAYS LLOYD WEBBER** Philips 4322911	**15**	13 wks

First two albums credit the London Symphony Orchestra, third credits the Royal Philharmonic Orchestra. See also the London Symphony Orchestra; Andrew Lloyd Webber; Royal Philharmonic Orchestra.

Los LOBOS *US, male vocal / instrumental group*   **9 wks**

6 Apr 85	**HOW WILL THE WOLF SURVIVE?** Slash SLMP 3	**77**	6 wks
7 Feb 87	**BY THE LIGHT OF THE MOON** Slash SLAP 13	**77**	3 wks

Tone LOC *US, male rapper*   **16 wks**

25 Mar 89	**LOC'ED AFTER DARK** Delicious BRLP 526	**22**	16 wks

L
191

Josef LOCKE *Ireland, male vocalist*   **20 wks**

28 Jun 69	**THE WORLD OF JOSEF LOCKE TODAY** Decca SPA 21 ....**29**	1	wk
21 Mar 92	● **HEAR MY SONG (THE BEST OF JOSEF LOCKE)** EMI CDGO 2034 ..**7**	17	wks
27 Jun 92	**TAKE A PAIR OF SPARKLING EYES** EMI CDGO 2038 ....**41**	2	wks

John LODGE *UK, male vocalist / instrumentalist – guitar*   **20 wks**

29 Mar 75	● **BLUE JAYS** Threshold THS 12 1 ....**4**	18	wks
19 Feb 77	**NATURAL AVENUE** Decca TXS 120......................................**38**	2	wks

1 Justin Hayward and John Lodge.

Lisa LOEB and NINE STORIES
US, female / male vocal / instrumental group   **2 wks**

7 Oct 95	**TAILS** Geffen GED 24734 ....**39**	2	wks

Nils LOFGREN *US, male vocalist / instrumentalist – guitar*   **30 wks**

17 Apr 76	● **CRY TOUGH** A & M AMLH 64573 ....**8**	11	wks
26 Mar 77	**I CAME TO DANCE** A & M AMLH 64628 ....**30**	4	wks
5 Nov 77	**NIGHT AFTER NIGHT** A & M AMLH 68439 ....**38**	2	wks
26 Sep 81	**NIGHT FADES AWAY** Backstreet MCF 3121 ....**50**	3	wks
1 May 82	**A RHYTHM ROMANCE** A & M AMLH 68543...................**100**	1	wk
6 Jul 85	**FLIP** Towerbell TOWLP 11 ....**36**	7	wks
5 Apr 86	**CODE OF THE ROAD** Towerbell TOWDLP 17 ....**86**	1	wk
27 Apr 91	**SILVER LINING** Essential ESSLP 145 ....**61**	1	wk

Johnny LOGAN *Ireland, male vocalist*   **1 wk**

22 Aug 87	**HOLD ME NOW** CBS 451 0731 ....**83**	1	wk

LONDON BOYS *UK, male vocal duo*   **29 wks**

29 Jul 89	● **THE TWELVE COMMANDMENTS OF DANCE** WEA WX 278...........**2**	29	wks

LONDON PHILHARMONIC CHOIR *UK, choir*   **20 wks**

3 Dec 60	● **THE MESSIAH** Pye Golden Guinea GGL 0062 1 ....**10**	7	wks
13 Nov 76	● **SOUND OF GLORY** Arcade ADEP 25 2 ....**10**	10	wks
13 Apr 91	**PRAISE – 18 CHORAL MASTERPIECES** Pop & Arts PATLP 301 3 ..**54**	3	wks

1 London Philharmonic Choir with the London Orchestra conducted by Peter Susskind
2 London Philharmonic Choir with the National Philharmonic Orchestra conducted by John Aldiss 3 London Philharmonic Choir with the National Philharmonic Orchestra

See also Adiemus.

LONDON PHILHARMONIC ORCHESTRA *UK, orchestra*   **5 wks**

23 Apr 60	**RAVEL'S BOLERO** London HAV 2189 ....**15**	4	wks
8 Apr 61	**VICTORY AT SEA** Pye GGL 0073 ....**12**	1	wk

See also Nigel Kennedy; Ennio Morricone; Justin Hayward.

LONDON SYMPHONY ORCHESTRA *UK, orchestra*   **192 wks**

18 Mar 72	**TOP TV THEMES** Studio Two STWO 372 ....**13**	7	wks
16 Dec 72	● **THE STRAUSS FAMILY** Polydor 2659 014 1 ....**2**	21	wks
5 Jul 75	**MUSIC FROM 'EDWARD VII'** Polydor 2659 041 ....**52**	1	wk
21 Jan 78	**STAR WARS (film soundtrack)** 20th Century BTD 541 ....**21**	12	wks
8 Jul 78	● **CLASSIC ROCK** K-Tel ONE 1009 ....**3**	39	wks
10 Feb 79	**CLASSIC ROCK - THE SECOND MOVEMENT** K-Tel NE 1039.........**26**	8	wks
5 Jan 80	**RHAPSODY IN BLACK** K-Tel ONE 1063 ....**34**	5	wks
1 Aug 81	● **CLASSIC ROCK – ROCK CLASSICS** K-Tel ONE 1123.......................**5**	23	wks
27 Nov 82	**THE BEST OF CLASSIC ROCK** K-Tel ONE 1080 ....**35**	11	wks
27 Aug 83	**ROCK SYMPHONIES** K-Tel ONE 1243 ....**40**	9	wks

16 Nov 85	**THE POWER OF CLASSIC ROCK** Portrait PRT 10049 ....**13**	15 wks
14 Nov 87	**CLASSIC ROCK COUNTDOWN** CBS MOOD 3 ....**32**	16 wks
18 Nov 89	**CLASSIC ROCK – THE LIVING YEARS** CBS MOOD 9 ....**51**	6 wks
18 Jan 92	**WIND OF CHANGE – CLASSIC ROCK** Columbia MOODCD 19 [2] **24**	8 wks
19 Nov 94	**THE WORKS OF RICE AND LLOYD WEBBER** Vision VISCD 4 ....**55**	2 wks
23 Sep 95	**BRAVEHEART (film soundtrack)** Decca 4482952 [3] **27**	9 wks

[1] London Symphony Orchestra conducted by Cyril Ornadel [2] London Symphony Orchestra and the Royal Choral Society [3] London Symphony Orchestra, conductor James Horner

See also Michael Crawford; Kimera; Julian Lloyd Webber; Spike Milligan.

LONDON WELSH MALE VOICE CHOIR UK, male choir   **10 wks**

5 Sep 81	**SONGS OF THE VALLEYS** K-Tel NE 1117...**61**	10 wks

LONDONBEAT UK/US, male vocal/instrumental group   **6 wks**

13 Oct 90	**IN THE BLOOD** AnXious ZL 74810 ....**34**	6 wks

LONE JUSTICE US, male/female vocal/instrumental group   **5 wks**

6 Jul 85	**LONE JUSTICE** Geffen GEF 26288.......................................**49**	2 wks
8 Nov 86	**SHELTER** Geffen WX 73 ....**84**	3 wks

LONE STAR UK, male vocal/instrumental group   **7 wks**

2 Oct 76	**LONE STAR** Epic EPC 81545..**47**	1 wk
17 Sep 77	**FIRING ON ALL SIX** CBS 82213 ....**36**	6 wks

LONG RYDERS US, male vocal/instrumental group   **1 wk**

16 Nov 85	**STATE OF OUR UNION** Island ILPS 9802 ....**66**	1 wk

Joe LONGTHORNE UK, male vocalist and impersonator   **32 wks**

3 Dec 88	**THE JOE LONGTHORNE SONGBOOK** Telstar STAR 2353 ....**16**	12 wks
29 Jul 89	**ESPECIALLY FOR YOU** Telstar STAR 2365 ....**22**	10 wks
9 Dec 89	**THE JOE LONGTHORNE CHRISTMAS ALBUM** Telstar STAR 2385..**44**	4 wks
13 Nov 93	**I WISH YOU LOVE** EMI CDEMC 3662 ....**47**	4 wks
8 Oct 94	**LIVE AT THE ROYAL ALBERT HALL** Premier CDDPR 126...............**57**	2 wks

LOOP UK, male vocal/instrumental group   **2 wks**

4 Feb 89	**FADE OUT** Chapter 22 CHAPLP 34 ....**51**	1 wk
3 Feb 90	**A GILDED ETERNITY** Situation Two SITU 27....................**39**	1 wk

LOOSE ENDS UK, male/female vocal/instrumental group   **41 wks**

21 Apr 84	**A LITTLE SPICE** Virgin V 2301..**46**	9 wks
20 Apr 85	**SO WHERE ARE YOU?** Virgin V 2340 ....**13**	13 wks
18 Oct 86	**ZAGORA** Virgin V 2384 ....**15**	8 wks
2 Jul 88	**THE REAL CHUCKEEBOO** Virgin V 2528 ....**52**	4 wks
22 Sep 90	**LOOK HOW LONG** Ten DIX 94 ....**19**	5 wks
19 Sep 92	**TIGHTEN UP VOLUME 1** Ten DIXCD 112 ....**40**	2 wks

Trini LOPEZ US, male vocalist   **42 wks**

26 Oct 63	● **TRINI LOPEZ AT P.J.'S** Reprise R 6093 ....**7**	25 wks
25 Mar 67	● **TRINI LOPEZ IN LONDON** Reprise RSLP 6238 ....**6**	17 wks

Jeff LORBER US, male vocalist/instrumentalist keyboards   **2 wks**

18 May 85	**STEP BY STEP** Club JABH 9..**97**	2 wks

LORDS OF THE UNDERGROUND US, male rap group   **1 wk**

12 Nov 94	**KEEPERS OF THE FUNK** Pendulum CDCHR 6088 ....**68**	1 wk

Sophia LOREN – *See Peter SELLERS*

Joe LOSS *UK, orchestra* 10 wks

30 Oct 71 **ALL–TIME PARTY HITS** *MFP 5227* ....**24** 10 wks
See also the George Mitchell Minstrels.

LOTUS EATERS *UK, male vocal / instrumental group* 1 wk

16 Jun 84 **NO SENSE OF SIN** *Sylvan 206 263* ....**96** 1 wk
James LOUGHRAN – *See BBC SYMPHONY ORCHESTRA*

Jacques LOUSSIER *France, male instrumentalist – piano* 3 wks

30 Mar 85 **THE BEST OF PLAY BACH** *Start STL 1* ....**58** 3 wks

LOVE *US, male vocal / instrumental group* 8 wks

24 Feb 68 **FOREVER CHANGES** *Elektra EKS7 4013* ....**24** 6 wks
16 May 70 **OUT HERE** *Harvest Show 3/4*..**29** 2 wks

Geoff LOVE *UK, orchestra* 28 wks

7 Aug 71 **BIG WAR MOVIE THEMES** *MFP 5171* ....**11** 20 wks
21 Aug 71 **BIG WESTERN MOVIE THEMES** *MFP 5204*.....................**38** 3 wks
30 Oct 71 **BIG LOVE MOVIE THEMES** *MFP 5221*.......................**28** 5 wks
See also Manuel and his Music of the Mountains.

L
194

Monie LOVE *UK, female rapper* 3 wks

20 Oct 90 **DOWN TO EARTH** *Cooltempo CTLP 14* ....**30** 3 wks

LOVE AND MONEY *UK, male vocal / instrumental group* 2 wks

29 Oct 88 **STRANGE KIND OF LOVE** *Fontana SFLP 7* ....**71** 1 wk
3 Aug 91 **DOGS IN THE TRAFFIC** *Fontana 8489931* ....**41** 1 wk

LOVE/HATE *US, male vocal / instrumental group* 5 wks

7 Mar 92 **WASTED IN AMERICA** *Columbia 4694532* ....**20** 4 wks
24 Jul 93 **LET'S RUMBLE** *RCA 74321153112* ....**24** 1 wk

Lyle LOVETT *US, male vocalist* 1 wk

8 Oct 94 **I LOVE EVERYBODY** *MCA MCD 10808* ....**54** 1 wk

Lene LOVICH *US, female vocalist* 17 wks

17 Mar 79 **STATELESS** *Stiff SEEZ 7* ....**35** 11 wks
2 Feb 80 **FLEX** *Stiff SEEZ 19* ....**19** 6 wks

LOVIN' SPOONFUL *US / Canada, male vocal / instrumental group* 11 wks

7 May 66 ● **DAYDREAM** *Pye NPL 28078* ....**8** 11 wks

Nick LOWE *UK, male vocalist* 17 wks

11 Mar 78 **THE JESUS OF COOL** *Radar RAD 1*...............................**22** 9 wks
23 Jun 79 **LABOUR OF LUST** *Radar RAD 21* ....**43** 6 wks
20 Feb 82 **NICK THE KNIFE** *F-Beat XXLP 14* ....**99** 2 wks

L7 *US, female vocal / instrumental group* 8 wks

2 May 92 **BRICKS ARE HEAVY** *Slash 8283072*.................................**24** 6 wks

British Hit Albums Part One

Date of chart entry/Title & catalogue no./Peak position reached/Weeks on chart

★ Number One   ● Top Ten   † still on chart at 30 Dec 1995   ☐ credited to act billed in footnote

| 23 Jul 94 | **HUNGRY FOR STINK** Slash 8285312 | **26** | 2 wks |

LULU UK, female vocalist — **7 wks**

| 25 Sep 71 | **THE MOST OF LULU** MFP 5215 | **15** | 6 wks |
| 6 Mar 93 | **INDEPENDENCE** Dôme DOMECD 1 | **67** | 1 wk |

Bob LUMAN US, male vocalist — **1 wk**

| 14 Jan 61 | **LET'S THINK ABOUT LIVING** Warner Bros. WM 4025 | **18** | 1 wk |

LURKERS UK, male vocal / instrumental group — **1 wk**

| 1 Jul 78 | **FULHAM FALLOUT** Beggars Banquet BEGA 2 | **57** | 1 wk |

LUSH UK, male / female vocal / instrumental group — **5 wks**

| 8 Feb 92 | ● **SPOOKY** 4AD CAD 2002CD | **7** | 3 wks |
| 25 Jun 94 | **SPLIT** 4AD CAD 4011CD | **19** | 2 wks |

LYLE – See GALLAGHER and LYLE

Vera LYNN UK, female vocalist — **15 wks**

| 21 Nov 81 | **20 FAMILY FAVOURITES** EMI EMTV 28 | **25** | 12 wks |
| 9 Sep 89 | **WE'LL MEET AGAIN** Telstar STAR 2369 | **44** | 3 wks |

Jeff LYNNE UK, male vocalist — **4 wks**

| 4 Aug 90 | **ARMCHAIR THEATRE** Reprise WX 347 | **24** | 4 wks |

Philip LYNOTT Ireland, male vocalist — **16 wks**

| 26 Apr 80 | **SOLO IN SOHO** Vertigo 9102 038 | **28** | 6 wks |
| 14 Nov 87 | **SOLDIER OF FORTUNE - THE BEST OF PHIL LYNOTT AND THIN LIZZY** Telstar STAR 2300 [1] | **55** | 10 wks |

[1] Phil Lynott and Thin Lizzy

See also Midge Ure.

LYNYRD SKYNYRD US, male vocal / instrumental group — **19 wks**

3 May 75	**NUTHIN' FANCY** MCA MCF 2700	**43**	1 wk
28 Feb 76	**GIMME BACK MY BULLETS** MCA MCF 2744	**34**	5 wks
6 Nov 76	**ONE MORE FOR THE ROAD** MCA MCPS 279	**17**	4 wks
12 Nov 77	**STREET SURVIVORS** MCA MCG 3525	**13**	4 wks
4 Nov 78	**SKYNYRD'S FIRST AND LAST** MCA MCG 3529	**50**	1 wk
9 Feb 80	**GOLD AND PLATINUM** MCA MCSP 308	**49**	4 wks

M PEOPLE UK, male / female vocal / instrumental group — **131 wks**

6 Mar 93	**NORTHERN SOUL** Deconstruction 74321117772	**53**	2 wks
16 Oct 93	● **ELEGANT SLUMMING** Deconstruction 74321166782	**2**	70 wks
26 Nov 94	● **BIZARRE FRUIT / BIZARRE FRUIT II** Deconstruction 74321240812	**4†**	56 wks

16 Sep 95   **NORTHERN SOUL (re-issue)** *RCA PD 75157* ....**26**   3 wks
From 9 Dec 95 Bizarre Fruit *was listed with the remix album* Bizarre Fruit II.

Lorin MAAZEL – *See Andrew LLOYD WEBBER*

MAC BAND featuring the McCAMPBELL BROTHERS
US, male vocal group   **3 wks**

20 Aug 88   **THE MAC BAND** *MCA MCC 6032* ....**61**   3 wks

McALMONT and BUTLER *UK, male vocal / instrumental duo*   **4 wks**

9 Dec 95   **THE SOUND OF MCALMONT AND BUTLER** *Hut CDHUT 32*........**33†**   4 wks

Frankie McBRIDE *Ireland, male vocalist*   **3 wks**

17 Feb 68   **FRANKIE MCBRIDE** *Emerald SLD 28* ....**29**   3 wks

MACC LADS *UK, male vocal / instrumental group*   **1 wk**

7 Oct 89   **FROM BEER TO ETERNITY** *Hectic House HHLP 12* ....**72**   1 wk

McCAMPBELL BROTHERS – *See MAC BAND featuring the McCAMPBELL BROTHERS*

Paul McCARTNEY *UK, male vocalist / multi–instrumentalist*   **522 wks**

2 May 70	● **MCCARTNEY** *Apple PCS 7102* **2**	32 wks
5 Jun 71	★ **RAM** *Apple PAS 10003* 1 ....**1**	24 wks
18 Dec 71	**WILD LIFE** *Apple PCS 7142* 2 ....**11**	9 wks
19 May 73	● **RED ROSE SPEEDWAY** *Apple PCTC 251* 3 ....**5**	16 wks
15 Dec 73	★ **BAND ON THE RUN** *Apple PAS 10007* 3 ....**1**	124 wks
21 Jun 75	★ **VENUS AND MARS** *Apple PCTC 254* 2 ....**1**	29 wks
17 Apr 76	● **WINGS AT THE SPEED OF SOUND** *Apple PAS 10010* 2 ....**2**	35 wks
15 Jan 77	● **WINGS OVER AMERICA** *Parlophone PAS 720* 2 ....**8**	22 wks
15 Apr 78	● **LONDON TOWN** *Parlophone PAS 10012* 2 ....**4**	23 wks
16 Dec 78	● **WINGS GREATEST HITS** *Parlophone PCTC 256* 2 ....**5**	32 wks
23 Jun 79	● **BACK TO THE EGG** *Parlophone PCTC 257* 2 ....**6**	15 wks
31 May 80	★ **MCCARTNEY II** *Parlophone PCTC 258* **1**	18 wks
7 Mar 81	**MCCARTNEY INTERVIEW** *EMI CHAT 1* **34**	4 wks
8 May 82	★ **TUG OF WAR** *Parlophone PCTC 259* **1**	27 wks
12 Nov 83	● **PIPES OF PEACE** *Parlophone PCTC 1652301* **4**	23 wks
3 Nov 84	★ **GIVE MY REGARDS TO BROAD STREET** *Parlophone PCTC 2*...**1**	21 wks
13 Sep 86	● **PRESS TO PLAY** *Parlophone PCSD 103*...........................**8**	6 wks
14 Nov 87	● **ALL THE BEST!** *Parlophone PMTV 1*...............................**2**	21 wks
17 Jun 89	★ **FLOWERS IN THE DIRT** *Parlophone PCSD 106* **1**	20 wks
17 Nov 90	**TRIPPING THE LIVE FANTASTIC** *Parlophone PCST 7346* **17**	11 wks
1 Jun 91	● **UNPLUGGED – THE OFFICIAL BOOTLEG** *Parlophone PCSD 116*.....**7**	3 wks
12 Oct 91	**CHOBA B CCCP (THE RUSSIAN ALBUM)** *Parlophone CDPCSD 117* **63**	1 wk
13 Feb 93	● **OFF THE GROUND** *Parlophone CDPCSD 125* **5**	4 wks
20 Nov 93	**PAUL IS LIVE** *Parlophone PDPCSD 147* **34**	2 wks

1 Paul and Linda McCartney 2 Wings 3 Paul McCartney and Wings

Kirsty MacCOLL *UK, female vocalist*   **49 wks**

20 May 89	**KITE** *Virgin KMLP 1* **34**	12 wks
6 Jul 91	**ELECTRIC LANDLADY** *Virgin V 2663*...............................**17**	8 wks
12 Mar 94	**TITANIC DAYS** *ZTT 4509947112* **46**	2 wks
18 Mar 95	● **GALORE** *Virgin CDV 2763* **6**	27 wks

Noel McKOY – *See James TAYLOR QUARTET*

Van McCOY and the SOUL CITY SYMPHONY
US, orchestra   **11 wks**

5 Jul 75   **DISCO BABY** *Avco 9109 004* ....**32**   11 wks

TOP 30 Nº 27

PAUL McCARTNEY (left), shown with a flight of Wings, is, with Phil Collins, one of the two artists to be in the all-time Top 30 both as a soloist and as a member of a group (Beatles and Genesis respectively).

(Barry Wentzell/LFI)

George McCRAE US, male vocalist — 29 wks

3 Aug 74	ROCK YOUR BABY Jayboy JSL 3	13	28 wks
13 Sep 75	GEORGE MCCRAE Jayboy JSL 10	54	1 wk

Ian McCULLOCH UK, male vocalist — 4 wks

7 Oct 89	CANDLELAND WEA WX 303	18	3 wks
21 Mar 92	MYSTERIO East West 9031762642	46	1 wk

Michael McDONALD US, male vocalist — 39 wks

22 Nov 86	● SWEET FREEDOM: BEST OF MICHAEL MCDONALD Warner Bros. WX 67	6	35 wks
26 May 90	TAKE IT TO HEART Reprise WX 285	35	4 wks

Bobby McFERRIN US, male vocalist — 1 wk

29 Oct 88	SIMPLE PLEASURES Manhattan MTL 1018	92	1 wk

Kate and Anna McGARRIGLE Canada, female vocal duo — 4 wks

26 Feb 77	DANCER WITH BRUISED KNEES Warner Bros. K 56356	35	4 wks

Shane MacGOWAN and the POPES
UK, male vocal / instrumental group — 2 wks

29 Oct 94	THE SNAKE ZTT 4509981042	37	2 wks

M 198

Mary MacGREGOR US, female vocalist — 1 wk

23 Apr 77	TORN BETWEEN TWO LOVERS Ariola America AAS 1504	59	1 wk

McGUINNESS FLINT UK, male vocal / instrumental group — 10 wks

23 Jan 71	● MCGUINNESS FLINT Capitol EAST 22625	9	10 wks

MACHINE HEAD UK, male vocal / instrumental group — 3 wks

20 Aug 94	BURN MY EYES Roadrunner RR 90169	25	3 wks

Duff McKAGAN US, male vocalist / instrumentalist – bass — 2 wks

9 Oct 93	BELIEVE IN ME Geffen GED 24605	27	2 wks

Maria McKEE US, female vocalist — 6 wks

24 Jun 89	MARIA MCKEE Geffen WX 270	49	3 wks
12 Jun 93	YOU GOTTA SIN TO GET SAVED Geffen GED 24508	26	3 wks

Kenneth McKELLAR UK, male vocalist — 10 wks

28 Jun 69	THE WORLD OF KENNETH MCKELLAR Decca SPA 11	27	7 wks
31 Jan 70	ECCO DI NAPOLI Decca SKL 5018	45	3 wks

Craig McLACHLAN and CHECK 1–2
Australia, male vocal / instrumental group — 11 wks

21 Jul 90	● CRAIG MCLACHLAN AND CHECK 1–2 Epic 4663471	10	11 wks

Malcolm McLAREN UK, male vocalist — 41 wks

4 Jun 83	DUCK ROCK Charisma MMLP 1	18	17 wks
26 May 84	WOULD YA LIKE MORE SCRATCHIN' Charisma CLAM 1 [1]	44	4 wks
29 Dec 84	FANS Charisma MMDL 2	47	8 wks

| 15 Jul 89 | **WALTZ DANCING** Epic 460736 1 [2] | **30** | 11 wks |
| 20 Aug 94 | **PARIS** No! NOCD 101 | **44** | 1 wk |

[1] Malcolm McLaren and the World's Famous Supreme Team [2] Malcolm McLaren and the Bootzilla Orchestra

Mahavishnu John McLAUGHLIN – See Carlos SANTANA; MAHAVISHNU ORCHESTRA

Bitty McLEAN   UK, male vocalist — **11 wks**

| 19 Feb 94 | **JUST TO LET YOU KNOW** Brilliant BRILCD 1 | **19** | 11 wks |

Don McLEAN   US, male vocalist — **89 wks**

11 Mar 72	● **AMERICAN PIE** United Artists UAS 29285	**3**	54 wks
17 Jun 72	**TAPESTRY** United Artists UAS 29350	**16**	12 wks
24 Nov 73	**PLAYIN' FAVORITES** United Artists UAG 29528	**42**	2 wks
14 Jun 80	**CHAIN LIGHTNING** EMI International INS 3025	**19**	9 wks
27 Sep 80	● **THE VERY BEST OF DON MCLEAN** United Artists UAG 30314	**4**	12 wks

Andy McNABB   UK, male soldier — **2 wks**

| 21 May 94 | **BRAVO TWO ZERO** PolyGram TV 5222002 | **45** | 2 wks |

Ian McNABB   UK, male vocalist — **3 wks**

| 30 Jan 93 | **TRUTH AND BEAUTY** This Way Up 5143782 | **51** | 1 wk |
| 16 Jul 94 | **HEAD LIKE A ROCK** This Way Up 5222982 | **29** | 2 wks |

Rita McNEIL   Canada, female vocalist — **4 wks**

| 24 Nov 90 | **REASON TO BELIEVE** Polydor 8471061 | **32** | 4 wks |

Ian McSHANE   UK, male vocalist — **7 wks**

| 21 Nov 92 | **FROM BOTH SIDES NOW** PolyGram TV 5176192 | **40** | 7 wks |

Ralph McTELL   UK, male vocalist — **17 wks**

18 Nov 72	**NOT TILL TOMORROW** Reprise K 44210	**36**	1 wk
2 Mar 74	**EASY** Reprise K 54013	**31**	4 wks
15 Feb 75	**STREETS** Warner Bros. K 56105	**13**	12 wks

Christine McVIE   UK, female vocalist — **4 wks**

| 11 Feb 84 | **CHRISTINE MCVIE** Warner Bros. 92 5059 | **58** | 4 wks |

David McWILLIAMS   UK, male vocalist — **9 wks**

10 Jun 67	**DAVID MCWILLIAMS SINGS** Major Minor MMLP 2	**38**	2 wks
4 Nov 67	**DAVID MCWILLIAMS VOLUME 2** Major Minor MMLP 10	**23**	6 wks
9 Mar 68	**DAVID MCWILLIAMS VOLUME 3** Major Minor MMLP 11	**39**	1 wk

MAD SEASON   UK, male vocal/instrumental group — **1 wk**

| 25 Mar 95 | **ABOVE** Columbia 4785072 | **41** | 1 wk |

MAD STUNTMAN – See REEL 2 REAL featuring the MAD STUNTMAN

MADDER ROSE   US, male/female vocal/instrumental group — **2 wks**

| 9 Apr 94 | **PANIC ON** Atlantic 7567825812 | **52** | 2 wks |

MADNESS   UK, male vocal/instrumental group — **396 wks**

| 3 Nov 79 | ● **ONE STEP BEYOND** Stiff SEEZ 17 | **2** | 78 wks |

4 Oct 80 ● **ABSOLUTELY** *Stiff SEEZ 29* **2**	46	wks
10 Oct 81 ● **MADNESS 7** *Stiff SEEZ 39* **5**	29	wks
1 May 82 ★ **COMPLETE MADNESS** *Stiff HIT-TV 1* **1**	88	wks
13 Nov 82 ● **THE RISE AND FALL** *Stiff SEEZ 46* **10**	22	wks
3 Mar 84 ● **KEEP MOVING** *Stiff SEEZ 53* **6**	19	wks
12 Oct 85 **MAD NOT MAD** *Zarjazz JZLP 1* **16**	9	wks
6 Dec 86 **UTTER MADNESS** *Zarjazz JZLP 2* **29**	8	wks
7 May 88 **THE MADNESS** *Virgin V 2507* **65**	1	wk
7 Mar 92 ★ **DIVINE MADNESS** *Virgin CDV 2692* **1**	87	wks
14 Nov 92 **MADSTOCK** *Go! Discs 8283672* **22**	9	wks

MADONNA US, female vocalist   677 wks

11 Feb 84 ● **MADONNA / THE FIRST ALBUM** *Sire 923867* **6**	123	wks
24 Nov 84 ★ **LIKE A VIRGIN** *Sire 925157* **1**	152	wks
12 Jul 86 ★ **TRUE BLUE** *Sire WX 54* **1**	85	wks
28 Nov 87 ● **YOU CAN DANCE** *Sire WX 76* **5**	16	wks
1 Apr 89 ★ **LIKE A PRAYER** *Sire WX 239* **1**	70	wks
2 Jun 90 ● **I'M BREATHLESS** *Sire WX 351* **2**	20	wks
24 Nov 90 ★ **THE IMMACULATE COLLECTION** *Sire WX 370* **1**	141	wks
24 Oct 92 ● **EROTICA** *Maverick 9362450312* **2**	38	wks
5 Nov 94 ● **BEDTIME STORIES** *Maverick 9362457672* **2**	25	wks
18 Nov 95 ● **SOMETHING TO REMEMBER** *Maverick 9362461002* ......**3†**	7	wks

From 22 Aug 85 Madonna was repackaged as The First Album Sire WX 22.
Like A Virgin changed label number to SIRE WX 20 during its chart run.

MAGAZINE UK, male vocal / instrumental group   24 wks

24 Jun 78 **REAL LIFE** *Virgin V 2100* **29**	8	wks
14 Apr 79 **SECONDHAND DAYLIGHT** *Virgin V 2121* **38**	8	wks
10 May 80 **CORRECT USE OF SOAP** *Virgin V 2156* **28**	4	wks
13 Dec 80 **PLAY** *Virgin V 2184* **69**	1	wk
27 Jun 81 **MAGIC, MURDER AND THE WEATHER** *Virgin V 2200* **39**	3	wks

MAGIC BAND – *See CAPTAIN BEEFHEART and his MAGIC BAND*

MAGNA CARTA UK, male vocal / instrumental group   2 wks

8 Aug 70 **SEASONS** *Vertigo 6360 003* **55**	2	wks

MAGNUM UK, male vocal / instrumental group   47 wks

16 Sep 78 **KINGDOM OF MADNESS** *Jet JETLP 210* **58**	1	wk
19 Apr 80 **MARAUDER** *Jet JETLP 230* **34**	5	wks
6 Mar 82 **CHASE THE DRAGON** *Jet JETLP 235* **17**	7	wks
21 May 83 **THE ELEVENTH HOUR** *Jet JETLP 240* **38**	4	wks
25 May 85 **ON A STORYTELLER'S NIGHT** *FM WKFM LP 34* **24**	7	wks
4 Oct 86 **VIGILANTE** *Polydor POLD 5198* **24**	5	wks
9 Apr 88 ● **WINGS OF HEAVEN** *Polydor POLD 5221* **5**	9	wks
21 Jul 90 ● **GOODNIGHT L.A.** *Polydor 8435681* **9**	5	wks
14 Sep 91 **THE SPIRIT** *Polydor 5111691* **50**	1	wk
24 Oct 92 **SLEEPWALKING** *Music For Nations CDMFN 143* **27**	2	wks
18 Jun 94 **ROCK ART** *EMI CDEMD 1066* **57**	1	wk

Sean MAGUIRE UK, male vocalist   1 wk

26 Nov 94 **SEAN MAGUIRE** *Parlophone CDPCSDX 164* **75**	1	wk

MAHAVISHNU ORCHESTRA UK / US, male instrumental group   14 wks

31 Mar 73 **BIRDS OF FIRE** *CBS 65321* **20**	5	wks
28 Jul 73 ● **LOVE DEVOTION SURRENDER** *CBS 69037* [1] **7**	9	wks

[1] Carlos Santana and Mahavishnu John McLaughlin

MAI TAI Holland, female vocal group   1 wk

6 Jul 85 **HISTORY** *Virgin V 2359* **91**	1	wk

MAJESTICS UK, male / female vocal group — **4 wks**

4 Apr 87	**TUTTI FRUTTI** BBC REN 629	64	4 wks

Tommy MAKEM – See CLANCY BROTHERS and Tommy MAKEM

Timmy MALLETT – See BOMBALURINA featuring Timmy MALLETT

Yngwie J. MALMSTEEN Sweden, male instrumentalist – guitar — **11 wks**

21 May 88	**ODYSSEY** Polydor POLD 5224	27	7 wks
4 Nov 89	**TRIAL BY FIRE – LIVE IN LENINGRAD** Polydor 839726 1	65	1 wk
28 Apr 90	**ECLIPSE** Polydor 8434611	43	2 wks
29 Feb 92	**FIRE AND ICE** Elektra 7559611372	57	1 wk

MAMA'S BOYS Ireland, male vocal / instrumental group — **4 wks**

6 Apr 85	**POWER AND PASSION** Jive HIP 24	55	4 wks

MAMAS and PAPAS US, male / female vocal group — **65 wks**

25 Jun 66	● **THE MAMAS AND PAPAS** RCA Victor RD 7803	3	18 wks
28 Jan 67	**CASS, JOHN, MICHELLE, DENNY** RCA Victor SF 7639	24	6 wks
24 Jun 67	● **MAMAS AND PAPAS DELIVER** RCA Victor SF 7880	4	22 wks
26 Apr 69	● **HITS OF GOLD** Stateside S 5007	7	2 wks
18 Jun 77	● **THE BEST OF THE MAMAS AND PAPAS** Arcade ADEP 30	6	13 wks
28 Jan 95	**CALIFORNIA DREAMIN' – THE VERY BEST OF THE MAMAS AND THE PAPAS** PolyGram TV 5239732	14	4 wks

MAN UK, male vocal / instrumental group — **11 wks**

20 Oct 73	**BACK INTO THE FUTURE** United Artists UAD 60053/4	23	3 wks
25 May 74	**RHINOS WINOS AND LUNATICS** United Artists UAG 29631	24	4 wks
11 Oct 75	**MAXIMUM DARKNESS** United Artists UAG 29872	25	2 wks
17 Apr 76	**WELSH CONNECTION** MCA MCF 2753	40	2 wks

MANCHESTER BOYS CHOIR UK, male choir — **2 wks**

21 Dec 85	**THE NEW SOUND OF CHRISTMAS** K-Tel ONE 1314	80	2 wks

Henry MANCINI US, orchestra / chorus — **23 wks**

16 Oct 76	**HENRY MANCINI** Arcade ADEP 24	26	8 wks
30 Jun 84	**MAMMA** Decca 411959 [1]	96	1 wk
8 Dec 84	**IN THE PINK** RCA Red Seal RL 85315 [2]	62	6 wks
13 Dec 86	**THE HOLLYWOOD MUSICALS** CBS 4502581 [3]	46	8 wks

[1] Luciano Pavarotti with the Henry Mancini Orchestra [2] James Galway and Henry Mancini and the National Philharmonic Orchestra [3] Johnny Mathis and Henry Mancini

MANFRED MANN South Africa / UK, male vocal / instrumental group — **101 wks**

19 Sep 64	● **FIVE FACES OF MANFRED MANN** HMV CLP 1731	3	24 wks
23 Oct 65	● **MANN MADE** HMV CLP 1911	7	11 wks
17 Sep 66	**MANN MADE HITS** HMV CLP 3559	11	18 wks
29 Oct 66	**AS IS** Fontana TL 5377	22	4 wks
21 Jan 67	**SOUL OF MANN** HMV CSD 3594	40	1 wk
17 Jun 78	**WATCH** Bronze BRON 507 [1]	33	6 wks
24 Mar 79	**ANGEL STATION** Bronze BRON 516 [1]	30	8 wks
15 Sep 79	● **SEMI–DETACHED SUBURBAN** EMI EMTV 19	9	14 wks
26 Feb 83	**SOMEWHERE IN AFRIKA** Bronze BRON 543 [1]	87	1 wk
18 Sep 86	● **THE ROARING SILENCE** Bronze ILPS 9357 [1]	10	9 wks
23 Jan 93	**AGES OF MANN** PolyGram TV 5143622	23	4 wks
10 Sep 94	**THE VERY BEST OF MANFRED MANN'S EARTH BAND** Arcade ARC 3100162 [1]	69	1 wk

[1] Manfred Mann's Earth Band

MANHATTAN TRANSFER US, male / female vocal group   85 wks

12 Mar 77	**COMING OUT** Atlantic K 50291 ....**12**	20 wks
19 Mar 77	**MANHATTAN TRANSFER** Atlantic K 50138.............**49**	7 wks
25 Feb 78	● **PASTICHE** Atlantic K 50444 ....**10**	34 wks
11 Nov 78	● **LIVE** Atlantic K 50540...**4**	17 wks
17 Nov 79	**EXTENSIONS** Atlantic K 50674 ....**63**	3 wks
18 Feb 84	**BODIES AND SOULS** Atlantic 780104 ....**53**	4 wks

MANHATTANS US, male vocal group   3 wks

14 Aug 76	**MANHATTANS** CBS 81513...**37**	3 wks

MANIC STREET PREACHERS UK, male vocal / instrumental group 24 wks

22 Feb 92	**GENERATION TERRORISTS** Columbia 4710602 ....**13**	10 wks
3 Jul 93	● **GOLD AGAINST THE SOUL** Columbia 4640642 ....**8**	11 wks
10 Sep 94	● **THE HOLY BIBLE** Epic 4774219 ....**6**	3 wks

Barry MANILOW US, male vocalist   336 wks

23 Sep 78	**EVEN NOW** Arista SPART 1047 ....**12**	28 wks
3 Mar 79	● **MANILOW MAGIC** Arista ARTV 2 ....**3**	151 wks
20 Oct 79	**ONE VOICE** Arista SPART 1106 ....**18**	7 wks
29 Nov 80	● **BARRY** Arista DLART 2...**5**	34 wks
25 Apr 81	**GIFT SET** Arista BOX 1..**62**	1 wk
3 Oct 81	● **IF I SHOULD LOVE AGAIN** Arista BMAN 1 ....**5**	26 wks
1 May 82	★ **BARRY LIVE IN BRITAIN** Arista ARTV 4.....................**1**	23 wks
27 Nov 82	● **I WANNA DO IT WITH YOU** Arista BMAN 2 ....**7**	9 wks
8 Oct 83	● **A TOUCH MORE MAGIC** Arista BMAN 3.................**10**	12 wks
1 Dec 84	**2.00 AM PARADISE CAFE** Arista 206 496 ....**28**	6 wks
16 Nov 85	**MANILOW** RCA PL 87044 ....**40**	6 wks
20 Feb 88	**SWING STREET** Arista 208860 ....**81**	1 wk
20 May 89	**SONGS TO MAKE THE WHOLE WORLD SING** Arista 209927......**20**	4 wks
17 Mar 90	**LIVE ON BROADWAY** Arista 303785 ....**19**	3 wks
30 Jun 90	**SONGS 1975–1990** Arista 303868 ....**13**	7 wks
2 Nov 91	**SHOWSTOPPERS** Arista 212091 ....**53**	3 wks
3 Apr 93	**HIDDEN TREASURES** Arista 74321135682....................**36**	7 wks
27 Nov 93	**THE PLATINUM COLLECTION** Arista 74321175452 ......**37**	6 wks
5 Nov 94	**SINGIN' WITH THE BIG BANDS** Arista 07822187712.......**54**	2 wks

Aimee MANN US, female vocalist   2 wks

18 Sep 93	**WHATEVER** Imago 72787210172 ....**39**	1 wk
11 Nov 95	**I'M WITH STUPID** Geffen GED 24951 ....**51**	1 wk

Roberto MANN UK, male orchestra leader   9 wks

9 Dec 67	**GREAT WALTZES** Deram SML 1010 ....**19**	9 wks

Shelley MANNE US, male instrumentalist – drums   1 wk

18 Jun 60	**MY FAIR LADY** Vogue LAC 12100 ....**20**	1 wk

MANOWAR US, male vocal / instrumental group   3 wks

18 Feb 84	**HAIL TO ENGLAND** Music For Nations MFN 19 ....**83**	2 wks
6 Oct 84	**SIGN OF THE HAMMER** 10 DIX 10............................**73**	1 wk

MANTOVANI UK, orchestra   151 wks

21 Feb 59	● **CONTINENTAL ENCORES** Decca LK 4298 ....**4**	12 wks
18 Feb 61	**CONCERT SPECTACULAR** Decca LK 4377 ....**16**	2 wks
16 Apr 66	● **MANTOVANI MAGIC** Decca LK 7949..........................**3**	15 wks
15 Oct 66	**MR. MUSIC – MANTOVANI** Decca LK 4809 ....**24**	3 wks
14 Jan 67	● **MANTOVANI'S GOLDEN HITS** Decca SKL 4818 ....**10**	43 wks
30 Sep 67	**HOLLYWOOD** Decca SKL 4887....................................**37**	1 wk

14 Jun 69	● THE WORLD OF MANTOVANI Decca SPA 1 6	31 wks
4 Oct 69	● THE WORLD OF MANTOVANI VOLUME 2 Decca SPA 36 4	19 wks
16 May 70	MANTOVANI TODAY Decca SKL 5003 16	8 wks
26 Feb 72	TO LOVERS EVERYWHERE Decca SKL 5112 44	1 wk
3 Nov 79	● 20 GOLDEN GREATS Warwick WW 5067 9	13 wks
16 Mar 85	MANTOVANI MAGIC Telstar STAR 2237 [1] 52	3 wks

[1] Mantovani Orchestra conducted by Roland Shaw

MANTRONIX Jamaica / US, male vocal / instrumental duo   17 wks

29 Mar 86	THE ALBUM 10 DIX 37..45	3 wks
13 Dec 86	MUSICAL MADNESS 10 DIX 50 66	3 wks
2 Apr 88	IN FULL EFFECT 10 DIX 74 39	3 wks
17 Feb 90	THIS SHOULD MOVE YA Capitol EST 2117 18	6 wks
30 Mar 91	THE INCREDIBLE SOUND MACHINE Capitol EST 2139 36	2 wks

MANUEL and his MUSIC OF THE MOUNTAINS
UK, orchestra conductor Geoff Love   38 wks

10 Sep 60	MUSIC OF THE MOUNTAINS Columbia 33SX 1212 17	1 wk
7 Aug 71	THIS IS MANUEL Studio Two STWO 5 18	19 wks
31 Jan 76	● CARNIVAL Studio Two TWO 337 3	18 wks

See also Geoff Love.

PHIL MANZANERA UK, male vocalist / instrumentalist guitar   1 wk

24 May 75	DIAMOND HEAD Island ILPS 9315 40	1 wk

MARC AND THE MAMBAS – See Marc ALMOND

MARILLION UK, male vocal / instrumental group   160 wks

26 Mar 83	● SCRIPT FOR A JESTER'S TEAR EMI EMC 3429 7	31 wks
24 Mar 84	● FUGAZI EMI EMC 2400851..5	20 wks
17 Nov 84	● REAL TO REEL EMI JEST 1 8	22 wks
29 Jun 85	★ MISPLACED CHILDHOOD EMI MRL 2 1	41 wks
4 Jul 87	● CLUTCHING AT STRAWS EMI EMD 1002 2	15 wks
23 Jul 88	B SIDES THEMSELVES EMI EMS 1295 64	6 wks
10 Dec 88	THE THIEVING MAGPIE EMI MARIL 1 25	6 wks
7 Oct 89	● SEASON'S END EMI EMD 1011 22 7	4 wks
6 Jul 91	● HOLIDAYS IN EDEN EMI EMD 1022....................................7	7 wks
20 Jun 92	A SINGLES COLLECTION 1982–1992 EMI CDEMD 1033...............27	2 wks
19 Feb 94	● BRAVE EMI CDEMC 1054 10	4 wks
8 Jul 95	AFRAID OF SUNLIGHT EMI CDEMD 1079 16	2 wks

Yannis MARKOPOULOS Greece, orchestra   8 wks

26 Aug 78	WHO PAYS THE FERRYMAN BBC REB 315 22	8 wks

MARKY MARK and the FUNKY BUNCH
US, male vocalist and dancers   1 wk

5 Oct 91	MUSIC FOR THE PEOPLE Interscope 7567917371 61	1 wk

Bob MARLEY and the WAILERS
Jamaica, male vocal / instrumental group   443 wks

4 Oct 75	NATTY DREAD Island ILPS 9281 43	5 wks
20 Dec 75	LIVE Island ILPS 9376 38	11 wks
8 May 76	RASTAMAN VIBRATION Island ILPS 9383 15	13 wks
11 Jun 77	● EXODUS Island ILPS 9498..8	56 wks
1 Apr 78	● KAYA Island ILPS 9517 4	24 wks
16 Dec 78	BABYLON BY BUS Island ISLD 11......................................40	11 wks
13 Oct 79	SURVIVAL Island ILPS 9542 20	6 wks
28 Jun 80	● UPRISING Island ILPS 9596 6	17 wks
28 May 83	● CONFRONTATION Island ILPS 9760 5	19 wks
19 May 84	★ LEGEND Tuff Gong BMWX 1..1	265 wks

MADONNA receives the news that Simple Minds have kept _Erotica_ from the number one spot.

(Nick Elgar/ LFI)

TOP 30 № 17

TOP 30 № 16

Fifteen years separated _Bat Out Of Hell_ and its number one sequel by MEAT LOAF.

(LFI)

28 Jul 86	**REBEL MUSIC** *Island ILPS 9843*	**54**	3	wks
3 Oct 92	● **SONGS OF FREEDOM** *Tuff Gong TGCBX 1*	**10**	5	wks
3 Jun 95	● **NATURAL MYSTIC** *Tuff Gong BMWCD 2*	**5**	8	wks

Live *Island ILPS 9376* returned to the chart in 1981 under the title Live At The Lyceum.

Neville MARRINER and the ACADEMY OF ST. MARTIN IN THE FIELDS *UK, male conductor with chamber orchestra*   **6 wks**

6 Apr 85	**AMADEUS (film soundtrack)** *London LONDP 6*	**64**	6	wks

Bernie MARSDEN *UK, male vocalist / instrumentalist – guitar*   **2 wks**

5 Sep 81	**LOOK AT ME NOW** *Parlophone PCF 7217*	**71**	2	wks

Lena MARTELL *UK, female vocalist*   **71 wks**

25 May 74	**THAT WONDERFUL SOUND OF LENA MARTELL** *Pye SPL 18427*	**35**	2	wks
8 Jan 77	**THE BEST OF LENA MARTELL** *Pye NSPL 18506*	**13**	16	wks
27 May 78	**THE LENA MARTELL COLLECTION** *Ronco RTL 2028*	**12**	19	wks
20 Oct 79	● **LENA'S MUSIC ALBUM** *Pye N 123*	**5**	18	wks
19 Apr 80	● **BY REQUEST** *Ronco RTL 2046*	**9**	9	wks
29 Nov 80	**BEAUTIFUL SUNDAY** *Ronco RTL 2052*	**23**	7	wks

MARTHA and the MUFFINS
Canada, male / female vocal / instrumental group   **6 wks**

15 Mar 80	**METRO MUSIC** *DinDisc DID 1*	**34**	6	wks

MARTIKA *US, female vocalist*   **52 wks**

16 Sep 89	**MARTIKA** *CBS 463355 1*	**11**	37	wks
7 Sep 91	**MARTIKA'S KITCHEN** *Columbia 4671891*	**15**	15	wks

M
205

Dean MARTIN *US, male vocalist*   **25 wks**

13 May 61	**THIS TIME I'M SWINGING** *Capitol T 1442*	**18**	1	wk
25 Feb 67	**AT EASE WITH DEAN** *Reprise RSLP 6322*	**35**	1	wk
4 Nov 67	**WELCOME TO MY WORLD** *Philips DBL 001*	**39**	1	wk
12 Oct 68	**GREATEST HITS VOLUME 1** *Reprise RSLP 6301*	**40**	1	wk
22 Feb 69	● **BEST OF DEAN MARTIN** *Capitol ST 21194*	**9**	1	wk
22 Feb 69	● **GENTLE ON MY MIND** *Reprise RSLP 6330*	**9**	8	wks
27 Nov 71	**WHITE CHRISTMAS** *MFP 524* ①	**45**	1	wk
13 Nov 76	● **20 ORIGINAL DEAN MARTIN HITS** *Reprise K 54066*	**7**	11	wks

① Nat 'King' Cole and Dean Martin.

George MARTIN ORCHESTRA – *See BEATLES*

Juan MARTIN and the ROYAL PHILHARMONIC ORCHESTRA *Spain, male instrumentalist – guitar with UK, orchestra*   **9 wks**

11 Feb 84	**SERENADE** *K-Tel NE 1267*	**21**	9	wks

See also Royal Philharmonic Orchestra.

John MARTYN *UK, male vocalist / instrumentalist – guitar*   **25 wks**

4 Feb 78	**ONE WORLD** *Island ILPS 9492*	**54**	1	wk
1 Nov 80	**GRACE AND DANGER** *Island ILPS 9560*	**54**	2	wks
26 Sep 81	**GLORIOUS FOOL** *Geffen K 99178*	**25**	7	wks
4 Sep 82	**WELL KEPT SECRET** *WEA K 99255*	**20**	7	wks
17 Nov 84	**SAPPHIRE** *Island ILPS 9779*	**57**	2	wks
8 Mar 86	**PIECE BY PIECE** *Island ILPS 9807*	**28**	4	wks
10 Oct 92	**COULDN'T LOVE YOU MORE** *Permanent PERMCD 9*	**65**	2	wks

Hank MARVIN *UK, male vocalist / instrumentalist – guitar*   **42 wks**

22 Nov 69	**HANK MARVIN** *Columbia SCX 6352*	**14**	2	wks

20 Mar 82	**WORDS AND MUSIC** Polydor POLD 5054 ....**66**	3 wks
31 Oct 92	**INTO THE LIGHT** Polydor 5171482 ....**18**	10 wks
20 Nov 93	**HEARTBEAT** PolyGram TV 52132222 ....**17**	9 wks
22 Oct 94	**THE BEST OF HANK MARVIN AND THE SHADOWS**	
	PolyGram TV 5238212 [1] **19**	11 wks
18 Nov 95	**HANK PLAYS CLIFF** PolyGram TV 5294262 ....**33†**	7 wks

[1] Hank Marvin and the Shadows

See also Marvin, Welch and Farrar.

MARVIN, WELCH and FARRAR
UK, male vocal / instrumental group　　　　　　　　　**4 wks**

| 3 Apr 71 | **MARVIN, WELCH AND FARRAR** Regal Zonophone SRZA 8502 ....**30** | 4 wks |

See also Hank Marvin.

Richard MARX *US, male vocalist*　　　　**39 wks**

9 Apr 88	**RICHARD MARX** Manhattan MTL 1017............................**68**	2 wks
20 May 89	● **REPEAT OFFENDER** EMI-USA MTL 1043 ....**8**	12 wks
16 Nov 91	● **RUSH STREET** Capitol ESTU 2158 ....**7**	20 wks
19 Feb 94	**PAID VACATION** Capitol CDESTU 2208 ....**11**	5 wks

MARXMAN *Ireland / UK, male rap group*　　　**1 wk**

| 3 Apr 93 | **33 REVOLUTIONS PER MINUTE** Talkin Loud 5145382..............**69** | 1 wk |

MARY JANE GIRLS *US, female vocal group*　　**9 wks**

| 28 May 83 | **MARY JANE GIRLS** Gordy STML 12189..............................**51** | 9 wks |

MASSED WELSH CHOIRS *UK, male voice choir*　　**7 wks**

| 9 Aug 69 | ● **CYMANSA GANN** BBC REC 53 M.......................................**5** | 7 wks |

MASSIVE ATTACK *UK, male / female vocal / instrumental group*　　**62 wks**

| 20 Apr 91 | **BLUE LINES** Wild Bunch WBRLP 1 ....**13** | 16 wks |
| 8 Oct 94 | ● **PROTECTION / NO PROTECTION** Wild Bunch WBRCD 2................**4** | 46 wks |

From 4 Mar 95 Protection was listed with the remix album No Protection.

MASTERMIXERS – *See JIVE BUNNY and the MASTERMIXERS*

MATCHBOX *UK, male vocal / instrumental group*　　**14 wks**

| 2 Feb 80 | **MATCHBOX** Magnet MAG 5031 ....**44** | 5 wks |
| 11 Oct 80 | **MIDNITE DYNAMOS** Magnet MAG 5036 ....**23** | 9 wks |

Mireille MATHIEU *France, female vocalist*　　**1 wk**

| 2 Mar 68 | **MIREILLE MATHIEU** Columbia SCX 6210............................**39** | 1 wk |

Johnny MATHIS *US, male vocalist*　　**228 wks**

8 Nov 58	● **WARM** Fontana TBA TFL 5015......................................**6**	2 wks
24 Jan 59	● **SWING SOFTLY** Fontana TBA TFL 5039 ....**10**	1 wk
13 Feb 60	● **RIDE ON A RAINBOW** Fontana TFL 5061 ....**10**	2 wks
10 Dec 60	● **RHYTHMS AND BALLADS OF BROADWAY** Fontana SET 101 ....**6**	10 wks
17 Jun 61	**I'LL BUY YOU A STAR** Fontana TFL 5143 ....**18**	1 wk
16 May 70	**RAINDROPS KEEP FALLING ON MY HEAD** CBS 63587 ....**23**	10 wks
3 Apr 71	**LOVE STORY** CBS 64334 ....**27**	5 wks
9 Sep 72	**FIRST TIME EVER I SAW YOUR FACE** CBS 64930 ....**40**	3 wks
16 Dec 72	**MAKE IT EASY ON YOURSELF** CBS 65161 ....**49**	1 wk
8 Mar 75	**I'M COMING HOME** CBS 65690 ....**18**	11 wks
5 Apr 75	**THE HEART OF A WOMAN** CBS 80533 ....**39**	2 wks
26 Jul 75	**WHEN WILL I SEE YOU AGAIN** CBS 80738.................**13**	10 wks

3 Jul 76	I ONLY HAVE EYES FOR YOU CBS 81329	14	12 wks
19 Feb 77	GREATEST HITS VOLUME IV CBS 86022	31	5 wks
18 Jun 77	★ THE JOHNNY MATHIS COLLECTION CBS 10003	1	40 wks
17 Dec 77	SWEET SURRENDER CBS 86036	55	1 wk
29 Apr 78	● YOU LIGHT UP MY LIFE CBS 86055	3	19 wks
26 Aug 78	THAT'S WHAT FRIENDS ARE FOR CBS 86068 [1]	16	11 wks
7 Apr 79	THE BEST DAYS OF MY LIFE CBS 86080	38	5 wks
3 Nov 79	MATHIS MAGIC CBS 86103	59	4 wks
8 Mar 80	★ TEARS AND LAUGHTER CBS 10019	1	15 wks
12 Jul 80	ALL FOR YOU CBS 86115	20	8 wks
19 Sep 81	● CELEBRATION CBS 10028	9	16 wks
15 May 82	FRIENDS IN LOVE CBS 85652	34	7 wks
17 Sep 83	● UNFORGETTABLE: A MUSICAL TRIBUTE TO NAT 'KING' COLE CBS 10042 [2]	5	16 wks
15 Sep 84	A SPECIAL PART OF ME CBS 25475	45	3 wks
13 Dec 86	THE HOLLYWOOD MUSICALS CBS 4502581 [3]	46	8 wks

[1] Johnny Mathis and Deniece Williams [2] Johnny Mathis and Natalie Cole [3] Johnny Mathis and Henry Mancini

MATT BIANCO *UK, male vocalist – Mark Riley*　　　　**67 wks**

8 Sep 84	WHOSE SIDE ARE YOU ON WEA WX 7	35	39 wks
22 Mar 86	MATT BIANCO WEA WX 35	26	13 wks
9 Jul 88	INDIGO WEA WX 181	23	13 wks
2 Nov 90	THE BEST OF MATT BIANCO East West WX 376	49	2 wks

For first album, act was a UK / Poland, male / female vocal / instrumental group.

Kathy MATTEA *US, female vocalist*　　　　**1 wk**

15 Apr 95	READY FOR THE STORM (FAVOURITE CUTS) Mercury 5280062	61	1 wk

MATTHEWS' SOUTHERN COMFORT
UK, male vocal / instrumental group　　　　**4 wks**

25 Jul 70	SECOND SPRING Uni UNLS 112	52	4 wks

MAX Q *Australia, male vocal / instrumental duo*　　　　**1 wk**

4 Nov 89	MAX Q Mercury 838942 1	69	1 wk

MAXX *UK / Sweden / Germany, male / female vocal / instrumental group*　　　　**1 wk**

23 Jul 94	TO THE MAXXIMUM Pulse 8 PULSE 15CD	66	1 wk

Brian MAY *UK, male vocalist / instrumentalist – guitar*　　　　**21 wks**

12 Nov 83	STAR FLEET PROJECT EMI SFLT 1078061 [1]	35	4 wks
10 Oct 92	● BACK TO THE LIGHT Parlophone CDPCSD 123	6	14 wks
19 Feb 94	LIVE AT THE BRIXTON ACADEMY Parlophone CDPCSD 150 [2]	20	3 wks

[1] Brian May and Friends [2] Brian May Band

Simon MAY ORCHESTRA *UK, orchestra*　　　　**7 wks**

27 Sep 86	SIMON'S WAY BBC REB 594	59	7 wks

John MAYALL *UK, male vocalist*　　　　**115 wks**

30 Jul 66	● BLUES BREAKERS Decca LK 4804 [1]	6	17 wks
4 Mar 67	● A HARD ROAD Decca SKL 4853	10	19 wks
23 Sep 67	● CRUSADE Decca SKL 4890	8	14 wks
25 Nov 67	BLUES ALONE Ace Of Clubs SCL 1243	24	5 wks
16 Mar 68	DIARY OF A BAND VOLUME 1 Decca SKL 4918	27	9 wks
16 Mar 68	DIARY OF A BAND VOLUME 2 Decca SKL 4919	28	5 wks
20 Jul 68	● BARE WIRES Decca SKL 4945	3	17 wks
18 Jan 69	BLUES FROM LAUREL CANYON Decca SKL 4972	33	3 wks
23 Aug 69	LOOKING BACK Decca SKL 5010	14	7 wks

15 Nov 69	**TURNING POINT** Polydor 583571	....	**11**	7 wks
11 Apr 70	● **EMPTY ROOMS** Polydor 583580	....	**9**	8 wks
12 Dec 70	**U.S.A. UNION** Polydor 2425020	....	**50**	1 wk
26 Jun 71	**BACK TO THE ROOTS** Polydor 2657005	....	**31**	2 wks
17 Apr 93	**WAKE UP CALL** Silvertone ORECD 527	....	**61**	1 wk

1 John Mayall and Eric Clapton

Curtis MAYFIELD *US, male vocalist* — **2 wks**

| 31 Mar 73 | **SUPERFLY** Buddah 2318 065 | .... | **26** | 2 wks |

MAZE featuring Frankie BEVERLY
US, male vocalist and male vocal / instrumental group — **25 wks**

7 May 83	**WE ARE ONE** Capitol EST 12262	....	**38**	6 wks
9 Mar 85	**CAN'T STOP THE LOVE** Capitol MAZE 1	....	**41**	12 wks
27 Sep 86	**LIVE IN LOS ANGELES** Capitol ESTSP 24	....	**70**	2 wks
16 Sep 89	**SILKY SOUL** Warner Bros. WX 301	....	**43**	5 wks

MAZZY STARR *US, male / female vocal / instrumental duo* — **1 wk**

| 9 Oct 93 | **SO TONIGHT THAT I MIGHT SEE** Capitol CDEST 2206 | .... | **68** | 1 wk |

MC HAMMER *US, male rapper* — **67 wks**

28 Jul 90	● **PLEASE HAMMER DON'T HURT 'EM** Capitol EST 2120	....	**8**	59 wks
6 Apr 91	**LET'S GET IT STARTED** Capitol EST 2140	....	**46**	2 wks
2 Nov 91	**TOO LEGIT TO QUIT** Capitol ESTP 26 1	....	**41**	6 wks

1 Hammer

MC TUNES *UK, male rapper* — **3 wks**

| 13 Oct 90 | **THE NORTH AT ITS HEIGHTS** ZTT ZTT 3 | .... | **26** | 3 wks |

Vaughn MEADER *US, male comedian* — **8 wks**

| 29 Dec 62 | **THE FIRST FAMILY** London HAA 8048 | .... | **12** | 8 wks |

MEAT LOAF *US, male vocalist* — **713 wks**

11 Mar 78	● **BAT OUT OF HELL** Cleveland International EPC 82419	....	**9**	472 wks
12 Sep 81	★ **DEAD RINGER** Epic EPC 83645	....	**1**	46 wks
7 May 83	● **MIDNIGHT AT THE LOST AND FOUND** Epic EPC 25243	....	**7**	23 wks
10 Nov 84	● **BAD ATTITUDE** Arista 206 619	....	**8**	16 wks
26 Jan 85	● **HITS OUT OF HELL** Epic EPC 26156	....	**2**	80 wks
11 Oct 86	**BLIND BEFORE I STOP** Arista 207 741	....	**28**	6 wks
7 Nov 87	**LIVE AT WEMBLEY** RCA 208599	....	**60**	2 wks
18 Sep 93	★ **BAT OUT OF HELL II – BACK INTO HELL** Virgin CDV 2710	....	**1**	56 wks
22 Oct 94	**ALIVE IN HELL** Pure Music PMCD 7002	....	**33**	4 wks
11 Nov 95	● **WELCOME TO THE NEIGHBOURHOOD** Virgin CDV 2799	....	**3†**	8 wks

Hits Out Of Hell *changed catalogue number to 4504471 during its chart run.*

MECHANICS – *See MIKE and the MECHANICS*

Glenn MEDEIROS *US, male vocalist* — **2 wks**

| 8 Oct 88 | **NOT ME** London LONLP 68 | .... | **63** | 2 wks |

MEDICS – *See DOCTOR and the MEDICS*

MEGA CITY FOUR *UK, male vocal / instrumental group* — **3 wks**

17 Jun 89	**TRANZOPHOBIA** Decoy DYL 3	....	**67**	1 wk
7 Mar 92	**SEBASTOPOL RD** Big Life MEGCD 1	....	**41**	1 wk
22 May 93	**MAGIC BULLETS** Big Life MEGCD 3	....	**57**	1 wk

MEGADETH *US, male vocal / instrumental group* **22 wks**

26 Mar 88	**SO FAR SO GOOD . . . SO WHAT!** *Capitol EST 2053* **18**	5 wks
6 Oct 90	● **RUST IN PEACE** *Capitol EST 2132* **8**	4 wks
18 Jul 92	● **COUNTDOWN TO EXTINCTION** *Capitol CDESTU 2175* **5**	8 wks
5 Nov 94	● **YOUTHANASIA / HIDDEN TREASURE** *Capitol CDEST 2244* **6**	5 wks

From 25 Mar 95 Youthanasia was listed with a bonus album Hidden Treasure.

MEL and KIM *UK, female vocal duo* **25 wks**

25 Apr 87	● **F.L.M.** *Supreme SU 2*..**3**	25 wks

See also Kim Appleby.

MELANIE *US, female vocalist* **69 wks**

19 Sep 70	● **CANDLES IN THE RAIN** *Buddah 2318009* **5**	27 wks
16 Jan 71	**LEFTOVER WINE** *Buddah 2318011*..**22**	11 wks
29 May 71	● **GOOD BOOK** *Buddah 2322 001* **9**	9 wks
8 Jan 72	**GATHER ME** *Buddah 2322 002* **14**	14 wks
1 Apr 72	**GARDEN IN THE CITY** *Buddah 2318 054*................................**19**	6 wks
7 Oct 72	**THE FOUR SIDES OF MELANIE** *Buddah 2659 013* **23**	2 wks

MELBOURNE SYMPHONY ORCHESTRA – *See Elton JOHN*

John Cougar MELLENCAMP *US, male vocalist* **27 wks**

6 Nov 82	**AMERICAN FOOL** *Riva RVLP 16* 1 ....**37**	6 wks
3 Mar 84	**UH–HUH** *Riva RIVL 1*..**92**	1 wk
3 Oct 87	**THE LONESOME JUBILEE** *Mercury MERH 109* **31**	12 wks
27 May 89	**BIG DADDY** *Mercury MERH 838220 1* **25**	4 wks
19 Oct 91	**WHENEVER WE WANTED** *Mercury 5101511* **39**	2 wks
18 Sep 93	**HUMAN WHEELS** *Mercury 5180882*......................................**37**	2 wks

1 John Cougar

MEMBERS *UK, male vocal / instrumental group* **5 wks**

28 Apr 79	**AT THE CHELSEA NIGHTCLUB** *Virgin V 2120* **45**	5 wks

MEN AT WORK *Australia, male vocal / instrumental group* **71 wks**

15 Jan 83	★ **BUSINESS AS USUAL** *Epic EPC 85669* **1**	44 wks
30 Apr 83	● **CARGO** *Epic EPC 25372* **8**	27 wks

MEN THEY COULDN'T HANG *UK, male vocal / instrumental group* **9 wks**

27 Jul 85	**NIGHT OF A THOUSAND CANDLES** *Imp FIEND 50* **91**	2 wks
8 Nov 86	**HOW GREEN IS THE VALLEY** *MCA MCF 3337* **68**	2 wks
23 Apr 88	**WAITING FOR BONAPARTE** *Magnet MAGL 5075* **41**	2 wks
6 May 89	**SILVER TOWN** *Silvertone ORELP 503* **39**	2 wks
1 Sep 90	**THE DOMINO CLUB** *Silvertone ORELP 512* **53**	1 wk

MEN WITHOUT HATS *Canada, male vocal / instrumental group* **1 wk**

12 Nov 83	**RHYTHM OF YOUTH** *Statik STATLP 10*...................................**96**	1 wk

MENSWEAR *UK, male vocal / instrumental group* **3 wks**

21 Oct 95	**NUISANCE** *Laurel 8286792* **11**	3 wks

Natalie MERCHANT *US, female vocalist* **2 wks**

1 Jul 95	**TIGERLILY** *Elektra 7559617452* **39**	2 wks

Freddie MERCURY *UK, male vocalist* **56 wks**

11 May 85	● **MR BAD GUY** *CBS 86312*..**6**	23 wks

M
209

| 22 Oct 88 | **BARCELONA** *Polydor POLH 44* [1] | **15** | 8 wks |
| 28 Nov 92 ● | **THE FREDDIE MERCURY ALBUM** *Parlophone CDPCSD 124* | **4** | 25 wks |

[1] Freddie Mercury and Montserrat Caballe

MERCURY REV UK, male/female vocal/instrumental group — **1 wk**

| 12 Jun 93 | **BOCES** *Beggars Banquet BBQCD 140* | **43** | 1 wk |

MERLE and ROY UK, female/male vocal/instrumental duo — **5 wks**

| 26 Sep 87 | **REQUESTS** *Mynod Mawr RMBR 8713* | **74** | 5 wks |

MERSEYBEATS UK, male vocal/instrumental group — **9 wks**

| 20 Jun 64 | **THE MERSEYBEATS** *Fontana TL 5210* | **12** | 9 wks |

METALLICA US/Denmark, male vocal/instrumental group — **84 wks**

11 Aug 84	**RIDE THE LIGHTNING** *Music For Nations MFN 27*	**87**	2 wks
15 Mar 86	**MASTER OF PUPPETS** *Music For Nations MFN 60*	**41**	4 wks
17 Sep 88 ●	**. . . AND JUSTICE FOR ALL** *Vertigo VERH 61*	**4**	6 wks
19 May 90	**THE GOOD THE BAD AND THE LIVE** *Vertigo 8754871*	**56**	1 wk
24 Aug 91 ★	**METALLICA** *Vertigo 5100221*	**1**	70 wks
11 Dec 93	**LIVE SHIT – BINGE AND PURGE** *Vertigo 5187250*	**54**	1 wk

Live Shit – Binge and Purge was a boxed set containing two CDs, three video cassettes and a book.

METEORS UK, male vocal/instrumental group — **3 wks**

| 26 Feb 83 | **WRECKIN' CREW** *I.D. NOSE 1* | **53** | 3 wks |

MEZZOFORTE Iceland, male instrumental group — **10 wks**

| 5 Mar 83 | **SURPRISE SURPRISE** *Steinar STELP 02* | **23** | 9 wks |
| 2 Jul 83 | **CATCHING UP WITH MEZZOFORTE** *Steinar STELP 03* | **95** | 1 wk |

MG'S – See Booker T. and the MG's

MIAMI SOUND MACHINE – See Gloria ESTEFAN

George MICHAEL UK, male vocalist — **133 wks**

| 14 Nov 87 ★ | **FAITH** *Epic 4600001* | **1** | 76 wks |
| 15 Sep 90 ★ | **LISTEN WITHOUT PREJUDICE VOLUME 1** *Epic 4672951* | **1** | 57 wks |

Keith MICHELL Australia, male vocalist — **12 wks**

| 9 Feb 80 | **CAPTAIN BEAKY AND HIS BAND** *Polydor 238 3462* | **28** | 12 wks |

Bette MIDLER US, female vocalist — **39 wks**

15 Jul 89	**BEACHES (film soundtrack)** *Atlantic 7819931*	**21**	9 wks
13 Jul 91 ●	**SOME PEOPLE'S LIVES** *Atlantic 7567821291*	**5**	11 wks
15 Feb 92	**FOR THE BOYS (film soundtrack)** *Atlantic 7567823292*	**75**	1 wk
30 Oct 93 ●	**EXPERIENCE THE DIVINE – GREATEST HITS** *Atlantic 7567824972*	**3**	15 wks
25 Nov 95	**BETTE OF ROSES** *Atlantic 7567828232*	**55†**	3 wks

MIDNIGHT OIL Australia, male vocal/instrumental group — **21 wks**

25 Jun 88	**DIESEL AND DUST** *CBS 4600051*	**19**	16 wks
10 Mar 90	**BLUE SKY MINING** *CBS 4656531*	**28**	3 wks
1 May 93	**EARTH AND SUN AND MOON** *Columbia 4736052*	**27**	2 wks

MIDNIGHT STAR US, male/female vocal/instrumental group — **6 wks**

| 2 Feb 85 | **PLANETARY INVASION** *Solar MCF 3251* | **85** | 2 wks |
| 5 Jul 86 | **HEADLINES** *Solar MCF 3322* | **42** | 4 wks |

MIGHTY LEMON DROPS *UK, male vocal / instrumental group* **5 wks**

4 Oct 86	**HAPPY HEAD** *Blue Guitar AZLP 1* **58**	2 wks
27 Feb 88	**THE WORLD WITHOUT END** *Blue Guitar AZLP 4* **34**	3 wks

MIGHTY MORPH'N POWER RANGERS
US, male / female vocal group **3 wks**

24 Dec 94	**POWER RANGERS – THE ALBUM** *RCA 74321252982* **50**	3 wks

MIGHTY WAH *UK, male vocal / instrumental group* **11 wks**

18 Jul 81	**NAH–POO = THE ART OF BLUFF** *Eternal CLASSIC 1* [1]..........**33**	5 wks
4 Aug 84	**A WORD TO THE WISE GUY** *Beggars Banquet BEGA 54*............**28**	6 wks

[1] Wah!

MIKE and the MECHANICS *UK, male vocal / instrumental group* **62 wks**

15 Mar 86	**MIKE AND THE MECHANICS** *WEA WX 49*.................**78**	3 wks
26 Nov 88	● **THE LIVING YEARS** *WEA WX 203* **2**	19 wks
27 Apr 91	**WORD OF MOUTH** *Virgin V 2662*...................**11**	7 wks
18 Mar 95	● **BEGGAR ON A BEACH OF GOLD** *Virgin CDV 2772* **9**	33 wks

See also Mike Rutherford.

Buddy MILES – *See SANTANA*

John MILES *UK, male vocalist / multi–instrumentalist* **25 wks**

27 Mar 76	● **REBEL** *Decca SKL 5231* **9**	10 wks
26 Feb 77	**STRANGER IN THE CITY** *Decca TXS 118* **37**	3 wks
1 Apr 78	**ZARAGON** *Decca TXS 126* **43**	5 wks
21 Apr 79	**MORE MILES PER HOUR** *Decca TXS 135*..............**46**	5 wks
29 Aug 81	**MILES HIGH** *EMI EMC 3374* **96**	2 wks

Paul MILES–KINGSTON – *See Andrew LLOYD WEBBER*

Frankie MILLER *UK, male vocalist* **1 wk**

14 Apr 79	**FALLING IN LOVE** *Chrysalis CHR 1220* **54**	1 wk

Glenn MILLER *US, orchestra* **80 wks**

28 Jan 61	● **GLENN MILLER PLAYS SELECTIONS FROM 'THE GLENN MILLER STORY' AND OTHER HITS** *RCA 27068 0023* **10**	18 wks
5 Jul 69	● **THE BEST OF GLENN MILLER** *RCA International 1002* **5**	14 wks
6 Sep 69	**NEARNESS OF YOU** *RCA International INTS 1019* **30**	2 wks
25 Apr 70	**A MEMORIAL 1944–1969** *RCA GM 1* **18**	17 wks
25 Dec 71	**THE REAL GLENN MILLER AND HIS ORCHESTRA PLAY THE ORIGINAL MUSIC OF THE FILM 'THE GLENN MILLER STORY' AND OTHER HITS** *RCA International NTS 1157* **28**	2 wks
14 Feb 76	**A LEGENDARY PERFORMER** *RCA Victor DPM 2065* **41**	5 wks
14 Feb 76	**A LEGENDARY PERFORMER VOLUME 2** *RCA Victor CPL 11349* ..**53**	2 wks
9 Apr 77	● **THE UNFORGETTABLE GLENN MILLER** *RCA Victor TVL 1*..............**4**	8 wks
20 Mar 93	**THE ULTIMATE GLENN MILLER** *Bluebird 74321131372*.................**11**	6 wks
25 Feb 95	**THE LOST RECORDINGS** *Happy Days CDHD 4012* **22**	6 wks

The Real Glenn Miller And His Orchestra Play . . . is a re–titled re–issue of the first album.

Steve MILLER BAND *US, male vocal / instrumental group* **50 wks**

12 Jun 76	**FLY LIKE AN EAGLE** *Mercury 9286 177*................**11**	17 wks
4 Jun 77	**BOOK OF DREAMS** *Mercury 9286 456* **12**	12 wks
19 Jun 82	● **ABRACADABRA** *Mercury 6302 204* **10**	16 wks
7 May 83	**STEVE MILLER BAND LIVE!** *Mercury MERL 18* **79**	2 wks
6 Oct 90	**THE BEST OF 1968–1973** *Capitol EST 2133*................**34**	3 wks

MILLI VANILLI France / Germany, male duo **25 wks**

21 Jan 89 ● **ALL OR NOTHING / 2X2** Cooltempo CTLP 11 ....**6**	25 wks

All Or Nothing was *repackaged and available with a free re–mix album, 2X2, from 16 Oct 89 onwards.*

MILLICAN and NESBIT UK, male vocal duo **24 wks**

23 Mar 74 ● **MILLICAN AND NESBIT** Pye NSPL 18428............................**3**	21 wks
4 Jan 75 **EVERYBODY KNOWS MILLICAN AND NESBIT** Pye NSPL 18446 ..**23**	3 wks

Spike MILLIGAN UK, male comedian **5 wks**

25 Nov 61 **MILLIGAN PRESERVED** Parlophone PMC 1152 ....**11**	4 wks
18 Dec 76 **THE SNOW GOOSE** RCA RS 1088 [1] **49**	1 wk

[1] Spike Milligan with the London Symphony Orchestra

See also *Harry Secombe, Peter Sellers and Spike Milligan; London Symphony Orchestra.*

Mrs. MILLS UK, female instrumentalist – piano **13 wks**

10 Dec 66 **COME TO MY PARTY** Parlophone PMC 7010 ....**17**	7 wks
28 Dec 68 **MRS. MILLS' PARTY PIECES** Parlophone PCS 7066 ....**32**	3 wks
13 Dec 69 **LET'S HAVE ANOTHER PARTY** Parlophone PCS 7035 ....**23**	2 wks
6 Nov 71 **I'M MIGHTY GLAD** MFP 5225 ....**49**	1 wk

MILLTOWN BROTHERS UK, male vocal / instrumental group **5 wks**

23 Mar 91 **SLINKY** A & M 3953461 ....**27**	5 wks

MINDBENDERS UK, male vocal / instrumental group **4 wks**

25 Jun 66 **THE MINDBENDERS** Fontana TL 5324.............................**28**	4 wks

See also *Wayne Fontana and the Mindbenders.*

MINDFUNK US, male vocal / instrumental group **1 wk**

15 May 93 **DROPPED** Megaforce CDZAZ 3 ....**60**	1 wk

Zodiac MINDWARP and the LOVE REACTION
UK, male vocal / instrumental group **5 wks**

5 Mar 88 **TATTOOED BEAT MESSIAH** Mercury ZODLP 1 ....**20**	5 wks

MINIPOPS UK, male / female vocal group **12 wks**

26 Dec 81 **MINIPOPS** K-Tel NE 1102....................................**63**	7 wks
19 Feb 83 **WE'RE THE MINIPOPS** K-Tel ONE 1187 ....**54**	5 wks

MINISTRY US, male vocal / instrumental group **5 wks**

25 Jul 92 **PSALM 69** Sire 7599267272 ....**33**	5 wks

Liza MINNELLI US, female vocalist **26 wks**

7 Apr 73 ● **LIZA WITH A 'Z'** CBS 65212 ....**9**	15 wks
16 Jun 73 **THE SINGER** CBS 65555 ....**45**	1 wk
21 Oct 89 ● **RESULTS** Epic 465511 1 ....**6**	10 wks

Dannii MINOGUE Australia, female vocalist **21 wks**

15 Jun 91 ● **LOVE AND KISSES** MCA MCA 10340......................**8**	20 wks
16 Oct 93 **GET INTO YOU** MCA MCD 10909 ....**52**	1 wk

Kylie MINOGUE *Australia, female vocalist*   **159 wks**

16 Jul 88 ★ **KYLIE** *PWL HF 3* **1**	67 wks
21 Oct 89 ★ **ENJOY YOURSELF** *PWL HF 9* **1**	33 wks
24 Nov 90 ● **RHYTHM OF LOVE** *PWL HF 18* **9**	22 wks
26 Oct 91 **LET'S GET TO IT** *PWL HF 21* **15**	12 wks
5 Sep 92 ★ **GREATEST HITS** *PWL International HFCD 25*....................**1**	10 wks
1 Oct 94 ● **KYLIE MINOGUE** *Deconstruction 74321227492* **4**	15 wks

MIRAGE *UK, male / female vocal / instrumental group*   **33 wks**

26 Dec 87 ● **THE BEST OF MIRAGE JACK MIX '88** *Stylus SMR 746* **7**	15 wks
25 Jun 88 ● **JACK MIX IN FULL EFFECT** *Stylus SMR 856* **7**	12 wks
7 Jan 89 **ROYAL MIX '89** *Stylus SMR 871* **34**	6 wks

MIRAGE *UK, male instrumental group*   **3 wks**

23 Sep 95 **CLASSIC GUITAR MOODS** *PolyGram TV 5290562* **25**	3 wks

MISSION *UK, male vocal / instrumental group*   **47 wks**

22 Nov 86 **GOD'S OWN MEDICINE** *Mercury MERH 102* **14**	20 wks
4 Jul 87 **THE FIRST CHAPTER** *Mercury MISH 1* **35**	4 wks
12 Mar 88 ● **LITTLE CHILDREN** *Mercury MISH 2*.................................**2**	9 wks
17 Feb 90 ● **CARVED IN SAND** *Mercury 8422511* **7**	8 wks
2 Nov 90 **GRAINS OF SAND** *Mercury 8469371* **28**	2 wks
4 Jul 92 **MASQUE** *Vertigo 5121212* **23**	2 wks
19 Feb 94 **SUM AND SUBSTANCE** *Vertigo 5184472* **49**	1 wk
25 Feb 95 **NEVERLAND** *Neverland SMEECD 001* **58**	1 wk

MR. BIG *US, male vocal / instrumental group*   **14 wks**

22 Jul 89 **MR. BIG** *Atlantic 781990 1* **60**	1 wk
13 Apr 91 **LEAN INTO IT** *Atlantic 7567822091* **28**	12 wks
2 Oct 93 **BUMP AHEAD** *Atlantic 7567824952*..........................**61**	1 wk

MR. BUNGLE *US, male vocal / instrumental group*   **1 wk**

21 Sep 91 **MR BUNGLE** *London 8282671* **57**	1 wk

MR. MISTER *US, male vocal / instrumental group*   **24 wks**

15 Feb 86 ● **WELCOME TO THE REAL WORLD** *RCA PL 89647* **6**	24 wks

Joni MITCHELL *Canada, female vocalist*   **115 wks**

6 Jun 70 ● **LADIES OF THE CANYON** *Reprise RSLP 6376* **8**	25 wks
24 Jul 71 ● **BLUE** *Reprise K 44128* **3**	18 wks
16 Mar 74 **COURT AND SPARK** *Asylum SYLA 8756* **14**	11 wks
1 Feb 75 **MILES OF AISLES** *Asylum SYSP 902*........................**34**	4 wks
27 Dec 75 **THE HISSING OF SUMMER LAWNS** *Asylum SYLA 8763* **14**	10 wks
11 Dec 76 **HEJIRA** *Asylum K 53053*......................................**11**	5 wks
21 Jan 78 **DON JUAN'S RECKLESS DAUGHTER** *Asylum K 63003* **20**	7 wks
14 Jul 79 **MINGUS** *Asylum K 53091* **24**	7 wks
4 Oct 80 **SHADOWS AND LIGHT** *Elektra K 62030* **63**	3 wks
4 Dec 82 **WILD THINGS RUN FAST** *Geffen GEF 25102* **32**	8 wks
30 Nov 85 **DOG EAT DOG** *Geffen GEF 26455* **57**	3 wks
2 Apr 88 **CHALK MARK IN A RAIN STORM** *Geffen WX 141* **26**	7 wks
9 Mar 91 **NIGHT RIDE HOME** *Geffen GEF 24302* **25**	5 wks
5 Nov 94 **TURBULENT INDIGO** *Reprise 9362457862*...................**53**	2 wks

George MITCHELL MINSTRELS *UK, male / female vocal group*   **292 wks**

26 Nov 60 ★ **THE BLACK AND WHITE MINSTREL SHOW** *HMV CLP 1399*...........**1**	142 wks
21 Oct 61 ★ **ANOTHER BLACK AND WHITE MINSTREL SHOW** *HMV CLP 1460* **1**	64 wks
20 Oct 62 ★ **ON STAGE WITH THE GEORGE MITCHELL MINSTRELS**	
HMV CLP 1599...**1**	26 wks

M
213

2 Nov 63 ● **ON TOUR WITH THE GEORGE MITCHELL MINSTRELS**
  HMV CLP 1667..**6**   18 wks
12 Dec 64 ● **SPOTLIGHT ON THE GEORGE MITCHELL MINSTRELS**
  HMV CLP 1803..**6**   7 wks
4 Dec 65 ● **MAGIC OF THE MINSTRELS** *HMV CLP 1917* ....**9**   7 wks
26 Nov 66   **HERE COME THE MINSTRELS** *HMV CLP 3579* ....**11**   11 wks
16 Dec 67   **SHOWTIME** *HMV CSD 3642* ....**26**   2 wks
14 Dec 68   **SING THE IRVING BERLIN SONGBOOK** *Columbia SCX 6267* ....**33**   1 wk
19 Dec 70   **THE MAGIC OF CHRISTMAS** *Columbia SCX 6431* ....**32**   4 wks
19 Nov 77 ● **30 GOLDEN GREATS** *EMI EMTV 7* 1 ....**10**   10 wks

1 George Mitchell Minstrels with the Joe Loss Orchestra

MN8 *UK / Trinidad, male vocal group*   **4 wks**

27 May 95   **TO THE NEXT LEVEL** *Columbia 4802802* ....**13**   4 wks

MOBY *US, male producer – Richard Hall*   **4 wks**

25 Mar 95   **EVERYTHING IS WRONG** *Mute LCDSTUMM 130* ....**21**   4 wks

MOCK TURTLES *UK, male / female vocal / instrumental group*   **4 wks**

25 May 91   **TURTLE SOUP** *Imaginary ILLUSION 012* ....**54**   1 wk
27 Jul 91   **TWO SIDES** *Siren SRNLP31* ....**33**   3 wks

MODERN EON *UK, male vocal / instrumental group*   **1 wk**

13 Jun 81   **FICTION TALES** *DinDisc DID 11*................................**65**   1 wk

MODERN LOVERS – *See Jonathan RICHMAN and the MODERN LOVERS*

MODERN ROMANCE *UK, male vocal / instrumental group*   **13 wks**

16 Apr 83   **TRICK OF THE LIGHT** *WEA X 0127*.............................**53**   7 wks
3 Dec 83   **PARTY TONIGHT** *Ronco RON LP 3* ....**45**   6 wks

MODERN TALKING *Germany, male vocal / instrumental group*   **3 wks**

11 Oct 86   **READY FOR ROMANCE** *RCA PL 71133* ....**76**   3 wks

MOIST *Canada, male vocal / instrumental group*   **3 wks**

26 Aug 95   **SILVER** *Chrysalis CDCHR 6080* ....**49**   3 wks

MOLLY HATCHET *US, male vocal / instrumental group*   **1 wk**

25 Jan 86   **DOUBLE TROUBLE – LIVE** *Epic EPC 88670* ....**94**   1 wk

MONEY MARK *US, male producer – Mark Ramos Nischita*   **2 wks**

9 Sep 95   **MARK'S KEYBOARD REPAIR** *Mo Wax MW 034CD* ....**35**   2 wks

Zoot MONEY and the BIG ROLL BAND
UK, male vocalist and male instrumental backing group   **3 wks**

15 Oct 66   **ZOOT** *Columbia SX 6075* ....**23**   3 wks

MONKEES *US / UK, male vocal / instrumental group*   **101 wks**

28 Jan 67 ★ **THE MONKEES** *RCA Victor SF 7844* ....**1**   36 wks
15 Apr 67 ★ **MORE OF THE MONKEES** *RCA Victor SF 7868* ....**1**   25 wks
8 Jul 67 ● **HEADQUARTERS** *RCA Victor SF 7886*......................**2**   19 wks
13 Jan 68 ● **PISCES, AQUARIUS, CAPRICORN & JONES LTD.**
  RCA Victor SF 7912 ....**5**   11 wks
28 Nov 81   **THE MONKEES** *Arista DARTY 12* ....**99**   1 wk
15 Apr 89   **HEY HEY IT'S THE MONKEES – GREATEST HITS** *K-Tel NE 1432* ..**12**   9 wks

The two albums titled The Monkees *are different.*

MONKS CHORUS SILOS – See *CORO DE MUNJES DEL MONASTERIO BENEDICTINO DE SANTO DOMINGO DE SILOS*

MONKS OF AMPLEFORTH ABBEY UK, monastic choir   **2 wks**

17 Jun 95	**VISION OF PEACE** Classic FM CFMCD 1783	73	2	wks

MONOCHROME SET UK, male vocal / instrumental group   **4 wks**

3 May 80	**STRANGE BOUTIQUE** DinDisc DID 4	62	4	wks

Tony MONOPOLY Australia, male vocalist   **4 wks**

12 Jun 76	**TONY MONOPOLY** BUK BULP 2000	25	4	wks

Matt MONRO UK, male vocalist   **15 wks**

7 Aug 65	**I HAVE DREAMED** Parlophone PMC 1250	20	1	wk
17 Sep 66	**THIS IS THE LIFE** Capitol T 2540	25	2	wks
26 Aug 67	**INVITATION TO THE MOVIES** Capitol ST 2730	30	1	wk
15 Mar 80	● **HEARTBREAKERS** EMI EMTV 23	5	11	wks

MONSTER MAGNET US, male vocal / instrumental group   **1 wk**

1 Apr 95	**DOPES TO INFINITY** A & M 5403152	51	1	wk

MONTROSE US, male vocal / instrumental group   **1 wk**

15 Jun 74	**MONTROSE** Warner Bros. K 46276	43	1	wk

MONTY PYTHON'S FLYING CIRCUS UK, male comedy group   **33 wks**

30 Oct 71	**ANOTHER MONTY PYTHON RECORD** Charisma CAS 1049	26	3	wks
27 Jan 73	**MONTY PYTHON'S PREVIOUS ALBUM** Charisma CAS 1063	39	3	wks
23 Feb 74	**MATCHING TIE AND HANDKERCHIEF** Charisma CAS 1080	49	2	wks
27 Jul 74	**LIVE AT DRURY LANE** Charisma CLASS 4	19	8	wks
9 Aug 75	**MONTY PYTHON** Charisma CAS 1003	45	4	wks
24 Nov 79	**THE LIFE OF BRIAN** Warner Bros. K 56751	63	3	wks
18 Oct 80	**CONTRACTUAL OBLIGATION ALBUM** Charisma CAS 1152	13	8	wks
16 Nov 91	**MONTY PYTHON SINGS** Virgin MONT 1	62	2	wks

MOODY BLUES UK, male vocal / instrumental group   **310 wks**

27 Jan 68	**DAYS OF FUTURE PASSED** Deram SML 707	27	16	wks
3 Aug 68	● **IN SEARCH OF THE LOST CHORD** Deram SML 711	5	32	wks
3 May 69	★ **ON THE THRESHOLD OF A DREAM** Deram SML 1035	1	73	wks
6 Dec 69	● **TO OUR CHILDREN'S CHILDREN'S CHILDREN** Threshold THS 1	2	44	wks
15 Aug 70	★ **A QUESTION OF BALANCE** Threshold THS 3	1	19	wks
7 Aug 71	★ **EVERY GOOD BOY DESERVES FAVOUR** Threshold THS 5	1	21	wks
2 Dec 72	● **SEVENTH SOJOURN** Threshold THS 7	5	18	wks
16 Nov 74	**THIS IS THE MOODY BLUES** Threshold MB 1/2	14	18	wks
24 Jun 78	● **OCTAVE** Decca TXS 129	6	18	wks
10 Nov 79	**OUT OF THIS WORLD** K–Tel NE 1051	15	10	wks
23 May 81	● **LONG DISTANCE VOYAGER** Threshold TXS 139	7	19	wks
10 Sep 83	**THE PRESENT** Threshold TXS 140	15	8	wks
10 May 86	**THE OTHER SIDE OF LIFE** Threshold POLD 5190	24	6	wks
25 Jun 88	**SUR LA MER** Polydor POLH 43	21	5	wks
20 Jan 90	**GREATEST HITS** Threshold 8406591	71	1	wk
13 Jul 91	**KEYS OF THE KINGDOM** Threshold 8494331	54	2	wks

Christy MOORE Ireland, male vocalist   **6 wks**

4 May 91	**SMOKE AND STRONG WHISKEY** Newberry CM 21	49	3	wks
21 Sep 91	**THE CHRISTY MOORE COLLECTION** East West WX 434	69	1	wk
6 Nov 93	**KING PUCK** Equator ATLASCD 003	66	2	wks

Dudley MOORE *UK, male instrumentalist   piano* **24 wks**

4 Dec 65	**THE OTHER SIDE OF DUDLEY MOORE** *Decca LK 4732* **11**	9 wks
11 Jun 66	**GENUINE DUD** *Decca LK 4788* **13**	10 wks
26 Jan 91	**ORCHESTRA!** *Decca 4308361* 1 ....**38**	5 wks

1 Sir George Solti and Dudley Moore

See also Peter Cook and Dudley Moore.

Gary MOORE *UK, male vocalist / instrumentalist – guitar* **100 wks**

3 Feb 79	**BACK ON THE STREETS** *MCA MCF 2853* **70**	1 wk
16 Oct 82	**CORRIDORS OF POWER** *Virgin V 2245* **30**	6 wks
18 Feb 84	**VICTIMS OF THE FUTURE** *10 DIX 2* **12**	7 wks
13 Oct 84	**WE WANT MOORE!** *10 GMDL 1* **32**	3 wks
14 Sep 85	**RUN FOR COVER** *10 DIX 16* **12**	8 wks
12 Jul 86	**ROCKIN' EVERY NIGHT** *10 XID 1* **99**	1 wk
14 Mar 87	● **WILD FRONTIER** *10 DIX 56* **8**	14 wks
11 Feb 89	**AFTER THE WAR** *Virgin V 2575* **23**	5 wks
7 Apr 90	**STILL GOT THE BLUES** *Virgin V 2612*................................**13**	26 wks
21 Mar 92	● **AFTER HOURS** *Virgin CDV 2684* **4**	13 wks
22 May 93	● **BLUES ALIVE** *Virgin CDVX 2716* **8**	5 wks
26 Nov 94	**BALLADS AND BLUES 1982–1994** *Virgin CDV 2768*.........**33**	6 wks
10 Jun 95	**BLUES FOR GREENEY** *Virgin CDV 2784* **14**	5 wks

Patrick MORAZ *Switzerland, male instrumentalist – keyboards* **8 wks**

10 Apr 76	**PATRICK MORAZ** *Charisma CDS 4002* **28**	7 wks
23 Jul 77	**OUT IN THE SUN** *Charisma CDS 4007*...............................**44**	1 wk

MORDRED *UK, male vocal / instrumental group* **1 wk**

16 Feb 91	**IN THIS LIFE** *Noise International NO 1591* **70**	1 wk

Alanis MORISSETTE *Canada, female vocalist* **19 wks**

26 Aug 95	**JAGGED LITTLE PILL** *Maverick 9362459012* ....**12†**	19 wks

Giorgio MORODER – *See Philip OAKEY and Giorgio MORODER*

Joseph MOROVITZ – *See SOUTH BANK ORCHESTRA*

Ennio MORRICONE *Italy, orchestra* **15 wks**

2 May 81	**THIS IS ENNIO MORRICONE** *EMI THIS 33*............................**23**	5 wks
9 May 81	**CHI MAI** *BBC REH 414* **29**	6 wks
7 Mar 87	**THE MISSION (film soundtrack)** *Virgin V 2402* 1 ....**73**	4 wks

1 Ennio Morricone and the London Philharmonic Orchestra

See also London Philharmonic Orchestra.

Van MORRISON *UK, male vocalist* **210 wks**

18 Apr 70	**MOONDANCE** *Warner Bros. WS 1835* **32**	2 wks
11 Aug 73	**HARD NOSE THE HIGHWAY** *Warner Bros. K 46242*.........**22**	3 wks
16 Nov 74	**VEEDON FLEECE** *Warner Bros. K 56068* **41**	1 wk
7 May 77	**A PERIOD OF TRANSITION** *Warner Bros. K 56322*............**23**	5 wks
21 Oct 78	**WAVELENGTH** *Warner Bros. K 56526* **27**	6 wks
8 Sep 79	**INTO THE MUSIC** *Vertigo 9120 852* **21**	9 wks
20 Sep 80	**THE COMMON ONE** *Mercury 6302 021* **53**	3 wks
27 Feb 82	**BEAUTIFUL VISION** *Mercury 6302 122* **31**	14 wks
26 Mar 83	**INARTICULATE SPEECH OF THE HEART** *Mercury MERL 16*...........**14**	8 wks
3 Mar 84	**LIVE AT THE GRAND OPERA HOUSE** *Mercury MERL 36*.............**47**	4 wks
9 Feb 85	**A SENSE OF WONDER** *Mercury MERH 54*...........................**25**	5 wks
2 Aug 86	**NO GURU, NO METHOD, NO TEACHER** *Mercury MERH 94* **27**	5 wks
19 Sep 87	**POETIC CHAMPIONS COMPOSE** *Mercury MERH 110* **26**	6 wks
2 Jul 88	**IRISH HEARTBEAT** *Mercury MERH 124* 1 ....**18**	7 wks

10 Jun 89	**AVALON SUNSET** *Polydor 839262 1*...............**13**	14 wks
7 Apr 90	● **THE BEST OF VAN MORRISON** *Polydor 8419701* **4**	66 wks
20 Oct 90	● **ENLIGHTENMENT** *Polydor 8471001* **5**	14 wks
21 Sep 91	● **HYMNS TO THE SILENCE** *Polydor 8490261* **5**	6 wks
27 Feb 93	**THE BEST OF VAN MORRISON VOLUME 2** *Polydor 5177602* **31**	3 wks
12 Jun 93	● **TOO LONG IN EXILE** *Exile 5192192* **4**	9 wks
30 Apr 94	● **A NIGHT IN SAN FRANCISCO** *Polydor 5212902*.........**8**	5 wks
24 Jun 95	● **DAYS LIKE THIS** *Exile 5273072* **5**	15 wks

1 Van Morrison and the Chieftains

MORRISSEY *UK, male vocalist*   **45 wks**

26 Mar 88	★ **VIVA HATE** *HMV CSD 3787* **1**	20 wks
27 Oct 90	● **BONA DRAG** *HMV CLP 3788* **9**	4 wks
16 Mar 91	● **KILL UNCLE** *HMV CSD 3789* **8**	4 wks
8 Aug 92	● **YOUR ARSENAL** *HMV CDCSD 3790* **4**	5 wks
22 May 93	**BEETHOVEN WAS DEAF** *HMV CDCSD 3791* **13**	2 wks
26 Mar 94	★ **VAUXHALL AND I** *Parlophone CDPCSD 148* **1**	5 wks
18 Feb 95	**WORLD OF MORRISSEY** *Parlophone CDPCSD 163*...........**15**	2 wks
9 Sep 95	● **SOUTHPAW GRAMMAR** *RCA Victor 74321299532* **4**	3 wks

MORRISSEY MULLEN *UK, male vocal / instrumental duo*   **11 wks**

18 Jul 81	**BADNESS** *Beggars Banquet BEGA 27* **43**	5 wks
3 Apr 82	**LIFE ON THE WIRE** *Beggars Banquet BEGA 33*...........**47**	5 wks
23 Apr 83	**IT'S ABOUT TIME** *Beggars Banquet BEGA 44* **95**	1 wk

MORRISTOWN ORPHEUS CHOIR – *See G.U.S. (FOOTWEAR) BAND and the MORRISTOWN ORPHEUS CHOIR*

Wendy MOTEN *US, female vocalist*   **2 wks**

| 19 Mar 94 | **WENDY MOTEN** *EMI CDMTL 1073*...........**42** | 2 wks |

MOTHER EARTH *UK, male vocal / instrumental group*   **2 wks**

| 5 Mar 94 | **THE PEOPLE TREE** *Acid Jazz JAZIDCD 083* ....**45** | 2 wks |

MOTHERS OF INVENTION *US, male vocal / instrumental group*   **12 wks**

29 Jun 68	**WE'RE ONLY IN IT FOR THE MONEY** *Verve SVLP 9199*...........**32**	5 wks
28 Mar 70	**BURNT WEENY SANDWICH** *Reprise RSLP 6370* **17**	3 wks
3 Oct 70	**WEASELS RIPPED MY FLESH** *Reprise RSLP 2028*...........**28**	4 wks

MOTLEY CRUE *US, male vocal / instrumental group*   **26 wks**

13 Jul 85	**THEATRE OF PAIN** *Elektra EKT 8* **36**	3 wks
30 May 87	**GIRLS GIRLS GIRLS** *Elektra EKT 39* **14**	11 wks
16 Sep 89	● **DR. FEELGOOD** *Elektra EKT 59*...........**4**	7 wks
19 Oct 91	**DECADE OF DECADENCE** *Elektra EKT 95*...........**20**	3 wks
26 Mar 94	**MOTLEY CRUE** *Elektra 7559615342* **17**	2 wks

MOTORHEAD *UK, male vocal / instrumental group*   **102 wks**

24 Sep 77	**MOTORHEAD** *Chiswick WIK 2*...........**43**	5 wks
24 Mar 79	**OVERKILL** *Bronze BRON 515*...........**24**	11 wks
27 Oct 79	**BOMBER** *Bronze BRON 523*...........**12**	13 wks
8 Dec 79	**ON PARADE** *United Artists LBR 1004* **65**	2 wks
8 Nov 80	● **ACE OF SPADES** *Bronze BRON 531* **4**	16 wks
27 Jun 81	★ **NO SLEEP TILL HAMMERSMITH** *Bronze BRON 535*...........**1**	21 wks
17 Apr 82	● **IRONFIST** *Bronze BRNA 539* **6**	9 wks
26 Feb 83	**WHAT'S WORDS WORTH** *Big Beat NED 2* **71**	2 wks
4 Jun 83	**ANOTHER PERFECT DAY** *Bronze BRON 546* **20**	4 wks
15 Sep 84	**NO REMORSE** *Bronze PROTV MOTOR 1* **14**	6 wks
9 Aug 86	**ORGASMATRON** *GWR GWLP 1* **21**	4 wks
5 Sep 87	**ROCK 'N' ROLL** *GWR GWLP 14*...........**34**	3 wks
15 Oct 88	**NO SLEEP AT ALL** *GWR GWR 31* **79**	1 wk

| 2 Feb 91 | **1916** *Epic 4674811* .... | **24** | 4 wks |
| 8 Aug 92 | **MARCH OR DIE** *Epic 4717232*.. | **60** | 1 wk |

MOTORS *UK, male vocal / instrumental group* **6 wks**

| 15 Oct 77 | **THE MOTORS** *Virgin V 2089* .... | **46** | 5 wks |
| 3 Jun 78 | **APPROVED BY THE MOTORS** *Virgin V 2101* .... | **60** | 1 wk |

MOTT THE HOOPLE *UK, male vocal / instrumental group* **32 wks**

2 May 70	**MOTT THE HOOPLE** *Island ILPS 9108*	**66**	1 wk
17 Oct 70	**MAD SHADOWS** *Island ILPS 9119*	**48**	2 wks
17 Apr 71	**WILD LIFE** *Island ILPS 9144*	**44**	2 wks
23 Sep 72	**ALL THE YOUNG DUDES** *CBS 65184*	**21**	4 wks
11 Aug 73	● **MOTT** *CBS 69038*..	**7**	15 wks
13 Apr 74	**THE HOOPLE** *CBS 69062*	**11**	5 wks
23 Nov 74	**LIVE** *BS 69093*..	**32**	2 wks
4 Oct 75	**DRIVE ON** *CBS 69154*...	**45**	1 wk

MOUNTAIN *US / Canada, male vocal / instrumental group* **4 wks**

| 5 Jun 71 | **NANTUCKET SLEIGHRIDE** *Island ILPS 9148*................... | **43** | 1 wk |
| 8 Jul 72 | **THE ROAD GOES EVER ON** *Island ILPS 9199* .... | **21** | 3 wks |

Nana MOUSKOURI *Greece, female vocalist* **208 wks**

7 Jun 69	● **OVER AND OVER** *Fontana S 5511*	**10**	105 wks
4 Apr 70	● **THE EXQUISITE NANA MOUSKOURI** *Fontana STL 5536*	**10**	25 wks
10 Oct 70	**RECITAL '70** *Fontana 6312 003*....................................	**68**	1 wk
3 Apr 71	**TURN ON THE SUN** *Fontana 6312 008*..........................	**16**	15 wks
29 Jul 72	**BRITISH CONCERT** *Fontana 6651 003*	**29**	11 wks
28 Apr 73	**SONGS FROM HER TV SERIES** *Fontana 6312 036*	**29**	11 wks
28 Sep 74	**SPOTLIGHT ON NANA MOUSKOURI** *Fontana 6641 197*	**38**	6 wks
10 Jul 76	● **PASSPORT** *Philips 9101 061*..	**3**	16 wks
22 Feb 86	**ALONE** *Philips PHH 3*	**19**	10 wks
8 Oct 88	**THE MAGIC OF NANA MOUSKOURI** *Philips NMTV 1*	**44**	8 wks

MOVE *UK, male vocal / instrumental group* **9 wks**

| 13 Apr 68 | **MOVE** *Regal Zonophone SLPZ 1002* .... | **15** | 9 wks |

Alison MOYET *UK, female vocalist* **170 wks**

17 Nov 84	★ **ALF** *CBS 26229*	**1**	84 wks
18 Apr 87	● **RAINDANCING** *CBS 450 1521*	**2**	52 wks
4 May 91	**HOODOO** *Columbia 4682721*	**11**	6 wks
2 Apr 94	**ESSEX** *Columbia 4759552*	**24**	4 wks
3 Jun 95	★ **SINGLES** *Columbia 4806632*	**1**	24 wks

MSG – *See Michael SCHENKER GROUP*

MTUME *US, male / female vocal / instrumental group* **1 wk**

| 6 Oct 84 | **YOU, ME AND HE** *Epic EPC 26077* .... | **85** | 1 wk |

MUD *UK, male vocal / instrumental group* **58 wks**

28 Sep 74	● **MUD ROCK** *RAK SRAK 508*	**8**	35 wks
26 Jul 75	● **MUD ROCK VOLUME 2** *RAK SRAK 513*	**6**	12 wks
1 Nov 75	**MUD'S GREATEST HITS** *RAK SRAK 6755*.........................	**25**	6 wks
27 Dec 75	**USE YOUR IMAGINATION** *Private Stock PVLP 1003*	**33**	5 wks

MUDHONEY *UK, male vocal / instrumental group* **5 wks**

31 Aug 91	**EVERY GOOD BOY DESERVES FUDGE** *Subpop SP 18160*	**34**	2 wks
17 Oct 92	**PIECE OF CAKE** *Reprise 9362450902*	**39**	2 wks
8 Apr 95	**MY BROTHER THE COW** *Reprise 9362458402*................	**70**	1 wk

Heather Small had big
success with M PEOPLE,
who won the Mercury
Music Prize with *Elegant
Slumming*.
(Solo/Joe Bangay Photography)

Nevermind by NIRVANA
has had more weeks on
the chart than any other
album during the 1990s.
(Kevin Mazur/LFI)

MUFFINS – See MARTHA and the MUFFINS

Gerry MULLIGAN and Ben WEBSTER
US, male instrumental duo   baritone and tenor sax   **1 wk**

24 Sep 60   **GERRY MULLIGAN MEETS BEN WEBSTER** HMV CLP 1373 ....**15**   1 wk

MUNGO JERRY UK, male vocal / instrumental group   **14 wks**

 8 Aug 70   **MUNGO JERRY** Dawn DNLS 3008.....................................**13**   6 wks
10 Apr 71   **ELECTRONICALLY TESTED** Dawn DNLS 3020 ....**14**   8 wks

MUPPETS US, puppets   **45 wks**

11 Jun 77 ★ **THE MUPPET SHOW** Pye NSPH 19 ....**1**   35 wks
25 Feb 78   **THE MUPPET SHOW VOLUME 2** Pye NSPH 21 ....**16**   10 wks

Peter MURPHY UK, male vocalist   **1 wk**

26 Jul 86   **SHOULD THE WORLD FAIL TO FALL APART**
              Beggars Banquet BEGA 69..**82**   1 wk

Anne MURRAY Canada, female vocalist   **10 wks**

 3 Oct 81   **VERY BEST OF ANNE MURRAY** Capitol EMTV 31 ....**14**   10 wks

Pauline MURRAY and the INVISIBLE GIRLS
UK, female vocalist with male vocal / instrumental group   **4 wks**

11 Oct 80   **PAULINE MURRAY AND THE INVISIBLE GIRLS**
              Elusive 2394 227 ....**25**   4 wks

MUSIC OF THE MOUNTAINS – See MANUEL and his MUSIC OF THE MOUNTAINS

MUSIC STUDENTS – See Ian DURY and the BLOCKHEADS

MUSICAL YOUTH UK, male vocal / instrumental group   **22 wks**

 4 Dec 82   **THE YOUTH OF TODAY** MCA YOULP 1 ....**24**   22 wks

MY BLOODY VALENTINE
UK, male / female vocal / instrumental group   **2 wks**

23 Nov 91   **LOVELESS** Creation CRELP 060 ....**24**   2 wks

Alannah MYLES Canada, female vocalist   **21 wks**

28 Apr 90 ● **ALANNAH MYLES** Atlantic 7819561 ....**3**   21 wks

Jimmy NAIL UK, male vocalist   **50 wks**

 8 Aug 92 ● **GROWING UP IN PUBLIC** East West 4509901442 ....**2**   12 wks
 3 Dec 94 ● **CROCODILE SHOES** East West 4509985562..**2**   31 wks
18 Nov 95 ● **BIG RIVER** East West 0630128232 ....**8†**   7 wks

NAILBOMB Brazil / US, male vocal / instrumental duo   **1 wk**

 2 Apr 94   **POINT BLANK** Roadrunner RR 90552...............................**62**   1 wk

NAPALM DEATH UK, male vocal / instrumental group · 2 wks

15 Sep 90	HARMONY OF CORRUPTION Earache MOSH 19	67	1 wk
30 May 92	UTOPIA BANISHED Earache MOSH 53CD	58	1 wk

NARADA US, male vocalist / instrumentalist / producer · 5 wks

14 May 88	DIVINE EMOTION Reprise WX 172	60	5 wks

Graham NASH UK, male vocalist · 13 wks

26 Jun 71	SONGS FOR BEGINNERS Atlantic 2401011	13	8 wks
13 May 72	GRAHAM NASH AND DAVID CROSBY Atlantic K 50011 [1]	13	5 wks

[1] Graham Nash and David Crosby

See also Crosby, Stills, Nash and Young.

Johnny NASH US, male vocalist · 17 wks

5 Aug 72	I CAN SEE CLEARLY NOW CBS 64860	39	6 wks
10 Dec 77	JOHNNY NASH COLLECTION Epic EPC 10008	18	11 wks

NASH THE SLASH Canada, male vocalist / multi–instrumentalist · 1 wk

21 Feb 81	CHILDREN OF THE NIGHT DinDisc DID 9	61	1 wk

NATASHA UK, female vocalist · 3 wks

9 Oct 82	CAPTURED Towerbell TOWLP 2	53	3 wks

NATIONAL BRASS BAND UK, orchestra · 10 wks

10 May 80	GOLDEN MELODIES K-Tel ONE 1075	15	10 wks

NATIONAL PHILHARMONIC ORCHESTRA – See LONDON PHILHARMONIC CHOIR; James GALWAY; Henry MANCINI

NAUGHTY BY NATURE US, male rap group · 5 wks

6 Mar 93	19 NAUGHTY III Big Life BLRCD 23	40	2 wks
27 May 95	POVERTY'S PARADISE Big Life BLRCD 28	20	3 wks

NAZARETH UK, male vocal / instrumental group · 51 wks

26 May 73	RAZAMANAZ Mooncrest CREST 1	11	25 wks
24 Nov 73	● LOUD 'N' PROUD Mooncrest CREST 4	10	7 wks
18 May 74	RAMPANT Mooncrest CREST 15	13	3 wks
13 Dec 75	GREATEST HITS Mountain TOPS 108	54	1 wk
3 Feb 79	NO MEAN CITY Mountain TOPS 123	34	9 wks
28 Feb 81	THE FOOL CIRCLE NEMS NEL 6019	60	3 wks
3 Oct 81	NAZARETH LIVE NEMS NELD 102	78	3 wks

NED'S ATOMIC DUSTBIN UK, male vocal / instrumental group · 8 wks

9 Feb 91	BITE (import) Rough Trade Germany RTD 14011831	72	1 wk
13 Apr 91	● GOD FODDER Furtive 4681121	4	5 wks
31 Oct 92	ARE YOU NORMAL Furtive 4726332	13	2 wks

Vince NEIL US, male vocalist · 1 wk

8 May 93	EXPOSED Warner Bros. 9362452602	44	1 wk

Bill NELSON UK, male vocalist / multi–instrumentalist · 21 wks

24 Feb 79	SOUND ON SOUND Harvest SHSP 4095 [1]	33	5 wks
23 May 81	● QUIT DREAMING AND GET ON THE BEAM Mercury 6359 055	7	6 wks

British Hit Albums Part One

Date of chart entry/Title & catalogue no./Peak position reached/Weeks on chart

★ Number One   ● Top Ten   † still on chart at 30 Dec 1995   □ credited to act billed in footnote

3 Jul 82	**THE LOVE THAT WHIRLS (DIARY OF A THINKING HEART** Mercury WHIRL 3	**28**	4 wks
14 May 83	**CHIMERA** Mercury MERB 19	**30**	5 wks
3 May 86	**GETTING THE HOLY GHOST ACROSS** Portrait PRT 26602	**91**	1 wk

1 Bill Nelson's Red Noise

Phyllis NELSON US, female vocalist   **10 wks**

| 20 Apr 85 | **MOVE CLOSER** Carrere CAL 203 | **29** | 10 wks |

Shara NELSON UK, female vocalist   **11 wks**

| 2 Oct 93 | **WHAT SILENCE KNOWS** Cooltempo CTCD 35 | **22** | 9 wks |
| 7 Oct 95 | **FRIENDLY FIRE** Cooltempo CTCD 48 | **44** | 2 wks |

NENA Germany, female / male vocal / instrumental group   **5 wks**

| 24 Mar 84 | **NENA** Epic EPC 25925 | **31** | 5 wks |

NESBIT – See MILLICAN and NESBIT

Robbie NEVIL US, male vocalist   **1 wk**

| 13 Jun 87 | **C'EST LA VIE** Manhattan MTL 1006 | **93** | 1 wk |

Aaron NEVILLE – See Linda RONSTADT; NEVILLE BROTHERS

N 222

NEVILLE BROTHERS US, male vocal / instrumental group   **3 wks**

| 18 Aug 90 | **BROTHER'S KEEPER** A & M 3953121 | **35** | 3 wks |

NEW BOHEMIANS – See Edie BRICKELL and the NEW BOHEMIANS

NEW FAST AUTOMATIC DAFFODILS
UK, male vocal / instrumental group   **2 wks**

| 17 Nov 90 | **PIGEON HOLE** Play It Again Sam BIAS 185 | **49** | 1 wk |
| 24 Oct 92 | **BODY EXIT MIND** Play It Again Sam BIAS 205CD | **57** | 1 wk |

NEW KIDS ON THE BLOCK US, male vocal group   **106 wks**

9 Dec 89	● **HANGIN' TOUGH** CBS 4608741	**2**	41 wks
30 Jun 90	★ **STEP BY STEP** CBS 4666861	**1**	31 wks
2 Nov 90	● **NEW KIDS ON THE BLOCK** CBS 4675041	**6**	13 wks
15 Dec 90	**MERRY MERRY CHRISTMAS** CBS 4659071	**13**	5 wks
2 Mar 91	**NO MORE GAMES – THE REMIX ALBUM** Columbia 4674941	**15**	11 wks
21 Dec 91	**H.I.T.S.** Columbia 4694381	**50**	4 wks
12 Mar 94	**FACE THE MUSIC** Columbia 4743592 1	**36**	1 wk

1 NKOTB

NEW MODEL ARMY UK, male vocal / instrumental group   **20 wks**

12 May 84	**VENGEANCE** Abstract ABT 008	**73**	5 wks
25 May 85	**NO REST FOR THE WICKED** EMI NMAL 1	**22**	3 wks
11 Oct 86	**THE GHOST OF CAIN** EMI EMC 3516	**45**	3 wks
18 Feb 89	**THUNDER AND CONSOLATION** EMI EMC 3552	**20**	3 wks
6 Oct 90	**IMPURITY** EMI EMC 3581	**23**	2 wks
22 Jun 91	**RAW MELODY MEN** EMI EMC 3595	**43**	2 wks
10 Apr 93	**THE LOVE OF HOPELESS CAUSES** Epic 4735622	**22**	2 wks

NEW MUSIK UK, male vocal / instrumental group — 11 wks

| 17 May 80 | **FROM A TO B** GTO GTLP 041 | 35 | 9 wks |
| 14 Mar 81 | **ANYWHERE** GTO GTLP 044 | 68 | 2 wks |

NEW ORDER UK, male / female vocal / instrumental group — 145 wks

28 Nov 81	**MOVEMENT** Factory FACT 50	30	10 wks
14 May 83	● **POWER, CORRUPTION AND LIES** Factory FACT 75	4	29 wks
25 May 85	● **LOW–LIFE** Factory FACT 100	7	10 wks
11 Oct 86	● **BROTHERHOOD** Factory FACT 150	9	5 wks
29 Aug 87	● **SUBSTANCE** Factory FACT 200	3	37 wks
11 Feb 89	★ **TECHNIQUE** Factory FACT 275	1	14 wks
22 Feb 92	**BBC RADIO 1 LIVE IN CONCERT**		
	Windsong International WINCD 011	33	2 wks
15 May 93	★ **REPUBLIC** London 8284132	1	19 wks
17 Jul 93	**SUBSTANCE (re-issue)** London 5200082	32	2 wks
3 Dec 94	● **? (THE BEST OF) / ? (THE REST OF)** Centredate Co. 8285802	4	17 wks

From 2 Sep 95 ? (The Best Of) was listed with the remix album ? (The Rest Of).

NEW POWER GENERATION
US, male / female vocal / instrumental group — 3 wks

| 8 Apr 95 | **EXODUS** NPG 0061032 | 11 | 3 wks |

See also Prince.

NEW SEEKERS UK, male / female vocal / instrumental group — 49 wks

5 Feb 72	**NEW COLOURS** Polydor 2383 066	40	4 wks
1 Apr 72	● **WE'D LIKE TO TEACH THE WORLD TO SING** Polydor 2883 103	2	25 wks
12 Aug 72	**NEVER ENDING SONG OF LOVE** Polydor 2383 126	35	4 wks
14 Oct 72	**CIRCLES** Polydor 2442 102	23	5 wks
21 Apr 73	**NOW** Polydor 2383 195	47	2 wks
30 Mar 74	**TOGETHER** Polydor 2383 264	12	9 wks

NEW WORLD THEATRE ORCHESTRA UK, orchestra — 1 wk

| 24 Dec 60 | **LET'S DANCE TO THE HITS OF THE 30'S AND 40'S** | | |
| | Pye Golden Guinea GGL 0026 | 20 | 1 wk |

NEWCLEUS US, male vocal / instrumental group — 2 wks

| 25 Aug 84 | **JAM ON REVENGE** Sunnyview SVLP 6600 | 84 | 2 wks |

Bob NEWHART US, male comedian — 37 wks

| 1 Oct 60 | ● **BUTTON–DOWN MIND OF BOB NEWHART** | | |
| | Warner Bros. WM 4010 | 2 | 37 wks |

Anthony NEWLEY UK, male vocalist — 14 wks

| 14 May 60 | **LOVE IS A NOW AND THEN THING** Decca LK 4343 | 19 | 2 wks |
| 8 Jul 61 | ● **TONY** Decca LK 4406 | 5 | 12 wks |

See also Anthony Newley, Peter Sellers, Joan Collins.

Anthony NEWLEY, Peter SELLERS, Joan COLLINS
UK, male / female comedians — 10 wks

| 28 Sep 63 | ● **FOOL BRITANNIA** Ember CEL 902 | 10 | 10 wks |

See also Anthony Newley; Peter Sellers.

NEWS – See Huey LEWIS and the NEWS

Olivia NEWTON–JOHN UK, female vocalist — 103 wks

| 2 Mar 74 | **MUSIC MAKES MY DAY** Pye NSPL 28186 | 37 | 3 wks |

29 Jun 74	**LONG LIVE LOVE** *EMI EMC 3028* **40**	2 wks
26 Apr 75	**HAVE YOU NEVER BEEN MELLOW** *EMI EMC 3069* **37**	2 wks
29 May 76	**COME ON OVER** *EMI EMC 3124* **49**	4 wks
27 Aug 77	**MAKING A GOOD THING BETTER** *EMI EMC 3192* **60**	1 wk
21 Jan 78	**GREATEST HITS** *EMI EMA 785* **19**	9 wks
9 Dec 78	**TOTALLY HOT** *EMI EMA 789* **30**	9 wks
31 Oct 81	**PHYSICAL** *EMI EMC 3386* **11**	22 wks
23 Oct 82 ●	**GREATEST HITS** *EMI EMTV 36* **8**	38 wks
8 Mar 86	**SOUL KISS** *Mercury MERH 77* **66**	3 wks
25 Jul 92	**BACK TO BASICS – THE ESSENTIAL COLLECTION 1971–1992** *Mercury 5126412*)...................**12**	6 wks
4 Feb 95	**GAIA (ONE WOMAN'S JOURNEY)** *D-Sharp DSHLCD 7017* **33**	4 wks

NICE *UK, male instrumental group*   **38 wks**

13 Sep 69 ●	**NICE** *Immediate IMSP 026* **3**	6 wks
27 Jun 70 ●	**FIVE BRIDGES** *Charisma CAS 1014* **2**	21 wks
17 Apr 71 ●	**ELEGY** *Charisma CAS 1030* **5**	11 wks

Paul NICHOLAS *UK, male vocalist*   **8 wks**

29 Nov 86	**JUST GOOD FRIENDS** *K-Tel ONE 1334*...................**30**	8 wks

Stevie NICKS *US, female vocalist*   **80 wks**

8 Aug 81	**BELLA DONNA** *WEA K 99169*...................**11**	16 wks
2 Jul 83	**THE WILD HEART** *WEA 2500711* **28**	19 wks
14 Dec 85	**ROCK A LITTLE** *Modern PCS 7300* **30**	22 wks
10 Jun 89 ●	**THE OTHER SIDE OF THE MIRROR** *EMI EMD 1008* **3**	14 wks
14 Sep 91	**TIMESPACE – THE BEST OF STEVIE NICKS** *EMI EMD 3595* **15**	6 wks
4 Jun 94	**STREET ANGEL** *EMI CDEMC 3671* **16**	3 wks

Hector NICOL *UK, male vocalist*   **1 wk**

28 Apr 84	**BRAVO JULIET** *Klub KLP 42* **92**	1 wk

NICOLE *Germany, female vocalist*   **2 wks**

2 Oct 82	**A LITTLE PEACE** *CBS 85011* **85**	2 wks

NIGHTCRAWLERS featuring John REID
UK, male vocal / instrumental duo   **5 wks**

30 Sep 95	**LET'S PUSH IT** *Final Vinyl 74321309702*...................**14**	5 wks

NILSSON *US, male vocalist*   **43 wks**

29 Jan 72	**THE POINT** *RCA Victor SF 8166* **46**	1 wk
5 Feb 72 ●	**NILSSON SCHMILSSON** *RCA Victor SF 8242* **4**	22 wks
19 Aug 72	**SON OF SCHMILSSON** *RCA Victor SF 8297* **41**	1 wk
28 Jul 73	**A LITTLE TOUCH OF SCHMILSSON IN THE NIGHT** *RCA Victor SF 8371* **20**	19 wks

NINA and FREDERICK *Denmark, female / male vocal duo*   **6 wks**

13 Feb 60 ●	**NINA AND FREDERICK** *Pye NPT 19023* **9**	2 wks
29 Apr 61	**NINA AND FREDERICK** *Columbia COL 1314*...................**11**	4 wks

These two albums, although identically named, are different.

9 BELOW ZERO *UK, male vocal / instrumental group*   **12 wks**

14 Mar 81	**DON'T POINT YOUR FINGER** *A & M AMLH 68521*...................**56**	6 wks
20 Mar 82	**THIRD DEGREE** *A & M AMLH 68537* **38**	6 wks

NINE INCH NAILS *US, male vocal / instrumental group*   **8 wks**

12 Oct 91	**PRETTY HATE MACHINE** *TVT ILPS 9973* **67**	1 wk

17 Oct 92 **BROKEN** *Island IMCD 8004* ....**18** 3 wks
19 Mar 94 ● **THE DOWNWARD SPIRAL** *Island CID 8012* ....**9** 4 wks

999 *UK, male vocal / instrumental group* **1 wk**

25 Mar 78 **999** *United Artists UAG 30199* ....**53** 1 wk

NINE STORIES – *See Lisa LOEB and NINE STORIES*

Los NINOS *UK, male instrumental group* **1 wk**

22 Jul 95 **FRAGILE – MYSTICAL SOUNDS OF THE PANPIPE**
Pearls DPWKF 4253 ....**74** 1 wk

NIRVANA *US, male vocal / instrumental group* **263 wks**

5 Oct 91 ● **NEVERMIND** *DGC DGC 24425* ....**7** 164 wks
7 Mar 92 **BLEACH** *Tupelo TUPCD 6* ....**33** 7 wks
26 Dec 92 **INCESTICIDE** *Geffen GED 24504* ....**14** 11 wks
25 Sep 93 ★ **IN UTERO** *Geffen GED 24536* ....**1** 41 wks
12 Nov 94 ★ **UNPLUGGED IN NEW YORK** *Geffen GED 24727* ....**1** 40 wks

NKOTB – *See NEW KIDS ON THE BLOCK*

NOLANS *Ireland, female vocal group* **84 wks**

20 Jul 78 ● **20 GIANT HITS** *Target TGS 502* [1] ....**3** 12 wks
19 Jan 80 **NOLANS** *Epic EPC 83892* ....**15** 13 wks
25 Oct 80 **MAKING WAVES** *Epic EPC 10023* ....**11** 33 wks
27 Mar 82 ● **PORTRAIT** *Epic EPC 10033* ....**7** 10 wks
20 Nov 82 **ALTOGETHER** *Epic EPC 10037* ....**52** 8 wks
17 Nov 84 **GIRLS JUST WANNA HAVE FUN** *Towerbell TOWLP 10* ....**39** 8 wks

[1] Nolan Sisters

NOMAD *UK, male / female vocal / instrumental duo* **2 wks**

22 Jun 91 **CHANGING CABINS** *Rumour RULP 100* ....**48** 2 wks

NORTHSIDE *UK, male vocal / instrumental group* **3 wks**

29 Jun 91 **CHICKEN RHYTHMS** *Factory FACT 310* ....**19** 3 wks

NOT THE 9 O'CLOCK NEWS CAST
UK / New Zealand, male / female comedians **51 wks**

8 Nov 80 ● **NOT THE 9 O'CLOCK NEWS** *BBC REB 400* ....**5** 23 wks
17 Oct 81 ● **HEDGEHOG SANDWICH** *BBC REB 421* ....**5** 24 wks
23 Oct 82 **THE MEMORY KINDA LINGERS** *BBC REF 453* ....**63** 4 wks

NOTTING HILLBILLIES *UK, male vocal / instrumental group* **14 wks**

17 Mar 90 ● **MISSING . . . PRESUMED HAVING A GOOD TIME**
Vertigo 8426711 ....**2** 14 wks

Heather NOVA *US, female vocalist* **1 wk**

8 Apr 95 **OYSTER** *Butterfly BFLCD 12* ....**72** 1 wk

NU SHOOZ *US, male / female vocal duo* **8 wks**

14 Jun 86 **POOLSIDE** *Atlantic WX 60* ....**32** 8 wks

NUCLEAR ASSAULT *US, male vocal / instrumental group* **1 wk**

7 Oct 89 **HANDLE WITH CARE** *Under One Flag FLAG 35* ....**60** 1 wk

NUCLEUS *UK, male instrumental group*   **1 wk**

| 11 Jul 70 | **ELASTIC ROCK** Vertigo 6360 006 | **46** | 1 | wk |

Ted NUGENT *US, male vocalist / instrumentalist – guitar*   **14 wks**

4 Sep 76	**TED NUGENT** Epic EPC 81268	**56**	1	wk
30 Oct 76	**FREE FOR ALL** Epic EPC 81397	**33**	2	wks
2 Jul 77	**CAT SCRATCH FEVER** Epic EPC 82010	**28**	5	wks
11 Mar 78	**DOUBLE LIVE GONZO** Epic EPC 88282	**47**	2	wks
14 Jun 80	**SCREAM DREAM** Epic EPC 86111	**37**	3	wks
25 Apr 81	**IN 10 CITIES** Epic EPC 84917	**75**	1	wk

Gary NUMAN *UK, male vocalist*   **139 wks**

9 Jun 79	★ **REPLICAS** Beggars Banquet BEGA 7 [1]	**1**	31	wks
25 Aug 79	**TUBEWAY ARMY** Beggars Banquet BEGA 4 [1]	**14**	10	wks
22 Sep 79	★ **THE PLEASURE PRINCIPLE** Beggars Banquet BEGA 10	**1**	21	wks
13 Sep 80	★ **TELEKON** Beggars Banquet BEGA 19	**1**	11	wks
2 May 81	● **LIVING ORNAMENTS 1979–1980** Beggars Banquet BOX 1	**2**	4	wks
2 May 81	**LIVING ORNAMENTS 1979** Beggars Banquet BEGA 24	**47**	3	wks
2 May 81	**LIVING ORNAMENTS 1980** Beggars Banquet BEGA 25	**39**	3	wks
12 Sep 81	● **DANCE** Beggars Banquet BEGA 28	**3**	8	wks
18 Sep 82	● **I, ASSASSIN** Beggars Banquet BEGA 40	**8**	6	wks
27 Nov 82	**NEW MAN NUMAN – THE BEST OF GARY NUMAN** TV TVA 7	**45**	7	wks
24 Sep 83	**WARRIORS** Beggars Banquet BEGA 47	**12**	6	wks
6 Oct 84	**THE PLAN** Beggars Banquet BEGA 55	**29**	4	wks
24 Nov 84	**BERSERKER** Numa NUMA 1001	**45**	3	wks
13 Apr 85	**WHITE NOISE – LIVE** Numa NUMAD 1002	**29**	5	wks
28 Sep 85	**THE FURY** Numa NUMA 1003	**24**	5	wks
8 Nov 86	**STRANGE CHARM** Numa NUMA 1005	**59**	2	wks
3 Oct 87	**EXHIBITION** Beggars Banquet BEGA 88	**43**	3	wks
8 Oct 88	**METAL RHYTHM** Illegal ILP 035	**48**	2	wks
8 Jul 89	**AUTOMATIC** Polydor 8395201 [2]	**59**	1	wk
28 Oct 89	**SKIN MECHANIC** IRS EIRSA 1019	**55**	1	wk
30 Mar 91	**OUTLAND** IRS EIRSA 1039	**39**	1	wk
22 Aug 92	**MACHINE AND SOUL** Numa NUMACD 1009	**42**	1	wk
2 Oct 93	**BEST OF GARY NUMAN 1978–83** Beggars Banquet BEGA 150CD	**70**	1	wk

[1] Tubeway Army [2] Sharpe and Numan

Living Ornaments 1979–1980 is a boxed set of Living Ornaments 1979 and Living Ornaments 1980.

NWA *US, male rap group*   **6 wks**

| 30 Sep 89 | **STRAIGHT OUTTA COMPTON** Fourth & Broadway BRLP 534 | **41** | 4 | wks |
| 15 Jun 91 | **EFIL4ZAGGIN** Fourth & Broadway BRLP 562 | **25** | 2 | wks |

Michael NYMAN *UK, male instrumentalist – piano*   **14 wks**

| 12 Feb 94 | **THE PIANO (film soundtrack)** Venture CDVE 919 | **31** | 14 | wks |

Philip OAKEY and Giorgio MORODER
UK / Italy, male vocal / instrumental duo   **5 wks**

| 10 Aug 85 | **PHILIP OAKEY AND GIORGIO MORODER** Virgin V 2351 | **52** | 5 | wks |

OASIS *UK, male / female vocal instrumental group*   **14 wks**

| 28 Apr 84 | **OASIS** WEA WX 3 | **23** | 14 | wks |

OASIS, with lead singer Liam Gallagher, was the top-selling act of 1995.

(Solo)

OASIS *UK, male vocal/instrumental group*   **81 wks**

10 Sep 94 ★ **DEFINITELY MAYBE** *Creation CRECD 169* ....**1†**   69 wks
14 Oct 95 ★ **(WHAT'S THE STORY) MORNING GLORY** *Creation CRECD 189* ....**1†**   12 wks

John OATES – *See Daryl HALL and John OATES*

OBITUARY *US, male vocal/instrumental group*   **2 wks**

18 Apr 92   **THE END COMPLETE** *Roadrunner RC 92012* ....**52**   1   wk
17 Sep 94   **WORLD DEMISE** *Roadrunner RR 89955*..**65**   1   wk

Billy OCEAN *UK, male vocalist*   **119 wks**

24 Nov 84 ● **SUDDENLY** *Jive JIP 12* ....**9**   59 wks
17 May 86 ● **LOVE ZONE** *Jive HIP 35* ....**2**   32 wks
19 Mar 88 ● **TEAR DOWN THESE WALLS** *Jive HIP 57* ....**3**   13 wks
28 Oct 89 ● **GREATEST HITS** *Jive BOTV 1* ....**4**   15 wks

OCEANIC *UK, male/female vocal/instrumental group*   **2 wks**

4 Jul 92   **THAT ALBUM BY OCEANIC** *Dead Dead Good 4509900832* ....**49**   2 wks

Des O'CONNOR *UK, male vocalist*   **45 wks**

7 Dec 68 ● **I PRETEND** *Columbia SCX 6295*...**8**   10 wks
5 Dec 70   **WITH LOVE** *Columbia SCX 6417* ....**40**   4 wks
2 Dec 72   **SING A FAVOURITE SONG** *Pye NSPL 18390* ....**25**   6 wks
2 Feb 80   **JUST FOR YOU** *Warwick WW 5071* ....**17**   7 wks
13 Oct 84   **DES O'CONNOR NOW** *Telstar STAR 2245* ....**24**   14 wks
5 Dec 92   **PORTRAIT** *Columbia 4727302* ....**63**   4 wks

Hazel O'CONNOR *UK, female vocalist*   **45 wks**

9 Aug 80 ● **BREAKING GLASS (film soundtrack)** *A & M AMLH 64820*............**5**   38 wks
12 Sep 81   **COVER PLUS** *Albion ALB 108* ....**32**   7 wks

Sinead O'CONNOR *Ireland, female vocalist*   **85 wks**

23 Jan 88   **THE LION AND THE COBRA** *Ensign CHEN 7* ....**27**   20 wks
24 Mar 90 ★ **I DO NOT WANT WHAT I HAVEN'T GOT** *Ensign CHEN 14* ....**1**   51 wks
26 Sep 92 ● **AM I NOT YOUR GIRL** *Ensign CCD 1952* ....**6**   6 wks
24 Sep 94   **UNIVERSAL MOTHER** *Ensign CDCHEN 34* ....**19**   8 wks

Daniel O'DONNELL *Ireland, male vocalist*   **89 wks**

15 Oct 88   **FROM THE HEART** *Telstar STAR 2327*..**56**   12 wks
28 Oct 89   **THOUGHTS OF HOME** *Telstar STAR 2372*..**43**   10 wks
21 Apr 90   **FAVOURITES** *Ritz RITZLP 052* ....**61**   3 wks
17 Nov 90   **THE LAST WALTZ** *Ritz RITZALP 058* ....**46**   7 wks
9 Nov 91   **THE VERY BEST OF DANIEL O'DONNELL** *Ritz RITZBLD 700* ....**34**   14 wks
21 Nov 92   **FOLLOW YOUR DREAM** *Ritz RITZBCD 701* ....**17**   9 wks
6 Nov 93   **A DATE WITH DANIEL LIVE** *Ritz RITZBCD 702* ....**21**   10 wks
22 Oct 94   **ESPECIALLY FOR YOU** *Ritz RITZBCD 703* ....**14**   11 wks
3 Dec 94   **CHRISTMAS WITH DANIEL** *Ritz RITZBCD 704* ....**34**   5 wks
11 Nov 95   **THE CLASSIC COLLECTION** *Ritz RITZBCD 705* ....**34†**   8 wks

ODYSSEY *US, male/female vocal group*   **32 wks**

16 Aug 80   **HANG TOGETHER** *RCA PL 13526* ....**38**   3 wks
4 Jul 81   **I'VE GOT THE MELODY** *RCA RCALP 5028*.....................................**29**   7 wks
3 Jul 82   **HAPPY TOGETHER** *RCA RCALP 6036* ....**21**   9 wks
20 Nov 82   **THE MAGIC TOUCH OF ODYSSEY** *Telstar STAR 2223* ....**69**   5 wks
26 Sep 87   **THE GREATEST HITS** *Stylus SMR 735*...**26**   8 wks

Esther and Abi OFARIM Israel, female / male vocal duo — 24 wks

24 Feb 68	● **2 IN 3** Philips SBL 7825	6	20 wks
12 Jul 69	**OFARIM CONCERT – LIVE '69** Philips XL 4	29	4 wks

OFFSPRING US, male vocal / instrumental group — 34 wks

4 Mar 95	**SMASH** Epitaph E 864322	21	34 wks

Mary O'HARA UK, female vocalist / instrumentalist – harp — 12 wks

8 Apr 78	**MARY O'HARA AT THE ROYAL FESTIVAL HALL** Chrysalis CHR 1159	37	3 wks
1 Dec 79	**TRANQUILLITY** Warwick WW 5072	12	9 wks

David OISTRAKH – See Herbert VON KARAJAN

Mike OLDFIELD UK, male multi–instrumentalist / vocalist — 526 wks

14 Jul 73	★ **TUBULAR BELLS** Virgin V 2001	1	271 wks
14 Sep 74	★ **HERGEST RIDGE** Virgin V 2013	1	17 wks
8 Feb 75	**THE ORCHESTRAL TUBULAR BELLS** Virgin V 2026 [1]	17	7 wks
15 Nov 75	● **OMMADAWN** Virgin V 2043	4	23 wks
20 Nov 76	**BOXED** Virgin V BOX 1	22	13 wks
9 Dec 78	**INCANTATIONS** Virgin VDT 101	14	17 wks
11 Aug 79	**EXPOSED** Virgin VD 2511	16	9 wks
8 Dec 79	**PLATINUM** Virgin V 2141	24	9 wks
8 Nov 80	**QE 2** Virgin V 2181	27	12 wks
27 Mar 82	● **FIVE MILES OUT** Virgin V 2222	7	27 wks
4 Jun 83	● **CRISES** Virgin V 2262	6	29 wks
7 Jul 84	**DISCOVERY** Virgin V 2308	15	16 wks
15 Dec 84	**THE KILLING FIELDS** Virgin V 2328	97	1 wk
2 Nov 85	**THE COMPLETE MIKE OLDFIELD** Virgin MOC 1	36	17 wks
10 Oct 87	**ISLANDS** Virgin V 2466	29	5 wks
22 Jul 89	**EARTH MOVING** Virgin V 2610	30	5 wks
9 Jun 90	**AMAROK** Virgin V 2640	49	2 wks
12 Sep 92	★ **TUBULAR BELLS II** WEA 4509906182	1	30 wks
25 Sep 93	● **ELEMENTS – THE BEST OF MIKE OLDFIELD** Virgin VTCD 18	5	10 wks
3 Dec 94	**THE SONGS OF DISTANT EARTH** WEA 4509985812	24	6 wks

[1] Mike Oldfield with the Royal Philharmonic Orchestra

OMAR UK, male vocalist — 13 wks

14 Jul 90	**THERE'S NOTHING LIKE THIS** Kongo Dance KDLP 2	54	4 wks
27 Jul 91	**THERE'S NOTHING LIKE THIS (re-issue)** Talkin Loud 5100211	19	6 wks
24 Oct 92	**MUSIC** Talkin Loud 5124012	37	2 wks
2 Jul 94	**FOR PLEASURE** RCA 74321208532	50	1 wk

OMNI TRIO UK, male producer – Rob Haigh — 1 wk

11 Feb 95	**THE DEEPEST CUT VOLUME 1** Moving Shadow ASHADOW 1CD	..60	1 wk

ONE DOVE UK, male / female vocal / instrumental group — 2 wks

25 Sep 93	**MORNING DOVE WHITE** London 8283522	30	2 wks

ONE HUNDRED & ONE STRINGS Germany, orchestra — 35 wks

26 Sep 59	● **GYPSY CAMPFIRES** Pye GGL 0009	9	7 wks
26 Mar 60	**SOUL OF SPAIN** Pye GGL 0017	17	1 wk
16 Apr 60	● **GRAND CANYON SUITE** Pye GGL 0048	10	1 wk
27 Aug 60	★ **DOWN DRURY LANE TO MEMORY LANE** Pye GGL 0061	1	21 wks
15 Oct 83	**MORNING, NOON AND NIGHT** Ronco RTL 2094	32	5 wks

The orchestra was American based for last album.

ONE WORLD UK, male vocal / instrumental group   3 wks

| 9 Jun 90 | ONE WORLD ONE VOICE Virgin V 2632 ....27 | 3 wks |

Alexander O'NEAL US, male vocalist   162 wks

1 Jun 85	ALEXANDER O'NEAL Tabu TBU 26485 19	18 wks
8 Aug 87	● HEARSAY / ALL MIXED UP Tabu 4509361 4	103 wks
17 Dec 88	MY GIFT TO YOU Tabu 463152 1 53	3 wks
2 Feb 91	● ALL TRUE MAN Tabu 4658821 2	16 wks
30 May 92	● THIS THING CALLED LOVE – THE GREATEST HITS Tabu 4717142..4	18 wks
20 Feb 93	LOVE MAKES NO SENSE Tabu 5495022 14	4 wks

All Mixed Up, a re-mixed album of Hearsay, was listed with Hearsay from 15 Jul 89.

ONLY ONES UK, male vocal / instrumental group   8 wks

3 Jun 78	THE ONLY ONES CBS 82830 56	1 wk
31 Mar 79	EVEN SERPENTS SHINE CBS 83451 42	2 wks
3 May 80	BABY'S GOT A GUN CBS 84089 37	5 wks

Yoko ONO Japan, female vocalist   2 wks

| 20 Jun 81 | SEASON OF GLASS Geffen K 99164 ....47 | 2 wks |

See also John Lennon.

ONSLAUGHT UK, male vocal / instrumental group   2 wks

| 20 May 89 | IN SEARCH OF SANITY London 828142 1 ....46 | 2 wks |

O

230

ONYX US, male rap group   3 wks

| 4 Sep 93 | BACDAFUCUP Columbia 4729802 ....59 | 3 wks |

ORANGE JUICE UK, male vocal / instrumental group   18 wks

6 Mar 82	YOU CAN'T HIDE YOUR LOVE FOREVER Polydor POLS 1057 21	6 wks
20 Nov 82	RIP IT UP Holden Caulfield Universal POLS 1076..39	8 wks
10 Mar 84	TEXAS FEVER Polydor OJMLP 1 34	4 wks

ORB UK, male instrumental / production duo   23 wks

27 Apr 91	ORB'S ADVENTURES BEYOND THE ULTRAWORLD Big Life BLRDLP 5 29	5 wks
18 Jul 92	★ U.F. ORB Big Life BLRCD 18 1	9 wks
4 Dec 93	LIVE 93 Island CIDD 8022 23	2 wks
25 Jun 94	● POMME FRITZ Inter-Modo ORBCD 1 6	4 wks
1 Apr 95	ORBVS TERRARVM Island CIDX 8037 20	3 wks

Roy ORBISON US, male vocalist   222 wks

8 Jun 63	LONELY AND BLUE London HAU 2342 15	8 wks
29 Jun 63	CRYING London HAU 2437 17	3 wks
30 Nov 63	● IN DREAMS London HAU 8108 6	57 wks
25 Jul 64	EXCITING SOUNDS OF ROY ORBISON Ember NR 5013 17	2 wks
5 Dec 64	● OH PRETTY WOMAN London HAU 8207..4	16 wks
25 Sep 65	● THERE IS ONLY ONE ROY ORBISON London HAU 8252..........10	12 wks
26 Feb 66	THE ORBISON WAY London HAU 8279..11	10 wks
24 Sep 66	THE CLASSIC ROY ORBISON London HAU 8297 12	8 wks
22 Jul 67	ORBISONGS Monument SMO 5004 40	1 wk
30 Sep 67	ROY ORBISON'S GREATEST HITS Monument SMO 5007 40	1 wk
27 Jan 73	ALL–TIME GREATEST HITS Monument MNT 67290..........................39	3 wks
29 Nov 75	★ THE BEST OF ROY ORBISON Arcade ADEP 19 1	20 wks
18 Jul 81	GOLDEN DAYS CBS 10026 63	1 wk
4 Jul 87	IN DREAMS: THE GREATEST HITS Virgin VGD 3514 86	2 wks
29 Oct 88	★ THE LEGENDARY ROY ORBISON Telstar STAR 2330 1	38 wks

11 Feb 89	● MYSTERY GIRL Virgin V 2576	2	23 wks
25 Nov 89	A BLACK AND WHITE NIGHT Virgin V 2601	51	3 wks
2 Nov 90	BALLADS Telstar STAR 2441	38	10 wks
28 Nov 92	KING OF HEARTS Virgin America CDVUS 58	23	4 wks

ORBITAL UK, male instrumental duo   9 wks

12 Oct 91	ORBITAL ffrr 8282481	71	1 wk
5 Jun 93	ORBITAL Internal TRUCD 2	28	2 wks
19 Mar 94	PEEL SESSIONS Internal LIECD 12	32	2 wks
20 Aug 94	● SNIVILISATION Internal TRUCD 5	4	4 wks

The identically titled albums are different.

ORCHESTRAL MANOEUVRES IN THE DARK
UK, male vocal / instrumental duo   220 wks

1 Mar 80	ORCHESTRAL MANOEUVRES IN THE DARK DinDisc DID 2	27	29 wks
1 Nov 80	● ORGANISATION DinDisc DID 6	6	25 wks
14 Nov 81	● ARCHITECTURE AND MORALITY DinDisc DID 12	3	39 wks
12 Mar 83	● DAZZLE SHIPS Telegraph V 2261	5	13 wks
12 May 84	● JUNK CULTURE Virgin V 2310	9	27 wks
29 Jun 85	CRUSH Virgin V 2349	13	12 wks
11 Oct 86	THE PACIFIC AGE Virgin V 2398	15	7 wks
12 Mar 88	● THE BEST OF O.M.D. Virgin OMD 1	2	33 wks
18 May 91	● SUGAR TAX Virgin V 2648	3	29 wks
26 Jun 93	LIBERATOR Virgin CDV 2715	14	6 wks

Group often known as O.M.D.

L'ORCHESTRE ELECTRONIQUE UK, male synthesized orchestra   1 wk

29 Oct 83	SOUND WAVES Nouveau Musique NML 1005	75	1 wk

ORCHESTRE NATIONALE DE LA RADIO DIFFUSION FRANÇAISE – See Sir Thomas BEECHAM

Cyril ORNADEL – See LONDON SYMPHONY ORCHESTRA

ORVILLE – See Keith HARRIS, ORVILLE and CUDDLES

Jeffrey OSBORNE US, male vocalist   10 wks

5 May 84	STAY WITH ME TONIGHT A & M AMLX 64940	56	7 wks
13 Oct 84	DON'T STOP A & M AMA 5017	59	3 wks

Ozzy OSBOURNE UK, male vocalist   60 wks

20 Sep 80	● OZZY OSBOURNE'S BLIZZARD OF OZ Jet JETLP 234 [1]	7	8 wks
7 Nov 81	DIARY OF A MADMAN Jet JETLP 237	14	12 wks
27 Nov 82	TALK OF THE DEVIL Jet JETDP 401	21	6 wks
10 Dec 83	BARK AT THE MOON Epic EPC 25739	24	7 wks
22 Feb 86	● THE ULTIMATE SIN Epic EPC 26404	8	10 wks
23 May 87	TRIBUTE Epic 450 4751	13	6 wks
22 Oct 88	NO REST FOR THE WICKED Epic 462581 1	23	4 wks
17 Mar 90	JUST SAY OZZY Epic 4659401	69	1 wk
19 Oct 91	NO MORE TEARS Epic 4678591	17	3 wks
4 Nov 95	OZZMOSIS Epic 4810222	22	3 wks

[1] Ozzy Osbourne's Blizzard Of Oz

OSIBISA Ghana / Nigeria, male vocal / instrumental group   17 wks

22 May 71	OSIBISA MCA MDKS 8001	11	10 wks
5 Feb 72	WOYAYA MCA MDKS 8005	11	7 wks

Donny OSMOND US, male vocalist   104 wks

23 Sep 72	● PORTRAIT OF DONNY MGM 2315 108	5	43 wks

O
231

16 Dec 72	● TOO YOUNG *MGM 2315 113*	7	24 wks
26 May 73	● ALONE TOGETHER *MGM 2315 210*	6	19 wks
15 Dec 73	● A TIME FOR US *MGM 2315 273*	4	13 wks
8 Feb 75	DONNY *MGM 2315 314*	16	4 wks
2 Oct 76	DISCOTRAIN *Polydor 2391 226*	59	1 wk

See also Osmonds; Donny and Marie Osmond.

Donny and Marie OSMOND *US, male / female vocal duo* **19 wks**

2 Nov 74	I'M LEAVING IT ALL UP TO YOU *MGM 2315 307*	13	15 wks
26 Jul 75	MAKE THE WORLD GO AWAY *MGM 2315 343*	30	3 wks
5 Jun 76	DEEP PURPLE *Polydor 2391 220*	48	1 wk

See also Donny Osmond; Marie Osmond.

Little Jimmy OSMOND *US, male vocalist* **12 wks**

| 17 Feb 73 | KILLER JOE *MGM 2315 157* | 20 | 12 wks |

Marie OSMOND *US, female vocalist* **1 wk**

| 9 Feb 74 | PAPER ROSES *MGM 2315 262* | 46 | 1 wk |

See also Donny and Marie Osmond.

OSMONDS *US, male vocal / instrumental group* **103 wks**

18 Nov 72	OSMONDS LIVE *MGM 2315 117*	13	22 wks
16 Dec 72	● CRAZY HORSES *MGM 2315 123*	9	19 wks
25 Aug 73	● THE PLAN *MGM 2315 251*	6	25 wks
17 Aug 74	● OUR BEST TO YOU *MGM 2315 300*	5	20 wks
7 Dec 74	LOVE ME FOR A REASON *MGM 2315 312*	13	9 wks
14 Jun 75	I'M STILL GONNA NEED YOU *MGM 2315 342*	19	7 wks
10 Jan 76	AROUND THE WORLD – LIVE IN CONCERT *MGM 2659 044*	41	1 wk

See also Donny Osmond.

Gilbert O'SULLIVAN *UK, male vocalist* **195 wks**

25 Sep 71	● HIMSELF *MAM 501*	5	82 wks
18 Nov 72	★ BACK TO FRONT *MAM 502*	1	64 wks
6 Oct 73	● I'M A WRITER NOT A FIGHTER *MAMS 505*	2	25 wks
26 Oct 74	● STRANGER IN MY OWN BACK YARD *MAM MAMS 506*	9	8 wks
18 Dec 76	GREATEST HITS *MAM MAMA 2003*	13	11 wks
12 Sep 81	20 GOLDEN GREATS *K-Tel NE 1133*	98	1 wk
11 May 91	NOTHING BUT THE BEST *Castle Communications CTVLP 107*	50	4 wks

John OTWAY and Wild Willy BARRETT
UK, male vocal / instrumental duo **1 wk**

| 1 Jul 78 | DEEP AND MEANINGLESS *Polydor 2382 501* | 44 | 1 wk |

OUI 3 *UK / US / Switzerland, male / female vocal / instrumental group* **3 wks**

| 7 Aug 93 | OUI LOVE YOU *MCA MCD 10833* | 39 | 3 wks |

OUTHERE BROTHERS *US, male vocal / instrumental duo* **6 wks**

| 27 May 95 | 1 POLISH 2 BISCUITS AND A FISH SANDWICH *Eternal 0630105852* | 56 | 5 wks |
| 30 Dec 95 | THE PARTY ALBUM *Eternal 0630127812* | 67† | 1 wk |

The Party Album is a sanitized version of 1 Polish 2 Biscuits And A Fish Sandwich.

OVERLORD X *UK, male rapper* **1 wk**

| 4 Feb 89 | WEAPON IS MY LYRIC *Mango Street ILPS 9924* | 68 | 1 wk |

OZRIC TENTACLES *UK, male instrumental / vocal group*   **7 wks**

31 Aug 91	**STRANGEITUDE** Dovetail DOVELP 3	70	1 wk
1 May 93	**JURASSIC SHIFT** Dovetail DOVECD 6	11	4 wks
9 Jul 94	**ARBORESCENCE** Dovetail DOVECD 7	18	2 wks

PACEMAKERS – *See GERRY and the PACEMAKERS*

Jimmy PAGE *UK, male instrumentalist – guitar*   **27 wks**

27 Feb 82	**DEATHWISH II (film soundtrack)** Swansong SSK 59415	40	4 wks
16 Mar 85	**WHATEVER HAPPENED TO JUGULA?**		
	Beggars Banquet BEGA 60 [1]	44	4 wks
2 Jul 88	**OUTRIDER** Geffen WX 155	27	6 wks
19 Nov 94	● **NO QUARTER** Fontana 5263622 [2]	7	13 wks

[1] Roy Harper with Jimmy Page [2] Jimmy Page and Robert Plant

Elaine PAIGE *UK, female vocalist*   **149 wks**

1 May 82	**ELAINE PAIGE** WEA K 58385	56	6 wks
5 Nov 83	● **STAGES** K-Tel NE 1262	2	48 wks
20 Oct 84	**CINEMA** K-Tel NE 1282	12	25 wks
16 Nov 85	● **LOVE HURTS** WEA WX 28	8	20 wks
29 Nov 86	**CHRISTMAS** WEA WX 80	27	6 wks
5 Dec 87	**MEMORIES – THE BEST OF ELAINE PAIGE** Telstar STAR 2313	14	15 wks
19 Nov 88	**THE QUEEN ALBUM** Siren SRNLP 22	51	8 wks
27 Apr 91	**LOVE CAN DO THAT** RCA PL 74932	36	4 wks
28 Nov 92	**THE BEST OF ELAINE PAIGE AND BARBARA DICKSON**		
	Telstar TCD 2632 [1]	22	9 wks
10 Apr 93	**ROMANCE AND THE STAGE** RCA 74321136152	71	1 wk
19 Nov 94	**PIAF** WEA 4509946412	46	3 wks
1 Jul 95	**ENCORE** WEA 0630104762	20	4 wks

[1] Elaine Paige and Barbara Dickson

PALE FOUNTAINS *UK, male vocal / instrumental group*   **3 wks**

10 Mar 84	**PACIFIC STREET** Virgin V 2274	85	2 wks
16 Feb 85	**FROM ACROSS THE KITCHEN TABLE** Virgin V 2333	94	1 wk

PALE SAINTS *UK, male / female vocal / instrumental group*   **3 wks**

24 Feb 90	**THE COMFORTS OF MADNESS** 4AD CAD 0002	40	2 wks
4 Apr 92	**IN RIBBONS** 4AD CAD 2004CD	61	1 wk

PALLAS *UK, male vocal / instrumental group*   **4 wks**

25 Feb 84	**SENTINEL** Harvest SHSP 2400121	41	3 wks
22 Feb 86	**THE WEDGE** Harvest SHVL 850	70	1 wk

Robert PALMER *UK, male vocalist*   **151 wks**

6 Nov 76	**SOME PEOPLE CAN DO WHAT THEY LIKE** Island ILPS 9420	46	1 wk
14 Jul 79	**SECRETS** Island ILPS 9544	54	4 wks
6 Sep 80	**CLUES** Island ILPS 9595	31	8 wks
3 Apr 82	**MAYBE IT'S LIVE** Island ILPS 9665	32	6 wks
23 Apr 83	**PRIDE** Island ILPS 9720	37	9 wks
16 Nov 85	● **RIPTIDE** Island ILPS 9801	5	37 wks
9 Jul 88	**HEAVY NOVA** EMI EMD 1007	17	25 wks
11 Nov 89	● **ADDICTIONS VOLUME 1** Island ILPS 9944	7	17 wks

TOP 30 № 26

A charting artist for over two decades, **MIKE OLDFIELD** has yet to amass the number of weeks on chart with all subsequent releases combined that his very first album enjoyed.

(Solo/Joe Bangay Photography)

Beth Gibbons nearly led **PORTISHEAD** to the head of the class in 1995.

(Tom Sheehan/LFI)

17 Nov 90	● **DON'T EXPLAIN** EMI EMDX 1018......................................**9**	20 wks
4 Apr 92	**ADDICTIONS VOLUME 2** Island CIDTV 4...........................**12**	7 wks
31 Oct 92	**RIDIN' HIGH** EMI CDEMD 1038.....................................**32**	3 wks
24 Sep 94	**HONEY** EMI CDEMD 1069 ....**25**	4 wks
28 Oct 95	● **THE VERY BEST OF ROBERT PALMER** EMI CDEMD 1088 ....**4†**	10 wks

PANTERA US, male vocal / instrumental group · **5 wks**

| 7 Mar 92 | **VULGAR DISPLAY OF POWER** Atco 7567917582.........................**64** | 1 wk |
| 2 Apr 94 | ● **FAR BEYOND DRIVEN** Atco 7567923752 ....**3** | 4 wks |

PAPAS – See MAMAS and PAPAS

Vanessa PARADIS France, female vocalist · **2 wks**

| 7 Nov 92 | **VANESSA PARADIS** Remark 5139542 ....**45** | 2 wks |

PARADISE LOST UK, male vocal / instrumental group · **3 wks**

| 24 Jun 95 | **DRACONIAN TIMES** Music For Nations CDMFNX 184 ....**16** | 3 wks |

Mica PARIS UK, female vocalist · **39 wks**

3 Sep 88	● **SO GOOD** Fourth & Broadway BRLP 525 ....**6**	32 wks
27 Oct 90	**CONTRIBUTION** Fourth & Broadway BRLP 558 ....**26**	3 wks
26 Jun 93	**WHISPER A PRAYER** Fourth & Broadway BRCD 591 ....**20**	4 wks

PARIS ANGELS Ireland, male vocal / instrumental duo · **2 wks**

| 17 Aug 91 | **SUNDEW** Virgin V 2667 ....**37** | 2 wks |

Graham PARKER and the RUMOUR
UK, male vocal / instrumental group · **35 wks**

27 Nov 76	**HEAT TREATMENT** Vertigo 6360 137 ....**52**	2 wks
12 Nov 77	**STICK TO ME** Vertigo 9102 017 ....**19**	4 wks
27 May 78	**PARKERILLA** Vertigo 6641 797 ....**14**	5 wks
7 Apr 79	**SQUEEZING OUT SPARKS** Vertigo 9102 030.........................**18**	8 wks
7 Jun 80	**THE UP ESCALATOR** Stiff SEEZ 23 ....**11**	10 wks
27 Mar 82	**ANOTHER GREY AREA** RCA RCALP 6029 [1] **40**	6 wks

[1] Graham Parker

Ray PARKER Jr. US, male vocalist · **7 wks**

| 10 Oct 87 | **AFTER DARK** WEA WX 122.........................**40** | 7 wks |

John PARR UK, male vocalist · **2 wks**

| 2 Nov 85 | **JOHN PARR** London LONLP 12 ....**60** | 2 wks |

Alan PARSONS PROJECT UK, male vocal / instrumental group · **38 wks**

28 Aug 76	**TALES OF MYSTERY AND IMAGINATION** Charisma CDS 4003 ....**56**	1 wk
13 Aug 77	**I ROBOT** Arista SPARTY 1016.........................**30**	1 wk
10 Jun 78	**PYRAMID** Arista SPART 1054 ....**49**	4 wks
29 Sep 79	**EVE** Arista SPARTY 1100 ....**74**	1 wk
15 Nov 80	**THE TURN OF A FRIENDLY CARD** Arista DLART 1.........................**38**	4 wks
29 May 82	**EYE IN THE SKY** Arista 204 666 ....**27**	11 wks
26 Nov 83	**THE BEST OF THE ALAN PARSONS PROJECT** Arista APP 1 ....**99**	1 wk
3 Mar 84	**AMMONIA AVENUE** Arista 206 100 ....**24**	8 wks
23 Feb 85	**VULTURE CULTURE** Arista 206 577 ....**40**	5 wks
14 Feb 87	**GAUDI** Arista 208 084 ....**66**	2 wks

PARTISANS UK, male vocal / instrumental group · **1 wk**

| 19 Feb 83 | **THE PARTISANS** No Future PUNK 4 ....**94** | 1 wk |

Dolly PARTON *US, female vocalist* **19 wks**

25 Nov 78	**BOTH SIDES** Lotus WH 5006	**45**	12 wks
7 Sep 85	**GREATEST HITS** RCA PL 84422	**74**	1 wk
14 Mar 87	**TRIO** Warner Bros. 9254911 [1]	**60**	4 wks
22 Oct 94	**THE GREATEST HITS** Telstar TCD 2739...............	**65**	2 wks

[1] Dolly Parton/Emmylou Harris/Linda Ronstadt

Alan PARTRIDGE *UK, male comedian – Steve Coogan* **3 wks**

18 Mar 95	**KNOWING ME KNOWING YOU 3**		
	BBC Canned Laughter ZBBC 1671CD...............	**41**	3 wks

PARTRIDGE FAMILY *US, male/female vocal group* **13 wks**

8 Jan 72	**UP TO DATE** Bell SBLL 143..	**46**	2 wks
22 Apr 72	**THE PARTRIDGE FAMILY SOUND MAGAZINE** Bell BELLS 206	**14**	7 wks
30 Sep 72	**SHOPPING BAG** Bell BELLS 212	**28**	3 wks
9 Dec 72	**CHRISTMAS CARD** Bell BELLS 214	**45**	1 wk

PASADENAS *UK, male vocal group* **32 wks**

22 Oct 88	● **TO WHOM IT MAY CONCERN** CBS 462877 1	**3**	21 wks
7 Mar 92	● **YOURS SINCERELY** Columbia 4712642	**6**	11 wks

PASSENGERS *Ireland/UK/Italy, male vocal/instrumental group* **5 wks**

18 Nov 95	**ORIGINAL SOUNDTRACKS 1** Island CID 8043	**12**	5 wks

PASSIONS *UK, male/female vocal/instrumental group* **1 wk**

3 Oct 81	**THIRTY THOUSAND FEET OVER CHINA** Polydor POLS 1041	**92**	1 wk

Luciano PAVAROTTI *Italy, male vocalist* **263 wks**

15 May 82	**PAVAROTTI'S GREATEST HITS** Decca D 2362	**95**	1 wk
30 Jun 84	**MAMMA** Decca 411959 [1]................................	**96**	1 wk
9 Aug 86	**THE PAVAROTTI COLLECTION** Stylus SMR 8617.............	**12**	34 wks
16 Jul 88	**THE NEW PAVAROTTI COLLECTION LIVE!** Stylus SMR 857	**63**	8 wks
17 Mar 90	★ **THE ESSENTIAL PAVAROTTI** Decca 4302101	**1**	72 wks
1 Sep 90	★ **IN CONCERT** Decca 4304331 [2]..........................	**1**	78 wks
20 Jul 91	★ **ESSENTIAL PAVAROTTI II** Decca 4304701.............	**1**	28 wks
15 Feb 92	**PAVAROTTI IN HYDE PARK** Decca 4363202	**19**	7 wks
4 Sep 93	**TI AMO – PUCCINI'S GREATEST LOVE SONGS** Decca 4250992	**23**	4 wks
12 Feb 94	**MY HEART'S DELIGHT** Decca 4432602	**44**	4 wks
10 Sep 94	★ **THE THREE TENORS IN CONCERT 1994** Teldec 4509962002 [3]	**1**	26 wks

[1] Luciano Pavarotti with the Henry Mancini Orchestra [2] Luciano Pavarotti, Placido Domingo and José Carreras [3] José Carreras, Placido Domingo and Luciano Pavarotti with Mehta

PAVEMENT *US, male vocal/instrumental group* **8 wks**

25 Apr 92	**SLANTED AND ENCHANTED** Big Cat ABB 34CD	**72**	1 wk
3 Apr 93	**WESTING (BY MUSKET AND SEXTANT)** Big Cat ABBCD 40	**30**	2 wks
26 Feb 94	**CROOKED RAIN CROOKED RAIN** Big Cat ABB 56CD	**15**	3 wks
22 Apr 95	**WOWEE ZOWEE** Big Cat ABB 84CD	**18**	2 wks

Tom PAXTON *US, male vocalist* **10 wks**

13 Jun 70	**NO. 6** Elektra 2469003	**23**	5 wks
3 Apr 71	**THE COMPLEAT TOM PAXTON** Elektra EKD 2003	**18**	4 wks
1 Jul 72	**PEACE WILL COME** Reprise K 44182	**47**	1 wk

PEARL JAM *US, male vocal/instrumental group* **100 wks**

7 Mar 92	**TEN** Epic 4688842	**18**	65 wks

23 Oct 93 ● VS *Epic 4745492*	....	**2**	24 wks
3 Dec 94 ● VITALOGY *Epic 4778611*	....	**4**	11 wks

David PEASTON *UK, male vocalist*   **1 wk**

26 Aug 89	**INTRODUCING . . . DAVID PEASTON** *Geffen 924228 1*	**66**	1 wk

PEBBLES *US, female vocalist*   **4 wks**

14 May 88	**PEBBLES** *MCA MCF 3418*	**56**	4 wks

PEDDLERS *UK, male vocal / instrumental group*   **16 wks**

16 Mar 68	**FREE WHEELERS** *CBS SBPG 63183*	**27**	13 wks
7 Feb 70	**BIRTHDAY** *CBS 63682*	**16**	3 wks

Kevin PEEK *UK, male instrumentalist – guitar*   **8 wks**

21 Mar 81	**AWAKENING** *Ariola ARL 5065*	**52**	2 wks
13 Oct 84	**BEYOND THE PLANETS** *Telstar STAR 2244* [1]	**64**	6 wks

[1] Kevin Peek and Rick Wakeman

Beyond the Planets *also features Jeff Wayne with narration by Patrick Allen.*

Teddy PENDERGRASS *US, male vocalist*   **8 wks**

21 May 88	**JOY** *Elektra 960775 1*	**45**	8 wks

PENETRATION *UK, male / female vocal / instrumental group*   **8 wks**

28 Oct 78	**MOVING TARGETS** *Virgin V 2109*	**22**	4 wks
6 Oct 79	**COMING UP FOR AIR** *Virgin V 2131*	**36**	4 wks

PENGUIN CAFE ORCHESTRA *UK, male instrumental group*   **5 wks**

4 Apr 87	**SIGNS OF LIFE** *Edition EG EGED 50*	**49**	5 wks

Ce Ce PENISTON *US, female vocalist*   **21 wks**

8 Feb 92 ● FINALLY *A & M 3971822*	....	**10**	19 wks
5 Feb 94	**THOUGHT YA KNEW** *A & M 5402012*	**31**	2 wks

Dawn PENN *Jamaica, female vocalist*   **2 wks**

9 Jul 94	**NO NO NO** *Big Beat 7567923652*	**51**	2 wks

PENTANGLE *UK, male / female vocal / instrumental group*   **39 wks**

15 Jun 68	**THE PENTANGLE** *Transatlantic TRA 162*	**21**	9 wks
1 Nov 69 ● BASKET OF LIGHT *Transatlantic TRA 205*	....	**5**	28 wks
12 Dec 70	**CRUEL SISTER** *Transatlantic TRA 228*	**51**	2 wks

PEPSI and SHIRLIE *UK, female vocal duo*   **2 wks**

7 Nov 87	**ALL RIGHT NOW** *Polydor POLH 38*	**69**	2 wks

Carl PERKINS *US, male vocalist*   **3 wks**

15 Apr 78	**OL' BLUE SUEDES IS BACK** *Jet UATV 30146*	**38**	3 wks

Steve PERRY *US, male vocalist*   **3 wks**

14 Jul 84	**STREET TALK** *CBS 25967*	**59**	2 wks
27 Aug 94	**FOR THE LOVE OF STRANGE MEDICINE** *Columbia 4771962*	**64**	1 wk

PESTALOZZI CHILDREN'S CHOIR
International, male / female vocal group **2 wks**

26 Dec 81	**SONGS OF JOY** K-Tel NE 1140	65	2 wks

PET SHOP BOYS UK, male vocal / instrumental duo **321 wks**

5 Apr 86	● **PLEASE** Parlophone PSB 1	3	82 wks
29 Nov 86	**DISCO** EMI PRG 1001	15	72 wks
19 Sep 87	● **ACTUALLY** Parlophone PCSD 104	2	59 wks
22 Oct 88	● **INTROSPECTIVE** Parlophone PCS 7325	2	39 wks
3 Nov 90	● **BEHAVIOUR** Parlophone PCSD 113	2	14 wks
16 Nov 91	● **DISCOGRAPHY** Parlophone PMTV 3	3	24 wks
9 Oct 93	★ **VERY** Parlophone CDPCSD 143	1	22 wks
24 Sep 94	● **DISCO 2** Parlophone CDPCSD 159	6	4 wks
19 Aug 95	● **ALTERNATIVE** Parlophone CDPCSD 166	2	5 wks

PETER and GORDON UK, male vocal duo **1 wk**

20 Jun 64	**PETER AND GORDON** Columbia 33SX 1630	18	1 wk

PETER, PAUL and MARY
US, male / female vocal / instrumental group **26 wks**

4 Jan 64	**PETER PAUL AND MARY** Warner Bros. WM 4064	18	1 wk
21 Mar 64	**IN THE WIND** Warner Bros. WM 8142	11	19 wks
13 Feb 65	**IN CONCERT VOLUME 1** Warner Bros. WM 8158	20	2 wks
5 Sep 70	**TEN YEARS TOGETHER** Warner Bros. WS 2552	60	4 wks

PETERS and LEE UK, male / female vocal duo **166 wks**

30 Jun 73	★ **WE CAN MAKE IT** Philips 6308 165	1	55 wks
22 Dec 73	● **BY YOUR SIDE** Philips 6308 192	9	48 wks
21 Sep 74	● **RAINBOW** Philips 6308 208	6	27 wks
4 Oct 75	● **FAVOURITES** Philips 9109 205	2	32 wks
18 Dec 76	**INVITATION** Philips 9101 027	44	4 wks

Tom PETTY and the HEARTBREAKERS
US, male vocal / instrumental group **94 wks**

4 Jun 77	**TOM PETTY AND THE HEARTBREAKERS** Shelter ISA 5014	24	12 wks
1 Jul 78	**YOU'RE GONNA GET IT** Island ISA 5017	34	5 wks
17 Nov 79	**DAMN THE TORPEDOES** MCA MCF 3044	57	4 wks
23 May 81	**HARD PROMISES** MCA MCF 3098	32	5 wks
20 Nov 82	**LONG AFTER DARK** MCA MCF 3155	45	4 wks
20 Apr 85	**SOUTHERN ACCENTS** MCA MCF 3260	23	6 wks
2 May 87	**LET ME UP (I'VE HAD ENOUGH)** MCA MCG 6014	59	2 wks
8 Jul 89	● **FULL MOON FEVER** MCA MCG 6034 [1]	8	16 wks
20 Jul 91	● **INTO THE GREAT WIDE OPEN** MCA MCA 10317	3	18 wks
13 Nov 93	● **GREATEST HITS** MCA MCD 10964	10	20 wks
12 Nov 94	**WILDFLOWERS** Warner Bros. 9362457592 [1]	36	2 wks

[1] Tom Petty

PHARCYDE US, male rap group **1 wk**

21 Aug 93	**BIZARRE RIDE II THE PHARCYDE** Atlantic 756792222	58	1 wk

PhD UK, male vocal / instrumental duo **8 wks**

1 May 82	**PhD** WEA K 99150	33	8 wks

Barrington PHELOUNG Australia, male conductor / arranger **53 wks**

2 Mar 91	● **INSPECTOR MORSE MUSIC FROM THE TV SERIES** Virgin Television VTLP 2	4	30 wks
7 Mar 92	**INSPECTOR MORSE VOLUME 2** Virgin Television VTCD 14	18	12 wks

16 Jan 93   **INSPECTOR MORSE VOLUME 3** *Virgin Television VTCD 16* ....**20**   11 wks

PHENOMENA *UK, male vocal / instrumental group*   **2 wks**

6 Jul 85   **PHENOMENA** *Bronze PM 1* ....**63**   2 wks

Arlene PHILLIPS *UK, female exercise instructor*   **24 wks**

28 Aug 82   **KEEP IN SHAPE SYSTEM** *Supershape SUP 01*..................................**41**   23 wks
18 Feb 84   **KEEP IN SHAPE SYSTEM VOLUME 2** *Supershape SUP 2* ....**100**   1 wk

Keep In Shape System *features music by Funk Federation.*

PHOTOS *UK, male / female vocal / instrumental group*   **9 wks**

21 Jun 80 ● **THE PHOTOS** *CBS PHOTO 5* ....**4**   9 wks

Edith PIAF *France, female vocalist*   **5 wks**

26 Sep 87   **HEART AND SOUL** *Stylus SMR 736*..................**58**   5 wks

PIGBAG *UK, male instrumental group*   **14 wks**

13 Mar 82   **DR HECKLE AND MR JIVE** *Y Y 17*......................**18**   14 wks

PILOT *UK, male vocal / instrumental group*   **1 wk**

31 May 75   **SECOND FLIGHT** *EMI EMC 3075*......................**48**   1 wk

Courtney PINE *UK, male instrumentalist – saxophone*   **13 wks**

25 Oct 86   **JOURNEY TO THE URGE WITHIN** *Island ILPS 9846*..........................**39**   11 wks
6 Feb 88   **DESTINY'S SONGS** *Antilles AN 8275*....................................**54**   2 wks

PINK FAIRIES *UK, male vocal / instrumental group*   **1 wk**

29 Jul 72   **WHAT A BUNCH OF SWEETIES** *Polydor 2383 132* ....**48**   1 wk

PINK FLOYD *UK, male vocal / instrumental group*   **859 wks**

19 Aug 67 ● **PIPER AT THE GATES OF DAWN** *Columbia SCX 6157* ....**6**   14 wks
13 Jul 68 ● **SAUCERFUL OF SECRETS** *Columbia SCX 6258* ....**9**   11 wks
28 Jun 69 ● **MORE (film soundtrack)** *Columbia SCX 6346* ....**9**   5 wks
15 Nov 69 ● **UMMAGUMMA** *Harvest SHDW 1/2* ....**5**   21 wks
24 Oct 70 ★ **ATOM HEART MOTHER** *Harvest SHVL 781* ....**1**   23 wks
7 Aug 71   **RELICS** *Starline SRS 5071* ....**32**   6 wks
20 Nov 71 ● **MEDDLE** *Harvest SHVL 795* ....**3**   82 wks
17 Jun 72 ● **OBSCURED BY CLOUDS (film soundtrack)** *Harvest SHSP 4020* ....**6**   14 wks
31 Mar 73 ● **THE DARK SIDE OF THE MOON** *Harvest SHVL 804* ....**2**   337 wks
19 Jan 74   **A NICE PAIR (double re-issue)** *Harvest SHDW 403* ....**21**   20 wks
27 Sep 75 ★ **WISH YOU WERE HERE** *Harvest SHVL 814* ....**1**   89 wks
19 Feb 77 ● **ANIMALS** *Harvest SHVL 815* ....**2**   33 wks
8 Dec 79 ● **THE WALL** *Harvest SHDW 411*...................................**3**   51 wks
5 Dec 81   **A COLLECTION OF GREAT DANCE SONGS** *Harvest SHVL 822*......**37**   10 wks
2 Apr 83 ★ **THE FINAL CUT** *Harvest SHPF 1983* ....**1**   25 wks
19 Sep 87 ● **A MOMENTARY LAPSE OF REASON** *EMI EMD 1003* ....**3**   34 wks
3 Dec 88   **DELICATE SOUND OF THUNDER** *EMI EQ 5009* ....**11**   12 wks
9 Apr 94 ★ **THE DIVISION BELL** *EMI CDEMD 1055* ....**1**   51 wks
10 Jun 95 ★ **PULSE** *EMI CDEMD 1078* ....**1**   21 wks

A Nice Pair *is a double re–issue of the first two albums.*

PIPS – *See Gladys KNIGHT and the PIPS*

PIRANHAS *UK, male vocal / instrumental group*   **3 wks**

20 Sep 80   **PIRANHAS** *Sire SRK 6098* ....**69**   3 wks

PIRATES UK, male vocal / instrumental group   **3 wks**

| 19 Nov 77 | OUT OF THEIR SKULLS Warner Bros. K 56411 ....**57** | 3 wks |

Gene PITNEY US, male vocalist   **73 wks**

11 Apr 64	● BLUE GENE United Artists ULP 1061 ....**7**	11 wks
6 Feb 65	GENE PITNEY'S BIG 16 Stateside SL 10118 ....**12**	6 wks
20 Mar 65	I'M GONNA BE STRONG Stateside SL 10120 ....**15**	2 wks
20 Nov 65	LOOKIN' THRU THE EYES OF LOVE Stateside SL 10148 ....**15**	5 wks
17 Sep 66	NOBODY NEEDS YOUR LOVE Stateside SL 10183 ....**13**	17 wks
4 Mar 67	YOUNG WARM AND WONDERFUL Stateside SSL 10194 ....**39**	1 wk
22 Apr 67	GENE PITNEY'S BIG SIXTEEN Stateside SSL 10199 ....**40**	1 wk
20 Sep 69	● BEST OF GENE PITNEY Stateside SSL 10286 ....**8**	9 wks
2 Oct 76	● HIS 20 GREATEST HITS Arcade ADEP 22..................**6**	14 wks
20 Oct 90	BACKSTAGE – THE GREATEST HITS AND MORE Polydor 8471191 ....**17**	7 wks

PIXIES US, male / female vocal / instrumental group   **22 wks**

29 Apr 89	● DOOLITTLE 4AD CAD 905 ....**8**	9 wks
25 Aug 90	● BOSSANOVA 4AD CAD 0010 ....**3**	8 wks
5 Oct 91	● TROMPE LE MONDE 4AD CAD 1014 ....**7**	5 wks

PJ and DUNCAN UK, male vocal duo   **27 wks**

| 19 Nov 94 | ● PSYCHE – THE ALBUM XSrhythm TCD 2746 ....**5** | 20 wks |
| 18 Nov 95 | TOP KATZ – THE ALBUM XSrhythm TCD 2793 ....**46†** | 7 wks |

P
240

Robert PLANT UK, male vocalist   **70 wks**

10 Jul 82	● PICTURES AT ELEVEN Swansong SSK 59418..................**2**	15 wks
23 Jul 83	● THE PRINCIPLES OF MOMENTS WEA 7901011 ....**7**	14 wks
1 Jun 85	SHAKEN 'N' STIRRED Es Paranza 7902651 ....**19**	4 wks
12 Feb 88	● NOW AND ZEN Es Paranza WX 149.......................**10**	7 wks
31 Mar 90	MANIC NIRVANA Es Paranza WX 339.......................**15**	9 wks
5 Jun 93	● FATE OF NATIONS Es Paranza 5148672 ....**6**	8 wks
19 Nov 94	● NO QUARTER Fontana 5263622 [1] **7**	13 wks

[1] Jimmy Page and Robert Plant

PLASMATICS US, male / female vocal / instrumental group   **3 wks**

| 11 Oct 80 | NEW HOPE FOR THE WRETCHED Stiff SEEZ 24 ....**55** | 3 wks |

PLASTIC ONO BAND – See John LENNON

PLASTIK MAN Canada, male instrumentalist – Richie Hawtin, keyboards   **1 wk**

| 19 Nov 94 | MUSIK Novamute NOMU 37CD ....**58** | 1 wk |

See also Fuse.

PLATTERS US, male / female vocal group   **13 wks**

| 8 Apr 78 | ● 20 CLASSIC HITS Mercury 9100 049 ....**8** | 13 wks |

PLAYERS ASSOCIATION
US, male / female vocal / instrumental group   **4 wks**

| 17 Mar 79 | TURN THE MUSIC UP Vanguard VSD 79421 ....**54** | 4 wks |

PLAYN JAYN UK, male vocal / instrumental group   **1 wk**

| 1 Sep 84 | FRIDAY THE 13TH (AT THE MARQUEE CLUB) A & M JAYN 13 ....**93** | 1 wk |

PM DAWN *US, male rap duo*   **17 wks**

14 Sep 91	● OF THE HEART OF THE SOUL AND OF THE CROSS	
	Gee Street GEEA 7 8	12 wks
3 Apr 93	● THE BLISS ALBUM . . . ? *Gee Street GEED 9*.....................9	5 wks

POGUES *Ireland, male vocal / instrumental group*   **64 wks**

3 Nov 84	RED ROSES FOR ME *Stiff SEEZ 55* 89	1 wk
17 Aug 85	RUM, SODOMY AND THE LASH *Stiff SEEZ 58* 13	14 wks
30 Jan 88	● IF I SHOULD FALL FROM GRACE WITH GOD *Stiff NYR 1* 3	16 wks
29 Jul 89	● PEACE AND LOVE *WEA WX 247* 5	8 wks
13 Oct 90	HELL'S DITCH *Pogue Mahone WX 366* 12	5 wks
12 Oct 91	BEST OF THE POGUES *PM WX 430* 11	17 wks
11 Sep 93	WAITING FOR HERB *PM 4509934632* 20	3 wks

Group was male / female for first two albums.

POINTER SISTERS *US, female vocal group*   **88 wks**

29 Aug 81	BLACK AND WHITE *Planet K 52300* 21	13 wks
5 May 84	● BREAK OUT *Planet PL 84705*.....................9	58 wks
27 Jul 85	CONTACT *Planet PL 85457*.....................34	7 wks
29 Jul 89	JUMP – THE BEST OF THE POINTER SISTERS *RCA PL 90319* 11	10 wks

POISON *US, male vocal / instrumental group*   **37 wks**

21 May 88	OPEN UP AND SAY . . . AAH! *Capitol EST 2059* 18	21 wks
21 Jul 90	● FLESH AND BLOOD *Enigma EST 2126*.....................3	11 wks
14 Dec 91	SWALLOW THIS LIVE *Capitol ESTU 2159* 52	2 wks
6 Mar 93	NATIVE TONGUE *Capitol CDSETU 2190*.....................20	3 wks

POLECATS *UK, male vocal / instrumental group*   **2 wks**

4 Jul 81	POLECATS *Vertigo 6359 057* 28	2 wks

P
241

POLICE *UK, male vocal / instrumental group*   **353 wks**

21 Apr 79	● OUTLANDOS D'AMOUR *A & M AMLH 68502*.....................6	96 wks
13 Oct 79	★ REGGATTA DE BLANC *A & M AMLH 64792* 1	74 wks
11 Oct 80	★ ZENYATTA MONDATTA *A & M AMLH 64831* 1	31 wks
10 Oct 81	★ GHOST IN THE MACHINE *A & M AMLK 63730*.....................1	27 wks
25 Jun 83	★ SYNCHRONICITY *A & M AMLX 63735* 1	48 wks
8 Nov 86	★ EVERY BREATH YOU TAKE – THE SINGLES *A & M EVERY 1* 1	55 wks
10 Oct 92	● GREATEST HITS *A & M 5400302* 10	19 wks
10 Jun 95	LIVE *A & M 540222* 25	3 wks

Su POLLARD *UK, female vocalist*   **3 wks**

22 Nov 86	SU *K-Tel NE 1327* 86	3 wks

Iggy POP *US, male vocalist*   **27 wks**

9 Apr 77	THE IDIOT *RCA Victor PL 12275* 30	3 wks
4 Jun 77	RAW POWER *Embassy 31464* [1] 44	2 wks
1 Oct 77	LUST FOR LIFE *RCA PL 12488* 28	5 wks
19 May 79	NEW VALUES *Arista SPART 1092* 60	4 wks
16 Feb 80	SOLDIER *Arista SPART 1117* 62	2 wks
11 Oct 86	BLAH–BLAH–BLAH *A & M AMA 5145* 43	7 wks
2 Jul 88	INSTINCT *A & M AMA 5198* 61	1 wk
21 Jul 90	BRICK BY BRICK *Virgin America VUSLP 19*.....................50	2 wks
25 Sep 93	AMERICAN CAESAR *Virgin CDVUS 64* 43	1 wk

[1] Iggy and the Stooges

POP WILL EAT ITSELF *UK, male vocal / instrumental group*   **14 wks**

13 May 89	THIS IS THE DAY, THIS IS THE HOUR *RCA PL 74141* 24	2 wks

2 Nov 90	**CURE FOR SANITY** RCA PL 74828	**33**	3 wks
19 Sep 92	**THE LOOKS OR THE LIFESTYLE** RCA 74321102652	**15**	3 wks
6 Mar 93	**WEIRD'S BAR AND GRILL** RCA 74321133432	**44**	1 wk
6 Nov 93	**16 DIFFERENT FLAVOURS OF HELL** RCA 74321153172	**73**	1 wk
1 Oct 94	**DOS DEDOS MIS AMIGOS** Infectious INFECT 10CDX	**11**	2 wks
18 Mar 95	**TWO FINGERS MY FRIENDS** Infectious INFECT 10CDRX	**25**	2 wks

Two Fingers My Friends *is a remixed version of* Dos Dedos Mis Amigos.

POPE JOHN PAUL II *Poland, male pontiff* **8 wks**

3 Jul 82	**JOHN PAUL II THE PILGRIM POPE** BBC REB445	**71**	4 wks
10 Dec 94	**THE ROSARY** Pure Music PMCD 7009	**50**	4 wks

The Rosary *is a double CD or cassette, one with the Rosary in Latin by the Pope, the other featuring its English reading by Father Kilcoyne.*

POPES – *See Shane MacGOWAN and the POPES*

PORNO FOR PYROS *US, male vocal/instrumental group* **3 wks**

8 May 93	**PORNO FOR PYROS** Warner Bros. 9362452282	**13**	3 wks

PORTISHEAD *UK, male/female vocal/instrumental duo* **53 wks**

3 Sep 94	● **DUMMY** Go.Beat 8285222	**2**	53 wks

Nick PORTLOCK – *See ROYAL PHILHARMONIC ORCHESTRA*

Sandy POSEY *US, female vocalist* **1 wk**

11 Mar 67	**BORN A WOMAN** MGM MGMCS 8035	**39**	1 wk

Frank POURCEL *France, male orchestra leader* **7 wks**

20 Nov 71	● **THIS IS POURCEL** Studio Two STWO 7	**8**	7 wks

P
242

Cozy POWELL *UK, male instrumentalist – drums* **8 wks**

26 Jan 80	**OVER THE TOP** Ariola ARL 5038	**34**	3 wks
19 Sep 81	**TILT** Polydor POLD 5047	**58**	4 wks
28 May 83	**OCTOPUSS** Polydor POLD 5093	**86**	1 wk

See also Emerson, Lake and Powell.

Peter POWELL *UK, male exercise instructor* **13 wks**

20 Mar 82	● **KEEP FIT AND DANCE** K-Tel NE 1167	**9**	13 wks

POWER STATION *UK/US, male vocal/instrumental group* **23 wks**

6 Apr 85	**THE POWER STATION** Parlophone POST 1	**12**	23 wks

PRAYING MANTIS *UK, male vocal/instrumental group* **2 wks**

11 Apr 81	**TIME TELLS NO LIES** Arista SPART 1153	**60**	2 wks

PREFAB SPROUT *UK, male/female vocal/instrumental group* **100 wks**

17 Mar 84	**SWOON** Kitchenware KWLP 1	**22**	7 wks
22 Jun 85	**STEVE MCQUEEN** Kitchenware KWLP 3	**21**	35 wks
26 Mar 88	● **FROM LANGLEY PARK TO MEMPHIS** Kitchenware KWLP 9	**5**	24 wks
1 Jul 89	**PROTEST SONGS** Kitchenware KWLP 4	**18**	4 wks
8 Sep 90	● **JORDAN: THE COMEBACK** Kitchenware KWLP 14	**7**	17 wks
11 Jul 92	● **A LIFE OF SURPRISES – THE BEST OF PREFAB SPROUT** Kitchenware 4718862	**3**	13 wks

Elvis PRESLEY *US, male vocalist* **1071 wks**

8 Nov 58	● **ELVIS' GOLDEN RECORDS** RCA RB 16069	**3**	44 wks

8 Nov 58	● KING CREOLE (film soundtrack) *RCA RD 27086* 4	14	wks
4 Apr 59	● ELVIS (ROCK 'N' ROLL NO. 1) *HMV CLP 1093* 4	9	wks
8 Aug 59	● A DATE WITH ELVIS *RCA RD 27128* 4	15	wks
18 Jun 60	★ ELVIS IS BACK *RCA RD 27171* 1	27	wks
18 Jun 60	● ELVIS' GOLDEN RECORDS VOLUME 2 *RCA RD 27159* 4	20	wks
10 Dec 60	★ G.I. BLUES (film soundtrack) *RCA RD 27192* 1	55	wks
20 May 61	● HIS HAND IN MINE *RCA RD 27211* 3	25	wks
4 Nov 61	● SOMETHING FOR EVERYBODY *RCA RD 27224* 2	18	wks
9 Dec 61	★ BLUE HAWAII (film soundtrack) *RCA RD 27238* 1	65	wks
7 Jul 62	★ POT LUCK *RCA RD 27265*...1	25	wks
8 Dec 62	● ROCK 'N' ROLL NO. 2 *RCA RD 7528* 3	17	wks
26 Jan 63	● GIRLS! GIRLS! GIRLS! (film soundtrack) *RCA RD 7534* 2	21	wks
11 May 63	● IT HAPPENED AT THE WORLD'S FAIR (film soundtrack)		
	RCA RD 7565 4	21	wks
28 Dec 63	● FUN IN ACAPULCO (film soundtrack) *RCA RD 7609* 9	14	wks
11 Apr 64	● ELVIS' GOLDEN RECORDS VOLUME 3 *RCA RD 7630* 6	13	wks
4 Jul 64	● KISSIN' COUSINS (film soundtrack) *RCA RD 7645* 5	17	wks
9 Jan 65	● ROUSTABOUT (film soundtrack) *RCA RD 7678* 12	4	wks
1 May 65	● GIRL HAPPY (film soundtrack) *RCA RD 7714* 8	18	wks
25 Sep 65	FLAMING STAR AND SUMMER KISSES *RCA RD 7723* 11	4	wks
4 Dec 65	● ELVIS FOR EVERYBODY *RCA RD 7782* 8	8	wks
15 Jan 66	HAREM HOLIDAY (film soundtrack) *RCA RD 7767* 11	5	wks
30 Apr 66	FRANKIE AND JOHNNY (film soundtrack) *RCA RD 7793*...........11	5	wks
6 Aug 66	● PARADISE HAWAIIAN STYLE (film soundtrack)		
	RCA Victor RD 7810 7	9	wks
26 Nov 66	CALIFORNIA HOLIDAY (film soundtrack) *RCA Victor RD 7820* ..17	6	wks
8 Apr 67	HOW GREAT THOU ART *RCA Victor SF 7867* 11	14	wks
2 Sep 67	DOUBLE TROUBLE (film soundtrack) *RCA Victor SF 7892* 34	1	wk
20 Apr 68	CLAMBAKE (film soundtrack) *RCA Victor SD 7917* 39	1	wk
3 May 69	● ELVIS – NBC TV SPECIAL *RCA RD 8011*..............................2	26	wks
5 Jul 69	● FLAMING STAR *RCA International INTS 1012* 2	14	wks
23 Aug 69	★ FROM ELVIS IN MEMPHIS *RCA SF 8029* 1	13	wks
28 Feb 70	PORTRAIT IN MUSIC (import) *RCA 558* 36	1	wk
14 Mar 70	● FROM MEMPHIS TO VEGAS – FROM VEGAS TO MEMPHIS		
	RCA SF 8080/1 3	16	wks
1 Aug 70	● ON STAGE *RCA SF 8128* 2	18	wks
5 Dec 70	ELVIS' GOLDEN RECORDS VOLUME 1 (re-issue) *RCA SF 8129*....21	11	wks
12 Dec 70	WORLDWIDE 50 GOLD AWARD HITS VOLUME 1		
	RCA LPM 6401 49	2	wks
30 Jan 71	THAT'S THE WAY IT IS *RCA SF 8162* 12	41	wks
10 Apr 71	● ELVIS COUNTRY *RCA SF 8172* 6	9	wks
24 Jul 71	● LOVE LETTERS FROM ELVIS *RCA SF 8202*.........................7	5	wks
7 Aug 71	● C'MON EVERYBODY *RCA International INTS 1286* 5	21	wks
7 Aug 71	YOU'LL NEVER WALK ALONE *RCA Camden CDM 1088* 20	4	wks
25 Sep 71	ALMOST IN LOVE *RCA International INTS 1206* 38	2	wks
4 Dec 71	● ELVIS' CHRISTMAS ALBUM *RCA International INTS 1126* 7	5	wks
18 Dec 71	I GOT LUCKY *RCA International INTS 1322* 26	3	wks
27 May 72	ELVIS NOW *RCA SF 8266* 12	8	wks
3 Jun 72	ROCK AND ROLL (RE-ISSUE OF ROCK 'N' ROLL NO. 1)		
	RCA Victor SF 8233 34	4	wks
3 Jun 72	ELVIS FOR EVERYONE *RCA Victor SF 8232* 48	1	wk
15 Jul 72	● ELVIS AT MADISON SQUARE GARDEN *RCA Victor SF 8296* 3	20	wks
12 Aug 72	HE TOUCHED ME *RCA Victor SF 8275* 38	3	wks
24 Feb 73	ALOHA FROM HAWAII VIA SATELLITE *RCA Victor DPS 2040* ...11	10	wks
15 Sep 73	ELVIS *RCA Victor SF 8378* 16	4	wks
2 Mar 74	A LEGENDARY PERFORMER VOLUME 1 *RCA Victor CPLI 0341*...20	3	wks
25 May 74	GOOD TIMES *RCA Victor APLI 0475* 42	1	wk
7 Sep 74	ELVIS PRESLEY LIVE ON STAGE IN MEMPHIS		
	RCA Victor APLI 0606 44	1	wk
22 Feb 75	PROMISED LAND *RCA Victor APLI 0873* 21	4	wks
14 Jun 75	TODAY *RCA Victor RS 1011* 48	3	wks
5 Jul 75	★ 40 GREATEST HITS *Arcade ADEP 12* 1	38	wks
6 Sep 75	THE ELVIS PRESLEY SUN COLLECTION *RCA Starcall HY 1001* 16	13	wks
19 Jun 76	FROM ELVIS PRESLEY BOULEVARD, MEMPHIS, TENNESSEE		
	RCA Victor RS 1060 29	5	wks
19 Feb 77	ELVIS IN DEMAND *RCA Victor PL 42003* 12	11	wks
27 Aug 77	● MOODY BLUE *RCA PL 12428* 3	15	wks
3 Sep 77	● WELCOME TO MY WORLD *RCA PL 12274* 7	9	wks
3 Sep 77	G.I. BLUES (re-issue) *RCA SF 5078* 14	10	wks
10 Sep 77	ELVIS' GOLDEN RECORDS VOLUME 2 (re-issue) *RCA SF 8151*....27	4	wks

10 Sep 77	HITS OF THE 70'S *RCA LPLI 7527*	30	4 wks
10 Sep 77	BLUE HAWAII (re-issue) *RCA SF 8145*	26	6 wks
10 Sep 77	ELVIS' GOLDEN RECORDS VOLUME 3 (re-issue) *RCA SF 7630*	49	2 wks
10 Sep 77	PICTURES OF ELVIS *RCA Starcall HY 1023*	52	1 wk
8 Oct 77	THE SUN YEARS *Charly SUN 1001*	31	2 wks
15 Oct 77	LOVING YOU *RCA PL 42358*	24	3 wks
19 Nov 77	ELVIS IN CONCERT *RCA PL 02578*	13	11 wks
22 Apr 78	HE WALKS BESIDE ME *RCA PL 12772*	37	1 wk
3 Jun 78	THE '56 SESSIONS VOLUME 1 *RCA PL 42101*	47	4 wks
2 Sep 78	TV SPECIAL *RCA PL 42370*	50	2 wks
11 Nov 78	40 GREATEST HITS (re-issue) *RCA PL 42691*	40	14 wks
3 Feb 79	A LEGENDARY PERFORMER VOLUME 3 *RCA PL 13082*	43	3 wks
5 May 79	OUR MEMORIES OF ELVIS *RCA PL 13279*	72	1 wk
24 Nov 79 ●	LOVE SONGS *K-Tel NE 1062*	4	13 wks
21 Jun 80	ELVIS PRESLEY SINGS LIEBER AND STOLLER		
	RCA International INTS 5031	32	5 wks
23 Aug 80	ELVIS ARON PRESLEY *RCA ELVIS 25*	21	4 wks
23 Aug 80	PARADISE HAWAIIAN STYLE (re-issue)		
	RCA International INTS 5037	53	2 wks
29 Nov 80 ●	INSPIRATION *K-Tel NE 1101*	6	8 wks
14 Mar 81	GUITAR MAN *RCA RCALP 5010*	33	5 wks
9 May 81	THIS IS ELVIS PRESLEY *RCA RCALP 5029*	47	4 wks
28 Nov 81	THE ULTIMATE PERFORMANCE *K-Tel NE 1141*	45	6 wks
13 Feb 82	THE SOUND OF YOUR CRY *RCA RCALP 3060*	31	12 wks
6 Mar 82	ELVIS PRESLEY EP PACK *RCA EP1*	97	1 wk
21 Aug 82	ROMANTIC ELVIS / ROCKIN' ELVIS *RCA RCALP 1000/1*	62	5 wks
18 Dec 82	IT WON'T SEEM LIKE CHRISTMAS WITHOUT YOU		
	RCA INTS 5235	80	1 wk
30 Apr 83	JAILHOUSE ROCK / LOVE IN LAS VEGAS *RCA RCALP 9020*	40	2 wks
20 Aug 83	I WAS THE ONE *RCA RCALP 3105*	83	1 wk
3 Dec 83	A LEGENDARY PERFORMER VOLUME 4 *RCA PL 84848*	91	1 wk
7 Apr 84	I CAN HELP *RCA PL 89287*	71	3 wks
21 Jul 84	THE FIRST LIVE RECORDINGS *RCA International PG 89387*	69	2 wks
26 Jan 85	20 GREATEST HITS VOLUME 2 *RCA International NL 89168*	98	1 wk
25 May 85	RECONSIDER BABY *RCA PL 85418*	92	1 wk
12 Oct 85	BALLADS *Telstar STAR 2264*	23	17 wks
29 Aug 87 ●	PRESLEY – THE ALL TIME GREATEST HITS *RCA PL 90100*	4	22 wks
28 Jan 89	STEREO '57 (ESSENTIAL ELVIS VOLUME 2) *RCA PL 90250*	60	2 wks
21 Jul 90	HITS LIKE NEVER BEFORE (VOLUME 3) *RCA PL 90486*	71	1 wk
1 Sep 90	THE GREAT PERFORMANCES *RCA PL 82227*	62	1 wk
24 Aug 91	COLLECTORS GOLD *RCA PL 90574*	57	1 wk
22 Feb 92 ●	FROM THE HEART – HIS GREATEST LOVE SONGS *RCA PD 90642*	4	18 wks
10 Sep 94 ●	THE ESSENTIAL COLLECTION *RCA 74321228712*	6	25 wks

PRETENDERS *UK / US, female / male vocal / instrumental group*   **153 wks**

19 Jan 80 ★	PRETENDERS *Real RAL 3*	1	35 wks
15 Aug 81 ●	PRETENDERS II *Real SRK 3572*	7	27 wks
21 Jan 84	LEARNING TO CRAWL *Real WX 2*	11	16 wks
1 Nov 86 ●	GET CLOSE *WEA WX 64*	6	28 wks
7 Nov 87 ●	THE SINGLES *WEA WX 135*	6	25 wks
26 May 90	PACKED! *WEA WX 346*	19	5 wks
21 May 94 ●	LAST OF THE INDEPENDENTS *WEA 4509958222*	8	13 wks
28 Oct 95	THE ISLE OF VIEW *WEA 0630120592*	23	4 wks

PRETTY THINGS *UK, male vocal / instrumental group*   **13 wks**

| 27 Mar 65 ● | PRETTY THINGS *Fontana TL 5239* | 6 | 10 wks |
| 27 Jun 70 | PARACHUTE *Harvest SHVL 774* | 43 | 3 wks |

Alan PRICE *UK, male vocalist / instrumentalist – keyboards*   **10 wks**

| 8 Jun 74 ● | BETWEEN TODAY AND YESTERDAY *Warner Bros. K 56032* | 9 | 10 wks |

Charley PRIDE *US, male vocalist*   **17 wks**

10 Apr 71	CHARLEY PRIDE SPECIAL *RCA SF 8171*	29	1 wk
28 May 77	SHE'S JUST AN OLD LOVE TURNED MEMORY		
	RCA Victor PL 12261	34	2 wks

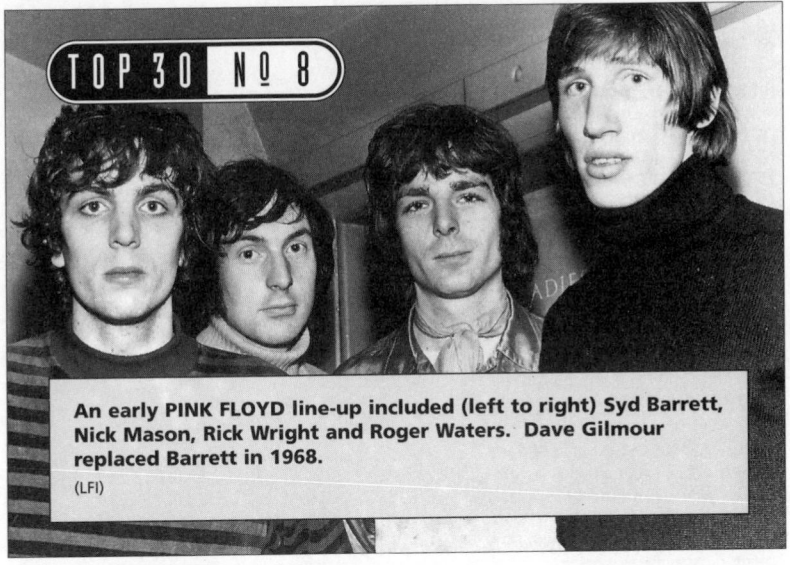

TOP 30 Nº 8

An early PINK FLOYD line-up included (left to right) Syd Barrett, Nick Mason, Rick Wright and Roger Waters. Dave Gilmour replaced Barrett in 1968.

(LFI)

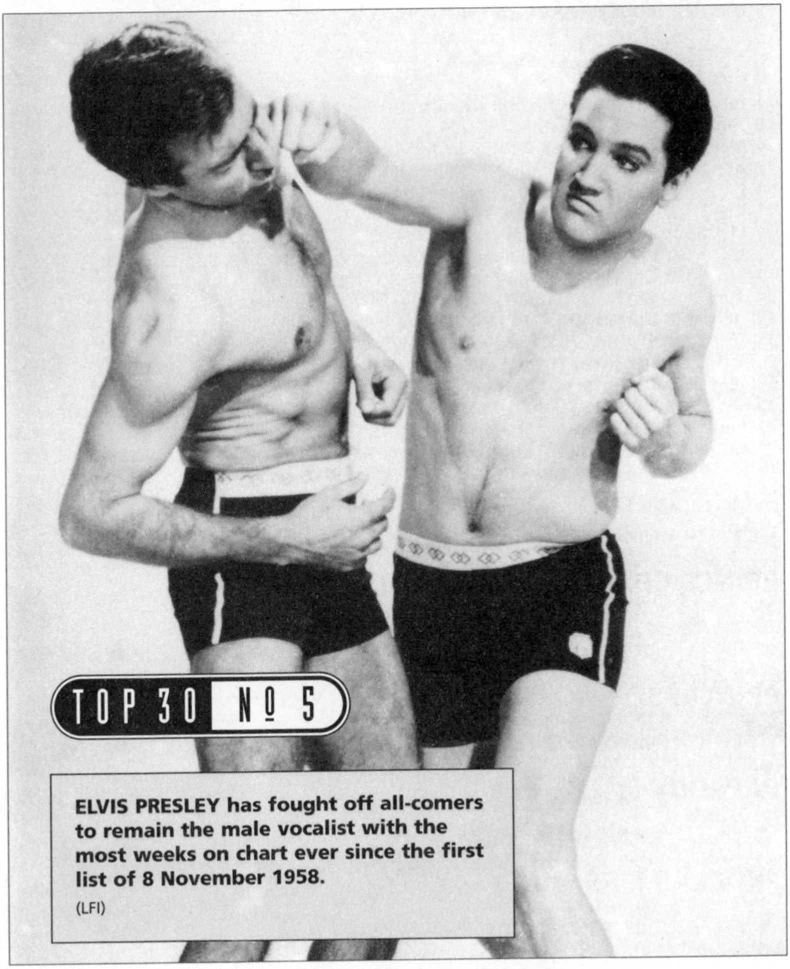

TOP 30 Nº 5

ELVIS PRESLEY has fought off all-comers to remain the male vocalist with the most weeks on chart ever since the first list of 8 November 1958.

(LFI)

P
245

3 Jun 78	**SOMEONE LOVES YOU HONEY** RCA PL 12478 48	2 wks
26 Jan 80 ●	**GOLDEN COLLECTION** K-Tel NE 1056 6	12 wks

Maxi PRIEST UK, male vocalist
35 wks

6 Dec 86	**INTENTIONS** 10 DIX 32 96	1 wk
5 Dec 87	**MAXI** 10 DIX 64 25	15 wks
15 Jul 90	**BONAFIDE** 10 DIX 92 11	13 wks
9 Nov 91	**BEST OF ME** 10 DIX 111 23	5 wks
14 Nov 92	**FE REAL** 10 DIXCD 113 60	1 wk

PRIMAL SCREAM UK, male vocal / instrumental group
36 wks

17 Oct 87	**SONIC FLOWER GROOVE** Elevation ELV 2 62	1 wk
5 Oct 91 ●	**SCREAMADELICA** Creation CRELP 076 8	17 wks
9 Apr 94 ●	**GIVE OUT BUT DON'T GIVE UP** Creation CRECD 146 2	18 wks

PRIMITIVES UK, male / female vocal / instrumental group
13 wks

9 Apr 88 ●	**LOVELY** RCA PL 71688 6	10 wks
2 Sep 89	**LAZY 86–88** Lazy 15 73	1 wk
28 Oct 89	**PURE** RCA PL 74252 33	2 wks

PRIMUS US, male vocal / instrumental group
1 wk

8 May 93	**PORK SODA** Interscope 75679922572 56	1 wk

⚥ PRINCE US, male vocalist
409 wks

P
246

21 Jul 84 ●	**PURPLE RAIN (film soundtrack)** Warner Bros. 9251101 [1] 7	91 wks
8 Sep 84	**1999** Warner Bros. 923720 30	21 wks
4 May 85 ●	**AROUND THE WORLD IN A DAY** Warner Bros. 92–5286–1 [1] 5	20 wks
12 Apr 86 ●	**PARADE – MUSIC FROM 'UNDER THE CHERRY MOON'** **(film soundtrack)** Warner Bros. WX 39 [1] 4	26 wks
11 Apr 87 ●	**SIGN 'O' THE TIMES** Paisley Park WX 88 4	32 wks
21 May 88 ★	**LOVESEXY** Paisley Park WX 164 1	32 wks
1 Jul 89 ★	**BATMAN (film soundtrack)** Warner Bros. WX 281 1	20 wks
1 Sep 90 ★	**GRAFFITI BRIDGE** Paisley Park WX 361 1	8 wks
24 Aug 91	**GETT OFF (import)** Paisley Park 9401382 33	3 wks
12 Oct 91 ●	**DIAMONDS AND PEARLS** Paisley Park WX 432 [2] 2	57 wks
17 Oct 92 ★	**SYMBOL** Paisley Park 9362450372 [2] 1	21 wks
25 Sep 93 ●	**THE HITS / THE B–SIDES** Paisley Park 9362454402 4	7 wks
25 Sep 93 ●	**THE HITS 1** Paisley Park 9362454312 5	27 wks
25 Sep 93 ●	**THE HITS 2** Paisley Park 9362454352 5	28 wks
27 Aug 94 ★	**COME** Warner Bros. 9362457002 1	8 wks
3 Dec 94	**THE BLACK ALBUM** Warner Bros. 9362457932 36	3 wks
7 Oct 95 ●	**THE GOLD EXPERIENCE** Warner Bros. 9362459992 [3] 4	5 wks

[1] Prince and the Revolution [2] Prince and the New Power Generation [3] ⚥

See also New Power Generation.

PRINCE CHARLES and the CITY BEAT BAND
US, male vocalist with male vocal / instrumental group
1 wk

30 Apr 83	**STONE KILLERS** Virgin V 2271 84	1 wk

PRINCESS UK, female vocalist
14 wks

17 May 86	**PRINCESS** Supreme SU1 15	14 wks

PJ PROBY US, male vocalist
3 wks

27 Feb 65	**I'M PJ PROBY** Liberty LBY 1235 16	3 wks

PROCLAIMERS UK, male vocal / instrumental duo
54 wks

9 May 87	**THIS IS THE STORY** Chrysalis CHR 1602 43	21 wks

| 24 Sep 88 | ● SUNSHINE ON LEITH Chrysalis CHR 1668 | 6 | 27 wks |
| 19 Mar 94 | ● HIT THE HIGHWAY Chrysalis CDCHR 6066 | 8 | 6 wks |

PROCOL HARUM UK, male vocal/instrumental group **11 wks**

19 Jul 69	A SALTY DOG Regal Zonophone SLRZ 1009	27	2 wks
27 Jun 70	HOME Regal Zonophone SLRZ 1014	49	1 wk
3 Jul 71	BROKEN BARRICADES Island ILPS 9158	42	1 wk
6 May 72	A WHITER SHADE OF PALE / A SALTY DOG (re-issue) Fly Double Back TOOFA 7/8	26	4 wks
6 May 72	PROCOL HARUM IN CONCERT WITH THE EDMONTON SYMPHONY ORCHESTRA Chrysalis CHR 1004	48	1 wk
30 Aug 75	PROCOL'S NINTH Chrysalis CHR 1080	41	2 wks

A Whiter Shade Of Pale / A Salty Dog *is a double re-issue, although* A Whiter Shade Of Pale *was not previously a hit. The Edmonton Symphony Orchestra is a Canadian orchestra.*

PRODIGY UK, male producer – Liam Howlett **75 wks**

| 10 Oct 92 | EXPERIENCE XL XLCD 110 | 12 | 25 wks |
| 16 Jul 94 | ★ MUSIC FOR THE JILTED GENERATION XL XLCD 114 | 1 | 50 wks |

PROJECT D UK, male instrumentalist **18 wks**

| 17 Feb 90 | THE SYNTHESIZER ALBUM Telstar STAR 2371 | 13 | 11 wks |
| 29 Sep 90 | THE SYNTHESIZER ALBUM 2 Telstar STAR 2428 | 25 | 7 wks |

PRONG US, male vocal/instrumental group **1 wk**

| 12 Feb 94 | CLEANSING Epic 4747962 | 71 | 1 wk |

PROPAGANDA Germany, male/female vocal/instrumental group **16 wks**

13 Jul 85	A SECRET WISH ZTT ZTTIQ 3	16	12 wks
23 Nov 85	WISHFUL THINKING ZTT ZTTIQ 20	82	2 wks
9 Jun 90	1234 Virgin V 2625	46	2 wks

Dorothy PROVINE US, female vocalist **49 wks**

| 2 Dec 61 | ● THE ROARING TWENTIES – SONGS FROM THE TV SERIES Warner Bros. WM 4035 | 3 | 42 wks |
| 10 Feb 62 | ● VAMP OF THE ROARING TWENTIES Warner Bros. WM 4053 | 9 | 7 wks |

PSYCHEDELIC FURS UK, male vocal/instrumental group **39 wks**

15 Mar 80	PSYCHEDELIC FURS CBS 84084	18	6 wks
23 May 81	TALK TALK TALK CBS 84892	30	9 wks
2 Oct 82	FOREVER NOW CBS 85909	20	6 wks
19 May 84	MIRROR MOVES CBS 25950	15	9 wks
14 Feb 87	MIDNIGHT TO MIDNIGHT CBS 450 2561	12	5 wks
13 Aug 88	ALL OF THIS AND NOTHING CBS 461101	67	2 wks
18 Nov 89	BOOK OF DAYS CBS 465982 1	74	1 wk
13 Jul 91	WORLD OUTSIDE East West WX 422	68	1 wk

PUBLIC ENEMY US, male rap group **32 wks**

30 Jul 88	● IT TAKES A NATION OF MILLIONS TO HOLD US BACK Def Jam 4624151	8	9 wks
28 Apr 90	● FEAR OF A BLACK PLANET Def Jam 4662811	4	10 wks
19 Oct 91	● APOCALYPSE '91 – THE ENEMY STRIKES BLACK Def Jam 4687511	8	7 wks
3 Oct 92	GREATEST MISSES Def Jam 4720312	14	3 wks
3 Sep 94	MUSE SICK-N-HOUR MESS AGE Def Jam 5233622	12	3 wks

PUBLIC IMAGE LTD. UK, male vocal/instrumental group **51 wks**

| 23 Dec 78 | PUBLIC IMAGE Virgin V 2114 | 22 | 11 wks |

Jarvis Cocker, a creative seed of PULP, poses with a source of pulp.
(Andrew Catlin/LFI)

British Hit Albums Part One

Date of chart entry/Title & catalogue no./Peak position reached/Weeks on chart

★ Number One   ● Top Ten   † still on chart at 30 Dec 1995   □ credited to act billed in footnote

8 Dec 79	**METAL BOX** *Virgin METAL 1*	**18**	8	wks
8 Mar 80	**SECOND EDITION OF PIL** *Virgin VD 2512*	**46**	2	wks
22 Nov 80	**PARIS IN THE SPRING** *Virgin V 2183*	**61**	2	wks
18 Apr 81	**FLOWERS OF ROMANCE** *Virgin V 2189*	**11**	5	wks
8 Oct 83	**LIVE IN TOKYO** *Virgin VGD 3508*	**28**	6	wks
21 Jul 84	**THIS IS WHAT YOU WANT . . . THIS IS WHAT YOU GET**			
	Virgin V 2309	**56**	2	wks
15 Feb 86	**ALBUM / CASSETTE** *Virgin V 2366*	**14**	6	wks
26 Sep 87	**HAPPY?** *Virgin V 2455*	**40**	2	wks
10 Jun 89	**9** *Virgin V 2588*	**36**	2	wks
10 Nov 90	**THE GREATEST HITS SO FAR** *Virgin V 2644*	**20**	3	wks
7 Mar 92	**THAT WHAT IS NOT** *Virgin CDV 2681*	**46**	2	wks

Gary PUCKETT and the UNION GAP
US, male vocalist, male vocal / instrumental group   **4 wks**

29 Jun 68	**UNION GAP** *CBS 63342*	**24**	4	wks

PULP *UK, male / female vocal / instrumental group*   **47 wks**

30 Apr 94	● **HIS 'N' HERS** *Island CID 8025*	**9**	39	wks
11 Nov 95	★ **DIFFERENT CLASS** *Island CID 8041*	**1†**	8	wks

Q-TIPS *UK, male vocal / instrumental group*   **1 wk**

30 Aug 80	**Q-TIPS** *Chrysalis CHR 1255*	**50**	1	wk

Suzi QUATRO *US, female vocalist / instrumentalist – guitar*   **13 wks**

13 Oct 73	**SUZI QUATRO** *RAK SRAK 505*	**32**	4	wks
26 Apr 80	● **SUZI QUATRO'S GREATEST HITS** *RAK EMTV 24*	**4**	9	wks

QUEDO BRASS – See CHAQUITO ORCHESTRA

QUEEN *UK, male vocal / instrumental group*   **1111 wks**

23 Mar 74	● **QUEEN 2** *EMI EMA 767*	**5**	29	wks
30 Mar 74	**QUEEN** *EMI EMC 3006*	**24**	18	wks
23 Nov 74	● **SHEER HEART ATTACK** *EMI EMC 3061*	**2**	42	wks
13 Dec 75	★ **A NIGHT AT THE OPERA** *EMI EMTC 103*	**1**	50	wks
25 Dec 76	★ **A DAY AT THE RACES** *EMI EMTC 104*	**1**	24	wks
12 Nov 77	● **NEWS OF THE WORLD** *EMI EMA 784*	**4**	20	wks
25 Nov 78	● **JAZZ** *EMI EMA 788*	**2**	27	wks
7 Jul 79	● **LIVE KILLERS** *EMI EMSP 330*	**3**	27	wks
12 Jul 80	★ **THE GAME** *EMI EMA 795*	**1**	18	wks
20 Dec 80	● **FLASH GORDON (film soundtrack)** *EMI EMC 3351*	**10**	15	wks
7 Nov 81	★ **GREATEST HITS** *Parlophone EMYV 30*	**1†**	426	wks
15 May 82	● **HOT SPACE** *EMI EMA 797*	**4**	19	wks
10 Mar 84	● **THE WORKS** *EMI EMC 240014*	**2**	93	wks
14 Jun 86	★ **A KIND OF MAGIC** *EMI EU 3509*	**1**	63	wks
13 Dec 86	● **LIVE MAGIC** *EMI EMC 3519*	**3**	43	wks
3 Jun 89	★ **THE MIRACLE** *Parlophone PCSD 107*	**1**	32	wks
16 Dec 89	**QUEEN AT THE BEEB** *Band Of Joy BOJLP 001*	**67**	1	wk
16 Feb 91	★ **INNUENDO** *Parlophone PCSD 115*	**1**	37	wks
9 Nov 91	★ **GREATEST HITS II** *Parlophone PMTV 2*	**1†**	98	wks

Since the death of Freddie Mercury in 1991, QUEEN have overtaken Simon and Garfunkel to become the all-time number two act.

(Hulton Deutsch)

TOP 30 N_0 2

6 Jun 92	● **LIVE AT WEMBLEY '86** Parlophone CDPCSP 725 ....**2**	15 wks
19 Nov 94	**GREATEST HITS I AND II (re-issue)** Parlophone CDPCSD 161 ......**37**	7 wks
18 Nov 95	★ **MADE IN HEAVEN** Parlophone CDPCSD 167 ....**1†**	7 wks

The Works changed label number during its run to EMI WORK 1.

QUEENSRYCHE US, male vocal/instrumental group   **11 wks**

29 Sep 84	**THE WARNING** EMI America EJ 2402201................................**100**	1 wk
26 Jul 86	**RAGE FOR ORDER** EMI America AML 3105 ....**66**	1 wk
4 Jun 88	**OPERATION MINDCRIME** Manhattan MTL 1023 ....**58**	3 wks
22 Sep 90	**EMPIRE** EMI-USA MTL 1058 ....**13**	3 wks
22 Oct 94	**PROMISED LAND** EMI CDMTL 1081................................**13**	3 wks

QUIET RIOT US, male vocal/instrumental group   **1 wk**

4 Aug 84	**CONDITION CRITICAL** Epic EPC 26075................................**71**	1 wk

QUINTESSENCE UK/Australia, male vocal/instrumental group   **6 wks**

27 Jun 70	**QUINTESSENCE** Island ILPS 9128 ....**22**	4 wks
3 Apr 71	**DIVE DEEP** Island ILPS 9143 ....**43**	1 wk
27 May 72	**SELF** RCA Victor SF 8273 ....**50**	1 wk

QUIREBOYS UK, male vocal/instrumental group   **17 wks**

10 Feb 90	● **A BIT OF WHAT YOU FANCY** Parlophone PCS 7335 ....**2**	15 wks
27 Mar 93	**BITTER SWEET AND TWISTED** Parlophone CDPCSD 120................**31**	2 wks

QUIVER – See SUTHERLAND BROTHERS and QUIVER

Harry RABINOWITZ – See ROYAL PHILHARMONIC ORCHESTRA

RACING CARS UK, male vocal/instrumental group   **6 wks**

19 Feb 77	**DOWNTOWN TONIGHT** Chrysalis CHR 1099 ....**39**	6 wks

RADIOHEAD UK, male vocal/instrumental group   **51 wks**

6 Mar 93	**PABLO HONEY** Parlophone CDPCS 7360 ....**25**	16 wks
25 Mar 95	● **THE BENDS** Parlophone CDPCS 7372 ....**6†**	36 wks

Gerry RAFFERTY UK, male vocalist   **89 wks**

25 Feb 78	● **CITY TO CITY** United Artists UAS 30104 ....**6**	37 wks
2 Jun 79	● **NIGHT OWL** United Artists UAK 30238 ....**9**	24 wks
26 Apr 80	**SNAKES AND LADDERS** United Artists UAK 30298 ....**15**	9 wks
25 Sep 82	**SLEEPWALKING** Liberty LBG 30352................................**39**	4 wks
21 May 88	**NORTH AND SOUTH** London LONLP 55................................**43**	4 wks
13 Feb 93	**A WING AND A PRAYER** A & M 5174952................................**73**	1 wk
28 Oct 95	**ONE MORE DREAM – THE VERY BEST OF GERRY RAFFERTY** PolyGram TV 5292792 ....**17**	9 wks

RAGE AGAINST THE MACHINE
US, male vocal/instrumental group   **42 wks**

13 Feb 93	**RAGE AGAINST THE MACHINE** Epic 4722242 ....**17**	42 wks

RAGGA TWINS UK, male vocal/instrumental duo   **5 wks**

1 Jun 91	**REGGAE OWES ME MONEY** Shut Up And Dance SUADLP 2 ....**26**	5 wks

RAH BAND UK, male/female vocal/instrumental group   **6 wks**

6 Apr 85	**MYSTERY** RCA PL 70640	60	6 wks

RAILWAY CHILDREN UK, male vocal/instrumental group   **3 wks**

21 May 88	**RECURRENCE** Virgin V 2525	96	1 wk
16 Mar 91	**NATIVE PLACE** Virgin V 2627	59	2 wks

RAIN PARADE US, male vocal/instrumental group   **1 wk**

29 Jun 85	**BEYOND THE SUNSET** Island IMA 17	78	1 wk

RAIN TREE CROW UK, male vocal/instrumental group   **3 wks**

20 Apr 91	**RAIN TREE CROW** Virgin V 2659	24	3 wks

RAINBOW UK, male vocal/instrumental group   **163 wks**

13 Sep 75	**RITCHIE BLACKMORE'S RAINBOW** Oyster OYA 2001 [1]	11	6 wks
5 Jun 76	**RAINBOW RISING** Polydor 2490 137 [1]	11	33 wks
30 Jul 77	● **ON STAGE** Polydor 2657 016...	7	10 wks
6 May 78	● **LONG LIVE ROCK 'N' ROLL** Polydor POLD 5002	7	12 wks
18 Aug 79	● **DOWN TO EARTH** Polydor POLD 5023	6	37 wks
21 Feb 81	● **DIFFICULT TO CURE** Polydor POLD 5036	3	22 wks
8 Aug 81	**RITCHIE BLACKMORE'S RAINBOW (re-issue)**		
	Polydor 2940141 [1]	91	2 wks
21 Nov 81	**BEST OF RAINBOW** Polydor POLDV 2	14	17 wks
24 Apr 82	● **STRAIGHT BETWEEN THE EYES** Polydor POLD 5056	5	14 wks
17 Sep 83	**BENT OUT OF SHAPE** Polydor POLD 5116................................	11	6 wks
8 Mar 86	**FINYL VINYL** Polydor PODV 8	31	4 wks

[1] Ritchie Blackmore's Rainbow

Bonnie RAITT US, female vocalist/instrumentalist – guitar   **14 wks**

28 Apr 90	**NICK OF TIME** Capitol EST 2095.....................................	51	5 wks
6 Jul 91	**LUCK OF THE DRAW** Capitol EST 2145	38	3 wks
16 Apr 94	**LONGING IN THEIR HEARTS** Capitol CDEST 2227	26	5 wks
25 Nov 95	**ROAD TESTED** Capitol CDEST 2274	69	1 wk

RAKIM – See Eric B. and RAKIM

RAMONES US, male vocal/instrumental group   **29 wks**

23 Apr 77	**LEAVE HOME** Philips 9103 254	45	1 wk
24 Dec 77	**ROCKET TO RUSSIA** Sire 9103 255....................................	60	2 wks
7 Oct 78	**ROAD TO RUIN** Sire SRK 6063	32	2 wks
16 Jun 79	**IT'S ALIVE** Sire SRK 26074..	27	8 wks
19 Jan 80	**END OF THE CENTURY** Sire SRK 6077	14	8 wks
26 Jan 85	**TOO TOUGH TO DIE** Beggars Banquet BEGA 59..................	63	3 wks
31 May 86	**ANIMAL BOY** Beggars Banquet BEGA 70	38	2 wks
10 Oct 87	**HALFWAY TO SANITY** Beggars Banquet BEGA 89..............	78	1 wk
19 Aug 89	**BRAIN DRAIN** Chrysalis CHR 1725	75	1 wk
8 Jul 95	**¡ADIOS AMIGOS!** Chrysalis CDCHR 6104	62	1 wk

RANCID US, male vocal/instrumental group   **1 wk**

2 Sep 95	**. . . AND OUT COME THE WOLVES** Epitaph 864442	55	1 wk

RANGE – See Bruce HORNSBY and the RANGE

Shabba RANKS Jamaica, male rapper   **10 wks**

22 Jun 91	**AS RAW AS EVER** Epic 4681021...	51	2 wks
22 Aug 92	**ROUGH AND READY VOLUME 1** Epic 4714422	71	2 wks
24 Apr 93	**X–TRA NAKED** Epic 4723332	38	6 wks

Roland RAT SUPERSTAR *UK, male rat vocalist* **3 wks**

15 Dec 84	**THE CASSETTE OF THE ALBUM** Rodent RATL 1001 ....**67**	3 wks

RATT *US, male vocal / instrumental group* **5 wks**

13 Jul 85	**INVASION OF YOUR PRIVACY** Atlantic 7812571 ....**50**	2 wks
25 Oct 86	**DANCING UNDERCOVER** Atlantic 781 6831 ....**51**	1 wk
12 Nov 88	**REACH FOR THE SKY** Atlantic 781929 ....**82**	1 wk
8 Sep 90	**DETONATOR** Atlantic 7567821271 ....**55**	1 wk

Mark RATTRAY *UK, male vocalist* **8 wks**

8 Dec 90	**SONGS OF THE MUSICALS** Telstar STAR 2458 ....**46**	7 wks
10 Oct 92	**THE MAGIC OF THE MUSICALS** Quality Television QTV 013 1 ..**55**	1 wk

1 Marti Webb and Mark Rattray

RAVEN *UK, male vocal / instrumental group* **3 wks**

17 Oct 81	**ROCK UNTIL YOU DROP** Neat NEAT 1001 ....**63**	3 wks

Simon RAYMOND – *See Harold BUDD/Liz FRASER/Robin GUTHRIE/Simon RAYMOND*

Chris REA *UK, male vocalist* **331 wks**

28 Apr 79	**DELTICS** Magnet MAG 5028 ....**54**	3 wks
12 Apr 80	**TENNIS** Magnet MAG 5032 ....**60**	1 wk
3 Apr 82	**CHRIS REA** Magnet MAGL 5040 ....**52**	4 wks
18 Jun 83	**WATER SIGN** Magnet MAGL 5048 ....**64**	2 wks
21 Apr 84	**WIRED TO THE MOON** Magnet MAGL 5057 ....**35**	7 wks
25 May 85	**SHAMROCK DIARIES** Magnet MAGL 5062 ....**15**	14 wks
26 Apr 86	**ON THE BEACH** Magnet MAGL 5069 ....**11**	37 wks
26 Sep 87	● **DANCING WITH STRANGERS** Magnet MAGL 5071 ....**2**	46 wks
13 Aug 88	**ON THE BEACH (re-issue)** WEA WX 191 ....**37**	10 wks
29 Oct 88	● **NEW LIGHT THROUGH OLD WINDOWS** WEA WX 200 ....**5**	51 wks
11 Nov 89	★ **THE ROAD TO HELL** WEA WX 317 ....**1**	76 wks
9 Mar 91	★ **AUBERGE** East West 9031735801 ....**1**	37 wks
14 Nov 92	● **GOD'S GREAT BANANA SKIN** East West 4509909952 ....**4**	15 wks
13 Nov 93	● **ESPRESSO LOGIC** East West 4509943112 ....**8**	10 wks
5 Nov 94	● **THE BEST OF CHRIS REA** East West 4509980402 ....**3**	18 wks

Eddi READER *UK, female vocalist* **14 wks**

7 Mar 92	**MIRMAMA** RCA PD 75156 ....**34**	2 wks
2 Jul 94	● **EDDI READER** Blanco Y Negro 4509961772 ....**4**	12 wks

REAL McCOY *Germany / US, male / female vocal / instrumental group* **5 wks**

20 May 95	● **ANOTHER NIGHT** Logic 74321280972 ....**6**	5 wks

REAL PEOPLE *UK, male vocal / instrumental group* **1 wk**

18 May 91	**THE REAL PEOPLE** Columbia 4680841 ....**59**	1 wk

REAL THING *UK, male vocal / instrumental group* **17 wks**

6 Nov 76	**REAL THING** Pye NSPL 18507 ....**34**	3 wks
7 Apr 79	**CAN YOU FEEL THE FORCE** Pye NSPH 18601 ....**73**	1 wk
10 May 80	**20 GREATEST HITS** K-Tel NE 1073 ....**56**	2 wks
12 Jul 86	**BEST OF THE REAL THING** West Five NRT 1 ....**24**	11 wks

REBEL MC *UK, male rapper* **11 wks**

28 Apr 90	**REBEL MUSIC** Desire LUVLP 5...**18**	7 wks
13 Jul 91	**BLACK MEANING GOOD** Desire LUVLP 12 ....**23**	4 wks

REBEL ROUSERS - See Cliff BENNETT and the REBEL ROUSERS

Ivan REBROFF USSR, male vocalist   **4 wks**

| 16 Jun 90 | **THE VERY BEST OF IVAN REBROFF** BBC REB 778 ....**57** | 4 wks |

RED BOX UK, male vocal / instrumental duo   **4 wks**

| 6 Dec 86 | **THE CIRCLE AND THE SQUARE** Sire WX 79 ....**73** | 4 wks |

RED HOT CHILI PEPPERS US, male vocal / instrumental group   **67 wks**

12 Oct 91	**BLOOD SUGAR SEX MAGIK** Warner Bros. WX 441 ....**25**	52 wks
17 Oct 92	**WHAT HITS!?** EMI USA CDMTL 1071 ....**23**	6 wks
19 Nov 94	**OUT IN L.A.** EMI CDMTL 1082 ....**61**	1 wk
23 Sep 95	● **ONE HOT MINUTE** Warner Bros. 9362457332 ....**2**	8 wks

RED HOUSE PAINTERS US, male vocal / instrumental group   **2 wks**

| 5 Jun 93 | **RED HOUSE PAINTERS** 4AD DAD 3008CD ....**63** | 1 wk |
| 30 Oct 93 | **RED HOUSE PAINTERS** 4AD CAD 3016CD....................**68** | 1 wk |

The identically titled albums are different.

RED NOISE – See Bill NELSON

Sharon REDD US, female vocalist   **5 wks**

| 23 Oct 82 | **REDD HOTT** Prelude PRL 25056 ....**59** | 5 wks |

Otis REDDING US, male vocalist   **220 wks**

19 Feb 66	● **OTIS BLUE** Atlantic ATL 5041 ....**6**	21 wks
23 Apr 66	**SOUL BALLADS** Atlantic ATL 5029....................**30**	1 wk
23 Jul 66	**SOUL ALBUM** Atlantic 587011 ....**22**	9 wks
21 Jan 67	**OTIS REDDING'S DICTIONARY OF SOUL** Atlantic 588050 ....**23**	16 wks
21 Jan 67	● **OTIS BLUE (re-issue)** Atlantic 587036 ....**7**	54 wks
29 Apr 67	**PAIN IN MY HEART** Atlantic 587042 ....**28**	9 wks
1 Jul 67	**KING AND QUEEN** Atlantic 589007 [1] **18**	17 wks
10 Feb 68	● **HISTORY OF OTIS REDDING** Volt S 418 ....**2**	43 wks
30 Mar 68	**OTIS REDDING IN EUROPE** Stax 589016 ....**14**	16 wks
1 Jun 68	★ **DOCK OF THE BAY** Stax 231001 ....**1**	15 wks
12 Oct 68	**IMMORTAL OTIS REDDING** Atlantic 588113 ....**19**	8 wks
11 Sep 93	**DOCK OF THE BAY – THE DEFINITIVE COLLECTION (re-issue)** Atlantic 9548317092 ....**50**	11 wks

[1] Otis Redding and Carla Thomas

Helen REDDY Australia, female vocalist   **27 wks**

| 8 Feb 75 | **FREE AND EASY** Capitol EST 11348....................**17** | 9 wks |
| 14 Feb 76 | ● **THE BEST OF HELEN REDDY** Capitol EST 11467................**5** | 18 wks |

REDHEAD KINGPIN and the FBI US, male vocalist   **3 wks**

| 9 Sep 89 | **A SHADE OF RED** 10 DIX 85................**35** | 3 wks |

REDSKINS UK, male vocal / instrumental duo   **4 wks**

| 22 Mar 86 | **NEITHER WASHINGTON, NOR MOSCOW** Decca FLP 1 ....**31** | 4 wks |

Dan REED NETWORK US, male vocal / instrumental group   **6 wks**

| 4 Nov 89 | **SLAM** Mercury 8388681................**66** | 2 wks |
| 27 Jul 91 | **THE HEAT** Mercury 8488551 ....**15** | 4 wks |

Lou REED US, male vocalist   **76 wks**

| 21 Apr 73 | **TRANSFORMER** RCA Victor LSP 4807................**13** | 25 wks |

ALPHABETICALLY BY ARTIST

British Hit Albums Part One

Date of chart entry/Title & catalogue no./Peak position reached/Weeks on chart

★ Number One   ● Top Ten   † still on chart at 30 Dec 1995   ☐ credited to act billed in footnote

20 Oct 73	● **BERLIN** *RCA Victor RS 1002* **7**	5 wks
16 Mar 74	**ROCK 'N' ROLL ANIMAL** *RCA Victor APLI 0472* **26**	1 wk
14 Feb 76	**CONEY ISLAND BABY** *RCA Victor RS 1035*.................**52**	1 wk
3 Jul 82	**TRANSFORMER (re-issue)** *RCA INTS 5061* **91**	2 wks
9 Jun 84	**NEW SENSATIONS** *RCA PL 84998* **92**	1 wk
24 May 86	**MISTRIAL** *RCA PL 87190* **69**	1 wk
28 Jan 89	● **NEW YORK** *Sire WX 246* **14**	22 wks
7 Oct 89	**RETRO** *RCA PL 90389* **29**	5 wks
5 May 90	**SONGS FOR DRELLA** *Sire WX 345* [1] **22**	5 wks
25 Jan 92	● **MAGIC AND LOSS** *Sire 7599266622* **6**	6 wks
28 Oct 95	**THE BEST OF LOU REED AND THE VELVET UNDERGROUND**	
	Global Television RADCD 21 [2] **56**	2 wks

[1] Lou Reed and John Cale [2] Lou Reed and the Velvet Underground

Don REEDMAN – *See Jeff JARRATT and Don REEDMAN*

REEF *UK, male vocal / instrumental group*   **11 wks**

1 Jul 95	● **REPLENISH** *Sony S2 4806982*.................**9**	11 wks

REEL 2 REAL featuring the MAD STUNTMAN
US, male vocal / instrumental duo   **8 wks**

22 Oct 94	● **MOVE IT!** *Positiva CDTIVA 1003* **8**	8 wks

Jim REEVES *US, male vocalist*   **391 wks**

28 Mar 64	● **GOOD 'N' COUNTRY** *RCA Camden CDN 5114* **10**	35 wks
9 May 64	● **GENTLEMAN JIM** *RCA RD 7541* **3**	23 wks
15 Aug 64	● **A TOUCH OF VELVET** *RCA RD 7521* **8**	9 wks
15 Aug 64	**INTERNATIONAL JIM REEVES** *RCA RD 7577* **11**	15 wks
22 Aug 64	**HE'LL HAVE TO GO** *RCA RD 27176* **16**	4 wks
29 Aug 64	**THE INTIMATE JIM REEVES** *RCA RD 27193* **12**	4 wks
29 Aug 64	● **GOD BE WITH YOU** *RCA RD 7636* **10**	10 wks
5 Sep 64	● **MOONLIGHT AND ROSES** *RCA RD 7639* **2**	52 wks
19 Sep 64	**COUNTRY SIDE OF JIM REEVES** *RCA Camden CDN 5100*.................**12**	5 wks
26 Sep 64	**WE THANK THEE** *RCA RD 7637* **17**	3 wks
28 Nov 64	● **TWELVE SONGS OF CHRISTMAS** *RCA RD 7663* **3**	17 wks
30 Jan 65	● **BEST OF JIM REEVES** *RCA RD 7666* **3**	47 wks
10 Apr 65	**HAVE I TOLD YOU LATELY THAT I LOVE YOU**	
	RCA Camden CDN 5122 ....**12**	5 wks
22 May 65	**THE JIM REEVES WAY** *RCA RD 7694*.................**16**	4 wks
5 Nov 66	● **DISTANT DRUMS** *RCA Victor RD 7814*.................**2**	34 wks
18 Jan 69	**A TOUCH OF SADNESS** *RCA SF 7978*.................**15**	5 wks
5 Jul 69	★ **ACCORDING TO MY HEART** *RCA International INTS 1013* **1**	14 wks
23 Aug 69	**JIM REEVES AND SOME FRIENDS** *RCA SF 8022* **24**	4 wks
29 Nov 69	**ON STAGE** *RCA SF 8047*.................**13**	4 wks
26 Dec 70	**MY CATHEDRAL** *RCA SF 8146* **48**	2 wks
3 Jul 71	**JIM REEVES WRITES YOU A RECORD** *RCA SF 8176* **47**	2 wks
7 Aug 71	● **JIM REEVES' GOLDEN RECORDS** *RCA International INTS 1070*......**9**	21 wks
14 Aug 71	● **THE INTIMATE JIM REEVES (re-issue)**	
	RCA International INTS 1256.................**8**	15 wks
21 Aug 71	**GIRLS I HAVE KNOWN** *RCA International INTS 1140* **35**	5 wks
27 Nov 71	● **TWELVE SONGS OF CHRISTMAS (re-issue)**	
	RCA International INTS 1188 ....**3**	6 wks
27 Nov 71	**A TOUCH OF VELVET (re-issue)** *RCA International INTS 1089*......**49**	2 wks
15 Apr 72	**MY FRIEND** *RCA SF 8258*.................**32**	5 wks
20 Sep 75	★ **40 GOLDEN GREATS** *Arcade ADEP 16*.................**1**	25 wks
6 Sep 80	**COUNTRY GENTLEMAN** *K-Tel NE 1088* **53**	4 wks
8 Aug 92	● **THE DEFINITIVE JIM REEVES** *Arcade ARC 94982*.................**9**	10 wks

---

Vic REEVES *UK, male vocalist*   **9 wks**

16 Nov 91	**I WILL CURE YOU** *Sense SIGH 111* **16**	9 wks

John REID – *See NIGHTCRAWLERS featuring John REID*

Neil REID *UK, male vocalist* **18 wks**

5 Feb 72 ★	**NEIL REID** *Decca SKL 5122*	**1**	16 wks
2 Sep 72	**SMILE** *Decca SKL 5136*	**47**	2 wks

R.E.M. *US, male vocal/instrumental group* **405 wks**

28 Apr 84	**RECKONING** *IRS A 7045*	**91**	2 wks
29 Jun 85	**FABLES OF THE RECONSTRUCTION** *IRS MIRF 1003*	**35**	4 wks
6 Sep 86	**LIFE'S RICH PAGEANT** *IRS MIRG 1014*	**43**	4 wks
16 May 87	**DEAD LETTER OFFICE** *IRS SP 70054*	**60**	2 wks
26 Sep 87	**DOCUMENT** *IRS MIRG 1025*	**28**	5 wks
29 Oct 88	**EPONYMOUS** *IRS MIRG 1038*	**69**	3 wks
19 Nov 88	**GREEN** *Warner Bros. WX 234*	**27**	20 wks
23 Mar 91 ★	**OUT OF TIME** *Warner Bros. WX 404*	**1**	153 wks
12 Oct 91 ●	**THE BEST OF R.E.M.** *IRS MIRH 1*	**7**	28 wks
10 Oct 92 ★	**AUTOMATIC FOR THE PEOPLE** *Warner Bros. 9362450552*	**1**	131 wks
8 Oct 94 ★	**MONSTER** *Warner Bros. 9362457632*	**1**	53 wks

REMBRANDTS *US, male vocal/instrumental group* **5 wks**

23 Sep 95	**LP** *East West 7559617522*	**14**	5 wks

RENAISSANCE *UK, male/female vocal/instrumental group* **10 wks**

21 Feb 70	**RENAISSANCE** *Island ILPS 9114*	**60**	1 wk
19 Aug 78	**A SONG FOR ALL SEASONS** *Warner Bros. K 56460*	**35**	8 wks
2 Jun 79	**AZUR D'OR** *Warner Bros. K 56633*	**73**	1 wk

RENATO *Italy, male vocalist* **14 wks**

25 Dec 82	**SAVE YOUR LOVE** *Lifestyle LEG 9*	**26**	14 wks

RENEGADE SOUNDWAVE *UK, male vocal/instrumental group* **1 wk**

24 Mar 90	**SOUNDCLASH** *Mute STUMM 63*	**74**	1 wk

REO SPEEDWAGON *US, male vocal/instrumental group* **36 wks**

25 Apr 81 ●	**HI INFIDELITY** *Epic EPC 84700*	**6**	29 wks
17 Jul 82	**GOOD TROUBLE** *Epic EPC 85789*	**29**	7 wks

REVOLTING COCKS *US, male vocal/instrumental group* **1 wk**

2 Oct 93	**LINGER FICKEN' GOOD** *Devotion CDDVN 22*	**39**	1 wk

REVOLUTION – *See PRINCE*

REZILLOS *UK, male/female vocal/instrumental group* **15 wks**

5 Aug 78	**CAN'T STAND THE REZILLOS** *Sire WEA K 56530*	**16**	10 wks
28 Apr 79	**MISSION ACCOMPLISHED BUT THE BEAT GOES ON** *Sire SRK 6069*	**30**	5 wks

Richie RICH *UK, male vocalist* **1 wk**

22 Jul 89	**I CAN MAKE YOU DANCE** *Gee St. GEEA 3*	**65**	1 wk

Charlie RICH *US, male vocalist* **28 wks**

23 Mar 74 ●	**BEHIND CLOSED DOORS** *Epic 65716*	**4**	26 wks
13 Jul 74	**VERY SPECIAL LOVE SONGS** *Epic 80031*	**34**	2 wks

The names are all there,
but only Michael (Stipe)
of R.E.M. is shown.
(Andrew Catlin/LFI)

RICH KIDS UK, male vocal / instrumental group | 1 wk

7 Oct 78	**GHOST OF PRINCES IN TOWERS** EMI EMC 3263 ....**51**	1	wk

Cliff RICHARD UK, male vocalist | 761 wks

18 Apr 59	● **CLIFF** Columbia 33SX 1147 ....**4**	31	wks
14 Nov 59	● **CLIFF SINGS** Columbia 33SX 1192 ....**2**	36	wks
15 Oct 60	● **ME AND MY SHADOWS** Columbia 33SX 1261 ....**2**	33	wks
22 Apr 61	● **LISTEN TO CLIFF** Columbia 33SX 1320.....................................**2**	28	wks
21 Oct 61	★ **21 TODAY** Columbia 33SX 1368 ....**1**	16	wks
23 Dec 61	★ **THE YOUNG ONES (film soundtrack)** Columbia 33SX 1384 ....**1**	42	wks
29 Sep 62	● **32 MINUTES AND 17 SECONDS** Columbia 33SX 1431 ....**3**	21	wks
26 Jan 63	★ **SUMMER HOLIDAY (film soundtrack)** Columbia 33SX 1472 ....**1**	36	wks
13 Jul 63	● **CLIFF'S HIT ALBUM** Columbia 33SX 1512 ....**2**	19	wks
28 Sep 63	● **WHEN IN SPAIN** Columbia 33SX 1541 ....**8**	10	wks
11 Jul 64	● **WONDERFUL LIFE (film soundtrack)** Columbia 33SX 1628..........**2**	23	wks
9 Jan 65	**ALADDIN (pantomime)** Columbia 33SX 1676 ....**13**	5	wks
17 Apr 65	● **CLIFF RICHARD** Columbia 33SX 1709......................................**9**	5	wks
14 Aug 65	**MORE HITS BY CLIFF** Columbia 33SX 1737..............................**20**	1	wk
8 Jan 66	**LOVE IS FOREVER** Columbia 33SX 1769 ....**19**	1	wk
21 May 66	● **KINDA LATIN** Columbia SX 6039 ....**9**	12	wks
17 Dec 66	● **FINDERS KEEPERS (film soundtrack)** Columbia SX 6079 ....**6**	18	wks
7 Jan 67	**CINDERELLA (pantomime)** Columbia 33SCX 6103 ....**30**	6	wks
15 Apr 67	**DON'T STOP ME NOW** . . . Columbia SCX 6133 ....**23**	9	wks
11 Nov 67	**GOOD NEWS** Columbia SCX 6167 ....**37**	1	wk
1 Jun 68	**CLIFF IN JAPAN** Columbia SCX 6244 ....**29**	2	wks
16 Nov 68	**ESTABLISHED 1958** Columbia SCX 6282 ....**30**	4	wks
12 Jul 69	● **BEST OF CLIFF** Columbia SCX 6343 ....**5**	17	wks
27 Sep 69	**SINCERELY** Columbia SCX 6357 ....**24**	3	wks
12 Dec 70	**TRACKS 'N' GROOVES** Columbia SCX 6435 ....**37**	2	wks
23 Dec 72	**BEST OF CLIFF VOLUME 2** Columbia SCX 6519 ....**49**	2	wks
19 Jan 74	**TAKE ME HIGH (film soundtrack)** EMI EMC 3016 ....**41**	4	wks
29 May 76	● **I'M NEARLY FAMOUS** EMI EMC 3122 ....**5**	21	wks
26 Mar 77	● **EVERY FACE TELLS A STORY** EMI EMC 3172 ....**8**	10	wks
22 Oct 77	★ **40 GOLDEN GREATS** EMI EMTV 6 ....**1**	19	wks
4 Mar 78	**SMALL CORNERS** EMI EMC 3219...**33**	5	wks
21 Oct 78	**GREEN LIGHT** EMI EMC 3231 ....**25**	3	wks
17 Feb 79	● **THANK YOU VERY MUCH – REUNION CONCERT AT THE**		
	LONDON PALLADIUM EMI EMTV 15...**5**	12	wks
15 Sep 79	● **ROCK 'N' ROLL JUVENILE** EMI EMC 3307.................................**3**	22	wks
13 Sep 80	● **I'M NO HERO** EMI EMA 796 ....**4**	12	wks
4 Jul 81	★ **LOVE SONGS** EMI EMTV 27 ....**1**	43	wks
26 Sep 81	● **WIRED FOR SOUND** EMI EMC 3377..**4**	25	wks
4 Sep 82	● **NOW YOU SEE ME, NOW YOU DON'T** EMI EMC 3415 ....**4**	14	wks
21 May 83	● **DRESSED FOR THE OCCASION** EMI EMC 3432 ....**7**	17	wks
15 Oct 83	● **SILVER** EMI EMC 1077871 ....**7**	24	wks
14 Jul 84	**20 ORIGINAL GREATS** EMI CRS 1 ....**43**	6	wks
1 Dec 84	**THE ROCK CONNECTION** EMI CLIF 2 ....**43**	5	wks
26 Sep 87	● **ALWAYS GUARANTEED** EMI EMD 1004 ....**5**	25	wks
19 Nov 88	★ **PRIVATE COLLECTION** EMI CRTV 30 ....**1**	26	wks
11 Nov 89	● **STRONGER** EMI EMD 1012 ....**7**	21	wks
17 Nov 90	● **FROM A DISTANCE . . . THE EVENT** EMI CRTV 31 ....**3**	15	wks
30 Nov 91	● **TOGETHER WITH CLIFF** EMI EMD 1028....................................**10**	7	wks
1 May 93	★ **THE ALBUM** EMI CDEMD 1043 ....**1**	15	wks
15 Oct 94	● **THE HIT LIST** EMI CDEMTV 84..**3**	19	wks
11 Nov 95	**SONGS FROM HEATHCLIFF** EMI CDEMD 1091 ....**15†**	8	wks

*The Shadows featured on all or some of the tracks of all albums up to and including
Aladdin and the following subsequent albums: More Hits By Cliff, Love Is Forever, Finders
Keepers, Cinderella, Established 1958, Best Of Cliff, Best Of Cliff Vol. 2, 40 Golden Greats,
Thank You Very Much, Love Songs, 20 Original Greats and The Hit List. Cliff is credited to
Cliff Richard and the Drifters, the original name used by the Shadows. See also the
Shadows.*

Keith RICHARDS UK, male vocalist / instrumentalist – guitar | 4 wks

15 Oct 88	**TALK IS CHEAP** Virgin V 2554 ....**37**	3	wks
31 Oct 92	**MAIN OFFENDER** Virgin America CDVUS 59.................................**45**	1	wk

Lionel RICHIE US, male vocalist · 366 wks

27 Nov 82 ● **LIONEL RICHIE** Motown STMA 8037 ....**9**	86 wks
29 Oct 83 ★ **CAN'T SLOW DOWN** Motown STMA 8041 ....**1**	154 wks
23 Aug 86 ● **DANCING ON THE CEILING** Motown ZL 72412 ....**2**	53 wks
6 Jun 92 ★ **BACK TO FRONT** Motown 5300182 ....**1**	73 wks

Jonathan RICHMAN and the MODERN LOVERS
US, male vocal / instrumental group · 3 wks

27 Aug 77 **ROCK 'N' ROLL WITH THE MODERN LOVERS** Beserkeley BSERK 9..**50**	3 wks

RICHMOND STRINGS/MIKE SAMMES SINGERS
UK, orchestra / male / female vocal group · 7 wks

19 Jan 76 **MUSIC OF AMERICA** Ronco TRD 2016 ....**18**	7 wks

Sviatoslav RICHTER – See Herbert VON KARAJAN

Frank RICOTTI ALL STARS UK, male instrumental group · 1 wk

26 Jun 93 **THE BEIDERBECKE COLLECTION** Dormouse DM 20CD **73**	1 wk

Album first entered the chart on 24 Dec 88 as a compilation.. See also Various Artists –
TV and Radio Soundtracks and Spin–Offs.

Nelson RIDDLE ORCHESTRA – See Shirley BASSEY; Linda RONSTADT; Kiri TE KANAWA

RIDE UK, male vocal / instrumental group · 14 wks

27 Oct 90 **NOWHERE** Creation CRELP 074...............................**11**	5 wks
21 Mar 92 ● **GOING BLANK AGAIN** Creation CRECD 124.....................**5**	5 wks
2 Jul 94 ● **CARNIVAL OF LIGHT** Creation CRECD 147 ....**5**	4 wks

RIGHT SAID FRED UK, male vocal / instrumental group · 53 wks

28 Mar 93 ★ **UP** Tug SNOGCD 1..**1**	49 wks
13 Nov 93 **SEX AND TRAVEL** Tug SNOGCD 2 ....**35**	4 wks

RIGHTEOUS BROTHERS US, male vocal duo · 17 wks

1 Dec 90 **THE VERY BEST OF THE RIGHTEOUS BROTHERS** Verve 8472481 ..**11**	17 wks

RIP RIG AND PANIC
UK / US, male / female vocal / instrumental group · 3 wks

26 Jun 82 **I AM COLD** Virgin V 2228 ....**67**	3 wks

Minnie RIPERTON US, female vocalist · 3 wks

17 May 75 **PERFECT ANGEL** Epic EPC 80426 ....**33**	3 wks

Angela RIPPON UK, female exercise instructor · 26 wks

17 Apr 82 ● **SHAPE UP AND DANCE (VOLUME II)** Lifestyle LEG 2.....................**8**	26 wks

RIVER CITY PEOPLE UK, male / female vocal / instrumental group · 10 wks

25 Aug 90 **SAY SOMETHING GOOD** EMI EMCX 3561..**23**	9 wks
2 Nov 91 **THIS IS THE WORLD** EMI EMC 3611...**56**	1 wk

RIVER DETECTIVES UK, male vocal / instrumental duo · 1 wk

23 Sep 89 **SATURDAY NIGHT SUNDAY MORNING** WEA WX 2955 ....**51**	1 wk

R
259

TOP 30 № 12

It has been star time in the album chart for CLIFF RICHARD since 1959.
(Hulton Deutsch Collection)

David ROACH *UK, male vocalist / instrumentalist – saxophone*   **1 wk**

14 Apr 84   **I LOVE SAX** *Nouveau Music NML 1006* ....**73**   1 wk

ROACHFORD *UK, male vocalist*   **53 wks**

23 Jul 88	**ROACHFORD** *CBS 460630 1*	**11**	27 wks
18 May 91	**GET READY** *Columbia 4681361*	**20**	5 wks
16 Apr 94	**PERMANENT SHADE OF BLUE** *Columbia 4758429*	**25**	21 wks

ROBBIE – *See SLY and ROBBIE*

Marty ROBBINS *US, male vocalist*   **15 wks**

13 Aug 60	**GUNFIGHTER BALLADS** *Fontana TFL 5063*	**20**	1 wk
10 Feb 79	● **MARTY ROBBINS COLLECTION** *Lotus WH 5009*	**5**	14 wks

Juliet ROBERTS *UK, female vocalist*   **1 wk**

2 Apr 94   **NATURAL THING** *Cooltempo CTCD 39* ....**65**   1 wk

Paddy ROBERTS *South Africa, male vocalist*   **6 wks**

26 Sep 59	● **STRICTLY FOR GROWN–UPS** *Decca LF 1322*	**8**	5 wks
17 Sep 60	**PADDY ROBERTS TRIES AGAIN** *Decca LK 4358*	**16**	1 wk

B.A. ROBERTSON *UK, male vocalist*   **10 wks**

29 Mar 80	**INITIAL SUCCESS** *Asylum K 52216*	**32**	8 wks
4 Apr 81	**BULLY FOR YOU** *Asylum K 52275*	**61**	2 wks

Robbie ROBERTSON *Canada, male vocalist*   **16 wks**

14 Nov 87	**ROBBIE ROBERTSON** *Geffen WX 133*	**23**	14 wks
12 Oct 91	**STORYVILLE** *Geffen GEF 24303*	**30**	2 wks

Smokey ROBINSON *US, male vocalist*   **21 wks**

20 Jun 81	**BEING WITH YOU** *Motown STML 12151*	**17**	10 wks
12 Nov 88	**LOVE SONGS** *Telstar STAR 2331* [1]	**69**	9 wks
14 Nov 92	**THE GREATEST HITS** *PolyGram TV 5301212* [2]	**65**	2 wks

[1] Marvin Gaye and Smokey Robinson [2] Smokey Robinson and the Miracles

Tom ROBINSON BAND *UK, male vocal / instrumental group*   **23 wks**

3 Jun 78	● **POWER IN THE DARKNESS** *EMI EMC 3226*	**4**	12 wks
24 Mar 79	**TRB2** *EMI EMC 3296*	**18**	6 wks
29 Sep 84	**HOPE AND GLORY** *Castaway ZL 70483* [1]	**21**	5 wks

[1] Tom Robinson

ROBSON and JEROME – *See Robson GREEN and Jerome FLYNN*

Pete ROCK and CL SMOOOTH *US, male vocal duo*   **1 wk**

19 Nov 94   **THE MAIN INGREDIENT** *Elektra 7559616612* ....**69**   1 wk

ROCK GODDESS *UK, female vocal / instrumental group*   **3 wks**

12 Mar 83	**ROCK GODDESS** *A & M AMLH 68554*	**65**	2 wks
29 Oct 83	**HELL HATH NO FURY** *A & M AMLX 68560*	**84**	1 wk

ROCKIN' BERRIES *UK, male vocal / instrumental group*   **1 wk**

19 Jun 65   **IN TOWN** *Pye NPL 38013* ....**15**   1 wk

R 261

ROCKPILE *UK, male vocal / instrumental group*   **5 wks**

18 Oct 80   **SECONDS OF PLEASURE** *F–Beat XXLP 7* ....**34**   5 wks

ROCKSTEADY CREW *US, male / female vocal group*   **1 wk**

16 Jun 84   **READY FOR BATTLE** *Charisma RSC LP1* ....**73**   1 wk

ROCKWELL *US, male vocalist*   **5 wks**

25 Feb 84   **SOMEBODY'S WATCHING ME** *Motown ZL 72147* ....**52**   5 wks

Clodagh RODGERS *Ireland, female vocalist*   **1 wk**

13 Sep 69   **CLODAGH RODGERS** *RCA SF 8033* ....**27**   1 wk

Paul RODGERS *UK, male vocalist*   **7 wks**

3 Jul 93 ● **MUDDY WATERS BLUES** *London 8284242* ....**9**   7 wks

RODS *US, male vocal / instrumental group*   **4 wks**

24 Jul 82   **WILD DOGS** *Arista SPART 1196* ....**75**   4 wks

Kenny ROGERS *US, male vocalist*   **98 wks**

18 Jun 77   **KENNY ROGERS** *United Artists UAS 30046* ....**14**   7 wks
6 Oct 79   **THE KENNY ROGERS SINGLES ALBUM**
            United Artists UAK 30263 ....**12**   22 wks
9 Feb 80 ● **KENNY** *United Artists UAG 30273* ....**7**   10 wks
31 Jan 81   **LADY** *Liberty LBG 30334* ....**40**   5 wks
1 Oct 83   **EYES THAT SEE IN THE DARK** *RCA RCALP 6088* ....**53**   19 wks
27 Oct 84   **WHAT ABOUT ME?** *RCA PL 85043* ....**97**   1 wk
27 Jul 85 ● **THE KENNY ROGERS STORY** *Liberty EMTV 39*.............**4**   29 wks
25 Sep 93   **DAYTIME FRIENDS – THE VERY BEST OF KENNY ROGERS**
            EMI CDEMTV 79 ....**16**   5 wks

ROLLING STONES *UK, male vocal / instrumental group*   **741 wks**

25 Apr 64 ★ **ROLLING STONES** *Decca LK 4605*................................**1**   51 wks
23 Jan 65 ★ **ROLLING STONES NO. 2** *Decca LK 4661* ....**1**   37 wks
2 Oct 65 ● **OUT OF OUR HEADS** *Decca LK 4733* ....**2**   24 wks
23 Apr 66 ★ **AFTERMATH** *Decca LK 4786* ....**1**   28 wks
12 Nov 66 ● **BIG HITS (HIGH TIDE AND GREEN GRASS)** *Decca TXS 101* ....**4**   43 wks
28 Jan 67 ● **BETWEEN THE BUTTONS** *Decca SKL 4852* ....**3**   22 wks
23 Dec 67 ● **THEIR SATANIC MAJESTIES REQUEST** *Decca TXS 103* ....**3**   13 wks
21 Dec 68 ● **BEGGARS BANQUET** *Decca SKL 4955* ....**3**   12 wks
27 Sep 69 ● **THROUGH THE PAST DARKLY (BIG HITS VOLUME 2)**
            Decca SKL 5019 ....**2**   37 wks
20 Dec 69 ★ **LET IT BLEED** *Decca SKL 5025*................................**1**   29 wks
19 Sep 70 ★ **'GET YOUR YA–YA'S OUT!'** *Decca SKL 5065* ....**1**   15 wks
3 Apr 71 ● **STONE AGE** *Decca SKL 5084* ....**4**   7 wks
8 May 71 ★ **STICKY FINGERS** *Rolling Stones COC 59100* ....**1**   25 wks
18 Sep 71   **GIMME SHELTER** *Decca SKL 5101* ....**19**   5 wks
11 Mar 72   **MILESTONES** *Decca SKL 5098* ....**14**   8 wks
10 Jun 72 ★ **EXILE ON MAIN STREET** *Rolling Stones COC 69100* ....**1**   16 wks
11 Nov 72   **ROCK 'N' ROLLING STONES** *Decca SKL 5149*.............**41**   1 wk
22 Sep 73 ★ **GOAT'S HEAD SOUP** *Rolling Stones COC 59101* ....**1**   14 wks
2 Nov 74 ● **IT'S ONLY ROCK 'N' ROLL** *Rolling Stones COC 59103* ....**2**   9 wks
28 Jun 75   **MADE IN THE SHADE** *Rolling Stones COC 59104* ....**14**   12 wks
28 Jun 75   **METAMORPHOSIS** *Decca SKL 5212* ....**45**   1 wk
29 Nov 75 ● **ROLLED GOLD – THE VERY BEST OF THE ROLLING STONES**
            Decca ROST 1/2 ....**7**   50 wks
8 May 76 ● **BLACK AND BLUE** *Rolling Stones COC 59106*............**2**   14 wks
8 Oct 77 ● **LOVE YOU LIVE** *Rolling Stones COC 89101* ....**3**   8 wks
5 Nov 77 ● **GET STONED** *Arcade ADEP 32* ....**8**   15 wks
24 Jun 78 ● **SOME GIRLS** *Rolling Stones CUN 39108* ....**2**   25 wks

ALPHABETICALLY BY ARTIST

5 Jul	80	★ **EMOTIONAL RESCUE** Rolling Stones CUN 39111 ....**1**	18 wks
12 Sep	81	● **TATTOO YOU** Rolling Stones CUNS 39114 ....**2**	29 wks
12 Jun	82	● **STILL LIFE (AMERICAN CONCERTS 1981)**	
		Rolling Stones CUN 39115 ....**4**	18 wks
31 Jul	82	**IN CONCERT (import)** Decca (Holland) 6640 037......................**94**	3 wks
11 Dec	82	**STORY OF THE STONES** K-Tel NE 1201 ....**24**	12 wks
19 Nov	83	● **UNDERCOVER** Rolling Stones CUN 1654361 ....**3**	18 wks
7 Jul	84	**REWIND 1971–1984 (THE BEST OF THE ROLLING STONES)**	
		Rolling Stones 4501991 ....**23**	18 wks
5 Apr	86	● **DIRTY WORK** Rolling Stones CUN 86321 ....**4**	10 wks
23 Sep	89	● **STEEL WHEELS** CBS 4657521 ....**2**	18 wks
7 Jul	90	● **HOT ROCKS 1964–1971** London 8201401.........................**3**	21 wks
20 Apr	91	● **FLASHPOINT** Rolling Stones 4681351..................................**6**	7 wks
4 Dec	93	**JUMP BACK – THE BEST OF THE ROLLING STONES 1971–1993**	
		Virgin CDV 2726 ....**16**	17 wks
2 Jul	94	**STICKY FINGERS (re-issue)** Virgin CDVX 2730 ....**74**	1 wk
23 Jul	94	★ **VOODOO LOUNGE** Virgin CDV 2750 ....**1**	24 wks
25 Nov	95	● **STRIPPED** Virgin CDV 2801 ....**9†**	6 wks

ROLLINS BAND US, male vocal / instrumental group　　　**2 wks**

23 Apr 94	**WEIGHT** Imago 72787210342 ....**22**	2 wks

ROMAN HOLIDAY UK, male vocal / instrumental group　　　**3 wks**

22 Oct 83	**COOKIN' ON THE ROOF** Jive HIP 9 ....**31**	3 wks

RONDO VENEZIANO UK, male / female orchestral group　　　**33 wks**

5 Nov 83	**VENICE IN PERIL** Ferroway RON 1.......................................**39**	13 wks
10 Nov 84	**THE GENIUS OF VENICE** Ferroway RON 2 ....**60**	13 wks
9 Jul 88	**VENICE IN PERIL (re-issue)** Fanfare RON 1 ....**34**	7 wks

Mick RONSON UK, male vocalist / instrumentalist – guitar　　　**10 wks**

16 Mar 74	● **SLAUGHTER ON TENTH AVENUE** RCA Victor APLI 0353 ....**9**	7 wks
8 Mar 75	**PLAY DON'T WORRY** RCA Victor APLI 0681 ....**29**	3 wks

Linda RONSTADT US, female vocalist　　　**43 wks**

4 Sep 76	**HASTEN DOWN THE WIND** Asylum K 53045 ....**32**	8 wks
25 Dec 76	**GREATEST HITS** Asylum K 53055 ....**37**	9 wks
1 Oct 77	**SIMPLE DREAMS** Asylum K 53065..**15**	5 wks
14 Oct 78	**LIVING IN THE USA** Asylum K 53085...................................**39**	2 wks
8 Mar 80	**MAD LOVE** Asylum K 52210 ....**65**	1 wk
28 Jan 84	**WHAT'S NEW** Asylum 96 0260 1 ....**31**	5 wks
19 Jan 85	**LUSH LIFE** Asylum 9603871 1 ....**100**	1 wk
14 Mar 87	**TRIO** Warner Bros. 9254911 2 ....**60**	4 wks
11 Nov 89	**CRY LIKE A RAINSTORM – HOWL LIKE THE WIND**	
	Elektra EKT 76..**43**	8 wks

1 Linda Ronstadt with the Nelson Riddle Orchestra 2 Dolly Parton/Emmylou Harris/
Linda Ronstadt

ROSE MARIE UK, female vocalist　　　**34 wks**

13 Apr 85	**ROSE MARIE SINGS JUST FOR YOU** A1 RMTV 1...........................**30**	13 wks
24 May 86	**SO LUCKY** A1–Spartan RMLP 2...**62**	3 wks
14 Nov 87	**SENTIMENTALLY YOURS** Telstar STAR 2302 ....**22**	11 wks
19 Nov 88	**TOGETHER AGAIN** Telstar STAR 2333 ....**52**	7 wks

ROSE ROYCE US, male / female vocal / instrumental group　　　**62 wks**

22 Oct 77	**IN FULL BLOOM** Warner Bros. K 56394..............................**18**	13 wks
30 Sep 78	● **STRIKES AGAIN** Whitfield K 56257 ....**7**	11 wks
22 Sep 79	**RAINBOW CONNECTION IV** Atlantic K 56714 ....**72**	2 wks
1 Mar 80	★ **GREATEST HITS** Whitfield K RRTV 1...................................**1**	34 wks
13 Oct 84	**MUSIC MAGIC** Streetwave MKL 2 ....**69**	2 wks

See also compilation albums – Dino.

TOP 30 No 15

It is 19 March 1964. The ROLLING STONES await the release the following month of their first album.

(Hulton Deutsch)

TOP 30 No 22

On the day before her first British solo tour begins in 1973, DIANA ROSS is the centre of attention at London's Inn on the Park.

(Hulton Deutsch)

ALPHABETICALLY BY ARTIST

ROSE TATTOO *Australia, male vocal / instrumental group* **4 wks**

26 Sep 81	**ASSAULT AND BATTERY** Carrere CAL 127 ....**40**	4 wks

Diana ROSS *US, female vocalist* **569 wks**

24 Oct 70	**DIANA ROSS** Tamla Motown SFTML 11159....................**14**	5 wks
19 Jun 71	**EVERYTHING IS EVERYTHING** Tamla Motown STML 11178 ....**31**	3 wks
9 Oct 71	● **I'M STILL WAITING** Tamla Motown STML 11193 ....**10**	11 wks
9 Oct 71	**DIANA** Tamla Motown STMA 8001 ....**43**	1 wk
11 Nov 72	**GREATEST HITS** Tamla Motown STMA 8006 ....**34**	10 wks
1 Sep 73	● **TOUCH ME IN THE MORNING** Tamla Motown STML 11239 ....**7**	35 wks
27 Oct 73	**LADY SINGS THE BLUES** Tamla Motown TMSP 1131 ....**50**	1 wk
19 Jan 74	● **DIANA AND MARVIN** Tamla Motown STMA 8015 [1] **6**	43 wks
2 Mar 74	**LAST TIME I SAW HIM** Tamla Motown STML 11255 ....**41**	1 wk
8 Jun 74	**LIVE** Tamla Motown STML 11248 ....**21**	8 wks
27 Mar 76	● **DIANA ROSS** Tamla Motown STML 12022.....................**4**	26 wks
7 Aug 76	● **GREATEST HITS 2** Tamla Motown STML 12036....................**2**	29 wks
19 Mar 77	**AN EVENING WITH DIANA ROSS** Motown TMSP 6005 ....**52**	1 wk
4 Aug 79	**THE BOSS** Motown STML 12118 ....**52**	2 wks
17 Nov 79	● **20 GOLDEN GREATS** Motown EMTV 21 ....**2**	29 wks
21 Jun 80	**DIANA** Motown STMA 8033 ....**12**	32 wks
28 Mar 81	**TO LOVE AGAIN** Motown STML 12152 ....**26**	10 wks
29 Aug 81	**DIANA AND MARVIN (re-issue)** Motown STMS 5001 [1] **78**	2 wks
7 Nov 81	**WHY DO FOOLS FALL IN LOVE** Capitol EST 26733 ....**17**	24 wks
21 Nov 81	**ALL THE GREAT HITS** Motown STMA 8036....................**21**	31 wks
13 Feb 82	**DIANA'S DUETS** Motown STML 12163 ....**43**	6 wks
23 Oct 82	**SILK ELECTRIC** Capitol EAST 27313 ....**33**	12 wks
4 Dec 82	● **LOVE SONGS** K-Tel NE 1200 ....**5**	17 wks
19 Jul 83	**ROSS** Capitol EST 1867051.....................**44**	5 wks
24 Dec 83	● **PORTRAIT** Telstar STAR 2238 ....**8**	31 wks
6 Oct 84	**SWEPT AWAY** Capitol ROSS 1.....................**40**	5 wks
28 Sep 85	**EATEN ALIVE** Capitol ROSS 2 ....**11**	19 wks
15 Nov 86	**DIANA ROSS. MICHAEL JACKSON. GLADYS KNIGHT.**	
	STEVIE WONDER. THEIR VERY BEST BACK TO BACK	
	PrioriTyV PTVR 2 [2] **21**	10 wks
30 May 87	**RED HOT RHYTHM 'N' BLUES** EMI EMC 3532 ....**47**	4 wks
31 Oct 87	**LOVE SONGS** Telstar STAR 2298 [3] **12**	24 wks
27 May 89	**WORKIN' OVERTIME** EMI EMD 1009.....................**23**	4 wks
25 Nov 89	**GREATEST HITS LIVE** EMI EMDC 1001.....................**34**	6 wks
14 Dec 91	**THE FORCE BEHIND THE POWER** EMI EMD 1023 ....**11**	31 wks
29 Feb 92	**MOTOWN'S GREATEST HITS** Motown 5300132.....................**20**	11 wks
24 Apr 93	**LIVE, STOLEN MOMENTS** EMI CDEMD 1044 ....**45**	2 wks
30 Oct 93	★ **ONE WOMAN – THE ULTIMATE COLLECTION** EMI CDONE 1 ....**1**	66 wks
25 Dec 93	**CHRISTMAS IN VIENNA** Sony Classical SK 53358 [4] **71**	2 wks
23 Apr 94	**DIANA EXTENDED – THE REMIXES** EMI CDDREX 1 ....**58**	1 wk
26 Nov 94	**A VERY SPECIAL SEASON** EMI CDEMD 1075.....................**37**	6 wks
16 Sep 95	● **TAKE ME HIGHER** EMI CDEMD 1085.....................**10**	3 wks

[1] Diana Ross and Marvin Gaye [2] Diana Ross/Michael Jackson/Gladys Knight/Stevie Wonder [3] Diana Ross and Michael Jackson [4] Placido Domingo, Diana Ross and José Carreras

The two Diana albums and the three Diana Ross titles are all different.From 14 Jan 89, when multi–artist albums were excluded from the main chart, Love Songs by Diana Ross and Michael Jackson was listed in the compilation albums chart. See also Supremes; Various Artists – Telstar.

ROSTAL and SCHAEFER *UK, male instrumental duo* **2 wks**

14 Jul 79	**BEATLES CONCERTO** Parlophone PAS 10014 ....**61**	2 wks

Mstilav ROSTROPOVICH – See Herbert VON KARAJAN

David Lee ROTH *US, male vocalist* **32 wks**

2 Mar 85	**CRAZY FROM THE HEAT** Warner Bros. 9252221 ....**91**	2 wks
19 Jul 86	**EAT 'EM AND SMILE** Warner Bros. WX 56.....................**28**	9 wks
6 Feb 88	**SKYSCRAPER** Warner Bros. 925671 1 ....**11**	12 wks
26 Jan 91	● **A LITTLE AIN'T ENOUGH** Warner Bros. WX 403.....................**4**	7 wks

19 Mar 94	**YOUR FILTHY LITTLE MOUTH** Reprise 9362453912 ....**28**	2 wks

Uli Jon ROTH and ELECTRIC SUN
Germany, male vocal / instrumental group   **2 wks**

23 Feb 85	**BEYOND THE ASTRAL SKIES** EMI ROTH 1 ....**64**	2 wks

Thomas ROUND – *See June BRONHILL and Thomas ROUND*

Demis ROUSSOS *Greece, male vocalist*   **143 wks**

22 Jun 74	● **FOREVER AND EVER** Philips 6325 021...............................**2**	68 wks
19 Apr 75	**SOUVENIRS** Philips 6325 201 ....**25**	18 wks
24 Apr 76	● **HAPPY TO BE** Philips 9101 027 ....**4**	34 wks
3 Jul 76	**MY ONLY FASCINATION** Philips 6325 094 ....**39**	6 wks
16 Apr 77	**THE MAGIC OF DEMIS ROUSSOS** Philips 9101 131.............**29**	6 wks
28 Oct 78	**LIFE AND LOVE** Philips 9199 873 ....**36**	11 wks

ROXETTE *Sweden, male / female vocal / instrumental duo*   **143 wks**

17 Jun 89	● **LOOK SHARP!** EMI EMC 3557..**4**	53 wks
13 Apr 91	● **JOYRIDE** EMI EMD 1019 ....**2**	48 wks
12 Sep 92	● **TOURISM** EMI CDEMD 1036 ....**2**	17 wks
23 Apr 94	● **CRASH BOOM BANG** EMI CDEMD 1056 ....**3**	16 wks
4 Nov 95	● **DON'T BORE US . . . GET TO THE CHORUS! – GREATEST HITS**	
	EMI CDXEMTV 98 ....**5†**	9 wks

ROXY MUSIC *UK, male vocal / instrumental group*   **414 wks**

29 Jul 72	● **ROXY MUSIC** Island ILPS 9200 ....**10**	16 wks
7 Apr 73	● **FOR YOUR PLEASURE** Island ILPS 9232 ....**4**	27 wks
1 Dec 73	★ **STRANDED** Island ILPS 9252 ....**1**	17 wks
30 Nov 74	● **COUNTRY LIFE** Island ILPS 9303 ....**3**	10 wks
8 Nov 75	● **SIREN** Island ILPS 9344 ....**4**	17 wks
31 Jul 76	● **VIVA ROXY MUSIC** Island ILPS 9400 ....**6**	12 wks
19 Nov 77	**GREATEST HITS** Polydor 2302 073 ....**20**	11 wks
24 Mar 79	● **MANIFESTO** Polydor POLH 001 ....**7**	34 wks
31 May 80	★ **FLESH AND BLOOD** Polydor POLH 002 ....**1**	60 wks
5 Jun 82	★ **AVALON** EG EGLP 50 ....**1**	57 wks
19 Mar 83	**THE HIGH ROAD (import)** EG EGMLP 1 ....**26**	7 wks
12 Nov 83	**ATLANTIC YEARS 1973–1980** EG EGLP 54.......................**23**	25 wks
26 Apr 86	★ **STREET LIFE 20 GREAT HITS** EG EGTV 1 [1] **1**	77 wks
19 Nov 88	● **THE ULTIMATE COLLECTION** EG EGTV 2 [1] **6**	35 wks
4 Nov 95	**MORE THAN THIS – THE BEST OF BRYAN FERRY AND**	
	ROXY MUSIC Virgin CDV 2791 [1] ....**15†**	9 wks

[1] Bryan Ferry and Roxy Music

ROYAL CHORAL SOCIETY – *See LONDON SYMPHONY ORCHESTRA*

ROYAL LIVERPOOL PHILHARMONIC ORCHESTRA – *See Carl DAVIS and the ROYAL LIVERPOOL PHILHARMONIC ORCHESTRA*

ROYAL PHILHARMONIC ORCHESTRA
UK, orchestra conducted by Louis Clark   **119 wks**

8 Jan 77	**CLASSICAL GOLD** Ronco RTD 42020 ....**24**	13 wk
23 Dec 78	**CLASSIC GOLD VOLUME 2** Ronco RTD 42032 ....**31**	4 wks
19 Sep 81	● **HOOKED ON CLASSICS** K-Tel ONE 1146 ....**4**	43 wks
31 Jul 82	**CAN'T STOP THE CLASSICS - HOOKED ON CLASSICS 2**	
	K-Tel ONE 1173 ....**13**	26 wks
9 Apr 83	**JOURNEY THROUGH THE CLASSICS – HOOKED ON CLASSICS 3**	
	K-Tel ONE 1266 ....**19**	15 wks
8 Oct 83	**LOVE CLASSICS** Nouveau Music NML 1003 [1] **30**	9 wks
10 Dec 83	**THE BEST OF HOOKED ON CLASSICS** K-Tel ONE 1266 ....**51**	6 wks
26 May 84	**AS TIME GOES BY** Telstar STAR 2240 [2] **95**	2 wks
26 Nov 88	**RHYTHM AND CLASSICS** Telstar STAR 2344.......................**96**	1 wk
22 Sep 90	**MUSIC FOR THE LAST NIGHT OF THE PROMS**	
	Cirrus TVLP 501 [3] **39**	4 wks

| 5 Oct 91 | **SERIOUSLY ORCHESTRAL** Virgin RPOLP 1 ....**31** | 6 wks |
| 30 Jul 94 | **BIG SCREEN CLASSICS** Quality Television GIGSCD 1 ....**49** | 2 wks |

[1] Royal Philharmonic Orchestra conducted by Nick Portlock [2] Royal Philharmonic Orchestra conducted by Harry Rabinowitz [3] Sir Charles Groves, Royal Philharmonic Orchestra and Chorus with Sarah Walker

See also Richard Clayderman; Julian Lloyd Webber; Juan Martin; Andy Williams.

ROZALLA Zimbabwe, female vocalist

4 wks

| 4 Apr 92 | **EVERYBODY'S FREE** Pulse 8 PULSECD 3 ....**20** | 4 wks |

RUBETTES UK, male vocal / instrumental group

1 wk

| 10 May 75 | **WE CAN DO IT** State ETAT 001 ....**41** | 1 wk |

David RUFFIN – *See Daryl HALL and John OATES*

Jimmy RUFFIN US, male vocalist

10 wks

| 13 May 67 | **THE JIMMY RUFFIN WAY** Tamla Motown STML 11048 ....**32** | 6 wks |
| 1 Jun 74 | **GREATEST HITS** Tamla Motown STML 11259 ....**41** | 4 wks |

RUFUS US, male instrumental group and female vocalist

7 wks

| 12 Apr 75 | **RUFUSIZED** ABC ABCL 5063 ....**48** | 2 wks |
| 21 Apr 84 | **STOMPIN' AT THE SAVOY** Warner Bros. 923679 [1] ....**64** | 5 wks |

[1] Rufus and Chaka Khan

RUMOUR – *See Graham PARKER and the RUMOUR*

RUN D.M.C. US, male rap group

33 wks

26 Jul 86	**RAISING HELL** Profile LONLP 21...........................**41**	26 wks
4 Jun 88	**TOUGHER THAN LEATHER** Profile LONLP 38 ....**13**	5 wks
15 May 93	**DOWN WITH THE KING** Profile FILECD 440 ....**44**	2 wks

Todd RUNDGREN US, male vocalist

9 wks

| 29 Jan 77 | **RA** Bearsville K 55514...........................**27** | 6 wks |
| 6 May 78 | **HERMIT OF MINK HOLLOW** Bearsville K 55521 ....**42** | 3 wks |

RUNRIG UK, male vocal / instrumental group

36 wks

26 Nov 88	**ONCE IN A LIFETIME** Chrysalis CHR 1695 ....**61**	2 wks
7 Oct 89	**SEARCHLIGHT** Chrysalis CHR 1713 ....**11**	4 wks
22 Jun 91	● **THE BIG WHEEL** Chrysalis CHR 1858...........**4**	15 wks
27 Mar 93	● **AMAZING THINGS** Chrysalis CDCHR 2000...........**2**	6 wks
26 Nov 94	**TRANSMITTING LIVE** Chrysalis CDCHR 6090...........**41**	3 wks
20 May 95	**THE CUTTER AND THE CLAN** Chrysalis CCD 1669 ....**45**	2 wks
18 Nov 95	**MARA** Chrysalis CDCHR 6111 ....**24**	4 wks

RUSH Canada, male vocal / instrumental group

95 wks

8 Oct 77	**FAREWELL TO KINGS** Mercury 9100 042 ....**22**	4 wks
25 Nov 78	**HEMISPHERES** Mercury 9100 059...........**14**	6 wks
26 Jan 80	● **PERMANENT WAVES** Mercury 9100 071 ....**3**	16 wks
21 Feb 81	● **MOVING PICTURES** Mercury 6337 160 ....**3**	11 wks
7 Nov 81	● **EXIT STAGE LEFT** Mercury 6619 053 ....**6**	14 wks
18 Sep 82	● **SIGNALS** Mercury 6337 243 ....**3**	9 wks
28 Apr 84	● **GRACE UNDER PRESSURE** Vertigo VERH 12 ....**5**	12 wks
9 Nov 85	● **POWER WINDOWS** Vertigo VERH 31 ....**9**	4 wks
21 Nov 87	● **HOLD YOUR FIRE** Vertigo VERH 47 ....**10**	4 wks
28 Jan 89	**A SHOW OF HANDS** Vertigo 836346...........**12**	4 wks
9 Dec 89	**PRESTO** Atlantic WX 327...........**27**	2 wks
13 Oct 90	**CHRONICLES** Vertigo CBTV 1 ....**42**	2 wks
14 Sep 91	● **ROLL THE BONES** Atlantic WX 436 ....**10**	4 wks

R
267

30 Oct 93   **COUNTERPARTS** *Atlantic 7567825282* ....**14**   3 wks

Jennifer RUSH *US, female vocalist*   **43 wks**

16 Nov 85 ● **JENNIFER RUSH** *CBS 26488*.......................**7**	35 wks
3 May 86 **MOVIN'** *CBS 26710*.......................**32**	5 wks
18 Apr 87 **HEART OVER MIND** *CBS 450 4701* **48**	3 wks

Patrice RUSHEN *US, female vocalist*   **17 wks**

1 May 82   **STRAIGHT FROM THE HEART** *Elektra K 52352*..................**24**   14 wks
16 Jun 84   **NOW** *Elektra 960360* ....**73**   3 wks

Brenda RUSSELL *US, female vocalist*   **4 wks**

23 Apr 88   **GET HERE** *A & M AMA 5178*..........................**77**   4 wks

Leon RUSSELL *US, male vocalist*   **1 wk**

3 Jul 71   **LEON RUSSELL AND THE SHELTER PEOPLE** *A & M AMLS 65003* ..**29**   1 wk

Mike RUTHERFORD *UK, male vocalist / instrumentalist – guitar*   **11 wks**

23 Feb 80   **SMALLCREEP'S DAY** *Charisma CAS 1149* ....**13**   7 wks
18 Sep 82   **ACTING VERY STRANGE** *WEA K 99249* ....**23**   4 wks

See also Mike and the Mechanics.

RUTLES *UK, male vocal / instrumental group*   **11 wks**

15 Apr 78   **THE RUTLES** *Warner Bros. K 56459* ....**12**   11 wks

RUTS *UK, male vocal / instrumental group*   **10 wks**

13 Oct 79   **THE CRACK** *Virgin V 2132*..........................**16**   6 wks
18 Oct 80   **GRIN AND BEAR IT** *Virgin V 2188* 1 ....**28**   4 wks

1 Ruts D.C.

S EXPRESS *UK, male / female vocal / instrumental group*   **9 wks**

1 Apr 89 ● **ORIGINAL SOUNDTRACK** *Rhythm King LEFTLP 8* ....**5**   9 wks

S.O.S. BAND *US, male / female vocal / instrumental group*   **19 wks**

1 Sep 84   **JUST THE WAY YOU LIKE IT** *Tabu TBU 26058* ....**29**   10 wks
17 May 86   **SANDS OF TIME** *Tabu TBU 26863* ....**15**   9 wks

Robin S *US, female vocalist*   **3 wks**

4 Sep 93   **SHOW ME LOVE** *Champion CHAMPCD 1028* ....**34**   3 wks

SABRES OF PARADISE *UK, male instrumental group*   **3 wks**

23 Oct 93   **SABRESONIC** *Warp WARPCD 16* ....**29**   2 wks
10 Dec 94   **HAUNTED DANCEHALL** *Warp WARPCD 26* ....**57**   1 wk

SACRED SPIRIT
Europe, anonymous producer, utilizing Native American chants   **13 wks**

1 Apr 95 ● **CHANTS AND DANCES OF THE NATIVE AMERICANS**
    Virgin CDV 2753 ....**9†**   13 wks

SAD CAFE   UK, male vocal / instrumental group   36 wks

1 Oct 77	**FANX TA RA** RCA PL 25101	56	1 wk
29 Apr 78	**MISPLACED IDEALS** RCA PL 25133	50	1 wk
29 Sep 79	● **FACADES** RCA PL 25249	8	23 wks
25 Oct 80	**SAD CAFE** RCA SADLP 4	46	5 wks
21 Mar 81	**LIVE** RCA SAD LP 5	37	4 wks
24 Oct 81	**OLE** Polydor POLD 5045	72	2 wks

SADE   UK, female vocalist   190 wks

28 Jul 84	● **DIAMOND LIFE** Epic EPC 26044	2	99 wks
16 Nov 85	★ **PROMISE** Epic EPC 86318	1	31 wks
14 May 88	● **STRONGER THAN PRIDE** Epic 460497 1	3	17 wks
7 Nov 92	● **LOVE DELUXE** Epic 4726262	10	27 wks
12 Nov 94	● **THE BEST OF SADE** Epic 4777932	6	16 wks

SAILOR   UK, male vocal / instrumental group   8 wks

7 Feb 76	**TROUBLE** Epic EPC 69192	45	8 wks

General SAINT – See Clint EASTWOOD and General SAINT

SAINT ETIENNE   UK, male / female vocal / instrumental group   20 wks

26 Oct 91	**FOXBASE ALPHA** Heavenly HVNLP 1	34	3 wks
6 Mar 93	● **SO TOUGH** Heavenly HVNLP 6CD	7	7 wks
12 Mar 94	● **TIGER BAY** Heavenly HVNLP 8CD	8	4 wks
25 Nov 95	**TOO YOUNG TO DIE – THE SINGLES** Heavenly HVNLP 10CD	17†	6 wks

ST. PAUL'S BOYS' CHOIR   UK, choir   8 wks

29 Nov 80	**REJOICE** K-Tel NE 1064	36	8 wks

Buffy SAINTE-MARIE   Canada, female vocalist   2 wks

21 Mar 92	**COINCIDENCE (AND LIKELY STORIES)** Ensign CCD 1920	39	2 wks

Ryuichi SAKAMOTO   Japan, male composer / multi–instrumentalist   9 wks

3 Sep 83	**MERRY CHRISTMAS MR LAWRENCE (film soundtrack)** Virgin V 2276	36	9 wks

SALAD   UK / Holland, male / female vocal / instrumental group   2 wks

27 May 95	**DRINK ME** Island Red CIRDX 1002	16	2 wks

SALT-N-PEPA   US, female rap group   57 wks

6 Aug 88	**A SALT WITH A DEADLY PEPA** ffrr FFRLP 3	19	27 wks
12 May 90	**BLACKS' MAGIC** ffrr 8281641	70	1 wk
6 Jul 91	**A BLITZ OF SALT-N-PEPA HITS** ffrr 8282491	70	2 wks
19 Oct 91	● **GREATEST HITS** ffrr 8282911	6	20 wks
25 Apr 92	**RAPPED IN REMIXES** ffrr 8282972	37	2 wks
23 Apr 94	**VERY NECESSARY** ffrr 8284542	36	5 wks

SALVATION ARMY   UK, brass band   5 wks

24 Dec 77	**BY REQUEST** Warwick WW 5038	16	5 wks

SAM and DAVE   US, male vocal duo   20 wks

21 Jan 67	**HOLD ON I'M COMIN'** Atlantic 588045	35	7 wks
22 Apr 67	**DOUBLE DYNAMITE** Stax 589003	28	5 wks
23 Mar 68	**SOUL MAN** Stax 589015	32	8 wks

S
269

Richie SAMBORA US, male vocalist / instrumentalist – guitar   **3 wks**

14 Sep 91   **STRANGER IN THIS TOWN** Mercury 8488951 ....**20**   3 wks

Mike SAMMES SINGERS – See RICHMOND STRINGS/Mike SAMMES SINGERS

SAMSON UK, male vocal / instrumental group   **6 wks**

26 Jul 80   **HEAD ON** Gem GEMLP 108 ....**34**   6 wks

David SANBORN US, male instrumentalist – saxophone   **1 wk**

14 Mar 87   **A CHANGE OF HEART** Warner Bros. 925 4791 ....**86**   1 wk

SANTANA US, male vocal / instrumental group   **220 wks**

2 May 70	**SANTANA** CBS 63815	**26**	11 wks
28 Nov 70	● **ABRAXAS** CBS 64807	**7**	52 wks
13 Nov 71	● **SANTANA 3** CBS 69015	**6**	14 wks
26 Aug 72	**CARLOS SANTANA AND BUDDY MILES LIVE** CBS 65142 [1]	**29**	4 wks
25 Nov 72	● **CARAVANSERAI** CBS 65299	**6**	11 wks
28 Jul 73	● **LOVE DEVOTION SURRENDER** CBS 69037 [2]	**7**	9 wks
8 Dec 73	● **WELCOME** CBS 69040	**8**	6 wks
21 Sep 74	**GREATEST HITS** CBS 69081	**14**	15 wks
2 Nov 74	**ILLUMINATIONS** CBS 69063 [3]	**40**	1 wk
30 Nov 74	**BARBOLETTA** CBS 69084	**18**	5 wks
10 Apr 76	**AMIGOS** CBS 86005	**21**	9 wks
8 Jan 77	**FESTIVAL** CBS 86020	**27**	3 wks
5 Nov 77	● **MOONFLOWER** CBS 88272	**7**	27 wks
11 Nov 78	**INNER SECRETS** CBS 86075	**17**	16 wks
24 Mar 79	**ONENESS – SILVER DREAMS GOLDEN REALITY** CBS 86037 [4]	**55**	4 wks
27 Oct 79	**MARATHON** CBS 86098	**28**	5 wks
20 Sep 80	**THE SWING OF DELIGHT** CBS 22075 [4]	**65**	2 wks
18 Apr 81	**ZE BOP** CBS 84946	**33**	4 wks
14 Aug 82	**SHANGO** CBS 85914	**35**	7 wks
30 Apr 83	**HAVANA MOON** BS 25350 [4]	**84**	3 wks
23 Mar 85	**BEYOND APPEARANCES** CBS 86307	**58**	3 wks
15 Nov 86	**VIVA! SANTANA – THE VERY BEST** K-Tel NE 1338	**50**	8 wks
14 Jul 90	**SPIRITS DANCING IN THE FLESH** CBS 4669131	**68**	1 wk

[1] Carlos Santana and Buddy Miles [2] Carlos Santana and Mahavishnu John McLaughlin
[3] Carlos Santana and Alice Coltran [4] Carlos Santana

Peter SARSTEDT UK, male vocalist   **4 wks**

15 Mar 69   ● **PETER SARSTEDT** United Artists SULP 1219 ....**8**   4 wks

SASHA UK, male producer   **2 wks**

12 Mar 94   **THE QAT COLLECTION** Deconstruction 74321191962 ....**55**   2 wks

Joe SATRIANI US, male instrumentalist – guitar   **11 wks**

15 Aug 92	**THE EXTREMIST** Epic 4716722	**13**	6 wks
6 Nov 93	**TIME MACHINE** Relativity 4745152	**32**	2 wks
14 Oct 95	**JOE SATRIANI** Relativity 4811022	**21**	3 wks

Telly SAVALAS US, male vocalist   **10 wks**

22 Mar 75   **TELLY** MCA MCF 2699 ....**12**   10 wks

SAVOY BROWN UK, male vocal / instrumental group   **1 wk**

28 Nov 70   **LOOKIN' IN** Decca SKL 5066 ....**50**   1 wk

SAW DOCTORS Ireland, male vocal / instrumental group   **4 wks**

8 Jun 91   **IF THIS IS ROCK AND ROLL I WANT MY OLD JOB**
      BACK Solid ROCK 7 ....**69**   2 wks

31 Oct 92   **ALL THE WAY FROM TUAM** Solid 4509911462 ....**33**   2 wks

SAXON *UK, male vocal / instrumental group*   **97 wks**

12 Apr 80 ● **WHEELS OF STEEL** Carrere CAL 115.....................**5**	29 wks
15 Nov 80 **STRONG ARM OF THE LAW** Carrere CAL 120 ....**11**	13 wks
3 Oct 81 ● **DENIM AND LEATHER** Carrere CAL 128 ....**9**	11 wks
22 May 82 ● **THE EAGLE HAS LANDED** Carrere CAL 157 ....**5**	19 wks
26 Mar 83 **POWER AND THE GLORY** Carrere CAL 147 ....**15**	9 wks
11 Feb 84 **CRUSADER** Carrere CAL 200 ....**18**	7 wks
14 Sep 85 **INNOCENCE IS NO EXCUSE** Parlophone SAXON 2 ....**36**	4 wks
27 Sep 86 **ROCK THE NATIONS** EMI EMC 3515 ....**34**	3 wks
9 Apr 88 **DESTINY** EMI EMC 3543 ....**49**	2 wks

Leo SAYER *UK, male vocalist*   **236 wks**

5 Jan 74 ● **SILVER BIRD** Chrysalis CHR 1050 ....**2**	22 wks
26 Oct 74 ● **JUST A BOY** Chrysalis CHR 1068 ....**4**	14 wks
20 Sep 75 ● **ANOTHER YEAR** Chrysalis CHR 1087 ....**8**	9 wks
27 Nov 76 ● **ENDLESS FLIGHT** Chrysalis CHR 1125.....................**4**	66 wks
22 Oct 77 ● **THUNDER IN MY HEART** Chrysalis CDL 1154 ....**8**	16 wks
2 Sep 78 **LEO SAYER** Chrysalis CDL 1198.....................**15**	25 wks
31 Mar 79 ★ **THE VERY BEST OF LEO SAYER** Chrysalis CDL 1222 ....**1**	37 wks
13 Oct 79 **HERE** Chrysalis CDL 1240 ....**44**	4 wks
23 Aug 80 **LIVING IN A FANTASY** Chrysalis CDL 1297.....................**15**	9 wks
8 May 82 **WORLD RADIO** Chrysalis CDL 1345 ....**30**	12 wks
12 Nov 83 **HAVE YOU EVER BEEN IN LOVE** Chrysalis LEOTV 1 ....**15**	18 wks
6 Mar 93 **ALL THE BEST** Chrysalis CDCHR 1980.....................**26**	4 wks

Alexei SAYLE *UK, male comedian*   **5 wks**

17 Mar 84   **THE FISH PEOPLE TAPES** Island IMA 9 ....**62**   5 wks

Boz SCAGGS *US, male vocalist*   **29 wks**

12 Mar 77 **SILK DEGREES** CBS 81193.....................**37**	24 wks
17 Dec 77 **DOWN TWO, THEN LEFT** CBS 86036 ....**55**	1 wk
3 May 80 **MIDDLE MAN** CBS 86094 ....**52**	4 wks

SCARLET *UK, female vocal / instrumental duo*   **2 wks**

11 Mar 95   **NAKED** WEA 4509976432 ....**59**   2 wks

SCARS *UK, male vocal / instrumental group*   **3 wks**

18 Apr 81   **AUTHOR AUTHOR** Pre PREX 5 ....**67**   3 wks

SCHAEFER – See ROSTAL and SCHAEFER

Michael SCHENKER GROUP
Germany / UK, male vocal / instrumental group   **44 wks**

6 Sep 80 ● **MICHAEL SCHENKER GROUP** Chrysalis CHR 1302 ....**8**	8 wks
19 Sep 81 **MICHAEL SCHENKER GROUP (re-issue)** Chrysalis CHR 1336........**14**	8 wks
13 Mar 82 ● **ONE NIGHT AT BUDOKAN** Chrysalis CTY 1375.....................**5**	11 wks
23 Oct 82 **ASSAULT ATTACK** Chrysalis CHR 1393.....................**19**	5 wks
10 Sep 83 **BUILT TO DESTROY** Chrysalis CHR 1441.....................**23**	5 wks
23 Jun 84 **ROCK WILL NEVER DIE** Chrysalis CUX 1470 ....**24**	5 wks
24 Oct 87 **PERFECT TIMING** EMI EMC 3539 [1] **65**	2 wks

[1] MSG

SCHON – See HAGAR, SCHON, AARONSON, SHRIEVE

SCHOOL OF EXCELLENCE *UK, male instrumental duo*   **2 wks**

28 Oct 95   **PIANO MOODS** Dino DINCD 114 ....**47**   2 wks

SCORPIONS *Germany, male vocal / instrumental group*   **56 wks**

21 Apr 79	**LOVE DRIVE** Harvest SHSP 4097	**36**	11 wks
3 May 80	**ANIMAL MAGNETISM** Harvest SHSP 4113	**23**	6 wks
10 Apr 82	**BLACKOUT** Harvest SHVL 823	**11**	11 wks
24 Mar 84	**LOVE AT FIRST STING** Harvest SHSP 2400071	**17**	6 wks
29 Jun 85	**WORLD WIDE LIVE** Harvest SCORP 1	**18**	8 wks
14 May 88	**SAVAGE AMUSEMENT** Harvest SHSP 4125	**18**	6 wks
17 Nov 90	**CRAZY WORLD** Vertigo 8469081	**27**	7 wks
25 Sep 93	**FACE THE HEAT** Mercury 5182802	**51**	1 wk

SCOTLAND WORLD CUP SQUAD 1974
UK, male football team vocalists   **9 wks**

25 May 74	● **EASY EASY** Polydor 2383 282	**3**	9 wks

Band of the SCOTS GUARDS *UK, military band*   **2 wks**

28 Jun 69	**BAND OF THE SCOTS GUARDS** Fontana SFXL 54	**25**	2 wks

Jack SCOTT *Canada, male vocalist*   **12 wks**

7 May 60	● **I REMEMBER HANK WILLIAMS** Top Rank BUY 034	**7**	11 wks
3 Sep 60	**WHAT IN THE WORLD'S COME OVER YOU** Top Rank 25/024	**11**	1 wk

Mike SCOTT *UK, male vocalist / multi–instrumentalist*   **2 wks**

30 Sep 95	**BRING 'EM ALL IN** Chrysalis CDCHR 6108	**23**	2 wks

SCREAMING BLUE MESSIAHS
UK, male vocal / instrumental group   **1 wk**

17 May 86	**GUN–SHY** WEA WX 41	**90**	1 wk

SCREEN II *UK, male vocal / instrumental group*   **1 wk**

9 Apr 94	**LET THE RECORD SPIN** Cleveland City CLE 13015	**36**	1 wk

SCRITTI POLITTI *UK, male vocal / instrumental group*   **37 wks**

11 Sep 82	**SONGS TO REMEMBER** Rough Trade ROUGH 20	**12**	7 wks
22 Jun 85	● **CUPID AND PSYCHE 85** Virgin V 2350	**5**	19 wks
18 Jun 88	● **PROVISION** Virgin V 2515	**8**	11 wks

SEAL *UK, male vocalist*   **118 wks**

1 Jun 91	★ **SEAL** ZTT ZTT 9	**1**	58 wks
4 Jun 94	★ **SEAL** ZTT 4509962562	**1†**	60 wks

The identically titled albums are different.

SEARCHERS *UK, male vocal / instrumental group*   **87 wks**

10 Aug 63	● **MEET THE SEARCHERS** Pye NPL 18086	**2**	44 wks
16 Nov 63	● **SUGAR AND SPICE** Pye NPL 18089	**5**	21 wks
30 May 64	● **IT'S THE SEARCHERS** Pye NPL 18092	**4**	17 wks
27 Mar 65	● **SOUNDS LIKE THE SEARCHERS** Pye NPL 18111	**8**	5 wks

SEBADOH *US, male vocal / instrumental group*   **3 wks**

8 May 93	**BUBBLE AND SCRAPE** Domino WIGCD 4	**63**	1 wk
3 Sep 94	**BAKESALE** Domino WIGCD 11	**40**	2 wks

Jon SECADA *US, male vocalist*   **16 wks**

5 Sep 92	**JON SECADA** SBK SBKCD 19	**20**	11 wks

SEAL unveiled his bald image at a low-key concert in a Sunset Boulevard cafe.
(LFI)

S
273

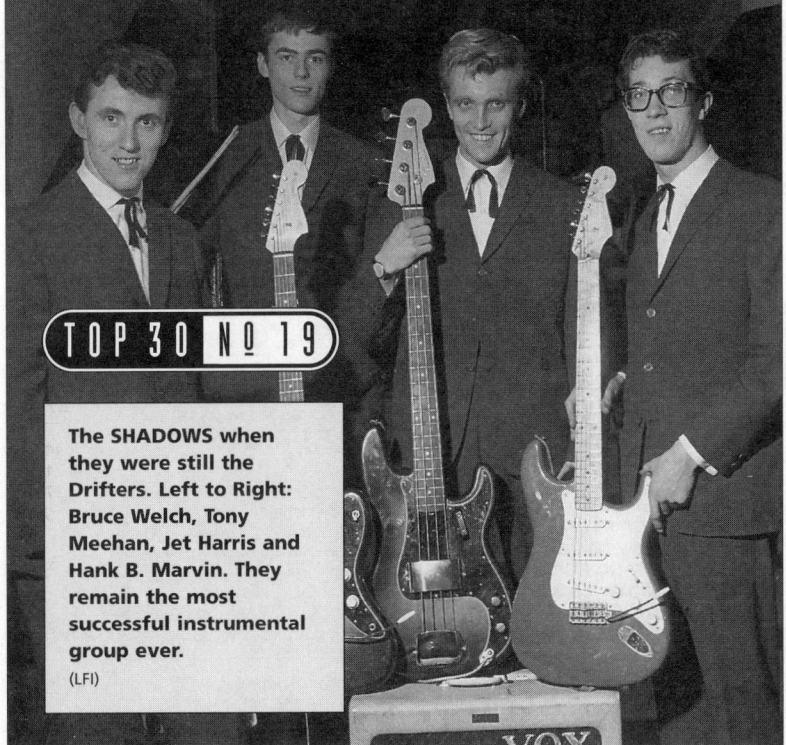

TOP 30 № 19

The **SHADOWS** when they were still the Drifters. Left to Right: Bruce Welch, Tony Meehan, Jet Harris and Hank B. Marvin. They remain the most successful instrumental group ever.
(LFI)

4 Jun 94	**HEART SOUL AND A VOICE** SBK SBKCD 29	**17**	5 wks

Harry SECOMBE *UK, male vocalist* — **61 wks**

31 Mar 62	**SACRED SONGS** Philips RBL 7501	**16**	1 wk
22 Apr 67	● **SECOMBE'S PERSONAL CHOICE** Philips BETS 707	**6**	13 wks
7 Aug 71	**IF I RULED THE WORLD** Contour 6870 501	**17**	20 wks
16 Dec 78	● **20 SONGS OF JOY** Warwick WW 5052	**8**	12 wks
5 Dec 81	**GOLDEN MEMORIES** Warwick WW 5107 [1]	**46**	5 wks
13 Dec 86	**HIGHWAY OF LIFE** Telstar STAR 2289	**45**	5 wks
30 Nov 91	**YOURS SINCERELY** Philips 5107321	**46**	5 wks

[1] Harry Secombe and Moira Anderson

See also Harry Secombe, Peter Sellers and Spike Milligan.

Harry SECOMBE, Peter SELLERS and Spike MILLIGAN
UK, male comedy group — **1 wk**

18 Apr 64	**HOW TO WIN AN ELECTION** Philips AL 3464	**20**	1 wk

See also Harry Secombe; Peter Sellers; Spike Milligan.

SECOND IMAGE *UK, male vocal / instrumental group* — **1 wk**

30 Mar 85	**STRANGE REFLECTIONS** MCA MCF 3255	**100**	1 wk

SECRET AFFAIR *UK, male vocal / instrumental group* — **15 wks**

1 Dec 79	**GLORY BOYS** I–Spy 1	**41**	8 wks
20 Sep 80	**BEHIND CLOSED DOORS** I–Spy 2	**48**	4 wks
13 Mar 82	**BUSINESS AS USUAL** I–Spy 3	**84**	3 wks

Neil SEDAKA *US, male vocalist* — **77 wks**

1 Sep 73	**THE TRA–LA DAYS ARE OVER** MGM 2315 248	**13**	10 wks
22 Jun 74	**LAUGHTER IN THE RAIN** Polydor 2383 265	**17**	10 wks
23 Nov 74	**LIVE AT THE ROYAL FESTIVAL HALL** Polydor 2383 299	**48**	1 wk
1 Mar 75	**OVERNIGHT SUCCESS** Polydor 2442 131	**31**	6 wks
10 Jul 76	● **LAUGHTER AND TEARS – THE BEST OF NEIL SEDAKA TODAY** Polydor 2383399	**2**	25 wks
2 Nov 91	● **TIMELESS – THE VERY BEST OF NEIL SEDAKA** Polydor 5114421	**10**	16 wks
4 Nov 95	**CLASSICALLY SEDAKA** Vision VISCD 5	**23†**	9 wks

SEEKERS *Australia, male / female vocal group* — **280 wks**

3 Jul 65	● **A WORLD OF OUR OWN** Columbia 33SX 1722	**5**	36 wks
3 Jul 65	**THE SEEKERS** Decca LK 4694	**16**	1 wk
19 Nov 66	● **COME THE DAY** Columbia SX 6093	**3**	67 wks
25 Nov 67	**SEEKERS – SEEN IN GREEN** Columbia SCX 6193	**15**	10 wks
14 Sep 68	● **LIVE AT THE TALK OF THE TOWN** Columbia SCX 6278	**2**	29 wks
16 Nov 68	★ **BEST OF THE SEEKERS** Columbia SCX 6268	**1**	125 wks
23 Apr 94	● **CARNIVAL OF HITS** EMI CDEMTV 83 [1]	**7**	12 wks

[1] Judith Durham and the Seekers

Bob SEGER and the SILVER BULLET BAND
US, male vocal / instrumental group — **52 wks**

3 Jun 78	**STRANGER IN TOWN** Capitol EAST 11698	**31**	6 wks
15 Mar 80	**AGAINST THE WIND** Capitol EAST 12041	**26**	6 wks
26 Sep 81	**NINE TONIGHT** Capitol ESTSP 23	**24**	10 wks
8 Jan 83	**THE DISTANCE** Capitol EST 12254	**45**	10 wks
26 Apr 86	**LIKE A ROCK** Capitol EST 2011	**35**	6 wks
21 Sep 91	**THE FIRE INSIDE** Capitol EST 2149	**54**	2 wks
18 Feb 95	● **GREATEST HITS** Capitol CDEST 2241	**6**	12 wks

SELECTER *UK, male / female vocal / instrumental group* — **17 wks**

23 Feb 80	● **TOO MUCH PRESSURE** 2-Tone CDL TT 5002	**5**	13 wks

7 Mar 81 **CELEBRATE THE BULLET** Chrysalis CHR 1306 ....**41**   4 wks

Peter SELLERS UK, male vocalist   **102 wks**

14 Feb 59 ● **THE BEST OF SELLERS** Parlophone PMD 1069 ....**3**   47 wks
12 Dec 59 ● **SONGS FOR SWINGING SELLERS** Parlophone PMC 1111 ....**3**   37 wks
3 Dec 60 ● **PETER AND SOPHIA** Parlophone PMC 1131 1 ....**5**   18 wks

1 Peter Sellers and Sophia Loren

See also Harry Secombe, Peter Sellers and Spike Milligan.

SENSATIONAL ALEX HARVEY BAND
UK, male vocal/instrumental group   **42 wks**

26 Oct 74   **THE IMPOSSIBLE DREAM** Vertigo 6360 112 ....**16**   4 wks
10 May 75 ● **TOMORROW BELONGS TO ME** Vertigo 9102 003 ....**9**   10 wks
23 Aug 75   **NEXT** Vertigo 6360 103 ....**37**   5 wks
27 Sep 75   **SENSATIONAL ALEX HARVEY BAND LIVE** Vertigo 6360 122 ......**14**   7 wks
10 Apr 76   **PENTHOUSE TAPES** Vertigo 9102 007 ....**14**   7 wks
31 Jul 76   **SAHB STORIES** Mountain TOPS 112.....................**11**   9 wks

SENSELESS THINGS UK, male vocal/instrumental group   **2 wks**

26 Oct 91   **THE FIRST OF TOO MANY** Epic 4691571.........................**66**   1 wk
13 Mar 93   **EMPIRE OF THE SENSELESS** Epic 4735252 ....**37**   1 wk

SENSER UK, male/female vocal/instrumental group   **5 wks**

7 May 94 ● **STACKED UP** Ultimate TOPPCD 008 ....**4**   5 wks

SEPULTURA Brazil, male vocal/instrumental group   **6 wks**

6 Apr 91   **ARISE** Roadracer RO 93281 ....**40**   2 wks
23 Oct 93   **CHAOS AD** Roadrunner RR 90002 ....**11**   4 wks

Taja SEVELLE US, female vocalist   **4 wks**

26 Mar 88   **TAJA SEVELLE** Paisley Park WX 165.................**48**   4 wks

SEX PISTOLS UK, male vocal/instrumental group   **101 wks**

12 Nov 77 ★ **NEVER MIND THE BOLLOCKS HERE'S THE SEX PISTOLS**
              Virgin V 2086...**1**   48 wks
10 Mar 79 ● **THE GREAT ROCK 'N' ROLL SWINDLE (film soundtrack)**
              Virgin VD 2410 ....**7**   33 wks
11 Aug 79 ● **SOME PRODUCT – CARRI ON SEX PISTOLS** Virgin VR 2 ....**6**   10 wks
16 Feb 80   **FLOGGING A DEAD HORSE** Virgin V 2142...................**23**   6 wks
17 Oct 92 ● **KISS THIS** Virgin CDV 2702 ....**10**   4 wks

SHADES OF RHYTHM UK, male/female vocal/instrumental group   **3 wks**

17 Aug 91   **SHADES** ZTT ZTT 8 ....**51**   3 wks

SHADOWS UK, male instrumental group   **461 wks**

16 Sep 61 ★ **THE SHADOWS** Columbia 33SX 1374....................**1**   57 wks
13 Oct 62 ★ **OUT OF THE SHADOWS** Columbia 33SX 1458 ....**1**   38 wks
22 Jun 63 ● **GREATEST HITS** Columbia 33SX 1522 ....**2**   49 wks
9 May 64 ● **DANCE WITH THE SHADOWS** Columbia 33SX 1619 ....**2**   27 wks
17 Jul 65 ● **SOUND OF THE SHADOWS** Columbia 33SX 1736...........**4**   17 wks
21 May 66 ● **SHADOW MUSIC** Columbia SX 6041 ....**5**   17 wks
15 Jul 67 ● **JIGSAW** Columbia SCX 6148 ....**8**   16 wks
24 Oct 70   **SHADES OF ROCK** Columbia SCX 6420 ....**30**   4 wks
13 Apr 74   **ROCKIN' WITH CURLY LEADS** EMI EMA 762 ....**45**   1 wk
11 May 74   **GREATEST HITS (re-issue)** Columbia SCX 1522 ....**48**   6 wks
29 Mar 75   **SPECS APPEAL** EMI EMC 3066 ....**30**   5 wks
12 Feb 77 ★ **20 GOLDEN GREATS** EMI EMTV 3 ....**1**   43 wks

S
275

15 Sep 79	★ STRING OF HITS *EMI EMC 3310* **1**	43 wks
26 Jul 80	ANOTHER STRING OF HITS *EMI EMC 3339*......................**16**	8 wks
13 Sep 80	CHANGE OF ADDRESS *Polydor 2442 179* **17**	6 wks
19 Sep 81	HITS RIGHT UP YOUR STREET *Polydor POLD 5046* **15**	16 wks
25 Sep 82	LIFE IN THE JUNGLE / LIVE AT ABBEY ROAD *Polydor SHADS 1* ..**24**	6 wks
22 Oct 83	XXV *Polydor POLD 5120* **34**	6 wks
17 Nov 84	GUARDIAN ANGEL *Polydor POLD 5169* **98**	1 wk
24 May 86	● MOONLIGHT SHADOWS *Polydor PROLP 8* **6**	19 wks
24 Oct 87	SIMPLY SHADOWS *Polydor SHAD 1* **11**	17 wks
20 May 89	STEPPIN' TO THE SHADOWS *Polydor SHAD 30* **11**	9 wks
16 Dec 89	AT THEIR VERY BEST *Polydor 8415201*..........................**12**	9 wks
13 Oct 90	● REFLECTION *Roll Over 8471201*....................................**5**	15 wks
16 Nov 91	THEMES AND DREAMS *Polydor 5113741*.........................**21**	11 wks
15 May 93	SHADOWS IN THE NIGHT *PolyGram TV 8437982*..............**22**	4 wks
22 Oct 94	THE BEST OF HANK MARVIN AND THE SHADOWS *PolyGram TV 5238212* 1 ....**19**	11 wks

1 Hank Marvin and the Shadows

See also Cliff Richard.

SHAGGY *Jamaica, male vocalist*   **4 wks**

| 24 Jul 93 | PURE PLEASURE *Greensleeves GRELCD 184* ....**67** | 1 wk |
| 14 Oct 95 | BOOMBASTIC *Virgin CDV 2782* ....**38** | 3 wks |

SHAKATAK *UK, male / female vocal / instrumental group*   **73 wks**

30 Jan 82	DRIVIN' HARD *Polydor POLS 1030*................................**35**	17 wks
15 May 82	● NIGHT BIRDS *Polydor POLS 1059* **4**	28 wks
27 Nov 82	INVITATIONS *Polydor POLD 5068*.................................**30**	11 wks
22 Oct 83	OUT OF THIS WORLD *Polydor POLD 5115*........................**30**	4 wks
25 Aug 84	DOWN ON THE STREET *Polydor POLD 5148*.....................**17**	9 wks
23 Feb 85	LIVE! *Polydor POLH 21* **82**	3 wks
22 Oct 88	THE COOLEST CUTS *K-Tel NE 1422* **73**	1 wk

SHAKESPEAR'S SISTER *UK / US, female vocal / instrumental duo*   **63 wks**

| 2 Sep 89 | ● SACRED HEART *London 828131 1* ....**9** | 8 wks |
| 29 Feb 92 | ● HORMONALLY YOURS *London 8282262*............................**3** | 55 wks |

SHAKIN' PYRAMIDS *UK, male vocal / instrumental group*   **4 wks**

| 4 Apr 81 | SKIN 'EM UP *Cuba Libra V 2199* ....**48** | 4 wks |

SHAKY – *See Shakin' STEVENS*

SHALAMAR *US, male / female vocal / instrumental group*   **121 wks**

27 Mar 82	● FRIENDS *Solar K 52345* **6**	72 wks
11 Sep 82	GREATEST HITS *Solar SOLA 3001* **71**	5 wks
30 Jul 83	● THE LOOK *Solar 960239*...**7**	20 wks
12 Apr 86	● THE GREATEST HITS *Stylus SMR 8615* **5**	24 wks

The two Greatest Hits *albums are different.*

SHAM 69 *UK, male vocal / instrumental group*   **27 wks**

11 Mar 78	TELL US THE TRUTH *Polydor 2383 491* **25**	8 wks
2 Dec 78	THAT'S LIFE *Polydor POLD 5010*...................................**27**	11 wks
29 Sep 79	● THE ADVENTURES OF THE HERSHAM BOYS *Polydor POLD 5025*....**8**	8 wks

SHAMEN *UK, male vocal / instrumental duo*   **50 wks**

2 Nov 90	EN–TACT *One Little Indian TPLP 22* **31**	10 wks
28 Sep 91	PROGENY *One Little Indian TPLP 32* **23**	2 wks
26 Sep 92	● BOSS DRUM / DIFFERENT DRUM *One Little Indian TPLP 42CD* **3**	35 wks
20 Nov 93	ON AIR *Band Of Joy BOJCD 006* **61**	1 wk
4 Nov 95	AXIS MUTATIS *One Little Indian TPLP 52CDL* **27**	2 wks

From 18 Dec 93 sales of Boss Drum *and the remix album,* Different Drum, *were amalgamated.*

SHAMPOO *UK, female vocal duo*   **2 wks**

5 Nov 94   **WE ARE SHAMPOO** *Food FOODCD 12* ....**45**   2 wks

Jimmy SHAND, HIS BAND AND GUESTS
UK, male instrumentalist – accordian, male / female vocal / instrumental group   **2 wks**

24 Dec 83   **FIFTY YEARS ON WITH JIMMY SHAND** *Ross WGR 062* ....**97**   2 wks

SHANICE *US, female vocalist*   **4 wks**

21 Mar 92   **INNER CHILD** *Motown 5300082* ....**21**   4 wks

SHANNON *US, female vocalist*   **12 wks**

10 Mar 84   **LET THE MUSIC PLAY** *Club JABL 1*.......................................**52**   12 wks

Del SHANNON *US, male vocalist*   **23 wks**

11 May 63 ● **HATS OFF TO DEL SHANNON** *London HAX 8071* ....**9**   17 wks
2 Nov 63   **LITTLE TOWN FLIRT** *London HAX 8091*...**15**   6 wks

Helen SHAPIRO *UK, female vocalist*   **25 wks**

10 Mar 62 ● **TOPS WITH ME** *Columbia 33SX 1397*.................................**2**   25 wks

Feargal SHARKEY *UK, male vocalist*   **24 wks**

23 Nov 85   **FEARGAL SHARKEY** *Virgin V 2360* ....**12**   20 wks
20 Apr 91   **SONGS FROM THE MARDI GRAS** *Virgin V 2642* ....**27**   4 wks

SHARPE and NUMAN – *See Gary NUMAN*

Roland SHAW – *See MANTOVANI*

Sandie SHAW *UK, female vocalist*   **14 wks**

6 Mar 65 ● **SANDIE** *Pye NPL 18110* ....**3**   13 wks
19 Nov 94   **NOTHING LESS THAN BRILLIANT** *Virgin VTCD 34* ....**64**   1 wk

George SHEARING *UK, male instrumentalist – piano*   **13 wks**

11 Jun 60   **BEAUTY AND THE BEAT** *Capitol T 1219* `1` ....**16**   6 wks
20 Oct 62 ● **NAT 'KING' COLE SINGS AND THE GEORGE SHEARING
              QUINTET PLAYS** *Capitol W 1675* `2` ....**8**   7 wks

`1` Peggy Lee and George Shearing `2` Nat 'King' Cole and the George Shearing Quintet

SHED SEVEN *UK, male vocal / instrumental group*   **2 wks**

17 Sep 94   **CHANGE GIVER** *Polydor 5236152* ....**16**   2 wks

SHEEP ON DRUGS *UK, male vocal / instrumental duo*   **1 wk**

10 Apr 93   **GREATEST HITS** *Transglobal CID 8006* ....**55**   1 wk

Pete SHELLEY *UK, male vocalist*   **4 wks**

2 Jul 83   **XL-1** *Genetic XL 1* ....**42**   4 wks

SHERRICK *US, male vocalist*   **6 wks**

29 Aug 87   **SHERRICK** *Warner Bros. WX 118* ....**27**   6 wks

Brendon SHINE *Ireland, male vocalist*   **29 wks**

12 Nov 83   **THE BRENDON SHINE COLLECTION** *Play PLAYTV 1* ....**51**   12 wks

S
277

British Hit Albums Part One

Date of chart entry/Title & catalogue no./Peak position reached/Weeks on chart

★ Number One   ● Top Ten   † still on chart at 30 Dec 1995   ☐ credited to act billed in footnote

3 Nov 84	**WITH LOVE** Play PLAYTV 2	**74**	4 wks
16 Nov 85	**MEMORIES** Play PLAYTV 3	**81**	7 wks
18 Nov 89	**MAGIC MOMENTS** Stylus SMR 991	**62**	6 wks

SHIRLIE – See PEPSI and SHIRLIE

Michelle SHOCKED US, female vocalist · **24 wks**

10 Sep 88	**SHORT SHARP SHOCKED** Cooking Vinyl CVLP 1	**33**	19 wks
18 Nov 89	**CAPTAIN SWING** Cooking Vinyl 838878 1	**31**	3 wks
11 Apr 92	**ARKANSAS TRAVELER** London 5121892	**46**	2 wks

SHOP ASSISTANTS UK, male/female vocal/instrumental group · **1 wk**

| 29 Nov 86 | **SHOP ASSISTANTS** Blue Guitar AZLP 2 | **100** | 1 wk |

SHOWADDYWADDY UK, male vocal/instrumental group · **126 wks**

7 Dec 74	● **SHOWADDYWADDY** Bell BELLS 248	**9**	19 wks
12 Jul 75	● **STEP TWO** Bell BELLS 256	**7**	17 wks
29 May 76	**TROCADERO** Bell SYBEL 8003	**41**	3 wks
25 Dec 76	● **GREATEST HITS** Arista ARTY 145	**4**	26 wks
3 Dec 77	**RED STAR** Arista SPARTY 1023	**20**	10 wks
9 Dec 78	★ **GREATEST HITS (1976–1978)** Arista ARTV 1	**1**	17 wks
10 Nov 79	● **CREPES AND DRAPES** Arista ARTV 3	**8**	14 wks
20 Dec 80	**BRIGHT LIGHTS** Arista SPART 1142	**54**	8 wks
7 Nov 81	**THE VERY BEST OF** Arista SPART 1178	**33**	11 wks
5 Dec 87	**THE BEST STEPS TO HEAVEN** Tiger SHTV 1	**90**	1 wk

SHRIEKBACK UK, male vocal/instrumental group · **1 wk**

| 11 Aug 84 | **JAM SCIENCE** Arista 206 416 | **85** | 1 wk |

SHRIEVE – See HAGAR, SCHON, AARONSON, SHRIEVE

SHUT UP AND DANCE
UK, male vocal/instrumental/sampling group · **2 wks**

| 27 Jun 92 | **DEATH IS NOT THE END** Shut Up And Dance SUADCD 005 | **38** | 2 wks |

SHY UK, male vocal/instrumental group · **2 wks**

| 11 Apr 87 | **EXCESS ALL AREAS** RCA PL 71221 | **74** | 2 wks |

Labi SIFFRE UK, male vocalist · **2 wks**

| 24 Jul 71 | **SINGER AND THE SONG** Pye NSPL 28147 | **47** | 1 wk |
| 14 Oct 72 | **CRYING, LAUGHING, LOVING, LYING** Pye NSPL 28163 | **46** | 1 wk |

SIGUE SIGUE SPUTNIK UK, male vocal/instrumental group · **7 wks**

| 9 Aug 86 | ● **FLAUNT IT** Parlophone PCS 7305 | **10** | 6 wks |
| 15 Apr 89 | **DRESS FOR EXCESS** Parlophone PCS 7328 | **53** | 1 wk |

SILENCERS UK, male vocal/instrumental group · **3 wks**

| 23 Mar 91 | **DANCE TO THE HOLY MAN** RCA PL 74924 | **39** | 2 wks |
| 5 Jun 93 | **SECONDS OF PLEASURE** RCA 74321141132 | **52** | 1 wk |

SILVER BULLET UK, male vocal/instrumental duo · **2 wks**

| 4 May 91 | **BRING DOWN THE WALLS NO LIMIT SQUAD** Parlophone PCS 7350 | **38** | 2 wks |

SILVER BULLET BAND – See Bob SEGER and the SILVER BULLET BAND

SILVER CONVENTION Germany / US, female vocal group   **3 wks**

25 Jun 77	**SILVER CONVENTION: GREATEST HITS** Magnet MAG 6001 ....**34**	3 wks

SILVERCHAIR Australia, male vocal / instrumental group   **1 wk**

23 Sep 95	**FROGSTOMP** Murmur 4803402 ....**49**	1 wk

SILVERFISH US, male vocal / instrumental group   **1 wk**

27 Jun 92	**ORGAN FAN** Creation CRECD 118 ....**65**	1 wk

Carly SIMON US, female vocalist   **61 wks**

20 Jan 73	● **NO SECRETS** Elektra K 42127 ....**3**	26 wks
16 Mar 74	**HOT CAKES** Elektra K 52005 ....**19**	9 wks
9 May 87	**COMING AROUND AGAIN** Arista 208 140 ....**25**	20 wks
3 Sep 88	**GREATEST HITS LIVE** Arista 209196 ....**49**	6 wks

Paul SIMON US, male vocalist   **261 wks**

26 Feb 72	★ **PAUL SIMON** CBS 69007 ....**1**	26 wks
2 Jun 73	● **THERE GOES RHYMIN' SIMON** CBS 69035 ....**4**	22 wks
1 Nov 75	**STILL CRAZY AFTER ALL THESE YEARS** CBS 86001 .....**6**	31 wks
3 Dec 77	● **GREATEST HITS, ETC.** CBS 10007 ....**6**	15 wks
30 Aug 80	**ONE–TRICK PONY** Warner Bros. K 56846 ....**17**	12 wks
12 Nov 83	**HEARTS AND BONES** Warner Bros. 9239421 ....**34**	8 wks
13 Sep 86	★ **GRACELAND** Warner Bros. WX 52 ....**1**	101 wks
24 Jan 87	**GREATEST HITS, ETC. (re-issue)** CBS 450 1661 ....**73**	2 wks
5 Nov 88	**NEGOTIATIONS AND LOVE SONGS 1971–1986** Warner Bros. WX 223 ....**17**	15 wks
27 Oct 90	★ **RHYTHM OF THE SAINTS** Warner Bros. WX 340 ....**1**	28 wks
23 Nov 91	**THE CONCERT IN THE PARK – AUGUST 15TH 1991** Warner Bros. WX 448 ....**60**	1 wk

See also Simon and Garfunkel.

SIMON and GARFUNKEL US, male vocal duo   **1083 wks**

16 Apr 66	**SOUNDS OF SILENCE** CBS 62690 ....**13**	104 wks
3 Aug 68	★ **BOOKENDS** CBS 63101 ....**1**	77 wks
31 Aug 68	**PARSLEY, SAGE, ROSEMARY AND THYME** CBS 62860 ....**13**	66 wks
26 Oct 68	● **THE GRADUATE (film soundtrack)** CBS 70042 ....**3**	71 wks
9 Nov 68	**WEDNESDAY MORNING 3 A.M.** CBS 63370 ....**24**	6 wks
21 Feb 70	★ **BRIDGE OVER TROUBLED WATER** CBS 63699 ....**1**	304 wks
22 Jul 72	● **GREATEST HITS** CBS 69003 ....**2**	283 wks
4 Apr 81	**SOUNDS OF SILENCE (re-issue)** CBS 32020 ....**68**	1 wk
21 Nov 81	● **THE SIMON AND GARFUNKEL COLLECTION** CBS 10029 ....**4**	80 wks
20 Mar 82	**THE CONCERT IN CENTRAL PARK** Geffen GEF 96008 ....**6**	43 wks
30 Nov 91	● **THE DEFINITIVE SIMON AND GARFUNKEL** Columbia MOODCD 21 ....**8**	48 wks

See also Paul Simon; Art Garfunkel.

Nina SIMONE US, female vocalist   **20 wks**

24 Jul 65	**I PUT A SPELL ON YOU** Philips BL 7671 ....**18**	3 wks
15 Feb 69	**'NUFF SAID** RCS SF 7979 ....**11**	1 wk
14 Nov 87	**MY BABY JUST CARES FOR ME** Charly CR 30217 ....**56**	8 wks
16 Jul 94	● **FEELING GOOD – THE VERY BEST OF NINA SIMONE** PolyGram TV 5226692 ....**9**	8 wks

SIMPLE MINDS UK, male vocal / instrumental group   **347 wks**

5 May 79	**A LIFE IN THE DAY** Zoom ZULP 1 ....**30**	6 wks
27 Sep 80	**EMPIRES AND DANCE** Arista SPART 1140 ....**41**	3 wks

S
279

TOP 30   № 3

Bridge Over Troubled Water by Simon and Garfunkel has the most weeks at number one (41) of any album that was not a film soundtrack.

(Hulton Deutsch)

12 Sep 81	**SONS AND FASCINATIONS / SISTERS FEELINGS CALL**		
	Virgin V 2207 ....**11**	7	wks
27 Feb 82	**CELEBRATION** *Arista SPART 1183* **45**	7	wks
25 Sep 82	● **NEW GOLD DREAM (81, 82, 83, 84)** *Virgin V 2230* **3**	52	wks
18 Feb 84	★ **SPARKLE IN THE RAIN** *Virgin V 2300* **1**	57	wks
2 Nov 85	★ **ONCE UPON A TIME** *Virgin V 2364* **1**	83	wks
6 Jun 87	★ **LIVE IN THE CITY OF LIGHT** *Virgin V SMDL 1* **1**	26	wks
13 May 89	★ **STREET FIGHTING YEARS** *Virgin MINDS 1* **1**	28	wks
20 Apr 91	● **REAL LIFE** *Virgin V 2660* **2**	25	wks
24 Oct 92	★ **GLITTERING PRIZE 81 / 92** *Virgin SMTVD 1* **1**	39	wks
11 Feb 95	● **GOOD NEWS FROM THE NEXT WORLD** *Virgin CDV 2760* **2**	14	wks

SIMPLY RED *UK, male vocal / instrumental group*   **410 wks**

26 Oct 85	● **PICTURE BOOK** *Elektra EKT 27* **2**	130	wks
21 Mar 87	● **MEN AND WOMEN** *WEA WX 85* **2**	60	wks
25 Feb 89	★ **A NEW FLAME** *Elektra WX 242* **1**	84	wks
12 Oct 91	★ **STARS** *East West WX 427*...........**1**	125	wks
21 Oct 95	★ **LIFE** *East West 0630120692* ....**1†**	11	wks

SIMPSON – *See ASHFORD and SIMPSON*

SIMPSONS *US, male / female cartoon group*   **30 wks**

2 Feb 91	● **THE SIMPSONS SING THE BLUES** *Geffen 7599243081* **6**	30	wks

Joyce SIMS *US, female vocalist*   **25 wks**

9 Jan 88	● **COME INTO MY LIFE** *London LONLP 47* **5**	24	wks
16 Sep 89	**ALL ABOUT LOVE** *London 828129 1* **64**	1	wk

Kym SIMS *US, female vocalist*   **2 wks**

18 Apr 92	**TOO BLIND TO SEE IT** *Atco 7567921042* **39**	2	wks

S 281

Frank SINATRA *US, male vocalist*   **662 wks**

8 Nov 58	● **COME FLY WITH ME** *Capitol LCT 6154* **2**	18	wks
15 Nov 58	● **SONGS FOR SWINGING LOVERS** *Capitol LCT 6106* **8**	8	wks
29 Nov 58	● **FRANK SINATRA STORY** *Fontana TFL 5030* **8**	1	wk
13 Dec 58	● **FRANK SINATRA SINGS FOR ONLY THE LONELY**		
	Capitol LCT 6168 ....**5**	13	wks
16 May 59	● **COME DANCE WITH ME** *Capitol LCT 6179* **2**	30	wks
22 Aug 59	● **LOOK TO YOUR HEART** *Capitol LCT 6181* **5**	8	wks
11 Jun 60	● **COME BACK TO SORRENTO** *Fontana TFL 5082* **6**	9	wks
29 Oct 60	● **SWING EASY** *Capitol W 587* **5**	17	wks
21 Jan 61	● **NICE 'N EASY** *Capitol W 1417* **4**	27	wks
15 Jul 61	**SINATRA SOUVENIR** *Fontana TFL 5138*...........**18**	1	wk
19 Aug 61	● **WHEN YOUR LOVER HAS GONE** *Encore ENC 101* **6**	10	wks
23 Sep 61	● **SINATRA'S SWINGING SESSION** *Capitol W 1491* **6**	8	wks
28 Oct 61	● **SINATRA SWINGS** *Reprise R 1002* **8**	8	wks
25 Nov 61	● **SINATRA PLUS** *Fontana SET 303* **7**	9	wks
16 Dec 61	● **RING-A-DING-DING** *Reprise R 1001* **8**	9	wks
17 Feb 62	**COME SWING WITH ME** *Capitol W 1594* **13**	4	wks
7 Apr 62	● **I REMEMBER TOMMY** *Reprise R 1003* **10**	12	wks
9 Jun 62	● **SINATRA AND STRINGS** *Reprise R 1004* **6**	20	wks
27 Oct 62	**GREAT SONGS FROM GREAT BRITAIN** *Reprise R 1006*...........**12**	9	wks
29 Dec 62	**SINATRA WITH SWINGING BRASS** *Reprise R 1005* **14**	11	wks
23 Feb 63	● **SINATRA – BASIE** *Reprise R 1008* 1 ....**2**	23	wks
27 Jul 63	● **CONCERT SINATRA** *Reprise R 1009* **8**	18	wks
5 Oct 63	● **SINATRA'S SINATRA** *Reprise R 1010* **9**	24	wks
19 Sep 64	**IT MIGHT AS WELL BE SWING** *Reprise R 1012* **17**	4	wks
20 Mar 65	**SOFTLY AS I LEAVE YOU** *Reprise R 1013* **20**	1	wk
22 Jan 66	● **A MAN AND HIS MUSIC** *Reprise R 1016*...........**9**	19	wks
21 May 66	**MOONLIGHT SINATRA** *Reprise R 1018*...........**18**	8	wks
2 Jul 66	● **STRANGERS IN THE NIGHT** *Reprise R 1017* **4**	18	wks
1 Oct 66	● **SINATRA AT THE SANDS** *Reprise RLP 1019* **7**	18	wks
3 Dec 66	**FRANK SINATRA SINGS SONGS FOR PLEASURE** *MFP 1120* **26**	2	wks

Mick Hucknall of SIMPLY RED is shown in concert during 1992, the second consecutive year in which *Stars* was Britain's best-selling album.

(Mirror Syndication)

TOP 30 Nº 18

FRANK SINATRA has reached the Top Ten in every decade except the 1980s.

(Hulton Deutsch)

25 Feb 67	**THAT'S LIFE** *Reprise RSLP 1020*..........................**22**	12 wks
7 Oct 67	**FRANK SINATRA** *Reprise RSLP 1022* **28**	5 wks
19 Oct 68 ●	**GREATEST HITS** *Reprise RSLP 1025*.....................**8**	38 wks
7 Dec 68	**BEST OF FRANK SINATRA** *Capitol ST 21140* **17**	10 wks
7 Jun 69 ●	**MY WAY** *Reprise RSLP 1029* **2**	59 wks
4 Oct 69	**A MAN ALONE** *Reprise RSLP 1030*.......................**18**	7 wks
9 May 70	**WATERTOWN** *Reprise RSLP 1031* **14**	9 wks
12 Dec 70 ●	**GREATEST HITS VOLUME 2** *Reprise RSLP 1032* **6**	40 wks
5 Jun 71 ●	**SINATRA AND COMPANY** *Reprise RSLP 1033* **9**	9 wks
27 Nov 71	**FRANK SINATRA SINGS RODGERS AND HART**	
	Starline SRS 5083 ....**35**	1 wk
8 Jan 72	**MY WAY (re-issue)** *Reprise K 44015*.....................**35**	1 wk
8 Jan 72	**GREATEST HITS VOLUME 2 (re-issue)** *Reprise K 44018*..............**29**	3 wks
1 Dec 73	**OL' BLUE EYES IS BACK** *Warner Bros. K 44249* **12**	13 wks
17 Aug 74	**SOME NICE THINGS I'VE MISSED** *Reprise K 54020* **35**	3 wks
15 Feb 75	**THE MAIN EVENT (TV SOUNDTRACK)** *Reprise K 54031*..............**30**	2 wks
14 Jun 75	**THE BEST OF OL' BLUE EYES** *Reprise K 54042*.........**30**	3 wks
19 Mar 77 ★	**PORTRAIT OF SINATRA** *Reprise K 64039*................**1**	18 wks
13 May 78 ●	**20 GOLDEN GREATS** *Capitol EMTV 10* **4**	11 wks
18 Aug 84	**L.A. IS MY LADY** *Qwest 925145* **41**	8 wks
22 Mar 86	**NEW YORK NEW YORK (GREATEST HITS)** *Warner Bros. WX 32*..**13**	12 wks
4 Oct 86	**THE FRANK SINATRA COLLECTION** *Capitol EMTV 41*..................**40**	5 wks
6 Nov 93 ●	**DUETS** *Capitol CDEST 2218* **5**	14 wks
26 Nov 94	**DUETS II** *Capitol CDEST 2245* **29**	6 wks
11 Mar 95	**THIS IS FRANK SINATRA 1953–1957**	
	Music For Pleasure CDDL 1275......................**56**	1 wk
2 Dec 95	**SINATRA 80TH – ALL THE BEST** *Capitol CDESTD 2* ....**49†**	5 wks

[1] Frank Sinatra and Count Basie

Nancy SINATRA *US, female vocalist*   **32 wks**

16 Apr 66	**BOOTS** *Reprise R 6202* **12**	9 wks
18 Jun 66	**HOW DOES THAT GRAB YOU** *Reprise R 6207* **17**	3 wks
29 Jun 68	**NANCY AND LEE** *Reprise RSLP 6273* [1] **17**	12 wks
10 Oct 70	**NANCY'S GREATEST HITS** *Reprise RSLP 6409* **39**	3 wks
25 Sep 71	**NANCY AND LEE (re-issue)** *Reprsie K 44126* [1] **42**	1 wk
29 Jan 72	**DID YOU EVER** *RCA Victor SF 8240* [1] **31**	4 wks

[1] Nancy Sinatra and Lee Hazlewood

SINFONIA OF LONDON – *See Howard BLAKE conducting the SINFONIA OF LONDON*

SINITTA *US, female vocalist*   **23 wks**

| 26 Dec 87 | **SINITTA!** *Fanfare BOYLP 1* ....**34** | 19 wks |
| 9 Dec 89 | **WICKED!** *Fanfare FARE 2* ....**52** | 4 wks |

SIOUXSIE and the BANSHEES
UK, female / male vocal / instrumental group   **119 wks**

2 Dec 78	**THE SCREAM** *Polydor POLD 5009* **12**	11 wks
22 Sep 79	**JOIN HANDS** *Polydor POLD 5024* **13**	5 wks
16 Aug 80 ●	**KALEIDOSCOPE** *Polydor 2442 177* **5**	6 wks
27 Jun 81 ●	**JU JU** *Polydor POLS 1034* **7**	17 wks
12 Dec 81	**ONCE UPON A TIME** *Polydor POLS 1056*...............**21**	26 wks
13 Nov 82	**A KISS IN THE DREAMHOUSE** *Polydor POLD 5064* **11**	11 wks
3 Dec 83	**NOCTURNE** *Wonderland SHAH 1* **29**	10 wks
16 Jun 84	**HYENA** *Wonderland SHELP 2* **15**	6 wks
26 Apr 86	**TINDERBOX** *Wonderland SHELP 3* **13**	6 wks
14 Mar 87	**THROUGH THE LOOKING GLASS** *Wonderland SHELP 4* **15**	8 wks
17 Sep 88	**PEEP SHOW** *Wonderland SHELP 5* **20**	5 wks
22 Jun 91	**SUPERSTITION** *Wonderland 8477311* **25**	4 wks
17 Oct 92	**TWICE UPON A TIME – THE SINGLES** *Wonderland 5171602* **26**	2 wks
28 Jan 95	**THE RAPTURE** *Wonderland 5237252* **33**	2 wks

SISSEL *Norway, female vocalist / instrumentalist – keyboards*   **1 wk**

| 20 May 95 | **DEEP WITHIN MY SOUL** *Mercury 5267752*..............**58** | 1 wk |

SISTER SLEDGE *US, female vocal group* **58 wks**

12 May 79	● **WE ARE FAMILY** Atlantic K 50587 ....**7**	39	wks
22 Jun 85	**WHEN THE BOYS MEET THE GIRLS** Atlantic 7812551 ....**19**	11	wks
5 Dec 87	**FREAK OUT** Telstar STAR 2319 [1] **72**	3	wks
20 Feb 93	**THE VERY BEST OF SISTER SLEDGE 1973–1993**		
	Atlantic 9548318132............................**19**	5	wks

[1] Chic and Sister Sledge

SISTERHOOD *UK, male vocal / instrumental group* **1 wk**

26 Jul 86	**GIFT** Merciful Release SIS 020 ....**90**	1	wk

SISTERS OF MERCY *UK, male / female vocal / instrumental duo* **42 wks**

23 Mar 85	**FIRST AND LAST AND ALWAYS** Merciful Release MR 337 L **14**	8	wks
28 Nov 87	● **FLOODLAND** Merciful Release MR 441 L **9**	20	wks
2 Nov 90	**VISION THING** Merciful Release **11**	4	wks
9 May 92	● **SOME GIRLS WANDER BY MISTAKE**		
	Merciful Release 9031764762..............................**5**	5	wks
4 Sep 93	**GREATEST HITS VOLUME 1** Merciful Release 4509935792 ....**14**	5	wks

Act was a male–only group for first album.

Peter SKELLERN *UK, male vocalist* **31 wks**

9 Sep 78	**SKELLERN** Mercury 9109 701 ....**48**	3	wks
8 Dec 79	**ASTAIRE** Mercury 9102 702........................**23**	20	wks
4 Dec 82	**A STRING OF PEARLS** Mercury MERL 10 ....**67**	5	wks
1 Apr 95	**STARDUST MEMORIES** WEA 4509981322........................**50**	3	wks

SKID ROW *UK, male vocal / instrumental group* **3 wks**

17 Oct 70	**SKID** CBS 63965 ....**30**	3	wks

SKID ROW *US, male vocal / instrumental group* **28 wks**

2 Sep 89	**SKID ROW** Atlantic 781936 1 ....**30**	16	wks
22 Jun 91	● **SLAVE TO THE GRIND** Atlantic WX 423 ....**5**	9	wks
8 Apr 95	● **SUBHUMAN RACE** Atlantic 7567827302 ....**8**	3	wks

SKIDS *UK, male vocal / instrumental group* **20 wks**

17 Mar 79	**SCARED TO DANCE** Virgin V 2116 ....**19**	10	wks
27 Oct 79	**DAYS IN EUROPA** Virgin V 2138 ....**32**	5	wks
27 Sep 80	● **THE ABSOLUTE GAME** Virgin V 2174 ....**9**	5	wks

SKIN *UK / Germany, male vocal / instrumental group* **3 wks**

14 May 94	● **SKIN** Parlophone CDPCSD 151........................**9**	3	wks

SKUNK ANANSIE *UK, female / male vocal / instrumental group* **3 wks**

30 Sep 95	● **PARANOID AND SUNBURNT** One Little Indian TPLP 55CD **8**	3	wks

SKY *UK / Australia, male instrumental group* **202 wks**

2 Jun 79	● **SKY** Ariola ARLH 5022 ....**9**	56	wks
26 Apr 80	★ **SKY 2** Ariola ADSKY 2 ....**1**	53	wks
28 Mar 81	● **SKY 3** Ariola ASKY 3 ....**3**	23	wks
3 Apr 82	● **SKY 4 – FORTHCOMING** Ariola ASKY 4 ....**7**	22	wks
22 Jan 83	**SKY FIVE LIVE** Ariola 302 171 ....**14**	14	wks
3 Dec 83	**CADMIUM** Ariola 205 885........................**44**	10	wks
12 May 84	**MASTERPIECES – THE VERY BEST OF SKY** Telstar STAR 2241......**15**	18	wks
13 Apr 85	**THE GREAT BALLOON RACE** Epic EPC 26419 ....**63**	6	wks

SKYY US, male vocal / instrumental group
1 wk

21 Jun 86   **FROM THE LEFT SIDE** Capitol EST 2014 ....**85**   1 wk

SLADE UK, male vocal / instrumental group
207 wks

8 Apr 72	● **SLADE ALIVE** Polydor 2383 101	**2**	58 wks
9 Dec 72	★ **SLAYED?** Polydor 2383 163	**1**	34 wks
6 Oct 73	★ **SLADEST** Polydor 2442 119	**1**	24 wks
23 Feb 74	★ **OLD NEW BORROWED AND BLUE** Polydor 2383 261	**1**	16 wks
14 Dec 74	● **SLADE IN FLAME** Polydor 2442 126	**6**	18 wks
27 Mar 76	**NOBODY'S FOOL** Polydor 2383 377	**14**	4 wks
22 Nov 80	**SLADE SMASHES** Polydor POLTV 13	**21**	15 wks
21 Mar 81	**WE'LL BRING THE HOUSE DOWN** Cheapskate SKATE 1	**25**	4 wks
28 Nov 81	**TILL DEAF US DO PART** RCA RCALP 6021	**68**	2 wks
18 Dec 82	**SLADE ON STAGE** RCA RCALP 3107	**58**	3 wks
24 Dec 83	**THE AMAZING KAMIKAZE SYNDROME** RCA PL 70116	**49**	13 wks
9 Jun 84	**SLADE'S GREATS** Polydor SLAD 1	**89**	1 wk
6 Apr 85	**ROGUES GALLERY** RCA PL 70604	**60**	2 wks
30 Nov 85	**CRACKERS – THE SLADE CHRISTMAS PARTY ALBUM** Telstar STAR 2271	**34**	7 wks
9 May 87	**YOU BOYZ MAKE BIG NOIZE** RCA PL 71260	**98**	1 wk
23 Nov 91	**WALL OF HITS** Polydor 5116121	**34**	5 wks

SLASH'S SNAKEPIT US, male vocal / instrumental group
4 wks

25 Feb 95   **IT'S FIVE O'CLOCK SOMEWHERE** Geffen GED 24730 ....**15**   4 wks

SLAUGHTER US, male vocal / instrumental group
1 wk

23 May 92   **THE WILD LIFE** Chrysalis CCD 1911 ....**64**   1 wk

SLAYER US, male vocal / instrumental group
16 wks

2 May 87	**REIGN IN BLOOD** Def Jam LONLP 34	**47**	3 wks
23 Jul 88	**SOUTH OF HEAVEN** London LONLP 63	**25**	4 wks
6 Oct 90	**SEASONS IN THE ABYSS** Def American 8468711	**18**	3 wks
2 Nov 91	**DECADE OF AGGRESSION LIVE** Def American 5106051	**29**	2 wks
15 Oct 94	**DIVINE INTERVENTION** American 74321236772	**15**	4 wks

Percy SLEDGE US, male vocalist
4 wks

14 Mar 87   **WHEN A MAN LOVES A WOMAN (THE ULTIMATE COLLECTION)** Atlantic WX 89 ....**36**   4 wks

SLEEPER UK, male / female vocal / instrumental group
11 wks

25 Feb 95   ● **SMART** Indolent SLEEPCD 007 ....**5**   11 wks

SLEIGHRIDERS UK, male vocal / instrumental group
1 wk

17 Dec 83   **A VERY MERRY DISCO** Warwick WW 5136 ....**100**   1 wk

Grace SLICK US, female vocalist
6 wks

31 May 80   **DREAMS** RCA PL 13544 ....**28**   6 wks

SLIK UK, male vocal / instrumental group
1 wk

12 Jun 76   **SLIK** Bell SYBEL 8004 ....**58**   1 wk

SLIM CHANCE – See Ronnie LANE

SLITS UK, female vocal / instrumental group
5 wks

22 Sep 79   **CUT** Island ILPS 9573 ....**30**   5 wks

SLOWDIVE UK, male vocal / instrumental group   **3 wks**

| 14 Sep 91 | **JUST FOR A DAY** Creation CRELP 094 | 32 | 2 wks |
| 12 Jun 93 | **SOUVLAKI** Creation CRECD 139 | 51 | 1 wk |

SLY and the FAMILY STONE
US, male / female vocal / instrumental group   **2 wks**

| 5 Feb 72 | **THERE'S A RIOT GOIN' ON** Epic EPC 64613 | 31 | 2 wks |

SLY and ROBBIE Jamaica, male vocal / instrumental duo   **5 wks**

| 9 May 87 | **RHYTHM KILLERS** Fourth & Broadway BRLP 512 | 35 | 5 wks |

SMALL FACES UK, male vocal / instrumental group   **66 wks**

14 May 66	● **SMALL FACES** Decca LK 4790	3	25 wks
17 Jun 67	**FROM THE BEGINNING** Decca LK 4879	17	5 wks
1 Jul 67	**SMALL FACES** Immediate IMSP 008	12	17 wks
15 Jun 68	★ **OGDEN'S NUT GONE FLAKE** Immediate IMLP 012	1	19 wks

The two albums titled Small Faces are different.

S*M*A*S*H UK, male vocal / instrumental group   **4 wks**

| 2 Apr 94 | **S*M*A*S*H** Hi-Rise FLATMCD 2 | 28 | 3 wks |
| 17 Sep 94 | **SELF ABUSED** Hi-Rise FLATCD 6 | 59 | 1 wk |

SMASHING PUMPKINS US, male vocal / instrumental group   **21 wks**

| 31 Jul 93 | ● **SIAMESE DREAM** Hut CDHUT 11 | 4 | 15 wks |
| 4 Nov 95 | ● **MELLON COLLIE AND THE INFINITE SADNESS** Hut CDHUTD 30 | 4 | 6 wks |

Brian SMITH and his HAPPY PIANO
UK, male instrumentalist – piano   **1 wk**

| 19 Sep 81 | **PLAY IT AGAIN** Deram DS 047 | 97 | 1 wk |

Jimmy SMITH US, male instrumentalist – organ   **3 wks**

| 18 Jun 66 | **GOT MY MOJO WORKING** Verve VLP 912 | 19 | 3 wks |

Keely SMITH US, female vocalist   **9 wks**

| 16 Jan 65 | **LENNON–McCARTNEY SONGBOOK** Reprise R 6142 | 12 | 9 wks |

O.C. SMITH US, male vocalist   **1 wk**

| 17 Aug 68 | **HICKORY HOLLER REVISITED** CBS 63362 | 40 | 1 wk |

Patti SMITH GROUP US, female / male vocal / instrumental group   **21 wks**

1 Apr 78	**EASTER** Arista SPART 1043	16	14 wks
19 May 79	**WAVE** Arista SPART 1086	41	6 wks
16 Jul 88	**DREAM OF LIFE** Arista 209172 [1]	70	1 wk

[1] Patti Smith

Steven SMITH and FATHER UK, male instrumental duo   **3 wks**

| 13 May 72 | **STEVEN SMITH AND FATHER AND 16 GREAT SONGS** Decca SKL 5128 | 17 | 3 wks |

SMITH and JONES UK, male comedy duo   **8 wks**

| 15 Nov 86 | **SCRATCH AND SNIFF** 10 DIX 51 | 62 | 8 wks |

British Hit Albums Part One
Date of chart entry/Title & catalogue no./Peak position reached/Weeks on chart
★ Number One   ● Top Ten   † still on chart at 30 Dec 1995   □ credited to act billed in footnote

SMITHS *UK, male vocal / instrumental group* **199 wks**

3 Mar 84	● THE SMITHS *Rough Trade ROUGH 61*	2	33 wks
24 Nov 84	● HATFUL OF HOLLOW *Rough Trade ROUGH 76*	7	46 wks
23 Feb 85	★ MEAT IS MURDER *Rough Trade ROUGH 81*	1	13 wks
28 Jun 86	● THE QUEEN IS DEAD *Rough Trade ROUGH 96*	2	22 wks
7 Mar 87	● THE WORLD WON'T LISTEN *Rough Trade ROUGH 101*	2	15 wks
30 May 87	LOUDER THAN BOMBS (import) *Rough Trade ROUGH 255*	38	5 wks
10 Oct 87	● STRANGEWAYS HERE WE COME *Rough Trade ROUGH 106*	2	17 wks
17 Sep 88	● RANK *Rough Trade ROUGH 126*	2	7 wks
29 Aug 92	★ BEST . . . I *WEA 4509903272*	1	9 wks
14 Nov 92	BEST . . . II *WEA 4509904062*	29	5 wks
4 Mar 95	● SINGLES *WEA 4509990902*	5	8 wks
4 Mar 95	HATFUL OF HOLLOW (re-issue) *WEA 4509918932*	26	3 wks
4 Mar 95	THE QUEEN IS DEAD (re-issue) *WEA 4509918962*	30	4 wks
4 Mar 95	STRANGEWAYS HERE WE COME (re-issue) *WEA 4509918992*	38	4 wks
4 Mar 95	MEAT IS MURDER (re-issue) *WEA 4509918952*	39	2 wks
4 Mar 95	THE SMITHS (re-issue) *WEA 4509918922*	42	4 wks
4 Mar 95	THE WORLD WON'T LISTEN (re-issue) *WEA 4509918982*	52	2 wks

SMOKIE *UK, male vocal / instrumental group* **42 wks**

1 Nov 75	SMOKIE / CHANGING ALL THE TIME *RAK SRAK 517*	18	5 wks
30 Apr 77	● GREATEST HITS *RAK SRAK 526*	6	22 wks
4 Nov 78	THE MONTREUX ALBUM *RAK SRAK 6757*	52	2 wks
11 Oct 80	SMOKIE'S HITS *RAK SRAK 540*	23	13 wks

CL SMOOTH – *See Pete ROCK and CL SMOOTH*

SMURFS – *See FATHER ABRAHAM and the SMURFS*

SNAP *US / Germany, male / female vocal / instrumental group* **55 wks**

26 May 90	● WORLD POWER *Arista 210682*	10	39 wks
8 Aug 92	● THE MADMAN'S RETURN *Logic 262552*	8	15 wks
15 Oct 94	WELCOME TO TOMORROW *Ariola 74321223842*	69	1 wk

The Madman's Return *changed catalogue number to 74321128512 during its chart run.*

SNOOP DOGGY DOGG *US, male rapper* **27 wks**

11 Dec 93	DOGGYSTYLE *Death Row 6544922792*	38	27 wks

SNOW *Canada, male rapper* **4 wks**

17 Apr 93	12 INCHES OF SNOW *East West America 7567922072*	41	4 wks

SOFT CELL *UK, male vocal / instrumental duo* **101 wks**

5 Dec 81	● NON–STOP EROTIC CABARET *Some Bizzare BZLP 2*	5	46 wks
26 Jun 82	● NON–STOP ECSTATIC DANCING *Some Bizzare BZX 1012*	6	18 wks
22 Jan 83	● THE ART OF FALLING APART *Some Bizzare BIZL 3*	5	10 wks
31 Mar 84	THE LAST NIGHT IN SODOM *Some Bizzare BIZL 6*	12	5 wks
20 Dec 86	THE SINGLES ALBUM *Some Bizzare BZLP 3*	58	9 wks
1 Jun 91	● MEMORABILIA – THE SINGLES *Mercury 8485121*	8	13 wks

SOFT MACHINE *UK, male vocal / instrumental group* **8 wks**

4 Jul 70	THIRD *CBS 66246*	18	6 wks
3 Apr 71	FOURTH *CBS 64280*	32	2 wks

SOLID SENDERS UK, male vocal / instrumental group   **3 wks**

23 Sep 78   **SOLID SENDERS** Virgin V 2105 42   3 wks

Diane SOLOMON UK, female vocalist   **6 wks**

9 Aug 75   **TAKE TWO** Philips 6308 236 26   6 wks

Sir George SOLTI – See Dudley MOORE

Jimmy SOMERVILLE UK, male vocalist   **42 wks**

9 Dec 89   **READ MY LIPS** London 8281661 29   14 wks
24 Nov 90 ● **THE SINGLES COLLECTION 1984–1990** London 8282261..............4   26 wks
24 Jun 95   **DARE TO LOVE** London 8285402 38   2 wks

SONIA UK, female vocalist   **14 wks**

5 May 90 ● **EVERYBODY KNOWS** Chrysalis CHR 1734 7   10 wks
19 Oct 91   **SONIA** IQ ZL 751675..33   2 wks
29 May 93   **BETTER THE DEVIL YOU KNOW** Arista 74321149802 32   2 wks

SONIC BOOM UK, male vocal / instrumental group   **1 wk**

17 Mar 90   **SPECTRUM** Silverstone ORELP 56..65   1 wk

SONIC YOUTH US, male / female vocal / instrumental group   **13 wks**

29 Oct 88   **DAYDREAM NATION** Blast First BFFP 34............................99   1 wk
4 Feb 89   **THE WHITEY ALBUM** Blast First BFFP 28 [1] 63   1 wk
7 Jul 90   **GOO** DGC 7599242971 32   2 wks
4 May 91   **DIRTY BOOTS – PLUS 5 LIVE TRACKS** DGC DGC 21634 69   1 wk
1 Aug 92 ● **DIRTY** DGC DGCD 24485 6   5 wks
21 May 94 ● **EXPERIMENTAL JET SET TRASH AND NO STAR**
          Geffen GED 24632 10   2 wks
14 Oct 95   **WASHING MACHINE** Geffen GED 24825 39   1 wk

[1] Ciccone Youth

SONNY and CHER US, male / female vocal duo   **20 wks**

16 Oct 65 ● **LOOK AT US** Atlantic ATL 5036..7   13 wks
14 May 66   **THE WONDROUS WORLD OF SONNY AND CHER**
          Atlantic 587006...15   7 wks

See also Cher.

David SOUL US, male vocalist   **51 wks**

27 Nov 76 ● **DAVID SOUL** Private Stock PVLP 1012 2   28 wks
17 Sep 77 ● **PLAYING TO AN AUDIENCE OF ONE** Private Stock PVLP 1026 8   23 wks

SOUL ASYLUM US, male vocal / instrumental group   **29 wks**

31 Jul 93   **GRAVE DANCERS UNION** Columbia 4722532 27   25 wks
1 Jul 95   **LET YOUR DIM LIGHT SHINE** Columbia 4803202 22   4 wks

SOUL CITY SYMPHONY – See Van McCOY and the SOUL CITY SYMPHONY

SOUL II SOUL
UK, male / female vocal / instrumental group and male producer   **108 wks**

22 Apr 89 ★ **CLUB CLASSICS VOLUME ONE** 10 DIX 82 1   60 wks
2 Jun 90 ★ **VOLUME II (1990 A NEW DECADE)** 10 DIX 90 1   20 wks
25 Apr 92 ● **VOLUME III JUST RIGHT** Ten DIXCD 100......................3   11 wks
27 Nov 93 ● **VOLUME IV THE CLASSIC SINGLES 88–93** Virgin CDV 2724........10   13 wks
12 Aug 95   **VOLUME V BELIEVE** Virgin CDV 2739...............................13   4 wks

SOUNDGARDEN US, male vocal / instrumental group — 26 wks

25 Apr 92	**BADMOTORFINGER** A & M 3953742	39	2 wks
19 Mar 94	● **SUPERUNKNOWN** A & M 5402152	4	24 wks

SOUNDS OF BLACKNESS UK, male / female gospel choir — 6 wks

30 Apr 94	**AFRICA TO AMERICA; THE JOURNEY OF THE DRUM** A & M 5490092	28	6 wks

SOUNDS ORCHESTRAL UK, orchestra — 1 wk

12 Jun 65	**CAST YOUR FATE TO THE WIND** Piccadilly NPL 38041	17	1 wk

SOUNDTRACKS (films, TV etc) – See VARIOUS ARTISTS

SOUP DRAGONS UK, male vocal / instrumental group — 17 wks

7 May 88	**THIS IS OUR ART** Sire WX 169	60	1 wk
5 May 90	● **LOVEGOD** Raw TV SOUPLP 2	7	15 wks
16 May 92	**HOTWIRED** Big Life BLRCD 15	74	1 wk

SOUTH BANK ORCHESTRA UK, orchestra — 6 wks

2 Dec 78	**LILLIE** Sounds MOR 516	47	6 wks

Album was conducted by Joseph Morovitz and Laurie Holloway.

SOUTHERN DEATH CULT – See CULT

SPACE France, male instrumental group — 9 wks

17 Sep 77	**MAGIC FLY** Pye NSPL 28232	11	9 wks

SPACEMEN UK, male instrumental group — 1 wk

9 Mar 91	**RECURRING** Fire FIRELP 23	46	1 wk

SPANDAU BALLET UK, male vocal / instrumental group — 251 wks

14 Mar 81	● **JOURNEY TO GLORY** Reformation CHR 1331	5	29 wks
20 Mar 82	**DIAMOND** Reformation CDL 1353	15	18 wks
12 Mar 83	★ **TRUE** Reformation CDL 1403	1	90 wks
7 Jul 84	● **PARADE** Reformation CDL 1473	2	39 wks
16 Nov 85	● **THE SINGLES COLLECTION** Chrysalis SBTV 1	3	50 wks
29 Nov 86	● **THROUGH THE BARRICADES** Reformation CBS 450 2591	7	19 wks
30 Sep 89	**HEART LIKE A SKY** CBS 4633181	31	3 wks
28 Sep 91	**THE BEST OF SPANDAU BALLET** Chrysalis CHR 1894	44	3 wks

SPARKS US / UK, male vocal / instrumental group — 42 wks

1 Jun 74	● **KIMONO MY HOUSE** Island ILPS 9272	4	24 wks
23 Nov 74	● **PROPAGANDA** Island ILPS 9312	9	13 wks
18 Oct 75	**INDISCREET** Island ILPS 9345	18	4 wks
8 Sep 79	**NUMBER ONE IN HEAVEN** Virgin V 2115	73	1 wk

SPEAR OF DESTINY UK, male vocal / instrumental group — 35 wks

23 Apr 83	**GRAPES OF WRATH** Epic EPC 25318	62	2 wks
28 Apr 84	**ONE EYED JACKS** Burning Rome EPC 25836	22	7 wks
7 Sep 85	**WORLD SERVICE** Burning Rome EPC 26514	11	7 wks
2 May 87	**OUTLAND** 10 DIX 59	16	13 wks
16 May 87	**S.O.D. – THE EPIC YEARS** Epic 450 8721	53	3 wks
22 Oct 88	**THE PRICE YOU PAY** Virgin V 2549	37	3 wks

Billie Jo SPEARS US, female vocalist   28 wks

11 Sep 76	**WHAT I'VE GOT IN MIND** United Artists UAS 29955 ....**47**	2 wks
19 May 79	● **THE BILLIE JO SPEARS SINGLES ALBUM**	
	United Artists UAK 30231...**7**	17 wks
21 Nov 81	**COUNTRY GIRL** Warwick WW 5109 ....**17**	9 wks

SPECIALS UK, male instrumental group   79 wks

3 Nov 79	● **SPECIALS** 2-Tone CDL TT 5001 ....**4**	45 wks
4 Oct 80	● **MORE SPECIALS** 2-Tone CHR TT 5003 ....**5**	19 wks
23 Jun 84	**IN THE STUDIO** 2-Tone CHR TT 5008 1 ....**34**	6 wks
7 Sep 91	● **THE SPECIALS SINGLES** 2-Tone CHRTT 5010 ....**10**	9 wks

1 Special A.K.A.

Group was male / female for the third and fourth albums..

Phil SPECTOR US, male producer   29 wks

23 Dec 72	**PHIL SPECTOR'S CHRISTMAS ALBUM** Apple SAPCOR 24 ....**21**	3 wks
15 Oct 77	**PHIL SPECTOR'S ECHOES OF THE 60'S**	
	Phil Spector International 2307 013 ....**21**	10 wks
25 Dec 82	**PHIL SPECTOR'S CHRISTMAS ALBUM (re-issue)**	
	Phil Spector International 2307 005 ....**96**	2 wks
10 Dec 83	**PHIL SPECTOR'S GREATEST HITS / PHIL SPECTOR'S**	
	CHRISTMAS ALBUM (2nd re–issue) Impression PSLP 1/2 ....**19**	8 wks
12 Dec 87	**PHIL SPECTOR'S CHRISTMAS ALBUM (3rd re-issue)**	
	Chrysalis CDL 1625 ....**69**	6 wks

SPEEDY J Holland, male producer – Jochem Paap   1 wk

| 10 Jul 93 | **GINGER** Warp WARPCD 14 ....**68** | 1 wk |

SPIDER UK, male vocal / instrumental group   2 wks

| 23 Oct 82 | **ROCK 'N' ROLL GYPSIES** RCA RCALP 3101....................**75** | 1 wk |
| 7 Apr 84 | **ROUGH JUSTICE** A & M AMLX 68563 ....**96** | 1 wk |

SPIN DOCTORS US, male vocal / instrumental group   57 wks

| 20 Mar 93 | ● **POCKET FULL OF KRYPTONITE** Epic 4682502.....................**2** | 48 wks |
| 9 Jul 94 | ● **TURN IT UPSIDE DOWN** Epic 4768862.............................**3** | 9 wks |

SPINAL TAP UK / US, male vocal / instrumental group   2 wks

| 11 Apr 92 | **BREAK LIKE THE WIND** MCA MCAD 10514 ....**51** | 2 wks |

SPINNERS UK, male vocal group   24 wks

5 Sep 70	**THE SPINNERS ARE IN TOWN** Fontana 6309 014 ....**40**	5 wks
7 Aug 71	**SPINNERS LIVE PERFORMANCE** Contour 6870 502 ....**14**	12 wks
13 Nov 71	**THE SWINGING CITY** Philips 6382 002 ....**20**	3 wks
8 Apr 72	**LOVE IS TEASING** Columbia SCX 6493 ....**33**	4 wks

SPIRIT US, male vocal / instrumental duo   2 wks

| 18 Apr 81 | **POTATO LAND** Beggars Banquet BEGA 23 ....**40** | 2 wks |

SPIRITUAL COWBOYS – See Dave STEWART and the SPIRITUAL COWBOYS

SPIRITUALIZED ELECTRIC MAINLINE
UK, male vocal / instrumental group   4 wks

| 11 Apr 92 | **LAZER GUIDED MELODIES** Dedicated DEDCD 004 1 ....**27** | 2 wks |
| 18 Feb 95 | **PURE PHASE** Dedicated DEDCD 017S..**20** | 2 wks |

1 Spiritualized

SPITTING IMAGE UK, puppets — **3 wks**

| 18 Oct 86 | **SPIT IN YOUR EAR** Virgin V 2403 | ....55 | 3 wks |

SPLIT ENZ New Zealand / UK, male vocal / instrumental group — **9 wks**

| 30 Aug 80 | **TRUE COLOURS** A & M AMLH 64822 | ....42 | 8 wks |
| 8 May 82 | **TIME AND TIDE** A & M AMLH 64894 | ....71 | 1 wk |

SPOTNICKS Sweden, male instrumental group — **1 wk**

| 9 Feb 63 | **OUT–A–SPACE** Oriole PS 40036 | ....20 | 1 wk |

Dusty SPRINGFIELD UK, female vocalist — **110 wks**

25 Apr 64	● **A GIRL CALLED DUSTY** Philips BL 7594	6	23 wks
23 Oct 65	● **EVERYTHING COMES UP DUSTY** Philips RBL 1002	6	12 wks
22 Oct 66	● **GOLDEN HITS** Philips BL 7737	2	36 wks
11 Nov 67	**WHERE AM I GOING** Philips SBL 7820	40	1 wk
21 Dec 68	**DUSTY . . . DEFINITELY** Philips SBL 7864	30	6 wks
2 May 70	**FROM DUSTY WITH LOVE** Philips SBL 7927	35	2 wks
4 Mar 78	**IT BEGINS AGAIN** Mercury 9109 607	41	2 wks
30 Jan 88	**DUSTY – THE SILVER COLLECTION** Phonogram DUSTV 1	14	10 wks
7 Jul 90	**REPUTATION** Parlophone PCSD 111	18	6 wks
14 May 94	● **GOIN' BACK – THE VERY BEST OF DUSTY SPRINGFIELD** Philips 8487892	5	11 wks
8 Jul 95	**A VERY FINE LOVE** Columbia 4785082	43	1 wk

Rick SPRINGFIELD Australia, male vocalist — **8 wks**

11 Feb 84	**LIVING IN OZ** RCA PL 84660	41	4 wks
25 May 85	**TAO** RCA PL 85370	68	3 wks
26 Mar 88	**ROCK OF LIFE** CA PL 86620	80	1 wk

**S
291**

Bruce SPRINGSTEEN US, male vocalist — **459 wks**

1 Nov 75	**BORN TO RUN** CBS 69170	17	50 wks
17 Jun 78	**DARKNESS ON THE EDGE OF TOWN** CBS 86061	16	40 wks
25 Oct 80	● **THE RIVER** CBS 88510	2	88 wks
2 Oct 82	● **NEBRASKA** CBS 25100	3	19 wks
16 Jun 84	★ **BORN IN THE USA** CBS 86304	1	128 wks
15 Jun 85	**THE WILD THE INNOCENT AND THE E STREET SHUFFLE** CBS 32363	33	12 wks
15 Jun 85	**GREETINGS FROM ASBURY PARK, N.J.** CBS 32210	41	10 wks
22 Nov 86	● **LIVE 1975–1985** CBS 450 2271 [1]	4	9 wks
17 Oct 87	★ **TUNNEL OF LOVE** CBS 460 2701	1	33 wks
4 Apr 92	★ **HUMAN TOUCH** Columbia 4714232	1	17 wks
4 Apr 92	● **LUCKY TOWN** Columbia 4714242	2	11 wks
24 Apr 93	● **IN CONCERT – MTV PLUGGED** Columbia 4738602	4	7 wks
11 Mar 95	★ **GREATEST HITS** Columbia 4785552	1	29 wks
25 Nov 95	**THE GHOST OF TOM JOAD** Columbia 4816502	........16†	6 wks

[1] Bruce Springsteen and the E Street Band

SPYRO GYRA US, male instrumental group — **23 wks**

| 14 Jul 79 | **MORNING DANCE** Infinity INS 2003 | ....11 | 16 wks |
| 23 Feb 80 | **CATCHING THE SUN** MCA MCG 4009 | ....31 | 7 wks |

SQUEEZE UK, male vocal / instrumental group — **122 wks**

28 Apr 79	**COOL FOR CATS** A & M AMLH 68503	45	11 wks
16 Feb 80	**ARGY BARGY** A & M AMLH 64802	32	15 wks
23 May 81	**EAST SIDE STORY** A & M AMLH 64854	19	26 wks
15 May 82	**SWEETS FROM A STRANGER** A & M AMLH 64899	20	7 wks
6 Nov 82	● **SINGLES - 45'S AND UNDER** A & M AMLH 68552	3	29 wks
7 Sep 85	**COSI FAN TUTTI FRUTTI** A & M AMA 5085	31	7 wks

BRUCE SPRINGSTEEN admires the off-camera Clarence Clemmons in a photo taken just after the release of *Born To Run*.
(Hulton Deutsch)

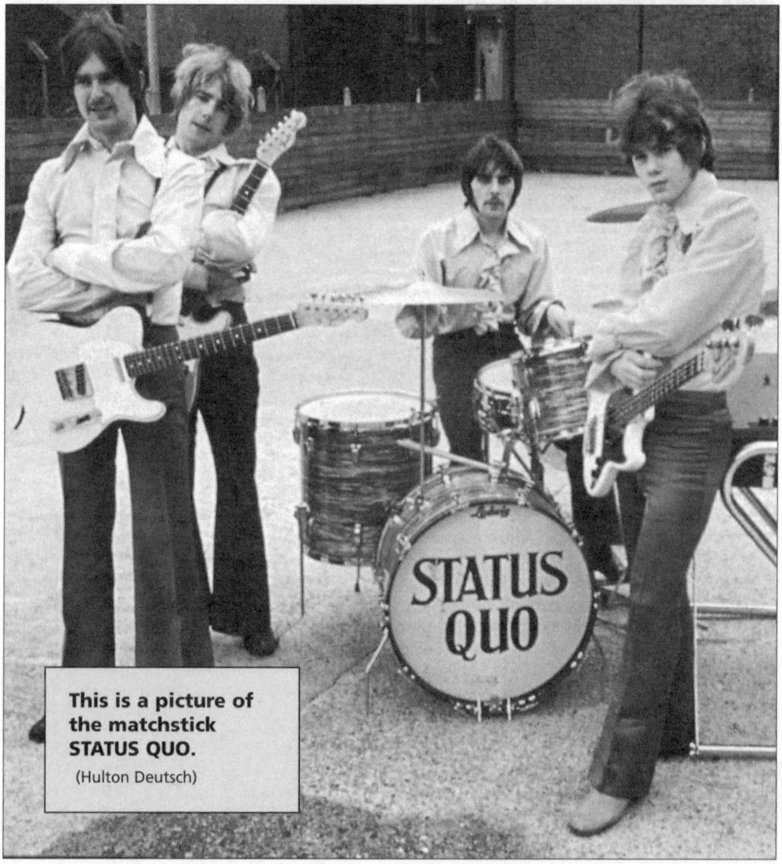

This is a picture of the matchstick STATUS QUO.
(Hulton Deutsch)

19 Sep 87	**BABYLON AND ON** *A & M AMA 5161*	**14**	8 wks
23 Sep 89	**FRANK** *A & M AMA 5278*	**58**	1 wk
7 Apr 90	**A ROUND AND A BOUT** *IRS DFCLP 1*	**50**	1 wk
7 Sep 91	**PLAY** *Reprise WX 428*	**41**	1 wk
23 May 92	● **GREATEST HITS** *A & M 3971812*	**6**	11 wks
25 Sep 93	**SOME FANTASTIC PLACE** *A & M 5401402*	**26**	4 wks
25 Nov 95	**RIDICULOUS** *A & M 5404402*	**50**	1 wk

Chris SQUIRE *UK, male vocalist / instrumentalist – bass*   **7 wks**

| 6 Dec 75 | **FISH OUT OF WATER** *Atlantic K 50203* | **25** | 7 wks |

STAGE CAST RECORDINGS – See *VARIOUS ARTISTS*

Lisa STANSFIELD *UK, female vocalist*   **94 wks**

2 Dec 89	● **AFFECTION** *Arista 210379*	**2**	31 wks
23 Nov 91	● **REAL LOVE** *Arista 212300*	**3**	49 wks
20 Nov 93	● **SO NATURAL** *Arista 74321172312*	**6**	14 wks

Alvin STARDUST *UK, male vocalist*   **17 wks**

16 Mar 74	● **THE UNTOUCHABLE** *Magnet MAG 5001*	**4**	12 wks
21 Dec 74	**ALVIN STARDUST** *Magnet MAG 5004*	**37**	3 wks
4 Oct 75	**ROCK WITH ALVIN** *Magnet MAG 5007*	**52**	2 wks

Ed STARINK *US, male instrumentalist*   **11 wks**

| 27 Oct 90 | **SYNTHESIZER GREATEST** *Arcade ARC 938101* | **22** | 5 wks |
| 9 Jan 93 | **SYNTHESIZER GOLD** *Arcade ARC 3100012* | **29** | 6 wks |

Freddie STARR *UK, male vocalist*   **16 wks**

| 18 Nov 89 | ● **AFTER THE LAUGHTER** *Dover ADD 10* | **10** | 9 wks |
| 17 Nov 90 | **THE WANDERER** *Dover ADD 17* | **33** | 7 wks |

Kay STARR *US, female vocalist*   **1 wk**

| 26 Mar 60 | **MOVIN'** *Capitol 1254* | **16** | 1 wk |

Ringo STARR *UK, male vocalist*   **28 wks**

18 Apr 70	● **SENTIMENTAL JOURNEY** *Apple PCS 7101*	**7**	6 wks
8 Dec 73	● **RINGO** *Apple PCTC 252*	**7**	20 wks
7 Dec 74	**GOODNIGHT VIENNA** *Apple PMC 7168*	**30**	2 wks

STARSHIP – See *JEFFERSON AIRPLANE*

STARSOUND *Holland, disco aggregation*   **28 wks**

16 May 81	★ **STARS ON 45** *CBS 86132*	**1**	21 wks
19 Sep 81	**STARS ON 45 VOLUME 2** *CBS 85181*	**18**	6 wks
3 Apr 82	**STARS MEDLEY** *CBS 85651*	**94**	1 wk

STARTRAX *UK, disco aggregation*   **7 wks**

| 1 Aug 81 | **STARTRAX CLUB DISCO** *Picksy KSYA 1001* | **26** | 7 wks |

Candi STATON *US, female vocalist*   **3 wks**

| 24 Jul 76 | **YOUNG HEARTS RUN FREE** *Warner Bros. K 56259* | **34** | 3 wks |

STATUS QUO *UK, male vocal / instrumental group*   **435 wks**

| 20 Jan 73 | ● **PILEDRIVER** *Vertigo 6360 082* | **5** | 37 wks |
| 9 Jun 73 | **THE BEST OF STATUS QUO** *Pye NSPL 18402* | **32** | 7 wks |

6 Oct 73	★ **HELLO** Vertigo 6360 098	1	28 wks
18 May 74	● **QUO** Vertigo 9102 001	2	16 wks
1 Mar 75	★ **ON THE LEVEL** Vertigo 9102 002	1	27 wks
8 Mar 75	**DOWN THE DUSTPIPE** Golden Hour CH 604	20	6 wks
20 Mar 76	★ **BLUE FOR YOU** Vertigo 9102 006	1	30 wks
12 Mar 77	● **LIVE** Vertigo 6641 580	3	14 wks
26 Nov 77	● **ROCKIN' ALL OVER THE WORLD** Vertigo 9102 014	5	15 wks
11 Nov 78	● **IF YOU CAN'T STAND THE HEAT** Vertigo 9102 027	3	14 wks
20 Oct 79	● **WHATEVER YOU WANT** Vertigo 9102 037	3	14 wks
22 Mar 80	● **12 GOLD BARS** Vertigo QUO TV 1	3	48 wks
25 Oct 80	● **JUST SUPPOSIN'** Vertigo 6302 057	4	18 wks
28 Mar 81	● **NEVER TOO LATE** Vertigo 6302 104	2	13 wks
10 Oct 81	**FRESH QUOTA** PRT DOW 2	74	1 wk
24 Apr 82	★ **1982** Vertigo 6302 169	1	20 wks
13 Nov 82	● **FROM THE MAKERS OF . . .** Vertigo PROLP 1	4	18 wks
3 Dec 83	● **BACK TO BACK** Vertigo VERH 10	9	22 wks
4 Aug 84	**STATUS QUO LIVE AT THE NEC** Vertigo (Holland) 8189 471	83	3 wks
1 Dec 84	**12 GOLD BARS VOLUME 2 (AND 1)** Vertigo QUO TV 2	12	18 wks
6 Sep 86	● **IN THE ARMY NOW** Vertigo VERH 36	7	23 wks
18 Jun 88	**AIN'T COMPLAINING** Vertigo VERH 58	12	5 wks
2 Dec 89	**PERFECT REMEDY** Vertigo 842098 1	49	2 wks
20 Oct 90	● **ROCKING ALL OVER THE YEARS** Vertigo 8467971	2	25 wks
5 Oct 91	● **ROCK 'TIL YOU DROP** Vertigo 5103411	10	7 wks
14 Nov 92	**LIVE ALIVE QUO** Polydor 5173672	37	1 wk
3 Sep 94	**THIRSTY WORK** Polydor 5236072	13	3 wks

STEEL PULSE UK, male vocal / instrumental group   18 wks

| 5 Aug 78 | ● **HANDSWORTH REVOLUTION** Island EMI ILPS 9502 .... | 9 | 12 wks |
| 14 Jul 79 | **TRIBUTE TO MARTYRS** Island ILPS 9568 .... | 42 | 6 wks |

STEELEYE SPAN UK, male / female vocal instrumental group   48 wks

10 Apr 71	**PLEASE TO SEE THE KING** B & C CAS 1029	45	2 wks
14 Oct 72	**BELOW THE SALT** Chrysalis CHR 1008	43	1 wk
28 Apr 73	**PARCEL OF ROGUES** Chrysalis CHR 1046	26	5 wks
23 Mar 74	**NOW WE ARE SIX** Chrysalis CHR 1053	13	13 wks
15 Feb 75	**COMMONER'S CROWN** Chrysalis CHR 1071	21	4 wks
25 Oct 75	● **ALL AROUND MY HAT** Chrysalis CHR 1091	7	20 wks
16 Oct 76	**ROCKET COTTAGE** Chrysalis CHR 1123	41	3 wks

STEELY DAN US, male vocal / instrumental group   83 wks

30 Mar 74	**PRETZEL LOGIC** Probe SPBA 6282	37	2 wks
3 May 75	**KATY LIED** ABC ABCL 5094	13	6 wks
20 Sep 75	**CAN'T BUY A THRILL** ABC ABCL 5024	38	1 wk
22 May 76	**ROYAL SCAM** ABC ABCL 5161	11	13 wks
8 Oct 77	● **AJA** ABC ABCL 5225	5	10 wks
2 Dec 78	**GREATEST HITS** ABC BLD 616	41	18 wks
29 Nov 80	**GAUCHO** MCA MCF 3090	27	12 wks
3 Jul 82	**GOLD** MCA MCF 3145	44	6 wks
26 Oct 85	**REELIN' IN THE YEARS – THE VERY BEST OF STEELY DAN** MCA DANTV 1	43	5 wks
10 Oct 87	**DO IT AGAIN – THE VERY BEST OF STEELY DAN** Telstar STAR 2297	64	4 wks
20 Nov 93	**REMASTERED – THE BEST OF STEELY DAN** MCA MCD 10967	42	5 wks
28 Oct 95	**ALIVE IN AMERICA** Giant 74321286912	62	1 wk

Wout STEENHUIS Holland, male instrumentalist – guitar   7 wks

| 21 Nov 81 | **HAWAIIAN PARADISE / CHRISTMAS** Warwick WW 5106 ..... | 28 | 7 wks |

Jim STEINMAN US, male vocalist   25 wks

| 9 May 81 | ● **BAD FOR GOOD** Epic EPC 84361 .... | 7 | 25 wks |

Martin STEPHENSON and the DAINTEES
UK, male vocal / instrumental group   11 wks

| 17 May 86 | **BOAT TO BOLIVIA** Kitchenware KWLP 5 .... | 85 | 3 wks |

16 Apr 88	**GLADSOME, HUMOUR AND BLUE** Kitchenware KWLP 8	39	4 wks
19 May 90	**SALUTATION ROAD** Kitchenware 8281981	35	3 wks
25 Jul 92	**THE BOY'S HEART** Kitchenware 8283242	68	1 wk

STEPPENWOLF Canada / US, male vocal / instrumental group   **20 wks**

28 Feb 70	**MONSTER** Stateside SSL 5021	43	4 wks
25 Apr 70	**STEPPENWOLF** Stateside SSL 5020	59	2 wks
4 Jul 70	**STEPPENWOLF LIVE** Stateside SSL 5029	16	14 wks

STEREO MCs UK, male vocal / instrumental group   **52 wks**

17 Oct 92	● **CONNECTED** Fourth & Broadway BRCD 589	2	52 wks

STEREOLAB UK / France, male / female vocal / instrumental group   **7 wks**

18 Sep 93	**TRANSIENT RANDOM NOISE BURSTS** Duophonic UHF DUHFCD 02	62	1 wk
20 Aug 94	**MARS AUDIAC QUINTET** Duophonic UHF DUHFCD 05X	16	3 wks
29 Apr 95	**MUSIC FOR AMORPHOUS BODY STUDY CENTRE** Duophonic UHF DUHFCD 08	59	1 wk
16 Sep 95	**REFRIED ECTOPLASM (SWITCHED ON VOLUME 2)** Duophonic UHF DUHFCD 09	30	2 wks

Cat STEVENS UK, male vocalist   **259 wks**

25 Mar 67	● **MATTHEW AND SON** Deram SML 1004	7	16 wks
11 Jul 70	**MONA BONE JAKON** Island ILPS 9118	63	4 wks
28 Nov 70	**TEA FOR THE TILLERMAN** Island ILPS 9135	20	39 wks
2 Oct 71	● **TEASER AND THE FIRECAT** Island ILPS 9154	3	93 wks
7 Oct 72	● **CATCH BULL AT FOUR** Island ILPS 9206	2	27 wks
21 Jul 73	● **FOREIGNER** Island ILPS 9240	3	10 wks
6 Apr 74	● **BUDDAH AND THE CHOCOLATE BOX** Island ILPS 9274	3	15 wks
19 Jul 75	● **GREATEST HITS** Island ILPS 9310	2	24 wks
14 May 77	**IZITSO** Island ILPS 9451	18	15 wks
3 Feb 90	● **THE VERY BEST OF CAT STEVENS** Island CATV 1	4	16 wks

Ray STEVENS US, male vocalist   **8 wks**

26 Sep 70	**EVERYTHING IS BEAUTIFUL** CBS 64074	62	1 wk
13 Sep 75	**MISTY** Janus 9109 401	23	7 wks

Shakin' STEVENS UK, male vocalist   **158 wks**

15 Mar 80	**TAKE ONE** Epic EPC 83978	62	2 wks
4 Apr 81	● **THIS OLE HOUSE** Epic EPC 84985	2	28 wks
8 Aug 81	**SHAKIN' STEVENS** Hallmark/Pickwick SHM 3065	34	5 wks
19 Sep 81	★ **SHAKY** Epic EPC 10027	1	28 wks
9 Oct 82	● **GIVE ME YOUR HEART TONIGHT** Epic EPC 10035	3	18 wks
26 Nov 83	**THE BOP WON'T STOP** Epic EPC 86301	21	27 wks
17 Nov 84	● **GREATEST HITS** Epic EPC 10047	8	22 wks
16 Nov 85	**LIPSTICK POWDER AND PAINT** Epic EPC 26646	37	9 wks
31 Oct 87	**LET'S BOOGIE** Epic 460 1261	59	7 wks
19 Nov 88	**A WHOLE LOTTA SHAKY** Epic MOOD 5	42	8 wks
20 Oct 90	**THERE'S TWO KINDS OF MUSIC: ROCK 'N' ROLL** Telstar STAR 2454	65	2 wks
31 Oct 92	**THE EPIC YEARS** Epic 4724222 [1]	57	2 wks

[1] Shaky

Al STEWART UK, male vocalist   **20 wks**

11 Apr 70	**ZERO SHE FLIES** CBS 63848	40	4 wks
5 Feb 77	**YEAR OF THE CAT** RCA RS 1082	38	7 wks
21 Oct 78	**TIME PASSAGES** RCA PL 25173	39	1 wk
6 Sep 80	**24 CARAT** RCA PL 25306	55	6 wks
9 Jun 84	**RUSSIANS AND AMERICANS** RCA PL 70307	83	2 wks

Andy STEWART *UK, male vocalist*   **2 wks**

3 Feb 62	**ANDY STEWART** *Top Rank 35116* **13**	2 wks

David A. STEWART *UK, male vocalist / instrumentalist*   **7 wks**

7 Apr 90	**LILY WAS HERE (film soundtrack)** *Anxious ZL 74233* **35**	5 wks
15 Sep 90	**DAVE STEWART AND THE SPIRITUAL COWBOYS** *RCA OB 74710* [1] **38**	2 wks

[1] Dave Stewart and the Spiritual Cowboys

Jermaine STEWART *US, male vocalist*   **12 wks**

4 Oct 86	**FRANTIC ROMANTIC** *10 DIX 26* **49**	4 wks
5 Mar 88	**SAY IT AGAIN** *Siren SRNLP 14* **32**	8 wks

Rod STEWART *UK, male vocalist*   **747 wks**

3 Oct 70	**GASOLINE ALLEY** *Vertigo 6360 500* **62**	1 wk
24 Jul 71	★ **EVERY PICTURE TELLS A STORY** *Mercury 6338 063* **1**	81 wks
5 Aug 72	★ **NEVER A DULL MOMENT** *Philips 6499 153* **1**	36 wks
25 Aug 73	★ **SING IT AGAIN ROD** *Mercury 6499 484* **1**	30 wks
19 Oct 74	★ **SMILER** *Mercury 9104 011*...............**1**	20 wks
30 Aug 75	★ **ATLANTIC CROSSING** *Warner Bros. K 56151* **1**	88 wks
3 Jul 76	★ **A NIGHT ON THE TOWN** *Riva RVLP 1* **1**	47 wks
16 Jul 77	**BEST OF ROD STEWART** *Mercury 6643 030* **18**	22 wks
19 Nov 77	● **FOOT LOOSE AND FANCY FREE** *Riva RVLP 5*...............**3**	26 wks
21 Jan 78	● **ATLANTIC CROSSING (re-issue)** *Riva RVLP 4* **60**	1 wk
9 Dec 78	● **BLONDES HAVE MORE FUN** *Riva RVLP 8* **3**	31 wks
10 Nov 79	★ **GREATEST HITS** *Riva ROD TV 1* **1**	74 wks
22 Nov 80	● **FOOLISH BEHAVIOUR** *Riva RVLP 11*...............**4**	13 wks
14 Nov 81	● **TONIGHT I'M YOURS** *Riva RVLP 14* **8**	21 wks
13 Nov 82	**ABSOLUTELY LIVE** *Riva RVLP 17* **35**	5 wks
18 Jun 83	● **BODY WISHES** *Warner Bros. K 923 8771* **5**	27 wks
23 Jun 84	● **CAMOUFLAGE** *Warner Bros. 925095* **8**	17 wks
5 Jul 86	● **EVERY BEAT OF MY HEART** *Warner Bros. WX 53* **5**	17 wks
4 Jun 88	● **OUT OF ORDER** *Warner Bros. WX 152* **11**	8 wks
25 Nov 89	● **THE BEST OF ROD STEWART** *Warner Bros. WX 314* **3**	106 wks
6 Apr 91	● **VAGABOND HEART** *Warner Bros. WX 408* **2**	27 wks
7 Nov 92	**THE BEST OF ROD STEWART AND THE FACES 1971–1975** *Mercury 5141802* [1] **58**	1 wk
6 Mar 93	● **ROD STEWART, LEAD VOCALIST** *Warner Bros. 9362452582* **3**	9 wks
5 Jun 93	● **UNPLUGGED . . . AND SEATED** *Warner Bros. 9362452892*.............**2**	27 wks
10 Jun 95	● **A SPANNER IN THE WORKS** *Warner Bros. 9362458672* **4**	12 wks

[1] Rod Stewart and the Faces

Greatest Hits *changed label / number to Warner Bros. K 56744 during its chart run. See also the Faces.*

STIFF LITTLE FINGERS *UK, male vocal / instrumental group*   **57 wks**

3 Mar 79	**INFLAMMABLE MATERIAL** *Rough Trade ROUGH 1* **14**	19 wks
15 Mar 80	● **NOBODY'S HEROES** *Chrysalis CHR 1270* **8**	10 wks
20 Sep 80	● **HANX** *Chrysalis CHR 1300* **9**	5 wks
25 Apr 81	**GO FOR IT** *Chrysalis CHX 1339* **14**	8 wks
2 Oct 82	**NOW THEN** *Chrysalis CHR 1400*...............**24**	6 wks
12 Feb 83	**ALL THE BEST** *Chrysalis CTY 1414* **19**	9 wks

Curtis STIGERS *US, male vocalist*   **52 wks**

29 Feb 92	● **CURTIS STIGERS** *Arista 261953*...............**7**	50 wks
1 Jul 95	**TIME WAS** *Arista 74321282792*...............**34**	2 wks

Stephen STILLS *US, male vocalist*   **19 wks**

19 Dec 70	**STEPHEN STILLS** *Atlantic 2401 004* **30**	1 wk
14 Aug 71	**STEPHEN STILLS 2** *Atlantic 2401 013* **22**	3 wks

TOP 30 №14

1993 was the first year in which ROD STEWART placed two new releases in the Top Ten.
(Solo/Joe Bangay Photography)

20 May 72	**MANASSAS** Atlantic K 60021 [1]	**30**	5 wks
19 May 73	**DOWN THE ROAD** Atlantic K 40440 [1]	**33**	2 wks
26 Jul 75	**STILLS** CBS 69146	**31**	1 wk
29 May 76	**ILLEGAL STILLS** CBS 81330	**54**	2 wks
9 Oct 76	**LONG MAY YOU RUN** Reprise K 54081 [2]	**12**	5 wks

[1] Stephen Stills' Manassas [2] Stills–Young Band

See also Crosby, Stills, Nash and Young.

STILTSKIN UK, male vocal / instrumental group   **4 wks**

29 Oct 94	**THE MIND'S EYE** White Water WWD 1	**17**	4 wks

STING UK, male vocalist   **229 wks**

29 Jun 85	● **THE DREAM OF THE BLUE TURTLES** A & M DREAM 1	**3**	64 wks
28 Jun 86	**BRING ON THE NIGHT** A & M BRING 1	**16**	12 wks
24 Oct 87	★ **NOTHING LIKE THE SUN** A & M AMA 6402	**1**	47 wks
2 Feb 91	★ **THE SOUL CAGES** A & M 3964051	**1**	16 wks
13 Mar 93	● **TEN SUMMONER'S TALES** A & M 5400752	**2**	60 wks
19 Nov 94	● **FIELDS OF GOLD – THE BEST OF STING** A & M 5403072	**2**	30 wks

Miriam STOCKLEY – See ADIEMUS

STONE ROSES UK, male vocal / instrumental group   **104 wks**

13 May 89	**THE STONE ROSES** Silvertone ORELP 502	**19**	69 wks
1 Aug 92	**TURNS INTO STONE** Silvertone ORECD 521	**32**	3 wks
17 Dec 94	● **SECOND COMING** Geffen GED 24503	**4**	21 wks
27 May 95	● **THE COMPLETE STONE ROSES** Silvertone ORECD 535	**4**	11 wks

STONE TEMPLE PILOTS US, male vocal / instrumental group   **17 wks**

4 Sep 93	**CORE** Atlantic 7567824182	**27**	8 wks
18 Jun 94	● **PURPLE** Atlantic 7567826072	**10**	9 wks

STONE THE CROWS UK, female / male vocal / instrumental group   **3 wks**

7 Oct 72	**ONTINUOUS PERFORMANCE** Polydor 2391 043	**33**	3 wks

STOOGES – See Iggy POP

STORYVILLE JAZZMEN – See Bob WALLIS and his STORYVILLE JAZZMEN

IZZY STRADLIN AND THE JU JU HOUNDS
US, male vocal / instrumental group   **1 wk**

24 Oct 92	**IZZY STRADLIN AND THE JU JU HOUNDS** Geffen GED 24490	**52**	1 wk

STRANGELOVE UK, male vocal / instrumental group   **1 wk**

13 Aug 94	**TIME FOR THE REST OF YOUR LIFE** Food FOODCD 11	**69**	1 wk

STRANGLERS UK, male vocal / instrumental group   **218 wks**

30 Apr 77	● **STRANGLERS IV (RATTUS NORVEGICUS)** United Artists UAG 30045	**4**	34 wks
8 Oct 77	● **NO MORE HEROES** United Artists UAG 30200	**2**	19 wks
3 Jun 78	● **BLACK AND WHITE** United Artists UAK 30222	**2**	18 wks
10 Mar 79	● **LIVE (X CERT)** United Artists UAG 30224	**7**	10 wks
6 Oct 79	● **THE RAVEN** United Artists UAG 30262	**4**	8 wks
21 Feb 81	● **THEMENINBLACK** Liberty LBG 30313	**8**	5 wks
21 Nov 81	**LA FOLIE** Liberty LBG 30342	**11**	18 wks
25 Sep 82	**THE COLLECTION 1977–1982** Liberty LBS 30353	**12**	16 wks
22 Jan 83	● **FELINE** Epic EPC 25237	**4**	11 wks
17 Nov 84	**AURAL SCULPTURE** Epic EPC 26220	**14**	10 wks
20 Sep 86	**OFF THE BEATEN TRACK** Liberty LBG 5001	**80**	2 wks

8 Nov 86	**DREAMTIME** Epic EPC 26648	16	6 wks
20 Feb 88	**ALL LIVE AND ALL OF THE NIGHT** Epic 465259	12	6 wks
18 Feb 89	**THE SINGLES** EMI EM 1314	57	2 wks
17 Mar 90	**10** Epic 4664831	15	4 wks
1 Dec 90	● **GREATEST HITS 1977–1990** Epic 4675411	4	47 wks
19 Sep 92	**STRANGLERS IN THE NIGHT** Psycho WOLCD 1030	33	1 wk
27 May 95	**ABOUT TIME** When! WENCD 001	31	1 wk

STRAWBERRY SWITCHBLADE UK, female vocal duo — 4 wks

| 13 Apr 85 | **STRAWBERRY SWITCHBLADE** Korova KODE 11 | 25 | 4 wks |

STRAWS UK, male vocal / instrumental group — 31 wks

21 Nov 70	**JUST A COLLECTION OF ANTIQUES AND CURIOS** A & M AMLS 994	27	2 wks
17 Jul 71	**FROM THE WITCHWOOD** A & M AMLH 64304	39	2 wks
26 Feb 72	**GRAVE NEW WORLD** A & M AMLH 68078	11	12 wks
24 Feb 73	● **BURSTING AT THE SEAMS** A & M AMLH 68144	2	12 wks
27 Apr 74	**HERO AND HEROINE** A & M AMLH 63607	35	3 wks

STRAY CATS US, male vocal / instrumental group — 32 wks

28 Feb 81	● **STRAY CATS** Arista STRAY 1	6	22 wks
21 Nov 81	**GONNA BALL** Arista STRAY 2	48	4 wks
3 Sep 83	**RANT 'N' RAVE WITH THE STRAY CATS** Arista STRAY 3	51	5 wks
8 Apr 89	**BLAST OFF** EMI MTL 1040	58	1 wk

STREETWALKERS UK, male vocal / instrumental group — 6 wks

| 12 Jun 76 | **RED CARD** Vertigo 9102 010 | 16 | 6 wks |

Barbra STREISAND US, female vocalist — 415 wks

22 Jan 66	● **MY NAME IS BARBRA, TWO** CBS BPG 62603	6	22 wks
4 Apr 70	**GREATEST HITS** CBS 63921	44	2 wks
17 Apr 71	**STONEY END** CBS 64269	28	2 wks
15 Jun 74	**THE WAY WE WERE** CBS 69057	49	1 wk
23 Jul 77	**STREISAND SUPERMAN** CBS 86030	32	9 wks
15 Jul 78	**SONGBIRD** CBS 86060	50	1 wk
17 Mar 79	★ **BARBRA STREISAND HITS VOLUME 2** CBS 10012	1	30 wks
17 Nov 79	**WET** CBS 86104	25	13 wks
11 Oct 80	★ **GUILTY** CBS 86122	1	82 wks
16 Jan 82	★ **LOVE SONGS** CBS 10031	1	129 wks
19 Nov 83	**YENTL (film soundtrack)** CBS 86302	21	35 wks
27 Oct 84	**EMOTION** CBS 86309	15	12 wks
18 Jan 86	● **THE BROADWAY ALBUM** CBS 86322	3	16 wks
30 May 87	**ONE VOICE** CBS 450 8901	27	7 wks
3 Dec 88	**TILL I LOVED YOU** CBS 462943 1	29	13 wks
25 Nov 89	**A COLLECTION – GREATEST HITS . . . AND MORE** CBS 465845 1	22	23 wks
10 Jul 93	● **BACK TO BROADWAY** Columbia 4738802	4	17 wks
29 Oct 94	**THE CONCERT** Columbia 4775992	63	1 wk

STRINGS FOR PLEASURE UK, orchestra — 1 wk

| 4 Dec 71 | **BEST OF BACHARACH** MFP 1334 | 49 | 1 wk |

Joe STRUMMER UK, male vocalist — 1 wk

| 14 Oct 89 | **EARTHQUAKE WEATHER** Epic 465347 1 | 58 | 1 wk |

STYLE COUNCIL UK, male vocal / instrumental duo — 94 wks

24 Mar 84	● **CAFE BLEU** Polydor TSCLP 1	2	38 wks
8 Jun 85	★ **OUR FAVOURITE SHOP** Polydor TSCLP 2	1	22 wks
17 May 86	● **HOME AND ABROAD** Polydor TSCLP 3	8	8 wks
14 Feb 87	● **THE COST OF LOVING** Polydor TSCLP 4	2	7 wks

S 299

2 Jul 88	**CONFESSIONS OF A POP GROUP** Polydor TSCMC 5 ....**15**	3 wks
18 Mar 89	● **SINGULAR ADVENTURES OF THE STYLE COUNCIL**	
	Polydor TSCTV 1 ....**3**	15 wks
10 Jul 93	**HERE'S SOME THAT GOT AWAY** Polydor 5193722 ....**39**	1 wk

STYLISTICS US, male vocal group   **142 wks**

24 Aug 74	**ROCKIN' ROLL BABY** Avco 6466 012......................................**42**	3 wks
21 Sep 74	**LET'S PUT IT ALL TOGETHER** Avco 6466 013 ....**26**	14 wks
1 Mar 75	**FROM THE MOUNTAIN** Avco 9109 002..................................**36**	1 wk
5 Apr 75	★ **THE BEST OF THE STYLISTICS** Avco 9109 003 ....**1**	63 wks
5 Jul 75	● **THANK YOU BABY** Avco 9109 005......................................**5**	23 wks
6 Dec 75	**YOU ARE BEAUTIFUL** Avco 9109 006 ....**26**	9 wks
12 Jun 76	**FABULOUS** Avco 9109 008..**21**	5 wks
18 Sep 76	★ **BEST OF THE STYLISTICS VOLUME 2** H & L 9109 010.......**1**	21 wks
17 Oct 92	**THE GREATEST HITS OF THE STYLISTICS** Mercury 5129852 ....**34**	3 wks

STYX US, male vocal / instrumental group   **24 wks**

3 Nov 79	**CORNERSTONE** A & M AMLK 63711 ....**36**	8 wks
24 Jan 81	● **PARADISE THEATER** A & M AMLH 63719 ....**8**	8 wks
12 Mar 83	**KILROY WAS HERE** A & M AMLX 63734.................................**67**	6 wks
5 May 84	**CAUGHT IN THE ACT** A & M AMLM 66704 ....**44**	2 wks

SUEDE UK, male vocal / instrumental group   **38 wks**

| 10 Apr 93 | ★ **SUEDE** Nude NUDE 1CD...**1** | 22 wks |
| 22 Oct 94 | ● **DOG MAN STAR** Nude 4778112 ....**3** | 16 wks |

SUGAR US, male vocal / instrumental group   **19 wks**

19 Sep 92	● **COPPER BLUE** Creation CRECD 129 ....**10**	11 wks
17 Apr 93	● **BEASTER** Creation CRECD 153 ....**3**	5 wks
17 Sep 94	● **FILE UNDER EASY LISTENING** Creation CRECD 172 ....**7**	3 wks

SUGARCUBES Iceland, male / female vocal / instrumental group   **14 wks**

7 May 88	**LIFE'S TOO GOOD** One Little Indian TPLP 5 ....**14**	6 wks
14 Oct 89	**HERE TODAY, TOMORROW, NEXT WEEK**	
	One Little Indian TPLP 15..**15**	3 wks
22 Feb 92	**STICK AROUND FOR JOY** One Little Indian TPLP 30CD.................**16**	4 wks
17 Oct 92	**IT'S IT** One Little Indian TPLP 40CD **47**	1 wk

SUGGS UK, male vocalist   **3 wks**

| 28 Oct 95 | **THE LONE RANGER** WEA 0630124782 ....**14** | 3 wks |

SUICIDAL TENDENCIES UK, male vocal / instrumental group   **2 wks**

| 9 May 87 | **JOIN THE ARMY** Virgin V 2424 ....**81** | 1 wk |
| 21 Jul 90 | **LIGHTS . . . CAMERA . . . REVOLUTION** Epic 4665691 ....**59** | 1 wk |

SULTANS OF PING Ireland, male vocal / instrumental group   **3 wks**

| 13 Feb 93 | **CASUAL SEX IN THE CINEPLEX** Rhythm King 4724952 [1] ....**26** | 2 wks |
| 5 Mar 94 | **TEENAGE DRUG** Epic 4747162 ....**57** | 1 wk |

[1] Sultans Of Ping FC

Donna SUMMER US, female vocalist   **198 wks**

31 Jan 76	**LOVE TO LOVE YOU BABY** GTO GTLP 008 ....**16**	9 wks
22 May 76	**A LOVE TRILOGY** GTO GTLP 010 ....**41**	10 wks
25 Jun 77	● **I REMEMBER YESTERDAY** GTO GTLP 025 ....**3**	23 wks
26 Nov 77	**ONCE UPON A TIME** Casablanca CALD 5003 ....**24**	13 wks
7 Jan 78	● **GREATEST HITS** GTO GTLP 028...**4**	18 wks
21 Oct 78	**LIVE AND MORE** Casablanca CALD 5006 ....**16**	16 wks
2 Jun 79	**BAD GIRLS** Casablanca CALD 5007 ....**23**	23 wks

10 Nov 79	**ON THE RADIO – GREATEST HITS VOLUMES 1 & 2**			
	Casablanca CALD 5008	**24**	22 wks
1 Nov 80	**THE WANDERER** *Geffen K 99124*	**55**	2 wks
31 Jul 82	**DONNA SUMMER** *Warner Bros. K 99163*	**13**	16 wks
16 Jul 83	**SHE WORKS HARD FOR THE MONEY** *Mercury MERL 21*	**28**	5 wks
15 Sep 84	**CATS WITHOUT CLAWS** *Warner Bros. 250806*	**69**	2 wks
25 Mar 89	**ANOTHER PLACE AND TIME** *Warner Bros. WX 219*	**17**	28 wks
24 Nov 90	**THE BEST OF DONNA SUMMER** *Warner Bros. WX 397*	**24**	9 wks
26 Nov 94	**ENDLESS SUMMER – GREATEST HITS** *Mercury 5262172*	**37**	2 wks

SUNDAYS *UK, male/female vocal/instrumental group* **11 wks**

27 Jan 90	● **READING, WRITING AND ARITHMETIC** *Rough Trade ROUGH 148*	**4**	8 wks
31 Oct 92	**BLIND** *Parlophone CDPCSD 121*	**15**	3 wks

SUNSCREEM *UK, male/female vocal/instrumental group* **5 wks**

13 Feb 93	**03** *Sony S2 4722182*	**33**	5 wks

SUNSHINE BAND – *See KC and the SUNSHINE BAND*

SUPERGRASS *UK, male vocal/instrumental group* **25 wks**

27 May 95	★ **I SHOULD COCO** *Parlophone CDPCS 7373*	**1**	25 wks

SUPERTRAMP *UK/US, male vocal/instrumental group* **174 wks**

23 Nov 74	● **CRIME OF THE CENTURY** *A & M AMLS 68258*	**4**	22 wks
6 Dec 75	**CRISIS? WHAT CRISIS?** *A & M AMLH 68347*	**20**	15 wks
23 Apr 77	**EVEN IN THE QUIETEST MOMENTS** *A & M AMLK 64634*	**12**	22 wks
31 Mar 79	● **BREAKFAST IN AMERICA** *A & M AMLK 63708*	**3**	53 wks
4 Oct 80	● **PARIS** *A & M AMLM 66702*	**7**	17 wks
6 Nov 82	● **FAMOUS LAST WORDS** *A & M AMLK 63732*	**6**	16 wks
25 May 85	**BROTHER WHERE YOU BOUND** *A & M AMA 5014*	**20**	5 wks
18 Oct 86	● **THE AUTOBIOGRAPHY OF SUPERTRAMP** *A & M TRAMP 1*	**9**	19 wks
31 Oct 87	**FREE AS A BIRD** *A & M AMA 5181*	**93**	1 wk
15 Aug 92	**THE VERY BEST OF SUPERTRAMP** *A & M TRACD 1992*	**24**	4 wks

SUPREMES *US, female vocal group* **222 wks**

5 Dec 64	● **MEET THE SUPREMES** *Stateside SL 10109*	**8**	6 wks
17 Dec 66	**SUPREMES A GO–GO** *Tamla Motown STML 11039*	**15**	21 wks
13 May 67	**SUPREMES SING MOTOWN** *Tamla Motown STML 11047*	**15**	16 wks
30 Sep 67	**SUPREMES SING RODGERS AND HART**		
	Tamla Motown STML 11054	**25**	7 wks
20 Jan 68	★ **GREATEST HITS** *Tamla Motown STML 11063*	**1**	60 wks
30 Mar 68	● **LIVE AT THE TALK OF THE TOWN** *Tamla Motown STML 11070*	**6**	18 wks
20 Jul 68	**REFLECTIONS** *Tamla Motown STML 11073*	**30**	2 wks
25 Jan 69	★ **DIANA ROSS AND THE SUPREMES JOIN THE TEMPTATIONS**		
	Tamla Motown STML 11096 [1]	**1**	15 wks
1 Feb 69	● **LOVE CHILD** *Tamla Motown STML 11095*	**8**	6 wks
28 Jun 69	**TCB** *Tamla Motown STML 11110* [1]	**11**	12 wks
14 Feb 70	**TOGETHER** *Tamla Motown STML 11122* [1]	**28**	4 wks
29 May 71	● **MAGNIFICENT SEVEN** *Tamla Motown STML 11179* [2]	**6**	11 wks
25 Sep 71	**TOUCH** *Tamla Motown STML 11189*	**40**	1 wk
17 Sep 77	★ **20 GOLDEN GREATS** *Motown EMTV 5*	**1**	34 wks
21 Jan 89	● **LOVE SUPREME** *Motown ZL 72701*	**10**	9 wks

[1] Diana Ross and the Supremes with the Temptations [2] Supremes and the Four Tops

All albums beginning with Greatest Hits, with the exception of Touch, credit Diana Ross and the Supremes. See also Diana Ross.

SURVIVOR *US, male vocal/instrumental group* **10 wks**

21 Aug 82	**EYE OF THE TIGER** *Scotti Bros SCT 85845*	**12**	10 wks

Walter SUSSKIND – *See LONDON PHILHARMONIC CHOIR*

SUPERGRASS are caught by the cameraman.
(Solo/Joe Bangay Photography)

TAKE THAT take advice on how to split without acrimony.
(Solo/Mail Newspapers)

SUTHERLAND BROTHERS and QUIVER
UK, male vocal / instrumental group   **11 wks**

| 15 May 76 | **REACH FOR THE SKY** CBS 69191 ....**26** | 8 wks |
| 9 Oct 76 | **SLIPSTREAM** CBS 81593 ....**49** | 3 wks |

SWANS WAY *UK, male / female vocal / instrumental group*   **1 wk**

| 3 Nov 84 | **THE FUGITIVE KIND** Balgier SWAN 1 ....**88** | 1 wk |

Keith SWEAT *US, male vocalist*   **29 wks**

16 Jan 88	**MAKE IT LAST FOREVER** Elektra 960763 1....................**41**	21 wks
23 Jun 90	**I'LL GIVE ALL MY LOVE TO YOU** Vintertainment EKT 60 ....**47**	4 wks
9 Jul 94	**GET UP ON IT** Elektra 7559615502....................................**20**	4 wks

SWEET *UK, male vocal / instrumental group*   **8 wks**

| 18 May 74 | **SWEET FANNY ADAMS** RCA LPI 5038.......................**27** | 2 wks |
| 22 Sep 84 | **SWEET 16 IT'S . . . IT'S . . . SWEET'S HITS** Anagram GRAM 16 ..**49** | 6 wks |

SWERVEDRIVER *UK, male vocal / instrumental group*   **2 wks**

| 12 Oct 91 | **RAISE** Creation CRELP 093......................................**44** | 1 wk |
| 9 Oct 93 | **MEZCAL HEAD** Creation CCRE 143 ....**55** | 1 wk |

SWING OUT SISTER *UK, male / female vocal / instrumental group*   **36 wks**

23 May 87	★ **IT'S BETTER TO TRAVEL** Mercury OUTLP 1 ....**1**	21 wks
20 May 89	● **KALEIDOSCOPE WORLD** Fontana 838293 1 ....**3**	11 wks
16 May 92	**GET IN TOUCH WITH YOURSELF** Fontana 5122412.....................**27**	4 wks

SWINGLE SINGERS *US / France, male / female vocal group*   **18 wks**

| 1 Feb 64 | **JAZZ SEBASTIAN BACH** Philips BL 7572 ....**13** | 18 wks |

SWV *US, female vocal group*   **17 wks**

| 17 Jul 93 | **IT'S ABOUT TIME** RCA 7863660742 ....**17** | 17 wks |

SYBIL *US, female vocalist*   **12 wks**

5 Sep 87	**LET YOURSELF GO** Champion CHAMP 1009....................**92**	1 wk
24 Feb 90	**WALK ON BY** PWL HF 10 ....**21**	5 wks
12 Jun 93	**GOOD 'N' READY** PWL International HFCD 28................**13**	6 wks

SYLVESTER *US, male vocalist*   **3 wks**

| 23 Jun 79 | **MIGHTY REAL** Fantasy FTA 3009 ....**62** | 3 wks |

David SYLVIAN *UK, male vocalist*   **24 wks**

7 Jul 84	● **BRILLIANT TREES** Virgin V 2290.........................**4**	14 wks
13 Sep 86	**GONE TO EARTH** Virgin VDL 1 ....**24**	5 wks
7 Nov 87	**SECRETS OF THE BEEHIVE** Virgin V 2471 ....**37**	2 wks
2 Apr 88	**PLIGHT AND PREMONITION** Virgin VE 11 [1] **71**	1 wk
17 Jul 93	**THE FIRST DAY** Virgin CDVX 2712 [2] **21**	2 wks

[1] David Sylvian and Holgar Czukay [2] David Sylvian and Robert Fripp

SYMPHONIQUE *UK, male instrumentalist – Chris Cozens, keyboards*   **4 wks**

| 1 Apr 95 | **MOODS SYMPHONIQUE 95** Vision VISCD 10 ....**21** | 4 wks |

SYNTHPHONIC VARIATIONS *UK, session musicians*   **1 wk**

| 1 Nov 86 | **SEASONS** CBS 450 1491.....................................**84** | 1 wk |

S
303

ALPHABETICALLY BY ARTIST

British Hit Albums Part One

Date of chart entry/Title & catalogue no./Peak position reached/Weeks on chart

★ Number One   ● Top Ten   † still on chart at 30 Dec 1995   □ credited to act billed in footnote

Stanislas SYREWICZ – *See Anthony WAY*

SYSTEM 7 *UK, male / female instrumental / vocal group*   **3 wks**

20 Jun 92	**ALTITUDE** *Ten TENG 403*	**75**	1 wk
20 Mar 93	**777** *Big Life BFLCD 1*	**30**	2 wks

T. REX *UK, male vocal / instrumental group*   **219 wks**

13 Jul 68	**MY PEOPLE WERE FAIR AND HAD SKY IN THEIR HAIR BUT NOW THEY'RE CONTENT TO WEAR STARS ON THEIR BROWS** *Regal Zonophone SLRZ 1003* [1]	**15**	9 wks
7 Jun 69	**UNICORN** *Regal Zonophone S 1007* [1]	**12**	3 wks
14 Mar 70	**A BEARD OF STARS** *Regal Zonophone SLRZ 1013* [1] ...	**21**	6 wks
16 Jan 71	**T. REX** *Fly HIFLY 2*	**13**	24 wks
7 Aug 71	**THE BEST OF T. REX** *Flyback TON 2*	**21**	7 wks
9 Oct 71	★ **ELECTRIC WARRIOR** *Fly HIFLY 6*	**1**	44 wks
29 Mar 72	★ **PROPHETS, SEERS AND SAGES THE ANGELS OF THE AGES / MY PEOPLE WERE FAIR . . .** *Fly Double Back TOOFA 3/4* [1]	**1**	12 wks
20 May 72	★ **BOLAN BOOGIE** *Fly HIFLY 8*	**1**	19 wks
5 Aug 72	● **THE SLIDER** *EMI BLN 5001*	**4**	18 wks
9 Dec 72	**A BEARD OF STARS / UNICORN (re-issue)** *Cube TOOFA 9/10* [1]	**44**	2 wks
31 Mar 73	● **TANX** *EMI BLN 5002*	**4**	12 wks
10 Nov 73	**GREAT HITS** *EMI BLN 5003*	**32**	3 wks
16 Mar 74	**ZINC ALLOY AND THE HIDDEN RIDERS OF TOMORROW** *EMI BLNA 7751* [2]	**12**	3 wks
21 Feb 76	**FUTURISTIC DRAGON** *EMI BLN 5004*	**50**	1 wk
9 Apr 77	**DANDY IN THE UNDERWORLD** *EMI BLN 5005*	**26**	3 wks
30 Jun 79	**SOLID GOLD** *EMI NUT 5*	**51**	3 wks
12 Sep 81	**T. REX IN CONCERT** *Marc ABOLAN 1*	**35**	6 wks
7 Nov 81	**YOU SCARE ME TO DEATH** *Cherry Red ERED 20* [3]	**88**	1 wk
24 Sep 83	**DANCE IN THE MIDNIGHT** *Marc On Wax MARCL 501* [3]	**83**	3 wks
4 May 85	● **BEST OF THE 20TH CENTURY BOY** *K-Tel NE 1297* [2]	**5**	21 wks
28 Sep 91	● **THE ULTIMATE COLLECTION** *Telstar TCD 2539* [2]	**4**	16 wks
7 Oct 95	**THE ESSENTIAL COLLECTION** *PolyGram TV 5259612* [2]	**24**	3 wks

[1] Tyrannosaurus Rex   [2] Marc Bolan and T. Rex   [3] Marc Bolan

Prophets /My People *is a double re-issue, although* Prophets *had not previously been a hit.*

TAKE THAT *UK, male vocal group*   **178 wks**

5 Sep 92	● **TAKE THAT AND PARTY** *RCA 74321109*	**2**	70 wks
23 Oct 93	★ **EVERYTHING CHANGES** *RCA 74321169262*	**1**	78 wks
13 May 95	★ **NOBODY ELSE** *RCA 74321279092*	**1**	26 wks
26 Aug 95	**NOBODY ELSE (import)** *Arista 07822188002*	**26**	4 wks

TALK TALK *UK, male vocal / instrumental group*   **84 wks**

24 Jul 82	**THE PARTY'S OVER** *EMI EMC 3413*	**21**	25 wks
25 Feb 84	**IT'S MY LIFE** *EMI EMC 2400021*	**35**	8 wks
1 Mar 86	● **THE COLOUR OF SPRING** *EMI EMC 3506*	**8**	21 wks
24 Sep 88	**SPIRIT OF EDEN** *Parlophone PCSD 105*	**19**	5 wks
9 Jun 90	● **THE VERY BEST OF TALK TALK – NATURAL HISTORY** *Parlophone PCSD 109*	**3**	21 wks
6 Apr 91	**HISTORY REVISITED** *Parlophone PCS 7349*	**35**	2 wks
28 Sep 91	**LAUGHING STOCK** *Verve 8477171*	**26**	2 wks

TALKING HEADS US/UK, male/female vocal/instrumental group 229 wks

25 Feb 78	TALKING HEADS '77 Sire 9103 328 60	1	wk
29 Jul 78	MORE SONGS ABOUT BUILDINGS AND FOOD Sire K 56531 21	3	wks
15 Sep 79	FEAR OF MUSIC Sire SRK 6076 33	5	wks
1 Nov 80	REMAIN IN LIGHT Sire SRK 6095 21	17	wks
10 Apr 82	THE NAME OF THIS BAND IS TALKING HEADS Sire SRK 23590 ..22	5	wks
18 Jun 83	SPEAKING IN TONGUES Sire K 923 8831 21	12	wks
27 Oct 84	STOP MAKING SENSE EMI TAH 1 37	81	wks
29 Jun 85	● LITTLE CREATURES EMI TAH 2 10	65	wks
27 Sep 86	● TRUE STORIES EMI EU 3511 7	9	wks
26 Mar 88	● NAKED EMI EMD 1005...3	15	wks
24 Oct 92	● ONCE IN A LIFETIME / SAND IN THE VASELINE EMI CDEQ 5010 ..7	16	wks

TANGERINE DREAM Germany, male instrumental group 77 wks

20 Apr 74	PHAEDRA Virgin V 2010 15	15	wks
5 Apr 75	RUBYCON Virgin V 2025 12	14	wks
20 Dec 75	RICOCHET Virgin V 2044 40	2	wks
13 Nov 76	STRATOSFEAR Virgin V 2068 39	4	wks
23 Jul 77	SORCERER (film soundtrack) MCA MCF 2806 25	7	wks
19 Nov 77	ENCORE Virgin VD 2506 55	1	wk
1 Apr 78	CYCLONE Virgin V 2097 37	4	wks
17 Feb 79	FORCE MAJEURE Virgin V 2111 26	7	wks
7 Jun 80	TANGRAM Virgin V 2147 36	5	wks
18 Apr 81	THIEF (film soundtrack) Virgin V 2198 43	3	wks
19 Sep 81	EXIT Virgin V 2212 43	5	wks
10 Apr 82	WHITE EAGLE Virgin V 2226..57	5	wks
5 Nov 83	HYPERBOREA Virgin V 2292...45	2	wks
10 Nov 84	POLAND Jive Electro HIP 22 90	1	wk
26 Jul 86	UNDERWATER SUNLIGHT Jive Electro HIP 40....................97	1	wk
27 Jun 87	TYGER Jive Electro HIP 47 88	1	wk

TANK UK, male vocal/instrumental group 5 wks

13 Mar 82	FILTH HOUNDS OF HADES Kamaflage KAMLP 1 33	5	wks

Bill TARMEY UK, male vocalist 23 wks

27 Nov 93	A GIFT OF LOVE EMI CDEMC 3665 15	14	wks
5 Nov 94	TIME FOR LOVE EMI CDEMTV 85....................................28	9	wks

TASTE Ireland, male vocal/instrumental group 12 wks

7 Feb 70	ON THE BOARDS Polydor 583083 18	11	wks
9 Sep 72	TASTE LIVE AT THE ISLE OF WIGHT Polydor 2383 120.................41	1	wk

Jeffrey TATE – See Nigel KENNEDY

TAVARES US, male vocal group 15 wks

21 Aug 76	SKY HIGH Capitol EST 11533 22	13	wks
1 Apr 78	THE BEST OF TAVARES Capitol EST 11701 39	2	wks

Andy TAYLOR UK, male vocalist/instrumentalist – guitar 1 wk

30 May 87	THUNDER MCA MCG 6018 61	1	wk

James TAYLOR US, male vocalist 111 wks

21 Nov 70	● SWEET BABY JAMES Warner Bros. ES 1843 7	53	wks
29 May 71	● MUD SLIDE SLIM AND THE BLUE HORIZON		
	Warner Bros. WS 2561 4	41	wks
8 Jan 72	SWEET BABY JAMES (re-issue) Warner Bros. K 46043 34	6	wks
18 Mar 72	MUD SLIDE SLIM AND THE BLUE HORIZON (re-issue)		
	Warner Bros. K 46085..49	1	wk
9 Dec 72	ONE MAN DOG Warner Bros. K 46185 27	5	wks

| 4 Apr 87 | **CLASSIC SONGS** CBS/WEA JTV 1 | **53** | 5 wks |

James TAYLOR QUARTET UK, male instrumental group — **5 wks**

1 May 93	**SUPERNATURAL FEELING** Big Life BLRCD 21 [1]	**36**	3 wks
29 OCT 94	**EXTENDED PLAY** Acid Jazz JAZID 110CD	**70**	1 wks
11 Mar 95	**IN THE HAND OF THE INEVITABLE** Acid Jazz JAZID CD115	**63**	1 wks

[1] JTQ with Noel McKoy

Roger TAYLOR UK, male vocalist / instrumentalist – drums — **10 wks**

18 Apr 81	**FUN IN SPACE** EMI EMC 3369	**18**	5 wks
7 Jul 84	**STRANGE FRONTIER** EMI RTA 1	**30**	4 wks
17 Sep 94	**HAPPINESS** Parlophone CDPCSD 157	**22**	1 wk

Kiri TE KANAWA New Zealand, female vocalist — **52 wks**

2 Apr 83	**CHANTS D'AUVERGNE VOLUME 1** Decca SXDL 7604 [1]	**57**	1 wk
26 Oct 85	**BLUE SKIES** London KTKT 1 [2]	**40**	29 wks
13 Dec 86	**CHRISTMAS WITH KIRI** Decca PROLP 12	**47**	4 wks
17 Dec 88	**KIRI** K-Tel NE 1424	**70**	3 wks
29 Feb 92	**THE ESSENTIAL KIRI** Decca 4362862	**23**	10 wks
23 May 92	**KIRI SIDETRACKS THE JAZZ ALBUM** Philips 4340922	**73**	1 wk
9 Apr 94	**KIRI!** PolyGram TV 4436002	**16**	4 wks

[1] Kiri Te Kanawa with the English Chamber Orchestra [2] Kiri Te Kanawa with the Nelson Riddle Orchestra

TEARDROP EXPLODES UK, male vocal / instrumental group — **45 wks**

18 Oct 80	**KILIMANJARO** Mercury 6359 035	**24**	35 wks
5 Dec 81	**WILDER** Mercury 6359 056	**29**	6 wks
14 Apr 90	**EVERYBODY WANTS TO SHAG THE TEARDROP EXPLODES** Fontana 8424391 72	**72**	1 wk
15 Aug 92	**FLOORED GENIUS THE BEST OF JULIAN COPE** Island CID 8000 [1]	**22**	3 wks

[1] Julian Cope and the Teardrop Explodes

T
306

TEARS FOR FEARS UK, male vocal / instrumental duo — **210 wks**

19 Mar 83	★ **THE HURTING** Mercury MERS 17	**1**	65 wks
9 Mar 85	● **SONGS FROM THE BIG CHAIR** Mercury MERH 58	**2**	81 wks
7 Oct 89	★ **THE SEEDS OF LOVE** Fontana 838730 1	**1**	30 wks
14 Mar 92	● **TEARS ROLL DOWN (GREATEST HITS 1982–1992)** Fontana 5109392	**2**	26 wks
19 Jun 93	● **ELEMENTAL** Mercury 5148752	**5**	7 wks
28 Oct 95	**RAOUL AND THE KINGS OF SPAIN** Epic 4809822	**41**	1 wk

Act was UK, male vocalist / instrumentalist for the last two albums.

TECHNOTRONIC
Belgium / UK, male / female vocal / instrumental group — **62 wks**

6 Jan 90	● **PUMP UP THE JAM** Swanyard SYRLP 1	**2**	44 wks
2 Nov 90	● **TRIP ON THIS – REMIXES** Telstar STAR 2461	**7**	14 wks
15 Jun 91	**BODY TO BODY** ARS 4683421	**27**	4 wks

TEENAGE FANCLUB UK, male vocal / instrumental group — **16 wks**

7 Sep 91	**KING** Creation CRELP 096	**53**	2 wks
16 Nov 91	**BANDWAGONESQUE** Creation CRELP 106	**22**	7 wks
16 Oct 93	**THIRTEEN** Creation CRECD 144	**14**	3 wks
10 Jun 95	● **GRAND PRIX** Creation CRECD 173	**7**	4 wks

TELEVISION US, male vocal / instrumental group — **17 wks**

| 26 Mar 77 | **MARQUEE MOON** Elektra K 52046 | **28** | 13 wks |
| 29 Apr 78 | ● **ADVENTURE** Elektra K 52072 | **7** | 4 wks |

TEMPERANCE SEVEN UK, male vocal / instrumental group   **10 wks**

13 May 61	**TEMPERANCE SEVEN PLUS ONE** Argo RG 11 19	1	wk
25 Nov 61	● **TEMPERANCE SEVEN 1961** Parlophone PMC 1152 8	9	wks

TEMPLE CHURCH CHOIR UK, male vocal / instrumental group   **3 wks**

16 Dec 61	● **CHRISTMAS CAROLS** HMV CLP 1309...8	3	wks

TEMPTATIONS US, male vocal group   **139 wks**

24 Dec 66	**GETTING READY** Tamla Motown STML 11035 40	2	wks
11 Feb 67	**TEMPTATIONS GREATEST HITS** Tamla Motown STML 11042 17	40	wks
22 Jul 67	**TEMPTATIONS LIVE** Tamla Motown STML 11053 20	4	wks
18 Nov 67	**TEMPTATIONS WITH A LOT OF SOUL**		
	Tamla Motown STML 11057...19	18	wks
25 Jan 69	★ **DIANA ROSS AND THE SUPREMES JOIN THE TEMPTATIONS**		
	Tamla Motown STML 11096 [1] 1	15	wks
28 Jun 69	**TCB** Tamla Motown STML 11110 [1] 11	12	wks
20 Sep 69	**CLOUD NINE** Tamla Motown STML 11109.............................32	1	wk
14 Feb 70	**PUZZLE PEOPLE** Tamla Motown STML 11133 20	4	wks
14 Feb 70	**TOGETHER** Tamla Motown STML 11122 [1] 28	4	wks
11 Jul 70	**PSYCHEDELIC SHACK** Tamla Motown STML 11147......................56	1	wk
26 Dec 70	**GREATEST HITS VOLUME 2** Tamla Motown STML 11170 35	12	wks
29 Apr 72	**SOLID ROCK** Tamla Motown STML 11202 34	2	wks
20 Jan 73	**ALL DIRECTIONS** Tamla Motown STML 11218 19	7	wks
7 Jul 73	**MASTERPIECE** Tamla Motown STML 11229 28	3	wks
8 Dec 84	**TRULY FOR YOU** Motown ZL 72342....................................75	5	wks
11 Apr 92	● **MOTOWN'S GREATEST HITS** Motown 5300152 8	9	wks

[1] Diana Ross and the Supremes with the Temptations

10 C.C. UK, male vocal / instrumental group   **215 wks**

1 Sep 73	**10 C.C.** UK UKAL 1005...36	5	wks
15 Jun 74	● **SHEET MUSIC** UK UKAL 1007 9	24	wks
22 Mar 75	● **THE ORIGINAL SOUNDTRACK** Mercury 9102 50Q 4	40	wks
7 Jun 75	● **GREATEST HITS OF 10 C.C.** Decca UKAL 1012 9	18	wks
31 Jan 76	● **HOW DARE YOU?** Mercury 9102 501 5	31	wks
14 May 77	● **DECEPTIVE BENDS** Mercury 9102 502................................3	21	wks
10 Dec 77	**LIVE AND LET LIVE** Mercury 6641 698 14	15	wks
23 Sep 78	● **BLOODY TOURISTS** Mercury 9102 503 3	15	wks
6 Oct 79	● **GREATEST HITS 1972–1978** Mercury 9102 504 5	21	wks
5 Apr 80	**LOOK HERE** Mercury 9102 505 35	5	wks
15 Oct 83	**WINDOW IN THE JUNGLE** Mercury MERL 28 70	2	wks
29 Aug 87	● **CHANGING FACES – THE VERY BEST OF 10 C.C. AND**		
	GODLEY AND CREME ProTV TGCLP 1 [1] 4	18	wks

[1] 10 C.C. and Godley and Creme

TEN CITY US, male vocal / instrumental group   **12 wks**

18 Feb 89	**FOUNDATION** Atlantic WX 249 22	12	wks

TEN POLE TUDOR UK, male vocal / instrumental group   **8 wks**

9 May 81	**EDDIE, OLD BOB, DICK & GARRY** Stiff SEEZ 31 44	8	wks

TEN SHARP Holland, male vocal / instrumental duo   **2 wks**

9 May 92	**UNDER THE WATER–LINE** Columbia 4690702 46	2	wks

10,000 MANIACS US, female / male vocal / instrumental group   **12 wks**

27 May 89	**BLIND MAN'S ZOO** Elektra EKT 57 18	8	wks
10 Oct 92	**OUR TIME IN EDEN** Elektra 7559613852............................33	2	wks
6 Nov 93	**UNPLUGGED** Elektra 7559615692 40	2	wks

TEN YEARS AFTER *UK, male vocal / instrumental group* **73 wks**

21 Sep 68	**UNDEAD** Deram SML 1023	26	7 wks
22 Feb 69	● **STONEDHENGE** Deram SML 1029	6	5 wks
4 Oct 69	● **SSSSH** Deram SML 1052	4	18 wks
2 May 70	● **CRICKLEWOOD GREEN** Deram SML 1065	4	27 wks
9 Jan 71	● **WATT** Deram SML 1078	5	12 wks
13 Nov 71	**SPACE IN TIME** Chrysalis CHR 1001	36	1 wk
7 Oct 72	**ROCK AND ROLL** Chrysalis CHR 1009	27	1 wk
28 Jul 73	**RECORDED LIVE** Chrysalis CHR 1049	36	2 wks

TENNILLE – *See CAPTAIN and TENNILLE*

TERRAPLANE *UK, male vocal / instrumental group* **1 wk**

25 Jan 86	**BLACK AND WHITE** Epic EPC 26439	74	1 wk

Tammi TERRELL – *See Marvin GAYE*

TERRORVISION *UK, male vocal / instrumental group* **26 wks**

15 May 93	**FORMALDEHYDE** Total Vegas VEGASCD 1	75	1 wk
30 Apr 94	**HOW TO MAKE FRIENDS AND INFLUENCE PEOPLE** Total Vegas VEGASCD 2	18	25 wks

Todd TERRY *US, male producer* **1 wk**

5 Aug 95	**A DAY IN THE LIFE OF TODD TERRY** Sound Of Ministry SOMCD 2	73	1 wk

TESLA *US, male vocal / instrumental group* **6 wks**

11 Feb 89	**THE GREAT RADIO CONTROVERSY** Geffen WX 244	34	2 wks
2 Mar 91	**FIVE MAN ACOUSTICAL JAM** Geffen 9243111	59	1 wk
21 Sep 91	**PSYCHOTIC SUPPER** Geffen GEF 24424	44	2 wks
3 Sep 94	**BUST A NUT** Geffen GED 24713	51	1 wk

TESTAMENT *US, male vocal / instrumental group* **6 wks**

28 May 88	**THE NEW ORDER** Megaforce 781849 1	81	1 wk
19 Aug 89	**PRACTICE WHAT YOU PREACH** Atlantic WX 297	40	2 wks
6 Oct 90	**SOULS OF BLACK** Megaforce 7567821431	35	2 wks
30 May 92	**THE RITUAL** Atlantic 7567823922	48	1 wk

TEXAS *UK, male / female vocal / instrumental group* **33 wks**

25 Mar 89	● **SOUTHSIDE** Mercury 838171 1	3	27 wks
5 Oct 91	**MOTHER'S HEAVEN** Mercury 8485781	32	4 wks
13 Nov 93	**RICK'S ROAD** Vertigo 5182522	18	2 wks

THA DOGG POUND *US, male rap group* **2 wks**

11 Nov 95	**DOGG FOOD** Death Row 5241772	66	2 wks

THAT PETROL EMOTION *UK, male vocal / instrumental group* **8 wks**

10 May 86	**MANIC POP THRILL** Demon FIEND 70	84	2 wks
23 May 87	**BABBLE** Polydor TPE LP 1	30	3 wks
24 Sep 88	**END OF MILLENNIUM PSYCHOSIS BLUES** Virgin V 2550	53	2 wks
21 Apr 90	**CHEMICRAZY** Virgin V 2618	62	1 wk

The THE *UK, male vocal / instrumental group* **51 wks**

29 Oct 83	**SOUL MINING** Some Bizzare EPC 25525	27	5 wks
29 Nov 86	**INFECTED** Some Bizzare EPC 26770	14	30 wks
27 May 89	● **MIND BOMB** Epic 463319 1	4	9 wks

T
308

British Hit Albums Part One

Date of chart entry/Title & catalogue no./Peak position reached/Weeks on chart

★ Number One   ● Top Ten   † still on chart at 30 Dec 1995   ☐ credited to act billed in footnote

---

6 Feb 93	● **DUSK** Epic 4724682 ....**2**	4 wks
19 Jun 93	**BURNING BLUE SOUL** 4AD HAD 113CD **65**	1 wk
25 Feb 95	**HANKY PANKY** Epic 4781392 ....**28**	2 wks

Matt Johnson leads The The, which is an informal group of his studio guests and friends.

THEATRE OF HATE *UK, male vocal/instrumental group*   **9 wks**

13 Mar 82	**WESTWORLD** Burning Rome TOH 1 ....**17**	6 wks
18 Aug 84	**REVOLUTION** Burning Rome TOH 2 ....**67**	3 wks

THEN JERICO *UK, male vocal/instrumental group*   **24 wks**

3 Oct 87	**FIRST (THE SOUND OF MUSIC)** London LONLP 26 ....**35**	7 wks
4 Mar 89	● **THE BIG AREA** London 828122 1 ....**4**	17 wks

THERAPY? *UK, male vocal/instrumental group*   **22 wks**

8 Feb 92	**PLEASURE DEATH** Wiiija WIJ 11 ....**52**	1 wk
14 Nov 92	**NURSE** A & M 5400442 ....**38**	3 wks
19 Feb 94	● **TROUBLEGUM** A & M 5401962 ....**5**	11 wks
24 Jun 95	● **INFERNAL LOVE** A & M 5403792 ....**9**	7 wks

THESE ANIMAL MEN *UK, male vocal/instrumental group*   **4 wks**

2 Jul 94	**TOO SUSSED** Hi-Rise FLATMCD 4 ....**39**	2 wks
8 Oct 94	**(COME ON JOIN) THE HIGH SOCIETY** Hi-Rise FLATCD 8...**62**	1 wk
25 Mar 95	**TAXI FOR THESE ANIMAL MEN** Hi-Rise FLATMCD 14 ....**64**	1 wk

THEY MIGHT BE GIANTS *US, male vocal/instrumental duo*   **12 wks**

7 Apr 90	**FLOOD** Elektra EKT 68 ....**14**	12 wks

THIN LIZZY *Ireland/UK/US, male vocal/instrumental group*   **239 wks**

27 Sep 75	**FIGHTING** Vertigo 6360 121 ....**60**	1 wk
10 Apr 76	● **JAILBREAK** Vertigo 9102 008 ....**10**	50 wks
6 Nov 76	**JOHNNY THE FOX** Vertigo 9102 012 ....**11**	24 wks
1 Oct 77	● **BAD REPUTATION** Vertigo 9102 016 ....**4**	9 wks
17 Jun 78	● **LIVE AND DANGEROUS** Vertigo 6641 807 ....**2**	62 wks
5 May 79	● **BLACK ROSE (A ROCK LEGEND)** Vertigo 9102 032 ....**2**	21 wks
18 Oct 80	● **CHINA TOWN** Vertigo 6359 030 ....**7**	7 wks
11 Apr 81	● **ADVENTURES OF THIN LIZZY** Vertigo LIZTV 1...........**6**	13 wks
5 Dec 81	**RENEGADE** Vertigo 6359 083 ....**38**	8 wks
12 Mar 83	● **THUNDER AND LIGHTNING** Vertigo VERL 3 ....**4**	11 wks
26 Nov 83	**LIFE** Vertigo VERD 6.....................................**29**	6 wks
14 Nov 87	**SOLDIER OF FORTUNE – THE BEST OF PHIL LYNOTT AND** **THIN LIZZY** Telstar STAR 2300 ☐1 ....**55**	10 wks
16 Feb 91	● **DEDICATION – THE VERY BEST OF THIN LIZZY** Vertigo 8481921..**8**	17 wks

☐1 Phil Lynott and Thin Lizzy

3RD BASS *US, male rap group*   **1 wk**

20 Jul 91	**DERELICTS OF DIALECT** Def Jam 4683171 ....**46**	1 wk

THIRD EAR BAND *UK, male instrumental group*   **2 wks**

27 Jun 70	**AIR, EARTH, FIRE, WATER** Harvest SHVL 773................**49**	2 wks

THIRD WORLD *Jamaica, male vocal/instrumental group*   **18 wks**

21 Oct 78	**JOURNEY TO ADDIS** Island ILPS 9554 ....**30**	6 wks

T

309

| 11 Jul 81 | **ROCKS THE WORLD** CBS 85027 | **37** | 9 wks |
| 15 May 82 | **YOU'VE GOT THE POWER** CBS 85563 | **87** | 3 wks |

THIS MORTAL COIL UK, male / female instrumental group **10 wks**

20 Oct 84	**IT'LL END IN TEARS** 4AD CAD 411	**38**	4 wks
11 Oct 86	**FILIGREE AND SHADOW** 4AD DAD 609	**53**	3 wks
4 May 91	**BLOOD** 4AD DAD 1005	**65**	3 wks

Carla THOMAS – See Otis REDDING

Kenny THOMAS UK, male vocalist **28 wks**

| 26 Oct 91 | ● **VOICES** Cooltempo CTLP 24 | **3** | 23 wks |
| 25 Sep 93 | ● **WAIT FOR ME** Cooltempo CTCD 36 | **10** | 5 wks |

Lillo THOMAS US, male vocalist **7 wks**

| 2 May 87 | **LILLO** Capitol EST 2031 | **43** | 7 wks |

Ray THOMAS UK, male vocalist **3 wks**

| 26 Jul 75 | **FROM MIGHTY OAKS** Threshold THS 16 | **23** | 3 wks |

Richard THOMPSON UK, male vocalist / instrumentalist – guitar **10 wks**

27 Apr 85	**ACROSS A CROWDED ROOM** Polydor POLD 5175	**80**	2 wks
18 Oct 86	**DARING ADVENTURES** Polydor POLD 5202	**92**	1 wk
29 Oct 88	**AMNESIA** Capitol EST 2075	**89**	1 wk
25 May 91	**RUMOUR AND SIGH** Capitol EST 2142	**32**	3 wks
29 Jan 94	**MIRROR BLUE** Capitol CDEST 2207	**23**	3 wks

THOMPSON TWINS
UK / New Zealand, male / female vocal / instrumental group **128 wks**

13 Mar 82	**SET** Tee TELP 2	**48**	3 wks
26 Feb 83	● **QUICK STEP AND SIDE KICK** Arista 204 924	**2**	56 wks
25 Feb 84	★ **INTO THE GAP** Arista 205 971	**1**	51 wks
28 Sep 85	● **HERE'S TO FUTURE DAYS** Arista 207 164	**5**	9 wks
2 May 87	**CLOSE TO THE BONE** Arista 208 143	**90**	1 wk
10 Mar 90	**GREATEST HITS** Stylus SMR 92	**23**	8 wks

George THOROGOOD and the DESTROYERS
US, male vocal / instrumental group **1 wk**

| 2 Dec 78 | **GEORGE THOROGOOD AND THE DESTROYERS** Sonet SNTF 781 | **67** | 1 wk |

THOUSAND YARD STARE UK, male vocal / instrumental group **2 wks**

| 7 Mar 92 | **HANDS ON** Polydor 5130012 | **38** | 2 wks |

THREE DEGREES US, female vocal group **91 wks**

10 Aug 74	**THREE DEGREES** Philadelphia International 65858	**12**	22 wks
17 May 75	● **TAKE GOOD CARE OF YOURSELF** Philadelphia International PIR 69137	**6**	16 wks
24 Feb 79	**NEW DIMENSIONS** Ariola ARLH 5012	**34**	13 wks
3 Mar 79	● **A COLLECTION OF THEIR 20 GREATEST HITS** Epic EPC 10013	**8**	18 wks
15 Dec 79	**3D** Ariola 3D 1	**61**	7 wks
27 Sep 80	● **GOLD** Ariola 3D 2	**9**	15 wks

THROWING MUSES US / UK, male / female vocal / instrumental group **12 wks**

4 Feb 89	**HUNKPAPA** 4AD CAD 901	**59**	1 wk
2 Mar 91	**THE REAL RAMONA** 4AD CAD 1002	**26**	4 wks
22 Aug 92	**RED HEAVEN** 4AD CAD 2013CD	**13**	3 wks

| 28 Nov 92 | **THE CURSE** 4AD TAD 2019CD | **74** | 1 | wk |
| 28 Jan 95 | ● **UNIVERSITY** 4AD CADD 5002CD | **10** | 3 | wks |

THUNDER UK / US, male vocal / instrumental group   **34 wks**

17 Mar 90	**BACKSTREET SYMPHONY** EMI EMC 3570	**21**	16	wks
5 Sep 92	● **LAUGHING ON JUDGEMENT DAY** EMI CDEMD 1035	**2**	10	wks
4 Feb 95	● **BEHIND CLOSED DOORS** EMI CDEMD 1076	**5**	5	wks
7 Oct 95	**BEST OF THUNDER – THEIR FINEST HOUR (AND A BIT)** EMI CDEMD 1086	**22**	3	wks

TIFFANY US, female vocalist   **27 wks**

| 27 Feb 88 | ● **TIFFANY** MCA MCF 3415 | **5** | 21 | wks |
| 17 Dec 88 | **HOLD AN OLD FRIEND'S HAND** MCA MCF 3437 | **56** | 6 | wks |

TIGERTAILZ US, male vocal / instrumental group   **2 wks**

| 7 Apr 90 | **BEZERK** Music For Nations MFN 96 | **36** | 2 | wks |

TIGHT FIT UK, male / female vocal group   **6 wks**

| 26 Sep 81 | **BACK TO THE SIXTIES** Jive HIP 1 | **38** | 4 | wks |
| 4 Sep 82 | **TIGHT FIT** Jive HIP 2 | **87** | 2 | wks |

TIJUANA BRASS – See Herb ALPERT and the TIJUANA BRASS

TIK and TOK UK, male vocal / instrumental duo   **2 wks**

| 4 Aug 84 | **INTOLERANCE** Survival SUR LP 008 | **89** | 2 | wks |

Tanita TIKARAM UK, female vocalist   **61 wks**

24 Sep 88	● **ANCIENT HEART** WEA WX 210	**3**	49	wks
10 Feb 90	● **THE SWEET KEEPER** East West WX 330	**3**	7	wks
16 Feb 91	**EVERYBODY'S ANGEL** East West WX 401	**19**	4	wks
25 Feb 95	**LOVERS IN THE CITY** East West 4509988042	**75**	1	wk

TILBROOK – See DIFFORD and TILBROOK

TIMBUK THREE US, male / female vocal / instrumental duo   **4 wks**

| 14 Feb 87 | **GREETINGS FROM TIMBUK THREE** IRS MIRF 1015 | **51** | 4 | wks |

TIME US, male vocal / instrumental group   **1 wk**

| 28 Jul 90 | **PANDEMONIUM** Paisley Park WX 336 | **66** | 1 | wk |

TIME FREQUENCY UK, male instrumental / production group   **4 wks**

| 18 Jun 94 | **DOMINATOR** Internal Affairs KGBD 500 | **23** | 4 | wks |

TIN MACHINE US / UK, male vocal / instrumental group   **12 wks**

| 3 Jun 89 | ● **TIN MACHINE** EMI–USA MTLS 1044 | **3** | 9 | wks |
| 14 Sep 91 | **TIN MACHINE II** London 8282721 | **23** | 3 | wks |

TINDERSTICKS UK, male vocal / instrumental group   **5 wks**

23 Oct 93	**TINDERSTICKS** This Way Up 5183064	**56**	1	wk
15 Apr 95	**THE SECOND TINDERSTICKS ALBUM** This Way Up 5263032	**13**	3	wks
28 Oct 95	**THE BLOOMSBURY THEATRE 12.3.95** This Way Up 5285972	**32**	1	wk

TLC US, female vocal group   **24 wks**

| 20 May 95 | ● **CRAZYSEXYCOOL** LaFace 73008260092 | **4†** | 24 | wks |

T
311

TOM TOM CLUB US, female / male vocal / instrumental group — **1 wk**

24 Oct 81	**TOM TOM CLUB** Island ILPS 9686 ....**78**	1 wk

TOMITA Japan, male instrumentalist – synthesizer — **33 wks**

7 Jun 75	**SNOWFLAKES ARE DANCING** RCA Red Seal ARL 10488 ....**17**	20 wks
16 Aug 75	**PICTURES AT AN EXHIBITION** RCA Red Seal ARL 10838 ....**42**	5 wks
7 May 77	**HOLST: THE PLANETS** RCA Red Seal RL 11919 ....**41**	6 wks
9 Feb 80	**TOMITA'S GREATEST HITS** RCA Red Seal RL 43076 ....**66**	2 wks

TONGUE 'N' CHEEK UK, male / female vocal / instrumental group — **3 wks**

22 Sep 90	**THIS IS TONGUE 'N' CHEEK** Syncopate SYLP 6006 ....**45**	3 wks

TONY! TONI! TONE! US, male vocal group — **1 wk**

2 Oct 93	**SONS OF SOUL** Polydor 5149332 ....**66**	1 wk

TOPOL Israel, male vocalist — **1 wk**

11 May 85	**TOPOL'S ISRAEL** BBC REH 529 ....**80**	1 wk

Bernie TORME UK, male vocalist / instrumentalist – guitar — **3 wks**

3 Jul 82	**TURN OUT THE LIGHTS** Kamaflage KAMLP 2 ....**50**	3 wks

Peter TOSH Jamaica, male vocalist — **1 wk**

25 Sep 76	**LEGALIZE IT** Virgin V 2061 ....**54**	1 wk

TOTAL CONTRAST UK, male vocal / instrumental duo — **3 wks**

8 Mar 86	**TOTAL CONTRAST** London LONLP 15 ....**66**	3 wks

TOTO US, male vocal / instrumental group — **39 wks**

31 Mar 79	**TOTO** CBS 83148 ....**37**	5 wks
26 Feb 83 ●	**TOTO IV** CBS 85529 ....**4**	30 wks
17 Nov 84	**ISOLATION** CBS 86305 ....**67**	2 wks
20 Sep 86	**FAHRENHEIT** CBS 57091 ....**99**	1 wk
9 Apr 88	**THE SEVENTH ONE** CBS 460465 1 ....**73**	1 wk

Ali Farka TOURE – See Ry COODER

TOURISTS UK, female / male vocal / instrumental group — **18 wks**

14 Jul 79	**THE TOURISTS** Logo GO 1018...**72**	1 wk
3 Nov 79	**REALITY EFFECT** Logo GO 1019..**23**	16 wks
22 Nov 80	**LUMINOUS BASEMENT** RCA RCALP 5001 ....**75**	1 wk

Pete TOWNSHEND UK, male vocalist / instrumentalist – guitar — **28 wks**

21 Oct 72	**WHO CAME FIRST** Track 2408 201 ....**30**	2 wks
15 Oct 77	**ROUGH MIX** Polydor 2442147 [1] **44**	3 wks
3 May 80	**EMPTY GLASS** Atco K 50699 ....**11**	14 wks
3 Jul 82	**ALL THE BEST COWBOYS HAVE CHINESE EYES** Atco K 50889 ..**32**	8 wks
30 Nov 85	**WHITE CITY** Atco 2523921 ....**70**	1 wk

[1] Pete Townshend and Ronnie Lane

TOY DOLLS UK, male vocal / instrumental group — **1 wk**

25 May 85	**A FAR OUT DISC** Volume VOLP 2...**71**	1 wk

TOYAH *UK, female vocalist*   97 wks

14 Jun 80	**THE BLUE MEANING** Safari IEYA 666	.40	4 wks
17 Jan 81	**TOYAH TOYAH TOYAH** Safari LIVE 2	.22	14 wks
30 May 81	● **ANTHEM** Safari VOOR 1	.2	46 wks
19 Jun 82	● **THE CHANGELING** Safari VOOR 9	.6	12 wks
13 Nov 82	**WARRIOR ROCK – TOYAH ON TOUR** Safari TNT 1	.20	6 wks
5 Nov 83	**LOVE IS THE LAW** Safari VOOR 10	.28	7 wks
25 Feb 84	**TOYAH! TOYAH! TOYAH!** K–Tel NE 1268	.43	4 wks
3 Aug 85	**MINX** Portrait PRT 26415	.24	4 wks

T'PAU *UK, female / male vocal / instrumental group*   85 wks

26 Sep 87	★ **BRIDGE OF SPIES** Siren SIRENLP 8	.1	59 wks
5 Nov 88	● **RAGE** Siren SRNLP 20	.4	17 wks
22 Jun 91	● **THE PROMISE** Siren SRNLP 32	.10	7 wks
27 Feb 93	**HEART AND SOUL – THE VERY BEST OF T'PAU** Virgin TPAUD 1	.35	2 wks

Ian TRACEY/LIVERPOOL CATHEDRALS' CHOIRS
UK, conductor and male / female choirs   3 wks

21 Mar 92	**YOUR FAVOURITE HYMNS** Virgin Classics 7912092	.62	3 wks

TRACIE *UK, female vocalist*   2 wks

30 Jun 84	**FAR FROM THE HURTING KIND** Respond RRL 502	.64	2 wks

TRAFFIC *UK, male vocal / instrumental group*   41 wks

30 Dec 67	● **MR. FANTASY** Island ILP 9061	.8	16 wks
26 Oct 68	● **TRAFFIC** Island ILPS 9081 T	.9	8 wks
8 Aug 70	**JOHN BARLEYCORN MUST DIE** Island ILPS 9116	.11	9 wks
24 Nov 73	**ON THE ROAD** Island ISLD 2	.40	3 wks
28 Sep 74	**WHEN THE EAGLE FLIES** Island ILPS 9273	.31	1 wk
21 May 94	**FAR FROM HOME** Virgin CDV 2727	.29	4 wks

TRANSGLOBAL UNDERGROUND
UK, male / female vocal / instrumental group   2 wks

30 Oct 93	**DREAM OF 100 NATIONS** Nation NR 021CD	.45	1 wk
29 Oct 94	**INTERNATIONAL TIMES** Nation NATCD 38	.40	1 wk

TRANSVISION VAMP *UK, male / female vocal / instrumental group*   58 wks

15 Oct 88	● **POP ART** MCA MCF 3421	.4	32 wks
8 Jul 89	★ **VELVETEEN** MCA MCG 6050	.1	26 wks

TRASH CAN SINATRAS *UK, male vocal / instrumental group*   2 wks

7 Jul 90	**CAKE** Go! Discs 82820211	.74	1 wk
15 May 93	**I'VE SEEN EVERYTHING** Go! Discs 8284082	.50	1 wk

TRAVELING WILBURYS *US / UK, male vocal / instrumental group*   44 wks

5 Nov 88	**THE TRAVELING WILBURYS VOLUME 1** Wilbury WX 224	.16	35 wks
10 Nov 90	**THE TRAVELING WILBURYS VOLUME 3** Wilbury WX 384	.14	9 wks

Pat TRAVERS *US, male instrumentalist – guitar*   3 wks

2 Apr 77	**MAKIN' MAGIC** Polydor 2383 436	.40	3 wks

Randy TRAVIS *US, male vocalist*   2 wks

6 Aug 88	**OLD 8 X 10** Warner Bros. WX 162	.64	2 wks

T
313

John TRAVOLTA US, male vocalist **6 wks**

23 Dec 78 **SANDY** Polydor POLD 5014..............................**40**   6 wks

TREMELOES UK, male vocal / instrumental group **7 wks**

3 Jun 67 **HERE COME THE TREMELOES** CBS SBPG 63017.............................**15**   7 wks

Ralph TRESVANT US, male vocalist **3 wks**

23 Feb 91 **RALPH TRESVANT** MCA MCG 6120 ....**37**   3 wks

A TRIBE CALLED QUEST US, male rap group **4 wks**

19 May 90 **PEOPLE'S INSTINCTIVE TRAVELS** Jive HIP 96 ....**54**   2 wks
12 Oct 91 **LOW END THEORY** Jive HIP 117.....................................**58**   1 wk
27 Nov 93 **MIDNIGHT MARAUDERS** Jive CHIP 143 ....**70**   1 wk

TRICKY UK, male multi–instrumentalist **27 wks**

4 Mar 95 ● **MAXINQUAYE** Fourth & Broadway BRCD 610...................**3**   27 wks

TRIFFIDS New Zealand, male vocal / instrumental group **1 wk**

22 Apr 89 **THE BLACK SWAN** Island ILPS 9928.....................**63**   1 wk

TRIUMPH Canada, male vocal / instrumental group **8 wks**

10 May 80 **PROGRESSIONS OF POWER** RCA PL 13524......................**61**   5 wks
3 Oct 81 **ALLIED FORCES** RCA RCALP 6002 ....**64**   3 wks

T
314

TROGGS UK, male vocal / instrumental group **35 wks**

30 Jul 66 ● **FROM NOWHERE . . . THE TROGGS** Fontana TL 5355.....................**6**   16 wks
25 Feb 67 ● **TROGGLODYNAMITE** Page One POL 001 ....**10**   11 wks
5 Aug 67 **BEST OF THE TROGGS** Page One FOR 001 ....**24**   5 wks
16 Jul 94 **GREATEST HITS** PolyGram TV 5227392 ....**27**   3 wks

TROUBADOURS DU ROI BAUDOUIN
Zaire, male / female vocal group **1 wk**

22 May 76 **MISSA LUBA** Philips SBL 7592 ....**59**   1 wk

TROUBLE FUNK US, male vocal / instrumental group **4 wks**

8 Nov 86 **SAY WHAT!** Fourth & Broadway DCLP 101 ....**75**   2 wks
5 Sep 87 **TROUBLE OVER HERE, TROUBLE OVER THERE**
          Fourth & Broadway BRLP 513 ....**54**   2 wks

Robin TROWER UK, male instrumentalist – guitar **16 wks**

1 Mar 75 **FOR EARTH BELOW** Chrysalis CHR 1073 ....**26**   4 wks
13 Mar 76 **LIVE** Chrysalis CHR 1089.....................................**15**   6 wks
30 Oct 76 **LONG MISTY DAYS** Chrysalis CHR 1107 ....**31**   1 wk
29 Oct 77 **IN CITY DREAMS** Chrysalis CHR 1148 ....**58**   1 wk
16 Feb 80 **VICTIMS OF THE FURY** Chrysalis CHR 1215....................**61**   4 wks

TUBES US, male vocal / instrumental group **7 wks**

4 Mar 78 **WHAT DO YOU WANT FROM LIFE** A & M AMS 68460 ....**38**   1 wk
2 Jun 79 **REMOTE CONTROL** A & M AMLH 64751 ....**40**   5 wks
4 Jun 83 **OUTSIDE INSIDE** Capitol EST 12260.......................**77**   1 wk

TUBEWAY ARMY – See Gary Numan

Ike and Tina TURNER
US, male instrumentalist – guitar and female vocalist **1 wk**

1 Oct 66	**RIVER DEEP – MOUNTAIN HIGH** London HAU 8298	27	1 wk

See also Tina Turner.

Ruby TURNER *UK, female vocalist* **19 wks**

18 Oct 86	**WOMEN HOLD UP HALF THE SKY** Jive HIP 36	47	11 wks
8 Oct 88	**THE MOTOWN SONGBOOK** Jive HIP 58	22	6 wks
17 Feb 90	**PARADISE** Jive HIP 89	74	2 wks

Tina TURNER *US, female vocalist* **450 wks**

30 Jun 84	● **PRIVATE DANCER** Capitol TINA 1	2	147 wks
20 Sep 86	● **BREAK EVERY RULE** Capitol EST 2018	2	49 wks
2 Apr 88	● **LIVE IN EUROPE** Capitol ESTD 1	8	13 wks
30 Sep 89	★ **FOREIGN AFFAIR** Capitol ESTU 2103	1	78 wks
12 Oct 91	● **SIMPLY THE BEST** Capitol ESTV 1	2	130 wks
19 Jun 93	★ **WHAT'S LOVE GOT TO DO WITH IT (film soundtrack)** Parlophone CDPCSD 128	1	33 wks

See also Ike and Tina Turner.

TURTLES *US, male vocal / instrumental group* **9 wks**

22 Jul 67	**HAPPY TOGETHER** London HAU 8330	18	9 wks

TWELFTH NIGHT *UK, male vocal / instrumental group* **2 wks**

27 Oct 84	**ART AND ILLUSION** Music For Nations MFN 36	83	2 wks

TWENTY 4 SEVEN
US / Holland / Switzerland / Germany / Italy, male / female vocal / instrumental group **2 wks**

19 Jan 91	**STREET MOVES** BCM BCM 3124	69	2 wks

TWIGGY *UK, female vocalist* **11 wks**

21 Aug 76	**TWIGGY** Mercury 9102 600	33	8 wks
30 Apr 77	**PLEASE GET MY NAME RIGHT** Mercury 9102 601	35	3 wks

TWISTED SISTER *US, male vocal / instrumental group* **20 wks**

25 Sep 82	**UNDER THE BLADE** Secret SECX 9	70	3 wks
7 May 83	**YOU CAN'T STOP ROCK 'N' ROLL** Atlantic A 0074	14	9 wks
16 Jun 84	**STAY HUNGRY** Atlantic 780156	34	5 wks
14 Dec 85	**COME OUT AND PLAY** Atlantic 7812751	95	1 wk
25 Jul 87	**LOVE IS FOR SUCKERS** Atlantic WX 120	57	2 wks

2 IN A ROOM *US, male vocal duo* **1 wk**

2 Mar 91	**WIGGLE IT** SBK SBKLP 11	73	1 wk

2 UNLIMITED *Holland, male / female vocal duo* **38 wks**

7 Mar 92	**GET READY** PWL Continental HFCD 23	37	3 wks
22 May 93	★ **NO LIMITS** PWL Continental HFCD 27	1	21 wks
18 Jun 94	★ **REAL THINGS** PWL Continental HFCD 38	1	9 wks
11 Nov 95	**HITS UNLIMITED** PWL International HF 47CD	27	5 wks

Tommy TYCHO – See David GRAY and Tommy TYCHO

TYGERS OF PAN TANG *UK, male vocal / instrumental group* **20 wks**

30 Aug 80	**WILD CAT** MCA MCF 3075	18	5 wks

18 Apr 81	**SPELLBOUND** MCA MCF 3104	**33**	4 wks
21 Nov 81	**CRAZY NIGHTS** MCA MCF 3123	**51**	3 wks
28 Aug 82	**THE CAGE** MCA MCF 3150	**13**	8 wks

Bonnie TYLER UK, female vocalist   **75 wks**

16 Apr 83 ★	**FASTER THAN THE SPEED OF NIGHT** CBS 25304	**1**	45 wks
17 May 86	**SECRET DREAMS AND FORBIDDEN FIRE** CBS 86319	**24**	12 wks
29 Nov 86	**THE GREATEST HITS** Telstar STAR 2291	**24**	17 wks
21 May 88	**HIDE YOUR HEART** CBS 460125 1	**78**	1 wk

Judie TZUKE UK, female vocalist   **61 wks**

4 Aug 79	**WELCOME TO THE CRUISE** Rocket TRAIN 7	**14**	17 wks
10 May 80 ●	**SPORTS CAR** Rocket TRAIN 9	**7**	11 wks
16 May 81	**I AM PHOENIX** Rocket TRAIN 15	**17**	10 wks
17 Apr 82	**SHOOT THE MOON** Chrysalis CDL 1382	**19**	10 wks
30 Oct 82	**ROAD NOISE – THE OFFICIAL BOOTLEG** Chrysalis CTY 1405	**39**	4 wks
1 Oct 83	**RITMO** Chrysalis CDL 1442	**26**	5 wks
15 Jun 85	**THE CAT IS OUT** Legacy LLP 102	**35**	3 wks
29 Apr 89	**TURNING STONES** Polydor 839087 1	**57**	1 wk

UB40 UK, male vocal / instrumental group   **541 wks**

6 Sep 80 ●	**SIGNING OFF** Graduate GRAD LP 2	**2**	71 wks
6 Jun 81 ●	**PRESENT ARMS** DEP International LPDEP 1	**2**	38 wks
10 Oct 81	**PRESENT ARMS IN DUB** DEP International LPDEP 2	**38**	7 wks
28 Aug 82	**THE SINGLES ALBUM** Graduate GRADLSP 3	**17**	8 wks
9 Oct 82 ●	**UB 44** DEP International LPDEP 3	**4**	8 wks
26 Feb 83	**UB 40 LIVE** DEP International LPDEP 4	**44**	5 wks
24 Sep 83 ★	**LABOUR OF LOVE** DEP International LPDEP 5	**1**	76 wks
20 Oct 84 ●	**GEFFREY MORGAN** DEP International DEP 6	**3**	14 wks
14 Sep 85	**BAGGARADDIM** DEP International LPDEP 10	**14**	23 wks
9 Aug 86 ●	**RAT IN THE KITCHEN** DEP International LPDEP 11	**8**	20 wks
7 Nov 87 ●	**THE BEST OF UB40 VOLUME 1** Virgin UBTV 1	**3**	130 wks
23 Jul 88	**UB40** DEP International LPDEP 13	**12**	12 wks
9 Dec 89 ●	**LABOUR OF LOVE II** DEP International LPDEP 14	**3**	69 wks
24 Jul 93 ★	**PROMISES AND LIES** DEP International DEPCD 15	**1**	37 wks
12 Nov 94 ●	**LABOUR OF LOVE VOLUMES I AND II (re-issue)** DEP International DEPDD 1	**5**	15 wks
11 Nov 95	**THE BEST OF UB40 VOLUME 2** DEP International DUBTV 2	**12†**	8 wks

UFO UK, male vocal / instrumental group   **48 wks**

4 Jun 77	**LIGHTS OUT** Chrysalis CHR 1127	**54**	2 wks
15 Jul 78	**OBSESSION** Chrysalis CDL 1182	**26**	7 wks
10 Feb 79 ●	**STRANGERS IN THE NIGHT** Chrysalis CJT 5	**8**	11 wks
19 Jan 80	**NO PLACE TO RUN** Chrysalis CDL 1239	**11**	7 wks
24 Jan 81	**THE WILD THE WILLING AND THE INNOCENT** Chrysalis CHR 1307	**19**	5 wks
20 Feb 82 ●	**MECHANIX** Chrysalis CHR 1360	**8**	6 wks
12 Feb 83	**MAKING CONTACT** Chrysalis CHR 1402	**32**	4 wks
3 Sep 83	**HEADSTONE - THE BEST OF UFO** Chrysalis CTY 1437	**39**	4 wks
16 Nov 85	**MISDEMEANOUR** Chrysalis CHR 1518	**74**	2 wks

UGLY KID JOE US, male vocal / instrumental group   **42 wks**

13 Jun 92 ●	**AS UGLY AS THEY WANNA BE** Mercury 8688232	**9**	13 wks
12 Sep 92	**AMERICA'S LEAST WANTED** Vertigo 5125712	**11**	24 wks
17 Jun 95	**MENACE TO SOBRIETY** Mercury 5282622	**25**	5 wks

TOP 30 № 24

UB40, with brothers
Robin and Ali Campbell,
climbed three places on
the all-time table during
1994–95.

(LFI)

U
317

TOP 30 № 7

U2 are shown in 1981,
the year of their chart
debut.

(Solo/Joe Bangay Photography)

UK *UK, male vocal / instrumental group*   **3 wks**

27 May 78   **U.K.** *Polydor 2302 080* .... **43**   3 wks

UK SUBS *UK, male vocal / instrumental group*   **26 wks**

13 Oct 79	**ANOTHER KIND OF BLUES** *Gem GEMLP 100*	**21**	6 wks
19 Apr 80	**BRAND NEW AGE** *Gem GEMLP 106*	**18**	9 wks
27 Sep 80	● **CRASH COURSE** *Gem GEMLP 111*	**8**	6 wks
21 Feb 81	**DIMINISHED RESPONSIBILITY** *Gem GEMLP 112*	**18**	5 wks

Tracey ULLMAN *UK, female vocalist*   **22 wks**

3 Dec 83	**YOU BROKE MY HEART IN 17 PLACES** *Stiff SEEZ 51*	**14**	20 wks
8 Dec 84	**YOU CAUGHT ME OUT** *Stiff SEEZ 56*	**92**	2 wks

ULTIMATE KAOS *UK, male vocal group*   **1 wk**

29 Apr 95   **ULTIMATE KAOS** *Polydor 5274442* .... **51**   1 wk

ULTRA VIVID SCENE *US, male vocalist*   **1 wk**

19 May 90   **JOY 1967–1990** *4AD CAD 005* .... **58**   1 wk

ULTRAMARINE *UK, male instrumental duo*   **1 wk**

4 Sep 93   **UNITED KINGDOMS** *Blanco Y Negro 4509934252* .... **49**   1 wk

ULTRA–SONIC *UK, male instrumental / production duo*   **1 wk**

11 Nov 95   **GLOBAL TEKNO** *Cluscene DCSR 007* .... **58**   1 wk

ULTRAVOX *UK / Canada, male vocal / instrumental group*   **225 wks**

19 Jul 80	● **VIENNA** *Chrysalis CHR 1296*	**3**	72 wks
19 Sep 81	● **RAGE IN EDEN** *Chrysalis CDL 1338*	**4**	23 wks
23 Oct 82	● **QUARTET** *Chrysalis CDL 1394*	**6**	30 wks
22 Oct 83	● **MONUMENT – THE SOUNDTRACK** *Chrysalis CUX 1452*	**9**	15 wks
14 Apr 84	● **LAMENT** *Chrysalis CDL 1459*	**8**	26 wks
10 Nov 84	● **THE COLLECTION** *Chrysalis UTV 1*	**2**	53 wks
25 Oct 86	● **U–VOX** *Chrysalis CDL 1545*	**9**	6 wks

See also Midge Ure.

UNDERCOVER *UK, male vocal / instrumental group*   **9 wks**

5 Dec 92   **CHECK OUT THE GROOVE** *PWL International HFCD 26* .... **26**   9 wks

UNDERTONES *UK, male vocal / instrumental group*   **50 wks**

19 May 79	**THE UNDERTONES** *Sire SRK 6071*	**13**	21 wks
26 Apr 80	● **HYPNOTISED** *Sire SRK 6088*	**6**	10 wks
16 May 81	**POSITIVE TOUCH** *Ardeck ARD 103*	**17**	6 wks
19 Mar 83	**THE SIN OF PRIDE** *Ardeck ARD 104*	**43**	5 wks
10 Dec 83	**ALL WRAPPED UP** *Ardeck ARD 1654281/3*	**67**	4 wks
14 Jun 86	**CHER O'BOWLIES: PICK OF UNDERTONES** *Ardeck EMS 1172*	**96**	1 wk
25 Sep 93	**TEENAGE KICKS** *Castle Communications CTVCD 121*	**45**	3 wks

UNDERWORLD *UK, male instrumental group*   **4 wks**

5 Feb 94   **DUBNOBASSWITHMYHEADMAN** *Junior Boy's Own JBOCD 1* ...... **12**   4 wks

UNION *UK, male instrumental group*   **6 wks**

26 Oct 91   **WORLD IN UNION** *Columbia 4690471* .... **17**   6 wks

UNION GAP – *See Gary PUCKETT and the UNION GAP*

U.N.K.L.E. *UK, male instrumental / production group*   **1 wk**

| 21 Jan 95 | **THE TIME HAS COME EP** *Mo Wax MW 028P* ....**73** | 1 wk |

UNTOUCHABLES *US, male vocal / instrumental group*   **7 wks**

| 13 Jul 85 | **WILD CHILD** *Stiff SEEZ 57* ....**51** | 7 wks |

Dawn UPSHAW (soprano)/LONDON SINFONIETTA/ David ZINMAN (conductor)

US, female vocalist with UK orchestra and US conductor   **18 wks**

| 23 Jan 93 | ● **GORECKI SYMPHONY NO.3** *Elektra Nonsuch 7559792822*.............**6** | 18 wks |

URBAN COOKIE COLLECTIVE

UK, male / female vocal / instrumental group   **2 wks**

| 26 Mar 94 | **HIGH ON A HAPPY VIBE** *Pulse 8 PULSE 13CD* ....**28** | 2 wks |

URBAN SPECIES *UK, male vocal / instrumental group*   **2 wks**

| 7 May 94 | **LISTEN** *Talkin Loud 5186482* ....**43** | 2 wks |

Midge URE *UK, male vocalist*   **26 wks**

19 Oct 85	● **THE GIFT** *Chrysalis CHR 1508*......................**2**	15 wks
10 Sep 88	**ANSWERS TO NOTHING** *Chrysalis CHR 1649* **30**	3 wks
28 Sep 91	**PURE** *Arista 211922* **36**	2 wks
6 Mar 93	● **IF I WAS: THE VERY BEST OF MIDGE URE**	
	Chrysalis CDCHR 1987......................**10**	6 wks

If I Was: The Very Best Of Midge Ure *includes tracks by Ultravox, Visage, Band Aid and Phil Lynott.*

URIAH HEEP *UK, male vocal / instrumental group*   **51 wks**

13 Nov 71	**LOOK AT YOURSELF** *Island ILPS 9169* **39**	1 wk
10 Jun 72	**DEMONS AND WIZARDS** *Bronze ILPS 9193* **20**	11 wks
2 Dec 72	**THE MAGICIAN'S BIRTHDAY** *Bronze ILPS 9213*...............**28**	3 wks
19 May 73	**LIVE** *Island ISLD 1* **23**	8 wks
29 Sep 73	**SWEET FREEDOM** *Island ILPS 9245* **18**	3 wks
29 Jun 74	**WONDERWORLD** *Bronze ILPS 9280* **23**	3 wks
5 Jul 75	● **RETURN TO FANTASY** *Bronze ILPS 9335* **7**	6 wks
12 Jun 76	**HIGH AND MIGHTY** *Island ILPS 9384*...............**55**	1 wk
22 Mar 80	**CONQUEST** *Bronze BRON 524*...............**37**	3 wks
17 Apr 82	**ABOMINOG** *Bronze BRON 538* **34**	6 wks
18 Jun 83	**HEAD FIRST** *Bronze BRON 545*...............**46**	4 wks
6 Apr 85	**EQUATOR** *Portrait PRT 261414* **79**	2 wks

---

USA FOR AFRICA *US, male / female vocal / instrumental group*   **5 wks**

| 25 May 85 | **WE ARE THE WORLD** *CBS USAID F1* ....**31** | 5 wks |

Album contains tracks by various artists in addition to the title track.

US3 *UK, male instrumental duo*   **6 wks**

| 31 Jul 93 | **HAND ON THE TORCH** *Capitol CDEST 2195* ....**40** | 6 wks |

UTAH SAINTS *UK, male instrumental / sampling / vocal duo*   **15 wks**

| 5 Jun 93 | ● **UTAH SAINTS** *ffrr 8283792* ....**10** | 15 wks |

UTFO *US, male vocal group*   **1 wk**

16 Mar 85	**ROXANNE ROXANNE (6 TRACK VERSION)**		
	Streetwave 6 Track XKHAN 506......................................**72**	1	wk

UTOPIA *UK, male vocal / instrumental group*   **3 wks**

1 Oct 77	**OOPS SORRY WRONG PLANET** Bearsville K 53517 ....**59**	1	wk
16 Feb 80	**ADVENTURES IN UTOPIA** Island ILPS 9602......................**57**	2	wks

U2 *Ireland, male vocal / instrumental group*   **861 wks**

29 Aug 81	**BOY** Island ILPS 9646 ....**52**	31	wks
24 Oct 81	**OCTOBER** Island ILPS 9680......................**11**	42	wks
12 Mar 83	★ **WAR** Island ILPS 9733 ....**1**	147	wks
3 Dec 83	● **U2 LIVE: UNDER A BLOOD RED SKY** Island IMA 3 ....**2**	203	wks
13 Oct 84	★ **THE UNFORGETTABLE FIRE** Island U 25 ....**1**	130	wks
27 Jul 85	**WIDE AWAKE IN AMERICA (import)** Island 902791A **11**	16	wks
21 Mar 87	★ **THE JOSHUA TREE** Island U 26 ....**1**	129	wks
20 Feb 88	**THE JOSHUA TREE SINGLES** Island U2 PK 1......................**100**	1	wk
22 Oct 88	★ **RATTLE AND HUM** Island U2 7......................**1**	54	wks
30 Nov 91	● **ACHTUNG BABY** Island U 28 ....**2**	77	wks
17 Jul 93	★ **ZOOROPA** Island CIDU 29 ....**1**	31	wks

Steve VAI *UK, male vocalist*   **18 wks**

2 Jun 90	● **PASSION AND WARFARE** Food For Thought GRUB 17 ....**8**	10	wks
7 Aug 93	**SEX AND RELIGION** Relativity 4729472 `1` **17**	6	wks
15 Apr 95	**ALIEN LOVE SECRETS** Relativity 4785862......................**39**	2	wks

`1` Vai

Frankie VALLI – *See FOUR SEASONS*

VAN DER GRAAF GENERATOR
UK, male vocal / instrumental group   **2 wks**

25 Apr 70	**THE LEAST WE CAN DO IS WAVE TO EACH OTHER**		
	Charisma CAS 1007......................**47**	2	wks

VAN HALEN *US / Holland, male vocal / instrumental group*   **99 wks**

27 May 78	**VAN HALEN** Warner Bros. K 56470 ....**34**	11	wks
14 Apr 79	**VAN HALEN II** Warner Bros. K 566116......................**23**	7	wks
5 Apr 80	**WOMEN AND CHILDREN FIRST** Warner Bros. K 56793......................**15**	7	wks
23 May 81	**FAIR WARNING** Warner Bros. K 56899 ....**49**	4	wks
1 May 82	**DIVER DOWN** Warner Bros. K 57003 ....**36**	5	wks
4 Feb 84	**1984** Warner Bros. 923985 ....**15**	24	wks
5 Apr 86	**5150** Warner Bros. WS 5150 ....**16**	18	wks
4 Jun 88	**OU812** Warner Bros. WX 177 ....**16**	12	wks
29 Jun 91	**FOR UNLAWFUL CARNAL KNOWLEDGE** Warner Bros. WX 420 ..**12**	5	wks
6 Mar 93	**LIVE: RIGHT HERE RIGHT NOW** Warner Bros. 9362451982..........**24**	3	wks
4 Feb 95	● **BALANCE** Warner Bros. 9362457602 ....**8**	3	wks

Luther VANDROSS *US, male vocalist*   **264 wks**

21 Jan 84	**BUSY BODY** Epic EPC 25608 ....**42**	8	wks
6 Apr 85	**THE NIGHT I FELL IN LOVE** Epic EPC 26387 ....**19**	10	wks
1 Nov 86	● **GIVE ME THE REASON** Epic EPC 4501341 ....**3**	99	wks
21 Feb 87	**NEVER TOO MUCH** Epic EPC 32807 ....**41**	30	wks

LUTHER VANDROSS with Jackie Collins at a Vandross party at Spago Restaurant in West Hollywood.
(Scott Downie/LFI)

4 Jul 87	**FOREVER, FOR ALWAYS, FOR LOVE** Epic EPC 25013 ....**23**	16	wks
16 Apr 88	**BUSY BODY (re-issue)** Epic 460183 1 ....**78**	4	wks
29 Oct 88	● **ANY LOVE** Epic 462908 1 ....**3**	22	wks
11 Nov 89	**BEST OF LUTHER VANDROSS – BEST OF LOVE** Epic 465801 1 ....**14**	23	wks
25 May 91	● **POWER OF LOVE** Epic 4680121 ....**9**	9	wks
12 Jun 93	**NEVER LET ME GO** Epic 4735982 ....**11**	5	wks
1 Oct 94	★ **SONGS** Epic 4766562 ....**1**	28	wks
28 Oct 95	**GREATEST HITS 1981–1995** Epic 4811002 ....**12†**	10	wks

VANESSA–MAE UK, female instrumentalist – violin   **21 wks**

25 Feb 95	**THE VIOLIN PLAYER** EMI Classics CDC 5550892 ....**11**	21	wks

VANGELIS Greece, male instrumentalist – keyboards   **151 wks**

10 Jan 76	**HEAVEN AND HELL** RCA Victor RS 1025 ....**31**	7	wks
9 Oct 76	**ALBEDO 0.39** RCA Victor RS 1080 ....**18**	6	wks
18 Apr 81	● **CHARIOTS OF FIRE (film soundtrack)** Polydor POLS 1026 ....**5**	97	wks
5 May 84	**CHARIOTS OF FIRE (film soundtrack) (re-issue)** Polydor POLD 5160 ....**39**	10	wks
13 Oct 84	**SOIL FESTIVITIES** Polydor POLH 11 ....**55**	4	wks
30 Mar 85	**MASK** Polydor POLH 19...**69**	2	wks
22 Jul 89	**THEMES** Polydor VGTV 1 ....**11**	13	wks
24 Oct 92	**1492 – THE CONQUEST OF PARADISE (film soundtrack)** East West 4509910142 ....**33**	6	wks
18 Jun 94	**BLADERUNNER (film soundtrack)** East West 4509965742 ....**20**	6	wks

See also Jon and Vangelis.

VANILLA FUDGE US, male vocal / instrumental group   **3 wks**

4 Nov 67	**VANILLA FUDGE** Atlantic 588086 ....**31**	3	wks

VANILLA ICE US, male rapper   **23 wks**

15 Dec 90	● **TO THE EXTREME** SBK SBKLP 9 ....**4**	20	wks
6 Jul 91	**EXTREMELY LIVE** SBK SBKLP 12...**35**	3	wks

VAPORS UK, male vocal / instrumental group   **6 wks**

7 Jun 80	**NEW CLEAR DAYS** United Artists UAG 30300 ....**44**	6	wks

VARDIS UK, male vocal / instrumental group   **1 wk**

1 Nov 80	**100 MPH** Logo MOGO 4012 ....**52**	1	wk

Frankie VAUGHAN UK, male vocalist   **20 wks**

5 Sep 59	● **FRANKIE VAUGHAN AT THE LONDON PALLADIUM** Philips BDL 7330 ....**6**	2	wks
4 Nov 67	**FRANKIE VAUGHAN SONGBOOK** Philips DBL 001 ....**40**	1	wk
25 Nov 67	**THERE MUST BE A WAY** Columbia SCX 6200................................**22**	8	wks
12 Nov 77	**100 GOLDEN GREATS** Ronco RTDX 2021 ....**24**	9	wks

Sarah VAUGHAN US, female vocalist   **1 wk**

26 Mar 60	**NO COUNT – SARAH** Mercury MMC 14021.....................................**19**	1	wk

Stevie Ray VAUGHAN and DOUBLE TROUBLE
US, male vocal / instrumental group   **1 wk**

15 Jul 89	**IN STEP** Epic 463395 1 ....**63**	1	wk

VAUGHAN BROTHERS US, male vocal / instrumental group   **1 wk**

20 Oct 90	**FAMILY STYLE** Epic 4670141 ....**63**	1	wk

British Hit Albums Part One

Date of chart entry/Title & catalogue no./Peak position reached/Weeks on chart

★ Number One ● Top Ten † still on chart at 30 Dec 1995 ☐ credited to act billed in footnote

---

Bobby VEE *US, male vocalist*   **73 wks**

24 Feb 62	● TAKE GOOD CARE OF MY BABY London HAG 2428 7	8 wks
31 Mar 62	HITS OF THE ROCKIN' 50'S London HAG 2406 20	1 wk
27 Oct 62	● BOBBY VEE MEETS THE CRICKETS Liberty LBY 1086 [1] 2	27 wks
12 Jan 63	● A BOBBY VEE RECORDING SESSION Liberty LBY 1084 10	11 wks
20 Apr 63	● BOBBY VEE'S GOLDEN GREATS Liberty LBY 1112 10	14 wks
5 Oct 63	THE NIGHT HAS A THOUSAND EYES Liberty LIB 1139 15	2 wks
19 Apr 80	● THE BOBBY VEE SINGLES ALBUM United Artists UAG 30253 5	10 wks

[1] Bobby Vee and the Crickets

Suzanne VEGA *US, female vocalist*   **121 wks**

19 Oct 85	SUZANNE VEGA A & M AMA 5072 11	71 wks
9 May 87	● SOLITUDE STANDING A & M SUZLP 2 2	39 wks
28 Apr 90	● DAYS OF OPEN HAND A & M 3952931 7	7 wks
19 Sep 92	99.9° F A & M 5400122 20	4 wks

Rosie VELA *US, female vocalist*   **11 wks**

| 31 Jan 87 | ZAZU A & M AMA 5016..20 | 11 wks |

VELVET UNDERGROUND
US, male / female vocal / instrumental group   **7 wks**

23 Feb 85	V.U. Polydor POLD 5167...47	4 wks
13 Nov 93	LIVE MCMXCIII Sire 9362454642 70	1 wk
28 Oct 95	THE BEST OF LOU REED AND THE VELVET UNDERGROUND Global Television RADCD 21 [1] 56	2 wks

[1] Lou Reed and the Velvet Underground

VENOM *UK, male vocal / instrumental group*   **2 wks**

| 21 Apr 84 | AT WAR WITH SATAN Neat NEAT 1015...............................64 | 1 wk |
| 13 Apr 85 | POSSESSED Neat NEAT 1024 ....99 | 1 wk |

Anthony VENTURA ORCHESTRA *Switzerland, orchestra*   **4 wks**

| 20 Jan 79 | DREAM LOVER Lotus WH 5007 ....44 | 4 wks |

Tom VERLAINE *US, male vocalist*   **1 wk**

| 14 Mar 87 | FLASH LIGHT Fontana SFLP 1 ....99 | 1 wk |

VERUCA SALT *US, male vocal / instrumental group*   **2 wks**

| 15 Oct 94 | AMERICAN THIGHS Hi-Rise FLATCD 9 ....47 | 2 wks |

VERVE *UK, male vocal / instrumental group*   **8 wks**

| 3 Jul 93 | A STORM IN HEAVEN Hut CDHUT 10 ....27 | 2 wks |
| 15 Jul 95 | A NORTHERN SOUL Hut DGHUT 27.................................13 | 6 wks |

VIBRATORS *UK, male vocal / instrumental group*   **7 wks**

| 25 Jun 77 | THE VIBRATORS Epic EPC 82907 ....49 | 5 wks |
| 29 Apr 78 | V2 Epic EPC 82495 ....33 | 2 wks |

VICE SQUAD *UK, male / female vocal / instrumental group*   **10 wks**

| 24 Oct 81 | NO CAUSE FOR CONCERN Zonophone ZEM 103...........................32 | 5 wks |
| 22 May 82 | STAND STRONG STAND PROUD Zonophone ZEM 104.................47 | 5 wks |

Sid VICIOUS *UK, male vocalist* **8 wks**

15 Dec 79	**SID SINGS** *Virgin V 2144*..................30	8 wks

VIENNA PHILHARMONIC ORCHESTRA – *See Aram KHATCHATURIAN/VIENNA PHILHARMONIC ORCHESTRA*

VIENNA SYMPHONY ORCHESTRA *Austria, orchestra* **4 wks**

4 Apr 87	**SYMPHONIC ROCK WITH THE VIENNA SYMPHONY ORCHESTRA** *Stylus SMR 730*..................43	4 wks

VILLAGE PEOPLE *US, male vocal group* **29 wks**

27 Jan 79	**CRUISIN'** *Mercury 9109 614*..................24	9 wks
12 May 79	**GO WEST** *Mercury 9109 621*..................14	19 wks
18 Dec 93	**THE BEST OF THE VILLAGE PEOPLE** *Bell 4321178312* 72	1 wk

Gene VINCENT *US, male vocalist* **2 wks**

16 Jul 60	**CRAZY TIMES** *Capitol T 1342*..................12	2 wks

Vinnie VINCENT *US, male vocalist / instrumentalist – guitar* **2 wks**

28 May 88	**ALL SYSTEMS GO** *Chrysalis CHR 1626*..................51	2 wks

Bobby VINTON *US, male vocalist* **2 wks**

17 Nov 90	**BLUE VELVET** *Epic 4675701*..................67	2 wks

VIOLENT FEMMES *US, male / female vocal / instrumental group* **1 wk**

1 Mar 86	**THE BLIND LEADING THE NAKED** *Slash SLAP 10* 81	1 wk

VIOLINSKI *UK, male instrumental group* **1 wk**

26 May 79	**NO CAUSE FOR ALARM** *Jet JETLU 219*..................49	1 wk

VISAGE *UK, male vocal / instrumental group* **58 wks**

24 Jan 81	**VISAGE** *Polydor 2490 157*..................13	29 wks
3 Apr 82	● **THE ANVIL** *Polydor POLD 5050*..................6	16 wks
19 Nov 83	**FADE TO GREY – THE SINGLES COLLECTION** *Polydor POLD 5117*..................38	11 wks
3 Nov 84	**BEAT BOY** *Polydor POLH 12*..................79	2 wks

See also Midge Ure.

VIXEN *US, female vocal / instrumental group* **5 wks**

8 Oct 88	**VIXEN** *Manhattan MTL 1028*..................66	1 wk
18 Aug 90	**REV IT UP** *EMI USA MTL 1054*..................20	4 wks

VOICE OF THE BEEHIVE
UK / US, male / female vocal / instrumental group **26 wks**

2 Jul 88	**LET IT BEE** *London LONLP 57*..................13	13 wks
24 Aug 91	**HONEY LINGERS** *London 8282591* 17	13 wks

Herbert VON KARAJAN *Austria, male conductor* **17 wks**

26 Sep 70	**BEETHOVEN TRIPLE CONCERTO** *HMV ASD 2582*..................51	2 wks
16 Apr 88	**THE ESSENTIAL KARAJAN** *Deutsche Grammophon HVKTV 1* 51	5 wks
3 Aug 91	**HOLST: THE PLANETS** *Deutsche Grammophon 4352891* 52	2 wks
7 Oct 95	**KARAJAN: ADAGIO** *Deutsche Grammophon 4452822* 30	8 wks

On the Beethoven concerto, the soloists were David Oistrakh (violin), Mstislav Rostropovich (cello) and Sviatoslav Richter (piano). Von Karajan conducted the Berlin Philharmonic Orchestra – Germany, orchestra.

VOW WOW *Japan / US, male vocal / instrumental group*   **1 wk**

18 Mar 89   **HELTER SKELTER** *Arista 209691* ....**75**   1   wk

VOYAGE *UK / France, disco aggregation*   **1 wk**

9 Sep 78   **VOYAGE** *GTO GTLP 030*..**59**   1   wk

WAH! – *See MIGHTY WAH!*

WAILERS – *See Bob MARLEY and the WAILERS*

John WAITE *UK, male vocalist*   **3 wks**

10 Nov 84   **NO BREAKS** *EMI America WAIT 1* ....**64**   3   wks

Tom WAITS *US, male vocalist*   **19 wks**

8 Oct 83   **SWORDFISHTROMBONE** *Island ILPS 9762*............................**62**   3   wks
19 Oct 85   **RAIN DOGS** *Island ILPS 9803*..**29**   5   wks
5 Sep 87   **FRANK'S WILD YEARS** *Island ITW 3* ....**20**   5   wks
8 Oct 88   **BIG TIME** *Island ITW 4* ....**84**   1   wk
19 Sep 92   **BONE MACHINE** *Island CID 9993* ....**26**   3   wks
20 Nov 93   **THE BLACK RIDER** *Island CID 8021* ....**47**   2   wks

Rick WAKEMAN *UK, male instrumentalist – keyboards*   **129 wks**

24 Feb 73 ● **THE SIX WIVES OF HENRY VIII** *A & M AMLH 64361* ....**7**   22   wks
18 May 74 ★ **JOURNEY TO THE CENTRE OF THE EARTH** *A & M AMLH 63621* ....**1**   30   wks
12 Apr 75 ● **THE MYTHS AND LEGENDS OF KING ARTHUR AND THE
            KNIGHTS OF THE ROUND TABLE** *A & M AMLH 645150022* ....**2**   28   wks
24 Apr 76 ● **NO EARTHLY CONNECTION** *A & M AMLK 64583*........................**9**   9   wks
12 Feb 77   **WHITE ROCK** *A & M AMLH 64614* ....**14**   9   wks
3 Dec 77   **CRIMINAL RECORD** *A & M AMLK 64660* ....**25**   5   wks
2 Jun 79   **RHAPSODIES** *A & M AMLX 68508* ....**25**   10   wks
27 Jun 81   **1984** *Charisma CDS 4022* ....**24**   9   wks
13 Oct 84   **BEYOND THE PLANETS** *Telstar STAR 2244* ⃞1 ....**64**   6   wks
16 May 87   **THE GOSPELS** *Stylus SMR 729*..**94**   1   wk

⃞1 Kevin Peek and Rick Wakeman

See also Anderson Bruford Wakeman Howe.

WALKER BROTHERS *US, male vocal group*   **108 wks**

18 Dec 65 ● **TAKE IT EASY** *Philips BL 7691*..**3**   36   wks
3 Sep 66 ● **PORTRAIT** *Philips BL 7691* ....**3**   23   wks
18 Mar 67 ● **IMAGES** *Philips SBL 7770*..**6**   15   wks
16 Sep 67 ● **WALKER BROTHERS' STORY** *Philips DBL 002*......................**9**   19   wks
21 Feb 76   **NO REGRETS** *GTO GTLP 007* ....**49**   3   wks
25 Jan 92 ● **NO REGRETS – THE BEST OF SCOTT WALKER AND THE
            WALKER BROTHERS** *Fontana 5108312* ⃞1 ....**4**   12   wks

⃞1 Scott Walker and the Walker Brothers

See also Scott Walker.

Scott WALKER *US, male vocalist*   **57 wks**

16 Sep 67 ● **SCOTT** *Philips SBL 7816* ....**3**   17   wks
20 Apr 68 ★ **SCOTT 2** *Philips SBL 7840*..**1**   18   wks
5 Apr 69 ● **SCOTT 3** *Philips S 7882*..**3**   4   wks

5 Jul 69	● SONGS FROM HIS TV SERIES *Philips SBL 7900* **7**	3 wks
31 Mar 84	CLIMATE OF HUNTER *Virgin V 2303* **60**	2 wks
25 Jan 92	● NO REGRETS – THE BEST OF SCOTT WALKER AND THE	
	WALKER BROTHERS *Fontana 5108312* 1 ....**4**	12 wks
20 May 95	TILT *Fontana 5268592* **27**	1 wk

1 Scott Walker and the Walker Brothers

See also Walker Brothers.

Bob WALLIS and his STORYVILLE JAZZMEN
UK, male vocal / instrumental group **1 wk**

11 Jun 60	EVERYBODY LOVES SATURDAY NIGHT *Top Rank BUY 023* **20**	1 wk

Joe WALSH *US, male vocalist* **20 wks**

17 Apr 76	YOU CAN'T ARGUE WITH A SICK MIND *Anchor ABCL 5156* **28**	3 wks
10 Jun 78	BUT SERIOUSLY FOLKS *Asylum K 53081* **16**	17 wks

WANG CHUNG *UK, male vocal / instrumental group* **5 wks**

21 Apr 84	POINTS ON THE CURVE *Geffen GEF 25589* **34**	5 wks

WAR – *Eric BURDON and WAR*

Clifford T. WARD *UK, male vocalist* **5 wks**

21 Jul 73	HOME THOUGHTS *Charisma CAS 1066* **40**	3 wks
16 Feb 74	MANTLE PIECES *Charisma CAS 1077* **42**	2 wks

Michael WARD *UK, male vocalist* **3 wks**

5 Jan 74	INTRODUCING MICHAEL WARD *Philips 6308 189* **26**	3 wks

WARLOCK *Germany, male / female vocal / instrumental group* **2 wks**

14 Nov 87	TRIUMPH AND AGONY *Vertigo VERH 50* **54**	2 wks

Jennifer WARNES *US, female vocalist* **12 wks**

18 Jul 87	FAMOUS BLUE RAINCOAT *RCA PL 90048* **33**	12 wks

WARRANT *US, male vocal / instrumental group* **1 wk**

19 Sep 92	DOG EAT DOG *Columbia 4720332* **74**	1 wk

Dionne WARWICK *US, female vocalist* **146 wks**

23 May 64	PRESENTING DIONNE WARWICK *Pye NPL 28037* **14**	10 wks
7 May 66	● BEST OF DIONNE WARWICK *Pye NPL 28078* **8**	11 wks
4 Feb 67	HERE WHERE THERE IS LOVE *Pye NPL 28096* **39**	2 wks
18 May 68	● VALLEY OF THE DOLLS *Pye NSPL 28114* **10**	13 wks
23 May 70	GREATEST HITS VOLUME 1 *Wand WNS 1* **31**	26 wks
6 Jun 70	GREATEST HITS VOLUME 2 *Wand WNS 2* **28**	14 wks
30 Oct 82	● HEARTBREAKER *Arista 204 974* **3**	33 wks
21 May 83	THE COLLECTION *Arista DIONE 1* **11**	17 wks
29 Oct 83	SO AMAZING *Arista 205 755* **60**	3 wks
23 Feb 85	WITHOUT YOUR LOVE *Arista 206 571* **86**	2 wks
6 Jan 90	● LOVE SONGS *Arista 410441* **6**	13 wks
10 Dec 94	CHRISTMAS IN VIENNA II *Sony Classical SK 64304* 1 ....**60**	2 wks

1 Dionne Warwick and Placido Domingo

WAS (NOT WAS) *US, male vocal / instrumental group* **15 wks**

9 Apr 88	WHAT UP DOG? *Fontana SFLP 4* **47**	6 wks
21 Jul 90	ARE YOU OKAY? *Fontana 8463511* **35**	6 wks

13 Jun 92	**HELLO DAD I'M IN JAIL** Fontana 5124642	**61**	3 wks

Geno WASHINGTON UK, male vocalist — **51 wks**

10 Dec 66	● **HAND CLAPPIN' – FOOT STOMPIN' – FUNKY BUTT – LIVE!** Piccadilly NPL 38026	**5**	38 wks
23 Sep 67	● **HIPSTERS, FLIPSTERS, AND FINGER POPPIN' DADDIES** Piccadilly NSPL 38032	**8**	13 wks

Grover WASHINGTON Jr US, male instrumentalist – saxophone — **10 wks**

9 May 81	**WINELIGHT** Elektra K 52262	**34**	9 wks
19 Dec 81	**COME MORNING** Elektra K 52337	**98**	1 wk

W.A.S.P. US, male vocal / instrumental group — **24 wks**

8 Sep 84	**W.A.S.P.** Capitol EJ 2401951	**51**	2 wks
9 Nov 85	**THE LAST COMMAND** Capitol WASP 2	**48**	1 wk
8 Nov 86	**INSIDE THE ELECTRIC CIRCUS** Capitol EST 2025	**53**	3 wks
26 Sep 87	**LIVE IN THE RAW** Capitol EST 2040	**23**	4 wks
15 Apr 89	● **THE HEADLESS CHILDREN** Capitol EST 2087	**8**	10 wks
20 Jun 92	**THE CRIMSON IDOL** Parlophone CDPCSD 118	**21**	2 wks
6 Nov 93	**FIRST BLOOD . . . LAST CUTS** Capitol CDESTFG 2217	**69**	1 wk
1 Jul 95	**STILL NOT BLACK ENOUGH** Raw Power RAWCD 103	**52**	1 wk

WATERBOYS UK, male vocal / instrumental group — **69 wks**

16 Jun 84	**A PAGAN PLACE** Ensign ENCL 3	**100**	1 wk
28 Sep 85	**THIS IS THE SEA** Ensign ENCL 5	**37**	17 wks
29 Oct 88	**FISHERMAN'S BLUES** Ensign CHEN 5	**13**	19 wks
22 Sep 90	● **ROOM TO ROAM** Ensign CHEN 16	**5**	6 wks
11 May 91	● **BEST OF THE WATERBOYS '81–'91** Ensign CHEN 19	**2**	16 wks
5 Jun 93	● **DREAM HARDER** Geffen GED 24476	**5**	10 wks

WATERFRONT UK, male vocal / instrumental duo — **3 wks**

12 Aug 89	**WATERFRONT** Polydor 837970 1	**45**	3 wks

Roger WATERS UK, male vocalist / instrumentalist – bass — **25 wks**

12 May 84	**THE PROS AND CONS OF HITCH–HIKING** Harvest SHVL 240105	**13**	11 wks
27 Jun 87	**RADIO K.A.O.S.** EMI KAOS 1	**25**	7 wks
22 Sep 90	**THE WALL – LIVE IN BERLIN** Mercury 8466111	**27**	3 wks
19 Sep 92	● **AMUSED TO DEATH** Columbia 4687612	**8**	4 wks

Jody WATLEY US, female vocalist — **4 wks**

5 Sep 87	**JODY WATLEY** MCA MCG 6024	**62**	2 wks
27 May 89	**LARGER THAN LIFE** MCA MCG 6044	**39**	2 wks

WAVES – KATRINA and the WAVES

WAX UK / US, male vocal / instrumental duo — **3 wks**

12 Sep 87	**AMERICAN ENGLISH** RCA PL 71430	**59**	3 wks

Anthony WAY UK, male vocalist — **16 wks**

8 Apr 95	● **THE CHOIR – MUSIC FROM THE BBC TV SERIES** Decca 4481652 [1]	**3**	12 wks
9 Dec 95	**THE CHOIRBOY** Permanent PERMCD 41	**61**	3 wks

[1] Anthony Way and Stanislas Syrewicz

Jeff WAYNE US / UK, orchestra and cast — **237 wks**

1 Jul 78	● **WAR OF THE WORLDS** CBS 96000	**5**	235 wks

W 327

3 Oct 92   **SPARTACUS** Columbia 4720302 ....**36**   2 wks

Both albums feature various artists but are commonly credited to Jeff Wayne, the creator and producer.

WAYSTED   UK, male vocal/instrumental group   **5 wks**

8 Oct 83   **VICES** Chrysalis CHR 1438 ....**78**   3 wks
22 Sep 84   **WAYSTED** Music For Nations MFN 31 ....**73**   2 wks

WEATHER PROPHETS   UK, male vocal/instrumental group   **2 wks**

9 May 87   **MAYFLOWER** Elevation ELV 1.................................**67**   2 wks

WEATHER REPORT   US, male instrumental group   **12 wks**

23 Apr 77   **HEAVY WEATHER** CBS 81775 ....**43**   6 wks
11 Nov 78   **MR. GONE** CBS 82775 ....**47**   3 wks
27 Feb 82   **WEATHER REPORT** CBS 85326 ....**88**   2 wks
24 Mar 84   **DOMINO THEORY** CBS 25839 ....**54**   1 wk

Marti WEBB   UK, female vocalist   **33 wks**

16 Feb 80 ● **TELL ME ON A SUNDAY** Polydor POLD 5031 ....**2**   23 wks
28 Sep 85   **ENCORE** Starblend BLEND 1 ....**55**   4 wks
6 Dec 86   **ALWAYS THERE** BBC REB 619 ....**65**   5 wks
10 Oct 92   **THE MAGIC OF THE MUSICALS** Quality Television QTV 013 [1] ..**55**   1 wk

[1] Marti Webb and Mark Rattray

Ben WEBSTER – *Gerry MULLIGAN and Ben WEBSTER*

WEDDING PRESENT   UK, male vocal/instrumental group   **19 wks**

24 Oct 87   **GEORGE BEST** Reception LEEDS 001 ....**47**   2 wks
23 Jul 88   **TOMMY** Reception LEEDS 2 ....**42**   3 wks
29 Apr 89   **UKRAINSKI VISTUIP V JOHNA PEELA** RCA PL 74104 ....**22**   3 wks
4 Nov 89   **BIZZARO** RCA PL 74302 ....**22**   3 wks
8 Jun 91   **SEA MONSTERS** RCA PL 75012 ....**13**   3 wks
20 Jun 92   **HIT PARADE 1** RCA PD 75343 ....**22**   2 wks
16 Jan 93   **HIT PARADE 2** RCA 74321127752.......................**19**   2 wks
24 Sep 94   **WATUSI** Island CID 8014 ....**47**   1 wk

WEE PAPA GIRL RAPPERS   UK, female vocal duo   **3 wks**

5 Nov 88   **THE BEAT, THE RHYME AND THE NOISE** Jive HIP 67 ....**39**   3 wks

Bert WEEDON   UK, male instrumentalist – guitar   **26 wks**

16 Jul 60   **KING SIZE GUITAR** Top Rank BUY 026 ....**18**   1 wk
23 Oct 76 ★ **22 GOLDEN GUITAR GREATS** Warwick WW 5019 ....**1**   25 wks

WEEZER   US, male vocal/instrumental group   **11 wks**

4 Mar 95   **WEEZER** Geffen GED 24629 ....**23**   11 wks

WELCH – *MARVIN, WELCH and FARRAR*

Paul WELLER   UK, male vocalist   **86 wks**

12 Sep 92 ● **PAUL WELLER** Go! Discs 8283432.........................**8**   7 wks
18 Sep 93 ● **WILD WOOD** Go! Discs 8284352...........................**2**   44 wks
24 Sep 94   **LIVE WOOD** Go! Discs 8285612...........................**13**   3 wks
27 May 95 ★ **STANLEY ROAD** Go! Discs 8286192.......................**1†**   32 wks

WENDY and LISA   US, female vocal duo   **7 wks**

10 Oct 87   **WENDY AND LISA** Virgin V 2444 ....**84**   2 wks

WET WET WET, fronted by Marti Pellow, have reached the Top Ten with their first seven albums.

(Solo/Joe Bangay Photography)

| 28 Mar 89 | **FRUIT AT THE BOTTOM** Virgin V 2580 | **45** | 2 wks |
| 4 Aug 90 | **EROICA** Virgin V 2633 | **33** | 3 wks |

WESTWORLD UK / US, male / female vocal / instrumental group **2 wks**

| 5 Sep 87 | **WHERE THE ACTION IS** RCA PL 71429 | **49** | 2 wks |

WET WET WET UK, male vocal / instrumental group **241 wks**

3 Oct 87	★ **POPPED IN SOULED OUT** Precious JWWWL 1	**1**	71 wks
19 Nov 88	● **THE MEMPHIS SESSIONS** Precious JWWWL 2	**3**	13 wks
11 Nov 89	● **HOLDING BACK THE RIVER** Precious 842011 1	**2**	26 wks
8 Feb 92	★ **HIGH ON THE HAPPY SIDE** Precious 5104272	**1**	25 wks
29 May 93	● **LIVE AT THE ROYAL ALBERT HALL** Precious 5147742 `1`	**10**	4 wks
20 Nov 93	★ **END OF PART ONE (THEIR GREATEST HITS)** Precious 5184772	**1**	65 wks
22 Apr 94	★ **PICTURE THIS** Precious 5268512	**1†**	37 wks

`1` Wet Wet Wet with the Wren Orchestra

WE'VE GOT A FUZZBOX AND WE'RE GONNA USE IT
UK, female vocal / instrumental group **6 wks**

| 26 Aug 89 | ● **BIG BANG** WEA WX 282 | **5** | 6 wks |

WHALE Sweden, male / female vocal / instrumental group **2 wks**

| 12 Aug 95 | **WE CARE** Hut DGHUT 25 | **42** | 2 wks |

WHAM! UK, male vocal / instrumental duo **233 wks**

9 Jul 83	★ **FANTASTIC!** Inner Vision IVL 25328	**1**	116 wks
17 Nov 84	★ **MAKE IT BIG** Epic EPC 86311	**1**	72 wks
19 Jul 86	● **THE FINAL** Epic EPC 88681	**2**	45 wks

CARON WHEELER UK, female vocalist **5 wks**

| 13 Oct 90 | **UK BLAK** RCA PL 74751 | **14** | 5 wks |

Bill WHELAN Ireland, male composer **27 wks**

| 25 Mar 95 | **MUSIC FROM RIVERDANCE – THE SHOW** Celtic Heartbeat 75678061112 | **31†** | 27 wks |

WHIGFIELD Denmark, female vocalist **7 wks**

| 1 Jul 95 | **WHIGFIELD** Systematic 8286512 | **13** | 7 wks |

WHISPERS US, male vocal group **9 wks**

| 14 Mar 81 | **IMAGINATION** Solar SOLA 7 | **42** | 5 wks |
| 6 Jun 87 | **JUST GETS BETTER WITH TIME** Solar MCF 3381 | **63** | 4 wks |

Snowy WHITE UK, male vocalist / instrumentalist – guitar **5 wks**

| 11 Feb 84 | **WHITE FLAMES** Towerbell TOWLP 3 | **21** | 4 wks |
| 9 Feb 85 | **SNOWY WHITE** Towerbell TOWLP 8 | **88** | 1 wk |

Tony Joe WHITE US, male vocalist **1 wk**

| 26 Sep 70 | **TONY JOE** CBS 63800 | **63** | 1 wk |

Alan WHITE UK, male instrumentalist – drums **4 wks**

| 13 Mar 76 | **RAMSHACKLED** Atlantic K 50217 | **41** | 4 wks |

Barry WHITE US, male vocalist **156 wks**

| 9 Mar 74 | **STONE GON'** Pye NSPL 28186 | **18** | 17 wks |

6 Apr 74	**RHAPSODY IN WHITE** Pye NSPL 28191 ....**50**	1 wk
2 Nov 74	● **CAN'T GET ENOUGH** 20th Century BT 444 ....**4**	34 wks
26 Apr 75	**JUST ANOTHER WAY TO SAY I LOVE YOU** 20th Century BT 466 ....**12**	15 wks
22 Nov 75	**GREATEST HITS** 20th Century BTH 8000 ....**18**	12 wks
21 Feb 76	**LET THE MUSIC PLAY** 20th Century BT 502 ....**22**	14 wks
9 Apr 77	**BARRY WHITE'S GREATEST HITS VOLUME 2** 20th Century BTH 8001 ....**17**	7 wks
10 Feb 79	**THE MAN** 20th Century BT 571.................................**46**	4 wks
21 Dec 85	**HEART AND SOUL** K–Tel NE 1316 ....**34**	10 wks
17 Oct 87	**THE RIGHT NIGHT AND BARRY WHITE** Breakout AMA 5154 ......**74**	6 wks
2 Jul 88	● **THE COLLECTION** Mercury BWTV 1 ....**5**	33 wks
11 Feb 95	**THE ICON IS LOVE** A & M 5402802 ....**44**	3 wks

Karyn WHITE US, female vocalist　　　　　　　　**30 wks**

11 Mar 89	**KARYN WHITE** Warner Bros. WX 235 ....**20**	27 wks
21 Sep 91	**RITUAL OF LOVE** Warner Bros. WX 411 ....**31**	3 wks

WHITE LION US, male vocal / instrumental group　　　　　**3 wks**

1 Jul 89	**BIG GAME** Atlantic WX 277 ....**47**	1 wk
20 Apr 91	**MANE ATTRACTION** Atlantic WX 415 ....**31**	2 wks

WHITE ZOMBIE US, male vocal / instrumental group　　　**3 wks**

27 May 95	**ASTRO CREEP 2000** Geffen GED 24806 ....**25**	3 wks

WHITEOUT UK, male vocal / instrumental group　　　　　**1 wk**

1 Jul 95	**BITE IT** Silvertone ORECD 536 ....**71**	1 wk

WHITESNAKE UK, male vocal / instrumental group　　　**157 wks**

18 Nov 78	**TROUBLE** EMI International INS 3022.........................**50**	2 wks
13 Oct 79	**LOVE HUNTER** United Artists UAG 30264 ....**29**	7 wks
7 Jun 80	● **READY AND WILLING** United Artists UAG 30302 ....**6**	15 wks
8 Nov 80	● **LIVE IN THE HEART OF THE CITY** United Artists SNAKE 1 ....**5**	15 wks
18 Apr 81	● **COME AND GET IT** Liberty LBG 30327........................**2**	23 wks
27 Nov 82	● **SAINTS 'N' SINNERS** Liberty LBG 30354 ....**9**	9 wks
11 Feb 84	● **SLIDE IT IN** Liberty LBG 2400001 ....**9**	7 wks
11 Apr 87	● **WHITESNAKE 1987** EMI EMC 3528 ....**8**	57 wks
25 Nov 89	● **SLIP OF THE TONGUE** EMI EMD 1013 ....**10**	10 wks
16 Jul 94	● **GREATEST HITS** EMI CDEMD 1065 ....**4**	12 wks

Slim WHITMAN US, male vocalist　　　　　　　　　**59 wks**

14 Dec 74	**HAPPY ANNIVERSARY** United Artists UAS 29670 ....**44**	2 wks
31 Jan 76	★ **THE VERY BEST OF SLIM WHITMAN** United Artists UAS 29898 ....**1**	17 wks
15 Jan 77	★ **RED RIVER VALLEY** United Artists UAS 29993 ....**1**	14 wks
15 Oct 77	● **HOME ON THE RANGE** United Artists UATV 30102 ....**2**	13 wks
13 Jan 79	**GHOST RIDERS IN THE SKY** United Artists UATV 30202.......**27**	6 wks
22 Dec 79	**SLIM WHITMAN'S 20 GREATEST LOVE SONGS** United Artists UAG 30270 ....**18**	7 wks

Roger WHITTAKER Kenya, male vocalist　　　　　　**110 wks**

27 Jun 70	**I DON'T BELIEVE IN IF ANYMORE** Columbia SCX 6404 ....**23**	1 wk
3 Apr 71	**NEW WORLD IN THE MORNING** Columbia SCX 6456 ....**45**	2 wks
6 Sep 75	● **THE VERY BEST OF ROGER WHITTAKER** Columbia SCX 6560 ....**5**	42 wks
15 May 76	**THE SECOND ALBUM OF THE VERY BEST OF ROGER WHITTAKER** EMI EMC 3117....................**27**	7 wks
9 Dec 78	**ROGER WHITTAKER SINGS THE HITS** Columbia SCX 6601 ....**52**	5 wks
4 Aug 79	**20 ALL TIME GREATS** Polydor POLTV 8 ....**24**	9 wks
7 Feb 81	**THE ROGER WHITTAKER ALBUM** K-Tel NE 1105 ....**18**	14 wks
27 Dec 86	**SKYE BOAT SONG AND OTHER GREAT SONGS** Tembo TMB 1138**9**	1 wk
23 May 87	**HIS FINEST COLLECTION** Tembo RWTV 1 ....**15**	19 wks
23 Sep 89	**HOME LOVIN' MAN** Tembo RWTV 2 ....**20**	10 wks

WHO *UK, male vocal / instrumental group*   205 wks

25 Dec 65	● **MY GENERATION** *Brunswick LAT 8616*	**5**	11 wks
17 Dec 66	● **A QUICK ONE** *Reaction 593002*	**4**	17 wks
13 Jan 68	**THE WHO SELL-OUT** *Track 613002*	**13**	11 wks
7 Jun 69	● **TOMMY** *Track 613013/4*	**2**	9 wks
6 Jun 70	● **LIVE AT LEEDS** *Track 2406001*	**3**	21 wks
11 Sep 71	★ **WHO'S NEXT** *Track 2408102*	**1**	13 wks
18 Dec 71	● **MEATY, BEATY, BIG AND BOUNCY** *Track 2406006*	**9**	8 wks
17 Nov 73	● **QUADROPHENIA** *Track 2647013*	**2**	13 wks
26 Oct 74	● **ODDS AND SODS** *Track 2406116*	**10**	4 wks
23 Aug 75	**TOMMY (film soundtrack)** *Track 2657 007*	**30**	2 wks
18 Oct 75	● **THE WHO BY NUMBERS** *Polydor 2490129*	**7**	6 wks
9 Oct 76	● **THE STORY OF THE WHO** *Polydor 2683069*	**2**	18 wks
9 Sep 78	● **WHO ARE YOU** *Polydor WHOD 5004*	**6**	9 wks
30 Jun 79	**THE KIDS ARE ALRIGHT** *Polydor 2675 174*	**26**	13 wks
25 Oct 80	**MY GENERATION (re-issue)** *Virgin V 2179*	**20**	7 wks
28 Mar 81	● **FACE DANCES** *Polydor WHOD 5037*	**2**	9 wks
11 Sep 82	**IT'S HARD** *Polydor WHOD 5066*	**11**	6 wks
17 Nov 84	**WHO'S LAST** *MCA WHO 1*	**48**	4 wks
12 Oct 85	**THE WHO COLLECTION** *Impression IMDP 4*	**44**	6 wks
19 Mar 88	● **WHO'S BETTER WHO'S BEST** *Polydor WTV 1*	**10**	11 wks
19 Nov 88	**THE WHO COLLECTION** *Stylus SMR 570*	**71**	4 wks
24 Mar 90	**JOIN TOGETHER** *Virgin VDT 102*	**59**	1 wk
16 Jul 94	**30 YEARS OF MAXIMUM R&B** *Polydor 5217512*	**48**	1 wk
4 Mar 95	**LIVE AT LEEDS (re-issue)** *Polydor 5271692*	**59**	1 wk

The two albums titled The Who Collection *are different.*

Jane WIEDLIN *US, female vocalist*   3 wks

24 Sep 88	**FUR** *Manhattan MTL 1029*	**48**	3 wks

WILD HORSES *UK, male vocal / instrumental group*   4 wks

26 Apr 80	**WILD HORSES** *EMI EMC 3324*	**38**	4 wks

Eugene WILDE *US, male vocalist*   4 wks

8 Dec 84	**EUGENE WILDE** *Fourth & Broadway BRLP 502*	**67**	4 wks

Kim WILDE *UK, female vocalist*   88 wks

11 Jul 81	● **KIM WILDE** *RAK SRAK 544*	**3**	14 wks
22 May 82	**SELECT** *RAK SRAK 548*	**19**	11 wks
26 Nov 83	**CATCH AS CATCH CAN** *RAK SRAK 165408*	**90**	1 wk
17 Nov 84	**TEASES AND DARES** *MCA MCF 3250*	**66**	2 wks
18 May 85	**THE VERY BEST OF KIM WILDE** *RAK WILDE 1*	**78**	4 wks
15 Nov 86	**ANOTHER STEP** *MCA MCF 3339*	**73**	5 wks
25 Jun 88	● **CLOSE** *MCA MCG 6030*	**8**	38 wks
26 May 90	**LOVE MOVES** *MCA MCG 6088*	**37**	3 wks
30 May 92	**LOVE IS** *MCA MCAD 10625*	**21**	3 wks
25 Sep 93	**THE SINGLES COLLECTION 1981–1993** *MCA MCD 10921*	**11**	7 wks

Another Step *changed label number to MCA KIML 1 during its chart run.*

WILDHEARTS *UK, male vocal / instrumental group*   5 wks

11 Sep 93	**EARTH VS THE WILDHEARTS** *East West 4509932871*	**46**	1 wk
3 Jun 95	● **PHUQ** *East West 0630104372*	**6**	4 wks

Colm WILKINSON *Ireland, male vocalist*   6 wks

10 Jun 89	**STAGE HEROES** *RCA BL 74105*	**27**	6 wks

Alyson WILLIAMS *US, female vocalist*   21 wks

25 Mar 89	**RAW** *Def Jam 463293 1*	**29**	21 wks

Andy WILLIAMS *US, male vocalist*   **442 wks**

26 Jun 65	● **ALMOST THERE** *CBS BPG 62533*	4	46 wks
7 Aug 65	**CAN'T GET USED TO LOSING YOU** *CBS BPG 62146*	16	1 wk
19 Mar 66	**MAY EACH DAY** *CBS BPG 62658*	11	6 wks
30 Apr 66	**GREAT SONGS FROM MY FAIR LADY** *CBS BPG 62430*	30	1 wk
23 Jul 66	**SHADOW OF YOUR SMILE** *CBS 62633*	24	4 wks
29 Jul 67	**BORN FREE** *CBS SBPG 63027*	22	11 wks
11 May 68	★ **LOVE ANDY** *CBS 63167*	1	22 wks
6 Jul 68	● **HONEY** *CBS 63311*	4	17 wks
26 Jul 69	**HAPPY HEART** *CBS 63614*	22	9 wks
27 Dec 69	**GET TOGETHER WITH ANDY WILLIAMS** *CBS 63800*	13	12 wks
24 Jan 70	**ANDY WILLIAMS' SOUND OF MUSIC** *CBS 63920*	22	10 wks
11 Apr 70	★ **GREATEST HITS** *CBS 63920*	1	116 wks
20 Jun 70	● **CAN'T HELP FALLING IN LOVE** *CBS 64067*	7	48 wks
5 Dec 70	● **ANDY WILLIAMS SHOW** *CBS 64127*	10	6 wks
3 Apr 71	★ **HOME LOVING MAN** *CBS 64286*	1	25 wks
31 Jul 71	**LOVE STORY** *CBS 64467*	11	11 wks
29 Apr 72	**THE IMPOSSIBLE DREAM** *CBS 67236*	26	3 wks
29 Jul 72	**LOVE THEME FROM 'THE GODFATHER'** *CBS 64869*	11	16 wks
16 Dec 72	**GREATEST HITS VOLUME 2** *CBS 65151*	23	10 wks
22 Dec 73	● **SOLITAIRE** *CBS 65638*	3	26 wks
15 Jun 74	● **THE WAY WE WERE** *CBS 80152*	7	11 wks
11 Oct 75	**THE OTHER SIDE OF ME** *CBS 69152*	60	1 wk
28 Jan 78	● **REFLECTIONS** *CBS 10006*	2	17 wks
27 Oct 84	**GREATEST LOVE CLASSICS** *EMI ANDY 1* [1]	22	10 wks
7 Nov 92	**THE BEST OF ANDY WILLIAMS** *Dino DINCD 50*	51	3 wks

[1] Andy Williams and the Royal Philharmonic Orchestra

Deniece WILLIAMS *US, female vocalist*   **23 wks**

21 May 77	**THIS IS NIECEY** *CBS 81869*	31	12 wks
26 Aug 78	**THAT'S WHAT FRIENDS ARE FOR** *CBS 86068* [1]	16	11 wks

[1] Johnny Mathis and Deniece Williams

Don WILLIAMS *US, male vocalist*   **136 wks**

10 Jul 76	**GREATEST HITS VOLUME 1** *ABC ABCL 5147*	29	15 wks
19 Feb 77	**VISIONS** *ABC ABCL 5200*	13	20 wks
15 Oct 77	**COUNTRY BOY** *ABC ABCL 5233*	27	5 wks
5 Aug 78	● **IMAGES** *K-Tel NE 1033*	2	38 wks
5 Aug 78	**YOU'RE MY BEST FRIEND** *ABC ABCD 5127*	58	1 wk
4 Nov 78	**EXPRESSIONS** *ABC ABCL 5253*	28	8 wks
22 Sep 79	**NEW HORIZONS** *K-Tel NE 1048*	29	12 wks
15 Dec 79	**PORTRAIT** *MCA MCS 3045*	58	4 wks
6 Sep 80	**I BELIEVE IN YOU** *MCA MCF 3077*	36	5 wks
18 Jul 81	**ESPECIALLY FOR YOU** *MCA MCF 3114*	33	7 wks
17 Apr 82	**LISTEN TO THE RADIO** *MCA MCF 3135*	69	3 wks
23 Apr 83	**YELLOW MOON** *MCA MCF 3159*	52	1 wk
15 Oct 83	**LOVE STORIES** *K-Tel NE 1252*	22	13 wks
26 May 84	**CAFE CAROLINA** *MCA MCF 3225*	65	4 wks

Iris WILLIAMS *UK, female vocalist*   **4 wks**

22 Dec 79	**HE WAS BEAUTIFUL** *Columbia SCX 6627*	69	4 wks

John WILLIAMS *UK, male instrumentalist – guitar*   **62 wks**

3 Oct 70	**PLAYS SPANISH MUSIC** *CBS 72860*	46	1 wk
8 Feb 76	**RODRIGO: CONCERTO DE ARANJUEZ** *CBS 79369* [1]	20	9 wks
7 Jan 78	**BEST OF FRIENDS** *RCA RS 1094* [2]	18	22 wks
17 Jun 78	**TRAVELLING** *Cube HIFLY 27*	23	5 wks
30 Jun 79	● **BRIDGES** *Lotus WH 5015*	5	22 wks
4 Aug 79	**CAVATINA** *Cube HIFLY 32*	64	3 wks

[1] John Williams with the English Chamber Orchestra conducted by Daniel Barenboim
[2] Cleo Laine and John Williams

John WILLIAMS *US, male conductor*   **17 wks**

25 Dec 82	**ET – THE EXTRATERRESTRIAL (film soundtrack)** *MCA MCF 3160* **47**	10 wks
31 Jul 93	**JURASSIC PARK (film soundtrack)** *MCA MCD 10859* **42**	5 wks
2 Apr 94	**SCHINDLER'S LIST (film soundtrack)** *MCA MCD 10969* **59**	2 wks

Vanessa WILLIAMS *US, female vocalist*   **4 wks**

25 Apr 92	**THE COMFORT ZONE** *Polydor 5112672* **24**	4 wks

Wendy O. WILLIAMS *US, female vocalist*   **1 wk**

30 Jun 84	**W.O.W.** *Music For Nations MFN 24* **100**	1 wk

Ann WILLIAMSON *UK, female vocalist*   **13 wks**

15 Feb 86	**PRECIOUS MEMORIES** *Emerald Gem ERTV 1* **16**	9 wks
6 Feb 88	**COUNT YOUR BLESSINGS** *Emerald Gem ERTV 2* **58**	4 wks

Sonny Boy WILLIAMSON
US, male vocalist / instrumentalist – guitar   **1 wk**

20 Jun 64	**DOWN AND OUT BLUES** *Pye NPL 28036*............................**20**	1 wk

Bruce WILLIS *US, male vocalist*   **28 wks**

18 Apr 87	● **THE RETURN OF BRUNO** *Motown ZL 72571* **4**	28 wks

Brian WILSON *US, male vocalist*   **1 wk**

16 Sep 95	**I JUST WASN'T MADE FOR THESE TIMES** *MCA MCD 11270* **59**	1 wk

Mari WILSON with the WILSATIONS *UK, female vocalist*   **9 wks**

26 Feb 83	**SHOW PEOPLE** *Compact COMP 2*......................................**24**	9 wks

WILSON PHILLIPS *US, female vocal group*   **38 wks**

30 Jun 90	● **WILSON PHILLIPS** *SBK SBKLP 5* **7**	32 wks
13 Jun 92	● **SHADOWS AND LIGHT** *SBK SBKCD 18* **6**	6 wks

WIN *UK, male / female vocal / instrumental group*   **1 wk**

25 Apr 87	**UH! TEARS BABY** *Swampland LONLP 31* **51**	1 wk

WINCHESTER CATHEDRAL CHOIR – *See Andrew LLOYD WEBBER*

WINDJAMMER *US, male vocal / instrumental group*   **1 wk**

25 Aug 84	**WINDJAMMER II** *MCA MCF 3231* **82**	1 wk

WINGS – *See Paul McCARTNEY*

Johnny WINTER *US, male / vocal instrumental group*   **12 wks**

16 May 70	**SECOND WINTER** *CBS 66321* **59**	2 wks
31 Oct 70	**JOHNNY WINTER AND . . .** *CBS 64117* **29**	4 wks
15 May 71	**JOHNNY WINTER AND LIVE** *CBS 64289* **20**	6 wks

Ruby WINTERS *US, female vocalist*   **16 wks**

10 Jun 78	**RUBY WINTERS** *Creole CRLP 512* **27**	7 wks
23 Jun 79	**SONGBIRD** *K-Tel NE 1045* **31**	9 wks

ALPHABETICALLY BY ARTIST

Steve WINWOOD UK, male vocalist   120 wks

9 Jul 77	**STEVE WINWOOD** Island ILPS 9494	12	9 wks
10 Jan 81	**ARC OF A DIVER** Island ILPS 9576	13	20 wks
14 Aug 82	● **TALKING BACK TO THE NIGHT** Island ILPS 9777	6	13 wks
12 Jul 86	● **BACK IN THE HIGH LIFE** Island ILPS 9844	8	42 wks
7 Nov 87	**CHRONICLES** Island SSW 1	12	17 wks
2 Jul 88	● **ROLL WITH IT** Virgin V 2532	4	16 wks
17 Nov 90	**REFUGEES OF THE HEART** Virgin V 2650	26	3 wks

WIRE UK, male vocal / instrumental group   3 wks

7 Oct 78	**CHAIRS MISSING** Harvest SHSP 4093	48	1 wk
13 Oct 79	**154** Harvest SHSP 4105	39	1 wk
9 May 87	**THE IDEAL COPY** Mute STUMM 42	87	1 wk

WISHBONE ASH UK, male vocal / instrumental group   75 wks

23 Jan 71	**WISHBONE ASH** MCA MKPS 2014	34	2 wks
9 Oct 71	**PILGRIMAGE** MCA MDKS 8004	14	9 wks
20 May 72	● **ARGUS** MCA MDKS 8006	3	20 wks
26 May 73	**WISHBONE FOUR** MCA MDKS 8011	12	10 wks
30 Nov 74	**THERE'S THE RUB** MCA MCF 2585	16	5 wks
3 Apr 76	**LOCKED IN** MCA MCF 2750	36	2 wks
27 Nov 76	**NEW ENGLAND** MCA MCG 3523	22	3 wks
29 Oct 77	**FRONT PAGE NEWS** CA MCG 3524	31	4 wks
28 Oct 78	**NO SMOKE WITHOUT FIRE** MCA MCG 3528	43	3 wks
2 Feb 80	**JUST TESTING** CA MCF 3052	41	4 wks
1 Nov 80	**LIVE DATES II** MCA MCG 4012	40	3 wks
25 Apr 81	**NUMBER THE BRAVE** MCA MCF 3103	61	5 wks
16 Oct 82	**BOTH BARRELS BURNING** A & M ASH 1	22	5 wks

Bill WITHERS US, male vocalist   10 wks

11 Feb 78	**MENAGERIE** CBS 82265	27	5 wks
15 Jun 85	**WATCHING YOU, WATCHING ME** CBS 26200	60	1 wk
17 Sep 88	**GREATEST HITS** CBS 32343	90	4 wks

WIZZARD UK, male vocal / instrumental group   11 wks

19 May 73	**WIZZARD BREW** Harvest SHSP 4025	29	7 wks
17 Aug 74	**INTRODUCING EDDY AND THE FALCONS** Warner Bros. K 52029	19	4 wks

Jah WOBBLE UK, male vocalist / multi–instrumentalist   6 wks

28 May 94	**TAKE ME TO GOD** Island CID 8017 [1]	13	5 wks
14 Oct 95	**SPINNER** All saints ASCD 023 [2]	71	1 wk

[1] Jah Wobble's Invaders Of The Heart [2] Brian Eno and Jah Wobble

WOLFGANG PRESS UK, male vocal / instrumental duo   1 wk

4 Feb 95	**FUNKY LITTLE DEMONS** 4AD CADD 4016CD	75	1 wk

WOLFSBANE UK, male vocal / instrumental group   3 wks

5 Aug 89	**LIVE FAST DIE FAST** Def American 838486 1	48	1 wk
20 Oct 90	**ALL HELL'S BREAKING LOOSE** Def American 8469671	48	1 wk
19 Oct 91	**DOWN FALL THE GOOD GUYS** Def American 5104131	53	1 wk

Bobby WOMACK US, male vocalist   15 wks

28 Apr 84	**THE POET II** Motown ZL 72205	31	8 wks
28 Sep 85	**SO MANY RIVERS** MCA MCF 3282	28	7 wks

See also Wilton Felder.

W 335

WOMACK and WOMACK *US, male / female vocal duo* **52 wks**

21 Apr 84	**LOVE WARS** *Elektra 960293*	**45**	13 wks
22 Jun 85	**RADIO M.U.S.I.C. MAN** *Elektra EKT 6*	**56**	2 wks
27 Aug 88	● **CONSCIENCE** *Fourth & Broadway BRLP 519*	**4**	37 wks

WOMBLES
UK, male vocalist / arranger / producer, Mike Batt under group name **55 wks**

2 Mar 74	**WOMBLING SONGS** *CBS 65803*	**19**	17 wks
13 Jul 74	**REMEMBER YOU'RE A WOMBLE** *CBS 80191*	**18**	31 wks
21 Dec 74	**KEEP ON WOMBLING** *CBS 80526*	**17**	6 wks
8 Jan 77	**20 WOMBLING GREATS** *Warwick PR 5022*	**29**	1 wk

Stevie WONDER *US, male vocalist / multi–instrumentalist* **340 wks**

7 Sep 68	**STEVIE WONDER'S GREATEST HITS** *Tamla Motown STML 11075*	**25**	10 wks
13 Dec 69	**MY CHERIE AMOUR** *Tamla Motown STML 11128*	**17**	2 wks
12 Feb 72	**GREATEST HITS VOLUME 2** *Tamla Motown STML 11196*	**30**	4 wks
3 Feb 73	**TALKING BOOK** *Tamla Motown STMA 8007*	**16**	48 wks
1 Sep 73	● **INNERVISIONS** *Tamla Motown STMA 8011*	**8**	55 wks
17 Aug 74	● **FULFILLINGNESS' FIRST FINALE** *Tamla Motown STMA 8019*	**5**	16 wks
16 Oct 76	● **SONGS IN THE KEY OF LIFE** *Tamla Motown TMSP 6002*	**2**	54 wks
10 Nov 79	● **JOURNEY THROUGH THE SECRET LIFE OF PLANTS** *Motown TMSP 6009*	**8**	15 wks
8 Nov 80	● **HOTTER THAN JULY** *Motown STMA 8035*	**2**	55 wks
22 May 82	● **ORIGINAL MUSIQUARIUM 1** *Motown TMSP 6012*	**8**	17 wks
22 Sep 84	● **WOMAN IN RED (film soundtrack)** *Motown ZL 72285*	**2**	19 wks
24 Nov 84	**LOVE SONGS – 16 CLASSIC HITS** *Telstar STAR 2251*	**20**	10 wks
28 Sep 85	● **IN SQUARE CIRCLE** *Motown ZL 72005*	**5**	16 wks
15 Nov 86	**DIANA ROSS. MICHAEL JACKSON. GLADYS KNIGHT. STEVIE WONDER. THEIR VERY BEST BACK TO BACK** *PrioriTyV PTVR 2* ▢1	**21**	10 wks
28 Nov 87	**CHARACTERS** *RCA ZL 72001*	**33**	4 wks
8 Jun 91	**JUNGLE FEVER (film soundtrack)** *Motown ZL 71750*	**56**	1 wk
25 Mar 95	● **CONVERSATION PEACE** *Motown 5302382*	**8**	4 wks

▢1 Diana Ross/Michael Jackson/Gladys Knight/Stevie Wonder

WONDER STUFF *UK, male vocal / instrumental group* **48 wks**

27 Aug 88	**THE EIGHT LEGGED GROOVE MACHINE** *Polydor GONLP 1*	**18**	7 wks
14 Oct 89	● **HUP** *Polydor 841187 1*	**5**	8 wks
8 Jun 91	● **NEVER LOVED ELVIS** *Polydor 8472521*	**3**	23 wks
16 Oct 93	● **CONSTRUCTION FOR THE MODERN IDIOT** *Polydor 5198942*	**4**	5 wks
8 Oct 94	● **IF THE BEATLES HAD READ HUNTER . . . THE SINGLES** *Polydor 5213972*	**8**	4 wks
29 Jul 95	**LIVE IN MANCHESTER** *Windsong WINCD 074X*	**74**	1 wk

Roy WOOD *UK, male vocalist / multi–instrumentalist* **14 wks**

| 18 Aug 73 | **BOULDERS** *Harvest SHVL 803* | **15** | 8 wks |
| 24 Jul 82 | **THE SINGLES** *Speed SPEED 1000* | **37** | 6 wks |

WOODENTOPS *UK, male vocal / instrumental group* **6 wks**

| 12 Jul 86 | **GIANT** *Rough Trade ROUGH 87* | **35** | 4 wks |
| 5 Mar 88 | **WOODENFOOT COPS ON THE HIGHWAY** *Rough Trade ROUGH 127* | **48** | 2 wks |

Edward WOODWARD *UK, male vocalist* **12 wks**

| 6 Jun 70 | **THIS MAN ALONE** *DJM DJLPS 405* | **53** | 2 wks |
| 19 Aug 72 | **THE EDWARD WOODWARD ALBUM** *Jam JAL 103* | **20** | 10 wks |

WORKING WEEK *UK, male / female vocal / instrumental group* **10 wks**

| 4 Jun 85 | **WORKING NIGHTS** *Virgin V 2343* | **23** | 9 wks |
| 27 Sep 86 | **COMPANEROS** *Virgin V 2397* | **72** | 1 wk |

WORLD OF TWIST UK, male vocal / instrumental group   **1 wk**

9 Nov 91	**QUALITY STREET** Circa CIRCA 17 ....**50**	1 wk

WORLD PARTY Ireland / UK, male vocal / instrumental group   **22 wks**

21 Mar 87	**PRIVATE REVOLUTION** Chrysalis CHEN 4.................................**56**	4 wks
19 May 90	**GOODBYE JUMBO** Ensign CHEN 10...................................**36**	10 wks
8 May 93	● **BANG!** Ensign CDCHEN 33..**2**	8 wks

WORLD'S FAMOUS SUPREME TEAM – See Malcolm McLAREN

WRECKLESS ERIC UK, male vocalist   **5 wks**

1 Apr 78	**WRECKLESS ERIC** Stiff SEEZ 6 ....**46**	1 wk
8 Mar 80	**BIG SMASH** Stiff SEEZ 21 ....**30**	4 wks

WREN ORCHESTRA – See WET WET WET

Klaus WUNDERLICH Germany, male instrumentalist – organ   **19 wks**

30 Aug 75	**THE HIT WORLD OF KLAUS WUNDERLICH** Decca SPA 434 ....**27**	8 wks
20 May 78	**THE UNIQUE KLAUS WUNDERLICH SOUND** Decca DBC 5/5 ....**28**	4 wks
26 May 79	**THE FANTASTIC SOUND OF KLAUS WUNDERLICH** Lotus LH 5013 ....**43**	5 wks
17 Mar 84	**ON THE SUNNY SIDE OF THE STREET** Polydor POLD 5133 ....**81**	2 wks

WURZELS UK, male vocal / instrumental group   **29 wks**

11 Mar 67	**ADGE CUTLER AND THE WURZELS** Columbia SX 6126 1 ....**38**	4 wks
3 Jul 76	**COMBINE HARVESTER** One Up OU 2138 ....**15**	20 wks
2 Apr 77	**GOLDEN DELICIOUS** EMI Note NTS 122 ....**32**	5 wks

 1 Adge Cutler and the Wurzels

WWF SUPERSTARS US / UK, male vocal group   **5 wks**

17 Apr 93	● **WRESTLEMANIA – THE ALBUM** Arista 74321138062 ....**10**	5 wks

Bill WYMAN UK, male vocalist / instrumentalist   bass   **7 wks**

8 Jun 74	**MONKEY GRIP** Rolling Stones COC 59102 ....**39**	1 wk
10 Apr 82	**BILL WYMAN** A & M AMLH 68540.......................................**55**	6 wks

Tammy WYNETTE US, female vocalist   **49 wks**

17 May 75	● **THE BEST OF TAMMY WYNETTE** Epic EPC 63578 ....**4**	23 wks
21 Jun 75	**STAND BY YOUR MAN** Epic EPC 69141 ....**13**	7 wks
17 Dec 77	● **20 COUNTRY CLASSICS** CBS PR 5040 ....**3**	11 wks
4 Feb 78	**COUNTRY GIRL MEETS COUNTRY BOY** Warwick PR 5039 ....**43**	3 wks
6 Jun 87	**ANNIVERSARY – 20 YEARS OF HITS** Epic 450 3931 ....**45**	5 wks

X MAL DEUTSCHLAND
UK / Germany, male / female vocal / instrumental group   **1 wk**

7 Jul 84	**TOCSIN** 4AD CAD 407 ....**86**	1 wk

X–RAY SPEX UK, female / male vocal / instrumental group   **14 wks**

9 Dec 78	**GERM FREE ADOLESCENTS** EMI International INS 3023 ....**30**	14 wks

X
337

XTC *UK, male vocal / instrumental group* — **47 wks**

11 Feb 78	**WHITE MUSIC** *Virgin V 2095*......38	4 wks
28 Oct 78	**GO 2** *Virgin V 2108* 21	3 wks
1 Sep 79	**DRUMS AND WIRES** *Virgin V 2129* 34	7 wks
20 Sep 80	**BLACK SEA** *Virgin V 2173*......16	7 wks
20 Feb 82 ●	**ENGLISH SETTLEMENT** *Virgin V 2223* 5	11 wks
13 Nov 82	**WAXWORKS – SOME SINGLES (1977–82)** *Virgin V 2251* 54	3 wks
10 Sep 83	**MUMMER** *Virgin V 2264* 51	4 wks
27 Oct 84	**THE BIG EXPRESS** *Virgin V 2325* 38	2 wks
8 Nov 86	**SKYLARKING** *Virgin V 2399* 90	1 wk
11 Mar 89	**ORANGES AND LEMONS** *Virgin V 2581* 28	3 wks
9 May 92	**NONSUCH** *Virgin CDV 2699* 28	2 wks

Y & T *US, male vocal / instrumental group* — **15 wks**

11 Sep 82	**BLACK TIGER** *A & M AMLH 64910*......53	8 wks
10 Sep 83	**MEAN STREAK** *A & M AMLX 64960* 35	4 wks
18 Aug 84	**IN ROCK WE TRUST** *A & M AMLX 65007* 33	3 wks

YARDBIRDS *UK, male vocal / instrumental group* — **8 wks**

23 Jul 66	**YARDBIRDS** *Columbia SX 6063*......20	8 wks

YAZOO *UK, female / male vocal / instrumental duo* — **83 wks**

4 Sep 82 ●	**UPSTAIRS AT ERIC'S** *Mute STUMM 7* 2	63 wks
16 Jul 83 ★	**YOU AND ME BOTH** *Mute STUMM 12* 1	20 wks

YAZZ *UK, female vocalist* — **32 wks**

26 Nov 88 ●	**WANTED** *Big Life YAZZLP 1*......3	32 wks

YELLO *Switzerland, male vocal / instrumental duo* — **15 wks**

21 May 83	**YOU GOTTA SAY YES TO ANOTHER EXCESS** *Stiff SEEZ 48* 65	2 wks
6 Apr 85	**STELLA** *Elektra EKT 1*......92	1 wk
4 Jul 87	**ONE SECOND** *Mercury MERH 100* 48	3 wks
10 Dec 88	**FLAG** *Mercury 836778 1*......56	7 wks
29 Jun 91	**BABY** *Mercury 8487911*......37	2 wks

Bryn YEMM *UK, male vocalist* — **14 wks**

9 Jun 84	**HOW DO I LOVE THEE** *Lifestyle LEG 17*......57	2 wks
7 Jul 84	**HOW GREAT THOU ART** *Lifestyle LEG 15* 67	8 wks
22 Dec 84	**THE BRYN YEMM CHRISTMAS COLLECTION** *Bay BAY 104* 95	2 wks
26 Oct 85	**MY TRIBUTE – BRYN YEMM INSPIRATIONAL ALBUM** *Word WSTR 9665* [1] 85	2 wks

[1] Bryn Yemm and the Gwent Chorale

YES *UK, male vocal / instrumental group* — **210 wks**

1 Aug 70	**TIME AND A WORD** *Atlantic 2400006* 45	3 wks
3 Apr 71 ●	**THE YES ALBUM** *Atlantic 2400101* 7	29 wks
4 Dec 71 ●	**FRAGILE** *Atlantic 2409019*......7	17 wks
23 Sep 72 ●	**CLOSE TO THE EDGE** *Atlantic K 50012* 4	13 wks
26 May 73 ●	**YESSONGS** *Atlantic K 60045*......7	13 wks
22 Dec 73 ★	**TALES FROM TOPOGRAPHIC OCEANS** *Atlantic K 80001* 1	15 wks
21 Dec 74 ●	**RELAYER** *Atlantic K 50096* 4	11 wks

29 Mar 75	**YESTERDAYS** Atlantic K 50048 ....**27**	7 wks
30 Jul 77	★ **GOING FOR THE ONE** Atlantic K 50379 ....**1**	28 wks
7 Oct 78	● **TORMATO** Atlantic K 50518 ....**8**	11 wks
30 Aug 80	● **DRAMA** Atlantic K 50736 ....**2**	8 wks
10 Jan 81	**YESSHOWS** Atlantic K 60142 ....**22**	9 wks
26 Nov 83	**90125** Atco 790125 ....**16**	28 wks
29 Mar 86	**9012 LIVE: THE SOLOS** Atco 790 4741 ....**44**	3 wks
10 Oct 87	**BIG GENERATOR** Atco WEX 70 ....**17**	5 wks
11 May 91	● **UNION** Arista 211558 ....**7**	6 wks
2 Apr 94	**TALK** London 8284892 ....**20**	4 wks

Dwight YOAKAM US, male vocalist / instrumentalist – guitar   **4 wks**

9 May 87	**HILLBILLY DELUXE** Reprise WX 106 ....**51**	3 wks
13 Aug 88	**BUENAS NOCHES FROM A LONELY ROOM** Reprise WX 193 ....**87**	1 wk

Faron YOUNG US, male vocalist   **5 wks**

28 Oct 72	**IT'S FOUR IN THE MORNING** Mercury 6338 095 ....**27**	5 wks

Neil YOUNG Canada, male vocalist   **229 wks**

31 Oct 70	● **AFTER THE GOLDRUSH** Reprise RSLP 6383 ....**7**	68 wks
4 Mar 72	★ **HARVEST** Reprise K 54005 ....**1**	34 wks
27 Oct 73	**TIME FADES AWAY** Warner Bros. K 54010 ....**20**	2 wks
10 Aug 74	**ON THE BEACH** Reprise K 54014 ....**42**	2 wks
5 Jul 75	**TONIGHT'S THE NIGHT** Reprise K 54040 ....**48**	1 wk
27 Dec 75	**ZUMA** Reprise K 54057 ....**44**	2 wks
9 Oct 76	**LONG MAY YOU RUN** Reprise K 54081 [1] **12**	5 wks
9 Jul 77	**AMERICAN STARS 'N' BARS** Reprise K 54088 ....**17**	8 wks
17 Dec 77	**DECADE** Reprise K 64037 ....**46**	4 wks
28 Oct 78	**COMES A TIME** Reprise K 54099 ....**42**	3 wks
14 Jul 79	**RUST NEVER SLEEPS** Reprise K 54105 [2] **13**	13 wks
1 Dec 79	**LIVE RUST** Reprise K 64041 [2] **55**	3 wks
15 Nov 80	**HAWKS AND DOVES** Reprise K 54109 ....**34**	3 wks
14 Nov 81	**RE–AC–TOR** Reprise K 54116 [2] **69**	3 wks
5 Feb 83	**TRANS** Geffen GEF 25019 ....**29**	5 wks
3 Sep 83	**EVERYBODY'S ROCKIN'** Geffen GEF 25590 [3] **50**	3 wks
14 Sep 85	**OLD WAYS** Geffen GEF 26377 ....**39**	3 wks
2 Aug 86	**LANDING ON WATER** Geffen 924 1091 ....**52**	2 wks
4 Jul 87	**LIFE** Geffen WX 109 [2] **71**	1 wk
30 Apr 88	**THIS NOTE'S FOR YOU** WEA WX 168 [4] **56**	3 wks
21 Oct 89	**FREEDOM** Reprise WX 257 ....**17**	5 wks
22 Sep 90	**RAGGED GLORY** Reprise WX 374 ....**15**	5 wks
2 Nov 91	**WELD** Reprise 7599266711 ....**20**	3 wks
14 Nov 92	● **HARVEST MOON** Reprise 9362450572 ....**9**	18 wks
23 Jan 93	**LUCKY THIRTEEN** Geffen GED 24452 ....**69**	1 wk
26 Jun 93	● **UNPLUGGED** Reprise 9362450342 ....**4**	13 wks
27 Aug 94	● **SLEEPS WITH ANGELS** Reprise 9362457492 [2] **2**	7 wks
8 Jul 95	● **MIRROR BALL** Reprise 9362459342 ....**4**	9 wks

[1] Stills–Young Band [2] Neil Young and Crazy Horse [3] Neil Young and the Shocking Pinks
[4] Neil Young and the Blue Notes

See also Crosby, Stills, Nash and Young.

Paul YOUNG UK, male vocalist   **227 wks**

30 Jul 83	★ **NO PARLEZ** CBS 25521 ....**1**	119 wks
6 Apr 85	★ **THE SECRET OF ASSOCIATION** CBS 26234 ....**1**	49 wks
1 Nov 86	● **BETWEEN TWO FIRES** CBS 450 1501 ....**4**	17 wks
16 Jun 90	● **OTHER VOICES** CBS 4669171 ....**4**	11 wks
14 Sep 91	★ **FROM TIME TO TIME – THE SINGLES COLLECTION**	
	Columbia 4688251 ....**1**	27 wks
23 Oct 93	**THE CROSSING** Columbia 4739282 ....**27**	2 wks
26 Nov 94	**REFLECTIONS** Vision VISCD 1 ....**64**	2 wks

Y
339

YOUNG DISCIPLES *UK / US, male / female vocal / instrumental group*   **5 wks**

31 Aug 91	**ROAD TO FREEDOM** *Talkin Loud 5100971* **21**	5 wks

YOUNG GODS *Switzerland, male vocal / instrumental group*   **1 wk**

15 Feb 92	**TV SKY** *Play It Again Sam BIAS 201CD*................................**54**	1 wk

Sydney YOUNGBLOOD *US, male vocalist*   **17 wks**

28 Oct 89	**FEELING FREE** *Circa CIRCA 9* **23**	17 wks

Frank ZAPPA *US, male vocalist / multi–instrumentalist*   **57 wks**

28 Feb 70	● **HOT RATS** *Reprise RSLP 6356* **9**	27 wks
19 Dec 70	**CHUNGA'S REVENGE** *Reprise RSLP 2030* **43**	1 wk
6 May 78	**ZAPPA IN NEW YORK** *Discreet K 69204* **55**	1 wk
10 Mar 79	**SHEIK YERBOUTI** *CBS 88339*................**32**	7 wks
13 Oct 79	**JOE'S GARAGE ACT 1** *CBS 86101* **62**	3 wks
19 Jan 80	**JOE'S GARAGE ACTS 2 & 3** *CBS 88475* **75**	1 wk
16 May 81	**TINSEL TOWN REBELLION** *CBS 88516*.................**55**	4 wks
24 Oct 81	**YOU ARE WHAT YOU IS** *CBS 88560* **51**	2 wks
19 Jun 82	**SHIP ARRIVING TOO LATE TO SAVE A DROWNING WITCH** *CBS 85804*................................**61**	4 wks
18 Jun 83	**THE MAN FROM UTOPIA** *CBS 25251*................**87**	1 wk
27 Oct 84	**THEM OR US** *EMI FZD 1* **53**	2 wks
30 Apr 88	**GUITAR** *Zappa ZAPPA 6* **82**	2 wks
2 Sep 95	**STRICTLY COMMERCIAL – THE BEST OF FRANK ZAPPA** *Rykodisc RCD 40600* **45**	2 wks

Lena ZAVARONI *UK, female vocalist*   **5 wks**

23 Mar 74	● **MA** *Philips 6308 201* **8**	5 wks

ZOE *UK, female vocalist*   **1 wk**

7 Dec 91	**SCARLET RED AND BLUE** *M & G 5114431* **67**	1 wk

ZUCCHERO *Italy, male vocalist*   **4 wks**

18 May 91	**ZUCCHERO** *A & M EVERY 1*................................**29**	4 wks

ZZ TOP *US, male vocal / instrumental group*   **207 wks**

12 Jul 75	**FANDANGO** *London SHU 8482*........................**60**	1 wk
8 Aug 81	**EL LOCO** *Warner Bros. K 56929* **88**	2 wks
30 Apr 83	● **ELIMINATOR** *Warner Bros. W 3774* **3**	135 wks
9 Nov 85	● **AFTERBURNER** *Warner Bros. WX 27* **2**	40 wks
27 Oct 90	● **RECYCLER** *Warner Bros. WX 390* **8**	7 wks
25 Apr 92	● **GREATEST HITS** *Warner Bros. 7599268462* **5**	17 wks
5 Feb 94	● **ANTENNA** *RCA 74321152602* **3**	5 wks

VARIOUS ARTISTS

CONTENTS

Compilation albums are listed alphabetically by label, for each label which has pro-duced at least three hit compilations. Other hit compilations are listed together at the end of this section. Multi-artist Film Soundtracks, TV and Radio Soundtracks and Spin-Offs, Stage and Studio Cast Recordings, Anonymous Cover Versions and Miscellaneous albums are then listed separately.

On 14 January 1989 the Compilation Albums chart was established, and all entries on this chart are listed in this section. A dotted line in each label listing indicates when the new chart began. Some albums will have entries both above and below the line, indicating that they appeared in the main chart before 14 January 1989, and the Compilation Chart thereafter.

VARIOUS ARTISTS

COMPILATIONS

A & M

2 May 87	**PRINCE'S TRUST TENTH ANNIVERSARY BIRTHDAY PARTY** *A & M AMA 3906*	**76**	3 wks
22 Aug 87	**THE PRINCE'S TRUST CONCERT 1987** *A & M PTA 1987*	**44**	3 wks
5 Dec 87	**SPECIAL OLYMPICS – A VERY SPECIAL CHRISTMAS** *A & M AMA 3911*	**40**	5 wks
23 Dec 89	**SPECIAL OLYMPICS – A VERY SPECIAL CHRISTMAS** *A & M AMA 3911*	**19**	1 wk
29 Sep 90	★ **SLAMMIN'** *A & M SLAMM 1*	**1**	6 wks
20 Apr 91	**RAGE – MAKE SOME NOISE VOLUME 1** *A & M AMTV 1*	**12**	3 wks
29 Jun 91	★ **WINGS OF LOVE** *A & M 8455062*	**1**	21 wks
4 Nov 95	**THE HACIENDA – PLAY BY 01 / 96** *A & M 5404452*	**18**	1 wk

Arcade

29 Jul 72	★ **20 FANTASTIC HITS** *Arcade 2891 001*	**1**	24 wks
29 Nov 72	● **20 FANTASTIC HITS VOLUME 2** *Arcade 2891 002*	**2**	14 wks
7 Apr 73	● **40 FANTASTIC HITS FROM THE 50'S AND 60'S** *Arcade ADEP 3/4*	**2**	15 wks
26 May 73	● **20 FANTASTIC HITS VOLUME 3** *Arcade ADEP 5*	**3**	8 wks
15 Nov 75	● **DISCO HITS '75** *Arcade ADEP 18*	**5**	11 wks
26 Mar 77	**ROCK ON** *Arcade ADEP 27*	**16**	10 wks
2 Jun 77	**RULE BRITANNIA** *Arcade ADEP 29*	**56**	1 wk
23 Feb 80	**FIRST LOVE** *Arcade ADEP 41*	**58**	2 wks
12 Jan 91	**POP CLASSICS – 28 CLASSIC TRACKS** *Arcade ARC 94421*	**19**	2 wks
30 Mar 91	● **SOFT METAL BALLADS** *Arcade ARC 933501*	**5**	10 wks
8 Jun 91	● **IT STARTED WITH A KISS** *Arcade ARC 910301*	**9**	8 wks
13 Jul 91	● **THE HEAT IS ON** *Arcade ARC 925401*	**4**	9 wks
31 Aug 91	● **DANCE CLASSICS VOLUME 1** *Arcade ARC 925501*	**8**	4 wks
31 Aug 91	● **DANCE CLASSICS VOLUME 2** *Arcade ARC 925511*	**7**	5 wks
21 Sep 91	★ **GROOVY GHETTO** *Arcade ARC 925601*	**1**	6 wks
2 Nov 91	**GROOVY GHETTO – ALL THE RAGE** *Arcade ARC 925701*	**15**	2 wks
14 Dec 91	**CHRISTMAS LOVE SONGS** *Arcade ARC 948201*	**11**	6 wks
29 Feb 92	● **GROOVY GHETTO 2** *Arcade ARC 948102*	**8**	4 wks
4 Apr 92	**THE ESSENTIAL CHILL** *Arcade 948902*	**16**	2 wks
18 Jul 92	● **ONE LOVE – THE VERY BEST OF REGGAE** *Arcade ARC 94962*	**7**	6 wks
13 Feb 93	● **ROCK ROMANCE** *Arcade 3100032*	**9**	5 wks
7 May 94	**WOW! – LET THE MUSIC LIFT YOU UP** *Arcade ARC 3100112*	**13**	3 wks
13 Aug 94	**COMMITED TO SOUL** *Arcade ARC 3100142*	**11**	7 wks

Atlantic

2 Apr 66	**SOLID GOLD SOUL** *Atlantic ATL 5048*	**12**	27 wks
5 Nov 66	**MIDNIGHT SOUL** *Atlantic 587-021*	**22**	19 wks
14 Jun 69	**THIS IS SOUL** *Atlantic 643-301*	**16**	15 wks
25 Mar 72	**THE NEW AGE OF ATLANTIC** *Atlantic K 20024*	**25**	1 wk
22 Jun 74	**ATLANTIC BLACK GOLD** *Atlantic K 40550*	**23**	7 wks
3 Apr 76	**BY INVITATION ONLY** *Atlantic K 60112*	**17**	6 wks
11 Apr 81	**CONCERTS FOR THE PEOPLE OF KAMPUCHEA** *Atlantic K 60153*	**39**	2 wks
2 Feb 85	**THIS IS SOUL** *Atlantic SOUL 1*	**78**	7 wks
6 Jun 87	● **ATLANTIC SOUL CLASSICS** *Atlantic WX 105*	**9**	23 wks
18 Jun 88	**ATLANTIC SOUL BALLADS** *Atlantic WX 98*	**84**	2 wks

Beggars Banquet

21 Nov 81	**SLIP STREAM** *Beggars Banquet BEGA 31*	**72**	3 wks
15 May 82	**SEX SWEAT AND BLOOD** *Beggars Banquet BEGA 34*	**88**	1 wk
11 Sep 82	**THE BEST OF BRITISH JAZZ FUNK VOLUME 2** *Beggars Banquet BEGA 41*	**44**	4 wks

Castle Communications

7 Jul 90	● **THE ULTIMATE 60s COLLECTION** *Castle Communications CTVLP 305*	**4**	11 wks
12 Jan 91	**THE ULTIMATE BLUES COLLECTION** *Castle Communications CTVLP 206*	**14**	6 wks

8 Aug 92	● JAZZ ON A SUMMER'S DAY Castle Communications CTVCD 108 ..4	8 wks
10 Oct 92	● BLOCKBUSTER! – THE SENSATIONAL 70s	
	Castle Communications CTVCD 209................................6	6 wks
5 Jun 93	● ONE ORIGINAL STEP BEYOND	
	Castle Communications CTVCD 115...........................7	5 wks
3 Jul 93	MONSTER HITS OF DANCE Castle Communications CTVCD 220 ..13	3 wks
30 Oct 93	GOING UNDERGROUND Castle Communications CTVCD 123.......18	2 wks

CBS/Columbia

20 May 67	THRILL TO THE SENSATIONAL SOUNDS OF SUPER STEREO	
	CBS PR 5...20	30 wks
28 Jun 69	THE ROCK MACHINE TURNS YOU ON CBS SPR 22 18	7 wks
28 Jun 69	ROCK MACHINE I LOVE YOU CBS SPR 26 15	5 wks
20 May 72	● THE MUSIC PEOPLE CBS 66315 10	9 wks
21 Oct 78	● SATIN CITY CBS 10010.....................................10	11 wks
2 Jun 79	● THIS IS IT CBS 10014 6	12 wks
19 Apr 80	FIRST LADIES OF COUNTRY CBS 10018 37	6 wks
21 Jun 80	KILLER WATTS CBS KW1 27	6 wks
4 Apr 81	BITTER SUITE CBS 22082 55	3 wks
16 Oct 82	● REFLECTIONS CBS 10034....................................4	91 wks
22 Oct 83	IMAGINATIONS CBS 10044....................................15	21 wks
20 Apr 85	CLUB CLASSICS VOLUME 2 CBS VAULT 2 90	2 wks
14 Mar 87	● MOVE CLOSER CBS MOOD 1 4	19 wks
27 Jun 87	THE HOLIDAY ALBUM CBS MOOD 2 13	9 wks
30 Apr 88	★ NITE FLITE CBS MOOD 4 1	26 wks
4 Mar 89	● CHEEK TO CHEEK CBS MOOD 6 2	32 wks
13 May 89	★ NITE FLITE 2 CBS MOOD 8 1	26 wks
30 Dec 89	LAMBADA CBS 466055 1......................................15	6 wks
24 Mar 90	★ JUST THE TWO OF US CBS MOOD 11 1	37 wks
9 Jun 90	● NITE FLITE 3 – BEING WITH YOU CBS MOOD 14.........3	11 wks
2 Feb 91	★ THINKING OF YOU Columbia MOOD 15 1	23 wks
2 Feb 91	● THE TREE AND THE BIRD Columbia 4678801 9	3 wks
30 Mar 91	EVERYBODY DANCE NOW Columbia 468501 12	3 wks
20 Apr 91	● FREE SPIRIT – 17 CLASSIC ROCK BALLADS Columbia MOODS 16 ..4	23 wks
20 Apr 91	● YOU'RE THE INSPIRATION Columbia MOOD 17 10	5 wks
10 Aug 91	● SIMPLY . . . LOVE Columbia MOOD 17 3	10 wks
17 Aug 91	★ THE SOUND OF THE SUBURBS Columbia MOOD 18 1	25 wks
29 Feb 92	THE SOUND OF THE CITY Columbia MOODCD 22 11	5 wks
27 Jun 92	● HARD FAX Columbia SETVCD 1 3	6 wks
4 Jul 92	THE BOYS ARE BACK IN TOWN Columbia MOODCD 23 ...11	6 wks
3 Oct 92	● SOMETHING IN THE AIR Columbia SETVCD 2 10	5 wks
31 Oct 92	★ THE ULTIMATE COUNTRY COLLECTION Columbia MOODCD 26 1	23 wks
21 Nov 92	● HARD FAX 2 – TWICE THE VICE! Columbia SETVCD 3 ...6	2 wks
29 May 93	★ ORIGINALS Columbia MOODCD 29 1	23 wks
21 Aug 93	● AFTER DARK Columbia SETVCD 5 8	4 wks
15 Jan 94	TRUE LOVE WAYS Columbia MOODCD 28 14	2 wks
12 Feb 94	● SECRET LOVERS Columbia SETVCD 4 8	4 wks
19 Mar 94	● ORIGINALS 2 Columbia MOODCD 31 4	10 wks
23 Jul 94	● SOUL SEARCHING Columbia MOODCD 34 6	5 wks
4 Mar 95	● THE AWARDS 1995 Columbia MOODCD 39 10	2 wks
27 May 95	● TOP GEAR 2 Columbia MOODCD 41 4	6 wks
1 Jul 95	● MUNDO LATINO Columbia SONYTV 2CD 3	5 wks
8 Jul 95	● PURE ATTRACTION Columbia SONYTV 1CD 5	3 wks
25 Nov 95	● THIS YEAR'S LOVE IS FOREVER Columbia MOODCD 42 ....4t	6 wks
26 Sep 95	HEAVEN & HELL (Re-issue) Columbia 4736662 ....?	? wks

Heaven & Hell was previously released on Telstar.

Champion

8 Nov 86	ULTIMATE TRAX VOLUME 1 Champion CHAMP 103................66	2 wks
7 Mar 87	ULTIMATE TRAX VOLUME 2 Champion CHAMP 1005...............50	2 wks
18 Jul 87	ULTIMATE TRAX 3 – BATTLE OF THE D.J.s	
	Champion CHAMP 1008..69	2 wks

Charm

21 Apr 90	PURE LOVERS VOLUME 1 Charm CLP 101 14	4 wks
22 Sep 90	PURE LOVERS VOLUME 2 Charm CLP 102 12	3 wks
6 Apr 91	PURE LOVERS VOLUME 3 Charm CLP 103 16	2 wks

VARIOUS ARTISTS

2 Nov 91	PURE LOVERS VOLUME 4 *Charm CLP 104*	19	1 wk
25 Jul 92	JUST RAGGA *Charm CDCD 14*	17	1 wk
29 Aug 92	PURE LOVERS VOLUME 5 *Charm CCDJS 105*	13	3 wks
27 Feb 93	JUST RAGGA VOLUME III *Charm CRCD 16*	19	1 wk
1 May 93	PURE LOVERS VOLUME 6 *Charm CCDJS 106*	17	1 wk

Cookie Jar

14 Dec 91	● STEAMIN' – HARDCORE 92 *Cookie Jar JARTV 1*	3	8 wks
21 Mar 92	● TECHNOSTATE *Cookie Jar JARCD 2*	2	9 wks
23 May 92	★ THE RAVE GENER8TOR *Cookie Jar JARCD 3*	1	8 wks
5 Sep 92	● THE RAVE GENER8TOR 2 *Cookie Jar JARCD 4*	2	7 wks
28 Nov 92	● RAVE 92 *Cookie Jar JARCD 5*	3	11 wks
27 Mar 93	● UNDERGROUND VOLUME 1 *Cookie Jar JARCD 6*	6	5 wks
7 Aug 93	● JAMMIN' *Cookie Jar JARCD 7*	7	5 wks
11 Sep 93	FULL ON DANCE *Cookie Jar JARCD 8*	12	2 wks
6 Nov 93	● SOUL BEAT *Cookie Jar JARCD 9*	8	2 wks
27 Nov 93	● FULL ON DANCE '93 *Cookie Jar JARCD 10*	3	9 wks

Decca

8 Feb 64	READY STEADY GO *Decca LK 4577*	20	1 wk
28 Jun 69	THE WORLD OF BLUES POWER *Decca SPA 14*	24	6 wks
5 Jul 69	THE WORLD OF BRASS BANDS *Decca SPA 20*	13	11 wks
6 Sep 69	● THE WORLD OF HITS VOLUME 2 *Decca SPA 35*	7	5 wks
20 Sep 69	THE WORLD OF PROGRESSIVE MUSIC (WOWIE ZOWIE) *Decca SPA 34*	17	2 wks
20 Sep 69	THE WORLD OF PHASE 4 STEREO *Decca SPA 32*	29	2 wks
7 Aug 71	● THE WORLD OF YOUR 100 BEST TUNES *Decca SPA 112*	10	22 wks
9 Oct 71	● THE WORLD OF YOUR 100 BEST TUNES VOLUME 2 *Decca SPA 155*	9	13 wks
27 Sep 75	THE WORLD OF YOUR 100 BEST TUNES VOLUME 10 *Decca SPA 400*	41	4 wks
13 Dec 75	THE TOP 25 FROM YOUR 100 BEST TUNES *Decca HBT 1112*	21	5 wks
26 Nov 83	● FORMULA 30 *Decca PROLP 4*	6	17 wks
1 Jun 91	★ THE ESSENTIAL MOZART *Decca 4333231*	1	23 wks
16 Nov 91	● ESSENTIAL OPERA *Decca 4338221*	2	28 wks
26 Sep 92	● ESSENTIAL BALLET *Decca 4366582*	9	4 wks
12 Jun 93	● CLASSIC COMMERCIALS *Decca 4406382*	8	6 wks
6 Nov 93	ESSENTIAL OPERA 2 *Decca 4409472*	17	2 wks

Deconstruction

14 Oct 89	● ITALIA – DANCE MUSIC FROM ITALY *Deconstruction 64289*	4	6 wks
27 Feb 93	FULL ON – A YEAR IN THE LIFE OF HOUSE *Deconstruction 74321128032*	18	2 wks
6 May 95	● CREAM LIVE *Deconstruction 74321272192*	3	17 wks
26 Aug 95	DECONSTRUCTION CLASSICS – A HISTORY OF DANCE MUSIC *Deconstruction 74321299002*	17	1 wk
11 Nov 95	● CREAM ANTHEMS *Deconstruction 74321328162*	2	3 wks

Deutsche Grammophon

13 Oct 90	● ESSENTIAL CLASSICS *Deutsche Grammophon 4315411*	6	9 wks
28 Mar 92	● LIVING CLASSICS *Deutsche Grammophon 4356432*	7	5 wks
24 Jun 95	TOP GEAR CLASSICS – TURBO CLASSICS *Deutsche Grammophon 4479412*	17	1 wk

Dino

2 Dec 89	● THAT LOVING FEELING *Dino DINTV 5*	3	14 wks
3 Mar 90	● THAT LOVING FEELING VOLUME 2 *Dino DINTV 7*	5	26 wks
23 Jun 90	● LEATHER AND LACE *Dino DINTV 9*	3	8 wks
11 Aug 90	● THE SUMMER OF LOVE *Dino DINTV 10*	9	9 wks
6 Oct 90	★ THAT LOVING FEELING VOLUME 3 *Dino DINTV 11*	1	31 wks
10 Nov 90	LEATHER AND LACE – THE SECOND CHAPTER *Dino DINTV 12*	14	4 wks
24 Nov 90	● ROCK 'N' ROLL LOVE SONGS *Dino DINTV 13*	4	29 wks
29 Dec 90	BACHARACH AND DAVID – THEY WRITE THE SONGS *Dino DINTV 16*	16	3 wks
9 Feb 91	● TRACKS OF MY TEARS (SMOKEY ROBINSON – WRITER AND PERFORMER) *Dino DINTV 17*	6	8 wks

30 Mar 91	● HARDCORE UPROAR *Dino DINTV 20*	2	9	wks
6 Apr 91	● THAT LOVING FEELING VOLUME 4 *Dino DINTV 18*	3	14	wks
1 Jun 91	● LOVE SUPREME *Dino DINTV 19*	4	5	wks
15 Jun 91	★ THE RHYTHM DIVINE *Dino DINTV 22*	1	15	wks
13 Jul 91	● HARDCORE DANCEFLOOR *Dino DINTV 24*	2	10	wks
27 Jul 91	● CHIC AND ROSE ROYCE – THEIR GREATEST HITS SIDE BY SIDE *Dino DINTV 23*	8	6	wks
3 Aug 91	● LA FREEWAY *Dino DINTV 25*	6	7	wks
12 Oct 91	● WE WILL ROCK YOU *Dino DINTV 26*	3	6	wks
19 Oct 91	● THAT LOVING FEELING VOLUME 5 *Dino DINTV 28*	2	15	wks
2 Nov 91	★ HARDCORE ECSTASY *Dino DINTV 29*	1	16	wks
2 Nov 91	● THE RHYTHM DIVINE VOLUME 2 *Dino DINTV 27*	6	5	wks
23 Nov 91	● MORE ROCK 'N' ROLL LOVE SONGS *Dino DINTV 30*	6	23	wks
7 Dec 91	● PARTY MIX *Dino DINTV 32*	8	9	wks
28 Dec 91	★ ESSENTIAL HARDCORE *Dino DINTV 33*	1	10	wks
14 Mar 92	● HEAVENLY HARDCORE *Dino DINCD 35*	2	9	wks
28 Mar 92	● BREAKING HEARTS *Dino DINCD 34*	3	10	wks
18 Apr 92	● COLD SWEAT *Dino DINCD 36*	2	7	wks
2 May 92	● HEARTLANDS *Dino DINCD 37*	4	11	wks
20 Jun 92	● LET'S TALK ABOUT LOVE *Dino DINCD 39*	3	4	wks
11 Jul 92	PRECIOUS *Dino DINCD 38*	12	2	wks
18 Jul 92	● MIDNIGHT CRUISING *Dino DINCD 37*	10	4	wks
1 Aug 92	● UNDER SPANISH SKIES *Dino DINCD 41*	5	7	wks
22 Aug 92	● THE ORIGINALS! *Dino DINCD 34*	8	6	wks
29 Aug 92	● TRANCE DANCE *Dino DINCD 45*	7	5	wks
19 Sep 92	★ SIXTIES BEAT *Dino DINCD 42*	1	13	wks
17 Oct 92	★ ENERGY RUSH *Dino DINCD 53*	1	6	wks
24 Oct 92	● THE GREATEST VOICES *Dino DINCD 44*	5	6	wks
14 Nov 92	SWING HITS *Dino DINCD 46*	19	1	wk
28 Nov 92	ROCK 'N' ROLL IS HERE TO STAY *Dino DINCD 48*	14	5	wks
12 Dec 92	● ENERGY RUSH II *Dino DINCD 55*	7	7	wks
12 Dec 92	● MEMORIES ARE MADE OF THIS *Dino DINCD 47*	8	8	wks
5 Dec 92	● STOMPIN' PARTY *Dino DINCD 52*	10	7	wks
13 Feb 93	★ BLUES BROTHER SOUL SISTER *Dino DINCD 56*	1	38	wks
30 Jan 93	● ENERGY RUSH LEVEL 3 *Dino DINCD 57*	3	6	wks
10 Apr 93	★ ENERGY RUSH PRESENTS DANCE HITS 93 *Dino DINCD 59*	1	12	wks
5 Jun 93	● ENERGY RUSH PHASE 4 *Dino DINCD 65*	2	6	wks
10 Jul 93	● HEART FULL OF SOUL *Dino DINCD 63*	9	8	wks
17 Jul 93	● BLUES BROTHER SOUL SISTER VOLUME 2 *Dino DINCD 61*	8	8	wks
24 Jul 93	● ENERGY RUSH DANCE HITS 93 (2ND DIMENSION) *Dino DINCD 62*	2	8	wks
4 Sep 93	● THAT LOVING FEELING VOLUME VI *Dino DINCD 64*	3	12	wks
11 Sep 93	● ENERGY RUSH FACTOR 5 *Dino DINCD 66*	3	5	wks
18 Sep 93	● RAVE GENERATION *Dino DINCD 68*	2	7	wks
25 Sep 93	MORE THAN UNPLUGGED *Dino DINCD 69*	11	3	wks
16 Oct 93	● ENERGY RUSH PRESENTS DANCE HITS OF THE YEAR *Dino DINCD 70*	3	13	wks
16 Oct 93	● PLANET ROCK *Dino DINCD 67*	8	2	wks
23 Oct 93	● FUTURESHOCK – 20 FURIOUS DANCE TUNES *Dino DINCD 71*	4	4	wks
23 Oct 93	COUNTRY WOMEN *Dino DINCD 72*	11	3	wks
27 Nov 93	AS TIME GOES BY *Dino DINCD 77*	14	5	wks
4 Dec 93	● THE VERY BEST OF THAT LOVING FEELING *Dino DINCD 78*	2	21	wks
4 Dec 93	● ENERGY RUSH – SAFE SIX *Dino DINCD 74*	5	7	wks
4 Dec 93	KEEP ON DANCING *Dino DINCD 80*	14	6	wks
25 Dec 93	LOVE IN THE SIXTIES *Dino DINCD 81*	11	9	wks
29 Jan 94	● RAVE GENERATION 2 *Dino DINCD 75*	5	3	wks
19 Feb 94	MEMORIES ARE MADE OF THIS *Dino DINCD 47*	14	3	wks
19 Feb 94	● SOUL MATE *Dino DINCD 82*	6	3	wks
12 Mar 94	● ENERGY RUSH – EURO DANCE HITS 94 *Dino DINCD 76*	5	4	wks
2 Apr 94	● ENERGY RUSH 7 *Dino DINCD 79*	2	5	wks
9 Apr 94	● IT'S ELECTRIC *Dino DINCD 73*	2	12	wks
7 May 94	● BLUES BROTHER SOUL SISTER VOLUME 3 *Dino DINCD 85*	5	12	wks
28 May 94	★ ENERGY RUSH – XTERMIN8 *Dino DINCD 84*	1	8	wks
4 Jun 94	● WONDERFUL WORLD *Dino DINCD 89*	8	6	wks
23 Jul 94	● THE BEST OF ROCK 'N' ROLL LOVE SONGS *Dino DINCD 91*	9	5	wks
30 Jul 94	START – THE BEST OF BRITISH *Dino DINCD 92*	13	3	wks
6 Aug 94	● ENERGY RUSH DANCE HITS 94 *Dino DINCD 95*	3	8	wks
13 Aug 94	● THAT LOVING FEELING VOLUME VII *Dino DINCD 83*	4	10	wks
3 Sep 94	● DANCE MASSIVE *Dino DINCD 94*	3	8	wks
17 Sep 94	● WHEN A MAN LOVES A WOMAN *Dino DINCD 88*	7	6	wks

10 Dec 94 ●	**ROCK ANTHEMS** *Dino DINCD 101*	3	17 wks
17 Dec 94 ●	**DANCE MASSIVE 2** *Dino DINCD 103*	8	6 wks
7 Jan 95	**THE ULTIMATE JUNGLE COLLECTION** *Dino DINCD 105*	17	2 wks
11 Feb 95 ●	**ENERGY RUSH K9** *Dino DINCD 102*	3	4 wks
11 Mar 95 ●	**PURE SWING** *Dino DINCD 97*	2	9 wks
8 Apr 95 ●	**DRIVE TIME** *Dino DINCD 96*	5	8 wks
27 May 95 ●	**SKA MANIA** *Dino DINCD 86*	4	5 wks
10 Jun 95 ●	**DANCE MASSIVE 95** *Dino DINCD 87*	2	5 wks
10 Jun 95 ●	**PURE SWING TWO** *Dino DINCD 98*	4	5 wks
24 Jun 95	**REGGAE MASSIVE** *Dino DINCD 93*	19	1 wk
15 Jul 95 ●	**RAVE ANTHEMS** *Dino DINCD 104*	7	5 wks
22 Jul 95 ●	**DRIVE TIME 2** *Dino DINCD 99*	4	7 wks
19 Aug 95 ●	**THE AMERICAN DINER** *Dino DINCD 107*	7	5 wks
2 Sep 95 ●	**PURE SWING III** *Dino DINCD 109*	3	8 wks
21 Oct 95 ●	**THE GREATEST DANCE ALBUM OF ALL TIME** *Dino DINCD 108*	7	4 wks
28 Oct 95	**SPIRITUALLY IBIZA** *Dino DINCD 111*	17	1 wk
18 Nov 95 ★	**PURE SWING IV** *Dino DINCD 116*	1	7 wks
25 Nov 95	**THE VERY BEST OF BLUES BROTHER SOUL SISTER** *Dino DINCD 115*	11	6 wks
9 Dec 95	**THE GREATEST SOUL ALBUM OF ALL TIME** *Dino DINCD 113*	16	4 wks

DJ International

20 Sep 86	**THE HOUSE SOUND OF CHICAGO** *DJ International LONLP 22*	52	12 wks
18 Apr 87	**THE HOUSE OF SOUND OF CHICAGO VOLUME 2** *DJ International LONLP 32*	38	7 wks
31 Oct 87	**JACKMASTER VOLUME 1** *DJ International JACKLP 501*	36	4 wks
13 Feb 88	**JACKMASTER VOLUME 2** *DJ International JACKLP 502*	38	3 wks

Dover

4 Mar 89 ●	**AND ALL BECAUSE THE LADY LOVES . . .** *Dover ADD 6*	2	10 wks
10 Feb 90 ●	**ALL BY MYSELF** *Dover ADD 12*	2	15 wks
22 Sep 90 ●	**JUST SEVENTEEN – GET KICKIN'** *Dover ADD 16*	2	6 wks
24 Nov 90 ●	**A TON OF HITS** *Dover ADD 19*	7	8 wks
20 Apr 91 ●	**RED HOT METAL – 18 ROCK CLASSICS** *Dover ADD 21*	4	6 wks
8 Jun 91	**ALL BY MYSELF 2** *Dover ADD 23*	13	5 wks
14 Sep 91 ●	**MOMENTS IN SOUL** *Dover ADD 25*	2	7 wks
16 May 92 ●	**THE GREATEST MOMENTS IN SOUL** *Dover CCD 33*	4	7 wks

Elevate

11 Apr 92	**RAVE 2 – STRICTLY HARDCORE** *Elevate ELVCD 02*	11	3 wks
8 Aug 92	**RAVING MAD** *Elevate CDELV 01*	17	2 wks
27 Feb 93	**THE WIND DOWN ZONE** *Elevate CDELV 04*	17	3 wks

EMI

21 Jun 69	**IMPACT** *EMI STWO 2*	15	14 wks
2 Jun 73 ★	**PURE GOLD** *EMI EMK 251*	1	11 wks
18 Nov 78 ★	**DON'T WALK BOOGIE** *EMI EMTV 13*	1	23 wks
21 Apr 79 ●	**COUNTRY LIFE** *EMI EMTV 16*	2	14 wks
2 Jun 79	**KNUCKLE SANDWICH** *EMI International EMYV 18*	19	6 wks
15 Dec 79	**ALL ABOARD** *EMI EMTX 101*	13	8 wks
23 Feb 80	**METAL FOR MUTHAS** *EMI EMC 3318*	16	7 wks
14 Jun 80	**METAL FOR MUTHAS VOLUME 2** *EMI EMC 3337*	58	1 wk
13 Mar 82	**20 WITH A BULLET** *EMI EMTV 32*	11	8 wks
26 May 84 ●	**THEN CAME ROCK 'N' ROLL** *EMI THEN 1*	5	15 wks
5 Mar 88 ●	**UNFORGETTABLE** *EMI EMTV 44*	5	21 wks
22 Oct 88	**THE CLASSIC EXPERIENCE** *EMI EMTVD 45*	27	12 wks
3 Dec 88	**HELLO CHILDREN . . . EVERYWHERE** *EMI EM 1307*	59	5 wks
14 Jan 89 ●	**THE CLASSIC EXPERIENCE** *EMI EMTVD 45*	8	58 wks
28 Jan 89	**UNFORGETTABLE** *EMI EMTV 44*	18	1 wk
18 Mar 89 ★	**UNFORGETTABLE 2** *EMI EMTV 46*	1	15 wks
30 Sep 89 ●	**IS THIS LOVE** *EMI EMTV 47*	2	10 wks
18 Nov 89 ★	**THE 80'S – ALBUM OF THE DECADE** *EMI EMTVD 48*	1	12 wks
9 Dec 89 ●	**IT'S CHRISTMAS** *EMI EMTV 49*	2	16 wks
26 May 90 ★	**THE CLASSIC EXPERIENCE II** *EMI EMTVD 50*	1	32 wks
4 Aug 90 ●	**THE WILD ONE** *EMI EMTV 52*	8	7 wks
20 Oct 90 ★	**MISSING YOU – AN ALBUM OF LOVE** *EMI EMTV 53*	1	18 wks

VARIOUS ARTISTS

17 Nov 90	● TRULY UNFORGETTABLE *EMI EMTVD 55* 6	9	wks
1 Dec 90	THE BEST FROM THE MGM MUSICALS *EMI EMTV 56* 12	4	wks
16 Feb 91	● MISSING YOU 2 – AN ALBUM OF LOVE *EMI EMTV 57* 2	11	wks
11 May 91	● THE CLASSIC EXPERIENCE III *EMI EMTVD 59* 3	14	wks
26 Oct 91	● SEXUAL HEALING *EMI EMTV 60* 7	6	wks
30 Nov 91	A CLASSICAL CHRISTMAS *EMI EMTV 62* 14	7	wks
22 Feb 92	● TENDER LOVE – 17 ROMANTIC LOVE SONGS *EMI CDEMTV 64* 2	11	wks
22 Feb 92	● THE CLASSIC ROMANCE *EMI CDEMTV 63* 5	7	wks
22 Aug 92	● MAXIMUM RAVE *EMI CDEMTV 65* 2	9	wks
17 Oct 92	● WICKED!! *EMI CDEMTV 66* 2	5	wks
31 Oct 92	● SMASHIE AND NICEY PRESENT LET'S ROCK! *EMI CDEMTV 67* 8	4	wks
21 Nov 92	● IT'S CHRISTMAS TIME *EMI CDEMTV 69* 3	15	wks
5 Dec 92	FOREVER *EMI CDEMTV 70* 17	2	wks
20 Feb 93	● SOUL MOODS *EMI CDEMTV 71* 4	8	wks
27 Mar 93	● CLASSIC EXPERIENCE IV *EMI CDEMTVD 72* 9	6	wks
3 Jul 93	INNA DANCEHALL STYLE *EMI CDEMTV 76* 11	4	wks
18 Sep 93	● BACK TO THE 70S *EMI CDEMTV 77* 8	6	wks
6 Nov 93	LET'S GO DISCO *EMI CDEMTV 78* 12	3	wks
27 Nov 93	IT TAKES TWO – LOVE'S GREATEST DUETS *EMI CDEMTV 80* 17	1	wk
26 Feb 94	● THE BRIT AWARDS *EMI CDAWARD 1* 6	3	wks
25 Jun 94	TRANQUILITY *EMI CDC 5552432* 14	5	wks
8 Oct 94	● CLUB TOGETHER *EMI CDEMC 3692* 10	4	wks
29 Oct 94	● MISSING YOU *EMI CDEMTVD 86* 8	4	wks
26 Nov 94	● THE BEST COUNTRY ALBUM IN THE WORLD...EVER! *EMI CDEMTV 87* 4	12	wks
10 Dec 94	● THAT'S CHRISTMAS *EMI CDEMTV 88* 10	4	wks
11 Mar 95	● UNLACED *EMI CDEMTV 90* 8	4	wks
15 Jul 95	● THE BEST CLASSICAL ALBUM IN THE WORLD. . . EVER! *EMI CDEMTVD 93* 6	6	wks
22 Jul 95	● MOST EXCELLENT DANCE *EMI CDMXD 1* 8	4	wks
29 Jul 95	DEDICATED TO PLEASURE *EMI CDEMTV 91* 18	3	wks
23 Sep 95	TECHNO NIGHTS AMBIENT DAWN *EMI CDEMTV 97* 16	3	wks
28 Oct 95	THAT'S ROCK 'N' ROLL *EMI CDEMTVD 100* 12	2	wks
4 Nov 95	THAT'S COUNTRY *EMI CDEMTVD 103* 11	6	wks
11 Nov 95	★ THE GREATEST PARTY ALBUM UNDER THE SUN *EMI TV CDEMTVD 107* 1	7	wks
16 Dec 95	THAT'S CHRISTMAS (Re-issue) *EMI TV CDEMTVD 105* 15	2	wks
29 Apr 95	● CLUB TOGETHER *EMI CDEMC 3704* 9	4	wks

EMI/Virgin/PolyGram

23 Feb 91	★ AWESOME! *EMI/Virgin/PolyGram EMTV 58*............1	12	wks
2 Nov 91	● AWESOME! 2 *EMI/Virgin/PolyGram EVP 1* 2	11	wks
25 Jan 92	★ THE ULTIMATE RAVE *EMI/Virgin/PolyGram CDEVP 2* 1	15	wks
30 Jan 93	● THE MEGA RAVE *EMI/Virgin/PolyGram CDEVP 3* 2	8	wks
13 Mar 93	● MEGA DANCE – THE POWER ZONE *EMI/Virgin/PolyGram CDEVP 4* 2	8	wks
10 Apr 93	● LOADED *EMI/Virgin/PolyGram CDEVP 5*............6	6	wks
17 Apr 93	● MEGA DANCE 2 – THE ENERGY ZONE *EMI/Virgin/PolyGram CDEVP 6* 3	6	wks

See also Now!

Epic

2 Jul 83	DANCE MIX – DANCE HITS VOLUME 1 *Epic EPC 25564*............85	2	wks
24 Sep 83	DANCE MIX – DANCE HITS VOLUME 2 *Epic DM 2* 51	3	wks
3 Mar 84	DANCE MIX – DANCE HITS VOLUME 3 *Epic DM 3*.......70	1	wk
3 Mar 84	ELECTRO SHOCK VOLTAGE *Epic VOLT 1* 73	1	wk
16 Jun 84	● AMERICAN HEARTBEAT *Epic EPC 10045*............4	22	wks
16 Jun 84	DANCE MIX – DANCE HITS VOLUME 4 *Epic DM 4*............99	1	wk
8 Mar 86	● HITS FOR LOVERS *Epic EPC 10050* 2	14	wks
9 Nov 91	MELLOW MADNESS *Epic MOOD 20* 14	2	wks
18 Jul 92	● RED HOT + DANCE *Epic 4718212* 6	5	wks
29 Aug 92	● ROMANCING THE SCREEN *Epic 4719012* 5	11	wks
4 Jun 94	● TOP GEAR *Epic MOODCD 33*............3	13	wks

Fantazia

5 Dec 92	FANTAZIA – THE FIRST TASTE *Fantazia FANTA 001* 13	5	wks

24 Jul 93	**FANTAZIA – TWICE AS NICE** *Fantazia FANTA 002CD* **17**	3 wks
25 Jun 94	**FANTAZI III – MADE IN HEAVEN** *Fantazia FANTA 005CD* **16**	2 wks
29 Apr 95	● **THE HOUSE COLLECTION VOLUME 2** *Fantazia FHC 002CD* **6**	6 wks
30 Sep 95	● **THE HOUSE COLLECTION VOLUME 3** *Fantazia FHC 3CDL* **4**	7 wks

ffrr

30 Jan 88	**THE HOUSE SOUND OF CHICAGO VOLUME 3** *ffrr FFRLP 1* **40**	4 wks
27 Aug 88	**THE HOUSE SOUND OF LONDON VOLUME 4** *ffrr FFRDP 4* **70**	7 wks
1 Oct 88	**BALEARIC BEATS VOLUME 1** *ffrr FFRLP 5* **58**	2 wks

Global Television

17 Dec 94	**SOUNDS OF THE SEVENTIES** *Global Television RADCD 01* **11**	5 wks
17 Dec 94	**HITS HITS AND MORE DANCE HITS** *Global Television RADCD 02* **13**	4 wks
21 Jan 95	● **SOFT REGGAE** *Global Television RADCD 04* **2**	7 wks
18 Feb 95	● **NEW SOUL REBELS** *Global Television RADCD 05* **6**	6 wks
25 Feb 95	★ **ON A DANCE TIP** *Global Television RADCD 07* **1**	9 wks
4 Mar 95	● **GIRLS AND GUITARS** *Global Television RADCD 06* **8**	4 wks
15 Apr 95	**FIFTY NUMBER ONES OF THE 60S** *Global Television RADCD 08* **8**	4 wks
22 Apr 95	● **CLUB CLASS** *Global Television RADCD 10* **4**	5 wks
22 Apr 95	● **INTO THE EIGHTIES** *Global Television RADCD 09* **5**	5 wks
20 May 95	★ **ON A DANCE TIP 2** *Global Television RADCD 12* **1**	7 wks
17 Jun 95	● **DANCE BUZZ** *Global Television RADCD 17* **3**	4 wks
1 Jul 95	● **CHARTBUSTERS** *Global Television RADCD 15* **2**	6 wks
1 Jul 95	**GREAT SEX** *Global Television RADCD 16* **13**	2 wks
15 Jul 95	**THEMES AND DREAMS** *Global Television RADCD 11* **11**	2 wks
29 Jul 95	● **NATURAL WOMAN** *Global Television RADCD 14* **7**	8 wks
12 Aug 95	● **SUMMER DANCE PARTY** *Global Television RADCD 18* **2**	5 wks
26 Aug 95	● **HITZ BLITZ** *Global Television RADCD 23* **2**	5 wks
23 Sep 95	● **DANCE TIP 3** *Global Television RADCD 20* **2**	6 wks
30 Sep 95	● **DRIVING ROCK** *Global Television RADCD 03* **9**	5 wks
28 Oct 95	● **NIGHTFEVER** *Global Television RADCD 24* **7**	3 wks
18 Nov 95	● **DANCE TIP 95** *Global Television RADCD 27* **3**	7 wks

348

Heart & Soul

28 Mar 87	**HEART OF SOUL VOLUME 1** *Mastersound HASL 001* **96**	1 wk
19 Aug 89	● **HEART AND SOUL** *Heart & Soul HASTV 1* **2**	12 wks
17 Feb 90	● **BODY AND SOUL – HEART AND SOUL II** *Heart & Soul 8407761*....**2**	14 wks
4 Aug 90	● **HEART AND SOUL III – HEART FULL OF SOUL**	
	Heart & Soul 8450091 ....**4**	9 wks
16 Feb 91	● **SOUL REFLECTION** *Heart & Soul 8453341* **2**	12 wks

The Hit Label

27 Jun 92	● **Q THE BLUES** *The Hit Label AHLCD 1* **6**	5 wks
28 Nov 92	**BIG! DANCE HITS OF 92** *The Hit Label AHLCD 4* **11**	7 wks
5 Dec 92	**REMEMBER WHEN SINGERS COULD REALLY SING**	
	The Hit Label AHLCD 3 ....**16**	2 wks
10 Apr 93	**Q RHYTHM AND BLUES** *The Hit Label AHLCD 7* **14**	4 wks
8 May 93	● **THE LEGENDARY JOE BLOGGS DANCE ALBUM**	
	The Hit Label AHLCD 10 ....**3**	8 wks
31 Jul 93	**GET IT ON – GREATEST HITS OF THE 70S**	
	The Hit Label AHLCD 12 ....**12**	5 wks
30 Oct 93	**THE LEGENDARY JOE BLOGGS DANCE ALBUM 2**	
	The Hit Label AHLCD 13 ....**15**	2 wks
13 Nov 93	**IT MUST BE LOVE** *The Hit Label AHLCD 17* **11**	4 wks
5 Mar 94	● **THE BOYZ WHO SOULED THE WORLD** *The Hit Label AHLCD 18*....**8**	4 wks
21 May 94	**Q COUNTRY** *The Hit Label AHLCD 16* **20**	1 wk
18 Jun 94	**KERRANG! THE ALBUM** *The Hit Label AHLCD 21* **12**	5 wks
27 Aug 94	**THE ULTIMATE GOLD COLLECTION** *The Hit Label AHLCD 22*........**12**	4 wks
4 Feb 95	**ULTIMATE LOVE** *The Hit Label AHLCD 24* **13**	4 wks
18 Feb 95	**FEEL LIKE MAKING LOVE** *The Hit Label AHLCD 25* **17**	2 wks
8 Jul 95	**REGGAE GROOVE** *The Hit Label ULTCD 020* **12**	1 wk

Hits

1 Dec 84	★ **THE HITS ALBUM** *CBS/WEA HITS 1* **1**	36 wks
13 Apr 85	★ **HITS 2** *CBS/WEA HITS 2* **1**	21 wks
7 Dec 85	● **HITS 3** *CBS/WEA HITS 3* **2**	21 wks

VARIOUS ARTISTS

29 Mar 86	★ **HITS 4** *CBS/WEA/RCA/Arista HITS 4*	1	21 wks
22 Nov 86	★ **HITS 5** *CBS/WEA/RCA/Arista HITS 5*	1	25 wks
25 Jul 87	★ **HITS 6** *CBS/WEA/BMG HITS 6*	1	19 wks
5 Dec 87	● **HITS 7** *CBS/WEA/BMG HITS 7*	2	17 wks
30 Jul 88	● **HITS 8** *CBS/WEA/BMG HITS 8*	2	13 wks
17 Dec 88	● **THE HITS ALBUM** *CBS/WEA/BMG HITS 9*	5	4 wks
14 Jan 89	● **THE HITS ALBUM** *CBS/WEA/BMG HITS 9*	4	7 wks
3 Jun 89	★ **HITS 10** *CBS/WEA/BMG HITS 10*	1	13 wks
2 Dec 89	● **MONSTER HITS** *CBS/WEA/BMG HITS 11*	2	14 wks
11 Aug 90	● **SNAP IT UP – MONSTER HITS 2** *CBS/WEA/BMG HITS 12*	2	10 wks
29 Dec 90	● **THE HIT PACK** *CBS/WEA/BMG COMPC 1*	2	8 wks
10 Aug 91	★ **THE HITS ALBUM** *CBS/WEA/BMG HITS 15*	1	9 wks
19 Mar 94	● **HITS 94 VOLUME 1** *Telstar/BMG CDHITS 941*	3	7 wks
15 Oct 94	**THE ULTIMATE HITS ALBUM** *Telstar?BMG CDHITS 942*	11	2 wks
20 Feb 93	★ **HITS 93 VOLUME 1** *Telstar TCD 2641*	1	15 wks
29 May 93	● **HITS 93 VOLUME 2** *Telstar TCD 2661*	2	8 wks
14 Aug 93	● **HITS 93 VOLUME 3** *Telstar TCD 2681*	2	9 wks
20 Nov 93	● **HITS 93 VOLUME 4** *Telstar CDHITS 934*	2	9 wks
23 Dec 95	● **HITS 96** *Global Television RADCD 30*	3†	2 wks

Impression

16 Oct 82	**BEST FRIENDS** *Impression LP IMP 1*	28	21 wks
3 Sep 83	**SUNNY AFTERNOON** *Impression LP IMP 2*	13	8 wks
26 Nov 83	**PRECIOUS MOMENTS** *Impression LP IMP 3*	77	5 wks
7 Apr 84	**ALWAYS AND FOREVER – THE COLLECTION** *Impression LP IMP 4*	24	12 wks
21 Jul 84	**WIPEOUT – 20 INSTRUMENTAL GREATS** *Impression LP IMP 5*	37	3 wks
28 Jul 84	**SUNNY AFTERNOON VOLUME TWO** *Impression LP IMP 7*	90	1 wk
22 Dec 84	**FRIENDS AGAIN** *Impression LP IMP 8*	91	1 wk

Island

26 Aug 67	**CLUB SKA '67** *Island ILP 956*	37	19 wks
14 Jun 69	**YOU CAN ALL JOIN IN** *Island IWPS 2*	18	10 wks
29 Mar 80	**CLUB SKA '67 (re–issue)** *Island IRSP 4*	53	6 wks
16 Jun 84	**CREW CUTS** *Island IMA 11*	71	4 wks
27 Oct 84	**CREW CUTS – LESSON 2** *Island IMA 14*	95	2 wks
18 Jul 87	● **THE ISLAND STORY** *Island ISL 25*	9	10 wks
3 Nov 90	● **HAPPY DAZE VOLUME 1** *Island ILPTV 1*	7	4 wks
6 Apr 91	● **HAPPY DAZE VOLUME 2** *Island ILPTV 3*	17	2 wks
30 Oct 93	● **REGGAE 93** *Island CIDTV 7*	5	6 wks
27 Aug 94	● **PURE REGGAE VOLUME 1** *Island CIDTV 8*	10	5 wks

Jack Trax

18 Jul 87	**JACK TRAX – THE FIRST ALBUM** *Jack Trax JTRAX 1*	83	2 wks
3 Oct 87	**JACK TRAX – THE SECOND ALBUM** *Jack Trax JTRAX 2*	61	2 wks
5 Mar 88	**JACK TRAX – THE FOURTH ALBUM** *Jack Trax JTRAX 4*	49	4 wks

Jetstar

30 Mar 85	**REGGAE HITS VOLUME 1** *Jetstar JETLP 1001*	32	11 wks
26 Oct 85	**REGGAE HITS VOLUME 2** *Jetstar JETLP 1002*	86	2 wks
4 Jun 88	**REGGAE HITS VOLUME 4** *Jetstar JETLP 1004*	56	7 wks
17 Dec 88	**REGGAE HITS VOLUME 5** *Jetstar JETLP 1005*	96	1 wk
5 Aug 89	**REGGAE HITS VOLUME 6** *Jetstar JETLP 1006*	13	6 wks
23 Dec 89	**REGGAE HITS VOLUME 7** *Jetstar JETLP 1007*	13	6 wks
30 Jun 90	● **REGGAE HITS VOLUME 8** *Jetstar JETLP 1008*	7	5 wks
20 Jul 91	● **REGGAE HITS VOLUME 10** *Jetstar JETLP 1010*	6	7 wks
18 Apr 92	● **REGGAE HITS VOLUME 12** *Jetstar JECD 1012*	5	6 wks
28 Aug 93	**REGGAE HITS VOLUME 14** *Jetstar JECD 1014*	13	1 wk
3 Sep 94	● **JUNGLE HITS VOLUME 1** *Jetstar STRCD 1*	9	8 wks

K-Tel

10 Jun 72	★ **20 DYNAMIC HITS** *K-Tel TE 292*	1	28 wks
7 Oct 72	★ **20 ALL TIME HITS OF THE 50'S** *K-Tel NE 490*	1	22 wks

29 Nov 72 ● **25 DYNAMIC HITS VOLUME 2** *K-Tel TE 291* 2	12	wks
2 Dec 72 ★ **25 ROCKIN' & ROLLIN' GREATS** *K-Tel NE 493* 1	18	wks
31 Mar 73 ★ **20 FLASHBACK GREATS OF THE SIXTIES** *K-Tel NE 494* 1	11	wks
21 Apr 73 ● **BELIEVE IN MUSIC** *K-Tel TE 294*.................2	8	wks
8 Nov 75 **GOOFY GREATS** *K-Tel NE 707*..............19	7	wks
13 Dec 75 ● **40 SUPER GREATS** *K-Tel NE 708*............9	8	wks
31 Jan 76 ● **MUSIC EXPRESS** *K-Tel TE 702*...............3	10	wks
10 Apr 76 ● **JUKE BOX JIVE** *K-Tel NE 709*...............3	13	wks
17 Apr 76 **GREAT ITALIAN LOVE SONGS** *K-Tel NE 303*............17	14	wks
15 May 76 ● **HIT MACHINE** *K-Tel TE 713* 4	10	wks
5 Jun 76 **EUROVISION FAVOURITES** *K-Tel NE 712*...........44	1	wk
2 Oct 76 **SUMMER CRUISING** *K-Tel NE 918*...........30	1	wk
16 Oct 76 ● **COUNTRY COMFORT** *K-Tel NE 294*...........8	12	wks
16 Oct 76 ★ **SOUL MOTION** *K-Tel NE 930* 1	14	wks
4 Dec 76 ● **DISCO ROCKET** *K-Tel NE 948*...............3	14	wks
11 Dec 76 **44 SUPERSTARS** *K-Tel NE 939* 14	10	wks
12 Feb 77 ● **HEARTBREAKERS** *K-Tel NE 954* 2	18	wks
19 Feb 77 ● **DANCE TO THE MUSIC** *K-Tel NE 957*............5	9	wks
7 May 77 **HIT ACTION** *K-Tel NE 993* 15	9	wks
29 Oct 77 **SOUL CITY** *K-Tel NE 1003* 12	7	wks
12 Nov 77 ● **FEELINGS** *K-Tel NE 1006* 3	24	wks
26 Nov 77 ★ **DISCO FEVER** *K-Tel NE 1014* 1	20	wks
21 Jan 78 **40 NUMBER ONE HITS** *K-Tel NE 1008* 15	7	wks
4 Mar 78 ● **DISCO STARS** *K-Tel NE 1022* 6	8	wks
10 Jun 78 ● **DISCO DOUBLE** *K-Tel NE 1024* 10	6	wks
8 Jul 78 **ROCK RULES** *K-Tel RL 001* 12	11	wks
8 Jul 78 **THE WORLD'S WORST RECORD SHOW** *Yuk/K-Tel NE 1023* 47	2	wks
19 Aug 78 ● **STAR PARTY** *K-Tel NE 1034* 4	9	wks
4 Nov 78 ● **EMOTIONS** *K-Tel NE 1035* 2	17	wks
25 Nov 78 ● **MIDNIGHT HUSTLE** *K-Tel NE 1037* 2	13	wks
20 Jan 79 ★ **ACTION REPLAY** *K-Tel NE 1040* 1	14	wks
7 Apr 79 **DISCO INFERNO** *K-Tel NE 1043* 11	9	wks
5 May 79 **HI ENERGY** *K-Tel NE 1044* 17	7	wks
22 Sep 79 **HOT TRACKS** *K-Tel NE 1049* 31	8	wks
24 Nov 79 ● **NIGHT MOVES** *K-Tel NE 1065* 10	10	wks
24 Nov 79 **TOGETHER** *K-Tel NE 1053* 35	8	wks
12 Jan 80 ● **VIDEO STARS** *K-Tel NE 1066* 5	10	wks
26 Jan 80 **THE SUMMIT** *K-Tel NE 1067* 17	5	wks
29 Mar 80 ● **STAR TRACKS** *K-Tel NE 1070* 6	8	wks
26 Apr 80 **GOOD MORNING AMERICA** *K-Tel NE 1072* 15	12	wks
17 May 80 **HAPPY DAYS** *K-Tel ONE 1076*..............32	6	wks
17 May 80 ● **MAGIC REGGAE** *K-Tel NE 1074* 9	17	wks
14 Jun 80 ● **HOT WAX** *K-Tel NE 1082* 3	10	wks
27 Sep 80 ● **MOUNTING EXCITEMENT** *K-Tel NE 1091* 2	8	wks
11 Oct 80 ● **THE LOVE ALBUM** *K-Tel NE 1062* 6	16	wks
25 Oct 80 **AXE ATTACK** *K-Tel NE 1100* 15	14	wks
15 Nov 80 ● **CHART EXPLOSION** *K-Tel NE 1103* 6	17	wks
27 Dec 80 **NIGHTLIFE** *K-Tel NE 1107* 25	10	wks
14 Feb 81 **HIT MACHINE** *K-Tel NE 1113* 17	6	wks
21 Mar 81 **RHYTHM 'N' REGGAE** *K-Tel NE 1115* 42	4	wks
25 Apr 81 ● **CHARTBUSTERS 81** *K-Tel NE 1118* 3	9	wks
2 May 81 **AXE ATTACK 2** *K-Tel NE 1120*...............31	6	wks
23 May 81 ● **THEMES** *K-Tel NE 1122* 6	15	wks
29 Aug 81 **CALIFORNIA DREAMING** *K-Tel NE 1126* 27	11	wks
19 Sep 81 **DANCE DANCE DANCE** *K-Tel NE 1143* 29	5	wks
3 Oct 81 **THE PLATINUM ALBUM** *K-Tel NE 1134* 32	11	wks
10 Oct 81 ● **LOVE IS . . .** *K-Tel NE 1129* 10	15	wks
21 Nov 81 ★ **CHART HITS 81** *K-Tel NE 1142* 1	17	wks
9 Jan 82 ● **MODERN DANCE** *K-Tel NE 1156* 6	10	wks
6 Feb 82 ● **DREAMING** *K-Tel NE 1159*................2	12	wks
6 Mar 82 ● **ACTION TRAX** *K-Tel NE 1162* 2	12	wks
1 May 82 **MIDNIGHT HOUR** *K-Tel NE 1157* 98	1	wk
3 Jul 82 **TURBO TRAX** *K-Tel NE 1176* 17	7	wks
4 Sep 82 **THE NO 1 SOUNDS OF THE SEVENTIES** *K-Tel NE 1172*.............83	1	wk
11 Sep 82 ● **CHARTBEAT / CHARTHEAT** *K-Tel NE 1180* 2	14	wks
30 Oct 82 **THE LOVE SONGS ALBUM** *K-Tel NE 1179*...........28	8	wks
6 Nov 82 **CHART HITS '82** *K-Tel NE 1195*...............11	17	wks
6 Nov 82 **DISCO DANCER** *K-Tel NE 1190*...............26	8	wks
18 Dec 82 **STREETSCENE** *K-Tel NE 1183* 42	6	wks
15 Jan 83 ● **VISIONS** *K-Tel ONE 1199* 5	21	wks

VARIOUS ARTISTS

12 Feb 83	HEAVY *K-Tel NE 1203*	46	12 wks
5 Mar 83 ●	HOTLINE *K-Tel NE 1207*	3	9 wks
11 Jun 83 ●	CHART STARS *K-Tel NE 1225*	7	9 wks
20 Aug 83	COOL HEAT *K-Tel NE 1231*	79	3 wks
10 Sep 83 ●	HEADLINE HITS *K-Tel NE 1253*	5	6 wks
8 Oct 83 ●	THE TWO OF US *K-Tel NE 1222*	3	16 wks
8 Oct 83	IMAGES *K-Tel ONE 1254*	33	6 wks
12 Nov 83 ●	CHART HITS '83 VOLUMES 1 AND 2 *K-Tel NE 1256*	6	11 wks
24 Mar 84	NIGHT MOVES *K-Tel NE 1255*	15	11 wks
26 May 84 ●	HUNGRY FOR HITS *K-Tel NE 1272*	4	11 wks
23 Jun 84	THE THEMES ALBUM *K-Tel ONE 1257*	43	3 wks
28 Jul 84	BREAKDANCE, YOU CAN DO IT *K-Tel ONE 1276*	18	12 wks
12 Sep 84 ●	ALL BY MYSELF *K-Tel NE 1273*	7	16 wks
1 Dec 84	HOOKED ON NUMBER ONES – 100 NON–STOP HITS *K-Tel ONE 1285*	25	15 wks
2 Feb 85	FOUR STAR COUNTRY *K-Tel NE 1278*	52	6 wks
2 Mar 85	MODERN LOVE *K-Tel NE 1286*	13	7 wks
5 Oct 85	EXPRESSIONS *K-Tel NE 1307*	11	8 wks
9 Nov 85 ●	ROCK ANTHEMS *K-Tel NE 1309*	10	11 wks
9 Nov 85	OVATION – THE BEST OF ANDREW LLOYD WEBBER *K-Tel ONE 1311*	34	12 wks
22 Mar 86	MASTERS OF METAL *K-Tel NE 1295*	38	4 wks
12 Apr 86 ●	HEART TO HEART *K-Tel NE 1318*	8	15 wks
19 Apr 86	ROCK ANTHEMS VOLUME TWO *K-Tel NE 1319*	43	9 wks
5 Jul 86	RAP IT UP – RAP'S GREATEST HITS *K-Tel NE 1324*	50	4 wks
19 Jul 86	DRIVE TIME USA *K-Tel NE 1321*	20	8 wks
18 Oct 86	DANCE HITS '86 *K-Tel NE 1344*	35	7 wks
1 Nov 86	TOGETHER *K-Tel NE 1345*	20	10 wks
7 Feb 87	IMPRESSIONS *K-Tel NE 1346*	15	14 wks
21 Mar 87	RHYTHM OF THE NIGHT *K-Tel NE 1348*	36	7 wks
21 Mar 87	HITS REVIVAL *K-Tel (Holland) KTLP 2351*	63	1 wk
13 Jun 87 ●	FRIENDS AND LOVERS *K-Tel NE 1352*	10	10 wks
27 Jun 87 ●	HITS REVIVAL *K-Tel NE 1363*	10	9 wks
17 Oct 87	TRUE LOVE *K-Tel NE 1359*	38	5 wks
31 Oct 87 ●	FROM MOTOWN WITH LOVE *K-Tel NE 1381*	9	21 wks
14 Nov 87	ALWAYS *K-Tel NE 1377*	65	4 wks
19 Dec 87	WOW WHAT A PARTY *K-Tel NE 1388*	97	2 wks
5 Mar 88	HORIZONS *K-Tel NE 1360*	13	10 wks
30 Apr 88	HITS REVIVAL 2: REPLAY *K-Tel NE 1405*	45	3 wks
14 May 88	TSOP – THE SOUND OF PHILADELPHIA *K-Tel NE 1406*	26	9 wks
11 Jun 88	THE HITS OF HOUSE ARE HERE *K-Tel NE 1419*	12	12 wks
15 Oct 88	MOTOWN IN MOTION *K-Tel NE 1410*	28	13 wks
15 Oct 88	THE RETURN OF SUPERBAD *K-Tel NE 1421*	83	4 wks
5 Nov 88	THE LOVERS *K-Tel NE 1426*	50	5 wks
26 Nov 88	RAPPIN' UP THE HOUSE *K-Tel NE 1428*	43	7 wks
14 Jan 89	RAPPIN' UP THE HOUSE *K-Tel NE 1428*	19	1 wk
4 Feb 89 ●	FROM MOTOWN WITH LOVE *K-Tel NE 1381*	6	7 wks
25 Mar 89 ●	HIP HOUSE – THE DEEPEST BEATS IN TOWN *K-Tel NE 1430*	10	5 wks
29 Jul 89 ●	GLAM SLAM *K-Tel NE 1434*	5	8 wks
23 Sep 89 ●	LOVE HOUSE *K-Tel NE 1446*	5	7 wks
30 Sep 89 ●	ETERNAL LOVE *K-Tel NE 1447*	5	7 wks
21 Oct 89 ●	RAP ATTACK *K-Tel NE 1450*	6	7 wks
25 Nov 89	SEDUCTION *K-Tel NE 1451*	15	4 wks
10 Mar 90	CAN U FEEL IT? – THE CHAMPION LEGEND *K-Tel ONE 1452*	12	3 wks
21 Apr 90 ●	HOOKED ON COUNTRY *K-Tel NE 1459*	6	12 wks

London

10 Jun 89 ●	FFRR – SILVER ON BLACK *London 8281551*	8	5 wks
11 Nov 89 ●	DANCE DECADE – DANCE HITS OF THE 80'S *London DDTV 1*	8	7 wks
16 Jun 90 ●	THE NORTHERN BEAT *London 8409681*	4	8 wks
7 Jul 90	MASSIVE 4 *London 8282101*	20	2 wks
8 Feb 92 ●	ONLY FOR THE HEADSTRONG *London 8283032*	10	1 wk
20 Jun 92	ONLY FOR THE HEADSTRONG II *London 8283162*	18	1 wk

Mastercuts

| 28 Sep 91 | CLASSIC MELLOW MASTERCUTS *Mastercuts CUTSLP 3* | 18 | 2 wks |
| 21 Mar 92 ● | CLASSIC NEW JACK SWING MASTERCUTS VOLUME 1 *Mastercuts CUTSCD 5* | 8 | 5 wks |

16 May 92	**CLASSIC FUNK MASTERCUTS VOLUME 1** *Mastercuts CUTSCD 6* **14**	3 wks
4 Jul 92	**CLASSIC JAZZ FUNK MASTERCUTS VOLUME 3**	
	Mastercuts CUTSCD 7 ....**18**	1 wk
15 Aug 92	**CLASSIC MELLOW MASTERCUTS VOLUME 2**	
	Mastercuts CUTSCD 8 ....**12**	3 wks
6 Mar 93	**CLASSIC SALSOUL MASTERCUTS VOLUME 1**	
	Mastercuts CUTSCD 10 ....**16**	3 wks
24 Apr 93	**CLASSIC RARE GROOVE MASTERCUTS VOLUME 1**	
	Mastercuts CUTSCD 11 ....**14**	3 wks
22 May 93	**CLASSIC P–FUNK MASTERCUTS VOLUME 1**	
	Mastercuts CUTSCD 12 ....**16**	1 wk
22 Jan 94	**CLASSIC JAZZ FUNK MASTERCUTS VOLUME 4**	
	Mastercuts CUTSCD 16 ....**19**	2 wks
26 Mar 94	**NEW JACK SWING VOLUME 3** *Mastercuts CUTSCD 18* **18**	1 wk
14 May 94	**CLASSIC ELECTRO MASTERCUTS VOLUME 1**	
	Mastercuts CUTSCD 19 ....**18**	1 wk
18 Jun 94	**CLASSIC HOUSE MASTERCUTS VOLUME 1**	
	Mastercuts CUTSCD 20 ....**11**	2 wks

Mercury

26 Nov 83	● **FORMULA 30** *Mercury PROLP 4* **6**	17 wks
14 Jun 86	**BEAT RUNS WILD** *Mercury WILD 1* **70**	2 wks
1 Nov 86	**FORMULA 30 2** *Mercury PROLP 9* **80**	3 wks

| 26 Oct 91 | ★ **TWO ROOMS — ELTON JOHN AND BERNIE TAUPIN** | |
| | *Mercury 8457491* ....**1** | 21 wks |

Ministry Of Sound

11 Sep 93	**MINISTRY OF SOUND – THE SESSIONS VOLUME 1**	
	Ministry Of Sound MINSTCD 1 ....**16**	2 wks
30 Apr 94	● **MINISTRY OF SOUND – THE SESSIONS VOLUME 2**	
	Ministry Of Sound MINSTCD 002 ....**6**	5 wks
22 Oct 94	● **MINISTRY OF SOUND – THE SESSIONS VOLUME 3**	
	Ministry Of Sound MINSTCD 003 ....**8**	3 wks
1 Apr 95	**THE FUTURE SOUND OF NEW YORK** *Sound Of Ministry SOMCD 1* **19**	1 wk
6 May 95	● **MINISTRY OF SOUND – THE SESSIONS VOLUME 4**	
	Ministry Of Sound MINCDB 4 ....**9**	5 wks
30 Sep 95	**MINISTRY OF SOUND – SESSIONS VOLUME 5**	
	Ministry Of Sound MINCD 5 ....**15**	5 wks
25 Nov 95	**THE ANNUAL** *Ministry Of Sound ANNCD 95* **16**	2 wks

Needle

4 Jul 87	**DANCE MANIA VOLUME 1** *Needle DAMA 1* **46**	4 wks
20 Feb 88	**MAD ON HOUSE VOLUME 1** *Needle MADD 1* **81**	2 wks
14 May 88	**HOUSE HITS** *Needle HOHI 88* **25**	8 wks

Nouveau Music

24 Sep 83	**CLASSIC THEMES** *Nouveau Music NML 1001* **61**	2 wks
2 Jun 84	**ESSENTIAL DISCO AND DANCE** *Nouveau Music NML 1010* **96**	1 wk
30 Mar 85	**DREAM MELODIES** *Nouveau Music NML 1013* **91**	1 wk

Now!

10 Dec 83	★ **NOW THAT'S WHAT I CALL MUSIC** *EMI/Virgin NOW 1* **1**	50 wks
7 Apr 84	★ **NOW THAT'S WHAT I CALL MUSIC 2** *EMI/Virgin NOW 2* **1**	38 wks
11 Aug 84	★ **NOW THAT'S WHAT I CALL MUSIC 3** *EMI/Virgin NOW 3* **1**	30 wks
8 Dec 84	● **NOW THAT'S WHAT I CALL MUSIC 4** *EMI/Virgin NOW 4* **2**	43 wks
1 Jun 85	● **NOW DANCE** *EMI/Virgin NOD 1* **3**	14 wks
17 Aug 85	★ **NOW THAT'S WHAT I CALL MUSIC 5** *EMI/Virgin NOW 5* **1**	21 wks
30 Nov 85	★ **NOW – THE CHRISTMAS ALBUM** *EMI/Virgin NOX 1* **1**	22 wks
7 Dec 85	★ **NOW THAT'S WHAT I CALL MUSIC 6** *EMI/Virgin NOW 6* **1**	40 wks
19 Jul 86	● **NOW – THE SUMMER ALBUM** *EMI/Virgin SUMMER 1* **7**	9 wks
23 Aug 86	★ **NOW THAT'S WHAT I CALL MUSIC 7** *EMI/Virgin NOW 7* **1**	21 wks
8 Nov 86	● **NOW DANCE '86** *EMI/Virgin NOD 2* **2**	13 wks
29 Nov 86	**NOW THAT'S WHAT I CALL MUSIC '86**	
	EMI/Virgin/PolyGram CDNOW 86 ....**65**	4 wks
6 Dec 86	★ **NOW THAT'S WHAT I CALL MUSIC 8**	
	EMI/Virgin/PolyGram NOW 8 ....**1**	23 wks

VARIOUS ARTISTS

Date	Title	Pos	Weeks
4 Apr 87	★ **NOW THAT'S WHAT I CALL MUSIC 9**		
	EMI/Virgin/PolyGram NOW 9 .... **1**		26 wks
3 Oct 87	● **NOW! SMASH HITS** *EMI/Virgin/PolyGram NOSH 1* **5**		10 wks
5 Dec 87	★ **NOW THAT'S WHAT I CALL MUSIC 10**		
	EMI/Virgin/PolyGram NOW 10 .... **1**		21 wks
2 Apr 88	★ **NOW THAT'S WHAT I CALL MUSIC 11**		
	EMI/Virgin/PolyGram NOW 11 .... **1**		17 wks
23 Jul 88	★ **NOW THAT'S WHAT I CALL MUSIC 12**		
	EMI/Virgin/PolyGram NOW 12 .... **1**		17 wks
3 Dec 88	★ **NOW THAT'S WHAT I CALL MUSIC 13**		
	EMI/Virgin/PolyGram NOW 13 .... **1**		6 wks
14 Jan 89	★ **NOW THAT'S WHAT I CALL MUSIC 13**		
	EMI/Virgin/PolyGram NOW 13 .... **1**		15 wks
1 Apr 89	★ **NOW THAT'S WHAT I CALL MUSIC 14**		
	EMI/Virgin/PolyGram NOW 14 .... **1**		18 wks
15 Jul 89	★ **NOW DANCE '89** *EMI/Virgin NOD 3* **1**		14 wks
26 Aug 89	★ **NOW THAT'S WHAT I CALL MUSIC 15**		
	EMI/Virgin/PolyGram NOW 15 .... **1**		13 wks
2 Dec 89	★ **NOW THAT'S WHAT I CALL MUSIC 16**		
	EMI/Virgin/PolyGram NOW 16 .... **1**		15 wks
10 Mar 90	★ **NOW DANCE 901** *EMI/Virgin/PolyGram NOD 4* **1**		14 wks
5 May 90	★ **NOW THAT'S WHAT I CALL MUSIC 17**		
	EMI/Virgin/PolyGram NOW 17 .... **1**		15 wks
28 Jul 90	★ **NOW DANCE 902** *EMI/Virgin/PolyGram NOD 5* **1**		13 wks
10 Nov 90	★ **NOW DANCE 903** *EMI/Virgin/PolyGram NOD 6* **1**		9 wks
1 Dec 90	★ **NOW THAT'S WHAT I CALL MUSIC 18**		
	EMI/Virgin/PolyGram NOW 18 .... **1**		18 wks
6 Apr 91	★ **NOW THAT'S WHAT I CALL MUSIC 19**		
	EMI/Virgin/PolyGram NOW 19 .... **1**		16 wks
5 Oct 91	★ **NOW DANCE 91** *EMI/Virgin/PolyGram NOD 7* **1**		9 wks
30 Nov 91	★ **NOW THAT'S WHAT I CALL MUSIC 20**		
	EMI/Virgin/PolyGram NOW 20 .... **1**		18 wks
25 Apr 92	★ **NOW THAT'S WHAT I CALL MUSIC 21**		
	EMI/Virgin/PolyGram CDNOW 21 .... **1**		13 wks
8 Aug 92	★ **NOW THAT'S WHAT I CALL MUSIC 22**		
	EMI/Virgin/PolyGram CDNOW 22 .... **1**		14 wks
14 Nov 92	● **NOW DANCE 92** *EMI/Virgin/PolyGram TCNOD 8* **3**		11 wks
28 Nov 92	★ **NOW THAT'S WHAT I CALL MUSIC 23**		
	EMI/Virgin/PolyGram CDNOW 23 .... **1**		18 wks
8 May 93	★ **NOW THAT'S WHAT I CALL MUSIC 24**		
	EMI/Virgin/PolyGram CDNOW 24 .... **1**		13 wks
26 Jun 93	★ **NOW DANCE 93** *EMI/Virgin/PolyGram CDNOD 9* **1**		9 wks
14 Aug 93	★ **NOW THAT'S WHAT I CALL MUSIC 25**		
	EMI/Virgin/PolyGram CDNOW 25 .... **1**		10 wks
4 Sep 93	● **NOW THAT'S WHAT I CALL MUSIC 1983**		
	EMI/Virgin/PolyGram CDNOW 1983 .... **10**		5 wks
4 Sep 93	**NOW THAT'S WHAT I CALL MUSIC 1984**		
	EMI/Virgin/PolyGram CDNOW 1984 .... **13**		4 wks
4 Sep 93	**NOW THAT'S WHAT I CALL MUSIC 1985**		
	EMI/Virgin/PolyGram CDNOW 1985 .... **15**		4 wks
4 Sep 93	**NOW THAT'S WHAT I CALL MUSIC 1986**		
	EMI/Virgin/PolyGram CDNOW 1986 .... **16**		2 wks
4 Sep 93	**NOW THAT'S WHAT I CALL MUSIC 1987**		
	EMI/Virgin/PolyGram CDNOW 1987 .... **17**		2 wks
25 Sep 93	**NOW THAT'S WHAT I CALL MUSIC 1988**		
	EMI/Virgin/PolyGram CDNOW 1988 .... **20**		1 wk
25 Sep 93	**NOW THAT'S WHAT I CALL MUSIC 1992**		
	EMI/Virgin/PolyGram CDNOW 1992 .... **14**		2 wks
9 Oct 93	★ **NOW THAT'S WHAT I CALL MUSIC 1993**		
	EMI/Virgin/PolyGram CDNOW 1993 .... **1**		8 wks
30 Oct 93	★ **NOW DANCE – THE BEST OF '93** *EMI/Virgin/PolyGram CDNOD 10* **1**		6 wks
27 Nov 93	★ **NOW THAT'S WHAT I CALL MUSIC 26**		
	EMI/Virgin/PolyGram CDNOW 26 .... **1**		15 wks
29 Jan 94	★ **NOW DANCE 94 VOLUME 1** *EMI/Virgin/PolyGram CDNOD 11* **1**		7 wks
19 Mar 94	● **NOW THAT'S WHAT I CALL LOVE** *EMI/Virgin/PolyGram CDEVP 7* .. **6**		6 wks
19 Mar 94	● **NOW DANCE 94 VOLUME 2** *EMI/Virgin/PolyGram CDNOD 12* **8**		5 wks
9 Apr 94	★ **NOW THAT'S WHAT I CALL MUSIC 27**		
	EMI/Virgin/PolyGram CDNOW 27 .... **1**		15 wks
2 Jul 94	★ **NOW DANCE – SUMMER 94** *EMI/Virgin CDNOD 13* **1**		8 wks

13 Aug 94 ★ **NOW THAT'S WHAT I CALL MUSIC 28**
EMI/Virgin/PolyGram CDNOW 28.................................**1**   13   wks

15 Oct 94 ★ **NOW THAT'S WHAT I CALL MUSIC 1994**
EMI/Virgin/PolyGram CDNOW 1994.................................**1**   8   wks

26 Nov 94 ★ **NOW THAT'S WHAT I CALL MUSIC 29**
EMI/Virgin/PolyGram CDNOW 29.................................**1**   13   wks

10 Dec 94 ● **NOW DANCE – THE BEST OF 94** *EMI/Virgin CDNOD 14* ....**4**   9   wks

1 Apr 95 ● **NOW DANCE 95** *EMI/Virgin CDNOD 15*...................**3**   6   wks

22 Apr 95 ★ **NOW THAT'S WHAT I CALL MUSIC 30**
EMI/Virgin/PolyGram CDNOW 30.................................**1**   12   wks

29 Jul 95 ● **NOW DANCE – SUMMER 95** *EMI/Virgin/PolyGram CDNOD 16*........**3**   5   wks

12 Aug 95 ★ **NOW THAT'S WHAT I CALL MUSIC 31**
EMI/Virgin/PolyGram CDNOW 31.................................**1**   12   wks

14 Oct 95 ● **NOW THAT'S WHAT I CALL MUSIC 1995**
EMI/Virgin/PolyGram CDNOW 1995.................................**2**   6   wks

25 Nov 95 ★ **NOW THAT'S WHAT I CALL MUSIC 32**
EMI/Virgin/PolyGram CDNOW 32.................................**1**   6   wks

See also EMI / Virgin / PolyGram.

Parlophone

22 Jun 91 ● **IT'S COOL** *Parlophone PCSTV 1*.................................**3**   7   wks

4 Jul 92 ● **DANCE ENERGY – FEEL THE RHYTHM** *Parlophone CDPMTV 4* ......**6**   4   wks

3 Sep 94 ● **60S SOUL 90S SOUL** *Parlophone CDPCSTV 4* ....**6**   5   wks

Philips

9 Mar 63 ● **ALL STAR FESTIVAL** *Philips DL 99500* ....**4**   19   wks

2 Jun 73 ● **20 ORIGINAL CHART HITS** *Philips TV 1*......................**9**   11   wks

2 Jun 73   **NICE 'N' EASY** *Philips 6441 076* ....**36**   1   wk

6 Aug 77   **NEW WAVE** *Philips 5300 902* ....**11**   12   wks

Polydor

10 Dec 66   **STEREO MUSICALE SHOWCASE** *Polydor 104450* ....**26**   2   wks

9 Oct 71   **THE A–Z OF EASY LISTENING** *Polydor 2661 005*...................**24**   4   wks

24 Feb 79   **20 OF ANOTHER KIND** *Polydor POLS 1006* ....**45**   3   wks

19 May 79   **BOOGIE BUS** *Polydor 9198 174*..................**23**   11   wks

3 May 80 ● **CHAMPAGNE AND ROSES** *Polydor ROSTV 1* ....**7**   14   wks

30 Aug 80   **I AM WOMAN** *Polydor WOMTV 1* ....**11**   13   wks

11 Oct 80   **COUNTRY ROUND UP** *Polydor KOWTV 1* ....**64**   3   wks

18 Oct 80   **MONSTERS OF ROCK** *Polydor 2488 810* ....**16**   5   wks

6 Dec 80   **THE HITMAKERS** *Polydor HOPTV 1* ....**45**   10   wks

4 Apr 81 ● **ROLL ON** *Polydor REDTV 1* ....**3**   13   wks

17 Oct 81   **MONSTER TRACKS** *Polydor HOPTV 2* ....**20**   8   wks

12 Nov 88 ● **THE PREMIER COLLECTION** *Polydor ALWTV 1* ....**3**   9   wks

14 Jan 89 ★ **THE PREMIER COLLECTION** *Polydor ALWTV 1* ....**1**   55   wks

4 Feb 89 ★ **THE MARQUEE – 30 LEGENDARY YEARS** *Polydor MOTV 1* ....**1**   21   wks

31 Mar 90 ● **SKINBEAT – THE FIRST TOUCH** *Polydor SKINL 101* ....**6**   8   wks

18 Aug 90 ★ **KNEBWORTH – THE ALBUM** *Polydor 843912* ....**1**   10   wks

5 Oct 91 ● **ABSOLUTION – ROCK THE ALTERNATIVE WAY** *Polydor 8457471*..**6**   5   wks

PolyGram TV

21 Mar 92 ★ **SOUL EMOTION** *PolyGram TV 5151882* ....**1**   10   wks

2 May 92 ● **COUNTRY MOODS** *PolyGram TV 5152992*..................**2**   10   wks

6 Jun 92 ● **POWER CUTS – ROCK'S GREATEST HITS** *PolyGram TV 5154152* ....**5**   9   wks

30 May 92 ● **BEATS RHYMES AND BASSLINES – THE BEST OF RAP**
PolyGram TV 5153842..................**7**   3   wks

20 Jun 92 ★ **MODERN LOVE** *PolyGram TV 5155182* ....**1**   20   wks

18 Jul 92 ● **DANCING ON SUNSHINE** *PolyGram TV 5155192* ....**4**   11   wks

1 Aug 92 ● **BLAME IT ON THE BOOGIE** *PolyGram TV 5155172* ....**5**   8   wks

5 Sep 92 ● **READING – THE INDIE ALBUM** *PolyGram TV 5156482* ....**5**   5   wks

27 Mar 93 ● **COUNTRY ROADS** *PolyGram TV 5161002* ....**3**   10   wks

17 Apr 93 ● **MEGA–LO–MANIA** *PolyGram TV 5158132*..................**8**   6   wks

24 Apr 93   **UNDER THE COVERS** *PolyGram TV 5160742*..................**11**   5   wks

8 May 93 ● **MIDNIGHT MOODS – THE LIGHTER SIDE OF JAZZ**
PolyGram TV 5158162..................**3**   8   wks

5 Jun 93 ● **WOMAN TO WOMAN** *PolyGram TV 5161632* ....**5**   10   wks

19 Jun 93 ● **THE GIFT OF SONG** *PolyGram TV 5160582* ....**7**   4   wks

26 Jun 93 ● **SOUL INSPIRATION** PolyGram TV 5162262 ......**4**	7	wks
3 Jul 93 ● **THE BLUES EXPERIENCE** PolyGram TV 5162282......**7**	6	wks
24 Jul 93 ● **TEMPTED** PolyGram TV 5163052 ......**10**	4	wks
14 Aug 93 ● **LEADERS OF THE PACK** PolyGram TV 5163762 ......**9**	9	wks
14 Aug 93 **ALL NIGHT LONG** PolyGram TV 5163752 ......**15**	3	wks
4 Sep 93 ● **PROGRESSION** PolyGram TV 5163982 ......**9**	3	wks
2 Oct 93 **'ROUND MIDNIGHT** PolyGram TV 5164712 ......**16**	2	wks
9 Oct 93 ● **DISCO DIVA** PolyGram TV 5164802 ......**4**	5	wks
19 Feb 94 ● **THE MOVIES' GREATEST LOVE SONGS** PolyGram TV 5166512 ......**4**	6	wks
5 Mar 94 ● **FACE THE MUSIC – TORVILL AND DEAN** PolyGram TV 8450652 ..**9**	3	wks
12 Mar 94 ★ **SOUL DEVOTION** PolyGram TV 5166242 ......**1**	14	wks
19 Mar 94 ● **I KNOW THEM SO WELL – TIM RICE** PolyGram TV 5166502 ......**2**	7	wks
9 Apr 94 ● **WOMAN 2 WOMAN TWO** PolyGram TV 5163302 ......**9**	4	wks
23 Apr 94 ● **ACOUSTIC MOODS** PolyGram TV 5166592 ......**4**	8	wks
7 May 94 ★ **DANCE ZONE LEVEL ONE** PolyGram TV 5167142 ......**1**	8	wks
21 May 94 ● **REMEMBER THEN – 30 DOO–WOP CLASSICS** PolyGram TV 5167922 ......**10**	3	wks
25 Jun 94 ● **THE ULTIMATE EIGHTIES** PolyGram TV 5168312 ......**2**	9	wks
2 Jul 94 ● **ROCK THERAPY** PolyGram TV 5168612 ......**9**	6	wks
16 Jul 94 ★ **DANCE ZONE LEVEL TWO** PolyGram TV 5169122 ......**1**	6	wks
23 Jul 94 ● **POWER AND SOUL** PolyGram TV 5168962 ......**5**	10	wks
27 Aug 94 ● **GROOVIN'** PolyGram TV 5169682 ......**2**	7	wks
10 Sep 94 ● **SATIN AND STEEL – WOMEN IN ROCK** PolyGram TV 5169712 ......**3**	7	wks
17 Sep 94 ● **SOUL NIGHTS** PolyGram TV 5250052 ......**3**	6	wks
1 Oct 94 ● **SENSES** PolyGram TV 5166272 ......**5**	5	wks
8 Oct 94 ★ **DANCE ZONE LEVEL THREE** PolyGram TV 5250732......**1**	6	wks
15 Oct 94 **AFTER MIDNIGHT** PolyGram TV 5168712 ......**17**	1	wk
22 Oct 94 **DR. HILARY'S CLASSIC RELAXATION** PolyGram TV 4458112 ......**13**	2	wks
29 Oct 94 ● **THE ULTIMATE 80S' BALLADS** PolyGram TV 5251132......**5**	3	wks
12 Nov 94 ● **DANCE ZONE 94** PolyGram TV 5251302 ......**2**	12	wks
11 Feb 95 ● **ENDLESS LOVE** PolyGram TV 5253412 ......**3**	6	wks
25 Feb 95 ● **ELECTRIC DREAMS** PolyGram TV 5254352 ......**3**	8	wks
11 Mar 95 **THE ESSENTIAL GROOVE** PolyGram TV 5254382......**11**	3	wks
25 Mar 95 ★ **DANCE ZONE LEVEL FOUR** PolyGram TV 5169612 ......**1**	8	wks
25 Mar 95 **EMERALD ROCK** PolyGram TV 5169442 ......**14**	3	wks
1 Apr 95 ● **TOGETHER** PolyGram TV 5254612......**2**	5	wks
8 Apr 95 **EVERY SONG TELLS A STORY** PolyGram TV 5251702......**17**	1	wk
15 Apr 95 ● **ROCKS OFF** PolyGram TV 5254872 ......**4**	5	wks
6 May 95 ● **LET'S HEAR IT FOR THE GIRLS** PolyGram TV 5165522 ......**8**	5	wks
13 May 95 ● **SHINE** PolyGram TV 5255672......**4**	5	wks
20 May 95 ● **SILK AND STEEL** PolyGram TV 5255692 ......**3**	6	wks
3 Jun 95 ● **TEENAGE KICKS** PolyGram TV 5253382 ......**8**	3	wks
10 Jun 95 ● **WORLD IN UNION – ANTHEMS** PolyGram TV 5278072......**8**	4	wks
24 Jun 95 ★ **DANCE ZONE LEVEL FIVE** PolyGram TV 5256332 ......**1**	10	wks
1 Jul 95 ● **SUNNY AFTERNOONS** PolyGram TV 5256002......**6**	3	wks
15 Jul 95 ● **THE NO. 1 CLASSIC SOUL ALBUM** PolyGram TV 5256562 ......**5**	4	wks
22 Jul 95 **THE NO. 1 REGGAE ALBUM** PolyGram TV 5256392 ......**14**	2	wks
19 Aug 95 ● **ACOUSTIC FREEWAY** PolyGram TV 5257352......**7**	4	wks
26 Aug 95 ● **THE NO. 1 70S ROCK ALBUM** PolyGram TV 5257172 ......**3**	5	wks
26 Aug 95 ● **SUMMERTIME SOUL** PolyGram TV 5258002 ......**5**	4	wks
2 Sep 95 ★ **DANCE ZONE LEVEL SIX** PolyGram TV 5258602 ......**1**	7	wks
2 Sep 95 ● **SHINE TOO** PolyGram TV 5258582 ......**4**	5	wks
23 Sep 95 ● **ACOUSTIC ROCK** PolyGram TV 5258962 ......**7**	5	wks
14 Oct 95 ● **KISS IN IBIZA 95** PolyGram TV 5259112 ......**3**	5	wks
4 Nov 95 ● **THE NO. 1 MOVIES ALBUM** PolyGram TV 5259622......**2†**	9	wks
11 Nov 95 ● **DANCE ZONE 95** PolyGram TV 5350452 ......**8**	3	wks
11 Nov 95 **THE NO. 1 ALL TIME ROCK ALBUM** PolyGram TV 5350542......**16**	2	wks
18 Nov 95 **SHINE 3** PolyGram TV 5259652 ......**13**	6	wks
9 Dec 95 ● **THE NO. 1 CHRISTMAS ALBUM** PolyGram TV 5259782 ......**4†**	4	wks
19 Feb 94 **DANCE DIVAS** PolyGram TV 5166522 ......**11**	3	wks

Pure Music

22 Oct 94 ● **THE LADY SINGS THE BLUES** Pure Music PMCD 7001 ......**9**	4	wks
5 Nov 94 **THE GREATEST NO. 1S OF THE 80S** Pure Music PMCD 7003 ......**11**	4	wks
11 Feb 95 ★ **DANCE MANIA 95 VOLUME 1** Pure Music PMCD 7008 ......**1**	11	wks
8 Apr 95 ★ **DANCE MANIA 95 VOLUME 2** Pure Music PMCD 7010 ......**1**	9	wks
15 Jul 95 ★ **DANCE MANIA 95 VOLUME 3** Pure Music PMCD 7013 ......**1**	7	wks
30 Sep 95 ● **DANCE MANIA 95 VOLUME 4** Pure Music PMCD 7015 ......**7**	4	wks
11 Nov 95 ● **THE BEST OF DANCE MANIA 95** Pure Music PMCD 7025 ......**5†**	8	wks

Pye

9 May 59 ● **CURTAIN UP** *Pye Nixa BRTH 0059* **4**	13	wks
23 Jun 62 **HONEY HIT PARADE** *Pye Golden Guinea GGL 0129*..........**13**	7	wks
30 Nov 62 **ALL THE HITS BY ALL THE STARS** *Pye Golden Guinea GGL 0162* **19**	2	wks
7 Sep 63 **HITSVILLE** *Pye Golden Guinea GGL 0202*.....................**11**	6	wks
14 Sep 63 **THE BEST OF RADIO LUXEMBOURG**		
Pye Golden Guinea GGL 0208 ....**14**	2	wks
23 Nov 63 **HITSVILLE VOLUME 2** *Pye Golden Guinea GGL 0233*.........**20**	1	wk
4 Jan 64 **THE BLUES VOLUME 1** *Pye NPL 28030*......................**15**	3	wks
22 Feb 64 **FOLK FESTIVAL OF THE BLUES (LIVE RECORDING)**		
Pye NPL 28033 ....**16**	4	wks
30 May 64 **THE BLUES VOLUME 2** *Pye NPL 28035*......................**16**	3	wks
10 Feb 68 **STARS OF '68** *Marble Arch MAL 762*.......................**23**	3	wks
16 Oct 71 **PYE CHARTBUSTERS** *Pye PCB 15000* **36**	1	wk
18 Dec 71 **PYE CHARTBUSTERS VOLUME 2** *Pye PCB 15001* **29**	3	wks

Quality Television

15 Feb 92 ● **HIT THE DECKS VOLUME 1 – BATTLE OF THE DJs**		
Quality Television QTVCD 003 ....**3**	7	wks
4 Apr 92 ★ **ALL WOMAN** *Quality Television QTVCD 004*..............**1**	15	wks
2 May 92 ● **TEMPTATION** *Quality Television QTVCD 005* **3**	8	wks
6 Jun 92 ● **THE SOUND OF SKA** *Quality Television QTVCD 007*........**4**	6	wks
20 Jun 92 ● **TO HAVE AND TO HOLD – THE WEDDING ALBUM**		
Quality Television QTVCD 006 ....**7**	4	wks
4 Jul 92 ● **HIT THE DECKS VOLUME 2 – BATTLE OF THE DJs**		
Quality Television QYVCD 008 ....**3**	6	wks
11 Jul 92 ● **CELEBRATION – THE BEST OF REGGAE**		
Quality Television QTVCD 0101 ....**5**	8	wks
18 Jul 92 **DANGER ZONE VOLUME 1** *Quality Television QTVCD 009*..........**16**	3	wks
12 Sep 92 ● **THREE STEPS TO HEAVEN** *Quality Television QTVCD 011* **6**	5	wks
10 Oct 92 ★ **ALL WOMAN 2** *Quality Television QTVCD 012* **1**	7	wks
7 Nov 92 ● **HIT THE DECKS III** *Quality Television QTVCD 017*.........**3**	4	wks
7 Nov 92 ● **THE POWER OF LOVE** *Quality Television QTVCD 015*.........**4**	7	wks
21 Nov 92 ● **RARE GROOVE** *Quality Television QTVCD 016* **7**	14	wks
16 Jan 93 **ALL WOMAN – THE COMPLETE WOMAN**		
Quality Television QTVCD 019 ....**19**	1	wk
30 Jan 93 ● **THE NASHVILLE DREAM** *Quality Television QTVCD 014*..........**10**	3	wks
8 May 93 ● **GLAM MANIA** *Quality Television MANIACD 1* **10**	4	wks
19 Mar 94 ● **ALL WOMAN 3** *Quality Television ALLWOCD 3* **2**	11	wks
3 Dec 94 **ALL WOMAN 4** *Quality Television ALLWOCD 4* **18**	4	wks
7 Oct 95 ● **THE BEST OF ALL WOMAN** *Quality Television BOWOCD 001*.........**6**	8	wks

RCA

28 May 83 **GET ON UP** *RCA BSLP5001* **35**	5	wks
5 Sep 86 **RARE** *RCA NL90010* **80**	1	wk
23 Apr 87 **RARE 2** *RCA PL71681* **88**	1	wk
24 Jun 89 ● **RAINBOW WORRIORS** *RCA PL74065* **2**	10	wks
1 Jul 95 **PRIDE – THE VERY BEST OF SCOTLAND** *RCA 74321284372* **13**	4	wks

React

22 Jun 91 **REACTIVATE VOLUME 1: BELGIAN TECHNO ANTHEMS**		
React REACTLP **13**	4	wks
5 Oct 91 ● **REACTIVATE VOLUME 2: PHASERS ON FULL** *React REACTLP 2* **9**	4	wks
16 May 92 **REACTIVATE VOLUME 4 — TECHNOVATION** *React REACTCD 6* ..**16**	2	wks
5 Sep 92 **REACTIVATE VOLUME 5 — PURE TRANCE** *React REACTCD 10* **18**	2	wks
4 Jun 94 **FRESKA!** *React REACTCD 39* **20**	1	wk
24 Sep 94 **HOUSE NATION 1** *React REACTCD 48* **20**	1	wk
3 Jun 95 **REACTIVATE 10** *React REACTCDX 060*......................**14**	1	wk
12 Aug 95 **CAFE DEL MAR IBIZA VOLUMEN DOS** *React REACTCDL 062* **17**	1	wk

Ronco

21 Oct 72 ● **20 STAR TRACKS** *Ronco PP 2001* **2**	13	wks
23 Jun 73 ★ **THAT'LL BE THE DAY** *Ronco MR 2002/3* **1**	8	wks
8 Nov 75 **BLAZING BULLETS** *Ronco RTI 2012* **17**	8	wks
6 Dec 75 **GREATEST HITS OF WALT DISNEY** *Ronco RTD 2013* **11**	12	wks
13 Dec 75 **A CHRISTMAS GIFT** *Ronco P 12430*.......................**39**	5	wks

24 Jan 76	● STAR TRACKIN' 76 Ronco RTL 2014	9	5 wks
8 Jan 77	CLASSICAL GOLD Ronco RTD 42020	24	12 wks
16 Jul 77	SUPERGROUPS Ronco RTL 2023	57	1 wk
26 Nov 77	BLACK JOY Ronco RTL 2025	26	13 wks
18 Mar 78	● BOOGIE NIGHTS Ronco RTL 2027	5	7 wks
18 Nov 78	BOOGIE FEVER Ronco RTL 2034	15	11 wks
9 Jun 79	ROCK LEGENDS Ronco RTL 2037	54	3 wks
3 Nov 79	● ROCK 'N' ROLLER DISCO Ronco RTL 2040	3	11 wks
8 Dec 79	● PEACE IN THE VALLEY Ronco RTL 2043	6	18 wks
22 Dec 79	MILITARY GOLD Ronco RTD 42042	62	3 wks
25 Oct 80	STREET LEVEL Ronco RTL 2048	29	5 wks
8 Nov 80	● COUNTRY LEGENDS Ronco RTL 2050	9	12 wks
15 Nov 80	RADIOACTIVE Ronco RTL 2049	13	9 wks
29 Nov 80	SPACE INVADERS Ronco RTL 2051	47	3 wks
6 Dec 80	THE LEGENDARY BIG BANDS Ronco RTL 2047	24	6 wks
9 May 81	★ DISCO DAZE AND DISCO NITES Ronco RTL 2056 A/B	1	23 wks
19 Sep 81	● SUPER HITS 1 & 2 Ronco RTL 2058 A/B	2	17 wks
24 Oct 81	COUNTRY SUNRISE / COUNTRY SUNSET Ronco RTL 2059 A/B	27	11 wks
14 Nov 81	ROCK HOUSE Ronco RTL 2061	44	4 wks
12 Dec 81	MISTY MORNINGS Ronco RTL 2066	44	5 wks
12 Dec 81	MEMORIES ARE MADE OF THIS Ronco RTL 2062	84	4 wks
26 Dec 81	● HITS HITS HITS Ronco RTL 2063	2	10 wks
24 Apr 82	● DISCO UK & DISCO USA Ronco RTL 2073	7	10 wks
15 May 82	● CHARTBUSTERS Ronco RTL 2074	3	10 wks
3 Jul 82	● OVERLOAD Ronco RTL 2079	10	8 wks
28 Aug 82	SOUL DAZE / SOUL NITES Ronco RTL 2080	25	10 wks
11 Sep 82	● BREAKOUT Ronco RTL 2081	4	8 wks
30 Oct 82	MUSIC FOR THE SEASONS Ronco RTL 2075	41	10 wks
27 Nov 82	CHART WARS Ronco RTL 2086	30	7 wks
27 Nov 82	THE GREAT COUNTRY MUSIC SHOW Ronco RTD 2083	38	7 wks
18 Dec 82	THE BEST OF BEETHOVEN / STRAUSS / TCHAIKOWSKY / MOZART Ronco RTL 2084	49	10 wks
25 Dec 82	★ RAIDERS OF THE POP CHARTS Ronco RTL 2088	1	17 wks
19 Mar 83	● CHART RUNNERS Ronco RTL 2090	4	13 wks
21 May 83	● CHART ENCOUNTERS OF THE HIT KIND Ronco RTL 2091	5	10 wks
18 Jun 83	LOVERS ONLY Ronco RTL 2093	12	13 wks
16 Jul 83	HITS ON FIRE Ronco RTL 2095	11	10 wks
17 Sep 83	● THE HIT SQUAD – CHART TRACKING Ronco RON LP 1	4	9 wks
17 Sep 83	THE HIT SQUAD – NIGHT CLUBBING Ronco RON LP 2	28	7 wks
12 Nov 83	HIT SQUAD – HITS OF '83 Ronco RON LP 4	12	11 wks
17 Dec 83	● GREEN VELVET Ronco RON LP 6	6	17 wks
7 Jan 84	CHART TREK VOLUMES 1 & 2 Ronco RON LP 8	20	9 wks
21 Jan 84	● SOMETIMES WHEN WE TOUCH Ronco RON LP 9	8	14 wks
24 Mar 84	BABY LOVE Ronco RON LP 11	47	6 wks
7 Apr 84	DREAMS AND THEMES Ronco RON LP 10	75	2 wks

Green Velvet was re-issued on Telstar STAR 2252.

Rumour

16 Sep 89	WAREHOUSE RAVES Rumour RUMLD 101	15	4 wks
31 Mar 90	WAREHOUSE RAVES 3 Rumour RUMLD 103	12	5 wks
29 Sep 90	WAREHOUSE RAVES 4 Rumour RUMLD 104	13	3 wks
11 May 91	WAREHOUSE RAVES 5 Rumour RUMLD 105	18	1 wk
20 Jul 91	BREAKS BASS AND BLEEPS Rumour RAID 504	20	1 wk
21 Mar 92	WAREHOUSE RAVES 6 Rumour CDRUMD 106	16	2 wks
18 Apr 92	BREAKS, BASS AND BLEEPS Rumour CDRAID 507	20	1 wk
27 Jun 92	MOVIN' ON Rumour RULCD 300	20	1 wk
29 Aug 92	WAREHOUSE RAVES 7 Rumour CDRUMD 107	20	1 wk
26 Sep 92	TRANCE Rumour CDRAID 508	18	1 wk
24 Oct 92	MOVIN' ON 2 Rumour RULCD 301	15	2 wks

Serious

7 Jun 86	UPFRONT 1 Serious UPFT 1	17	10 wks
23 Aug 86	UPFRONT 2 Serious UPFT 2	27	6 wks
1 Nov 86	UPFRONT 3 Serious UPFT 3	37	5 wks
31 Jan 87	UPFRONT 4 Serious UPFT 4	21	5 wks
28 Mar 87	SERIOUS HIP-HOP 2 Serious SHOP 2	95	1 wk
28 Mar 87	UPFRONT 5 Serious UPFT 5	21	6 wks
23 May 87	UPFRONT 6 Serious UPFT 6	22	6 wks

VARIOUS ARTISTS

4 Jul 87	**BEST OF HOUSE VOLUME 1** *Serious BEHO 1*	**55**	12 wks
15 Aug 87	**UPFRONT 7** *Serious UPFT 7*	**31**	4 wks
12 Sep 87	**BEST OF HOUSE VOLUME 2** *Serious BEHO 2*	**30**	7 wks
17 Oct 87	**HIP–HOP '87** *Serious HHOP 87*	**81**	1 wk
17 Oct 87	**UPFRONT 8** *Serious UPFT 8*	**22**	6 wks
14 Nov 87	**BEST OF HOUSE VOLUME 3** *Serious BEHO 3*	**61**	3 wks
12 Dec 87	**BEST OF HOUSE MEGAMIX** *Serious BOIT 1*	**77**	4 wks
19 Dec 87	**UPFRONT 9** *Serious UPFT 9*	**92**	1 wk
20 Feb 88	**DANCE MANIA VOLUME 2** *Serious DAMA 2*	**59**	2 wks
12 Mar 88	**BEST OF HOUSE VOLUME 4** *Serious BEHO 4*	**27**	8 wks
9 Apr 88	**UPFRONT 10** *Serious UPFT 10*	**45**	5 wks
14 May 88	**BEST OF HOUSE MEGAMIX VOLUME 2** *Serious BOIT 2*	**73**	2 wks
29 Oct 88	**ACID TRAX MEGAMIX VOLUME 1** *Serious DUIX 1*	**93**	1 wk
18 Feb 89	**UPFRONT '89** *Serious UPFT 89*	**15**	1 wk

Smash Hits

29 Oct 88	**SMASH HITS PARTY '88** *Dover ADD 5*	**6**	11 wks
14 Jan 89	**SMASH HITS PARTY '88** *Dover ADD 5*	**12**	5 wks
28 Oct 89	★ **SMASH HITS PARTY '89** *Dover ADD 8*	**1**	14 wks
14 Jul 90	★ **SMASH HITS – RAVE!** *Dover ADD 14*	**1**	10 wks
3 Nov 90	● **SMASH HITS 1990** *Dover ADD 18*	**2**	14 wks
25 May 91	★ **SMASH HITS – MASSIVE!** *Dover ADD 24*	**1**	9 wks
26 Oct 91	● **SMASH HITS 1991** *Dover ADD 28*	**3**	16 wks
22 Aug 92	● **SMASH HITS – PARTY ON!** *Dover CCD 34*	**9**	5 wks
12 Dec 92	● **SMASH HITS '92** *Dover ADDCD 35*	**5**	8 wks
13 Nov 93	● **SMASH HITS '93 – 40 TOP CHARTIN' GROOVES** *Chrysalis CDCHR 6058*	**4**	10 wks
3 Dec 94	● **SMASH HITS 94** *Telstar TCD 2750*	**9**	7 wks
18 Mar 95	★ **SMASH HITS 95 VOLUME 1** *Telstar TCD 2764*	**1**	7 wks
24 Jun 95	● **SMASH HITS 95 VOLUME 2** *Telstar TCD 2768*	**4**	5 wks

358

Starblend

12 Nov 83	**IN TOUCH** *Starblend STD 9*	**89**	2 wks
23 Jun 84	**BROKEN DREAMS** *Starblend SLTD 1*	**48**	7 wks
27 Apr 85	**12 X 12 MEGA MIXES** *Starblend INCH 1*	**77**	2 wks
3 Aug 85	**AMERICAN DREAMS** *Starblend SLTD 12*	**43**	8 wks
21 Dec 85	**CHRISTMAS AT THE COUNTRY STORE** *Starblend NOEL 1*	**94**	1 wk
12 Jul 86	**DISCOVER COUNTRY / DISCOVER NEW COUNTRY** *Starblend DNC 1*	**60**	3 wks
16 Aug 86	**HEARTBREAKERS** *Starblend BLEND 3*	**38**	8 wks
20 Sep 86	**ABSOLUTE ROCK 'N' ROLL** *Starblend SLTD 15*	**88**	1 wk

Street Sounds

19 Feb 83	**STREET SOUNDS EDITION 2** *Street Sounds STSND 002*	**35**	6 wks
23 Apr 83	**STREET SOUNDS EDITION 3** *Street Sounds STSND 003*	**21**	5 wks
25 Jun 83	**STREET SOUNDS EDITION 4** *Street Sounds STSND 004*	**14**	8 wks
13 Aug 83	**STREET SOUNDS EDITION 5** *Street Sounds STSND 005*	**16**	8 wks
8 Oct 83	**STREET SOUNDS EDITION 6** *Street Sounds STSND 006*	**23**	5 wks
22 Oct 83	**STREET SOUNDS ELECTRO 1** *Street Sounds ELCST 1*	**18**	8 wks
17 Dec 83	**STREET SOUNDS EDITION 7** *Street Sounds STSND 007*	**48**	4 wks
7 Jan 84	**STREET SOUNDS ELECTRO 2** *Street Sounds ELCST 2*	**49**	7 wks
3 Mar 84	**STREET SOUNDS HI ENERGY 1** *Street Sounds HINRG 16*	**71**	1 wk
10 Mar 84	**STREET SOUNDS CRUCIAL ELECTRO** *Street Sounds ELCST 999*	**24**	10 wks
10 Mar 84	**STREET SOUNDS EDITION 8** *Street Sounds STSND 008*	**22**	7 wks
7 Apr 84	**STREET SOUNDS ELECTRO 3** *Street Sounds ELCST 3*	**25**	9 wks
12 May 84	**STREET SOUNDS EDITION 9** *Street Sounds STSND 009*	**22**	5 wks
9 Jun 84	**STREET SOUNDS ELECTRO 4** *Street Sounds ELCST 4*	**25**	9 wks
30 Jun 84	**STREET SOUNDS UK ELECTRO** *Street Sounds ELCST 1984*	**60**	4 wks
21 Jul 84	**LET THE MUSIC SCRATCH** *Street Sounds MKL 1*	**91**	3 wks
11 Aug 84	**STREET SOUNDS CRUCIAL ELECTRO 2** *Street Sounds ELCST 1000*	**35**	6 wks
18 Aug 84	**STREET SOUNDS EDITION 10** *Street Sounds STSND 010*	**24**	6 wks
6 Oct 84	**STREET SOUNDS ELECTRO 5** *Street Sounds ELCST 5*	**17**	6 wks
10 Nov 84	**STREET SOUNDS EDITION 11** *Street Sounds STSND 011*	**48**	4 wks
9 Mar 85	**STREET SOUNDS ELECTRO 6** *Street Sounds ELCST 6*	**24**	10 wks
9 Mar 85	**THE ARTISTS VOLUME 1** *Street Sounds ARTIS 1*	**65**	4 wks

VARIOUS ARTISTS

18 May 85	**STREET SOUNDS ELECTRO 7** Street Sounds ELCST 7 ....**12**	7 wks
18 May 85	**STREET SOUNDS EDITION 12** Street Sounds STSND 12 ....**23**	4 wks
13 Jul 85	**STREET SOUNDS ELECTRO 8** Street Sounds ELCST 8 ....**23**	5 wks
13 Jul 85	**THE ARTISTS VOLUME 2** Street Sounds ARTIS 2 ....**45**	4 wks
17 Aug 85	**STREET SOUNDS EDITION 13** Street Sounds STSND 13 ....**19**	9 wks
17 Aug 85	**STREET SOUNDS NY VS LA BEATS** Street Sounds ELCST 1001 ....**65**	4 wks
5 Oct 85	**STREET SOUNDS ELECTRO 9** Street Sounds ELCST 9 ....**18**	6 wks
12 Oct 85	**THE ARTISTS VOLUME 3** Street Sounds ARTIS 3 ....**87**	2 wks
16 Nov 85	**STREET SOUNDS EDITION 14** Street Sounds STSND 14 ....**43**	3 wks
21 Dec 85	**STREET SOUNDS ELECTRO 10** Street Sounds ELCST 10 ....**72**	6 wks
21 Dec 85	**STREET SOUNDS EDITION 15** Street Sounds STSND 15 ....**58**	8 wks
29 Mar 86	**STREET SOUNDS HIP–HOP ELECTRO 11** Street Sounds ELCST 11 **19**	5 wks
5 Apr 86	**STREET SOUNDS EDITION 16** Street Sounds STSND 16 ....**17**	7 wks
21 Jun 86	**JAZZ JUICE 2** Street Sounds SOUND 4 ....**96**	1 wk
28 Jun 86	**STREET SOUNDS HIP–HOP ELECTRO 12** Street Sounds ELCST 12 **28**	4 wks
19 Jul 86	**STREET SOUNDS EDITION 17** Street Sounds STSND 17 ....**35**	5 wks
6 Sep 86	**STREET SOUNDS HIP–HOP ELECTRO 13** Street Sounds ELCST 13 **23**	5 wks
11 Oct 86	**STREET SOUNDS EDITION 18** Street Sounds STSND 18 ....**20**	5 wks
11 Oct 86	**JAZZ JUICE 3** Street Sounds SOUND 5 ....**88**	1 wk
11 Oct 86	**STREET SOUNDS HIP–HOP ELECTRO 14** Street Sounds ELCST 14 **40**	3 wks
15 Nov 86	**STREET SOUNDS HIP–HOP ELECTRO 15** Street Sounds ELCST 15 **46**	2 wks
6 Dec 86	**STREET SOUNDS EDITION 19** Street Sounds STSND 19 ....**61**	3 wks
24 Jan 87	**STREET SOUNDS ELECTRO 3** Street Sounds ELCST 1002 ....**41**	3 wks
7 Feb 87	**STREET SOUNDS ANTHEMS VOLUME 1** Street Sounds MUSIC 5 **61**	3 wks
14 Feb 87	**STREET SOUNDS EDITION 20** Street Sounds STSND 20 ....**25**	4 wks
13 Jun 87	**STREET SOUNDS HIP–HOP ELECTRO 16** Street Sounds ELCST 16 **40**	3 wks
4 Jul 87	**STREET SOUNDS DANCE MUSIC '87** Street Sounds STSND 871 ..**40**	5 wks
15 Aug 87	**STREET SOUNDS HIP–HOP 17** Street Sounds ELCST 17 ....**38**	3 wks
15 Aug 87	**JAZZ JUICE 5** Street Sounds SOUND 8 ....**97**	1 wk
12 Sep 87	**BEST OF WEST COAST HIP HOP** Street Sounds MACA 1 ....**80**	2 wks
12 Sep 87	**STREET SOUNDS '87 VOLUME 2** Street Sounds STSND 872 ....**47**	3 wks
24 Oct 87	**STREET SOUNDS HIP–HOP 18** Street Sounds ELCST 18 ....**67**	1 wk
19 Mar 88	**STREET SOUNDS HIP–HOP 20** Street Sounds ELCST 20 ....**39**	4 wks
19 Mar 88	**STREET SOUNDS 88–1** Street Sounds STSND 881 ....**73**	2 wks
4 Jun 88	**STREET SOUNDS HIP–HOP 21** Street Sounds ELCST 21 ....**87**	1 wk

Studio Two

21 Oct 67	● **BREAKTHROUGH** Studio Two STWO 1 ....**2**	11 wks
4 Sep 71	**TOTAL SOUND** Studio Two STWO 4 ....**39**	4 wks
30 Oct 71	**STUDIO TWO CLASSICS** Studio Two STWO 6 ....**16**	4 wks

Stylus

3 Aug 85	**THE MAGIC OF TORVILL AND DEAN** Stylus SMR 8502 ....**35**	9 wks
17 Aug 85	**NIGHT BEAT** Stylus SMR 8501 ....**15**	8 wks
24 Aug 85	**DISCO BEACH PARTY** Stylus SMR 8503 ....**29**	10 wks
14 Dec 85	**VELVET WATERS** Stylus SMR 8507 ....**54**	4 wks
28 Dec 85	**CHOICES OF THE HEART** Stylus SMR 8511 ....**87**	2 wks
8 Mar 86	● **NIGHT BEAT 2** Stylus SMR 8613 ....**7**	9 wks
17 May 86	**LET'S HEAR IT FROM THE GIRLS** Stylus SMR 8614 ....**17**	10 wks
1 Nov 86	**BLACK MAGIC** Stylus SMR 619 ....**26**	9 wks
8 Nov 86	● **HIT MIX '86** Stylus SMR 624 ....**10**	14 wks
22 Nov 86	**CLASSICS BY CANDLELIGHT** Stylus SMR 620 ....**74**	4 wks
14 Mar 87	**BANDS OF GOLD – THE SWINGING SIXTIES** Stylus SMR 726 ......**48**	6 wks
21 Mar 87	**BANDS OF GOLD – THE SENSATIONAL SEVENTIES** Stylus SMR 727 ....**75**	4 wks
28 Mar 87	**BANDS OF GOLD – THE ELECTRIC EIGHTIES** Stylus SMR 728 ......**82**	1 wk
11 Jul 87	● **SIXTIES MIX** Stylus SMR 733 ....**3**	44 wks
24 Oct 87	**HIT FACTORY** Stylus SMR 740 ....**18**	17 wks
21 Nov 87	**HIT MIX – HITS OF THE YEAR** Stylus SMR 744 ....**29**	11 wks
2 Apr 88	● **HIP HOP AND RAPPING IN THE HOUSE** Stylus SMR 852 ....**5**	13 wks
30 Apr 88	**THE WORLDS OF FOSTER AND ALLEN** Stylus SMR 861 ....**21**	15 wks
7 May 88	**SIXTIES MIX 2** Stylus SMR 855 ....**14**	20 wks
4 Jun 88	**BACK ON THE ROAD** Stylus SMR 854 ....**29**	11 wks
30 Jul 88	● **THE GREATEST EVER ROCK 'N' ROLL MIX** Stylus SMR 858 ....**8**	15 wks
3 Sep 88	● **RAP TRAX** Stylus SMR 859 ....**3**	13 wks
1 Oct 88	**RARE GROOVE MIX** Stylus SMR 863 ....**20**	10 wks
17 Oct 88	**THE GREATEST HITS OF HOUSE** Stylus SMR 867 ....**26**	4 wks
22 Oct 88	● **SOFT METAL** Stylus SMR 862 ....**7**	12 wks

26 Nov 88	**HIT MIX '88** *Stylus SMR 865* **48**	7	wks

14 Jan 89	● **THE GREATEST HITS OF HOUSE** *Stylus SMR 867* **5**	9	wks
14 Jan 89	● **SOFT METAL** *Stylus SMR 862*....................................**7**	27	wks
14 Jan 89	**HIT MIX '88** *Stylus SMR 865* **15**	2	wks
14 Jan 89	**THE WORLDS OF FOSTER AND ALLEN** *Stylus SMR 861* **16**	3	wks
18 Feb 89	● **BEAT THIS – 20 HITS OF RHYTHM KING** *Stylus SMR 973* **9**	8	wks
11 Mar 89	**NEW ROOTS** *Stylus SMR 972*.....................................**18**	1	wk
25 Mar 89	● **HIP HOUSE** *Stylus SMR 974* **3**	8	wks
22 Apr 89	● **THE SINGER AND THE SONG** *Stylus SMR 975* **5**	11	wks
27 May 89	● **PRECIOUS METAL** *Stylus SMR 976* **2**	29	wks
24 Jun 89	● **DON'T STOP THE MUSIC** *Stylus SMR 977* **7**	6	wks
15 Jul 89	● **HOT SUMMER NIGHTS** *Stylus SMR 980* **4**	11	wks
19 Aug 89	● **SUNSHINE MIX** *Stylus SMP 986* **9**	7	wks
26 Aug 89	● **THE GREATEST EVER ROCK 'N' ROLL MIX** *Stylus SMR 858* **5**	9	wks
2 Sep 89	● **MIDNIGHT LOVE** *Stylus SMR 981* **7**	6	wks
16 Sep 89	● **LEGENDS AND HEROES** *Stylus SMR 987*.....................**6**	10	wks
21 Oct 89	● **THE RIGHT STUFF – REMIX '89** *Stylus SMR 990* **2**	11	wks
25 Nov 89	**JUKE BOX JIVE MIX – ROCK 'N' ROLL GREATS** *Stylus SMR 993*..**13**	8	wks
30 Dec 89	**WARE'S THE HOUSE** *Stylus SMR 997* **15**	1	wk
13 Jan 90	★ **PURE SOFT METAL** *Stylus SMR 996* **1**	23	wks
10 Mar 90	● **RIGHT STUFF 2 – NOTHING BUT A HOUSEPARTY** *Stylus SMR 998* **2**	15	wks
26 May 90	● **SIXTIES MIX 3** *Stylus SMR 021* **4**	9	wks
1 Oct 90	**THE WORDS OF FOSTER & ALLEN** *Stylus SMR 863* **21**	15	wks
22 Oct 90	● **MOMENTS IN SOUL** *Stylus SMR 023* **9**	2	wks

Tamla Motown

3 Apr 65	**A COLLECTION OF TAMLA MOTOWN HITS** *Tamla Motown TML 11001* **16**	4	wks
4 Mar 67	**16 ORIGINAL BIG HITS VOLUME 4** *Tamla Motown TML 11043* ..**33**	3	wks
17 Jun 67	**TAMLA MOTOWN HITS VOLUME 5** *Tamla Motown TML 11050* ..**11**	40	wks
21 Oct 67	● **BRITISH MOTOWN CHARTBUSTERS** *Tamla Motown TML 11055* **2**	54	wks
10 Feb 68	**MOTOWN MEMORIES** *Tamla Motown TML 11064* **21**	13	wks
24 Aug 68	**TAMLA MOTOWN HITS VOLUME 6** *Tamla Motown STML 11074*.....................................**32**	2	wks
30 Nov 68	● **BRITISH MOTOWN CHARTBUSTERS VOLUME 2** *Tamla Motown STML 11082*.....................................**8**	11	wks
25 Oct 69	★ **BRITISH MOTOWN CHARTBUSTERS VOLUME 3** *Tamla Motown STML 11121*.....................................**1**	93	wks
21 Feb 70	**COLLECTION OF BIG HITS VOLUME 8** *Tamla Motown STML 11130*.....................................**56**	1	wk
24 Oct 70	★ **MOTOWN CHARTBUSTERS VOLUME 4** *Tamla Motown STML 11162*.....................................**1**	40	wks
17 Apr 71	★ **MOTOWN CHARTBUSTERS VOLUME 5** *Tamla Motown STML 11181*.....................................**1**	36	wks
23 Oct 71	● **MOTOWN CHARTBUSTERS VOLUME 6** *Tamla Motown STML 11191*.....................................**2**	36	wks
26 Feb 72	**MOTOWN MEMORIES** *Tamla Motown STML 11200*......................**22**	4	wks
18 Mar 72	**MOTOWN STORY** *Tamla Motown TMSP 1130*...............................**21**	8	wks
29 Nov 72	● **MOTOWN CHARTBUSTERS VOLUME 7** *Tamla Motown STML 11215*.....................................**9**	16	wks
3 Nov 73	● **MOTOWN CHARTBUSTERS VOLUME 8** *Tamla Motown STML 11246*.....................................**9**	15	wks
26 Oct 74	**MOTOWN CHARTBUSTERS VOLUME 9** *Tamla Motown STML 11270*.....................................**14**	15	wks
1 Nov 75	● **MOTOWN GOLD** *Tamla Motown STML 12003*....................**8**	35	wks
5 Nov 77	**MOTOWN GOLD VOLUME 2** *Motown STML 12070* **28**	4	wks
7 Oct 78	● **BIG WHEELS OF MOTOWN** *Motown EMTV 12*......................**2**	18	wks
2 Feb 80	★ **THE LAST DANCE** *Motown EMTV 20*...............................**1**	23	wks
2 Aug 80	**THE 20TH ANNIVERSARY ALBUM** *Motown TMSP 6010*...............**53**	2	wks
21 May 88	● **MOTOWN DANCE PARTY** *Motown ZC 72700*.....................**3**	18	wks

19 May 90	● **MOTOWN DANCE PARTY 2** *Motown ZL 72703* **10**	7	wks
6 Oct 90	● **SOUL DECADE: THE SIXTIES** *Motown ZL 74816* **3**	10	wks
24 Oct 92	● **MOTOWN'S GREATEST LOVE SONGS** *Motown 5300062* **5**	5	wks
12 Nov 94	● **MOTOWN – THE ULTIMATE HITS COLLECTION** *Motown 5304652* **6**	13	wks
4 Nov 95	**MOTOWN – THE HITS COLLECTION VOLUME 2** *Motown 5306042* **19**	1	wk

360

Telstar

16 Oct 82 ●	CHART ATTACK Telstar STAR 2221	7	6 wks
6 Nov 82	MIDNIGHT IN MOTOWN Telstar STAR 2222	34	16 wks
18 Dec 82	DIRECT HITS Telstar STAR 2226	89	1 wk
8 Jan 83	DANCIN' – 20 ORIGINAL MOTOWN MOVERS Telstar STAR 2225	97	1 wk
5 Feb 83	INSTRUMENTAL MAGIC Telstar STAR 2227	68	5 wks
30 Apr 83	20 GREAT ITALIAN LOVE SONGS Telstar STAR 2230	28	6 wks
4 Jun 83	IN THE GROOVE — THE 12 INCH DISCO PARTY Telstar STAR 2228	20	12 wks
12 Nov 83	ROOTS REGGAE 'N' REGGAE ROCK Telstar STAR 2233	34	6 wks
19 Nov 83	SUPERCHART '83 Telstar STAR 2236	22	9 wks
4 Feb 84 ●	THE VERY BEST OF MOTOWN LOVE SONGS Telstar STAR 2239	10	22 wks
26 May 84	DON'T STOP DANCING Telstar STAR 2242	11	12 wks
13 Oct 84 ●	HITS HITS HITS – 18 SMASH ORIGINALS Telstar STAR 2243	6	9 wks
8 Dec 84	LOVE SONGS – 16 CLASSIC LOVE SONGS Telstar STAR 2246	20	12 wks
15 Dec 84 ●	GREEN VELVET Telstar STAR 2252	10	10 wks
7 Sep 85	OPEN TOP CARS AND GIRLS IN T-SHIRTS Telstar STAR 2257	13	9 wks
16 Nov 85 ★	THE GREATEST HITS OF 1985 Telstar STAR 2269	1	17 wks
16 Nov 85 ●	THE LOVE ALBUM Telstar STAR 2268	7	18 wks
30 Nov 85	THE PRINCE'S TRUST COLLECTION Telstar STAR 2275	64	5 wks
7 Dec 85	PERFORMANCE – THE VERY BEST OF TIM RICE AND ANDREW LLOYD WEBBER Telstar STAR 2262	33	7 wks
7 Dec 85	MORE GREEN VELVET Telstar STAR 2267	42	5 wks
12 Oct 86 ●	THE CHART Telstar STAR 2278	6	12 wks
1 Nov 86	ROCK LEGENDS Telstar STAR 2290	54	7 wks
8 Nov 86	LOVERS Telstar STAR 2279	14	16 wks
8 Nov 86 ●	THE GREATEST HITS OF 1986 Telstar STAR 2286	8	13 wks
22 Nov 86	SIXTIES MANIA Telstar STAR 2287	19	22 wks
6 Dec 86	MOTOWN CHARTBUSTERS Telstar STAR 2283	25	12 wks
28 Mar 87	THE DANCE CHART Telstar STAR 2285	23	8 wks
3 Oct 87	TRACKS OF MY TEARS Telstar STAR 2295	27	7 wks
21 Nov 87	THE GREATEST HITS OF 1987 Telstar STAR 2309	12	11 wks
28 Nov 87	DANCE MIX '87 Telstar STAR 2314	39	10 wks
28 Nov 87	ALWAYS AND FOREVER Telstar STAR 2301	41	10 wks
28 Nov 87	SIXTIES PARTY MEGAMIX ALBUM Telstar STAR 2307	46	7 wks
26 Dec 87 ●	LIFE IN THE FAST LANE Telstar STAR 2315	10	12 wks
26 Dec 87	THE GREATEST LOVE Telstar STAR 2316	11	40 wks
1 Oct 88	. . . AND THE BEAT GOES ON Telstar STAR 2338	12	8 wks
5 Nov 88	THE HEART AND SOUL OF ROCK 'N' ROLL Telstar STAR 2351	60	6 wks
12 Nov 88	THE LOVE ALBUM '88 Telstar STAR 2332	51	9 wks
19 Nov 88	BEST OF HOUSE '88 Telstar STAR 2347	33	8 wks
19 Nov 88	INSTRUMENTAL GREATS Telstar STAR 2341	79	5 wks
19 Nov 88	THE GREATEST HITS OF 1988 Telstar STAR 2334	11	8 wks
3 Dec 88	HYPERACTIVE Telstar STAR 2328	78	4 wks
3 Dec 88	BACK TO THE SIXTIES Telstar STAR 2348	47	6 wks
17 Dec 88	MORNING HAS BROKEN Telstar STAR 2337	88	2 wks
31 Dec 88	THE GREATEST LOVE 2 Telstar STAR 2352	37	2 wks
14 Jan 89	BEST OF HOUSE 1988 Telstar STAR 2347	11	5 wks
14 Jan 89	BACK TO THE SIXTIES Telstar STAR 2348	14	4 wks
14 Jan 89	LOVE SONGS Telstar STAR 2298	18	2 wks
14 Jan 89 ●	THE GREATEST HITS OF 1988 Telstar STAR 2334	8	8 wks
14 Jan 89 ●	THE GREATEST LOVE 2 Telstar STAR 2352	3	23 wks
14 Jan 89 ●	THE GREATEST LOVE Telstar STAR 2316	7	31 wks
25 Feb 89 ★	THE AWARDS Telstar STAR 2346	1	8 wks
4 Mar 89 ★	DEEP HEAT Telstar STAR 2345	1	15 wks
22 Apr 89 ●	DEEP HEAT – THE SECOND BURN Telstar STAR 2356	2	13 wks
15 Jul 89 ●	PROTECT THE INNOCENT Telstar STAR 2363	9	9 wks
15 Jul 89	RHYTHM OF THE SUN Telstar STAR 2362	12	4 wks
22 Jul 89 ●	THIS IS SKA Telstar STAR 2366	6	10 wks
22 Jul 89 ●	DEEP HEAT 3 – THE THIRD DEGREE Telstar STAR 2364	2	13 wks
23 Sep 89 ★	DEEP HEAT 4 – PLAY WITH FIRE Telstar STAR 2388	1	11 wks
11 Oct 89 ●	THE GREATEST LOVE 3 Telstar STAR 2384	4	18 wks
14 Oct 89 ●	MOTOWN HEARTBREAKERS Telstar STAR 2343	4	10 wks
18 Nov 89 ●	NUMBER ONES OF THE EIGHTIES Telstar STAR 2382	2	19 wks
18 Nov 89 ●	THE GREATEST HITS OF 1989 Telstar STAR 2389	4	11 wks
18 Nov 89 ●	THE GREATEST HITS OF THE 80S Telstar STAR 2382	2	18 wks
25 Nov 89 ●	DEEP HEAT 1989 – FIGHT THE FLAME Telstar STAR 2380	4	17 wks
25 Nov 89 ●	HEAVEN AND HELL Telstar STAR 2361	9	12 wks

V A R I O U S   A R T I S T S

9 Dec 89   **SOFT ROCK** *Telstar STAR 2397* 15   5 wks
3 Feb 90 ★ **DEEP HEAT 5 – FEED THE FEVER** *Telstar STAR 2411* 1   11 wks
3 Feb 90   **NEW TRADITIONS** *Telstar STAR 2399* 13   4 wks
10 Feb 90 ● **MILESTONES – 20 ROCK OPERAS** *Telstar STAR 2379* 6   11 wks
24 Feb 90 ● **THE AWARDS 1990** *Telstar STAR 2368* 3   10 wks
17 Mar 90   **PRODUCT 2378** *Telstar STAR 2378* 16   3 wks
31 Mar 90 ★ **DEEP HEAT 6 – THE SIXTH SENSE** *Telstar STAR 2412* 1   14 wks
12 May 90 ● **GET ON THIS! – 30 DANCE HITS VOLUME 1** *Telstar STAR 22420* ..2   12 wks
19 May 90 ● **A NIGHT AT THE OPERA** *Telstar STAR 2414* 2   12 wks
7 Jul 90 ★ **DEEP HEAT 7 – SEVENTH HEAVEN** *Telstar STAR 2422* 1   9 wks
18 Aug 90 ★ **MEGABASS** *Telstar STAR 2425* 1   12 wks
25 Aug 90   **MOLTEN METAL** *Telstar STAR 2429* 13   5 wks
25 Aug 90 ● **GET ON THIS!!! 2** *Telstar STAR 2424* 3   9 wks
15 Sep 90 ● **COUNTRY'S GREATEST HITS** *Telstar STAR 2433* 9   7 wks
27 Oct 90 ● **DEEP HEAT 8 – THE HAND OF FATE** *Telstar STAR 2447* 5   5 wks
27 Oct 90 ● **FINAL COUNTDOWN – BEST OF SOFT METAL** *Telstar STAR 2431* ..9   6 wks
27 Oct 90 ● **THE GREATEST LOVE 4** *Telstar STAR 2400* 4   19 wks
3 Nov 90 ● **RAVE** *Telstar STAR 2453* 10   4 wks
17 Nov 90 ● **THE GREATEST HITS OF 1990** *Telstar STAR 2439* 4   14 wks
24 Nov 90 ● **DEEP HEAT 90** *Telstar STAR 2438* 3   12 wks
24 Nov 90 ● **THE MOTOWN COLLECTION** *Telstar STAR 2375* 8   12 wks
1 Dec 90 ● **60 NUMBER ONES OF THE SIXTIES** *Telstar STAR 2432* 7   11 wks
8 Dec 90 ● **MEGABASS 2** *Telstar STAR 2448* 6   8 wks
8 Dec 90 ● **THE VERY BEST OF THE GREATEST LOVE** *Telstar STAR 2443* 5   17 wks
26 Jan 91 ★ **DEEP HEAT 9 – NINTH LIFE** *Telstar STAR 2470* 1   7 wks
23 Feb 91 ★ **UNCHAINED MELODIES** *Telstar STAR 2480* 1   20 wks
23 Mar 91   **DON'T STOP – DOOWOP** *Telstar STAR 2485* 15   4 wks
30 Mar 91 ● **THIN ICE – THE FIRST STEP** *Telstar STAR 2500* 2   9 wks
13 Apr 91   **AFTER THE DANCE** *Telstar STAR 2501* 16   3 wks
11 May 91 ● **MASSIVE HITS** *Telstar STAR 2505* 2   6 wks
18 May 91 ● **UNCHAINED MELODIES II** *Telstar STAR 2515* 3   8 wks
1 Jun 91 ● **DEEP HEAT 10 – THE AWAKENING** *Telstar STAR 2490* 2   7 wks
8 Jun 91 ● **MEGABASS 3** *Telstar STAR 2483* 3   8 wks
22 Jun 91 ● **FAST FORWARD** *Telstar STAR 2502* 4   8 wks
3 Aug 91 ★ **THIN ICE 2 – THE SECOND SHIVER** *Telstar STAR 2535* 1   9 wks
14 Sep 91 ● **Q – THE ALBUM VOLUME 1** *Telstar STAR 2522* 10   4 wks
28 Sep 91 ● **MAKE YOU SWEAT** *Telstar STAR 2542* 4   6 wks
12 Oct 91 ● **BORN TO BE WILD** *Telstar STAR 2524* 8   5 wks
2 Nov 91 ● **BURNING HEARTS** *Telstar STAR 2492* 7   10 wks
9 Nov 91 ● **BEST OF DANCE 91** *Telstar STAR 2537* 2   15 wks
16 Nov 91 ● **THE GREATEST HITS OF 1991** *Telstar STAR 2536* 4   13 wks
23 Nov 91 ● **LOVE AT THE MOVIES** *Telstar STAR 2545* 6   14 wks
23 Nov 91   **PUNK AND DISORDERLY – NEW WAVE** *Telstar STAR 2520* 18   2 wks
30 Nov 91   **CLASSICAL MASTERS** *Telstar STAR 2549* 13   15 wks
19 Oct 91 ● **IN LOVE – GREATEST LOVE 5** *Telstar STAR 2510* 5   9 wks
7 Dec 91   **LEGENDS OF SOUL – A WHOLE STACK OF SOUL**
          Telstar STAR 2489 15   10 wks
21 Dec 91 ● **DEEP HEAT 11 – SPIRIT OF ECSTASY** *Telstar STAR 2555* 3   8 wks
15 Feb 92 ● **KAOS THEORY** *Telstar STAR 2562* 2   7 wks
15 Feb 92 ● **ALL THE BEST – LOVE DUETS VOLUME 1** *Telstar STAR 2557* ..5   6 wks
29 Feb 92   **GOLD – 18 EPIC SPORTING ANTHEMS** *Telstar TCD 2563* 15   3 wks
7 Mar 92 ★ **THE ULTIMATE HARDCORE** *Telstar TCD 2561* 1   10 wks
11 Apr 92 ● **CLUB FOR HEROES** *Telstar TCD 2566* 3   10 wks
2 May 92 ● **KAOS THEORY 2** *Telstar STAR 2583* 2   8 wks
2 May 92   **INDIE HITS** *Telstar TCD 2578* 13   3 wks
9 May 92   **FLIGHT OF THE CONDOR** *Telstar TCD 2576* 11   6 wks
23 May 92 ● **GARAGE CITY** *Telstar TCD 2584* 8   5 wks
6 Jun 93 ● **RAVING WE'RE RAVING** *Telstar TCD 2567* 2   6 wks
18 Jul 92 ★ **KT3 – KAOS THEORY 3** *Telstar TCD 2593* 1   8 wks
1 Aug 92 ● **THE DIVAS OF DANCE** *Telstar TCD 2592* 9   4 wks
8 Aug 92 ● **RAVE ALERT** *Telstar TCD 2594* 2   10 wks
19 Sep 92 ● **BLUE EYED SOUL** *Telstar TCD 2591* 4   6 wks
10 Oct 92 ● **KAOS THEORY 4** *Telstar TCD 2605* 2   5 wks
17 Oct 92 ● **RAVE NATION** *Telstar TCD 2607* 2   6 wks
17 Oct 92 ● **MORE THAN LOVE** *Telstar TCD 2606* 4   9 wks
7 Nov 92 ★ **THE BEST OF DANCE 92** *Telstar TCD 2610* 1   17 wks
14 Nov 92 ● **CLASSIC LOVE** *Telstar TCD 2620* 4   15 wks
14 Nov 92 ● **THE GREATEST HITS OF 1992** *Telstar TCD 2611* 4   16 wks
21 Nov 92   **ROCK 'N' ROLL HEARTBEATS** *Telstar TCD 2628* 13   1 wk
21 Nov 92   **MY GENERATION** *Telstar TCD 2609* 16   1 wk

VARIOUS ARTISTS

Date	Title		Pos	Wks
28 Nov 92	● **THE GREATEST HITS OF DANCE** *Telstar TCD 2616*		5	11 wks
19 Dec 92	**SONIC SYSTEM** *Telstar TCD 2624*		17	3 wks
23 Jan 93	**MOVIE HITS** *Telstar TCD 2615*		19	1 wk
6 Feb 93	**IN LOVE – GREATEST LOVE 5** *Telstar TCD 2510*		12	2 wks
27 Feb 93	● **COUNTRY LOVE** *Telstar TCD 2645*		5	15 wks
3 Apr 93	**CLASSICAL MASTERS** *Telstar TCD 2549*		18	1 wk
10 Apr 93	● **DEEP HEAT 93 VOLUME 1** *Telstar TCD 2651*		2	7 wks
12 Jun 93	**THE PIG ATTRACTION FEATURING PINKY AND PERKY**			
	Telstar TCD 2668		19	2 wks
26 Jun 93	★ **100% DANCE** *Telstar TCD 2667*		1	15 wks
3 Jul 93	● **RAGGA HEAT REGGAE BEAT** *Telstar TCD 2666*		4	14 wks
17 Jul 93	● **FRESH DANCE 93** *Telstar TCD 2665*		4	7 wks
18 Sep 93	★ **DANCE ADRENALIN** *Telstar TCD 2688*		1	7 wks
2 Oct 93	★ **100% DANCE VOLUME 2** *Telstar TCD 2681*		1	9 wks
9 Oct 93	● **LOVE IS RHYTHM** *Telstar TCD 2683*		5	5 wks
9 Oct 93	**COUNTRY LOVE** *Telstar TCD 2682*		11	4 wks
6 Nov 93	★ **THE BEST OF DANCE '93** *Telstar TCD 2662*		1	14 wks
13 Nov 93	● **THE GREATEST HITS OF 1993** *Telstar TCD 2663*		4	13 wks
20 Nov 93	**THE ALL TIME GREATEST HITS OF DANCE** *Telstar TCD 2679*		11	7 wks
20 Nov 93	**THE GREATEST LOVE 6 – WITH LOVE FROM . . .**			
	Telstar TCD 2686		16	8 wks
11 Dec 93	● **100% REGGAE** *Telstar TCD 2659*		2	17 wks
11 Dec 93	● **100% DANCE VOLUME 3** *Telstar TCD 2705*		7	9 wks
18 Dec 93	● **A HEART OF GOLD** *Telstar TCD 2692*		9	4 wks
8 Jan 94	**NO. 1S OF DANCE** *Telstar TCD 2701*		16	3 wks
19 Feb 94	★ **DANCE HITS 94 VOLUME 1** *Telstar TCD 2693*		1	10 wks
19 Feb 94	● **LOVE OVER GOLD** *Telstar TCD 2684*		2	6 wks
12 Mar 94	● **100% RAP** *Telstar TCD 2694*		3	10 wks
9 Apr 94	**LOVE ON FILM** *Telstar TCD 2545*		17	2 wks
16 Apr 94	**MOVIE HITS** *Telstar TCD 2615*		20	1 wk
23 Apr 94	● **100% DANCE VOLUME 4** *Telstar TCD 2714*		2	7 wks
30 Apr 94	● **100% REGGAE VOLUME 2** *Telstar TCD 2716*		4	14 wks
7 May 94	● **AWESOME DANCE** *Telstar TCD 2721*		2	7 wks
11 Jun 94	★ **DANCE HITS 94 VOLUME 2** *Telstar TCD 2720*		1	8 wks
2 Jul 94	● **JAZZ MOODS** *Telstar TCD 2722*		3	8 wks
23 Jul 94	★ **IT'S THE ULTIMATE DANCE ALBUM** *Telstar TCD 2725*		1	11 wks
23 Jul 94	● **100% SUMMER** *Telstar TCD 2730*		4	7 wks
6 Aug 94	● **100% REGGAE 3** *Telstar TCD 2724*		6	7 wks
24 Sep 94	● **100% HITS** *Telstar TCD 2726*		2	8 wks
8 Oct 94	● **100% ACID JAZZ** *Telstar TCD 2733*		5	14 wks
29 Oct 94	● **JUNGLE MANIA 94** *Telstar TCD 2735*		7	6 wks
29 Oct 94	**THE ULTIMATE REGGAE PARTY ALBUM** *Telstar TCD 2731*		14	2 wks
29 Oct 94	**JAZZ MOODS 2** *Telstar TCD 2740*		18	1 wk
5 Nov 94	● **THE BEST OF DANCE 94** *Telstar TCD 2743*		10	5 wks
5 Nov 94	● **100% PURE LOVE** *Telstar TCD 2737*		7	7 wks
12 Nov 94	● **THE GREATEST HITS OF 1994** *Telstar TCD 2744*		9	5 wks
10 Dec 94	● **100% CHRISTMAS** *Telstar TCD 2754*		9	6 wks
24 Dec 94	● **JUNGLE MANIA 2** *Telstar TCD 2756*		5	8 wks
7 Jan 95	**THE BEST OF 100% DANCE** *Telstar TCD 2752*		11	3 wks
7 Jan 95	● **THE GREATEST LOVE EVER** *Telstar TCD 2747*		6	5 wks
14 Jan 95	● **100% CLASSICS** *Telstar TCD 2757*		8	6 wks
28 Jan 95	**THE GREATEST HITS OF THE 90S PART 1** *Telstar TCD 2749*		19	2 wks
18 Feb 95	**100% HOUSE CLASSICS VOLUME 1** *Telstar TCD 2759*		16	4 wks
25 Mar 95	● **JUNGLE MANIA 3** *Telstar TCD 2762*		5	6 wks
6 May 95	● **WARNING! DANCE BOOM** *Telstar TCD 2763*		2	6 wks
17 Jun 95	**100% ACID JAZZ VOLUME 2** *Telstar TCD 2767*		14	4 wks
8 Jul 95	● **100% SUMMER 95** *Telstar TCD 2777*		7	2 wks
5 Aug 95	● **CLUB ZONE** *Telstar TCD 2779*		4	5 wks
5 Aug 95	**100% SUMMER JAZZ** *Telstar TCD 2781*		11	4 wks
2 Sep 95	● **WARNING! DANCE BOOM 2** *Telstar TCD 2783*		7	4 wks
2 Sep 95	**100% CARNIVAL** *Telstar TCD 2782*		16	2 wks
7 Oct 95	● **CLUB ZONE 2** *Telstar TCD 2787*		10	3 wks
4 Nov 95	● **BEST SWING 95** *Telstar TCD 2789*		10	3 wks
18 Nov 95	● **THE GREATEST HITS OF 95** *Telstar TCD 2792*		9†	7 wks

Green Velvet was a re-issue of Ronco RON LP 6. Heaven & Hell was re-issued in 1995 on Columbia.

Towerbell

28 Sep 85	**THE TV HITS ALBUM** *Towerbell TVLP 3*		26	13 wks

8 Feb 86	● THE DANCE HITS ALBUM Towerbell TVLP 8	10	11	wks
15 Mar 86	THE CINEMA HITS ALBUM Towerbell TVLP 9	44	9	wks
12 Apr 86	THE TV HITS ALBUM TWO Towerbell TVLP 10	19	7	wks
17 May 86	SISTERS ARE DOIN' IT Towerbell TVLP 11	27	9	wks
7 Jun 86	TWO'S COMPANY Towerbell TVLP 12	51	5	wks
28 Jun 86	DANCE HITS II Towerbell TVLP 13	25	8	wks
2 Aug 86	THE ORIGINALS Towerbell TBDLP 14	15	9	wks
9 Aug 86	YOU'VE GOT TO LAUGH Towerbell TVLP 15	51	3	wks

Trax

17 Dec 88	NOEL – CHRISTMAS SONGS AND CAROLS Trax TRXLP 701	89	2	wks
22 Jul 89	DREAMS OF IRELAND Trax MODEM 1035	19	1	wk
17 Feb 90	● ROCK OF AMERICA Trax MODEM 1036	7	6	wks
19 May 90	● FREEDOM TO PARTY – FIRST LEGAL RAVE Trax MODEM 1048	4	10	wks
28 Jul 90	● SUMMER CHART PARTY Trax BWTX 1	9	6	wks
3 Nov 90	FREEDOM 2 – THE ULTIMATE RAVE Trax BWTX 4	16	2	wks
17 Nov 90	KARAOKE PARTY Trax BETX 5	20	1	wk
16 Mar 91	● KARAOKE PARTY II Trax TXTV 1	7	9	wks

Trojan

7 Aug 71	TIGHTEN UP VOLUME 4 Trojan TBL 163	20	7	wks
21 Aug 71	CLUB REGGAE Trojan TBL 159	25	4	wks
16 Jun 84	20 REGGAE CLASSICS Trojan TRLS 222	89	1	wk

TV

2 Oct 82	MODERN HEROES TV TVA 1	24	7	wks
9 Oct 82	ENDLESS LOVE TV TV 2	26	8	wks
6 Nov 82	FLASH TRACKS TV PTVL 1	19	7	wks
25 Dec 82	PARTY FEVER / DISCO MANIA TV TVA 5	71	3	wks

2 Tone

26 Nov 83	THIS ARE TWO TONE 2-Tone CHRTT 5007	51	9	wks
5 Aug 89	THE 2 TONE STORY 2-Tone CHRTT 5009	16	5	wks
23 Oct 93	● THE BEST OF 2 TONE 2-Tone CDCHRTT 5012	10	4	wks

Urban

14 Nov 87	URBAN CLASSICS Urban URBLP 4	96	1	wk
24 Sep 88	URBAN ACID Urban URBLP 15	51	8	wks
8 Oct 88	ACID JAZZ AND OTHER ILLICIT GROOVES Urban URBLP 16	86	3	wks

Vertigo

21 Jun 86	HEAR 'N' AID Vertigo VERH 35	50	2	wks
27 Aug 88	★ HOT CITY NIGHTS Vertigo PROVTV 15	1	14	wks
4 Nov 89	● ROCK CITY NIGHTS Vertigo RCNTV 1	3	14	wks

Virgin

22 Nov 80	CASH COWS Virgin MILK 1	49	1	wk
17 Apr 82	MUSIC OF QUALITY AND DISTINCTION (VOLUME 1) Virgin V 2219	25	6	wks
1 Jun 85	MASSIVE Virgin V 2346	61	3	wks

Virgin Television

19 Jan 91	DANCE ENERGY Virgin Television VTDLP 3	20	2	wks
1 Jun 91	● DANCE ENERGY VOLUME 2 Virgin Television VTLP 4	6	5	wks
19 Oct 91	● MOODS Virgin Television VTLP 5	2	22	wks
30 Nov 91	● DANCE ENERGY VOLUME 3 Virgin Television VTLP 6	10	6	wks
29 Feb 92	● THREE MINUTE HEROES Virgin Television VTCD 9	4	10	wks
16 May 92	● MOODS 2 Virgin Television VTCD 12	3	8	wks
25 Jul 92	● THE GREATEST DANCE ALBUM IN THE WORLD! Virgin Television VTCD 13	2	12	wks
31 Oct 92	● NEW ROMANTIC CLASSICS Virgin Television VTCD 15	7	5	wks

VARIOUS ARTISTS

17 Jul 93 ★ THE BEST DANCE ALBUM IN THE WORLD ... EVER!		
Virgin Television VTDCD 17 ....**1**	19 wks	
23 Oct 93 ● THE SINGER AND THE SONG *Virgin Television VTDCD 21* **5**	6 wks	
20 Nov 93 ● THE BEST DANCE ALBUM IN THE WORLD ... EVER! 2		
Virgin Television VTDCD 22 ....**3**	12 wks	
4 Dec 93 ● THE BEST CHRISTMAS ALBUM IN THE WORLD... EVER!		
Virgin Television VTDCD 23 ....**2**	9 wks	
29 Jan 94 ★ SWEET SOUL HARMONIES *Virgin Television VTCD 20*................**1**	9 wks	
26 Feb 94 ● DANCE TO THE MAX *Virgin Television VTCD 24* **2**	10 wks	
12 Mar 94 ● RAP TO THE MAX *Virgin Television VTCD 25* **10**	4 wks	
30 Apr 94 ● IN THE AIR TONIGHT *Virgin Television VTCD 26* **8**	10 wks	
7 May 94 ★ PURE MOODS *Virgin Television VTCD 28*..........................**1**	31 wks	
28 May 94 ● DANCE TO THE MAX 2 *Virgin Television VTCD 29*.................**4**	8 wks	
4 Jun 94 ● THE BEST REGGAE ALBUM IN THE WORLD...EVER!		
Virgin Television VTCD 27 ....**4**	10 wks	
9 Jul 94 ● SUPERFUNK *Virgin Television VTDCD 30* **8**	5 wks	
30 Jul 94 ● THE BEST DANCE ALBUM IN THE WORLD...EVER! 3		
Virgin Television VTDCD 32 ....**2**	11 wks	
20 Aug 94 ● SWEET SOUL HARMONIES 2 *Virgin Television VTCD 31* **10**	2 wks	
3 Sep 94 ★ THE BEST ROCK ALBUM IN THE WORLD...EVER!		
Virgin Television VTDCD 35 ....**1**	24 wks	
3 Sep 94 ● DANCE TO THE MAX 3 *Virgin Television VTCD 33*.................**12**	3 wks	
29 Oct 94 ● THE BEST ROCK 'N' ROLL ALBUM IN THE WORLD...EVER!		
Virgin Television VTDCD 37 ....**2**	10 wks	
19 Nov 94 ★ THE LOVE ALBUM *Virgin Television VTDCD 38*....................**1**	18 wks	
19 Nov 94 ● THE BEST DANCE ALBUM IN THE WORLD...EVER! 4		
Virgin Television VTDCD 40 ....**5**	4 wks	
4 Feb 95 ★ THE BEST PUNK ALBUM IN THE WORLD...EVER!		
Virgin Television VTDCD 42 ....**1**	13 wks	
18 Feb 95 ● DANCE 95 *Virgin Television VTCD 43* **8**	5 wks	
4 Mar 95 ● THE BEST FUNK ALBUM IN THE WORLD...EVER!		
Virgin Television VTDCD 44 ....**11**	3 wks	
25 Mar 95 ● CELTIC MOODS *Virgin Television VTCD 45* **8**	2 wks	
15 Apr 95 ● THE BEST ROCK ALBUM IN THE WORLD...EVER! II		
Virgin Television VTDCD 47 ....**3**	8 wks	
6 May 95 ● STREET SOUL *Virgin Television VTDCD 41* **2**	9 wks	
10 Jun 95 ● DANCE HEAT 95 *Virgin Television VTCD 50* **8**	3 wks	
17 Jun 95 ● CELTIC MOODS 2 *Virgin Television VTCD 52* **6**	5 wks	
15 Jul 95 ● THE BEST DANCE ALBUM IN THE WORLD...EVER! 5		
Virgin Television VTCD 55 ....**4**	7 wks	
15 Jul 95 ● THE BLUES ALBUM *Virgin Television VTDCD 54*....................**8**	3 wks	
22 Jul 95 ★ THE BEST SUMMER...EVER! *Virgin Television VTCD 57* **1**	8 wks	
29 Jul 95 ● SUMMER SWING *Virgin Television VTDCD 53* **18**	1 wk	
19 Aug 95 ● SERVE CHILLED *Virgin Television VTCD 56* **16**	1 wk	
2 Sep 95 ● THE BEST ROCK BALLADS ALBUM IN THE WORLD...EVER!		
Virgin Television VTDCD 60 ....**2**	18 wks	
2 Sep 95 ● THIS IS CULT FICTION *Virgin Television VTCD 59* **9**	4 wks	
16 Sep 95 ● THE BEST...ALBUM IN THE WORLD...EVER!		
Virgin Television VTCD 58 ....**2†**	8 wks	
21 Oct 95 ● THE BEST DANCE ALBUM IN THE WORLD...95!		
Virgin Television VTCD 67 ....**3**	4 wks	
11 Nov 95 ● THE BEST 80S ALBUM IN THE WORLD...EVER!		
Virgin Television VTCD 68 ....**7**	4 wks	
18 Nov 95 ● THE LOVE ALBUM II *Virgin Television VTCD 69* ....**2†**	7 wks	
18 Nov 95 ● INSTRUMENTAL MOODS *Virgin Television VTCD 65* **14**	5 wks	
25 Nov 95 ● THE BEST PARTY...EVER! *Virgin Television VTCD 71* ....**5†**	6 wks	
2 Dec 95 ● THE BEST 60S ALBUM IN THE WORLD...EVER!		
Virgin Television VTCD 66 ....**2†**	5 wks	

Vision

4 Mar 95 FLARED HITS AND PLATFORM SOUL *Vision VISCD 7* **13**	5 wks	
13 May 95 ● DANCE NATION 95 *Vision VISCD 11* **6**	5 wks	
10 Jun 95 LOVE WITH A REGGAE RHYTHM *Vision VISCD 13* **18**	2 wks	
9 Sep 95 ● THE BEST DANCE ALBUM OF THE YEAR *Vision VISCD 15* **5**	6 wks	

Vital Sounds

4 Jul 92 RED HOT AND WHITE LABELS *Vital Sounds CDVIT 1* **17**	2 wks	
26 Sep 92 RED HOT AND WHITE 2 *Vital Sounds CDVIT 2* **13**	2 wks	
29 May 93 STRICTLY RAGGA *Vital Sounds CDVIT 3* **12**	2 wks	

VARIOUS ARTISTS

Warner Bros.

25 Mar 78	**HOPE AND ANCHOR FRONT ROW FESTIVAL**		
	Warner Bros. K 66077	**28**	3 wks
21 Jul 79	★ **THE BEST DISCO ALBUM IN THE WORLD**		
	Warner Bros. K 58062	**1**	17 wks
4 Aug 90	**NOBODY'S CHILD – ROMANIAN ANGEL APPEAL**		
	Warner Bros. WX 353	**18**	3 wks
15 Aug 92	**BARCELONA GOLD** Warner Bros. 9362450462	**15**	2 wks

Warner Music

18 Feb 95	● **THE ULTIMATE SOUL COLLECTION** Warner Music 9548333402	**4**	9 wks
5 Aug 95	**DISCO INFERNO** Warner Music 548319632	**16**	1 wk
28 Oct 95	**THE ULTIMATE SOUL COLLECTION VOLUME 2**		
	Warner Music 9548338402	**11**	2 wks

Warwick

29 Nov 75	**ALL–TIME PARTY HITS** Warwick WW 5001	**21**	8 wks
17 Apr 76	● **INSTRUMENTAL GOLD** Warwick WW 5012	**3**	24 wks
29 May 76	**HAMILTON'S HOT SHOTS** Warwick WW 5014	**15**	5 wks
8 Jan 77	**SONGS OF PRAISE** Warwick WW 5020	**31**	2 wks
29 Jan 77	**HIT SCENE** Warwick PR 5023	**19**	5 wks
11 Mar 78	● **FONZIE'S FAVOURITES** Warwick WW 5037	**8**	16 wks
25 Nov 78	**LOVE SONGS** Warwick WW 5046	**47**	7 wks
2 Dec 78	**BLACK VELVET** Warwick WW 5047	**72**	3 wks
31 Mar 79	**LEMON POPSICLE** Warwick WW 5050	**42**	6 wks
7 Apr 79	**COUNTRY PORTRAITS** Warwick WW 5057	**14**	10 wks
10 Nov 79	**20 SMASH DISCO HITS (THE BITCH)** Warwick WW 5061	**42**	5 wks
16 Feb 80	**COUNTRY GUITAR** Warwick WW 5070	**46**	3 wks
14 Nov 81	**DISCO EROTICA** Warwick WW 5108	**35**	8 wks
10 Apr 82	**PS I LOVE YOU** Warwick WW 5121	**68**	3 wks
6 Nov 82	**HITS OF THE SCREAMING 60'S** Warwick WW 5124	**24**	10 wks
22 Dec 84	**MERRY CHRISTMAS TO YOU** Warwick WW 5141	**64**	2 wks

OTHER COMPILATION ALBUMS

10 Mar 62	**GREAT MOTION PICTURE THEMES** HMV CLP 1508	**19**	1 wk
24 Aug 63	**THE MERSEY BEAT VOLUME 1** Oriole PS 40047	**17**	5 wks
16 May 64	**OUT CAME THE BLUES** Ace of Hearts AH 72	**19**	1 wk
11 Sep 66	● **STARS CHARITY FANTASIA SAVE THE CHILDREN FUND**		
	SCF PL 145	**6**	16 wks
8 Apr 67	● **HIT THE ROAD STAX** Stax 589005	**10**	16 wks
11 May 68	**BLUES ANYTIME** Immediate IMLP 014	**40**	1 wk
4 Dec 71	**BREAKTHROUGH** MFP 1334	**49**	1 wk
22 Jan 72	★ **CONCERT FOR BANGLADESH** Apple STCX 3385	**1**	13 wks
15 Mar 75	**SOLID SOUL SENSATIONS** Disco Diamond DDLP 5001	**30**	1 wk
16 Aug 75	**NEVER TOO YOUNG TO ROCK** GTO GTLP 004	**30**	5 wks
31 Jan 76	**REGGAE CHARTBUSTERS 75** Cactus CTLP 114	**53**	1 wk
22 May 76	● **A TOUCH OF COUNTRY** Topaz TOC 1976	**7**	7 wks
3 Jul 76	**GOLDEN FIDDLE AWARDS 1976** Mountain TOPC 5002	**45**	2 wks
3 Jul 76	**A TOUCH OF CLASS** Topaz TOC 1976	**57**	1 wk
27 Nov 76	**ALL THIS AND WORLD WAR II** Riva RVLP 2	**23**	7 wks
16 Jul 77	**THE ROXY LONDON WC 2** Harvest SHSP 4069	**24**	5 wks
11 Mar 78	**STIFF'S LIVE STIFFS** Stiff GET 1	**28**	7 wks
28 Oct 78	**ECSTASY** Lotus WH 5003	**24**	6 wks
26 May 79	**A MONUMENT TO BRITISH ROCK** Harvest EMTV 17	**13**	12 wks
9 Jun 79	**THAT SUMMER** Arista SPART 1088	**36**	8 wks
3 Nov 79	**MODS MAYDAY 79** Arista FOUR 1	**75**	1 wk
24 May 80	**PRECIOUS METAL** MCA MCF 3069	**60**	2 wks
14 Mar 81	**THE SOME BIZARRE ALBUM** Some Bizzare BZLP 1	**58**	1 wk
4 Apr 81	**REMIXTURE** Champagne CHAMP 1	**32**	5 wks
30 May 81	**STRENGTH THROUGH OI!** Skin SKIN 1	**51**	5 wks
31 Oct 81	**CARRY ON OI!** Secret SEC 2	**60**	4 wks
12 Dec 81	**LIVE AND HEAVY** NEMS NEL 6020	**100**	2 wks
19 Dec 81	**WE ARE MOST AMUSED** Ronco/Charisma RTD 2067	**30**	9 wks
27 Mar 82	● **JAMES BOND'S GREATEST HITS** Liberty EMTV 007	**4**	13 wks
27 Mar 82	**PUNK AND DISORDERLY** Abstract AABT 100	**48**	8 wks

Date	Title	Pos	Weeks
14 Aug 82	**SOWETO** *Rough Trade ROUGH 37* **66**		3 wks
4 Sep 82	**PUNK AND DISORDERLY – FURTHER CHARGES**		
	Anagram GRAM 001 ....**91**		2 wks
25 Sep 82	**OI OI THAT'S YOUR LOT** *Secret SEC 5* **54**		4 wks
23 Oct 82	**STREET NOISE VOLUME 1** *Streetware STR 32234* **51**		4 wks
14 May 83	**THE LAUGHTER AND TEARS COLLECTION** *WEA LTC 1* **19**		16 wks
18 Jun 83	**TEARDROPS** *Ritz RITZSP 399* **37**		6 wks
2 Jul 83	**WIRED FOR CLUBS (CLUB TRACKS VOLUME 1)**		
	Club CLUBL 1001 ....**58**		4 wks
3 Sep 83	**COME WITH CLUB (CLUB TRACKS VOLUME 2)** *Club CLUBL 002* **55**		2 wks
15 Oct 83	**RESPOND PACKAGE – LOVE THE REASON** *Respond RRL 501* **50**		3 wks
26 Nov 83	**TWELVE INCHES OF PLEASURE** *Proto PROTO 1* **100**		1 wk
16 Jun 84	● **EMERALD CLASSICS** *Stoic SRTV 1* **10**		14 wks
21 Jul 84	**ROCKABILLY PSYCHOSIS AND THE GARAGE DISEASE**		
	Big Beat WIK 18 ....**88**		3 wks
11 Aug 84	**CHUNKS OF FUNK** *Loose End CHUNK 1* **46**		5 wks
8 Sep 84	**RECORD SHACK PRESENTS – VOLUME ONE**		
	Record Shack RSTV 1 ....**41**		4 wks
8 Dec 84	**THE CHRISTMAS CAROL COLLECTION** *Fame WHS 413000* **75**		3 wks
16 Feb 85	**STARGAZERS** *Kasino KTV 1* **69**		3 wks
6 Apr 85	**TOMMY BOY GREATEST BEATS** *Tommy Boy ILPS 9825* **44**		6 wks
25 May 85	● **OUT NOW!** *Chrysalis/MCA OUTV 1* **2**		16 wks
13 Jul 85	**KERRANG! KOMPILATION** *EMI/Virgin KER 1* **84**		2 wks
24 Aug 85	**20 HOLIDAY HITS** *Creole CTV 1* **48**		6 wks
19 Oct 85	**IQ6: ZANG TUMB TUUM SAMPLED** *ZTT IQ 6* **40**		3 wks
26 Oct 85	● **OUT NOW! 2** *Chrysalis/MCA OUTV 2* **3**		12 wks
22 Mar 86	**NUMA RECORDS YEAR 1** *Numa NUMA1004* **94**		1 wk
16 Aug 86	● **THE HEAT IS ON** *Portrait PRT 10051* **9**		12 wks
16 Aug 86	**SUMMER DAYS, BOOGIE NIGHTS** *Portrait PRT 10052* **40**		6 wks
18 Oct 86	**THE POWER OF LOVE** *West Five WEF 4* **33**		7 wks
28 Mar 87	**HEART OF SOUL VOLUME 1** *Mastersounds MASL 001* **96**		1 wk
30 May 87	**THE SOLAR SYSTEM** *Solar MCG 3338* **70**		1 wk
6 Jun 87	**CHICAGO JACKBEAT VOLUME 2** *Rhythm King LEFTLP 2* **67**		2 wks
11 Jul 87	**LONELY IS AN EYESORE** *4AD CAD 703* **53**		2 wks
1 Aug 87	**FIERCE** *Cooltempo CTLP 4* **37**		6 wks
8 Aug 87	**KICK IT! – THE DEF JAM SAMPLER ALBUM** *Def Jam KICKIT 1* ...**19**		7 wks
24 Oct 87	**THE WORD** *Zomba HOP 217* **86**		1 wk
26 Mar 88	**THE WORD VOLUME 2** *Jive HOP 220* **70**		2 wks
9 Apr 88	**SERGEANT PEPPER KNEW MY FATHER** *NME PELP 100* **37**		8 wks
3 Sep 88	**HOUSE HALLUCINATIONS (PUMP UP LONDON)**		
	Breakout HOSA 9002 ....**90**		2 wks
8 Oct 88	**BROTHERS IN RHYTHM** *Ariola 303374* **35**		5 wks
12 Nov 88	**THE HIT FACTORY VOLUME 2** *Fanfare/PWL HF 4* **16**		9 wks
14 Jan 89	**THE HIT FACTORY VOLUME 2** *Fanfare/PWL HF 4* **13**		3 wks
11 Feb 89	**RARE 3** *Ariola 209498* **15**		2 wks
18 Feb 89	**CAPITOL CLASSICS VOLUME 1** *Capitol EMS 1316* **16**		2 wks
15 Apr 89	**THE SONGS OF BOB DYLAN** *Start STDL 20* **13**		5 wks
1 Jul 89	**THIS IS GARAGE** *Cooltempo CTLP 12* **18**		2 wks
15 Jul 89	● **THE HIT FACTORY VOLUME 3** *Fanfare/PWL HF 8* **3**		10 wks
23 Sep 89	● **JUST SEVENTEEN – HEARTBEATS** *Fanfare FARE 1* **3**		6 wks
24 Mar 90	**EMERALD CLASSICS VOLUMES I & 11** *Westmoor WMTV 1* **14**		2 wks
7 Apr 90	**LET'S DANCE – SOUND OF THE SIXTIES PART 1**		
	Old Gold OG 1702 ....**18**		1 wk
21 Apr 90	● **THE EARTHQUAKE ALBUM** *Live Aid Armenia AIDLP 001* **3**		10 wks
16 Jun 90	**LOVERS FOR LOVERS VOLUME 3** *Business WBRLP 903* **18**		1 wk
28 Jul 90	**NOTHING COMPARES TO THIS** *Parkfield PMLP 5020* **13**		2 wks
3 Nov 90	● **RED HOT AND BLUE** *Chrysalis CHR 1799* **6**		3 wks
22 Dec 90	**CHRISTMAS GREATEST HITS** *Legends In LELP 501* **16**		1 wk
16 Mar 91	● **PETER HETHERINGTON: SONGS FROM THE HEART**		
	Mawson And Wareham PHMC 2 ....**10**		3 wks
4 May 91	● **MARQUEE METAL** *Marquee 8454171* **5**		6 wks
11 May 91	● **THE BEST OF INDIE TOP 20** *Beechwood BOTT 1* **10**		3 wks
18 May 91	**SOUTHERN KNIGHTS** *Knight KTVLP 1* **13**		2 wks
13 Jul 91	★ **PURPLE RAINBOWS** *Polydor/EMI 8455341* **1**		13 wks
14 Sep 91	● **XL RECORDINGS – THE SECOND CHAPTER** *XL XLLP 108* **5**		9 wks
28 Sep 91	● **THE POWER AND THE GLORY** *Vertigo 5103601* **2**		9 wks
12 Oct 91	**I'M YOUR FAN – THE SONGS OF LEONARD COHEN**		
	East West WX 444 ....**16**		2 wks
9 Nov 91	**RAVE** *Reachin' REMULP 01* **18**		2 wks
16 Nov 91	**R & S RECORDS – ORDER TO DANCE** *R & S RSLP 1* **18**		1 wk

Date	Title	Pos	Weeks
18 Jan 92	**NOISE** *Jumpin' & Pumpin' CDTOT 3*	20	1 wk
1 Feb 92	**CLOSET CLASSICS VOLUME 1** *More Protein CMMD 1*	20	1 wk
22 Feb 92	**SHUT UP AND DANCE** *Shut Up And Dance SUADCOMPCD 001*	20	1 wk
7 Mar 92	**THE REBIRTH OF COOL, TOO** *Fourth & Broadway BRCD 582*	13	2 wks
11 Apr 92	**DISCOVER THE CLASSICS VOLUME 1** *Imp Classics CDBOXD 21*	15	3 wks
11 Apr 92	**DISCOVER THE CLASSICS VOLUME 2** *Imp Classics CDBOXD 22*	12	3 wks
25 Apr 92	● **THE THIRD CHAPTER** *XL XLCD 109*	6	8 wks
9 May 92	**VIRUS 100 – ALTERNATIVE TENTACLES** *Alternative Tentacles VIRUS 100CD*	15	1 wk
16 May 92	**NOISE 2** *Jumpin' & Pumpin' CDTOT 4*	11	3 wks
13 Jun 92	★ **EARTHRISE – THE RAINFOREST ALBUM** *ELF 5154192*	1	6 wks
27 Jun 92	**JUNGLE TEKNO** *Debut CDTOT 5*	18	1 wk
11 Jul 92	**THE ULTIMATE OPERA COLLECTION** *Erato 2292457972*	14	5 wks
1 Aug 92	**HARDCORE DJS . . . TAKE CONTROL** *Perfecto 74321101812*	15	4 wks
19 Sep 92	**ILLEGAL RAVE** *Strictly Underground STHCCD 1*	20	1 wk
26 Sep 92	**VOLUME FOUR** *Worlds End V 4CD*	17	1 wk
21 Nov 92	**SENSUAL CLASSICS** *Teldec 4509900552*	19	2 wks
28 Nov 92	● **THE PREMIERE COLLECTION ENCORE** *Really Useful 5173362*	2	11 wks
5 Dec 92	**TAKE 2: OPERA FAVOURITES / ORCHESTRAL CLASSICS** *Masterworks S2K 48226*	18	3 wks
30 Jan 92	● **TALKIN LOUD TWO** *Talkin Loud 5159362*	6	3 wks
13 Feb 93	● **CELTIC HEART** *RCA 74321131662*	6	10 wks
6 Mar 93	**AMBIENT DUB VOLUME 2 – EARTH JUICE** *Beyond RABDCD 3*	20	1 wk
13 Mar 93	● **D–FROST – 20 GLOBAL DANCE WARNINGS** *Touchdown CTVCD 114*	8	4 wks
20 Mar 93	**YEAH YEAH YEAH / OUR TROUBLES YOUTH** *Catcall/Wiiija TUSS 001*	12	2 wks
17 Apr 93	**DUB HOUSE DISCO 2000** *Guerilla GRCD 7*	18	1 wk
24 Apr 93	**WINNER'S CIRCLE** *Expansion CDEXP 2*	20	1 wk
1 May 93	**VOLUME SIX** *Volume 6VCD 6*	19	1 wk
8 May 93	**COWBOY COMPILATION** *Cowboy RODEOCD 1*	18	1 wk
15 May 93	● **THE REBIRTH OF COOL III** *Fourth & Broadway BRCD 590*	9	4 wks
15 May 93	**UNIVERSE** *Universe VERSECD 1*	13	2 wks
29 May 93	**THE BEST OF ACID JAZZ VOLUME 2** *Acid Jazz JAZIDCD 66*	16	1 wk
29 May 93	**INFORCERS 3** *Reinforced RIVET1242CD*	18	1 wk
26 Jun 93	**DISCO INFERNO** *East West 9548319632*	17	1 wk
3 Jul 93	● **ON A REGGAE TIP** *Mango CIDTV 5*	3	9 wks
2 Oct 93	● **TRANCE EUROPE EXPRESS** *Volume TEEXCD 1*	14	5 wks
12 Mar 94	★ **RAP ATTACK** *Concept MOODCD 32*	9	7 wks
12 Mar 94	**JOURNEYS BY DJ VOLUME 4** *Music Unites JDJCD 4*	19	1 wk
2 Apr 94	**PHASE ONE** *Positiva CDTIVA 1002*	15	1 wk
11 Jun 94	**ARTIFICIAL INTELLIGENCE II** *Warp WARPLTDCD 23*	16	2 wks
23 Apr 94	**RHYTHM COUNTRY AND BLUES** *MCA MCD 10965*	19	2 wks
12 Jun 94	**TRANCE EUROPE EXPRESS 2** *Volume TEEXCD2*	65	3 wks
13 Aug 94	**JUNIOR BOY'S OWN COLLECTION** *Junior Boy's Own JBOCD 2*	20	1 wk
20 Aug 94	**1–800 NEW FUNK** *NPG BR 710062*	15	1 wk
17 Sep 94	**DRUM AND BASS SELECTION 2** *Break Down BDRCD 003*	14	3 wks
24 Sep 94	**IN ORDER TO DANCE 5** *R & S RS 94003CDXX*	16	1 wk
1 Oct 94	● **RENAISSANCE** *Six6 REMNIX 1CD*	9	5 wks
5 Nov 94	● **THE VERY BEST OF ANDREW LLOYD WEBBER** *Really Useful 5238602*	3	13 wks
4 Mar 95	**BORN TO BE WILD** *Mo Music MUSCD 001*	20	1 wk
4 Feb 95	● **LOVE ETERNAL** *Miracle MIRCD 0001*	5	4 wks
13 May 95	**YOU MUST REMEMBER THIS** *Happy Days CDHD 2656*	16	1 wk
27 May 95	● **MORE BUMP N' GRIND** *MCA MCD 11286*	9	3 wks
3 Jun 95	**FRESHEN UP** *Fresh FRSHCD 1*	20	1 wk
10 Jun 95	**UNIVERSE PRESENTS THE TRIBAL GATHERING** *Universe 8284522*	19	1 wk
17 Jun 95	**RADIO DREAMSCAPE VOLUME 1** *Dreamscape DREAMCD 01*	20	1 wk
15 Jul 95	**THE HOUSE OF HANDBAG** *Ultrasound USCD 3*	13	3 wks
5 Aug 95	● **A RETROSPECTIVE OF HOUSE 91–95 VOLUME 1** *Sound Dimension SDIMCD 3*	10	10 wks
16 Sep 95	★ **HELP – WAR CHILD** *Go! Discs 8286822*	1	7 wks
16 Sep 95	**TRADE** *Feverpitch FVRCD 1001*	14	2 wks
4 Nov 95	**CLUB IBIZA** *Quality Price Music QPMCD 1*	15	1 wk
4 Nov 95	**THE HOUSE OF HANDBAG – AUTUMN / WINTER** *Ultrasound USCD 4*	16	2 wks

368

FILM SOUNDTRACKS

| 8 Nov 58 | ★ **SOUTH PACIFIC** *RCA RB 16065* | 1 | 286 wks |

8 Nov 58	● THE KING AND I *Capitol LCT 6108*	**4**	103	wks
8 Nov 58	● OKLAHOMA *Capitol LCT 6100*	**4**	90	wks
6 Dec 58	● CAROUSEL *Capitol LCT 6105*	**8**	15	wks
31 Jan 59	● GIGI *MGM C 770*	**2**	88	wks
10 Oct 59	● PORGY AND BESS *Philips ABL 3282*	**7**	5	wks
23 Jan 60	● THE FIVE PENNIES *London HAU 2189*	**2**	15	wks
7 May 60	● CAN CAN *Capitol W 1301*	**2**	31	wks
28 May 60	PAL JOEY *Capitol LCT 6148*	**20**	1	wk
23 Jul 60	HIGH SOCIETY *Capitol LCT 6116*	**16**	1	wk
5 Nov 60	BEN HUR *MGM C 802*	**15**	3	wks
21 Jan 61	NEVER ON SUNDAY *London HAT 2309*	**17**	1	wk
18 Feb 61	● SONG WITHOUT END *Pye GGL 30169*	**9**	10	wks
29 Apr 61	● SEVEN BRIDES FOR SEVEN BROTHERS *MGM C 853*	**6**	22	wks
3 Jun 61	EXODUS *RCA RD 27210*	**17**	1	wk
11 Nov 61	GLENN MILLER STORY *Ace Of Hearts AH 12*	**12**	7	wks
24 Mar 62	★ WEST SIDE STORY *Philips BBL 7530*	**1**	175	wks
28 Apr 62	● IT'S TRAD DAD *Columbia 33SX 1412*	**3**	21	wks
22 Sep 62	THE MUSIC MAN *Warner Bros. WB 4066*	**14**	9	wks
3 Nov 62	PORGY AND BESS *CBS APG 60002*	**14**	7	wks
15 Jun 63	JUST FOR FUN *Decca LK 4524*	**20**	2	wks
31 Oct 64	● MY FAIR LADY *CBS BPG 72237*	**9**	51	wks
31 Oct 64	GOLDFINGER *United Artists ULP 1076*	**14**	5	wks
16 Jan 65	● MARY POPPINS *HMV CLP 1794*	**2**	82	wks
10 Apr 65	★ SOUND OF MUSIC *RCA RB 6616*	**1**	381	wks
30 Apr 66	FUNNY GIRL *Capitol W 2059*	**19**	3	wks
11 Sep 66	● DR ZHIVAGO *MGM C 8007*	**3**	106	wks
22 Jul 67	CASINO ROYALE *RCA Victor SF 7874*	**35**	1	wk
29 Jul 67	A MAN AND A WOMAN *United Artists SULP 1155*	**31**	11	wks
28 Oct 67	● THOROUGHLY MODERN MILLIE *Brunswick STA 8685*	**9**	19	wks
9 Mar 68	● THE JUNGLE BOOK *Disney ST 3948*	**5**	51	wks
21 Sep 68	STAR *Stateside SSL 10233*	**36**	1	wk
12 Oct 68	● THE GOOD, THE BAD AND THE UGLY *United Artists SULP 1197*	**2**	18	wks
23 Nov 68	● OLIVER *RCA Victor SB 6777*	**4**	107	wks
23 Nov 68	CAMELOT *Warner Bros. WS 1712*	**37**	1	wk
8 Feb 69	● CHITTY CHITTY BANG BANG *United Artists SULP 1200*	**10**	4	wks
10 May 69	FUNNY GIRL *CBS 70044*	**11**	22	wks
14 Jun 69	● 2001 – A SPACE ODYSSEY *MGM CS 8078*	**3**	67	wks
20 Dec 69	● EASY RIDER *Stateside SSL 5018*	**2**	67	wks
24 Jan 70	JUNGLE BOOK (re–issue)*Disney BVS 4041*	**25**	26	wks
7 Feb 70	● PAINT YOUR WAGON *Paramount SPFL 257*	**2**	102	wks
14 Mar 70	HELLO DOLLY *Stateside SSL 10292*	**45**	2	wks
18 Jul 70	WOODSTOCK *Atlantic 2662 001*	**35**	19	wks
24 Apr 71	LOVE STORY *Paramount SPFL 267*	**10**	33	wks
12 Feb 72	● CLOCKWORK ORANGE *Warner Bros. K 46127*	**4**	46	wks
8 Apr 72	FIDDLER ON THE ROOF *United Artists UAD 60011/2*	**26**	2	wks
13 May 72	2001 – A SPACE ODYSSEY (re–issue)*MGM 2315 034*	**20**	2	wks
29 Nov 72	SOUTH PACIFIC (re–issue)*RCA Victor SB 2011*	**25**	2	wks
31 Mar 73	CABARET *Probe SPB 1052*	**13**	22	wks
14 Apr 73	LOST HORIZON *Bell SYBEL 8000*	**36**	3	wks
22 Sep 73	JESUS CHRIST SUPERSTAR *MCA MDKS 8012/3*	**23**	18	wks
23 Mar 74	● THE STING *MCA MCF 2537*	**7**	35	wks
27 Apr 74	AMERICAN GRAFFITI *MCA MCSP 253*	**37**	1	wk
8 Jun 74	A TOUCH OF CLASS *Philips 6612 040*	**32**	1	wk
5 Oct 74	SUNSHINE *MCA MCF 2566*	**47**	3	wks
5 Apr 75	TOMMY *Polydor 2657 014*	**21**	9	wks
31 Jan 76	JAWS *MCA MCF 2716*	**55**	1	wk
5 Mar 77	MOSES *Pye 28503*	**43**	2	wks
9 Apr 77	★ A STAR IS BORN *CBS 86021*	**1**	54	wks
2 Jul 77	THE BEST OF CAR WASH *MCA MCF 2799*	**59**	1	wk
11 Mar 78	★ SATURDAY NIGHT FEVER *RSO 2658 123*	**1**	65	wks
22 Apr 78	● THE STUD *Ronco RTD 2029*	**2**	19	wks
29 Apr 78	CLOSE ENCOUNTERS OF THE THIRD KIND *Arista DLART 2001*	**40**	6	wks
6 May 78	THE LAST WALTZ *Warner Bros. K 66076*	**39**	4	wks
20 May 78	THANK GOD IT'S FRIDAY *Casablanca TGIF 100*	**40**	5	wks
27 May 78	FM *MCA MCSP 284*	**37**	7	wks
8 Jul 78	★ GREASE *RSO RSD 2001*	**1**	47	wks
12 Aug 78	SGT PEPPER'S LONELY HEARTS CLUB BAND *A & M AMLZ 66600*	**38**	2	wks
7 Oct 78	CONVOY *Capitol EST 24590*	**52**	1	wk
30 Jun 79	THE WORLD IS FULL OF MARRIED MEN *Ronco RTD 2038*	**25**	9	wks

369

VARIOUS ARTISTS

14 Jul 79	THE WARRIORS A & M AMLH 64761	53	7	wks
6 Oct 79	QUADROPHENIA Polydor 2625 037	23	16	wks
5 Jan 80	THE SECRET POLICEMAN'S BALL Island ILPS 9601	33	6	wks
9 Feb 80	SUNBURN Warwick RTL 2044	45	7	wks
16 Feb 80	GOING STEADY Warwick WW 5078	25	10	wks
8 Mar 80	THE ROSE Atlantic K 50681	68	1	wk
7 Jun 80	THE GREAT ROCK 'N' ROLL SWINDLE Virgin V 2168	16	11	wks
19 Jul 80	● XANADU Jet JET LX 526	2	17	wks
16 Aug 80	● CAN'T STOP THE MUSIC Mercury 6399 051	9	8	wks
6 Sep 80	★ FAME RSO 2479 253	1	25	wks
14 Feb 81	● DANCE CRAZE 2-Tone CHRTT 5004	5	15	wks
12 Dec 81	THE SECRET POLICEMAN'S OTHER BALL Springtime HAHA 6003	69	4	wks
20 Mar 82	THE SECRET POLICEMAN'S OTHER BALL (THE MUSIC) Springtime HAHA 6004	29	5	wks
17 Jul 82	THE SOUND OF MUSIC (re–issue) RCA Ints 5134	98	1	wk
4 Sep 82	ROCKY III Liberty LBG 30351	42	7	wks
4 Sep 82	ANNIE CBS 70219	83	2	wks
11 Sep 82	BRIMSTONE AND TREACLE A & M AMLH 64915	67	3	wks
12 Feb 83	AN OFFICER AND A GENTLEMAN Island ISTA 3	40	14	wks
25 Jun 83	RETURN OF THE JEDI RSO RSD 5023	85	5	wks
2 Jul 83	● FLASHDANCE Casablanca CANH 5	9	30	wks
1 Oct 83	STAYING ALIVE RSO RSBG 3	14	8	wks
21 Apr 84	● FOOTLOOSE CBS 70246	7	25	wks
21 Apr 84	AGAINST ALL ODDS Virgin V 2313	29	10	wks
16 Jun 84	● BREAKDANCE Polydor POLD 5147	6	29	wks
7 Jul 84	BEAT STREET Atlantic 780154	30	13	wks
18 Aug 84	ELECTRIC DREAMS Virgin V 2318	46	7	wks
29 Sep 84	GHOSTBUSTERS Arista 206 559	24	25	wks
16 Feb 85	BEVERLY HILLS COP MCA MCF 3253	24	32	wks
22 Jun 85	A VIEW TO A KILL Parlophone BOND 1	81	1	wk
11 Jan 86	BACK TO THE FUTURE MCA MCF 3285	66	8	wks
1 Feb 86	MISTRAL'S DAUGHTER Carrere CAL 221	53	3	wks
1 Feb 86	● ROCKY IV Scotti Bros. SCT 70272	3	22	wks
5 Apr 86	ABSOLUTE BEGINNERS Virgin V 2386	19	9	wks
26 Apr 86	OUT OF AFRICA MCA MCF 3310	81	2	wks
5 Jul 86	LABYRINTH EMI America AML 3104	38	2	wks
11 Oct 86	● TOP GUN CBS 70296	4	46	wks
11 Apr 87	THE BLUES BROTHERS Atlantic K 50715	59	26	wks
2 May 87	PLATOON WEA WX 95	90	2	wks
18 Jul 87	BEVERLY HILLS COP 2 MCA MCF 3383	71	5	wks
1 Aug 87	THE LIVING DAYLIGHTS Warner Bros. WX 111	57	6	wks
1 Aug 87	● WHO'S THAT GIRL Sire WX 102	4	25	wks
22 Aug 87	LA BAMBA London LONLP 36	24	15	wks
3 Oct 87	FULL METAL JACKET Warner Bros. 925 6131	60	4	wks
31 Oct 87	● DIRTY DANCING RCA BL 86408	4	63	wks
16 Jan 88	FLASHDANCE (re–issue) Mercury PRICE 111	93	2	wks
20 Feb 88	CRY FREEDOM MCA MCG 6029	73	2	wks
14 May 88	● MORE DIRTY DANCING RCA BL 86965	3	27	wks
24 Sep 88	● BUSTER Virgin V 2544	6	16	wks
22 Oct 88	GOOD MORNING VIETNAM A & M AMA 3913	50	9	wks
14 Jan 89	● BUSTER Virgin V 2544	2	36	wks
14 Jan 89	★ DIRTY DANCING RCA BL 86408	1	148	wks
21 Jan 89	● GOOD MORNING VIETNAM A & M AMA 3913	7	29	wks
21 Jan 89	● THE BLUES BROTHERS Atlantic K 50715	4	80	wks
28 Jan 89	★ THE LOST BOYS Atlantic 7817671	1	61	wks
4 Feb 89	● COCKTAIL Elektra EKT 54	2	15	wks
4 Feb 89	MORE DIRTY DANCING RCA BL 86965	14	17	wks
18 Mar 89	SCANDAL Parlophone PCS 7331	13	3	wks
22 Apr 89	● TOP GUN CBS 70296	4	34	wks
13 May 89	DIRTY DANCING – LIVE IN CONCERT RCA BL 90336	19	2	wks
15 Jul 89	LICENCE TO KILL MCA MCG 6051	17	2	wks
22 Jul 89	GHOSTBUSTERS 2 MCA MCG 6056	15	4	wks
10 Mar 90	THE DELINQUENTS PWL HF 11	16	1	wk
26 May 90	● PRETTY WOMAN EMI USA MTL 1052	2	72	wks
23 Jun 90	● TEENAGE MUTANT NINJA TURTLES SBK SBKLP 6	6	18	wks
11 Aug 90	● DAYS OF THUNDER Epic 4671591	4	15	wks
27 Oct 90	GHOST Milan A 620	15	4	wks
2 Feb 91	● ROCKY V Capitol EST 2137	9	9	wks

 370

VARIOUS ARTISTS

2 Mar 91	● GREASE (re–issue)*Polydor 8179981*	.........**8**	11	wks
23 Mar 91	THE GODFATHER III *Columbia 4678131*	.........**19**	1	wk
27 Apr 91	NEW JACK CITY *Giant 7599244091*	.........**16**	5	wks
1 Jun 91	● MERMAIDS *Epic 467874*	.........**6**	15	wks
27 Jul 91	● ROBIN HOOD – PRINCE OF THIEVES *Polydor 5110502*	.........**3**	14	wks
18 Jan 92	● BILL AND TED'S BOGUS JOURNEY *Interscope 7567917252*	.........**3**	8	wks
29 Feb 92	MY GIRL *Epic 4692134*	.........**13**	7	wks
30 May 92	● WAYNE'S WORLD *Reprise 7599258052*	.........**5**	11	wks
12 Sep 92	● THE BEST OF JAMES BOND – 30TH ANNIVERSARY			
	EMI CDBOND 007	.........**2**	11	wks
19 Sep 92	MO' MONEY *Perspective 3610042*	.........**16**	1	wk
14 Nov 92	BOOMERANG *LaFace 73008260062*	.........**17**	2	wks
28 Nov 92	★ THE BODYGUARD *Arista 07822186992*	.........**1**	78	wks
30 Jan 93	SISTER ACT *Hollywood HWCD 29*	.........**14**	4	wks
13 Feb 93	● BRAM STOKER'S DRACULA *Columbia 4727462*	.........**10**	6	wks
20 Mar 93	RESERVOIR DOGS *MCA MCD 10793*	.........**16**	3	wks
5 Jun 93	INDECENT PROPOSAL *MCA MCD 10863*	.........**13**	3	wks
24 Jul 93	THE LAST ACTION HERO *Columbia 4739902*	.........**16**	6	wks
18 Sep 93	SLIVER *Virgin CDVMMX 11*	.........**20**	1	wk
16 Oct 93	● SLEEPLESS IN SEATTLE *Epic 4735942*	.........**10**	6	wks
16 Oct 93	JUDGEMENT NIGHT *Epic 4741832*	.........**16**	3	wks
20 Nov 93	● THE VERY BEST OF DISNEY *Pickwick DISCD 471*	.........**4**	13	wks
8 Jan 94	ALADDIN *Pickwick DSTCD 470*	.........**11**	5	wks
5 Mar 94	WAYNE'S WORLD 2 *Warner Bros. WB 45485*	.........**17**	1	wk
12 Mar 94	● PHILADELPHIA *Epic 4749982*	.........**5**	14	wks
7 May 94	ABOVE THE RIM *Interscope 6544923592*	.........**18**	1	wk
28 May 94	● FOUR WEDDINGS AND A FUNERAL *Vertigo 5167512*	.........**5**	21	wks
25 Jun 94	THE CROW *Atlantic 7567825192*	.........**13**	5	wks
6 Aug 94	THE FLINTSTONES *MCA MCD 11045*	.........**18**	1	wk
22 Oct 94	● THE LION KING *Mercury 5226902*	.........**4**	20	wks
22 Oct 94	● FORREST GUMP *Epic 4769412*	.........**5**	13	wks
5 Nov 94	THE LION KING SING–ALONG *Disney DSMCD 477*	.........**16**	3	wks
5 Nov 94	● PULP FICTION *MCA MCD 11103*	.........**5**	50	wks
19 Nov 94	● THE VERY BEST OF DISNEY 2 *Disney DISCD 480*	.........**9**	4	wks
11 Mar 95	● NATURAL BORN KILLERS *Interscope 6544924602*	.........**10**	6	wks
8 Jul 95	BAD BOYS *Work 4804532*	.........**19**	1	wk
29 Jul 95	BATMAN FOREVER *Atlantic 7567827592*	.........**11**	4	wks

During its chart run, West Side Story changed label and number from Philips BBL 7530 to CBS BPG 62058.

STAGE CAST RECORDINGS

These albums still qualify for inclusion on the main chart, not the Compilation Albums chart.

8 Nov 58	● MY FAIR LADY (BROADWAY) *Philips RBL 1000*	.........**2**	129	wks
24 Jan 59	● WEST SIDE STORY (BROADWAY) *Philips BBL 7277*	.........**3**	27	wks
26 Mar 60	● AT THE DROP OF A HAT (LONDON) *Parlophone PMC 1033*	.........**9**	1	wk
26 Mar 60	● FINGS AIN'T WOT THEY USED TO BE (LONDON) *Decca LK 4346*	.........**5**	11	wks
2 Apr 60	● FLOWER DRUM SONG (BROADWAY) *Philips ABL 3302*	.........**2**	27	wks
7 May 60	● FOLLOW THAT GIRL (LONDON) *HMV CLP 1366*	.........**5**	9	wks
21 May 60	● MOST HAPPY FELLA (BROADWAY) *Philips BBL 7374*	.........**6**	13	wks
21 May 60	MAKE ME AN OFFER (LONDON) *HMV CLP 1333*	.........**18**	1	wk
28 May 60	● FLOWER DRUM SONG (LONDON) *HMV CLP 1359*	.........**10**	3	wks
9 Jul 60	MOST HAPPY FELLA (LONDON) *HMV CLP 1365*	.........**19**	1	wk
30 Jul 60	WEST SIDE STORY (BROADWAY) *Philips SBBL 504*	.........**14**	1	wk
10 Sep 60	● OLIVER (LONDON) *Decca LK 4359*	.........**4**	91	wks
11 Mar 61	KING KONG (SOUTH AFRICA) *Decca LK 4392*	.........**12**	8	wks
6 May 61	● MUSIC MAN (LONDON) *JMH CLP 1444*	.........**8**	13	wks
24 Jun 61	● SOUND OF MUSIC (BROADWAY) *Philips ABL 3370*	.........**4**	19	wks
22 Jul 61	BYE–BYE BIRDIE (LONDON) *Philips ABL 3385*	.........**17**	3	wks
22 Jul 61	BEYOND THE FRINGE (LONDON) *Parlophone PMC 1145*	.........**13**	17	wks
29 Jul 61	● SOUND OF MUSIC (LONDON) *HMV CLP 1453*	.........**4**	68	wks
9 Sep 61	● STOP THE WORLD I WANT TO GET OFF (LONDON)			
	Decca LK 4408	.........**8**	14	wks
14 Jul 62	● BLITZ (LONDON) *HMV CLP 1569*	.........**7**	21	wks
18 May 63	HALF A SIXPENCE (LONDON) *Decca LK 4521*	.........**20**	2	wks
3 Aug 63	PICKWICK (LONDON) *Philips AL 3431*	.........**12**	10	wks
4 Jan 64	MY FAIR LADY (BROADWAY) *CBS BPG 68001*	.........**19**	1	wk

22 Feb 64	**AT THE DROP OF ANOTHER HAT (LONDON)**	
	Parlophone PMC 1216 ....**12**	11 wks
3 Oct 64	● **CAMELOT (BROADWAY)** *CBS APG 60001* **10**	12 wks
16 Jan 65	**CAMELOT (LONDON)** *HMV CLP 1756* **19**	1 wk
11 Mar 67	● **FIDDLER ON THE ROOF (LONDON)** *CBS SBPG 70030* **4**	50 wks
28 Dec 68	● **HAIR (LONDON)** *Polydor 583043* **3**	94 wks
30 Aug 69	**OLIVER (LONDON) (re–issue)** *Decca SPA 30* **23**	4 wks
6 Sep 69	**HAIR (BROADWAY)** *RCA SF 7959* **29**	3 wks
19 Feb 72	**GODSPELL (LONDON)** *Bell BELLS 203* **25**	17 wks
18 Nov 78	**EVITA (LONDON)** *MCA MCF 3257* **24**	18 wks
1 Aug 81	● **CATS (LONDON)** *Polydor CATX 001* **6**	26 wks
6 Nov 82	**MACK AND MABEL (BROADWAY)** *MCA MCL 1728* **38**	7 wks
7 Aug 84	**STARLIGHT EXPRESS (LONDON)** *Starlight/Polydor LNER 1* **21**	9 wks
15 Feb 86	**LES MISERABLES (LONDON)** *First Night ENCORE 1* **72**	4 wks
21 Feb 87	★ **THE PHANTOM OF THE OPERA (LONDON)** *Really Useful PODV 3* **1**	141 wks
16 Sep 89	★ **ASPECTS OF LOVE (LONDON)** *Polydor 841126 1*...................**1**	29 wks
24 Feb 90	● **MISS SAIGON (LONDON)** *Geffen WX329*........................**4**	11 wks
29 Jun 91	**FIVE GUYS NAMED MOE (LONDON)** *First Night CAST 23* **59**	1 wk
31 Aug 91	★ **JOSEPH AND THE AMAZING TECHNICOLOUR DREAMCOAT**	
	Really Useful 511301...**1**	38 wks
10 Apr 93	**THE NEW STARLIGHT EXPRESS (LONDON)**	
	Really Useful 5190412 ....**42**	2 wks
11 Sep 93	**SUNSET BOULEVARD (LONDON)** *Really Useful 5197672* **11**	4 wks
2 Oct 93	**GREASE (LONDON)** *Epic 4746322* **20**	3 wks
1 Apr 95	**OLIVER! (LONDON)** *First Night CASTCD 47* **36**	3 wks

The Really Useful label was given credit midway through The Phantom of the Opera's *chart run.*

STUDIO CAST RECORDINGS

25 Jun 60	**SHOWBOAT** *HMV CLP 1310*...................................**12**	1 wk
8 Feb 72	● **JESUS CHRIST SUPERSTAR** *MCA MKPS 2011/2*.................**6**	20 wks
22 Jan 77	● **EVITA** *MCA MCX 503* **4**	35 wks
17 Jun 78	**WHITE MANSIONS** *A & M AMLX 64691* **51**	3 wks
10 Nov 84	● **CHESS** *RCA PL 70500* **10**	16 wks
18 May 85	**WEST SIDE STORY** *Deutsche Grammophon 41525* **11**	32 wks
2 Nov 85	**CHESS PIECES** *Telstar STAR 2274* **87**	3 wks
10 May 86	**WEST SIDE STORY – HIGHLIGHTS**	
	Deutsche Grammophon 45963 ....**72**	6 wks
17 May 86	**DAVE CLARK'S 'TIME'** *EMI AMPH 1* **21**	6 wks
11 Oct 86	● **SOUTH PACIFIC** *CBS SM 42205* **5**	24 wks
27 Jun 87	**MATADOR** *Epic VIVA 1* **26**	5 wks
21 Nov 87	**MY FAIR LADY** *Decca MFL 1* **41**	12 wks
10 Oct 92	**THE KING AND I** *Philips 4380072* **57**	2 wks
10 Apr 93	**LEONARD BERNSTEIN'S WEST SIDE STORY** *IMG IMGCD 1801*....**33**	5 wks

TV and RADIO SOUNDTRACKS and SPIN-OFFS

13 Dec 58	● **OH BOY!** *Parlophone PMC 1072* **9**	14 wks
4 Mar 61	● **HUCKLEBERRY HOUND** *Pye GGL 004* **10**	12 wks
28 Feb 63	**THAT WAS THE WEEK THAT WAS** *Parlophone PMC 1197* **11**	9 wks
28 Mar 64	**STARS FROM STARS AND GARTERS** *Pye GGL 0252* **17**	2 wks
4 Nov 72	**THE BBC 1922–1972 (TV AND RADIO EXTRACTS)** *BBC 50* ...**16**	7 wks
4 Jan 75	**BBC TV'S BEST OF TOP OF THE POPS** *Super Beeb BELP 001* **21**	5 wks
6 Dec 75	**SUPERSONIC** *Stallion SSM 001* **21**	6 wks
10 Apr 76	★ **ROCK FOLLIES** *Island ILPS 9362* **1**	15 wks
22 Oct 77	**10 YEARS OF HITS – RADIO ONE** *Super Beeb BEDP 002* **39**	3 wks
8 Apr 78	● **PENNIES FROM HEAVEN** *World Records SH 266* **10**	17 wks
1 Jul 78	**MORE PENNIES FROM HEAVEN** *World Records SH 267* **31**	4 wks
9 Dec 78	**STARS ON SUNDAY BY REQUEST** *Curzon Sounds CSL 0081* **65**	3 wks
15 Dec 79	**FAWLTY TOWERS** *BBC REB 377* **25**	10 wks
7 Feb 81	**FAWLTY TOWERS VOLUME 2** *BBC REB 405* **26**	7 wks
14 Feb 81	**HITCHHIKERS GUIDE TO THE GALAXY VOLUME 2**	
	Original ORA 54 ....**47**	4 wks
1 Aug 81	**MUSIC OF COSMOS** *RCA RCALP 5032* **43**	10 wks
21 Nov 81	**BRIDESHEAD REVISITED** *Chrysalis CDL 1367* **50**	12 wks
23 Oct 82	**ON THE AIR – 60 YEARS OF BBC THEME MUSIC** *BBC REF 454*....**85**	3 wks
26 Nov 83	**REILLY ACE OF THEMES** *Red Bus BUSLP 1004* **54**	6 wks

Date	Title	Pos	Weeks
4 Feb 84	**AUF WIEDERSEHEN PET** Towerbell AUF 1	21	6 wks
18 Feb 84	**THE TUBE** K-Tel NE 1261	30	6 wks
8 Sep 84	**SONG AND DANCE** RCA BL 70480	46	4 wks
12 Jan 85	**BREAKDANCE 2 – ELECTRIC BOOGALOO** Polydor POLD 5168	34	20 wks
18 May 85	**VICTORY IN EUROPE – BROADCASTS FROM BBC CORRESPONDENTS** BBC REC 562	61	1 wk
28 Sep 85	**THE TV HITS ALBUM** Towerbell TVLP 3	26	13 wks
26 Oct 85	**MIAMI VICE** BBC/MCA REMV 584	11	9 wks
16 Nov 85	**THE EASTENDERS SING–A–LONG ALBUM** BBC REB 586	33	10 wks
23 Nov 85	**TELLY HITS – 16 TOP TV THEMES** Stylus BBSR 508	34	6 wks
15 Feb 86	● **JONATHAN KING'S ENTERTAINMENT U.S.A.** Stylus SMR 6812	6	11 wks
12 Apr 86	**THE TV HITS ALBUM TWO** Towerbell TVLP 10	19	7 wks
5 Jul 86	**TELLY HITS 2** Stylus BBSR 616	68	2 wks
18 Oct 86	**THE VERY BEST OF ENTERTAINMENT U.S.A. VOLUME 2** Priority UPTVR 1	44	4 wks
1 Nov 86	**SIMON BATES – OUR TUNE** Polydor PROLP 10	58	5 wks
26 Dec 86	● **THE SINGING DETECTIVE** BBC REN 608	10	24 wks
27 Jun 87	**THE ROCK 'N' ROLL YEARS 1956–59** BBR REN 631	80	2 wks
27 Jun 87	**THE ROCK 'N' ROLL YEARS 1960–63** BBC REN 632	84	1 wk
27 Jun 87	**THE ROCK 'N' ROLL YEARS 1964–67** BBC REN 633	71	2 wks
27 Jun 87	**THE ROCK 'N' ROLL YEARS 1968–71** BBC REN 634	77	1 wk
3 Oct 87	**MOONLIGHTING** MCA MCF 3386	50	6 wks
17 Oct 87	**MIAMI VICE 2** MCA MCG 6019	71	4 wks
28 Nov 87	**THE CHART SHOW – DANCE HITS '87** Chrysalis ADD 1	39	6 wks
26 Mar 88	**THE CHART SHOW – ROCK THE NATION** Dover ADD 2	16	8 wks
1 Oct 88	● **MOONLIGHTING 2** WEA WX 202	5	9 wks
1 Oct 88	**MIAMI VICE 3** MCA MCG 6033	95	1 wk
8 Oct 88	● **ONES ON 1** BBC REF 693	10	7 wks
24 Dec 88	**THE BEIDERBECKE COLLECTION** Dormouse DM 20	89	2 wks
14 Jan 89	**THE BEIDERBECKE COLLECTION** Dormouse DM 20	14	5 wks
20 May 89	● **THE CHART SHOW – ROCK THE NATION 2** Dover ADD 4	8	4 wks
3 Jun 89	● **THE CHART SHOW – DANCE MASTERS** Dover ADD 7	4	7 wks
17 Jun 89	● **RAY MOORE – A PERSONAL CHOICE** BBC STAR 2352	7	4 wks
23 Sep 89	**TV TUNES** K-Tel NE 1429	17	3 wks
17 Feb 90	● **PENNIES FROM HEAVEN** BBC REF 768	8	13 wks
16 Feb 91	● **BRITS 1991 – THE MAGIC OF BRITISH MUSIC** Telstar STAR 2481	7	6 wks
21 Sep 91	**THE OLD GREY WHISTLE TEST – BEST OF THE TEST** Windsong International OGWTLP 1	13	3 wks
22 Feb 92	★ **THE AWARDS 1992** PolyGram TV 5152072	1	9 wks
27 Jun 92	★ **HEARTBEAT** Columbia 4719002	1	14 wks
18 Jul 92	**DOCTOR WHO – THE EVIL OF THE DALEKS** BBC ZBBC 1303	72	1 wk
25 Jul 92	● **32 ONES ON ONE – RADIO 1'S 25TH BIRTHDAY** Connoisseur Collection ONECD 32	8	10 wks
17 Oct 92	**BEST OF CAPITAL GOLD** The Hit Label AHLCD 2	20	1 wk
28 Nov 92	**GLADIATORS** PolyGram TV 5158772	11	10 wks
30 Jan 93	● **THE BEST OF THE CLASSICAL BITS** Philips/PolyGram TV 4381662	7	10 wks
13 Feb 93	● **HEAD OVER HEELS** Telstar TCD 2649	3	9 wks
20 Feb 93	● **THE AWARDS 1993** PolyGram TV 5160752	3	7 wks
13 Mar 93	● **LIPSTICK ON YOUR COLLAR** PolyGram TV 51608642	2	13 wks
17 Apr 93	● **THE CHART SHOW ULTIMATE ROCK ALBUM** The Hit Label AHLCD 9	4	11 wks
3 Jul 93	**ROADSHOW HITS** Connoisseur Collection RSHCD 20	18	2 wks
7 Aug 93	● **THE BIG BREAKFAST ALBUM** Arcade ARC 3100082	8	5 wks
14 Aug 93	**DOCTOR WHO – THE POWER OF THE DALEKS** BBC ZBBC 1433	71	1 wk
18 Sep 93	**DOCTOR WHO – THE PARADISE OF DEATH** BBC ZBBC 1494	48	1 wk
2 Oct 93	● **THE CHART SHOW... ULTIMATE ROCK 2** The Hit Label AHLCD 13	10	3 wks
23 Oct 93	**TALES FROM THE CITY** PolyGram TV 5165152	17	2 wks
20 Nov 93	**RETURN OF THE GLADIATORS** PolyGram TV 5165172	20	1 wk
22 Jan 94	★ **THE SOUND OF KISS 100FM** PolyGram TV 5164862	1	4 wks
16 Jul 94	**THE CHART SHOW – THE ULTIMATE BLUES ALBUM** The Hit label AHLCD 19	13	3 wks
28 Jan 95	★ **THE BEST OF HEARTBEAT** Columbia MOODCD 37	1	6 wks
20 May 95	**THE CHART SHOW PRESENTS CHART MACHINE** PolyGram TV 5250392	18	2 wks
10 Jun 95	★ **TOP OF THE POPS 1** Columbia MOODCD 40	1	6 wks
5 Aug 95	● **THE CHART SHOW DANCE ALBUM** PolyGram TV 5257682	6	3 wks
30 Sep 95	★ **HEARTBEAT – FOREVER YOURS** Columbia SONYTV 8CD	1†	14 wks
18 Nov 95	**THE CORONATION STREET ALBUM** EMI Premier CDCOROTV 1	20	1 wk

373

VARIOUS ARTISTS

2 Dec 95   **TOP OF THE POPS 2** *Columbia SONYTV 9CD* ....**14**   5 wks

ANONYMOUS COVER VERSIONS

29 Feb 64	**BEATLEMANIA** *Top Six TSL 1* **19**	2	wks
7 Aug 71	**HOT HITS 5** *MFP 5208* **48**	1	wk
7 Aug 71	★ **HOT HITS 6** *MFP 5214* **1**	7	wks
7 Aug 71	**TOP OF THE POPS VOLUME 17** *Hallmark SHM 740*.....................**16**	3	wks
7 Aug 71	★ **TOP OF THE POPS VOLUME 18** *Hallmark SHM 745* **1**	12	wks
7 Aug 71	**MILLION SELLER HITS** *MFP 5203*......................................**46**	2	wks
21 Aug 71	**SMASH HITS SUPREMES STYLE** *MFP 5184* **36**	3	wks
2 Oct 71	● **TOP OF THE POPS VOLUME 19** *Hallmark SHM 750*......................**3**	9	wks
23 Oct 71	● **HOT HITS 7** *MFP 5236* **3**	9	wks
6 Nov 71	**SMASH HITS COUNTRY STYLE** *MFP 5228* **38**	1	wk
13 Nov 71	★ **TOP OF THE POPS VOLUME 20** *Hallmark SHM 739*.......................**1**	8	wks
27 Nov 71	**NON STOP 20 VOLUME 4** *Plexium PXMS 1006* **35**	2	wks
4 Dec 71	**SMASH HITS 71** *MFP 5229* **21**	3	wks
11 Dec 71	● **HOT HITS 8** *MFP 5243* **2**	4	wks
27 Sep 75	**40 SINGALONG PUB SONGS** *K-Tel NE 509*....................**21**	7	wks
6 Nov 76	**FORTY MANIA** *Ronco RDT 2018*....................................**21**	6	wks

MISCELLANEOUS

12 Sep 70	**EDINBURGH MILITARY TATTOO 1970** *Waverley SZLP 2121* **34**	4	wks
18 Sep 71	**EDINBURGH MILITARY TATTOO 1971** *Waverley SZLP 2128* **44**	1	wk
11 Dec 71	**ELECTRONIC ORGANS TODAY** *Ad-Rhythm ADBS 1*.......................**48**	1	wk
8 Dec 73	● **MUSIC FOR A ROYAL WEDDING** *BBC REW 163* **7**	6	wks
27 Dec 75	**STRINGS OF SCOTLAND** *Philips 6382 108*....................................**50**	1	wk
1 Aug 81	**ROYAL ROMANCE** *Windosor WIN001* **84**	1	wk
8 Aug 81	★ **THE OFFICIAL BBC ALBUM OF THE ROYAL WEDDING**		
	BBC REP 413 ....**1**	11	wks
9 Aug 86	**ROYAL WEDDING** *BBC REP 596* **55**	1	wk

28 Dec 91	**TRIVIAL PURSUIT – THE MUSIC MASTER GAME**		
	Telstar STAC 2550 ....**20**	1	wk

HIT ALBUMS

ALPHABETICALLY BY TITLE

We have listed all albums alphabetically, together with the name of the recording act and the year the album first hit the chart. For 'Various Artists' albums the label is listed in brackets, to help you locate the album in the main section. All albums with the same title are, obviously, different. When two or more albums have the same title, they are listed chronologically by recording artist.

Ron Wolfson/LFI

PAUL WELLER had number one albums with the Jam and Style Council before *Stanley Road* **became his first solo effort to hit the top.**

INDEX

405

FACTS AND FEATS

BLIND FAITH (left to right: Steve Winwood, Rick Grech, Ginger Baker and Eric Clapton) made number one with their only album. (LFI)

CONTENTS

MOST WEEKS ON CHART

The following table lists the 181 recording acts that have spent 150 weeks or more on the British albums chart from the first chart on 8 Nov 1958 up to and including the chart of 31 Dec 1995. It is, of course, possible for an act to be credited with two or more chart weeks in the same week if the act has more than one album on the chart in any one week.

Beatles 1160	Led Zeppelin 441
Queen 1111	Status Quo 435
Simon and Garfunkel 1083	James Last 431
Dire Straits 1082	*(includes 15 weeks with Richard Clayderman)*
Elvis Presley 1071	Eurythmics 425
David Bowie 903	Tom Jones 422
U2 861	Barbra Streisand 415
Pink Floyd 859	Roxy Music 414
Elton John 801	*(includes 121 weeks with Bryan Ferry)*
Fleetwood Mac 795	Simply Red 410
Michael Jackson 770	Prince 409
(includes 58 weeks with Jackson Five,	*(plus 3 weeks with New Power Generation)*
10 weeks with Diana Ross, Gladys Knight	R.E.M. 405
and Stevie Wonder, and 24 weeks with	Madness 396
Diana Ross)	Jim Reeves 391
Cliff Richard 761	The Sound Of Music (*Original*
Phil Collins 756	*Soundtrack*) 382
Rod Stewart 747	Electric Light Orchestra 381
Rolling Stones 741	Duran Duran 372
Meat Loaf 713	Lionel Richie 366
Madonna 677	Police 353
Frank Sinatra 662	Guns N' Roses 351
(includes 23 weeks with Count Basie)	Simple Minds 347
Abba 635	Bon Jovi 340
Bob Dylan 575	Eagles 340
(includes 3 weeks with the Grateful Dead)	Stevie Wonder 340
Carpenters 574	*(includes 10 weeks with Diana Ross,*
Diana Ross 569	*Gladys Knight and Michael Jackson)*
(includes 45 weeks with Marvin Gaye,10	Barry Manilow 336
weeks with Michael Jackson, Gladys Knight	Chris Rea 331
and Stevie Wonder, 3 weeks with Placido	Buddy Holly and the Crickets 328
Domingo and José Carreras, and 24 weeks	*(Crickets +7 alone; + 27 with Bobby Vee)*
with Michael Jackson)	Pet Shop Boys 321
Beach Boys 558	Billy Joel 316
UB40 541	Herb Alpert 312
Neil Diamond 535	Erasure 311
Mike Oldfield 526	Moody Blues 310
Paul McCartney/Wings 522	John Lennon 297
Eric Clapton 475	Blondie 294
(includes 1 week as Derek and the	*(includes 26 with Debbie Harry)*
Dominoes, 17 weeks with John Mayall and	Bryan Ferry 293
104 weeks with Cream)	*(includes 121 weeks with Roxy Music)*
Genesis 468	George Mitchell Minstrels 292
Shadows 461	Johnny Cash 290
Bruce Springsteen 459	South Pacific (*Original Soundtrack*) 288
Tina Turner 450	Cream 286
(includes 1 week with Ike and Tina Turner)	*(includes 104 weeks with Eric Clapton)*
Bob Marley and the Wailers 443	Shirley Bassey 284
Andy Williams 442	

FACTS AND FEATS

Neil Young (229 weeks on chart)

Donny Osmond has racked up 104 weeks as a solo act, 103 as part of the Osmonds, and 19 with his sister Marie, a total of **226** weeks.

Steve Winwood has clocked up 120 weeks on the chart as a solo act, 47 weeks as a member of the Spencer Davis Group, 41 playing in Traffic and 10 as part of Blind Faith, a total of **218** weeks.

Graham Nash has had 8 weeks on the chart as a soloist, 5 weeks as half of a duo with David Crosby, 14 weeks as one third of Crosby, Stills and Nash, 79 weeks as one quarter of Crosby, Stills, Nash and Young and 106 weeks as one fifth of the Hollies, a total of **212** weeks.

New Order have spent 145 weeks on the chart, while Joy Division, mainly the same line up, have a further 32 weeks on chart, a total of **177** weeks.

The Royal Philharmonic Orchestra have enjoyed 119 weeks on the chart, plus 25 more with Richard Clayderman, 13 with Julian Lloyd Webber, 10 with Andy Williams, and 9 with Juan Martin a total of **176** weeks.

Jimmy Somerville has 42 solo chart weeks, 74 as a member of the Communards and 59 as part of Bronski Beat, a total of **175** weeks.

Dionne Warwick has 144 solo chart weeks, 2 with Placido Domingo and 19 more on Stevie Wonder's soundtrack album, *Woman In Red*. This is a total of **165** weeks.

David Sylvian has 21 solo weeks on the chart, 3 in partnership with Holgar Czukay and 136 as a member of Japan, a total of **160** weeks.

Boy George has 9 solo weeks to his credit, 1 week as Jesus Loves You and 149 more as lead vocalist with Culture Club, a total of **159** weeks.

Nat 'King' Cole has 118 weeks of solo chart action, plus 7 with the George Shearing Quintet and one with Dean Martin. He is also the uncredited duettist with his daughter on her 29-week chart resident *Unforgettable – With Love* album, a total of **155** weeks.

Scott Walker has charted for 45 weeks as a solo artist, 96 weeks as a Walker Brother and 12 weeks on an album of both his and the Walker Brothers' hits, a total of **153** weeks.

Belinda Carlisle has spent 149 solo weeks on the chart, and another 4 weeks as part of the Go-Gos, a total of **153** weeks.

There are 14 people who have been on the albums charts in total for over 1000 weeks, if we count their solo albums and albums by groups of which they were fully paid-up members. They are, in order:

Paul McCartney	**1682** weeks	Art Garfunkel	**1141** weeks
John Lennon	**1457** weeks	Brian May	**1132** weeks
Paul Simon	**1344** weeks	Roger Taylor	**1123** weeks
George Harrison	**1293** weeks	Mark Knopfler	**1116** weeks
Phil Collins	**1224** weeks	John Deacon	**1111** weeks
Ringo Starr	**1188** weeks	John Illsley	**1082** weeks
Freddie Mercury	**1167** weeks	Elvis Presley	**1071** weeks

FACTS AND FEATS

MOST WEEKS ON CHART IN A YEAR

There have been 54 instances of one act clocking up 100 or more chart weeks in one year, including most recently both Queen and Guns N' Roses in 1992. Dire Straits' record score in 1986 is the equivalent of four albums on the chart every week throughout the year.

217	Dire Straits	1986	112	Bob Dylan	1965
198	David Bowie	1983	112	Abba	1978
182	David Bowie	1973	112	Electric Light Orchestra	1979
177	Bruce Springsteen	1985	111	Andy Williams	1971
168	U2	1985	109	George Mitchell Minstrels	1962
167	Simon and Garfunkel	1970	108	Pink Floyd	1977
158	Dire Straits	1985	107	David Bowie	1974
136	Michael Jackson	1984	107	Dire Straits	1983
135	Tom Jones	1968	107	Queen	1986
131	Phil Collins	1985	107	Fleetwood Mac	1988
128	Queen	1992	106	Carpenters	1974
127	Madonna	1987	106	Abba	1977
126	U2	1987	105	Elton John	1975
125	Johnny Cash	1970	105	Duran Duran	1983
125	Madonna	1986	104	Beatles	1964
123	Michael Jackson	1983	104	Simon and Garfunkel	1973
122	Beatles	1970	104	Beatles	1974
121	Otis Redding	1968	103	Four Tops	1968
121	Guns N' Roses	1992	102	Led Zeppelin	1970
117	Queen	1987	102	Simon and Garfunkel	1971
116	Beach Boys	1968	102	Human League	1982
116	Police	1980	101	Herb Alpert	1967
116	Dire Straits	1984	101	Simon and Garfunkel	1974
116	Michael Jackson	1988	100	Simon and Garfunkel	1975
115	Jim Reeves	1964	100	Blondie	1979
115	Moody Blues	1970	100	U2	1984
113	Phil Collins	1986	100	Pet Shop Boys	1988

Simon and Garfunkel have racked up 100 chart weeks in a year five times. Dire Straits have done it four times, in consecutive years (1983 to 1986 inclusive). The Beatles, David Bowie, Michael Jackson, U2 and Queen have topped the century in three years, while Abba, Phil Collins and Madonna have done it twice.

MOST WEEKS ON CHART IN EACH CHART YEAR

1958	Elvis Presley	16*	1967	Herb Alpert	101
1959	Frank Sinatra	56*	1968	Tom Jones	135*
1960	Elvis Presley	51	1969	Seekers	66
1961	Elvis Presley	91*	1970	Simon and Garfunkel	167*
1962	George Mitchell Minstrels	109*	1971	Andy Williams	111
1963	Cliff Richard	72	1972	Cat Stevens	89
1964	Jim Reeves	115*	1973	David Bowie	182*
1965	Bob Dylan	112	1974	David Bowie	107
1966	Beach Boys	95	1975	Elton John	105

1976	Demis Roussos	.84	1986	Dire Straits	.217*
1977	Pink Floyd	.108	1987	Madonna	.127
1978	Abba	.112	1988	Michael Jackson	.116
1979	Electric Light Orchestra	.112	1989	Guns N' Roses	.85
1980	Police	.116	1990	Phil Collins	.85
1981	Barry Manilow	.92	1991	Michael Bolton	.63
1982	Human League	.102	1992	Queen	.128
1983	David Bowie	.198*	1993	R.E.M.	.97
1984	Michael Jackson	.136	1994	Meat Loaf	.75
1985	Bruce Springsteen	.177	1995	Cranberries	.96

(* denotes record annual total at the time)

In 1960, the soundtrack album *South Pacific* was on the charts for all 53 chart weeks of the year, a greater total than that of the year's individual champion, Elvis Presley.

Elvis Presley and David Bowie have each been the year's chart champions three times, and Michael Jackson has won twice. No other act has been chart champion more than once.

MOST WEEKS ON CHART IN 1994

434

75	Meat Loaf
69	Nirvana
65	R.E.M.
64	Mariah Carey
58	Take That
57	M People
56	Pink Floyd
	Diana Ross
53	Cranberries
52	Enigma

Meat Loaf, Nirvana, R.E.M. and Take That displayed great consistency in being among the Top Ten album chart acts for a second consecutive year. For R.E.M. and Nirvana it was actually a third consecutive year among the leaders, but for Take That it marked a remarkable triumph over the industry cynics who had written them off as a teeny-bop band who could not sell albums. For Meat Loaf, it was an astonishing comeback to the very top after several years with no new chart hits. Old hands Diana Ross and Pink Floyd also made long overdue returns to the top of the chart ladder, but there was also much promising new blood, especially the American Mariah Carey, the British M People, the Irish Cranberries and the Romanian Enigma.

MOST WEEKS ON CHART IN 1995

The Cranberries, who built on their success in 1994 to top the consistency ratings in 1995, became the first Irish act to outscore all-comers on the annual albums chart. The well-established consistency of R.E.M. and Bon Jovi took the next two places, but then it was two new British bands, Blur and Oasis, who confirmed what Take That had shown, that singles acts can sell albums too. Oasis' album, *(What's The Story) Morning Glory?*, looked to be the biggest-selling album of the year until it was pipped in Christmas week by the freakishly successful Robson and Jerome debut album. Celine Dion also made the big breakthrough, while M People remained consistent sellers without ever topping the weekly chart. Beautiful South owed their weeks total to just one album, *Carry On Up The Charts – The Best Of The Beautiful South*, which spent all year on the chart.

96	Cranberries
85	R.E.M.
80	Bon Jovi
73	Blur
64	Oasis
63	Celine Dion
61	M People
60	Nirvana
52	Beautiful South
49	Take That
	Wet Wet Wet

FACTS AND FEATS

MOST WEEKS ON CHART BY ONE ALBUM

This is a list of all the albums that have spent a total of 100 weeks or more on the chart to the end of 1995. Re-releases and re-issues are counted, provided that the re-issue is the same as the original release.

Bat Out Of Hell Meat Loaf...472
Rumours Fleetwood Mac..443
Greatest Hits Queen..433
The Sound Of Music Original Film Soundtrack.............382
Dark Side Of The Moon Pink Floyd............................337
Bridge Over Troubled Water Simon and Garfunkel.........304
South Pacific Original Film Soundtrack.......................288
Greatest Hits Simon and Garfunkel...........................283
Face Value Phil Collins..274
Tubular Bells Mike Oldfield.......................................271
Legend Bob Marley and the Wailers............................265
Makin' Movies Dire Straits..249
Jeff Wayne's War Of The Worlds Various....................235
Brothers In Arms Dire Straits....................................203
U2 Live: Under A Blood Red Sky U2...........................203
Love Over Gold Dire Straits......................................198
Off The Wall Michael Jackson...................................178
No Jacket Required Phil Collins.................................176
West Side Story Original Film Soundtrack....................175
Sergeant Pepper's Lonely Hearts Club Band Beatles......174
Thriller Michael Jackson...173
**The Rise And Fall Of Ziggy Stardust And The Spiders
From Mars** David Bowie...172
The Beatles 1962–1966 Beatles.................................171
Nevermind Nirvana 164
Alchemy – Dire Straits Live Dire Straits.....................163
Hello I Must Be Going Phil Collins.............................163
The Buddy Holly Story Buddy Holly...........................156
Can't Slow Down Lionel Richie..................................154
Out Of Time R.E.M...153
Like A Virgin Madonna...152
Manilow Magic Barry Manilow...................................151
Private Dancer Tina Turner.......................................147
War U2..147
Best Of The Beach Boys Beach Boys..........................142
Black And White Minstrel Show George Mitchell Minstrels.....142
The Immaculate Collection Madonna.........................141
Going Places Herb Alpert 138
Led Zeppelin II Led Zeppelin 138
Appetite For Destruction Guns N' Roses 137
Eliminator ZZ Top..135
The Beatles 1967–1970 Beatles.................................133
Automatic For The People R.E.M. 131
The Best Of UB40 Volume 1 UB40.............................130
Dire Straits Dire Straits 130
Greatest Hits Abba 130
Picture Book Simply Red...130
Simply The Best Tina Turner 130
The Unforgettable Fire U2..130
The Joshua Tree U2...129

435

Of these albums, only the three Beatles albums and the two Queen albums were on the chart in the final week of 1995.

Five Dire Straits albums are in this list. Three albums each by the Beatles, Phil Collins, Simon and Garfunkel, Michael Jackson, Madonna and U2 have spent over 100 weeks on the chart, as well as two each by Abba, David Bowie, Duran Duran, Electric Light Orchestra, Fleetwood Mac, Whitney Houston, Queen, R.E.M., Simply Red and Tina Turner. Paul Simon, John Lennon and Paul McCartney each feature in four albums which have enjoyed at least 100 weeks of chart life.

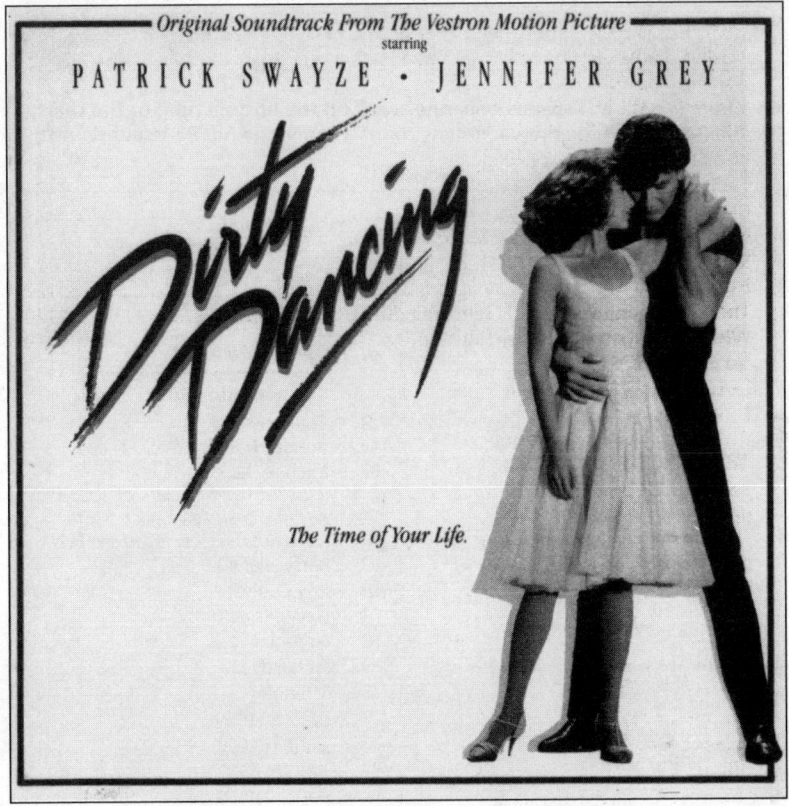

The sales of a record are not necessarily reflected in the length of its chart run. *Off The Wall* and *Thriller* have both had longer chart runs than Michael Jackson's best seller in Britain, *Bad*, while Dire Straits' biggest seller, *Brothers In Arms*, still has some way to go before its chart life overtakes that of *Makin' Movies*.

Dirty Dancing Original Film Soundtrack spent 63 weeks on the main chart up to the beginning of 1989, and a further 148 weeks on the compilations chart to the end of 1995, a total of 211 weeks of chart action. *The Blues Brothers Original Film Soundtrack* spent 26 weeks on the main chart up to the beginning of 1989, and a further 80 weeks on the compilations chart, a total of 106 weeks of chart action.

No other album has totalled over 100 weeks on the Compilation Albums chart, nor by a combination of appearances on the two charts.

The leading performers on the Compilation Albums chart in its first five years of existence are:

Dirty Dancing Original Film Soundtrack	148
The Blues Brothers Original Film Soundtrack	80
The Bodyguard Original Soundtrack	78
Pretty Woman Original Film Soundtrack	72
The Lost Boys Original Film Soundtrack	61
The Classic Experience Various Artists	57
The Premiere Collection Various Artists	53
Pulp Fiction Original Film Soundtrack	50

437

MOST HIT ALBUMS

An album is a hit if it spends only one week on the bottom rung of the chart. Double, treble and quadruple albums count as only one hit. Re-issues do not count as new hits.

96	Elvis Presley
61	James Last
	(includes 2 with Richard Clayderman)
54	Frank Sinatra
	(includes 1 with Count Basie)
50	Cliff Richard
41	Rolling Stones
39	Diana Ross
	(includes 1 with Marvin Gaye, 1 with Michael Jackson, 1 with Placido Domingo and José Carreras, and 1 with Gladys Knight, Stevie Wonder and Michael Jackson; plus 13 as a Supreme)
38	Bob Dylan
	(includes 1 with Grateful Dead)
34	Elton John
32	Shirley Bassey
31	David Bowie
29	Neil Diamond
27	Beach Boys
27	Beatles
27	Johnny Mathis
	(includes 1 with Natalie Cole, 1 with Deniece Williams and 1 with Henry Mancini)
27	Jim Reeves
27	Status Quo
27	Neil Young
	(plus 1 with Stills-Young Band and 3 with Crosby, Stills, Nash and Young)
26	Shadows
	(plus 24 more backing Cliff Richard)
25	Jethro Tull
25	Andy Williams
24	Iron Maiden
24	Tom Jones
24	Paul McCartney/Wings
24	Rod Stewart
	(plus 1 with the Faces)
23	Jimi Hendrix
	(includes 1 with Curtis Knight)
23	Gary Numan/Tubeway Army
	(includes 1 with Sharpe and Numan)
22	Eric Clapton
	(includes 1 as Derek and the Dominoes, 1 with John Mayall and 1 with Cream)
22	Hawkwind
	(includes 1 as Hawklords)
22	Van Morrison
22	Who
21	Black Sabbath
21	Marc Bolan/ T. Rex/Tyrannosaurus Rex
21	Deep Purple
21	Queen
20	Mike Oldfield
20	Santana
	Carlos Santana has 3 more with various other partners)
19	Elvis Costello
	includes 1 as the Costello Show)
19	Michael Jackson
	(includes 1 with Diana Ross, Gladys Knight and Stevie Wonder, 1 with Diana Ross and 1 with Jackson Five)
19	Barry Manilow
19	Roy Orbison
18	David Essex
18	Genesis
18	Pink Floyd
18	Stranglers
18	Barbra Streisand
17	Carpenters
17	Johnny Cash
17	Alice Cooper
17	Cure
17	Foster and Allen
17	Prince
17	Stevie Wonder
	(includes 1 with Diana Ross, Gladys Knight and Michael Jackson)
17	Yes
16	Herb Alpert
16	John Denver
	(includes 1 with Placido Domingo)
16	Fleetwood Mac
16	Kiss
16	London Symphony Orchestra
16	Moody Blues
16	Slade
16	Tangerine Dream
16	Temptations
	(includes 3 with Diana Ross and the Supremes)
15	Motorhead
15	Roxy Music
	(includes 3 with Bryan Ferry)
15	Donna Summer
15	Supremes
	(includes 1 with Four Tops, 3 with Diana Ross and the Temptations)
15	UB40
14	Abba

14	Joan Armatrading
14	Bee Gees
14	Richard Clayderman
	(includes 2 with James Last)
14	Barbara Dickson
	(includes 1 with Elaine Paige)
14	Placido Domingo
	(includes 1 with John Denver, 2 with Luciano Pavarotti and José Carreras, 1 with José Carreras and Montserrat Caballé, 1 with Diana Ross and José Carreras, and 1 with Dionne Warwick)
14	Fall
14	John Mayall
	(includes 1 with Eric Clapton)
14	Joni Mitchell
14	Chris Rea
14	Rush
14	Siouxsie and the Banshees
14	Bruce Springsteen
14	Don Williams
13	AC/DC
13	George Benson
	(includes 1 with Earl Klugh)
13	Elkie Brooks
13	Chris De Burgh
13	Electric Light Orchestra
13	Marvin Gaye
	(includes 1 with Smokey Robinson, 1 with Diana Ross and 1 with Tammi Terrell)
13	Hollies
13	Jean-Michel Jarre
13	Billy Joel
13	Judas Priest
13	Led Zeppelin
13	Bob Marley and the Wailers
13	Gary Moore
13	Robert Palmer
13	Squeeze
13	Thin Lizzy
	(includes 1 with Phil Lynott)
13	Wishbone Ash
13	Frank Zappa
12	Mr. Acker Bilk
	(includes 2 with Chris Barber and 1 with Chris Barber and Kenny Ball)
12	Max Bygraves
12	Everly Brothers
	(Phil Everly has 1 more solo)
12	Bryan Ferry
	(includes 3 with Roxy Music)
12	Four Tops
	(includes 1 with Supremes)
12	Engelbert Humperdinck
12	Jacksons
	(4 as Jackson Five, including 1 with Michael Jackson, 8 as Jacksons)
12	Kinks

12	John Lennon/Plastic Ono Band
12	Level 42
12	Manfred Mann
	(7 as Manfred Mann, 5 as Manfred Mann's Earth Band)
12	Mantovani
12	Marillion
12	Olivia Newton-John
12	Elaine Paige
	(includes 1 with Barbara Dickson)
12	Public Image Ltd.
12	Leo Sayer
12	Simple Minds
12	Steely Dan
12	Shakin' Stevens
12	10 C.C.
	(includes 1 with Godley and Creme)
12	Uriah Heep
12	Dionne Warwick
	(includes 1 with Placido Domingo)
12	Barry White
11	Ray Conniff
11	Val Doonican
11	Doors
11	Peter Gabriel
11	Hall and Oates
	(Daryl Hall has 1 more solo)
11	Buddy Holly and the Crickets
	(Crickets plus 1 with Bobby Vee and 1 solo)
11	Joe Jackson
11	Jam
11	King Crimson
11	Madness
11	Magnum
11	George Mitchell Minstrels
11	Luciano Pavarotti
	(includes 2 with José Carreras and Placido Domingo, and 1 with Henry Mancini)
11	Tom Petty and the Heartbreakers
11	Rainbow
11	Lou Reed
	(includes 1 with John Cale, 1 with Velvet Underground, plus 2 more as part of Velvet Underground)
11	R.E.M.
11	Royal Philharmonic Orchestra
11	Smiths
11	Dusty Springfield
11	U2
11	Luther Vandross
11	Van Halen
11	XTC
10	Barclay James Harvest
10	Blondie
	(includes 2 with Deborah Harry)
10	Byrds

439

FACTS AND FEATS

10	José Carreras		10	Meat Loaf
	(includes 2 more with Luciano		10	Nana Mouskouri
	Pavarotti and Placido Domingo,		10	Daniel O'Donnell
	1 with Placido Domingo and		10	Orchestral Manoeuvres In
	Monserrat Caballé, 1 with Placido			The Dark
	Domingo and Diana Ross, and 1 with		10	Ozzy Osbourne
	Sarah Brightman)		10	Alan Parsons Project
10	Leonard Cohen		10	Gene Pitney
10	Nat 'King' Cole		10	Ramones
	(includes 1 with George Shearing and		10	Otis Redding
	1 with Dean Martin)			*(includes 1 with Carla Thomas)*
10	Commodores		10	Showaddywaddy
10	Cream		10	Paul Simon
	(includes 1 with Eric Clapton)		10	Simon and Garfunkel
10	Depeche Mode			*(Art Garfunkel 6 more solo;*
10	Dire Straits			*Paul Simon 10 more solo)*
10	Duran Duran		10	Cat Stevens
10	Eagles		10	Supertramp
10	Eurythmics		10	Talking Heads
10	Rory Gallagher		10	Rick Wakeman
10	James Galway			*(includes 1 with Kevin Peek, plus 1*
	(includes 1 with Cleo Laine, 1 with			*with Anderson Bruford Wakeman*
	Henry Mancini and 1 with			*Howe)*
	Chieftains)		10	Whitesnake
10	Julio Iglesias		10	Roger Whittaker
10	Bert Kaempfert		10	Kim Wilde
10	Madonna			

440

Marc Almond has six solo hit albums to his credit, six more as vocalist with Soft Cell and two as Marc and the Mambas, a total of 14.

Ginger Baker has had one hit as leader of Ginger Baker's Air Force, one as co-general in the Baker-Gurvitz Army, eight as drummer with Cream and one more as part of the *Cream Of Eric Clapton*, a total of 11.

Boy George has had three solo hit albums, one more as Jesus Loves You, a Greatest Hits package with Culture Club and five others as lead vocalist with Culture Club, a total of ten.

Jack Bruce has one solo hit album, eight as bassist with Cream and one more as part of the *Cream Of Eric Clapton*, a total of ten.

David Cassidy has had six hit albums and four more as part of the Partridge Family, a total of ten.

Julian Cope has had eight solo hit albums, three more with the Teardrop Explodes, and a hits package with the Teardrop Explodes, a total of 12.

David Crosby has had one solo hit album, one as half of Graham Nash and David Crosby, two as one third of Crosby, Stills and Nash, three as one quarter of Crosby, Stills, Nash and Young, and six more as part of the Byrds, a total of 12 hit albums.

Emerson, Lake and Palmer have had nine hit albums, Emerson, Lake and Powell one more, and Greg Lake one on his own.

Graham Nash has had one solo hit album, one with David Crosby, two with Crosby, Stills and Nash, three with Crosby, Stills, Nash and Young, and was one of the Hollies on eight of their hit albums, a total of 15.

New Order have had nine hit albums, while the band from which they evolved, Joy Division, have had five, a total of 14.

Donny Osmond has had six solo hit albums, three more with Marie Osmond and seven as one of the Osmonds, a total of 16.

Harry Secombe has had six solo hit albums, one with Moira Anderson, and four with Peter Sellers and Spike Milligan, three as the Goons; a total of 11.

Stephen Stills has had four solo hit albums, two as leader of Stephen Stills' Manassas, two as part of Crosby, Stills and Nash, three as one quarter of Crosby, Stills, Nash and Young, and one as half of the Stills-Young Band, giving him a share in 12 hit albums.

Midge Ure has had four solo hit albums, one as a member of Slik, seven as part of Ultravox and four involved with Visage, a total of 16.

Vangelis has amassed eight solo hit albums, plus four more with Jon Anderson, making 12 hit albums in all.

Scott Walker has had six solo hit albums and five more as part of the Walker Brothers, as well as one which is a combination of his own solo hits and the group's hits, a total of 12.

Steve Winwood has had seven solo hit albums, three more as lead vocalist of the Spencer Davis Group, five with Traffic and one with Blind Faith, a total of 16.

MOST TOP TEN HIT ALBUMS

The rules for this category are the same as for **Most Hit Albums, except that the album must have made the Top Ten for at least one week.**

37	Elvis Presley		10	Eric Clapton
33	Cliff Richard			*(includes 1 with Cream and 1 with*
31	Rolling Stones			*John Mayall)*
29	Frank Sinatra		10	Depeche Mode
	(includes 1 with Count Basie)		10	Jimi Hendrix
25	Bob Dylan		10	Madonna
22	David Bowie		10	Diana Ross
21	Elton John			*(includes 1 with Marvin Gaye)*
20	Beatles		10	Andy Williams
19	Iron Maiden		10	Yes
19	Paul McCartney		9	Abba
19	Queen		9	AC/DC
19	Rod Stewart		9	Black Sabbath
	(plus 1 with the Faces)		9	Cure
18	Status Quo		9	Deep Purple
15	Genesis		9	Dire Straits
15	Pink Floyd		9	Fleetwood Mac
14	Beach Boys		9	Buddy Holly and the Crickets
14	Prince			*(Crickets plus 1 with Bobby Vee)*
14	Jim Reeves		9	Johnny Mathis
13	Who			*(includes 1 with Natalie Cole)*
12	Elvis Costello		9	Smiths
12	Tom Jones		9	Bruce Springsteen
11	Led Zeppelin		9	UB40
11	Roxy Music		9	Stevie Wonder
	(includes 2 with Bryan Ferry)		8	Bee Gees
11	Shadows		8	Kate Bush
	(plus 16 with Cliff Richard)		8	Carpenters

8	Cream
	(includes 1 with Eric Clapton)
8	Electric Light Orchestra
8	Bryan Ferry
	(includes 2 with Roxy Music)
8	Peter Gabriel
8	Marillion
8	Moody Blues
8	Pet Shop Boys
8	Rush
8	Simple Minds
8	Stranglers
8	Supremes
	(includes 1 with the Four Tops, 1 with the Temptations)
8	10 C.C.
	(includes 1 with Godley and Creme)
8	Thin Lizzy
8	Whitesnake
7	Blondie
	(includes 1 as Deborah Harry and Blondie; Debbie Harry has 1 more solo)
7	Marc Bolan/T. Rex/ Tyrannosaurus Rex
7	Neil Diamond
7	Duran Duran
7	Emerson, Lake and Palmer
7	Eurythmics
7	Michael Jackson
	(includes 1 with Jacksons)
7	Jam
7	John Lennon/Plastic Ono Band
7	Level 42
7	Madness
7	Bob Marley and the Wailers
7	Meat Loaf
7	George Mitchell Minstrels
7	New Order
7	Mike Oldfield
7	Police
7	Chris Rea
7	Simon and Garfunkel
	(Paul Simon has 6 more solo, Art Garfunkel has 2 more solo)
7	Cat Stevens
7	U2
7	Ultravox
7	Wet Wet Wet
6	Shirley Bassey
6	Acker Bilk
	(includes 2 with Chris Barber and 1 with Chris Barber and Kenny Ball)
6	Phil Collins
6	Russ Conway
6	Chris De Burgh
6	Eagles
6	Erasure
6	Four Tops
	(includes 1 with Supremes)

442

6	Free
6	Hollies
6	Human League
	(includes 1 as League Unlimited Orchestra)
6	Engelbert Humperdinck
6	INXS
6	Jethro Tull
6	Billy Joel
6	Barry Manilow
6	Mantovani
6	Van Morrison
6	Morrissey
6	Gary Numan/Tubeway Army
6	Roy Orbison
6	Orchestral Manoeuvres In The Dark
6	Leo Sayer
6	Paul Simon
	(plus 7 with Simon and Garfunkel)
6	Barbra Streisand
6	Tina Turner
6	Neil Young
	(plus 2 with Crosby, Stills, Nash and Young)
5	Herb Alpert
5	Joan Armatrading
5	Beautiful South
5	Big Country
5	Michael Bolton
5	Bon Jovi
	(Jon Bon Jovi has 1 more solo)
5	Max Bygraves
5	Mariah Carey
5	Belinda Carlisle
5	Johnny Cash
5	Alice Cooper
5	Randy Crawford
5	Cult
5	Culture Club
5	Deacon Blue
5	John Denver
5	Val Doonican
5	Echo and the Bunnymen
5	Duane Eddy
5	Gloria Estefan/ Miami Sound Machine
5	Everly Brothers
5	Jean-Michel Jarre
5	Jack Jones
5	Kinks
5	James Last
5	John Mayall
	(includes 1 with Eric Clapton)
5	Kylie Minogue
5	Robert Plant
	(includes 1 with Jimmy Page)
5	Pretenders
5	Rainbow

5	Roxette	5	Supertramp	
5	Sade	5	Tears For Fears	
5	Santana *(Carlos Santana plus 1 with Mahavishnu John McLaughlin)*	5	Bobby Vee *(includes 1 with the Crickets)*	
5	Seekers	5	Scott Walker *(includes one with the Walker Brothers)*	
5	Showaddywaddy			
5	Slade	5	Walker Brothers *(includes 1 with Scott Walker)*	
5	Spandau Ballet			
5	Sting	5	Paul Young	
5	Style Council	5	ZZ Top	

Cher has had four solo Top Ten hits, and one more with Sonny and Cher, a total of five.

Alison Moyet has had three solo Top Ten hits, and two more as vocalist with Yazoo, a total of five.

Depeche Mode and **Madonna** are the acts with the best 100% Top Ten album record, each with ten Top Ten hits out of ten releases.

MOST HITS WITHOUT A TOP TEN HIT

Only seven acts have had ten or more hit albums without ever reaching the Top Ten. They are **Foster and Allen** (17 hits), **Tangerine Dream** (16), **Public Image Ltd.** (12), **Doors** (11), **Barclay James Harvest** (10), **Ramones** (10) and **Alan Parsons Project** (10). The Alan Parsons Project has never even hit the Top 20, their most successful album being their eighth hit, *Ammonia Avenue*, which reached number 24 in 1984.

James Last has hit the Top Ten only five times out of 61 chart entries, a hit-making career which includes a run of 31 consecutive hit albums (his second to 32nd hits inclusive) which all missed the Top Ten. **Neil Young** clocked up 20 consecutive hit albums between Top Ten hits, a gap of just over 20 years. **Hawkwind** have hit the charts 19 times since their last brief taste of Top Ten glory, in 1973, as have **Jethro Tull**, whose first six albums were all Top Ten hits.

There were 57 hit compilation albums on the **Street Sounds** label totalling 269 weeks on the charts, but the highest placing for any of them was 12 by *Street Sounds Electro 7* in March 1985.

443

MOST HITS WITHOUT A NUMBER ONE HIT

61	**James Last** (who has had one number 2 hit)
32	**Shirley Bassey** (who has had one number 2 hit)
23	**Jimi Hendrix** (who has had two number 2 hits)
22	**Hawkwind** (who have had one number 9 hit)
22	**Van Morrison** (who has had two number 4 hits)
20	**Santana** (who have had two number 6 hits; Carlos Santana has made three hit albums with other partners, none of which hit the top)
19	**Elvis Costello** (who has had two number 2 hits)
18	**David Essex** (who has had one number 2 hit)
18	**Stranglers** (who have had two number 2 hits)
17	**Johnny Cash** (who has had one number 2 hit)

MOST HITS WITHOUT A NUMBER ONE HIT *continued*

17	**Foster and Allen** (who have had one number 11 hit)
17	**Stevie Wonder** (who has hit number 2 three times)
16	**Herb Alpert** (who has had one number 2 hit)
16	**John Denver** (who has had one number 2 hit)
16	**Kiss** (who have had one number 4 hit)
16	**Tangerine Dream** (whose biggest hit reached number 12)
15	**Donna Summer** (who has had one number 3 hit)

MOST ALBUMS ON THE CHART IN ONE WEEK

Dire Straits' record total of 217 weeks on the chart in one year (1986) is the equivalent of an average of four albums in the top 100 in every week of the year. Only six acts in the history of the albums chart have charted seven albums in one week, as follows:

14 albums in a chart of	60 . . . . .Elvis Presley	. . . . .10 Sep 1977
12 albums in a chart of	60 . . . . .Elvis Presley	. . . . .17 Sep 1977
11 albums in a chart of	60 . . . . .Elvis Presley	. . . . 1 Oct 1977
11 albums in a chart of	60 . . . . .Elvis Presley	. . . . 8 Oct 1977
10 albums in a chart of	100 . . . . .David Bowie	. . . . .16 Jul 1983
9 albums in a chart of	60 . . . . .Elvis Presley	. . . . .24 Sep 1977
9 albums in a chart of	100 . . . . .David Bowie	. . . . .11 Jun 1983
9 albums in a chart of	100 . . . . .David Bowie	. . . . 9 Jul 1983
8 albums in a chart of	20 . . . . .Jim Reeves	. . . . .26 Sep 1964
8 albums in a chart of	100 . . . . .David Bowie	. . . . .27 Aug 1983
7 albums in a chart of	20 . . . . .Jim Reeves	. . . . .29 Aug 1964
7 albums in a chart of	20 . . . . .Jim Reeves	. . . . 5 Sep 1964
7 albums in a chart of	20 . . . . .Jim Reeves	. . . . 3 Oct 1964
7 albums in a chart of	20 . . . . .Jim Reeves	. . . . .10 Oct 1964
7 albums in a chart of	60 . . . . .Elvis Presley	. . . . .15 Oct 1977
7 albums in a chart of	75 . . . . .U2	. . . . .13 Jun 1992
7 albums in a chart of	75 . . . . .Smiths	. . . . 4 Mar 1995
7 albums in a chart of	75 . . . . .Smiths	. . . . .11 Mar 1995
7 albums in a chart of	100 . . . . .David Bowie	. . . . .14 May 1983
7 albums in a chart of	100 . . . . .David Bowie	. . . . .21 May 1983
7 albums in a chart of	100 . . . . .David Bowie	. . . . .28 May 1983
7 albums in a chart of	100 . . . . .David Bowie	. . . . 4 Jun 1983
7 albums in a chart of	100 . . . . .David Bowie	. . . . .18 Jun 1983
7 albums in a chart of	100 . . . . .David Bowie	. . . . .30 Jul 1983
7 albums in a chart of	100 . . . . .David Bowie	. . . . .20 Aug 1983
7 albums in a chart of	100 . . . . . .Bruce Springsteen	. . . . .15 Jun 1985
	(nine consecutive weeks) to 10 Aug 1985	

Of all these instances, only Elvis Presley on 10 September 1977 and Bruce Springsteen for four weeks from 6 July 1985 held the top spot. The most complete chart domination was by Jim Reeves on 26 September 1964, when he accounted for 40% of the albums chart. Bruce Springsteen's achievement in the summer of 1985 is the only example of an artist who has released as many as seven albums charting all his albums at once. In 1986, Dire Straits charted all six of their albums (one of which was a double album) for a total of 12 weeks. For seven of those weeks they held the number one spot.

LEAST SUCCESSFUL CHART ACT

Between 8 August 1981 and 14 January 1989, when the chart was extended to a Top 100, eight acts achieved the minor distinction of a chart career consisting of only one week at no. 100. These acts, in chronological order, were:

17 Oct 81	Ronnie Laws	*Solid Ground*
17 Dec 83	Sleighriders	*A Very Merry Disco*
11 Feb 84	Europeans	*Live!*
30 Jun 84	Wendy O. Williams	*WOW*
30 Mar 85	Second Image	*Strange Reflections*
12 Oct 85	Alien Sex Fiend	*Maximum Security*
29 Nov 86	Shop Assistants	*Shop Assistants*
3 Oct 87	Bolshoi	*Lindy's Party*

There is also a compilation album which lasted at number 100 for just one week:

26 Nov 83	Various Artists	*Twelve Inches Of Pleasure*

Before 8 August 1981 and since 14 January 1989, 23 acts achieved the slightly less negative ultimate of one week of chart life on the bottom rung of a smaller chart:

			Chart Size
11 Jun 60	Bob Wallis and his Storyville Jazzmen	*Everybody Loves Saturday Night*	20
18 Jun 60	Shelley Manne	*My Fair Lady*	20
25 Jun 60	Knightsbridge Strings	*String Sway*	20
17 Dec 60	Big Ben Banjo Band	*More Minstrel Melodies*	20
24 Dec 60	New World Theatre Orchestra	*Let's Dance To The Hits Of The 30s and 40s*	20
14 Jul 62	Erroll Garner	*Close Up In Swing*	20
9 Feb 63	Spotnicks	*Out-A-Space*	20
18 Apr 64	Harry Secombe, Peter Sellers & Spike Milligan	*How To Win An Election*	20
20 Jun 64	Sonny Boy Williamson	*Down And Out Blues*	20
29 Jul 67	Manitas De Plata	*Flamenco Guitar*	40
22 Jun 68	Solomon King	*She Wears My Ring*	40
17 Aug 68	O.C. Smith	*Hickory Holler Revisited*	40
28 Feb 70	Bobbie Gentry and Glen Campbell	*Bobbie Gentry And Glen Campbell*	50
20 Jun 70	Moira Anderson	*These Are My Songs*	50
28 Nov 70	Savoy Brown	*Lookin' In*	50
13 Apr 74	Deke Leonard	*Kamikaze*	50
1 Apr 78	Culture	*Two Sevens Clash*	60
30 Sep 78	Cerrone	*Supernature*	60
18 Mar 89	Vow Wow	*Helter Skelter*	75
16 Jul 91	Fishbone	*The Reality Of My Surroundings*	75
26 Nov 94	Sean Maguire	*Sean Maguire*	75
4 Feb 95	Wolfgang Press	*Funky Little Demons*	75

Harry Secombe, Peter Sellers and Spike Milligan, and Bobbie Gentry and Glen Campbell have all charted with solo albums. Moira Anderson has also enjoyed chart success in duet with Harry Secombe.

Five compilation albums have also spent just one week at the bottom of the smaller charts, as follows:

28 May 60	'Pal Joey' Original Film Soundtrack	20
23 Nov 63	Hitsville Vol 2	20
8 Feb 64	Ready Steady Go!	20
11 May 68	Blues Anytime	40
3 Nov 79	Mods Mayday 79	75

The Adicts spent one week at number 99 with their only hit album, *The Sound Of Music*, and one week on the bottom rung, number 75, with their only hit single, 'Bad Boy'. This is the nearest to the ultimate least successful chart double so far.

Since the establishment of a separate Top 20 compilations albums chart, there have been 25 albums which have spent just one week on the bottom rung:

23 Dec 89	Reggae Hits Vol 7	20
17 Nov 90	Karaoke Party	20
20 Jul 91	Breaks, Bass and Bleeps	20
28 Dec 91	Trivial Pursuit – The Music Master Game	20
18 Jan 92	Noise	20
1 Feb 92	Closet Classics Volume 1	20
22 Feb 92	Shut Up And Dance	20
18 Apr 92	Breaks, Bass and Bleeps	20
27 Jun 92	Movin' On	20
29 Aug 92	Warehouse Raves 7	20
19 Sep 92	Illegal Rave	20
17 Oct 92	The Best Of Capital Gold	20
6 Mar 93	Ambient Dub Volume 2 – Earth Juice	20
24 Apr 93	Winner's Circle	20
18 Sep 93	Sliver (Original Soundtrack)	20
25 Sep 93	Now! That's What I Call Music 1988	20
20 Nov 93	The Return Of The Gladiators	20
16 Apr 94	Movie Hits	20
21 May 94	Q Country	20
4 Jun 94	Freska!	20
13 Aug 94	Junior Boy's Own Collection	20
24 Sep 94	House Nation 1	20
3 Jun 95	Freshen Up	20
17 Jun 95	Radio Dreamscape – Volume 1	20
18 Nov 95	The Coronation Street Album	20

The two albums entitled *Breaks, Bass and Bleeps* are different albums, both issued on the same label, Rumour.

Wolfgang Press. One week at number 75 in 1995. Photo: Dennis Keeley

FACTS AND FEATS

THE NUMBER ONE ALBUMS

8 NOVEMBER 1958 – 30 DECEMBER 1995

There have been 526 albums which have topped the charts in the 37 years since it was first compiled. In the first ten years of the albums charts, only 44 albums headed the lists, but over the past two years there have been 51 new chart-topping albums. The full list is as follows:

		Weeks
8 Nov 58	**South Pacific** *Film Soundtrack (RCA)*	70
12 Mar 60	**The Explosive Freddy Cannon** *Freddy Cannon (Top Rank)*	1
19 Mar 60	**South Pacific** *Film Soundtrack (RCA)*	19
30 Jul 60	**Elvis Is Back** *Elvis Presley (RCA)*	1
6 Aug 60	**South Pacific** *Film Soundtrack (RCA)*	5
10 Sep 60	**Down Drury Lane To Memory Lane** *101 Strings (Pye)*	5
15 Oct 60	**South Pacific** *Film Soundtrack (RCA)*	13
14 Jan 61	**GI Blues** *Elvis Presley (RCA)*	7
4 Mar 61	**South Pacific** *Film Soundtrack (RCA)*	1
11 Mar 61	**GI Blues** *Elvis Presley (RCA)*	3
1 Apr 61	**South Pacific** *Film Soundtrack (RCA)*	1
8 Apr 61	**GI Blues** *Elvis Presley (RCA)*	12
1 Jul 61	**South Pacific** *Film Soundtrack (RCA)*	4
29 Jul 61	**Black And White Minstrel Show** *George Mitchell Minstrels (HMV)*	4
26 Aug 61	**South Pacific** *Film Soundtrack (RCA)*	1
2 Sep 61	**Black And White Minstrel Show** *George Mitchell Minstrels (HMV)*	1
9 Sep 61	**South Pacific** *Film Soundtrack (RCA)*	1
16 Sep 61	**Black And White Minstrel Show** *George Mitchell Minstrels (HMV)*	1
23 Sep 61	**The Shadows** *Shadows (Columbia)*	4
21 Oct 61	**Black And White Minstrel Show** *George Mitchell Minstrels (HMV)*	1
28 Oct 61	**The Shadows** *Shadows (Columbia)*	1
4 Nov 61	**21 Today** *Cliff Richard (Columbia)*	1
11 Nov 61	**Another Black And White Minstrel Show** *George Mitchell Minstrels (HMV)*	8
6 Jan 62	**Blue Hawaii** *Elvis Presley (RCA)*	1
13 Jan 62	**The Young Ones** *Cliff Richard (Columbia)*	6
24 Feb 62	**Blue Hawaii** *Elvis Presley (RCA)*	17
23 Jun 62	**West Side Story** *Film Soundtrack (Philips/CBS)*	5
28 Jul 62	**Pot Luck** *Elvis Presley (RCA)*	5
1 Sep 62	**West Side Story** *Film Soundtrack (CBS)*	1
8 Sep 62	**Pot Luck** *Elvis Presley (RCA)*	1
15 Sep 62	**West Side Story** *Film Soundtrack (CBS)*	1
22 Sep 62	**The Best Of Ball, Barber And Bilk** *Kenny Ball, Chris Barber and Acker Bilk (Pye)*	1
29 Sep 62	**West Side Story** *Film Soundtrack (CBS)*	3
20 Oct 62	**The Best Of Ball, Barber And Bilk** *Kenny Ball, Chris Barber and Acker Bilk (Pye)*	1

27 Oct 62   **Out Of The Shadows** *Shadows (Columbia)* 3
17 Nov 62   **West Side Story** *Film Soundtrack (CBS)* 1
24 Nov 62   **Out Of The Shadows** *Shadows (Columbia)* 1
1 Dec 62   **On Stage With The Black And White Minstrels**
        George Mitchell Minstrels (HMV) 2
15 Dec 62   **West Side Story** *Film Soundtrack (CBS)* 1
22 Dec 62   **Out Of The Shadows** *Shadows (Columbia)* 1
29 Dec 62   **Black And White Minstrel Show**
        George Mitchell Minstrels (HMV) 2

12 Jan 63   **West Side Story** *Film Soundtrack (CBS)* 1
19 Jan 63   **Out Of The Shadows** *Shadows (Columbia)* 2
2 Feb 63   **Summer Holiday**
        Cliff Richard and the Shadows (Columbia) 14
11 May 63   **Please Please Me** *Beatles (Parlophone)* 30
7 Dec 63   **With The Beatles** *Beatles (Parlophone)* 21

2 May 64   **Rolling Stones** *Rolling Stones (Decca)* 12
25 Jul 64   **A Hard Day's Night** *Beatles (Parlophone)* 21
19 Dec 64   **Beatles For Sale** *Beatles (Parlophone)* 7

6 Feb 65   **Rolling Stones No. 2** *Rolling Stones (Decca)* 3
27 Feb 65   **Beatles For Sale** *Beatles (Parlophone)* 1
6 Mar 65   **Rolling Stones No. 2** *Rolling Stones (Decca)* 6
17 Apr 65   **Freewheelin' Bob Dylan** *Bob Dylan (CBS)* 1
24 Apr 65   **Rolling Stones No. 2** *Rolling Stones (Decca)* 1
1 May 65   **Beatles For Sale** *Beatles (Parlophone)* 3
22 May 65   **Freewheelin' Bob Dylan** *Bob Dylan (CBS)* 1
29 May 65   **Bringing It All Back Home** *Bob Dylan (CBS)* 1
5 Jun 65   **The Sound Of Music** *Soundtrack (RCA)* 10
14 Aug 65   **Help** *Beatles (Parlophone)* 9
16 Oct 65   **The Sound Of Music** *Soundtrack (RCA)* 10
25 Dec 65   **Rubber Soul** *Beatles (Parlophone)* 9

19 Feb 66   **The Sound Of Music** *Soundtrack (RCA)* 10
30 Apr 66   **Aftermath** *Rolling Stones (Decca)* 8
25 Jun 66   **The Sound Of Music** *Soundtrack (RCA)* 7
13 Aug 66   **Revolver** *Beatles (Parlophone)* 7
1 Oct 66   **The Sound Of Music** *Soundtrack (RCA)* 18

4 Feb 67   **Monkees** *Monkees (RCA)* 7
25 Mar 67   **The Sound Of Music** *Soundtrack (RCA)* 7
13 May 67   **More Of The Monkees** *Monkees (RCA)* 1
20 May 67   **The Sound Of Music** *Soundtrack (RCA)* 1
27 May 67   **More Of The Monkees** *Monkees (RCA)* 1
3 Jun 67   **The Sound Of Music** *Soundtrack (RCA)* 1
10 Jun 67   **Sergeant Pepper's Lonely Hearts Club Band**
        Beatles (Parlophone) 23
18 Nov 67   **The Sound Of Music** *Soundtrack (RCA)* 1
25 Nov 67   **Sergeant Pepper's Lonely Hearts Club Band**
        Beatles (Parlophone) 1
2 Dec 67   **The Sound Of Music** *Soundtrack (RCA)* 3
23 Dec 67   **Sergeant Pepper's Lonely Hearts Club Band**
        Beatles (Parlophone) 2

6 Jan 68   **Val Doonican Rocks But Gently** *Val Doonican (Pye)* 3
27 Jan 68   **The Sound Of Music** *Soundtrack (RCA)* 1

448

FACTS AND FEATS

3 Feb 68	**Sergeant Pepper's Lonely Hearts Club Band** *Beatles (Parlophone)* 1
10 Feb 68	**Greatest Hits** *Four Tops (Tamla Motown)* 1
17 Feb 68	**Greatest Hits** *Diana Ross and the Supremes (Tamla Motown)* 3
9 Mar 68	**John Wesley Harding** *Bob Dylan (CBS)* 10
18 May 68	**Scott 2** *Scott Walker (Philips)* 1
25 May 68	**John Wesley Harding** *Bob Dylan (CBS)* 3
15 Jun 68	**Love Andy** *Andy Williams (CBS)* .1
22 Jun 68	**Dock Of The Bay** *Otis Redding (Stax)* 1
29 Jun 68	**Ogden's Nut Gone Flake** *Small Faces (Immediate)* 6
10 Aug 68	**Delilah** *Tom Jones (Decca)* 1
17 Aug 68	**Bookends** *Simon and Garfunkel (CBS)* 5
21 Sep 68	**Delilah** *Tom Jones (Decca)* 1
28 Sep 68	**Bookends** *Simon and Garfunkel (CBS)* 2
12 Oct 68	**Greatest Hits** *Hollies (Parlophone)* 6
23 Nov 68	**The Sound Of Music** *Soundtrack (RCA)* 1
30 Nov 68	**Greatest Hits** *Hollies (Parlophone)* 1
7 Dec 68	**The Beatles** *Beatles (Apple)* 7
25 Jan 69	**Best Of The Seekers** *Seekers (Columbia)* 1
1 Feb 69	**The Beatles** *Beatles (Apple)* 1
8 Feb 69	**Best Of The Seekers** *Seekers (Columbia)* 1
15 Feb 69	**Diana Ross And The Supremes Join The Temptations** *Diana Ross/Supremes/Temptations (Tamla Motown)* 4
15 Mar 69	**Goodbye** *Cream (Polydor)* 2
29 Mar 69	**Best Of The Seekers** *Seekers (Columbia)* 2
12 Apr 69	**Goodbye** *Cream (Polydor)* 1
19 Apr 69	**Best Of The Seekers** *Seekers (Columbia)* 1
26 Apr 69	**Goodbye** *Cream (Polydor)* 1
3 May 69	**Best Of The Seekers** *Seekers (Columbia)* 1
10 May 69	**On The Threshold Of A Dream** *Moody Blues (Deram)* 2
24 May 69	**Nashville Skyline** *Bob Dylan (CBS)* 4
21 Jun 69	**His Orchestra, His Chorus, His Singers, His Sound** *Ray Conniff (CBS)* 3
12 Jul 69	**According To My Heart** *Jim Reeves (RCA International)* 4
9 Aug 69	**Stand Up** *Jethro Tull (Island)* 3
30 Aug 69	**From Elvis In Memphis** *Elvis Presley (RCA)* 1
6 Sep 69	**Stand Up** *Jethro Tull (Island)* 2
20 Sep 69	**Blind Faith** *Blind Faith (Polydor)* 2
4 Oct 69	**Abbey Road** *Beatles (Apple)* 11
20 Dec 69	**Let It Bleed** *Rolling Stones (Decca)* 1
27 Dec 69	**Abbey Road** *Beatles (Apple)* 6
7 Feb 70	**Led Zeppelin 2** *Led Zeppelin (Atlantic)* 1
14 Feb 70	**Motown Chartbusters Vol. 3** *Various (Tamla Motown)* 1
21 Feb 70	**Bridge Over Troubled Water** *Simon and Garfunkel (CBS)* 13
23 May 70	**Let It Be** *Beatles (Parlophone)* .3
13 Jun 70	**Bridge Over Troubled Water** *Simon and Garfunkel (CBS)* 4
11 Jul 70	**Self Portrait** *Bob Dylan (CBS)* 1
18 Jul 70	**Bridge Over Troubled Water** *Simon and Garfunkel (CBS)* 5
22 Aug 70	**Question Of Balance** *Moody Blues (Threshold)* 3

449

12 Sep 70	**Cosmo's Factory** *Creedence Clearwater Revival (Liberty)*	1
19 Sep 70	**Get Your Ya-Yas Out** *Rolling Stones (Decca)*	2
3 Oct 70	**Bridge Over Troubled Water** *Simon and Garfunkel (CBS)*	1
10 Oct 70	**Paranoid** *Black Sabbath (Vertigo)*	1
17 Oct 70	**Bridge Over Troubled Water** *Simon and Garfunkel (CBS)*	1
24 Oct 70	**Atom Heart Mother** *Pink Floyd (Harvest)*	1
31 Oct 70	**Motown Chartbusters Vol. 4** *Various (Tamla Motown)*	1
7 Nov 70	**Led Zeppelin 3** *Led Zeppelin (Atlantic)*	3
28 Nov 70	**New Morning** *Bob Dylan (CBS)*	1
5 Dec 70	**Greatest Hits** *Andy Williams (CBS)*	1
12 Dec 70	**Led Zeppelin 3** *Led Zeppelin (Atlantic)*	1
19 Dec 70	**Greatest Hits** *Andy Williams (CBS)*	4
16 Jan 71†	**Bridge Over Troubled Water** *Simon and Garfunkel (CBS)*	11
3 Apr 71	**Home Loving Man** *Andy Williams (CBS)*	2
17 Apr 71	**Motown Chartbusters** Vol. 5 *Various (Tamla Motown)*	3
8 May 71	**Sticky Fingers** *Rolling Stones (Rolling Stones)*	4
5 Jun 71	**Ram** *Paul and Linda McCartney (Apple)*	2
19 Jun 71	**Sticky Fingers** *Rolling Stones (Rolling Stones)*	1
26 Jun 71	**Tarkus** *Emerson, Lake and Palmer (Island)*	1
3 Jul 71	**Bridge Over Troubled Water** *Simon and Garfunkel (CBS)*	5
7 Aug 71	**Hot Hits 6** *Various (MFP)*	1
14 Aug 71	**Every Good Boy Deserves Favour** *Moody Blues (Threshold)*	1
21 Aug 71	**Top Of The Pops Vol. 18** *Various (Hallmark)*	3
11 Sep 71	**Bridge Over Troubled Water** *Simon and Garfunkel (CBS)*	1
18 Sep 71	**Who's Next** *Who (Track)*	1
25 Sep 71	**Fireball** *Deep Purple (Harvest)*	1
2 Oct 71	**Every Picture Tells A Story** *Rod Stewart (Mercury)*	4
30 Oct 71	**Imagine** *John Lennon/Plastic Ono Band (Apple)*	2
13 Nov 71	**Every Picture Tells A Story** *Rod Stewart (Mercury)*	2
27 Nov 71	**Top Of The Pops Vol. 20** *Various (Hallmark)*	1
4 Dec 71	**Four Symbols** *Led Zeppelin (Atlantic)*	2
18 Dec 71	**Electric Warrior** *T. Rex (Fly)*	6
29 Jan 72	**Concert For Bangladesh** *Various (Apple)*	1
5 Feb 72	**Electric Warrior** *T. Rex (Fly)*	2
19 Feb 72	**Neil Reid** *Neil Reid (Decca)*	3
11 Mar 72	**Harvest** *Neil Young (Reprise)*	1
18 Mar 72	**Paul Simon** *Paul Simon (CBS)*	1
25 Mar 72	**Fog On The Tyne** *Lindisfarne (Charisma)*	4
22 Apr 72	**Machine Head** *Deep Purple (Purple)*	2
6 May 72	**Prophets, Seers And Sages And The Angels Of The Ages/My People Were Fair And Had Sky In Their Hair But Now They're Content To Wear Stars On Their Brows** *Tyrannosaurus Rex (Fly Double Back)*	1

† This includes eight weeks at number one when charts were not published due to a postal strike.

13 May 72	**Machine Head** Deep Purple (Purple)	.1
20 May 72	**Bolan Boogie** T. Rex (Fly)	.3
10 Jun 72	**Exile On Main Street**	
	Rolling Stones (Rolling Stones)	.1
17 Jun 72	**20 Dynamic Hits** Various (K-Tel)	.8
12 Aug 72	**20 Fantastic Hits** Various (Arcade)	.5
16 Sep 72	**Never A Dull Moment** Rod Stewart (Philips)	.2
30 Sep 72	**20 Fantastic Hits** Various (Arcade)	.1
7 Oct 72	**20 All Time Hits Of The Fifties** Various (K-Tel)	.8
2 Dec 72	**25 Rockin' And Rollin' Greats** Various (K-Tel)	.3
23 Dec 72	**20 All Time Hits Of The Fifties** Various (K-Tel)	.3
13 Jan 73	**Slayed?** Slade (Polydor)	.1
20 Jan 73	**Back To Front** Gilbert O'Sullivan (MAM)	.1
27 Jan 73	**Slayed?** Slade (Polydor)	.2
10 Feb 73	**Don't Shoot Me, I'm Only The Piano Player**	
	Elton John (DJM)	.6
24 Mar 73	**Billion Dollar Babies** Alice Cooper (Warner Bros.)	.1
31 Mar 73	**20 Flashback Great Hits Of The Sixties**	
	Various (K-Tel)	.2
14 Apr 73	**Houses Of The Holy** Led Zeppelin (Atlantic)	.2
28 Apr 73	**Ooh La La** Faces (Warner Bros.)	.1
5 May 73	**Aladdin Sane** David Bowie (RCA Victor)	.5
9 Jun 73	**Pure Gold** Various (EMI)	.3
30 Jun 73	**That'll Be The Day** Various (Ronco)	.7
18 Aug 73	**We Can Make It** Peters and Lee (Philips)	.2
1 Sep 73	**Sing It Again** Rod Stewart (Mercury)	.3
22 Sep 73	**Goat's Head Soup** Rolling Stones (Rolling Stones)	.2
6 Oct 73	**Sladest** Slade (Polydor)	.3
27 Oct 73	**Hello** Status Quo (Vertigo)	.1
3 Nov 73	**Pin Ups** David Bowie (RCA)	.5
8 Dec 73	**Stranded** Roxy Music (Island)	.1
15 Dec 73	**Dreams Are Nothin' More Than Wishes**	
	David Cassidy (Bell)	.1
22 Dec 73	**Goodbye Yellow Brick Road** Elton John (DJM)	.2
5 Jan 74	**Tales From Topographic Oceans** Yes (Atlantic)	.2
19 Jan 74	**Sladest** Slade (Polydor)	.1
26 Jan 74	**And I Love You So** Perry Como (RCA)	.1
2 Feb 74	**The Singles 1969–73** Carpenters (A & M)	.4
2 Mar 74	**Old, New, Borrowed And Blue** Slade (Polydor)	.1
9 Mar 74	**The Singles 1969–73** Carpenters (A & M)	.11
25 May 74	**Journey To The Centre Of The Earth**	
	Rick Wakeman (A & M)	.1
1 Jun 74	**The Singles 1969–73** Carpenters (A & M)	.1
8 Jun 74	**Diamond Dogs** David Bowie (RCA)	.4
6 Jul 74	**The Singles 1969–73** Carpenters (A & M)	.1
13 Jul 74	**Caribou** Elton John (DJM)	.2
27 Jul 74	**Band On The Run** Wings (Apple)	.7
14 Sep 74	**Hergest Ridge** Mike Oldfield (Virgin)	.3
5 Oct 74	**Tubular Bells** Mike Oldfield (Virgin)	.1
12 Oct 74	**Rollin'** Bay City Rollers (Bell)	.1
19 Oct 74	**Smiler** Rod Stewart (Mercury)	.1
26 Oct 74	**Rollin'** Bay City Rollers (Bell)	.1
2 Nov 74	**Smiler** Rod Stewart (Mercury)	.1
9 Nov 74	**Rollin'** Bay City Rollers (Bell)	.2
23 Nov 74	**Elton John's Greatest Hits** Elton John (DJM)	.11
8 Feb 75	**His Greatest Hits** Engelbert Humperdinck (Decca)	.3

1 Mar 75	**On The Level** Status Quo (Vertigo)	.2
15 Mar 75	**Physical Graffiti** Led Zeppelin (Swansong)	.1
22 Mar 75	**20 Greatest Hits** Tom Jones (Decca)	.4
19 Apr 75	**The Best Of The Stylistics** Stylistics (Avco)	.2
3 May 75	**Once Upon A Star** Bay City Rollers (Bell)	.3
24 May 75	**The Best Of The Stylistics** Stylistics (Avco)	.5
28 Jun 75	**Venus And Mars** Wings (Apple)	.1
5 Jul 75	**Horizon** Carpenters (A & M)	.2
19 Jul 75	**Venus And Mars** Wings (Apple)	.1
26 Jul 75	**Horizon** Carpenters (A & M)	.3
16 Aug 75	**The Best Of The Stylistics** Stylistics (Avco)	.2
30 Aug 75	**Atlantic Crossing** Rod Stewart (Warner Bros.)	.5
4 Oct 75	**Wish You Were Here** Pink Floyd (Harvest)	.1
11 Oct 75	**Atlantic Crossing** Rod Stewart (Warner Bros.)	.2
25 Oct 75	**40 Golden Greats** Jim Reeves (Arcade)	.3
15 Nov 75	**We All Had Doctors' Papers** Max Boyce (EMI)	.1
22 Nov 75	**40 Greatest Hits** Perry Como (K-Tel)	.5
27 Dec 75	**A Night At The Opera** Queen (EMI)	.2
10 Jan 76	**40 Greatest Hits** Perry Como (K-Tel)	.1
17 Jan 76	**A Night At The Opera** Queen (EMI)	.2
31 Jan 76	**The Best Of Roy Orbison** Roy Orbison (Arcade)	.1
7 Feb 76	**The Very Best Of Slim Whitman**	
	Slim Whitman (United Artists)	.6
20 Mar 76	**Blue For You** Status Quo (Vertigo)	.3
10 Apr 76	**Rock Follies** TV Soundtrack (Island)	.2
24 Apr 76	**Presence** Led Zeppelin (Swansong)	.1
1 May 76	**Rock Follies** TV Soundtrack (Island)	.1
8 May 76	**Greatest Hits** Abba (Epic)	.9
10 Jul 76	**A Night On The Town** Rod Stewart (Riva)	.2
24 Jul 76	**20 Golden Greats** Beach Boys (Capitol)	.10
2 Oct 76	**Best Of The Stylistics Vol. 2** Stylistics (H & L)	.1
9 Oct 76	**Stupidity** Dr Feelgood (United Artists)	.1
16 Oct 76	**Greatest Hits** Abba (Epic)	.2
30 Oct 76	**Soul Motion** Various (K-Tel)	.2
13 Nov 76	**The Song Remains The Same**	
	Led Zeppelin (Swansong)	.1
20 Nov 76	**22 Golden Guitar Greats** Bert Weedon (Warwick)	.1
27 Nov 76	**20 Golden Greats** Glen Campbell (Capitol)	.6
8 Jan 77	**Day At The Races** Queen (EMI)	.1
15 Jan 77	**Arrival** Abba (Epic)	.1
22 Jan 77	**Red River Valley** Slim Whitman (United Artists)	.4
19 Feb 77	**20 Golden Greats** Shadows (EMI)	.6
2 Apr 77	**Portrait** Frank Sinatra (Reprise)	.2
16 Apr 77	**Arrival** Abba (Epic)	.9
18 Jun 77	**Live At The Hollywood Bowl** Beatles (Parlophone)	.1
25 Jun 77	**The Muppet Show** Muppets (Pye)	.1
2 Jul 77	**A Star Is Born** Soundtrack (CBS)	.2
16 Jul 77	**Johnny Mathis Collection** Johnny Mathis (CBS)	.4
13 Aug 77	**Going For The One** Yes (Atlantic)	.2
27 Aug 77	**20 All Time Greats** Connie Francis (Polydor)	.2
10 Sep 77	**Elvis Presley's 40 Greatest Hits**	
	Elvis Presley (Arcade)	.1
17 Sep 77	**20 Golden Greats**	
	Diana Ross and the Supremes (Tamla Motown)	.7
5 Nov 77	**40 Golden Greats** Cliff Richard (EMI)	.1

452

FACTS AND FEATS

12 Nov 77	**Never Mind The Bollocks Here's The Sex Pistols** *Sex Pistols (Virgin)* 2
26 Nov 77	**The Sound Of Bread** *Bread (Elektra)* 2
10 Dec 77	**Disco Fever** *Various (K-Tel)* .6
21 Jan 78	**The Sound Of Bread** *Bread (Elektra)* 1
28 Jan 78	**Rumours** *Fleetwood Mac (Warner Bros.)* 1
4 Feb 78	**The Album** *Abba (Epic)* 7
25 Mar 78	**20 Golden Greats** *Buddy Holly/Crickets (MCA)* 3
15 Apr 78	**20 Golden Greats** *Nat 'King' Cole (Capitol)* 3
6 May 78	**Saturday Night Fever** *Various (RSO)* 18
9 Sep 78	**Night Flight To Venus** *Boney M (Atlantic/Hansa)* 4
7 Oct 78	**Grease** *Soundtrack (RSO)* .13
6 Jan 79	**Greatest Hits** *Showaddywaddy (Arista)* 2
27 Jan 79	**Don't Walk – Boogie** *Various (EMI)* 3
10 Feb 79	**Action Replay** *Various (K-Tel)* 1
17 Feb 79	**Parallel Lines** *Blondie (Chrysalis)* 4
17 Mar 79	**Spirits Having Flown** *Bee Gees (RSO)* 2
31 Mar 79	**Greatest Hits Vol. 2** *Barbra Streisand (CBS)* 4
28 Apr 79	**The Very Best Of Leo Sayer** *Leo Sayer (Chrysalis)* 3
19 May 79	**Voulez-Vous** *Abba (Epic)* 4
16 Jun 79	**Discovery** *Electric Light Orchestra (Jet)* 5
21 Jul 79	**Replicas** *Tubeway Army (Beggars Banquet)* 1
28 Jul 79	**The Best Disco Album In The World** *Various (Warner Bros.)* 6
8 Sep 79	**In Through The Out Door** *Led Zeppelin (Swansong)* 2
22 Sep 79	**The Pleasure Principle** *Gary Numan (Beggars Banquet)* 1
29 Sep 79	**Oceans Of Fantasy** *Boney M (Atlantic/Hansa)* 1
6 Oct 79	**The Pleasure Principle** *Gary Numan (Beggars Banquet)* 1
13 Oct 79*	**Eat To The Beat** *Blondie (Chrysalis)* 1
13 Oct 79*	**Reggatta De Blanc** *Police (A & M)* 4
10 Nov 79	**Tusk** *Fleetwood Mac (Warner Bros.)* 1
17 Nov 79	**Greatest Hits Vol. 2** *Abba (Epic)* 3
8 Dec 79	**Greatest Hits** *Rod Stewart (Riva)* 5
12 Jan 80	**Greatest Hits Vol. 2** *Abba (Epic)* 1
19 Jan 80	**Pretenders** *Pretenders (Real)* 4
16 Feb 80	**The Last Dance** *Various (Motown)* 2
1 Mar 80	**String Of Hits** *Shadows (EMI)* 3
22 Mar 80	**Tears And Laughter** *Johnny Mathis (CBS)* 2
5 Apr 80	**Duke** *Genesis (Charisma)* 2
19 Apr 80	**Greatest Hits** *Rose Royce (Whitfield)* 2
3 May 80	**Sky 2** *Sky (Ariola)* 2
17 May 80	**The Magic Of Boney M** *Boney M (Atlantic/Hansa)* 2
31 May 80	**McCartney II** *Paul McCartney (Parlophone)* 2
14 Jun 80	**Peter Gabriel** *Peter Gabriel (Charisma)* 2
28 Jun 80	**Flesh And Blood** *Roxy Music (Polydor)* 1
5 Jul 80	**Emotional Rescue** *Rolling Stones (Rolling Stones)* 2
19 Jul 80	**The Game** *Queen (EMI)* 2
2 Aug 80	**Deepest Purple** *Deep Purple (Harvest)* 1
9 Aug 80	**Back In Black** *AC/DC (Atlantic)* 2
23 Aug 80	**Flesh And Blood** *Roxy Music (Polydor)* 3
13 Sep 80	**Telekon** *Gary Numan (Beggars Banquet)* 1
20 Sep 80	**Never For Ever** *Kate Bush (EMI)* 1

* Two charts published this week because of a change in chart collation.

453

27 Sep 80	**Scary Monsters And Super Creeps** *David Bowie (RCA)*	2
11 Oct 80	**Zenyatta Mondatta** *Police (A & M)*	4
8 Nov 80	**Guilty** *Barbra Streisand (CBS)*	2
22 Nov 80	**Super Trouper** *Abba (Epic)*	9
24 Jan 81	**Kings Of The Wild Frontier** *Adam and the Ants (CBS)*	2
7 Feb 81	**Double Fantasy** *John Lennon (Geffen)*	2
21 Feb 81	**Face Value** *Phil Collins (Virgin)*	3
14 Mar 81	**Kings Of The Wild Frontier** *Adam and the Ants (CBS)*	10
23 May 81	**Stars On 45** *Starsound (CBS)*	5
27 Jun 81	**No Sleep Til Hammersmith** *Motorhead (Bronze)*	1
4 Jul 81	**Disco Daze & Disco Nites** *Various (Ronco)*	1
11 Jul 81	**Love Songs** *Cliff Richard (EMI)*	5
15 Aug 81	**The Official BBC Album Of The Royal Wedding** *Soundtrack (BBC)*	2
29 Aug 81	**Time** *Electric Light Orchestra (Jet)*	2
12 Sep 81	**Dead Ringer** *Meat Loaf (Epic)*	2
26 Sep 81	**Abacab** *Genesis (Charisma)*	2
10 Oct 81	**Ghost In The Machine** *Police (A & M)*	3
31 Oct 81	**Dare** *Human League (Virgin)*	1
7 Nov 81	**Shaky** *Shakin' Stevens (Epic)*	1
14 Nov 81	**Greatest Hits** *Queen (EMI)*	4
12 Dec 81	**Chart Hits '81** *Various (K-Tel)*	1
19 Dec 81	**The Visitors** *Abba (Epic)*	3
9 Jan 82	**Dare Human** *League (Virgin)*	3
30 Jan 82	**Love Songs** *Barbra Streisand (CBS)*	7
20 Mar 82	**The Gift** *Jam (Polydor)*	1
27 Mar 82	**Love Songs** *Barbra Streisand (CBS)*	2
10 Apr 82	**The Number Of The Beast** *Iron Maiden (EMI)*	2
24 Apr 82	**1982** *Status Quo (Vertigo)*	1
1 May 82	**Barry Live In Britain** *Barry Manilow (Arista)*	1
8 May 82	**Tug Of War** *Paul McCartney (Parlophone)*	2
22 May 82	**Complete Madness** *Madness (Stiff)*	2
5 Jun 82	**Avalon** *Roxy Music (Polydor)*	1
12 Jun 82	**Complete Madness** *Madness (Stiff)*	1
19 Jun 82	**Avalon** *Roxy Music (Polydor)*	2
3 Jul 82	**The Lexicon Of Love** *ABC (Neutron)*	3
24 Jul 82	**=The Lexicon Of Love** *ABC (Neutron)*	1
	=Fame *Original Soundtrack (RSO)*	1
31 Jul 82	**Fame** *Original Soundtrack (RSO)*	1
7 Aug 82	**Kids From Fame** *Kids from Fame (BBC)*	8
2 Oct 82	**Love Over Gold** *Dire Straits (Vertigo)*	4
30 Oct 82	**Kids From Fame** *Kids from Fame (BBC)*	4
27 Nov 82	**The Singles – The First Ten Years** *Abba (Epic)*	1
4 Dec 82	**The John Lennon Collection** *John Lennon (Parlophone)*	6
15 Jan 83	**Raiders Of The Pop Charts** *Various Artists (Ronco)*	2
29 Jan 83	**Business As Usual** *Men At Work (Epic)*	5
5 Mar 83	**Thriller** *Michael Jackson (Epic)*	1
12 Mar 83	**War** *U2 (Island)*	1
19 Mar 83	**Thriller** *Michael Jackson (Epic)*	1
26 Mar 83	**The Hurting** *Tears For Fears (Mercury)*	1

FACTS AND FEATS

2 Apr 83	**The Final Cut** *Pink Floyd (Harvest)*	.2
16 Apr 83	**Faster Than The Speed Of Night** *Bonnie Tyler (CBS)*	.1
23 Apr 83	**Let's Dance** *David Bowie (EMI America)*	.3
14 May 83	**True** *Spandau Ballet (Reformation)*	.1
21 May 83	**Thriller** *Michael Jackson (Epic)*	.5
25 Jun 83	**Synchronicity** *Police (A & M)*	.2
9 Jul 83	**Fantastic!** *Wham! (Inner Vision)*	.2
23 Jul 83	**You And Me Both** *Yazoo (Mute)*	.2
6 Aug 83	**The Very Best Of The Beach Boys** *Beach Boys (Capitol)*	.2
20 Aug 83	**18 Greatest Hits** *Michael Jackson plus the Jackson Five (Telstar)*	.3
10 Sep 83	**The Very Best Of The Beach Boys** *Beach Boys (Capitol)*	.1
17 Sep 83	**No Parlez** *Paul Young (CBS)*	.1
24 Sep 83	**Labour Of Love** *UB 40 (DEP International)*	.1
1 Oct 83	**No Parlez** *Paul Young (CBS)*	.2
15 Oct 83	**Genesis** *Genesis (Charisma/Virgin)*	.1
22 Oct 83	**Colour By Numbers** *Culture Club (Virgin)*	.3
12 Nov 83	**Can't Slow Down** *Lionel Richie (Motown)*	.1
19 Nov 83	**Colour By Numbers** *Culture Club (Virgin)*	.2
3 Dec 83	**Seven And The Ragged Tiger** *Duran Duran (EMI)*	.1
10 Dec 83	**No Parlez** *Paul Young (CBS)* . . . . . . ˙	.1
17 Dec 83	**Now! That's What I Call Music** *Various Artists (EMI/Virgin)*	.4
14 Jan 84	**No Parlez** *Paul Young (CBS)*	.1
21 Jan 84	**Now! That's What I Call Music** *Various Artists (EMI/Virgin)*	.1
28 Jan 84	**Thriller** *Michael Jackson (Epic)*	.1
4 Feb 84	**Touch** *Eurythmics (RCA)*	.2
18 Feb 84	**Sparkle In The Rain** *Simple Minds (Virgin)*	.1
25 Feb 84	**Into The Gap** *Thompson Twins (Arista)*	.3
17 Mar 84	**Human's Lib** *Howard Jones (WEA)*	.2
31 Mar 84	**Can't Slow Down** *Lionel Richie (Motown)*	.2
14 Apr 84	**Now! That's What I Call Music 2** *Various Artists (EMI/Virgin)*	.5
19 May 84	**Legend** *Bob Marley and the Wailers (Island)*	.12
11 Aug 84	**Now! That's What I Call Music 3** *Various Artists (EMI/Virgin)*	.8
6 Oct 84	**Tonight** *David Bowie (EMI America)*	.1
13 Oct 84	**The Unforgettable Fire** *U2 (Island)*	.2
27 Oct 84	**Steel Town** *Big Country (Mercury)*	.1
3 Nov 84	**Give My Regards To Broad Street** *Paul McCartney (Parlophone)*	.1
10 Nov 84	**Welcome To The Pleasure Dome** *Frankie Goes To Hollywood (ZTT)*	.1
17 Nov 84	**Make It Big** *Wham! (Epic)*	.2
1 Dec 84	**The Hits Album/The Hits Tape** *Various Artists (CBS/WEA)*	.7
19 Jan 85	**Alf** *Alison Moyet (CBS)*	.1
26 Jan 85	**Agent Provocateur** *Foreigner (Atlantic)*	.3
16 Feb 85	**Born In The USA** *Bruce Springsteen (CBS)*	.1
23 Feb 85	**Meat Is Murder** *Smiths (Rough Trade)*	.1
2 Mar 85	**No Jacket Required** *Phil Collins (Virgin)*	.5
6 Apr 85	**The Secret Of Association** *Paul Young (CBS)*	.1

Date	Album	Weeks
13 Apr 85	**The Hits Album 2/The Hits Tape 2** Various Artists (CBS/WEA)	6
25 May 85	**Brothers In Arms** Dire Straits (Vertigo)	2
8 Jun 85	**Our Favourite Shop** Style Council (Polydor)	1
15 Jun 85	**Boys And Girls** Bryan Ferry (EG)	2
29 Jun 85	**Misplaced Childhood** Marillion (EMI)	1
6 Jul 85	**Born In The USA** Bruce Springsteen (CBS)	4
3 Aug 85	**Brothers In Arms** Dire Straits (Vertigo)	2
17 Aug 85	**Now! That's What I Call Music 5** Various Artists (EMI/Virgin)	5
21 Sep 85	**Like A Virgin** Madonna (Sire)	1
28 Sep 85	**Hounds Of Love** Kate Bush (EMI)	2
12 Oct 85	**Like A Virgin** Madonna (Sire)	1
19 Oct 85	**Hounds Of Love** Kate Bush (EMI)	1
26 Oct 85	**The Love Songs** George Benson (K-Tel)	1
2 Nov 85	**Once Upon A Time** Simple Minds (Virgin)	1
9 Nov 85	**The Love Songs** George Benson (K-Tel)	1
16 Nov 85	**Promise** Sade (Epic)	2
30 Nov 85	**The Greatest Hits Of 1985** Various Artists (Telstar)	1
7 Dec 85	**Now! That's What I Call Music 6** Various Artists (EMI/Virgin)	2
21 Dec 85	**Now! – The Christmas Album** Various Artists (EMI/Virgin)	2
4 Jan 86	**Now! That's What I Call Music 6** Various Artists (EMI/Virgin)	2
18 Jan 86	**Brothers In Arms** Dire Straits (Vertigo)	10
29 Mar 86	**Hits 4** Various Artists (CBS/WEA/RCA Ariola)	4
26 Apr 86	**Street Life – 20 Great Hits** Bryan Ferry/Roxy Music (EG)	5
31 May 86	**So** Peter Gabriel (Virgin)	2
14 Jun 86	**A Kind Of Magic** Queen (EMI)	1
21 Jun 86	**Invisible Touch** Genesis (Charisma)	3
12 Jul 86	**True Blue** Madonna (Sire)	6
23 Aug 86	**Now! That's What I Call Music 7** Various Artists (EMI/Virgin)	5
27 Sep 86	**Silk And Steel** Five Star (Tent)	1
4 Oct 86	**Graceland** Paul Simon (Warner Bros.)	5
8 Nov 86	**Every Breath You Take – The Singles** Police (A & M)	2
22 Nov 86	**Hits 5** Various Artists (CBS/WEA/RCA Ariola)	2
6 Dec 86	**Now! That's What I Call Music 8** Various Artists (EMI/Virgin)	6
17 Jan 87	**The Whole Story** Kate Bush (EMI)	2
31 Jan 87	**Graceland** Paul Simon (Warner Bros.)	3
21 Feb 87	**Phantom Of The Opera** Original London Cast (Polydor)	3
14 Mar 87	**The Very Best Of Hot Chocolate** Hot Chocolate (RAK)	1
21 Mar 87	**The Joshua Tree** U2 (Island)	2
4 Apr 87	**Now! That's What I Call Music 9** Various Artists (EMI/Virgin/Phonogram)	5
9 May 87	**Keep Your Distance** Curiosity Killed The Cat (Mercury)	2
23 May 87	**It's Better To Travel** Swing Out Sister (Mercury)	2
6 Jun 87	**Live In The City Of Light** Simple Minds (Virgin)	1

13 Jun 87	**Whitney** *Whitney Houston (Arista)*	.6
25 Jul 87	**Introducing The Hardline According To Terence**	
	Trent D'Arby Terence Trent D'Arby (CBS)	.1
1 Aug 87	**Hits 6** *Various Artists (CBS/WEA/BMG)*	.4
29 Aug 87	**Hysteria** *Def Leppard (Bludgeon Riffola)*	.1
5 Sep 87	**Hits 6** *Various Artists (CBS/WEA/BMG)*	.1
12 Sep 87	**Bad** *Michael Jackson (Epic)*	.5
17 Oct 87	**Tunnel Of Love** *Bruce Springsteen (CBS)*	.1
24 Oct 87	**Nothing Like The Sun** *Sting (A & M)*	.1
31 Oct 87	**Tango In The Night** *Fleetwood Mac (Warner Bros.)*	.2
14 Nov 87	**Faith** *George Michael (Epic)*	.1
21 Nov 87	**Bridge Of Spies** *T'Pau (Siren)*	.1
28 Nov 87	**Whenever You Need Somebody** *Rick Astley (RCA)*	.1
5 Dec 87	**Now! That's What I Call Music 10**	
	Various Artists (EMI/Virgin/Polygram)	.6
16 Jan 88	**Popped In Souled Out** *Wet Wet Wet (Precious)*	.1
23 Jan 88	**Turn Back The Clock** *Johnny Hates Jazz (Virgin)*	.1
30 Jan 88	**Introducing The Hardline According To Terence**	
	Trent D'Arby Terence Trent D'Arby (CBS)	.8
26 Mar 88	**Viva Hate** *Morrissey (HMV)*	.1
2 Apr 88	**Now! That's What I Call Music 11**	
	Various Artists (EMI/Virgin/Polygram)	.3
23 Apr 88	**Seventh Son Of A Seventh Son** *Iron Maiden (EMI)*	.1
30 Apr 88	**The Innocents** *Erasure (Mute)*	.1
7 May 88	**Tango In The Night** *Fleetwood Mac (Warner Bros.)*	.2
21 May 88	**Lovesexy** *Prince (Paisley Park)*	.1
28 May 88	**Tango In The Night** *Fleetwood Mac (Warner Bros.)*	.1
4 Jun 88	**Nite Flite** *Various Artists (CBS)*	.4
2 Jul 88	**Tracy Chapman** *Tracy Chapman (Elektra)*	.3
23 Jul 88	**Now! That's What I Call Music 12**	
	Various Artists (EMI/Virgin/Polygram)	.5
27 Aug 88	**Kylie** *Kylie Minogue (PWL)*	.4
24 Sep 88	**Hot City Nights** *Various Artists (Vertigo)*	.1
1 Oct 88	**New Jersey** *Bon Jovi (Vertigo)*	.2
15 Oct 88	**Flying Colours** *Chris De Burgh (A & M)*	.1
22 Oct 88	**Rattle And Hum** *U2 (Island)*	.1
29 Oct 88	**Money For Nothing** *Dire Straits (Vertigo)*	.3
19 Nov 88	**Kylie** *Kylie Minogue (PWL)*	.2
3 Dec 88	**Now! That's What I Call Music 13**	
	Various Artists (EMI/Virgin/Polygram)	.3
24 Dec 88	**Private Collection** *Cliff Richard (EMI)*	.2
7 Jan 89	**Now! That's What I Call Music 13**	
	Various Artists (EMI/Virgin/Polygram)	.1

(From 14 January 1989, compilation albums were excluded from the main chart)

14 Jan 89	**The Innocents** *Erasure (Mute)*	.1
21 Jan 89	**The Legendary Roy Orbison** *Roy Orbison (Telstar)*	.3
11 Feb 89	**Technique** *New Order (Factory)*	.1
18 Feb 89	**The Raw And The Cooked**	
	Fine Young Cannibals (London)	.1
25 Feb 89	**A New Flame** *Simply Red (Elektra)*	.4
25 Mar 89	**Anything For You**	
	Gloria Estefan and Miami Sound Machine (Epic)	.1
1 Apr 89	**Like A Prayer** *Madonna (Sire)*	.2
15 Apr 89	**When The World Knows Your Name**	
	Deacon Blue (CBS)	.2

457

Date	Album	Weeks
29 Apr 89	**A New Flame** *Simply Red (Elektra)*	1
6 May 89	**Blast** *Holly Johnson (MCA)*	1
13 May 89	**Street Fighting Years** *Simple Minds (Virgin)*	1
20 May 89	**Ten Good Reasons** *Jason Donovan (PWL)*	2
3 Jun 89	**The Miracle** *Queen (Parlophone)*	1
10 Jun 89	**Ten Good Reasons** *Jason Donovan (PWL)*	2
24 Jun 89	**Flowers In The Dirt** *Paul McCartney (Parlophone)*	1
1 Jul 89	**Batman** *Prince (Warner Bros.)*	1
8 Jul 89	**Velveteen** *Transvision Vamp (MCA)*	1
15 Jul 89	**Club Classics** *Volume One Soul II Soul (10)*	1
22 Jul 89	**A New Flame** *Simply Red (Elektra)*	2
5 Aug 89	**Cuts Both Ways** *Gloria Estefan (Epic)*	6
16 Sep 89	**Aspects Of Love** *Original London Cast (Polydor)*	1
23 Sep 89	**We Too Are One** *Eurythmics (RCA)*	1
30 Sep 89	**Foreign Affair** *Tina Turner (Capitol)*	1
7 Oct 89	**The Seeds Of Love** *Tears For Fears (Fontana)*	1
14 Oct 89	**Crossroads** *Tracy Chapman (Elektra)*	1
21 Oct 89	**Enjoy Yourself** *Kylie Minogue (PWL)*	1
28 Oct 89	**Wild!** *Erasure (Mute)*	2
11 Nov 89	**The Road To Hell** *Chris Rea (WEA)*	3
2 Dec 89	**. . . But Seriously** *Phil Collins (Virgin)*	8
27 Jan 90	**Colour** *Christians (Island)*	1
3 Feb 90	**. . . But Seriously** *Phil Collins (Virgin)*	7
24 Mar 90	**I Do Not Want What I Haven't Got** *Sinead O'Connor (Ensign)*	1
31 Mar 90	**Changesbowie** *David Bowie (EMI)*	1
7 Apr 90	**Only Yesterday** *Carpenters (A & M)*	2
21 Apr 90	**Behind The Mask** *Fleetwood Mac (Warner Bros.)*	1
28 Apr 90	**Only Yesterday** *Carpenters (A & M)*	5
2 Jun 90	**Vol II (1990 A New Decade)** *Soul II Soul (10)*	3
23 Jun 90	**The Essential Pavarotti** *Luciano Pavarotti (Decca)*	1
30 Jun 90	**Step By Step** *New Kids On The Block (CBS)*	1
7 Jul 90	**The Essential Pavarotti** *Luciano Pavarotti (Decca)*	3
28 Jul 90	**Sleeping With The Past** *Elton John (Rocket)*	5
1 Sep 90	**Graffiti Bridge** *Prince (Paisley Park)*	1
8 Sep 90	**In Concert** *Luciano Pavarotti, Placido Domingo and José Carreras (Decca)*	1
15 Sep 90	**Listen Without Prejudice Vol. 1** *George Michael (Epic)*	1
22 Sep 90	**In Concert** *Luciano Pavarotti, Placido Domingo and José Carreras (Decca)*	4
20 Oct 90	**Some Friendly** *Charlatans (Situation Two)*	1
27 Oct 90	**The Rhythm Of The Saints** *Paul Simon (Warner Bros.)*	2
10 Nov 90	**The Very Best Of Elton John** *Elton John (Rocket)*	2
24 Nov 90	**The Immaculate Collection** *Madonna (Sire)*	9
26 Jan 91	**MCMXC AD** *Enigma (Virgin International)*	1
2 Feb 91	**The Soul Cages** *Sting (A & M)*	1
9 Feb 91	**Doubt** *Jesus Jones (Food)*	1
16 Feb 91	**Innuendo** *Queen (Parlophone)*	2
2 Mar 91	**Circle Of One** *Oleta Adams (Fontana)*	1
9 Mar 91	**Auberge** *Chris Rea (East West)*	1
16 Mar 91	**Spartacus** *Farm (Produce)*	1
23 Mar 91	**Out Of Time** *R.E.M. (Warner Bros.)*	1
30 Mar 91	**Greatest Hits** *Eurythmics (RCA)*	9

Date	Title	Weeks
1 Jun 91	**Seal** Seal (ZTT)	3
22 Jun 91	**Greatest Hits** Eurythmics (RCA)	1
29 Jun 91	**Love Hurts** Cher (Geffen)	6
10 Aug 91	**The Essential Pavarotti II** Luciano Pavarotti (Decca)	2
24 Aug 91	**Metallica** Metallica (Vertigo)	1
31 Aug 91	**Joseph And The Amazing Technicolour Dreamcoat** Jason Donovan/ Original London Cast (Really Useful)	2
14 Sep 91	**From Time To Time – The Singles Collection** Paul Young (Columbia)	1
21 Sep 91	**On Every Street** Dire Straits (Vertigo)	1
28 Sep 91	**Use Your Illusion II** Guns N' Roses (Geffen)	1
5 Oct 91	**Waking Up The Neighbours** Bryan Adams (A & M)	1
12 Oct 91	**Stars** Simply Red (East West)	2
26 Oct 91	**Chorus** Erasure (Mute)	1
2 Nov 91	**Stars** Simply Red (East West)	1
9 Nov 91	**Greatest Hits II** Queen (Parlophone)	1
16 Nov 91	**Shepherd Moons** Enya (WEA)	1
23 Nov 91	**We Can't Dance** Genesis (Virgin)	1
30 Nov 91	**Dangerous** Michael Jackson (Epic)	1
7 Dec 91	**Greatest Hits II** Queen (Parlophone)	4
4 Jan 92	**Stars** Simply Red (East West)	5
8 Feb 92	**High On The Happy Side** Wet Wet Wet (Precious)	2
22 Feb 92	**Stars** Simply Red (East West)	3
14 Mar 92	**Divine Madness** Madness (Virgin)	3
4 Apr 92	**Human Touch** Bruce Springsteen (Columbia)	1
11 Apr 92	**Adrenalize** Def Leppard (Bludgeon Riffola)	1
18 Apr 92	**Diva** Annie Lennox (RCA)	1
25 Apr 92	**Up** Right Said Fred (Tug)	1
2 May 92	**Wish** Cure (Fiction)	1
9 May 92	**Stars** Simply Red (East West)	1
16 May 92	**1992 – The Love Album** Carter The Unstoppable Sex Machine (Chrysalis)	1
23 May 92	**Fear Of The Dark** Iron Maiden (EMI)	1
30 May 92	**Michael Ball** Michael Ball (Polydor)	1
6 Jun 92	**Back To Front** Lionel Richie (Motown)	6
18 Jul 92	**U.F. Orb** Orb (Big Life)	1
25 Jul 92	**The Greatest Hits 1966–1992** Neil Diamond (Columbia)	3
15 Aug 92	**Welcome To Wherever You Are** INXS (Mercury)	1
22 Aug 92	**We Can't Dance** Genesis (Virgin)	1
29 Aug 92	**Best . . . 1** Smiths (WEA)	1
5 Sep 92	**Greatest Hits** Kylie Minogue (PWL)	1
12 Sep 92	**Tubular Bells II** Mike Oldfield (WEA)	2
26 Sep 92	**The Best Of Belinda Volume I** Belinda Carlisle (Virgin)	1
3 Oct 92	**Gold – Greatest Hits** Abba (Polydor)	1
10 Oct 92	**Automatic For The People** R.E.M. (Warner Bros)	1
17 Oct 92	**Symbol** Prince (Paisley Park)	1
24 Oct 92	**Glittering Prize 81–92** Simple Minds (Virgin)	3
14 Nov 92	**Keep The Faith** Bon Jovi (Jambco)	1
21 Nov 92	**Cher's Greatest Hits 1965–1992** Cher (Geffen)	1
28 Nov 92	**Pop! The First 20 Hits** Erasure (Mute)	2
12 Dec 92	**Cher's Greatest Hits 1965–1992** Cher (Geffen)	6

459

23 Jan 93	**Live – The Way We Walk Volume II – The Longs** *Genesis (Virgin)*	.2
6 Feb 93	**Jam** *Little Angels (Polydor)*	.1
13 Feb 93	**Pure Cult** *Cult (Beggars Banquet)*	.1
20 Feb 93	**Words Of Love** *Buddy Holly and the Crickets (Polygram)*	.1
27 Feb 93	**Walthamstow** *East 17 (London)*	.1
6 Mar 93	**Diva** *Annie Lennox (RCA)*	.1
13 Mar 93	**Are You Gonna Go My Way** *Lenny Kravitz (Virgin)*	.2
27 Mar 93	**Their Greatest Hits** *Hot Chocolate (EMI)*	.1
3 Apr 93	**Songs Of Faith And Devotion** *Depeche Mode (Mute)*	.1
10 Apr 93	**Suede** *Suede (Nude)*	.1
17 Apr 93	**Black Tie White Noise** *David Bowie (Arista)*	.1
24 Apr 93	**Automatic For The People** *R.E.M. (Warner Bros)*	.1
1 May 93	**The Album** *Cliff Richard (EMI)*	.1
8 May 93	**Automatic For The People** *R.E.M. (Warner Bros)*	.1
15 May 93	**Republic** *New Order (London)*	.1
22 May 93	**Automatic For The People** *R.E.M. (Warner Bros)*	.1
29 May 93	**Janet** *Janet Jackson (Virgin)*	.2
12 Jun 93	**No Limits** *2 Unlimited (PWL Continental)*	.1
19 Jun 93	**What's Love Got To Do With It** *Tina Turner (Parlophone)*	.1
26 Jun 93	**Emergency On Planet Earth** *Jamiroquai (Sony)*	.3
17 Jul 93	**Zooropa** *U2 (Island)*	.1
24 Jul 93	**Promises And Lies** *UB40 (DEP International)*	.7
11 Sep 93	**Music Box** *Mariah Carey (Columbia)*	.1
18 Sep 93	**Bat Out Of Hell II – Back Into Hell** *Meat Loaf (Virgin)*	.1
25 Sep 93	**In Utero** *Nirvana (Geffen)*	.1
2 Oct 93	**Bat Out Of Hell II – Back Into Hell** *Meat Loaf (Virgin)*	.1
9 Oct 93	**Very** *Pet Shop Boys (Parlophone)*	.1
16 Oct 93	**Bat Out Of Hell II – Back Into Hell** *Meat Loaf (Virgin)*	.1
23 Oct 93	**Everything Changes** *Take That (RCA)*	.1
30 Oct 93	**Bat Out Of Hell II – Back Into Hell** *Meat Loaf (Virgin)*	.3
20 Nov 93	**Both Sides** *Phil Collins (Virgin)*	.1
27 Nov 93	**Bat Out Of Hell II – Back Into Hell** *Meat Loaf (Virgin)*	.5
1 Jan 94	**One Woman – The Ultimate Collection** *Diana Ross (EMI)*	.1
8 Jan 94	**Everything Changes** *Take That (RCA)*	.1
15 Jan 94	**So Far So Good** *Bryan Adams (A&M)*	.1
22 Jan 94	**One Woman – The Ultimate Collection** *Diana Ross (EMI)*	.1
29 Jan 94	**Tease Me** *Chaka Demus and Pliers (Mango)*	.2
12 Feb 94	**Under The Pink** *Tori Amos (East West)*	.1
19 Feb 94	**The Cross Of Changes** *Enigma (Virgin)*	.1
26 Feb 94	**Music Box** *Mariah Carey (Columbia)*	.4
26 Mar 94	**Vauxhall And I** *Morrissey (Parlophone)*	.1
2 Apr 94	**Music Box** *Mariah Carey (Columbia)*	.1
9 Apr 94	**The Division Bell** *Pink Floyd (EMI)*	.4
7 May 94	**Parklife** *Blur (Food)*	.1

FACTS AND FEATS

14 May 94	**Our Town – Greatest Hits** *Deacon Blue (Columbia)*	2
28 May 94	**I Say I Say I Say** *Erasure (Mute)*	. . .1
4 Jun 94	**Seal** *Seal (ZTT)*	. .2
18 Jun 94	**Real Things** *2 Unlimited (PWL Continental)*	. . .1
25 Jun 94	**Everybody Else Is Doing It, So Why Can't We?**	
	Cranberries (Island)	. . .1
2 Jul 94	**Happy Nation** *Ace Of Base (Metronome)*	. . .2
16 Jul 94	**Music For The Jilted Generation** *Prodigy (XL)*	. . .1
23 Jul 94	**Voodoo Lounge** *Rolling Stones (Virgin)*	. . .1
30 Jul 94	**End Of Part One (Their Greatest Hits)**	
	Wet Wet Wet (Precious Organisation)	. . .4
27 Aug 94	**Come** *Prince (Warner Bros)*	. . .1
3 Sep 94	**End Of Part One (Their Greatest Hits)**	
	Wet Wet Wet (Precious Organisation)	. . .1
10 Sep 94	**Definitely Maybe** *Oasis (Creation)*	. . .1
17 Sep 94	**Three Tenors In Concert 1994** *José Carreras,*	
	Placido Domingo and Luciano Pavarotti (Teldec)	. .1
24 Sep 94	**From The Cradle** *Eric Clapton (Duck)*	. . .1
1 Oct 94	**Songs** *Luther Vandross (Epic)*	. . .1
8 Oct 94	**Monster** *R.E.M. (Warner Bros)*	. . .2
22 Oct 94	**Cross Road – The Best Of** *Bon Jovi (Jambco)*	. . .3
12 Nov 94	**Unplugged In New York** *Nirvana (Geffen)*	. . .1
19 Nov 94	**Cross Road – The Best Of** *Bon Jovi (Jambco)*	. . .2
3 Dec 94	**Carry On Up The Charts – The Best Of**	
	Beautiful South (Go! Discs)	. . .1
10 Dec 94	**Live At The BBC** *Beatles (Apple)*	. . .1
17 Dec 94	**Carry On Up The Charts – The Best Of**	
	Beautiful South (Go! Discs)	. . .6

461

28 Jan 95	**The Colour Of My Love** *Celine Dion (Epic)*	. . .6
11 Mar 95	**Greatest Hits** *Bruce Springsteen (Columbia)*	. . .1
18 Mar 95	**Medusa** *Annie Lennox (RCA)*	. . .1
25 Mar 95	**Elastica** *Elastica (Deceptive)*	. . .1
1 Apr 95	**The Colour Of My Love** *Celine Dion (Epic)*	. . .1
8 Apr 95	**Wake Up!** *Boo Radleys (Creation)*	. . .1
15 Apr 95	**Greatest Hits** *Bruce Springsteen (Columbia)*	. . .1
22 Apr 95	**Picture This** *Wet Wet Wet (Precious Organisation)*	. . .3
13 May 95	**Nobody Else** *Take That (RCA)*	. . .2
27 May 95	**Stanley Road** *Paul Weller (Go! Discs)*	. . .1
3 Jun 95	**Singles** *Alison Moyet (Columbia)*	. . .1
10 Jun 95	**Pulse** *Pink Floyd (EMI)*	. .2
24 Jun 95	**HIStory – Past Present And Future Book 1**	
	Michael Jackson (Epic)	. . .1
1 Jul 95	**These Days** *Bon Jovi (Mercury)*	. . .4
29 Jul 95	**I Should Coco** *Supergrass (Parlophone)*	. . .3
19 Aug 95	**It's Great When You're Straight . . . Yeah!**	
	Black Grape (Radioactive)	. . .2
2 Sep 95	**Said And Done** *Boyzone (Polydor)*	. . .1
9 Sep 95	**Charlatans** *Charlatans (Beggars Banquet)*	. . .1
16 Sep 95	**Zeitgeist** *Levellers (China)*	. . .1
23 Sep 95	**The Great Escape** *Blur (Food)*	. . .2
7 Oct 95	**Daydream** *Mariah Carey (Columbia)*	. . .1
14 Oct 95	**(What's The Story) Morning Glory?** *Oasis (Creation)*	. . .1
21 Oct 95	**Life** *Simply Red (East West)*	. . .3
11 Nov 95	**Different Class** *Pulp (Island)*	. . .1
18 Nov 95	**Made In Heaven** *Queen (Parlophone)*	. . .1
25 Nov 95	**Robson And Jerome** *Robson Green and Jerome*	
	Flynn (RCA)	. .6+

Since 14 January 1989, the albums charts have been split into a Top 75 'Artist Albums' and a Top 20 'Compilation Albums'. The 126 number one hits on the Compilation Albums are as follows:

14 Jan 89	**Now! That's What I Call Music 13**	
	(EMI/Virgin/Polygram) .1	
21 Jan 89	**The Premiere Collection** (Really Useful/Polydor) 2	
4 Feb 89	**The Marquee – Thirty Legendary Years** (Polydor) 4	
4 Mar 89	**The Awards** (Telstar) 1	
11 Mar 89	**The Premiere Collection** (Really Useful/Polydor) 1	
18 Mar 89	**Deep Heat** (Telstar) 1	
25 Mar 89	**Unforgettable 2** (EMI) 1	
1 Apr 89	**Now! That's What I Call Music 14**	
	(EMI/Virgin/Polygram) .7	
20 May 89	**Nite Flite 2** (CBS) 2	
3 Jun 89	**The Hits Album 10** (CBS/WEA/BMG) 6	
15 Jul 89	**Now! Dance '89** (EMI/Virgin) 6	
26 Aug 89	**Now! That's What I Call Music 15**	
	(EMI/Virgin/Polygram) .5	
30 Sep 89	**Deep Heat 4 – Play With Fire** (Telstar) 5	
4 Nov 89	**Smash Hits Party '89** (Dover) 3	
25 Nov 89	**The 80s – The Album Of The Decade** (EMI) 1	
2 Dec 89	**Now! That's What I Call Music 16**	
	(EMI/Virgin/Polygram) .7	
20 Jan 90	**Pure Soft Metal** (Stylus) 2	
3 Feb 90	**Deep Heat 5 – Feed The Fever** (Telstar) 2	
17 Feb 90	**Pure Soft Metal** (Stylus) 3	
10 Mar 90	**Now Dance 901** (EMI/Virgin/Polygram) 4	
7 Apr 90	**Deep Heat 6 – The Sixth Sense** (Telstar) 2	
21 Apr 90	**Just The Two Of Us** (CBS) 2	
5 May 90	**Now! That's What I Call Music 17**	
	(EMI/Virgin/Polygram) .5	
9 Jun 90	**The Classic Experience II** (EMI) 4	
7 Jul 90	**Deep Heat 7 – Seventh Heaven** (Telstar) 1	
14 Jul 90	**Smash Hits – Rave!** (Dover) 2	
28 Jul 90	**Now Dance 902** (EMI/Virgin/Polygram) 3	
18 Aug 90	**Knebworth – The Album** (Polydor) 2	
1 Sep 90	**Megabass** (Telstar) 4	
29 Sep 90	**Slammin'** (A&M) 1	
6 Oct 90	**That Loving Feeling Vol. 3** (Dino) 3	
27 Oct 90	**Missing You – An Album Of Love** (EMI) 3	
17 Nov 90	**Now Dance 903** (EMI/Virgin/Polygram) 2	
1 Dec 90	**Now! That's What I Call Music 18**	
	(EMI/Virgin/Polygram) .7	
19 Jan 91	**Dirty Dancing** (Original Soundtrack) (RCA) 2	
2 Feb 91	**Deep Heat 9 – The Ninth Life** (Telstar) 2	
16 Feb 91	**The Lost Boys** (Original Soundtrack) (Atlantic) 1	
23 Feb 91	**Awesome!!** (EMI) 3	
16 Mar 91	**Unchained Melodies** (Telstar) 3	
6 Apr 91	**Now! That's What I Call Music 19**	
	(EMI/Virgin/Polygram) .5	
11 May 91	**Thinking Of You** (Columbia) 2	
25 May 91	**Smash Hits – Massive** (Dover) 2	
8 Jun 91	**The Essential Mozart** (Decca) 1	
15 Jun 91	**The Rhythm Divine** (Dino) 1	
22 Jun 91	**The Essential Mozart** (Decca) 1	

Date	Title	Weeks
29 Jun 91	**Wings Of Love** *(A&M)*	5
3 Aug 91	**Thin Ice 2 – The Second Shiver** *(Telstar)*	1
10 Aug 91	**Purple Rainbows** *(Polydor)*	1
17 Aug 91	**The Hits Album** *(Sony/BMG)*	2
31 Aug 91	**The Sound Of The Suburbs** *(Columbia)*	3
21 Sep 91	**Groovy Ghetto** *(Arcade)*	2
5 Oct 91	**Now! Dance 91** *(EMI/Virgin/Polygram)*	3
26 Oct 91	**Two Rooms – Elton John & Bernie Taupin** *(Mercury)*	1
2 Nov 91	**Hardcore Ecstasy** *(Dino)*	4
30 Nov 91	**Now! That's What I Call Music 20** *(EMI/Virgin/Polygram)*	7
18 Jan 92	**Essential Hardcore** *(Dino)*	1
25 Jan 92	**The Ultimate Rave** *(EMI/Virgin/Polygram)*	4
22 Feb 92	**The Awards 1992** *(Polygram TV)*	2
7 Mar 92	**The Ultimate Hardcore** *(Telstar)*	2
21 Mar 92	**Soul Emotion** *(Polygram)*	3
11 Apr 92	**All Woman** *(Quality Television)*	2
25 Apr 92	**Now! That's What I Call Music 21** *(EMI/Virgin/Polygram)*	5
30 May 92	**The Rave Gener8tor** *(Cookie Jar)*	2
13 Jun 92	**Earthrise – The Rainforest Album** *(ELF)*	1
20 Jun 92	**Modern Love** *(Polygram)*	1
27 Jun 92	**Heartbeat** *(Columbia)*	4
25 Jul 92	**KT3 – The Kaos Theory** *(Telstar)*	2
8 Aug 92	**Now! That's What I Call Music 22** *(EMI/Virgin/Polygram)*	8
3 Oct 92	**Sixties Beat** *(Dino)*	1
10 Oct 92	**All Woman 2** *(Quality Television)*	1
17 Oct 92	**Energy Rush** *(Dino)*	2
31 Oct 92	**The Ultimate Country Collection** *(Columbia)*	1
7 Nov 92	**The Best Of Dance '92** *(Telstar)*	1
14 Nov 92	**The Ultimate Country Collection** *(Columbia)*	1
21 Nov 92	**The Best Of Dance '92** *(Telstar)*	1
28 Nov 92	**Now! That's What I Call Music 23** *(EMI/Virgin/Polygram)*	5
2 Jan 93	**The Bodyguard** *(Original Soundtrack) (Arista)*	8
27 Feb 93	**Hits '93 Volume 1** *(Telstar/BMG)*	3
20 Mar 93	**The Bodyguard** *(Original Soundtrack) (Arista)*	2
3 Apr 93	**Blues Brother Soul Sister** *(Dino)*	1
10 Apr 93	**Energy Rush Presents Dance Hits '93** *(Dino)*	3
1 May 93	**The Bodyguard** *(Original Soundtrack) (Arista)*	1
8 May 93	**Now! That's What I Call Music 24** *(EMI/Virgin/Polygram)*	6
19 Jun 93	**Originals** *(Columbia)*	1
26 Jun 93	**Now! Dance '93** *(EMI/Virgin/Polygram)*	2
10 Jul 93	**100% Dance** *(Telstar)*	1
17 Jul 93	**The Best Dance Album In The World . . . Ever!** *(Virgin)*	4
14 Aug 93	**Now! That's What I Call Music 25** *(EMI/Virgin/Polygram)*	5
18 Sep 93	**Dance Adrenalin** *(Telstar)*	2
2 Oct 93	**100% Dance Volume 2** *(Telstar)*	2
16 Oct 93	**Now! 1993** *(EMI/Virgin/Polygram)*	1
23 Oct 93	**100% Dance Volume 2** *(Telstar)*	2

463

FACTS AND FEATS

6 Nov 93	**Now! Dance – The Best Of '93** *(EMI/Virgin/Polygram)*	1
13 Nov 93	**The Best Of Dance '93** *(Telstar)*	2
27 Nov 93	**Now! That's What I Call Music 26** *(EMI/Virgin/Polygram)*	8
22 Jan 94	**Sound Of Kiss FM** *(Polygram)*	1
29 Jan 94	**Now! Dance 94 Volume 1** *(EMI/Virgin/Polygram)*	2
12 Feb 94	**Sweet Soul Harmonies** *(Virgin)*	1
19 Feb 94	**Dance Hits 94 – Vol 1** *(Telstar)*	3
12 Mar 94	**Soul Devotion** *(Polygram)*	4
9 Apr 94	**Now! That's What I Call Music 27** *(EMI/Virgin/Polygram)*	4
7 May 94	**Dance Zone Level One** *(Polygram)*	4
4 Jun 94	**Energy Rush – Xtermin8** *(Dino)*	1
11 Jun 94	**Dance Hits 94 – Vol 2** *(Telstar)*	1
18 Jun 94	**Pure Moods** *(Virgin)*	2
2 Jul 94	**Now! Dance – Summer 94** *(EMI/Virgin)*	2
16 Jul 94	**Dance Zone Level Two** *(Polygram)*	2
30 Jul 94	**It's The Ultimate Dance Album** *(Telstar)*	2
13 Aug 94	**Now! That's What I Call Music 28** *(EMI/Virgin/Polygram)*	5
17 Sep 94	**Best Rock Album In The World Ever** *(Virgin)*	3
8 Oct 94	**Dance Zone Level Three** *(Polygram)*	1
15 Oct 94	**Now! That's What I Call Music 1994** *(EMI/Virgin/Polygram)*	4
12 Nov 94	**Best Rock Album In The World Ever** *(Virgin)*	1
19 Nov 94	**The Love Album** *(Virgin)*	1
26 Nov 94	**Now! That's What I Call Music 29** *(EMI/Virgin/Polygram)*	9
28 Jan 95	**Best Of Heartbeat** *(Columbia)*	1
4 Feb 95	**Best Punk Album In The World . . . Ever!** *(Virgin)*	1
11 Feb 95	**Dance Mania 95 – Volume One** *(Pure Music)*	2
25 Feb 95	**On A Dance Tip** *(Global Television)*	3
18 Mar 95	**Smash Hits 95 – Volume 1** *(Telstar)*	1
25 Mar 95	**Dance Zone Level Four** *(Polygram)*	2
8 Apr 95	**Dance Mania 95 – Volume Two** *(Pure Music)*	2
22 Apr 95	**Now! That's What I Call Music 30** *(EMI/Virgin/Polygram)*	4
20 May 95	**On A Dance Tip 2** *(Global Television)*	3
10 Jun 95	**Top Of The Pops 1** *(Columbia)*	2
24 Jun 95	**Dance Zone Level Five** *(Polygram)*	3
15 Jun 95	**Dance Mania 95 – Volume Three** *(Pure Music)*	3
5 Aug 95	**The Best Summer . . . Ever!** *(Virgin)*	1
12 Aug 95	**Now! That's What I Call Music 31** *(EMI/Virgin/Polygram)*	4
9 Sep 95	**Dance Zone Level Six** *(Polygram)*	1
16 Sep 95	**Help – War Child** *(Go! Discs)*	2
30 Sep 95	**Heartbeat – Forever Yours** *(Columbia)*	6
11 Nov 95	**The Greatest Party Album Under The Sun** *(EMI)*	1
18 Nov 95	**Pure Swing IV** *(Dino)*	1
25 Nov 95	**Now! That's What I Call Music 32** *(EMI/Virgin/Polygram)*	6+

All albums were, of course, credited to 'Various Artists'.

464

MOST NUMBER ONE ALBUMS

When *Live At The BBC* became the Beatles thirteenth chart-topper at the end of 1994, over 17 years after they previously hit the very top, they restored their three-album lead over the Rolling Stones, who became only the second act to achieve ten number one albums when *Voodoo Lounge* hit the top in July 1994. The leading chart-toppers are:

13	Beatles	4	Shadows
10	Rolling Stones	4	Bruce Springsteen
9	Abba	4	Status Quo
9	Queen	4	Wet Wet Wet
8	David Bowie	3	Boney M
8	Led Zeppelin	3	Kate Bush
7	Genesis	3	Carpenters
7	Paul McCartney/Wings	3	Deep Purple
7	Cliff Richard	3	Eurythmics
7	Rod Stewart	3	Iron Maiden
6	Bob Dylan	3	John Lennon
6	Elton John	3	Kylie Minogue
6	Elvis Presley	3	George Mitchell Minstrels
5	Erasure	3	Moody Blues
5	Michael Jackson *(includes 1 with Jacksons)*	3	Gary Numan/Tubeway Army
		3	Mike Oldfield
5	Pink Floyd	3	R.E.M.
5	Police	3	Diana Ross and the Supremes *(includes 1 with the Temptations)*
5	Prince		
5	Simple Minds	3	Paul Simon *(+ 2 with Simon & Garfunkel)*
5	U2		
4	Bon Jovi	3	Simply Red
4	Phil Collins	3	Slade
4	Dire Straits	3	Barbra Streisand
4	Fleetwood Mac	3	T. Rex
4	Madonna	3	Andy Williams
4	Roxy Music *(includes 1 with Bryan Ferry)*	3	Paul Young

Bryan Ferry has one solo number one to go with the four Roxy Music chart toppers, on all of which he sang lead and one of which he was given equal billing with Roxy Music as it also featured several solo Ferry tracks.

Annie Lennox has two solo number one hit albums, as well as three with Eurythmics.

Sting has two solo number one albums as well as five as lead singer of the Police.

Morrissey has had two solo number one hit albums and two as a member of the Smiths.

Alison Moyet has had two solo number one albums, and one more as vocalist with Yazoo.

George Michael has two solo chart-topping albums and two more as half of Wham!

Luciano Pavarotti has had two number one albums as a soloist, plus two in collaboration with José Carreras and Placido Domingo.

Paul Weller has topped the charts once as a soloist, once as half of the Style Council and once as one third of Jam.

MOST WEEKS AT NUMBER ONE

164	Beatles	16	Diana Ross and the Supremes
115	Cast of *South Pacific* Film Soundtrack		*(includes 4 with the Temptations)*
		15	Police
70	Cast of *The Sound Of Music* Film Soundtrack	15	Barbra Streisand
		14	Led Zeppelin
50	Abba	13	Beach Boys
49	Elvis Presley	13	Cher
48	Simon and Garfunkel	13	Cast of *Grease* Film Soundtrack
44	Rolling Stones	13	Eurythmics
30	Cliff Richard	13	Meat Loaf
29	Carpenters	13	Roxy Music
28	Elton John	13	Broadway Cast Of *West Side Story*
27	Rod Stewart		
24	Phil Collins	12	Adam and the Ants
22	David Bowie	12	Bon Jovi
22	Dire Straits	12	Genesis
22	Bob Dylan	12	Kids From 'Fame'
22	Simply Red	12	Bob Marley and the Wailers
21	Shadows	12	T. Rex
	(plus 22 weeks backing Cliff Richard)	12	Luciano Pavarotti
21	Queen		*(includes 6 with José Carreras and Placido Domingo)*
19	Madonna		
19	George Mitchell Minstrels	11	Paul Simon
18	Cast of *Saturday Night Fever* Film Soundtrack	11	Wet Wet Wet
		10	John Lennon
18	Michael Jackson	10	Pink Floyd
	(includes 3 with Jackson Five)	10	Stylistics
16	Paul McCartney/Wings	10	Slim Whitman

This list excludes individual appearances on compilations and soundtracks, except where the soundtrack is credited to one artist, for example Elvis Presley's *Blue Hawaii*.

MOST WEEKS AT NUMBER ONE IN A CALENDAR YEAR

Only five acts have spent more than 20 weeks on top of the charts in any one year. Two of these were film soundtrack casts. The feat has not been achieved since 1970.

52	Cast of *South Pacific*	1959
45	Cast of *South Pacific*	1960
40	Beatles	1964
34	Beatles	1963
30	Cast of *The Sound Of Music*	1966
26	Beatles	1967
24	Elvis Presley	1962
	Simon and Garfunkel	1970
22	Elvis Presley	1961
20	Cast of *The Sound Of Music*	1965

FACTS AND FEATS

Only two acts have achieved the feat of getting three albums to number one in one calendar year. They are:

1965   Beatles
        (Beatles For Sale, Help, Rubber Soul)
1972   T. Rex
        (Electric Warrior, Prophets Seers . . ./My People Were Fair . . ., Bolan Boogie)

The second of T. Rex's three number ones was a re-issued double album of Tyrannosaurus Rex material, so Marc Bolan's achievement could be considered even better than the Beatles, whose chart-topping albums were all single discs.

Sixteen acts have had two new number one hits in a year, as follows:

5 times	Beatles	(1963, 1964, 1965, 1969, 1970)
4 times	Abba	(1979, 1980, 1981, 1982)
3 times	Elton John	(1973, 1974, 1990)
2 times	Bob Dylan	(1965, 1970)
	Led Zeppelin	(1970, 1976)
	George Mitchell Minstrels	(1961, 1962)
Once	David Bowie	(1973)
	Erasure	(1989)
	Monkees	(1967)
	Gary Numan/Tubeway Army	(1979)
	Mike Oldfield	(1974)
	Elvis Presley	(1962)
	Queen	(1991)
	Slade	(1973)
	T. Rex	(1972)
	Andy Williams	(1971)

In 1981 and 1993, Phil Collins had number one hits as a soloist and as part of Genesis. In 1983 Michael Jackson hit the top with *Thriller* and also with a Greatest Hits package featuring tracks by the Jackson Five as well as some solo tracks by Michael. In 1990, Luciano Pavarotti was on top of the charts with *The Essential Pavarotti* and, seven weeks later, *In Concert* with José Carreras and Placido Domingo.

The longest title to hit the top of the charts is *My People Were Fair And Had Sky In Their Hair But Now They're Content To Wear Stars On Their Brows*, the 78-letter title by Tyrannosaurus Rex. The second-longest number one hit title is the album that was coupled with the longest title when they were re-issued, the 42-letter *Prophets Seers And Sages And The Angels Of The Ages*, also by Tyrannosaurus Rex. Only two other albums with 40 letters in their title have hit the top – *Diana Ross And The Supremes Join The Temptations* (41 letters) and *Joseph And The Amazing Technicolour Dreamcoat* (40 letters).

The shortest album title to top the charts is the two-lettered *Up* by Right Said Fred. Prince has hit number one with an album called ⚥, and Led Zeppelin ruled the roost with *Four Symbols*, neither of which titles had any letters at all.

SELF-REPLACEMENT AT THE TOP

Only three acts have ever knocked themselves off the top of the charts. They are:

Beatles: . . . . . . *With The Beatles* replaced *Please Please Me* on 7 Dec 63
Beatles: . . . . *Beatles For Sale* replaced *A Hard Day's Night* on 19 Dec 64
Bob Dylan: . . . . *Bringing It All Back Home* replaced *Freewheelin' Bob Dylan* on 29 May 65
Mike Oldfield: . . *Tubular Bells* replaced *Hergest Ridge* on 5 Oct 74

On 7 Aug 82 *Kids From Fame* replaced *Fame* at the top, but the TV spin-off featured an entirely different cast from the album soundtrack.

Hergest Ridge was released after *Tubular Bells* but got to number one first. Bob Dylan had two Top Ten hit albums released between *Freewheelin'* and *Bringing It All Back Home*.

MOST WEEKS AT NUMBER ONE IN TOTAL

115	*South Pacific*	Film Soundtrack
70	*The Sound Of Music*	Film Soundtrack
41	*Bridge Over Troubled Water*	Simon and Garfunkel
30	*Please Please Me*	Beatles
27	*Sergeant Pepper's Lonely Hearts Club Band*	Beatles
22	*GI Blues*	Elvis Presley (Film Soundtrack)
21	*With The Beatles*	Beatles
21	*A Hard Day's Night*	Beatles (Film Soundtrack)
18	*Blue Hawaii*	Elvis Presley (Film Soundtrack)
18	*Saturday Night Fever*	Film Soundtrack
17	*Abbey Road*	Beatles
17	*The Singles 1969–1973*	Carpenters
15	*. . . But Seriously*	Phil Collins
14	*Brothers In Arms*	Dire Straits
14	*Summer Holiday*	Cliff Richard and the Shadows (Film Soundtrack)
13	*John Wesley Harding*	Bob Dylan
13	*Grease*	Film Soundtrack
13	*West Side Story*	Film Soundtrack
12	*Kings Of The Wild Frontier*	Adam and the Ants
12	*The Kids From 'Fame'*	Kids From Fame
12	*Legend*	Bob Marley and the Wailers
12	*The Rolling Stones*	Rolling Stones
12	*Stars*	Simply Red
11	*Greatest Hits*	Abba
11	*Bat Out Of Hell II – Back Into Hell*	Meat Loaf
11	*Beatles For Sale*	Beatles
11	*Elton John's Greatest Hits*	Elton John
11	*20 All Time Hits Of The Fifties*	Various Artists
10	*Arrival*	Abba
10	*20 Golden Greats*	Beach Boys
10	*Greatest Hits*	Eurythmics
10	*Rolling Stones No 2*	Rolling Stones

The Bodyguard (Original Soundtrack) has spent 11 weeks at number one in the Compilations Album chart.

MOST CONSECUTIVE WEEKS AT NUMBER ONE BY ONE ALBUM

70	*South Pacific* Film Soundtrack	from 8 Nov 58
30	*Please Please Me* Beatles	from 11 May 63
23	*Sergeant Pepper's Lonely Hearts Club Band* Beatles	from 10 Jun 67
21	*With The Beatles* Beatles	from 7 Dec 63
21	*A Hard Day's Night* Beatles	from 25 Jul 64
19	*South Pacific* Film Soundtrack	from 19 Mar 60
18	*The Sound of Music* Film Soundtrack	from 1 Oct 66
18	*Saturday Night Fever* Film Soundtrack	from 6 May 78
17	*Blue Hawaii* Elvis Presley	from 24 Feb 62
14	*Summer Holiday* Cliff Richard and the Shadows	from 2 Feb 63
13	*South Pacific* Film Soundtrack	from 15 Oct 60
13	*Bridge Over Troubled Water* Simon and Garfunkel	from 21 Feb 70
13	*Grease* Film Soundtrack	from 7 Oct 78
12	*G.I. Blues* Elvis Presley	from 8 Apr 61
12	*Rolling Stones* Rolling Stones	from 2 May 64
12	*Legend* Bob Marley and the Wailers	from 19 May 84
11	*Abbey Road* Beatles	from 4 Oct 69
11	*Bridge Over Troubled Water* Simon and Garfunkel	from 16 Jan 71
11	*The Singles 1969–1973* Carpenters	from 9 Mar 74
11	*Elton John's Greatest Hits* Elton John	from 23 Nov 74
10	*The Sound Of Music* Film Soundtrack	from 5 Jun 65
10	*The Sound Of Music* Film Soundtrack	from 16 Oct 65
10	*The Sound Of Music* Film Soundtrack	from 19 Feb 66
10	*John Wesley Harding* Bob Dylan	from 9 Mar 68
10	*20 Golden Greats* Beach Boys	from 24 Jul 76
10	*Kings Of The Wild Frontier* Adam and the Ants	from 14 Mar 81
10	*Brothers In Arms* Dire Straits	from 18 Jan 86

The run of 11 weeks by *Bridge Over Troubled Water* includes eight weeks at number one when charts were not published because of a postal strike.

No album has spent more than nine consecutive weeks at number one in the Compilations Album chart, a record held by *Now! That's What I Call Music 29*, from 26 November 1994.

GAP BETWEEN SPELLS AT NUMBER ONE

Sixteen albums have returned to number one more than ten weeks after dropping from the top. Two albums have done this twice. The longest gaps between spells at number one are:

61 wks	*Black And White Minstrel Show* George Mitchell Minstrels	28 Oct 61 to 29 Dec 62
45 wks	*Diva* Annie Lennox	25 Apr 92 to 6 Mar 93
42 wks	*The Sound Of Music* Film Soundtrack	3 Feb 68 to 23 Nov 68

GAP BETWEEN SPELLS AT NUMBER ONE *continued*

38 wks	*We Can't Dance* Genesis	30 Nov 91 to 22 Aug 92
31 wks	*Thriller* Michael Jackson	25 Jun 83 to 28 Jan 84
27 wks	*Automatic For The People* R.E.M.	17 Oct 92 to 24 Apr 93
26 wks	*Introducing The Hardline . . .* Terence Trent D'Arby	1 Aug 87 to 30 Jan 88
25 wks	*Tango In The Night* Fleetwood Mac	14 Nov 87 to 7 May 88
23 wks	*The Sound Of Music* Film Soundtrack	10 Jun 67 to 18 Nov 67
23 wks	*Music Box* Mariah Carey	18 Sep 93 to 26 Feb 94
22 wks	*Brothers In Arms* Dire Straits	17 Aug 85 to 18 Jan 86
19 wks	*Can't Slow Down* Lionel Richie	19 Nov 83 to 31 Mar 84
19 wks	*Born In the USA* Bruce Springsteen	23 Feb 85 to 6 Jul 85
13 wks	*Bridge Over Troubled Water* Simon and Garfunkel	3 Apr 71 to 3 Jul 71
12 wks	*South Pacific* Film Soundtrack	8 Apr 61 to 1 Jul 61
12 wks	*Bridge Over Troubled Water* Simon and Garfunkel	24 Oct 70 to 16 Jan 71
12 wks	*Graceland* Paul Simon	8 Nov 86 to 31 Jan 87
11 wks	*A New Flame* Simply Red	6 May 89 to 22 Jul 89

Between *Diva's* first and second weeks at number one, 26 other albums topped the chart.

470

The longest span of any record's run at the top, from its first week of chart supremacy to its last, is 3 years 177 days by *The Sound Of Music* (Film Soundtrack) between 5 June 1965 and 29 November 1968. *South Pacific* (Film Soundtrack) topped the first chart of all, on 8 November 1958, and enjoyed its final stint at number one on 9 September 1961, a total span at the top of 2 years 311 days.

LONGEST CLIMB TO NUMBER ONE

Six albums have taken more than one year from their original date of chart entry to climb to the number one position on the regular chart, as follows:

3 years 298 days . . . .(from 13 Jul 68 to 6 May 72)
Tyrannosaurus Rex . . . .*My People Were Fair And Had Sky In Their Hair, But . . . . .Now They're Content To Wear Stars On Their Brows*

2 years 67 days . . . . .(from 5 Jul 75 to 10 Sep 77)
Elvis Presley . . . .*40 Greatest Hits*

1 year 321 days . . . .(from 6 Sep 80 to 24 Jul 82)
Film Soundtrack . . . . .*Fame*

1 year 104 days . . . .(from 13 Mar 93 to 25 Jun 94)
Cranberries . . . .*Everybody Else Is Doing It, So Why Can't We?*

1 year 83 days . . . .(from 14 Jul 73 to 5 Oct 74)
Mike Oldfield . . . .*Tubular Bells*

1 year 13 days . . . . .(from 19 Jun 93 to 2 Jul 94)
Ace Of Base . . . .*Happy Nation*

Twelve other albums have taken 30 weeks or more to reach the top, as follows:

Rumours	Fleetwood Mac	.49 weeks
The Freewheelin' Bob Dylan	Bob Dylan	.48 weeks
The Colour Of My Love	Celine Dion	.47 weeks
Sleeping With The Past	Elton John	.44 weeks
Like A Virgin	Madonna	.44 weeks
Circle Of One	Oleta Adams	.40 weeks
Black And White	George Mitchell	
Minstrel Show	Minstrels	.36 weeks
Born In The USA	Bruce Springsteen	.36 weeks
End Of Part One		
(Their Greatest Hits)	Wet Wet Wet	.36 weeks
Greatest Hits	Andy Williams	.35 weeks
Band On The Run	Wings	.33 weeks
And I Love You So	Perry Como	.30 weeks

Tyrannosaurus Rex hit number one with the longest-titled album ever to hit the top only after it was re-released in 1972 as a double album with *Prophets, Seers, Sages And The Angels Of The Ages*. Presley's album hit the top in the period immediately following his death. *Tubular Bells* spent 11 weeks at number two before replacing its follow-up at the very top, and *Rumours* remained 32 weeks in the Top Ten before hitting the number one slot. *The Freewheelin' Bob Dylan* climbed to the top during its seventh chart run. Oleta Adams became the first chart act ever to re-enter the charts at number one, 38 weeks after an original two-week run for *Circle Of One*, during which it peaked at number 49. This feat was duplicated by Chaka Demus and Pliers, whose *Tease Me* re-entered the charts at number one on 29 January 94, having previously peaked at number 26.

The soundtrack album of the film *Dirty Dancing* came on to the main chart on 31 October 1987, before the formation of the Compilation Albums chart. It spent 63 weeks on the main chart without ever climbing higher than number four, before being switched to the Compilations Chart on 14 January 1989. On 19 January 1991, 3 years and 80 days after its first entry on the main chart and 2 years and 5 days after it first came on to the Compilations Chart, it topped the Compilation Albums chart for the first time.

MOST CONSECUTIVE NUMBER ONE HIT ALBUMS

Twenty-two different acts have hit the very top of the albums chart with three or more consecutive official album releases, as follows:

8	Abba	(From 1976 to 1982: *Greatest Hits* to *The Singles – The First Ten Years* inclusive)
8	Led Zeppelin	(From 1970 to 1979: *Led Zeppelin 2* to *In Through The Out Door* inclusive)
7	Beatles	(From *Please Please Me* in 1963 to *Revolver* in 1966)
6	Rod Stewart	(From 1971 to 1976: *Every Picture Tells A Story* to *A Night On The Town* inclusive)
5	Erasure	(from 1988 to 1994: *The Innocents* to *I Say I Say I Say* inclusive)
5	Police	(From 1979 to 1986: *Reggatta De Blanc* to *Every Breath You Take – The Singles* inclusive)
5	Rolling Stones	(from 1969 to 1973: *Let It Bleed* to *Goat's Head Soup*. Their last two official releases on Decca and their first three on Rolling Stones Records)

4	Beatles	(from 1967 to 1970: *Sergeant Pepper's Lonely Hearts Club Band* to *Let It Be*. During this run *Magical Mystery Tour* (import) and *Yellow Submarine* hit the charts, but cannot be considered part of the offical sequence of Beatles albums)
4	Bon Jovi	(from 1988 to 1995: *New Jersey* to *These Days* inclusive)
4	Bob Dylan	(from 1968 to 1970: *John Wesley Harding* to *New Morning* inclusive)
4	Michael Jackson	(from 1982 to 1995: *Thriller* to *HIStory – Past Present and Future Book 1*. No fewer than seven other albums under the Jackson name hit the charts during this run, but there is no doubt that these were consecutive official releases by Jacko)
4	Elton John	(from 1973 to 1975: *Don't Shoot Me, I'm Only The Piano Player* to *Elton John's Greatest Hits* inclusive)
4	Simple Minds	(from 1984 to 1989: *Sparkle In The Rain* to *Street Fighting Years* inclusive. Each album spent only one week at the top of the charts)
3	Boney M	(from 1978 to 1980: *Night Flight To Venus, Oceans Of Fantasy* and *The Magic Of Boney M*)
3	David Bowie	(from 1973 to 1974: *Aladdin Sane, Pin-Ups* and *Diamond Dogs*)
3	Dire Straits	(from 1985 to 1991: *Brothers In Arms, Money For Nothing* and *On Every Street*)
3	Genesis	(from 1983 to 1991: *Genesis, Invisible Touch* and *We Can't Dance*. These were three consecutive official releases, although their 1970 album *Trespass* charted for the first time between the success of *Genesis* and *Invisible Touch*)
3	George Mitchell Minstrels	(from 1961 to 1963, the first album chart hat-trick: *The Black And White Minstrel Show, Another Black And White Minstrel Show* and *On Stage With The George Mitchell Minstrels*)
3	Gary Numan	(from 1979 to 1980: *Replicas, The Pleasure Principle* and *Telekon*. *Tubeway Army* was released before *Replicas*, even though it hit the charts later)
3	Prince	(from 1988 to 1991: *Lovesexy, Batman* and *Graffiti Bridge*)
3	Queen	(from 1989 to 1991: *Miracle, Innuendo* and *Greatest Hits Vol. 2*)
3	R.E.M.	(from 1991 to 1994: *Out Of Time, Automatic For The People* and *Monster*. A hits package from their previous label also charted during this run)
3	Simply Red	(from 1989 to 1995: *A New Flame, Stars* and *Life*)
3	Slade	(from 1973 to 1974: *Slayed?, Sladest* and *Old New Borrowed And Blue*)
3	T. Rex	(from 1971 to 1972: *Electric Warrior, Prophets Seers And Sages The Angels Of The Ages/My People Were Fair And Had Sky In Their Hair But Now They're Content To Wear Stars On Their Brows* and *Bolan Boogie*. The second of the three was a double album re-issue, but it had never been issued in that format, and one half of the double album had never been a hit before)
3	U2	(from 1984 to 1988: *The Unforgettable Fire, The Joshua Tree* and *Rattle And Hum*)

STRAIGHT IN AT NUMBER ONE

After the first chart on 8 November 1958, no album made its chart debut at number one until the Beatles' fifth album, *Help!*, did so on 14 August 1965. However, it is now a routine event in the albums charts, so much so that of 51 number one hits in 1994 and 1995, 38 came on to the charts at number one. 24 acts have achieved this feat at least three times, as follows:

8	David Bowie	5	Police	4	Paul McCartney
		5	Prince	4	Pink Floyd
7	Rolling Stones	5	Queen		
		5	Simple Minds	3	Michael Jackson
6	Beatles	5	U2	3	Madonna
6	Genesis			3	R.E.M.
		4	Bon Jovi	3	Simply Red
5	Abba	4	Phil Collins	3	Bruce Springsteen
5	Erasure	4	Dire Straits	3	Status Quo
5	Led Zeppelin	4	Elton John		

Phil Collins has therefore achieved the feat ten times, six times with Genesis and four times solo. Paul McCartney has also done it ten times, six times with the Beatles and four times solo.

NO.1 SINGLE AND ALBUM IN THE SAME WEEK

Many acts over the years have claimed the top spot in the singles charts, and many acts have claimed the number one position in the albums charts. But only 41 different acts have achieved the feat of holding the top placing in both charts in the same week. The first was Elvis Presley, in the week ending 26 January 1961, and the 41st was Robson Green and Jerome Flynn, in the week ending 2 December 1995.

The full list of acts, in alphabetical order, is: **Abba, Adam and the Ants, Bryan Adams, Beatles, Blondie, David Bowie, Mariah Carey, Culture Club, Celine Dion, Jason Donovan, Foreigner, Robson Green and Jerome Flynn, Whitney Houston, Human League, Michael Jackson, John Lennon, Madness, Madonna, Meat Loaf, Men At Work, Monkees, Gary Numan/Tubeway Army, Police, Elvis Presley, Pretenders, Queen, Cliff Richard, Lionel Richie, Right Said Fred, Rolling Stones, Shadows, Simon and Garfunkel, Simply Red, Soul II Soul, Spandau Ballet, Rod Stewart, Barbra Streisand, Stylistics, T. Rex, T'Pau, Wet Wet Wet.**

In addition, both Paul McCartney and Phil Collins have held top spot in the albums charts in the same week that they have duetted at the top of the singles charts, while Irene Cara and John Travolta & Olivia Newton-John have had singles at the top in the same week that the various artists soundtrack album featuring their number one hit single has led the album charts.

John Lennon, Gary Numan and the Shadows have all achieved the double top in more than one way. Lennon has done it solo and as a Beatle, Numan managed it first as Tubeway Army, and then nine weeks later as Gary Numan. The Shadows did the double in October 1961, before doing it again with Cliff Richard in 1962 and again in 1963. Cliff Richard has the longest span of double top weeks, over almost 27 years between January 1962 and December 1988. Both Elvis Presley (1961 to 1977) and Queen (1975 to 1991) have each topped both charts over a span of over 16 years.

Most weeks at the top of both charts:

45 ....Beatles (15 different runs)
22 ....Elvis Presley (7 different runs)
13 ....Abba (4 different runs)
11 ......Cliff Richard (4 different runs)

The 14 acts to have topped both charts more than once (i.e. with different singles and albums) are:

Beatles (14 times), Elvis Presley (6 times), Abba (4 times), Police (3 times), Queen (3 times), Cliff Richard (3 times), Rolling Stones (3 times), Michael Jackson (twice), Madonna twice), Gary Numan/Tubeway Army (twice), Shadows (twice), Rod Stewart (twice), T. Rex (twice), Wet Wet Wet (twice).

Cliff Richard. Photo: Lisa Hooley

Most consecutive weeks at the top of both charts:

		SINGLE	ALBUM	FROM
SIX	Cliff Richard and the Shadows	The Young Ones	*The Young Ones*	11 Jan 62
	Beatles	From Me To You	*Please Please Me*	11 May 63
	John Travolta and Olivia Newton-John	Summer Nights	*Grease (OST)*	7 Oct 78
FIVE	Beatles	I Want To Hold Your Hand	*With The Beatles*	12 Dec 63
	Celine Dion	Think Twice	*The Colour Of My Love*	4 Feb 95
FOUR	Elvis Presley	Are You Lonesome Tonight	*GI Blues*	26 Jan 61
	Elvis Presley	Surrender	*GI Blues*	1 Jun 61
	Elvis Presley	Rock-A-Hula Baby/ Can't Help Falling In Love	*Blue Hawaii*	22 Feb 62
	Elvis Presley	Good Luck Charm	*Blue Hawaii*	24 May 62
	Beatles	She Loves You	*Please Please Me*	12 Sep 63
	Beatles	I Feel Fine	*Beatles For Sale*	17 Dec 64
	Beatles	Day Tripper/We Can Work It Out	*Rubber Soul*	23 Dec 65
	Beatles	Yellow Submarine/ Eleanor Rigby	*Revolver*	18 Aug 66
	Rod Stewart	Sailing	*Atlantic Crossing*	6 Sep 75
	Abba	Fernando	*Greatest Hits*	8 May 76
	Wet Wet Wet	Love Is All Around	*End Of Part One*	30 Jul 94

FACTS AND FEATS

The week before the 'I Feel Fine'/*Beatles For Sale* combination topped both charts for four weeks in 1963, the Beatles' *A Hard Day's Night* was the top album and 'I Feel Fine' the top single, so they held both top spots for five consecutive weeks. In the two weeks before 'I Want To Hold Your Hand'/*With The Beatles* topped the charts for five weeks, the Beatles were also at number one on both charts, with, in the week ending 28 November 1963, 'She Loves You' and *Please Please Me*, and the following week with 'She Loves You' and *With The Beatles*. Thus they topped both charts for seven consecutive weeks, a record. Just to add to their chart domination, for three weeks from 12 December 1963, they had the top two singles, the top two albums and the top two EPs in the separate EP chart that existed at the time. Never has any other act approached this extraordinary chart domination.

In the week ending 23 July 1964, the Beatles knocked the Rolling Stones off the top of both charts, the only time that one act has ever dethroned another from both charts in the same week.

THE ONE-HIT WONDERS

It may be comparatively easy to hit the top with your only hit single – a feat that has been performed almost 40 times over the years – but it is far more difficult to hit the very top of the album charts with your only hit album. After 37 years, the list remains very short.

Kenny Ball, Chris Barber and Acker Bilk ....
....*The Best Of Ball, Barber and Bilk* ....(1962)

Blind Faith ....*Blind Faith* ....(1969)

Freddy Cannon ....*The Explosive Freddy Cannon* ....(1960)

Chaka Demus and Pliers.........*Tease Me*..(1994)

Farm ....*Spartacus* ....(1991)

Johnny Hates Jazz ....*Turn Back The Clock*....................................(1988)

Holly Johnson ....*Blast*..(1989)

Kenny Ball, Chris Barber and Acker Bilk all had solo hit albums. Blind Faith consisted of Eric Clapton, Ginger Baker, Steve Winwood and Rick Grech, all of whom had hit albums solo and/or in other combinations. Holly Johnson was the lead singer of Frankie Goes To Hollywood, who had three hit albums.

There are five other acts whose first chart album hit number one in 1995, but who will in all probability follow up their chart-topping debut albums very soon. They are Black Grape (*It's Great When You're Straight . . . Yeah!*), Boyzone (*Said And Done*), Elastica (*Elastica*), Robson Green and Jerome Flynn (*Robson and Jerome*), and Supergrass (*I Should Coco*).

There are also seven film soundtrack albums which topped the charts, making their casts in theory one-hit wonders. They are *Fame, Grease, Saturday Night Fever, The Sound Of Music, South Pacific, A Star Is Born* and *West Side Story*. The television soundtrack *Rock Follies*, as well as *The Official BBC Album Of The Royal Wedding* add to this bizarre list, along with three London stage cast recordings, *Aspects Of Love, Joseph And The Amazing Technicolour Dreamcoat* and *The Phantom Of The Opera*. Finally, there are 44 other Various Artists compilation albums which topped the main albums chart before the separate compilations chart was initiated in 1989.

THE TOP 20 ALBUMS ACTS

A table showing the comparative achievements of the 20 most charted albums acts of all time.

ACT	Year First Charted	Total Weeks	Total Hits	Top Tens	Number Ones	Most charted Album
Beatles	1963	1160	27	20	13	*Sgt. Pepper's Lonely Hearts Club Band* (174 wks)
Queen	1974	1111	21	19	9	*Greatest Hits* (433 wks)
Simon and Garfunkel	1966	1083	10	7	2	*Bridge Over Troubled Water* (304 wks)
Dire Straits	1978	1082	10	9	4	*Makin' Movies* (249 wks)
Elvis Presley	1958	1071	96	37	6	*Blue Hawaii* (71 wks)
David Bowie	1972	903	31	22	8	*The Rise And Fall Of Ziggy Stardust And The Spiders From Mars* (172 wks)
U2	1981	862	11	7	5	*Live: Under A Blood Red Sky* (203 wks)
Pink Floyd	1967	859	18	15	5	*Dark Side Of The Moon* (337 wks)
Elton John	1970	801	34	21	6	*Very Best Of Elton John* (94 wks)
Fleetwood Mac	1968	795	16	9	4	*Rumours* (443 wks)
Michael Jackson	1972	770	19	7	5	*Off The Wall* (178 wks)
Cliff Richard	1959	761	50	33	7	*Love Songs* (43 wks)
Phil Collins	1981	756	6	6	4	*Face Value* (274 wks)
Rod Stewart	1970	747	24	19	7	*Best Of Rod Stewart* (106 wks)
Rolling Stones	1964	741	41	31	10	*Rolling Stones* (51 wks)
Meat Loaf	1978	713	10	7	2	*Bat Out Of Hell* (472 wks)
Madonna	1984	677	10	10	4	*Like A Virgin* (152 wks)
Frank Sinatra	1958	662	54	29	1	*My Way* (59 wks)
Abba	1974	635	14	9	9	*Greatest Hits* (130 wks)
Bob Dylan	1964	575	38	25	6	*Greatest Hits* (84 wks)

Madonna

Over the past two years since *British Hit Albums 6* was published, there have been no changes to the top 20 acts. All the top acts have appeared in the charts over the past two years, with U2 and Bob Dylan the least impressive performers, each only having been on the charts for seven weeks in that period. Pink Floyd have added most to their total in 1994 and 1995, a further 104 weeks, which moved them up to eighth on the overall weeks on chart listing.

Both Elvis Presley and Frank Sinatra featured in the very first albums chart. Elvis is the only act to have appeared on the album charts for at least one week in every year of the chart's existence. The most recent arrival to the charts of any of the Top 20 acts is by Madonna, whose first album chart action came in the week ending 11 February 1984.

FACTS AND FEATS

Of the 20 leading acts, ten are British, seven are American, one is a transatlantic mixture (Fleetwood Mac), one is Swedish and one is Irish. There are ten male solo acts, but only one female soloist. Diana Ross, Barbra Streisand and Tina Turner are the next female soloists in the rankings, all with over 400 weeks of chart action.

If we look at the top acts on the basis of the average number of weeks each album has spent in the charts (i.e. total weeks divided by total hits), seven acts prove to have spent an average of more than one year on the charts with each album:

Phil Collins	126.0 weeks on chart per album
Simon and Garfunkel	108.3 weeks on chart per album
Dire Straits	108.2 weeks on chart per album
U2	78.4 weeks on chart per album
Meat Loaf	71.3 weeks on chart per album
Madonna	67.7 weeks on chart per album
Queen	52.9 weeks on chart per album

At the other end of the scale, each album hit by Elvis Presley has lasted on average only 11.2 weeks on the chart, each Frank Sinatra hit lasts only 12.3 weeks, and each Bob Dylan album hangs around for no more than 15.1 weeks. Cliff Richard's average stay is only 15.2 weeks and the Rolling Stones a mere 18.1 weeks. No other acts average fewer than 20 weeks of chart action per hit.

In terms of consistent chart success, we can rank these acts in terms of the percentage of their albums which reach the Top Ten, and the percentage which go all the way to the number one slot. In these terms, the top acts are:

	% of albums reaching Top Ten
Madonna	100.0
Phil Collins	100.0
Queen	90.5
Dire Straits	90.0
Pink Floyd	83.3
Rod Stewart	79.2
Rolling Stones	75.6

The lowest ranking in this list is, surprisingly, Michael Jackson, only 36.8% of whose albums have reached the Top Ten.

	% of albums reaching number one
Phil Collins	66.7
Abba	64.3
Beatles	48.1
U2	45.5
Queen	42.9
Madonna	40.0
Dire Straits	40.0

Only 1.9% of Frank Sinatra's hit albums have topped the charts, and only 6.25% of Elvis Presley's.

Ranking acts purely on the basis of weeks on chart is not a perfect solution, but in the case of the albums charts, overall success equates far more closely with chart life than on the singles charts. Long-running chart successes are what both the performers and their record companies are looking for. These charts are not meant to reflect total sales, but merely the relative chart success of the biggest album acts in British chart history.

| British Hit Singles | 0-85112-633-2 | £11.99 |
| British Hit Albums | 0-85112-619-7 | £12.99 |

The Complete Chart Package

| Top 40 Charts | 0-85112-834-0 | £14.99 |
| No.1 Hits | 0-85112-769-X | £11.99 |

BIOGRAPHIES

Jonathan Rice has finally got round to cataloguing his album collection. It began in 1965 with *The Golden Hits Of The Everly Brothers* and *The Eddie Cochran Memorial Album*, and now includes contributions from such unknowns as Eric Mercury, Tananas and Mariya Takeuchi, as well as rarities from the Vipers, Stan Freberg and the Big Three. He is happy to admit that his shelves contain the sounds of Mantovani and Doris Day as well as Elvis, Queen, Elmore James, and Madonna, but the George Mitchell Minstrels and Michael Bolton seem to be missing altogether. He mourns the passing of the sound of vinyl, but enjoys the convenience of the CD.

In stark contrast to his brother, **Tim Rice** finds CDs extraordinarily inconvenient. American-packaged CDs are a particular menace. They are impossible to open in under 20 minutes and, in the unlikely event of progress being made to the disc itself the naff plastic casing will have disintegrated or have been dismantled by hands driven to violence as they wrestle with Fort Knox-proof taping and skin-tight shrink wrapping. The artwork of a CD is unavoidably sad – in keeping with the feeble dimensions of the little bastard – and frankly only a hi-fi anorak gives a toss or even notices the CD's miniscule sound superiority over vinyl. Nonetheless the elder Rice follows the album charts with undimmed enthusiasm.

480

Paul Gambaccini's peak performance in the British album chart is as the Bad Samaritan on the Godley and Creme album *L*, which peaked at 47. This is still better than his American chart best, 121 for his Amnesty International benefit compilation *Conspiracy Of Hope*, renamed *Rock For Amnesty* for the States. Paul has yet to crack the Japanese chart in any way.